COMPUTER
ORGANIZATION

McGraw-Hill Series in Computer Organization and Architecture

McGraw-Hill Computer Science Series

COMPUTER ORGANIZATION

Second Edition

V. Carl Hamacher
Professor of Electrical Engineering and Computer Science
University of Toronto

Zvonko G. Vranesic
Professor of Electrical Engineering and Computer Science
University of Toronto

Safwat G. Zaky
Associate Professor of Electrical Engineering
University of Toronto

McGraw-Hill Book Company

New York   St. Louis   San Francisco   Auckland   Bogotá   Hamburg
Johannesburg   London   Madrid   Mexico   Montreal   New Delhi
Panama   Paris   São Paulo   Singapore   Sydney   Tokyo   Toronto

This book was set in Times Roman by Black Dot, Inc.
The editors were Eric M. Munson and Linda A. Mittiga;
the production supervisor was Charles Hess.
New drawings were done by Wellington Studios Ltd.
Halliday Lithograph Corporation was printer and binder.

COMPUTER ORGANIZATION

34567890 HALHAL 898765

ISBN 0-07-025683-7

Library of Congress Cataloging in Publication Data

Hamacher, V. Carl.
    Computer organization.

    Bibliography: p.
    Includes index.
    1. Computer architecture.   I. Vranesic, Zvonko G.
II. Zaky, Safwat G.   III. Title.
QA76.9.A73H35   1984   621.3819'52   83-24858
ISBN 0-07-025683-7

To Liz, Anne, and Shirley

CONTENTS

PREFACE

This book is intended for use in a first-level course on "computer organization" in computer science and electrical engineering curricula. The book is self-contained, assuming only that the reader has a basic knowledge of computer programming in a high-level language. Many students who study computer organization will have had an introductory course on digital logic circuits. Therefore, this subject is not covered in the main body of the book. However, we have provided an extensive appendix on logic circuits for those students who need it.

Our resolve to write a book stems from our experience in teaching computer organization to three distinct types of undergraduates: computer science specialists, electrical engineering undergraduates, and engineering science undergraduates. We have always approached the teaching of courses in this area from as practical a point of view as possible. Thus, a major choice in shaping the contents of the book was to illustrate the principles of computer organization by using a number of extensive examples drawn from commercially available computers.

Second, we feel that it is important to recognize that digital system design is not a straightforward process of applying "optimal design" algorithms. Many design decisions are based largely on heuristic judgment and tend to be a compromise between extreme alternatives. Thus it is our goal to convey these notions to the reader.

Third, we have endeavoured to provide sufficient details to force the student to dig beyond the surface when dealing with ideas that seem to be intuitively obvious. We believe that this is best accomplished by giving real examples that are adequately documented. Block diagrams are a powerful means of describing organizational features of a computer. However, they can easily lead to an oversimplified view of the problems involved. Hence, they must be accompanied by the details of implementation alternatives.

We use a number of real machines for illustrative purposes. Our main examples are drawn from the following computers: PDP-11, VAX-11, IBM 370,

HP3000, M6800, M6809, M68000, and Intel 8085. The PDP-11 is used for examples in many parts of the book. Its manageable size and complexity make it suitable for teaching purposes. Moreover, it has had considerable influence on instruction set and addressing mode design in small computers.

The book is aimed at a one-semester course in computer science or electrical engineering programs. It is suitable for both hardware- and software-oriented students. There is a greater emphasis on hardware since we feel that this is the way computer organization should be taught. It is a mistake to describe computer structures solely through the eyes of a programmer, particularly for people who work with systems that involve a variety of equipment, interfacing, and communication facilities. However, although the emphasis is on computer hardware, we have addressed a number of software issues and discussed representative instances of software-hardware trade-offs in the implementation of various components of a computing system.

Let us review the topics covered in sequence, chapter by chapter. The first eight chapters cover the basic principles of computer organization. The remaining four chapters deal with peripheral devices, system software, microprocessors, and computer communications.

Chapter 1 provides an overview of computer structure and informally introduces a number of terms that are dealt with in more depth in the remainder of the book. A discussion is included of the basic ways that the standard functional units can be interconnected to form a complete computing system.

Chapter 2 gives a methodical treatment of addressing techniques and instruction sequencing. The PDP-11 minicomputer is used to illustrate the basic concepts. Numerous programs and program segments at the machine instruction level are used to discuss loops, subroutines, and simple input-output programming.

Chapter 3 continues the discussion of instruction sets that was begun in Chapter 2 and focuses on some of the problems encountered because of the "bit-space" limitations of short word-length machines. Instruction sets in the VAX-11, the IBM 370, and the HP3000 are introduced. They illustrate the possibilities afforded by longer word lengths and stack-oriented design. The influence of high-level language programming on the design of these machines is discussed.

Chapter 4 begins with a register-transfer-level treatment of the implementation of instruction fetching and execution in a processor. The constraints imposed by various busing arrangements are explained, followed by a discussion of both hardwired and microprogrammed control.

Chapter 5 extends the discussion of microprogrammed control. The alternatives of fully decoded command words and partially encoded command words are treated, followed by a rather detailed analysis of the "next-address" generation problem in microprogram sequencing. The use of bit slices in designing microprogrammed machines is discussed.

Input-output organization is developed in Chapter 6. The basics of I/O data transfer synchronization are presented, and then a series of increasingly complex I/O structures is explained. Direct-memory access methods and interrupts are introduced, and then these ideas are extended to a discussion of channels. Three popular bus standards, multibus, S-100, and IEEE-488, are also presented.

Chapter 7 treats the arithmetic unit of a computer. It begins with a discussion of fixed-point add, subtract, multiply, and divide hardware, operating on 2's-complement numbers. Lookahead adders and high-speed array multipliers are included. Floating-point number representations and operations, including the IEEE standard, are presented.

Semiconductor memories are discussed in Chapter 8. Multiple-module memory systems and caches are explained as ways of increasing main memory bandwidth. Various cache mapping methods are presented and virtual-memory systems are discussed in some detail.

A variety of peripheral devices are dealt with in Chapter 9. Cathode-ray tube terminals and graphics displays are analyzed in detail. This is followed by a discussion of magnetic disks, drums, and tapes.

Chapter 10 gives an introduction to the subject of operating-system software, including linkers, loaders, and scheduling techniques.

An extensive treatment of microprocessors is provided in Chapter 11. Complete instruction sets, together with some comparative analyses, are given for Motorola's 6800, 6809, and 68000 and for Intel's 8085. Input-output aspects of microcomputer systems are emphasized.

Chapter 12 is an introduction to a number of topics in computer communications. Synchronous and asynchronous protocols for data transmission are considered. This is followed by a brief description of local area and wide area networks.

Most of the material in this book can be covered in a 12-to-15 week course, with 3 lecture hours per week. However, as well as being suited for the usual undergraduate class teaching environment, we feel that the material is appropriate for self-study by graduates who have not specialized in computers but who have taken introductory courses or have work experience in the area. The use of real (commercially available) computers in our examples makes the book attractive to the latter readership.

This second edition of the book contains substantial additions that update and extend the material of the first edition. The additional material includes the following:

- VAX-11 instruction set and addressing modes in Chapter 3
- Discussion of bit slices in Chapter 5
- Bus standards in Chapter 6
- IEEE floating-point standard in Chapter 7
- Dynamic memories and the VAX-11 virtual-memory system in Chapter 8
- M6809 and M68000 microprocessors in Chapter 11 and Appendix C
- Local area networks in Chapter 12

We should note that all of the material on I/O and buses has been consolidated in Chapter 6. A number of sections have also been extensively rewritten in order to update the material to be consistent with technology changes in the past few years.

The authors wish to express their thanks to all the people who have helped during the preparation of this second edition. We are especially grateful for the detailed, constructive criticism of the complete manuscript by Professors Harold Stone and Alfred Weaver. Professors Mary Jane Irwin and Henry Chuang provided useful suggestions in the planning stages for the second edition. Professor Tom Hull gave helpful advice on the floating-point section in Chapter 7. We also wish to acknowledge the typing work of Cathy Cheung.

V. Carl Hamacher
Zvonko G. Vranesic
Safwat G. Zaky

COMPUTER
ORGANIZATION

BASIC STRUCTURE OF COMPUTERS

The objective of this chapter is to introduce some basic concepts and associated terminology. We will give only a broad overview of the fundamental characteristics of computers, leaving the more detailed and precise discussion to the subsequent chapters.

Let us first define the meaning of the word "digital computer" or simply "computer," which is often misunderstood, despite the fact that most people take it for granted. In its simplest form, a contemporary *computer* is a fast electronic calculating machine, which accepts digitized "input" information, processes it according to a "program" stored in its "memory," and produces the resultant "output" information.

1.1 FUNCTIONAL UNITS

The word computer encompasses a large variety of machines, widely differing in size, speed, and cost. It is fashionable to use more specific words to represent some subclasses of computers. Smaller machines are usually called *minicomputers*, which is a reflection on their relatively lower cost, size, and computing power. In the early 1970s the term *microcomputer* was coined to describe a very small computer, low in price, and consisting of only a few very large-scale integrated (VLSI) circuit packages.

Large computers, sometimes called *mainframes*, are quite different from minicomputers and microcomputers in size, processing power, cost, and the complexity and sophistication of their design. Yet the basic concepts are essentially the same for all classes of computers, relying on a few well-defined ideas which we will attempt to explain.

In its simplest form, a computer consists of five functionally independent main parts: input, memory, arithmetic and logic, output, and control units, as

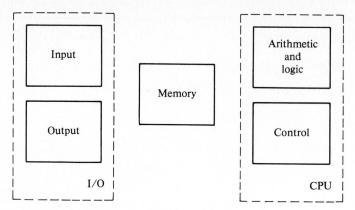

Figure 1.1 Basic functional units of a computer.

indicated in Figure 1.1. The input unit accepts coded information from human operators, from electromechanical devices, or from other computers connected to it over digital communication lines. The information is either stored in the memory for later reference or immediately handled by the arithmetic and logic circuitry, which performs the desired operations. The processing steps are determined by a program stored in the memory. Finally, the results are sent back to the outside world through the output unit. All these actions are coordinated by the control unit. The diagram in Figure 1.1 does not show the connections between the various functional units. Of course, such connections must exist. However, there are a number of ways in which the connections can be made, and they will be discussed in many places throughout the book. Although we will generally refer to a single computer when illustrating basic principles, many modern computing systems involve a number of computers interconnected by means of a communication network. The term *distributed computing* is often used to denote such an environment.

It has been traditional to refer to the arithmetic and logic circuits in conjunction with the main control circuits as a *central processing unit* (CPU), or simply a *processor*. The word central is used to indicate that most of the control functions in a given computer are centralized in a single unit. Modern systems often contain many processors, each assigned to perform a particular function. Input and output equipment is usually combined under the term *input-output unit* (I/O). This is reasonable in view of the fact that some standard equipment provides both input and output functions. The simplest such example is the often encountered cathode-ray tube (CRT) terminal, consisting of a keyboard for input and a CRT display for output. We must emphasize that input and output functions are separated within the terminal. Thus a computer sees two distinct devices, even though the human operator associates them as being part of the same unit.

In large computers the main functional units may comprise a number of separate, and often sizeable, physical parts. Figure 1.2 is a photograph of such a

Figure 1.2 A typical large computer—IBM S370/3031 *(IBM Corp. Ltd.)*

computer. Minicomputers and microcomputers are much smaller in size, often of desktop dimensions. Even a fairly complex minicomputer system, such as the one shown in Figure 1.3, tends to be small in comparison with large computers.

At this point we should take a closer look at the "information" fed into a computer. It is convenient to consider such information as being of two types, namely, *instructions* and *data*. Instructions are explicit commands which:

Figure 1.3 A minicomputer system. *(Digital Equipment Corp.)*

- Govern the transfer of information within a computer, as well as between the computer and its I/O devices
- Specify the arithmetic and logic operations to be performed

A set of instructions which perform a task is called a *program*. The usual mode of operation is to store a program (or several programs) in the memory. Then, the processor fetches the instructions comprising the program from the memory and performs the desired operations. Instructions are normally executed in the sequential order in which they are stored, although it is possible to have deviations from this order as in the case where branching is required. Thus the actual behavior of a computer is under the complete control of the *stored program*, except for the possibility of external interruption by the operator or by digital devices connected to the machine.

Data are numbers and encoded characters which are used as operands by the instructions. This should not be interpreted as a hard definition, since the term is often used to symbolize any digital information. Even within our definition of data, it is quite feasible that an entire program (that is, a set of instructions) may be considered as data if it is to be processed by another program. An example of this is the task of *compilation* of a high-level language source program into machine instructions and data. The source program is the input data for the compiler program. The compiler translates the source program into a machine language program.

Information handled by a computer must be encoded in a suitable format. Since most present-day hardware (that is, electronic and electromechanical equipment) employs digital circuits which have only two naturally stable states, namely, ON and OFF (see Appendix A), binary coding is used. That is, each number, character of text, or instruction is encoded as a string of binary digits (*bits*), each having one of two possible values. Numbers are usually represented in the positional binary notation, as will be discussed in detail in Chapter 7. Occasionally, the *binary-coded decimal* (BCD) format is employed, where each decimal digit is encoded by 4 bits.

Alphanumeric characters are also expressed in terms of binary codes. Several appropriate coding schemes have been developed. Two of the most widely encountered ones are ASCII (American Standard Code for Information Interchange), where each character is represented as a 7-bit code, and EBCDIC (extended binary-coded decimal interchange code), where 8 bits are used to denote a character. A more detailed description of binary notation and coding schemes is given in Appendix D.

Input unit Computers accept coded information by means of input units, which consist of devices capable of "reading" such data. The simplest of these is the keyboard of a CRT terminal. It is electronically connected to the processing part of a computer. The keyboard is wired so that whenever a key is depressed, the corresponding letter or digit is automatically translated into its corresponding code, which may then be sent directly to either the memory or the CPU. Figure 1.4 shows a CRT terminal.

Figure 1.4 A CRT terminal.
(Lanpar)

Many other kinds of input devices are available. These include light pens, joysticks, and trackballs. They are often used as graphic input devices in conjunction with CRT displays. Detailed discussion of input devices and their operation can be found in Chapter 9.

Memory unit The sole function of the memory unit is to store programs and data. Again, this function can be accomplished with a variety of equipment. It is useful to distinguish between two classes of memory devices, which comprise the primary and secondary storage.

Primary storage, or the *main memory*, is a fast memory capable of operating at electronic speeds, where programs and data are stored during their execution. The main memory contains a large number of semiconductor storage cells, each capable of storing 1 bit of information. These cells are rarely read or written as individual cells. Instead, they are processed in groups of fixed size called *words*. The main memory is organized so that the contents of one word, containing n bits, can be stored or retrieved in one basic operation.

To provide easy access to any word in the main memory, it is useful to associate a distinct name with each word location. These names are numbers that identify successive locations, which are hence called *addresses*. A given word is accessed by specifying its address and issuing a control command that starts the storage or retrieval process.

The number of bits in each word is often referred to as the *word length* of the given computer. Large computers usually have 32 or more bits in a word, while microcomputer and minicomputer word lengths range from 8 to 32 bits. The capacity of the main memory is one of the factors that characterize the size of a computer. Small machines may have only a few thousand words, whereas large machines often have millions of words. Data is usually manipulated within a machine in units of words, multiples of words, or submultiples of words. A typical access to the main memory results in one word of data being read from the memory or written into it.

As mentioned above, programs and data must reside in the main memory during execution. Instructions and data can be written into it or read out under control of the processing unit. It is essential to be able to access any word location within the main memory as quickly as possible. Memories where any location can be reached by specifying its address are called *random-access memories* (RAM). The time required to access one word is called the *memory access time*. This is a fixed time, usually 100 to 500 nanoseconds (ns) for most modern computers.

While primary storage is essential, it tends to be expensive. Thus additional, cheaper *secondary storage* is used when large amounts of data have to be stored, particularly if some of the data need not be accessed very frequently. Indeed, a wide selection of suitable devices is available. These include *magnetic disks*, *drums*, and *tapes*. Figures 1.5 and 1.6 show a bank of disk units and a tape unit, respectively.

Chapter 8 provides a detailed description of main memory components and their usage, while secondary storage devices are discussed in Chapter 9.

Arithmetic and logic unit Execution of most operations within a computer takes place in the arithmetic and logic unit (ALU). Consider a typical example. Suppose two numbers located in the main memory are to be added. They are brought into the arithmetic unit where the actual addition is carried out. The sum may then be stored in the memory.

Similarly, any other arithmetic or logic operation (for example, multiplication, division, or comparison of numbers) is done by bringing the required operands into the ALU, where the necessary operation is performed. We should point out that not all operands in an ongoing computation reside in the main memory, since processors normally contain a number of high-speed storage elements called *registers*, which may be used for temporary storage of often used operands. Each such register can store one word of data. Access times to registers are typically 5 to 10 times faster than memory access times.

The control and arithmetic units are usually many times faster in basic cycle time than other devices connected to a computer system. It is thus possible to design relatively complex computer systems containing a number of external devices controlled by a single processor. These devices can be CRT terminals, magnetic tape and disk memories, sensors, displays, mechanical controllers, etc. Of course, this is possible only because of the vast difference in speed, enabling the fast processor to organize and control the activity of many slower devices.

Output unit The output unit is the counterpart of the input unit. Its function is to return the processed results to the outside world.

A number of devices provide both an output function and an input function. This is the case with CRT terminals and graphic displays. This dual role of some devices is the reason for combining input and output units under the single name of I/O unit.

Of course, there exist devices used for output only, the most familiar example being a high-speed *printer*. It is possible to produce printers capable of

Figure 1.5 Magnetic disk storage. *(IBM Corp. Ltd.)*

Figure 1.6 A magnetic tape unit. *(IBM Corp. Ltd.)*

Figure 1.7 A line printer. *(IBM Corp. Ltd.)*

printing as many as 10,000 lines per minute. These are tremendous speeds in the mechanical sense, but are still very slow compared to the electronic speeds of a processor unit. A line printer is shown in Figure 1.7.

Control unit The previously described units provide the necessary tools for storing and processing information. Their operation must be coordinated in some organized way, which is the task of a control unit. It is effectively the nerve center, used to send control signals to other units.

A line printer will print a line only if it is specifically instructed to do so. This may typically be effected by an appropriate Write instruction executed by the processor. Processing of this instruction involves the sending of *timing signals* to and from the printer, which is the function of the control unit.

We can say, in general, that I/O transfers are controlled by software instructions which identify the devices involved and the type of transfer. However, the actual timing signals which govern the transfers during execution are generated by the control circuits. Data transfers between the processor and memory are also controlled by the control unit in a similar fashion.

Conceptually it is reasonable to think of a control unit as a well-defined, physically separate unit which somehow interacts with other parts of a machine. In practice this is seldom the case. Much of the control circuitry is physically distributed throughout the machine. A rather large set of control lines (wires) carry the signals used for timing and synchronization of events in all units.

In summary, the operation of a computer can be described as follows:

• It accepts information (programs and data) through an input unit and transfers it to the memory.
• Information stored in the memory is fetched, under program control, into an arithmetic and logic unit to be processed.

- Processed information leaves the computer through an output unit.
- All activities inside the machine are directed by a control unit.

1.2 BASIC OPERATIONAL CONCEPTS

In the previous section it was stated that the activity within a computer is governed by means of instructions. To perform a given task, an appropriate program consisting of a set of instructions is stored in the main memory. Individual instructions are brought from the memory into the processor, which executes the specified operations. In addition to the instructions, it is necessary to use some data as operands, which are also stored in the memory. A typical instruction may be

Add   LOCA,R0

which adds the operand at memory location LOCA to the operand in a register in the processor called R0, and places the sum into register R0. This instruction requires several steps to be performed. First, the instruction must be transferred from the main memory into the processor. Then, the operand from LOCA must be fetched. This operand is added to the contents of R0. Finally, the resultant sum is stored in register R0.

Transfers between the main memory and the processor start by sending the address of the memory location to be accessed to the memory unit and issuing the appropriate control signals. Then data is transferred from or to the memory.

Figure 1.8 shows how the connection between the main memory and the processor can be made. It also shows a few details of the processor that have not been discussed yet, but which are operationally essential. The interconnection pattern for these components is not shown explicitly, since at this point we will discuss their functional characteristics only. Chapter 4 will deal with the interconnection details as part of processor design.

The processor contains arithmetic and logic circuitry as the main processing elements. It also contains a number of registers used for temporary storage of data. Two registers are of particular interest. The *instruction register* (IR) contains the instruction that is being executed. Its output is available to the control circuits, which generate the timing signals for control of the actual processing circuits needed to execute the instruction. The *program counter* (PC) is a register which keeps track of the execution of a program. It contains the memory address of the instruction currently being executed. During the execution of the current instruction, the contents of the PC are updated to correspond to the address of the next instruction to be executed. It is customary to say that the PC *points* to the instruction that is to be fetched from the memory.

Besides the IR and PC there are usually several other *general-purpose registers*. Their role will be explained in Chapter 2.

Finally, there are two registers that facilitate communication with the main memory. These are the *memory address register* (MAR) and the *memory data*

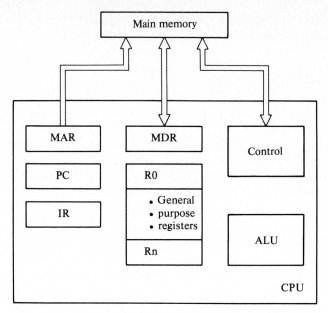

Figure 1.8 Connections between the CPU and the main memory.

register (MDR). As the name implies, the MAR is used to hold the address of the location to or from which data is to be transferred. The MDR contains the data to be written into or read out of the addressed location.

Let us now consider some typical operating steps. Programs reside in the main memory and usually get there via the input unit. Execution of a program starts by setting the PC to point to the first instruction of the program. The contents of the PC are transferred to the MAR and a Read control signal is sent to the memory. After a certain elapsed time (corresponding to the memory access time), the addressed word (in this case the first instruction of our program) is read out of the memory and loaded into the MDR. Next, the contents of the MDR are transferred to the IR, at which point the instruction is ready to be decoded and executed.

If the instruction involves an operation to be performed by the ALU, it will be necessary to obtain the required operands. If an operand resides in the memory (it could also be in a general register in the processor), it will have to be fetched by sending its address to the MAR and initiating a Read cycle. When the operand has been read from the memory into the MDR, it may be transferred from the MDR to the ALU. Having fetched one or more operands in this way, the ALU can perform the desired operation. If the result of this operation is to be stored in the memory, it must be sent to the MDR. The address of the location where the result is to be stored is sent to the MAR and a Write cycle is initiated. In the meantime the contents of the PC are incremented to point to the next instruction to be executed. Thus, as soon as the execution of the current instruction is completed, a new instruction fetch may be started.

In addition to transferring data between the main memory and the processor, it is necessary to have the ability to accept data from input devices and to send data to output devices. Thus some machine instructions with the capability of handling I/O transfers must be provided.

Normal execution of programs may sometimes be altered. It is often the case that some device requires urgent servicing. For example, a monitoring device in a computer-controlled industrial process may have detected a dangerous condition. To deal with such situations sufficiently quickly, the normal flow of the program that is being executed by the processor must be interrupted. To achieve this, the device can raise an *interrupt signal*. An interrupt is a request from the I/O device for service by the processor. The processor provides the requested service by executing an appropriate *interrupt-service routine*. Since such diversions may alter the internal state of the processor, it is essential that its state be saved in the main memory before servicing the interrupt. This normally involves storing the contents of the PC, the general registers, and some control information. Upon termination of the interrupt-service routine, the state of the processor is restored so that execution of the interrupted program may continue.

The processor unit shown in Figure 1.8 can be implemented in a variety of ways. In the case of a microprocessor, all elements are realized as a single VLSI chip. In larger machines, several VLSI chips may be needed.

1.3 BUS STRUCTURES

So far we have discussed the functional characteristics of individual parts that constitute a computer. To form an operational system they must be connected together in some organized way. There are many ways of doing this. We will consider three popular structures.

If a computer is to achieve a reasonable speed of operation, it must be organized in a *parallel* fashion. This means that all units can handle one full word of data at a given time. It also means that data transfers between units are to be done in parallel, which implies that a considerable number of wires (lines) are needed to establish the necessary connections. A collection of such wires, which have some common identity, is called a *bus*. In addition to the wires which carry the data, it is essential to have some lines for addressing and control purposes.

Figure 1.9 shows the simplest form of a *two-bus* structured computer. The processor interacts with the memory via a *memory bus*. Input and output functions are handled by means of an *I/O bus* so that data passes through the processor on route to the memory. In such configurations the I/O transfers are usually under direct control of the processor, which initiates transfers and monitors their progress until completion.

A somewhat different version of a two-bus structure is given in Figure 1.10. The relative positions of the processor and memory are reversed. Again, a

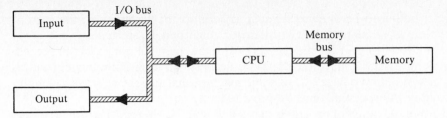

Figure 1.9 A two-bus structure.

memory bus exists for communication between them. However, I/O transfers are made directly to or from the memory. Since the memory has little in the way of circuitry capable of controlling such transfers, it is necessary to establish a different control mechanism. A standard technique is to provide *I/O channels* as part of the I/O equipment. An I/O channel has the necessary capability to control the transfers. In fact, it is a special-purpose processor, often called a peripheral processor. A typical procedure is to have the processor initiate a transfer by passing the required information to the I/O channel, which then takes over and controls the actual transfer.

We have already mentioned that a bus consists of a collection of distinct lines, serving different purposes. There are three main groupings of lines: *data*, *address*, and *control*. The data lines are used for transmission of data. Hence, the number of such lines corresponds to the number of bits in the word. To access data in the memory the address lines indicate its location. Control lines are used to indicate the direction of data transfer and to coordinate the timing of events during a transfer.

Many machines have several distinct buses, so that one could in fact treat them as *multiple-bus* machines. However, their operation is adequately represented by the two-bus examples, since the main reason for inclusion of additional buses is to improve the operating speed through further parallelism.

A significantly different structure, which has a *single bus*, is shown in Figure 1.11. All units are connected to this bus, so that it provides the sole means of interaction. Since the bus can be used for only one transfer at a time, it follows that only two units can be actively using the bus at any given instant. Bus control

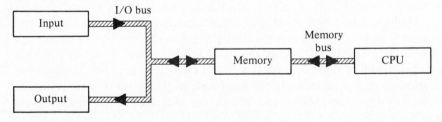

Figure 1.10 An alternative two-bus structure.

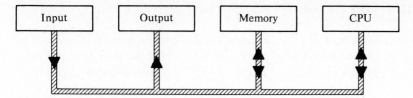

Figure 1.11 Single-bus structure.

lines are used to arbitrate among requesters for use of the bus. The main virtue of the single-bus structure is its low cost and flexibility for attaching peripheral devices. The trade-off is lower operating speed. It is not surprising that a single-bus structure is primarily found in small machines, namely, minicomputers and microcomputers.

Differences in bus structure have a pronounced effect on the performance of computers. Yet from the conceptual point of view (at least at this level of detail) they are not crucial in any functional description. Indeed, the fundamental principles of computer operation are essentially independent of the particular bus structure.

Transfer of information on a bus cannot, in general, be done at a speed directly comparable to the operating speed of all devices connected to the bus. Some electromechanical devices are relatively slow, for example, CRT terminals and printers. Others, such as disks and tapes, are considerably faster. Main memory and processors operate at electronic speeds, making them the fastest parts of a computer. Since all these devices must communicate with each other via a bus, it is necessary to provide an efficient transfer mechanism that is not constrained by the slow devices and can be used to smooth out the differences in timing among processors, memories, and external devices.

A common approach is to include *buffer registers* with the devices to hold the information during transfers. To illustrate this technique, consider the transfer of an encoded character from a processor to a character printer where it is to be printed. The processor effects the transfer by sending the character via the bus to the printer output buffer. Since the buffer is an electronic register, this transfer requires relatively little time. Once the buffer is loaded, the printer can start printing without further intervention by the processor. At this time the bus and the processor are no longer needed and can be released for other activity. The printer proceeds with the printing of the character in its buffer and is not available for further transfers until this process is completed. To summarize, buffer registers smooth out timing differences among the various processors, memories, and I/O devices that must communicate with each other in a complete computer system. Such registers prevent a high-speed processor from being locked to a slow I/O device during a sequence of data transfers. This allows the processor to switch rapidly from one device to another, interleaving its processing activity with data transfers to and from various devices.

1.4 DISTRIBUTED COMPUTING

Earlier in this chapter we briefly mentioned that computer systems have evolved from a structure centered on a single processing unit into multiple-processor configurations. Various processors may be linked by a communication network. Such a network is called a local area network if it is limited to a small geographical area (for example, within a building).

Many computer work loads can be partitioned into a set of tasks, some of which can be executed in parallel. If multiple processors are available, the total work load can be executed more rapidly by processing some tasks simultaneously. Consider, for example, a computer-aided design (CAD) environment. A computer system for such an environment may consist of one large computer and a number of work stations. Each work station is a computer in its own right with graphics input and output capability. A designer working at one of these stations generates a digitized description of a desired object using these graphics capabilities. The large computer provides facilities for simulation and test generation, which may require a large amount of computing power. Since the large computer is not involved in the time-consuming interactive graphics tasks, it can support a number of work stations.

The purpose of this book is to explain the fundamentals of the design and operation of various component units that exist in all computer systems, both centralized and decentralized, large and small. As well as discussing processors, input-output units, and storage devices, we will also introduce the basic principles of computer communication networks.

1.5 CONCLUDING REMARKS

The preceding discussion considered many aspects of computer structures and operation. Much of the terminology needed to deal with the subject was introduced quickly, and many important design concepts were only sketched superficially. The subsequent chapters will provide complete definitions of the terms used. It is hoped that this chapter has provided readers with an overall impression of what constitutes a computer and how it works. We fully realize that readers will not be able to place the various parts of this chapter into proper perspective until they have read the remainder of the book.

ADDRESSING METHODS AND MACHINE PROGRAM SEQUENCING

This chapter will consider the way in which programs are executed in a computer. The discussion is presented from the programmer's viewpoint. Chapter 1 introduced the general concept that both program instructions and data are stored in the main memory. We will study the ways in which sequences of instructions are brought from the main memory into the CPU (central processing unit) and executed to perform a given task. Most instructions specify operations to be performed on data located either in the main memory or in general-purpose registers in the CPU. We refer to such data, whether it be numeric or character data, as operands for these instructions.

The techniques that are in common use for addressing main memory locations and CPU registers will be discussed in general, followed by the specific example of the way that addressing is implemented in the PDP-11[1] computers. The PDP-11 is also used to illustrate instruction formats, program branching, subroutine entry and exit, and stack manipulation. A simple example of program-controlled I/O (input-output) for a teletypewriter is discussed. A number of programs at the assembly language level are used to illustrate the principles introduced.

2.1 MEMORY LOCATIONS, ADDRESSES, AND ENCODING OF INFORMATION

The main memory consists of a large number, usually many thousands, of storage *cells*, each of which can store a binary digit, or *bit*, having the value 0 or

---

[1]Manufactured by Digital Equipment Corporation (DEC).

1. Since 1 bit represents only a very small amount of information, bits are seldom handled individually. The usual approach is to deal with them in groups of fixed size. For this purpose, the main memory is organized so that a group of n bits can be stored or retrieved in a single basic operation. Each group of n bits is referred to as a *word* of information, and n is called the *word length*. As mentioned in Chapter 1, word lengths in microcomputers and minicomputers range from 8 to 32 bits, while large computers usually have 32 or more bits in a word.

To access the main memory to store or retrieve a single word of information, it is necessary to have distinct names or *addresses* for each word location. It is customary to use the numbers from 0 to *M-1* as the addresses of successive locations in a memory consisting of M words (see Figure 2.1).

The contents of memory locations can represent either instructions or operands. The latter may be either numbers or characters. Figure 2.2 illustrates three possible ways in which a 16-bit word can be used to represent information. Figure 2.2a shows the most straightforward way that a 16-bit pattern can be used to represent a signed integer. The leftmost bit, b_{15}, is called the *sign bit*. It is 0 for

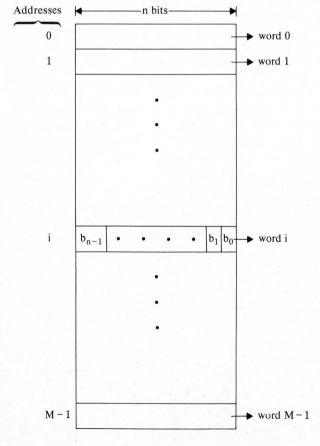

Figure 2.1 Main memory addresses.

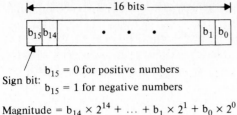

$b_{15} = 0$ for positive numbers

Sign bit: $b_{15} = 1$ for negative numbers

Magnitude $= b_{14} \times 2^{14} + \ldots + b_1 \times 2^1 + b_0 \times 2^0$

(*a*) A signed integer

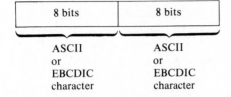

(*b*) Two characters

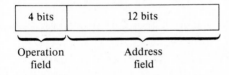

(*c*) A machine instruction

Figure 2.2 Examples of encoded information in a 16-bit word.

positive numbers and 1 for negative numbers. The magnitude of the number is determined from bits b_{14} through b_0 by the formula

$$\text{Magnitude} = b_{14} \times 2^{14} + \cdots + b_1 \times 2^1 + b_0 \times 2^0$$

Values represented in this way are said to be in the binary positional notation. The range of magnitudes that can be represented in this way is from 0 to $2^{15} - 1$ ($= 32,767$).

The above number representation is called the sign and magnitude representation. Two other binary number representations are frequently used. These are the 1's-complement and 2's-complement representations. In both these schemes, the representation of positive numbers is the same as in the sign and magnitude method. The differences among the three methods are in the ways in which negative numbers are represented. However, in all three schemes, the leftmost bit, which is b_{15} in our example, is the sign bit. Its interpretation always remains the same; that is, it is 0 for positive numbers and 1 for negative numbers.

The choice of number representation has a direct influence on the ease of implementation of the arithmetic operations by logic circuits in the CPU. In fact, the 2's-complement representation is the most suitable one to use. Details of number representations and their influence on the design of logic circuits for performing arithmetic operations will be discussed in Chapter 7.

In this chapter, we will use the decimal sign and magnitude representation when we wish to give numerical examples. Of course, these values are represented in the computer by binary patterns based on one of the schemes named above. The only technical detail about the binary representations that we will need in this chapter is that the sign bit is always the leftmost bit. This is true for 8-bit numbers, which we will have occasion to use, as well as for 16-bit numbers or numbers of any other length.

In addition to numbers, computers must be able to handle characters. Characters are used to denote letters of the alphabet, decimal digits, punctuation marks, etc. They are represented by codes that are usually 6 to 8 bits long. Figure 2.2*b* indicates how two characters in either the ASCII or EBCDIC codes can be stored in a 16-bit word. These codes are described in Appendix D.

A main memory word can also be used to encode an instruction. In this case, a part of the word specifies the operation to be performed. Other parts may be used to specify operand addresses. It is customary to use the name *field* for each of these parts. An example of a format that a 16-bit machine instruction might have is given in Figure 2.2*c*. The 4-bit operation field can encode $2^4(=16)$ distinct instructions, and the 12-bit address field can encode an address in the range 0 through $2^{12} - 1 (= 4095)$.

In general, it is not possible to determine whether a main memory location contains an instruction or an operand merely by inspecting its contents, because a given binary pattern may be interpreted according to any of the formats given in Figure 2.2. The additional information required is available inside the CPU. The interpretation of a given word is dependent upon the state, or the mode of operation of the CPU at the time the word is fetched from the main memory. It was pointed out in Chapter 1 that one of the important elements inside the CPU is the program counter (PC) (see Figure 1.8). All memory words that are pointed at by the PC are interpreted as instructions. Memory words whose addresses are specified by the instructions are interpreted as operands. Whether an operand is a character or a numeric data item is determined by the operation field of the instruction.

2.2 MAIN MEMORY OPERATIONS

To execute an instruction, it is necessary for the CPU control circuits to cause the transfer of the instruction from the main memory to the CPU. It is also necessary to move operands and results between the main memory and the CPU. Thus there is an obvious need for two basic operations involving the main memory, namely, *Fetch* (or *Read*) and *Store* (or *Write*).

The Fetch operation transfers the contents of a specific main memory location to the CPU. The word in the main memory remains unchanged. To start the Fetch operation, the CPU must send the address of the desired location to the main memory.

The Store operation transfers a word of information from the CPU to a specific main memory location, destroying the former contents of that location.

Again, as in the case of a Fetch, the CPU must send the address of the desired location to the main memory.

The details of the hardware implementation of the above operations will be treated in Chapters 4, 5, and 8. In this chapter, we are taking the programmer's viewpoint. Thus we will concentrate on the logical handling of instructions and operands. Specific hardware components, such as CPU registers, will be discussed only to the extent necessary to aid the reader in understanding the execution of machine instructions and programs.

2.3 INSTRUCTION FORMATS AND INSTRUCTION SEQUENCING

A typical program involves a number of functionally different steps to be performed. It is reasonable to assume that different classes of instructions should be available. We might roughly describe the classes as corresponding to:

- Data transfers between the main memory and the CPU registers
- Arithmetic and logic operations on data
- Program sequencing and control
- I/O transfers

We will begin by discussing possible formats for instructions in the first two classes.

The operation of adding two numbers is a fundamental capability in any computer. We will use an Add instruction to illustrate some possibilities for instruction formats. From the programmer's viewpoint, the simplest form of addition is $C \leftarrow A + B$, where A, B, and C are the names of three variables. Let the values of these variables be stored in distinct memory locations. We will associate the variable names A, B, and C with the addresses of these locations. The above expression then has the following meaning. The summands in memory locations A and B are to be fetched from the memory and transferred into the CPU where they will be added in the ALU (arithmetic and logic unit). Then, the resulting sum is to be stored into memory location C.

If the complete process is to be specified by a single machine instruction, three address fields, specifying A, B, and C, will be needed, together with the operation field that specifies the addition operation. This *three-address* instruction can be represented symbolically as

Add   A,B,C

A problem with this approach is that the inclusion of three address fields in an instruction may require a large number of bits. If A, B, and C are arbitrary addresses in the memory space 0 to $2^m - 1$, then m bits are needed to specify each address. Therefore, the instruction must contain $3m$ bits for addressing purposes, in addition to the bits needed to denote the operation to be performed.

An alternative approach is to perform the desired calculation by using a sequence of instructions, each of which requires fewer than three memory address fields. Suppose we use only two addresses. If they are used in an Add instruction to specify the two operands A and B, an implicit assumption will need to be made about where the sum is to be sent. A number of computers have *two-address* Add instructions that send the sum back into memory to one of the operand locations, thus destroying the original operand. The instruction

Add   A,B

performs the operation B ← A + B. A single, two-address Add instruction cannot be used to solve our original problem, which was to add the contents of locations A and B, destroying neither of them, and place the sum in location C. However, the problem can be solved through the use of another two-address instruction that moves the contents of one memory location into another location. The desired instruction

Move   B,C

performs the operation C ← B. Thus the operation C ← A + B can be performed by executing the two instructions

Move   B,C

Add   A,C

The next possibility is to consider using only *one-address* instructions. Of course, since addition is a two-operand operation, an implicit assumption must be made regarding the location of one of the operands as well as the result. A general-purpose CPU register, usually called an *accumulator*, may be used for this purpose. The machine instruction

Add   A

then means add the contents of memory location A to the contents of the accumulator and place the sum into the accumulator. Let us also introduce the one-address instructions

Load   A

and
Store   A

Execution of the Load instruction moves the contents of memory location A into the accumulator, and execution of the Store instruction moves the contents of the accumulator into memory location A. The operation C ← A + B can then be performed by executing the sequence of instructions

Load   A

Add   B

Store   C

Many computers have a number of general-purpose CPU registers, each of which can be used as an accumulator. If there are 8 (or 16) registers, then 3 (or

4) bits will be needed in a field of an instruction to address the register that is to take part in the operation. This is considerably less than the number of bits needed to address a location in the main memory. Let R_i represent a CPU general-purpose register. Then, the instructions

$$\text{Load} \quad A,R_i$$

$$\text{Store} \quad A,R_i$$

and $\qquad\qquad\qquad$ $\text{Add} \quad A,R_i$

are generalizations of the earlier Load, Store, and Add instructions of the single-accumulator case. In particular, execution of

$$\text{Load} \quad A,R_i$$

moves the contents of memory location A into register R_i. Execution of

$$\text{Store} \quad A,R_i$$

moves the contents of register R_i into memory location A, and execution of

$$\text{Add} \quad A,R_i$$

adds the contents of memory location A to the contents of register R_i and then places the result in register R_i. This type of instruction, in which one address always refers to a location in the main memory, and the other, shorter address always refers to a CPU register, has a format intermediate to the one- and two-address formats discussed earlier. Because of this property, it is often called a *1½-address* format. Machines with multiple CPU registers also include instruction formats that permit operations among the registers themselves. Thus

$$\text{Add} \quad R_i,R_j$$

adds the contents of register R_i to those of register R_j and places the answer in register R_j.

A number of general-purpose registers are often used in computers with two-address instruction formats. In general, the registers improve processing efficiency by reducing the number of main memory accesses required when a particular data item is used repeatedly in a computation. In machines that have the two-address format, there is usually a way to specify a register instead of a main memory location in either of the address fields. Thus the instructions

$$\text{Move} \quad A,R_i$$

and $\qquad\qquad\qquad$ $\text{Move} \quad R_i,A$

achieve the same results as the instructions

$$\text{Load} \quad A,R_i$$

and $\qquad\qquad\qquad$ $\text{Store} \quad A,R_i$

in the more restrictive 1½-address format discussed earlier.

We have discussed instructions that use three-, two-, and one-address fields. It is also possible to use instructions where the locations of all operands are defined implicitly. They depend upon the use of a method for storing operands in what is called a *pushdown stack*, which will be discussed in Section 3.6. Such instructions are sometimes referred to as *zero-address* instructions.

2.3.1 Instruction Execution and Straight-Line Sequencing

In the above discussion of instruction formats, the various possibilities have been illustrated with the aid of the simple task $C \leftarrow A + B$. A possible program for this task as it appears in the main memory of a computer with a two-address instruction format and a number of general-purpose CPU registers is shown in Figure 2.3. The four instructions of the program are placed in successive memory locations with increasing addresses, starting at location i, in the order in which they are to be executed.

Let us consider in detail how this program is executed. The CPU contains a register called the *program counter* (PC) that contains the address of the instruction to be executed. To begin the execution of a program, the address of its first instruction (i in our example) must be placed into the PC. The CPU control circuits automatically proceed to fetch and execute instructions, one at a time, and in the order of increasing addresses. While each instruction is executed, the PC is updated to point to the next instruction. This is called *straight-line sequencing*. The execution of a Halt instruction stops the automatic fetching of further instructions.

Execution of a given instruction consists of a two-phase procedure. In the first phase, called *instruction fetch*, the instruction is fetched from the main memory location whose address is in the PC. This instruction is placed in the instruction register (IR) in the CPU. At the start of the second phase, called *instruction execute*, the operation field of the instruction in the IR is examined to determine which operation is to be performed. The specified operation is then performed by the CPU. This may involve fetching operands from the main memory to the CPU, performing an arithmetic or logic operation, and storing the result into the main memory. Sometime during this two-phase procedure, the contents of the PC are updated to point at the next instruction. In our example, the contents of the PC are incremented by 1. Therefore, when the execute phase of an instruction is completed, the PC contains the address of the next instruction, and a new instruction fetch phase can begin.

2.3.2 Branching

Now consider a program for adding a list of n numbers. A generalization of the program in Figure 2.3 leads to the program outlined in Figure 2.4a. The addresses of the memory locations containing the n numbers are symbolically given as NUM_1, NUM_2, . . . , NUM_n, and the resulting sum is to be placed in

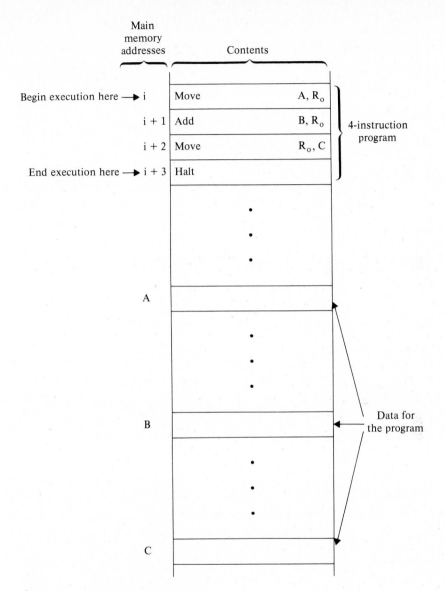

Figure 2.3 A program for $C \leftarrow A + B$.

memory location SUM. Instead of using a long list of Add instructions, it is possible to place a single Add instruction in a program loop and arrange to have it executed the required number of times. This is illustrated in Figure 2.4b.

The fundamental idea in program loops is to cause a straight-line sequence of instructions to be executed repeatedly. The number of repetitions, which

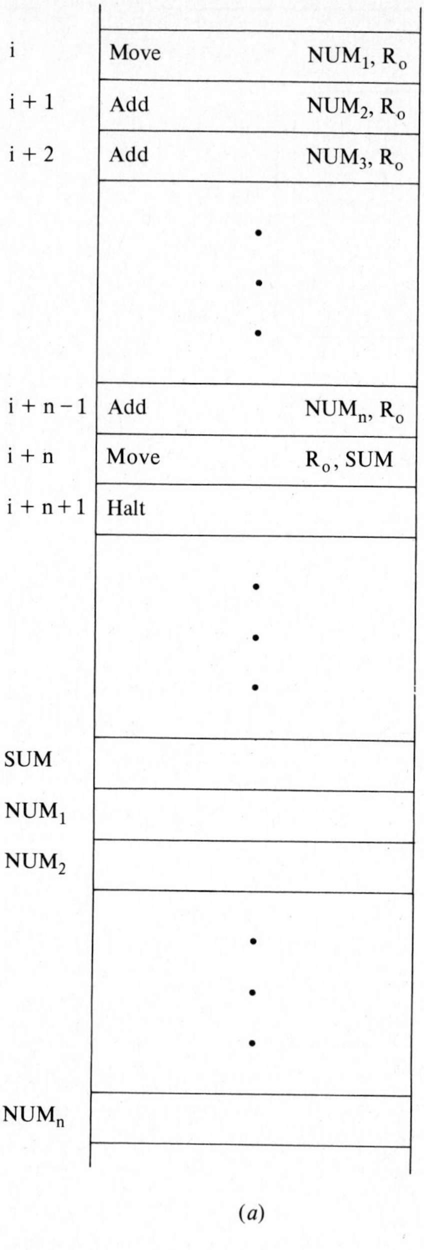

i	Move	NUM_1, R_o
i + 1	Add	NUM_2, R_o
i + 2	Add	NUM_3, R_o
		.
		.
		.
i + n − 1	Add	NUM_n, R_o
i + n	Move	R_o, SUM
i + n + 1	Halt	
		.
		.
		.
SUM		
NUM_1		
NUM_2		
		.
		.
		.
NUM_n		

(a)

Figure 2.4 Two programs for adding n numbers.

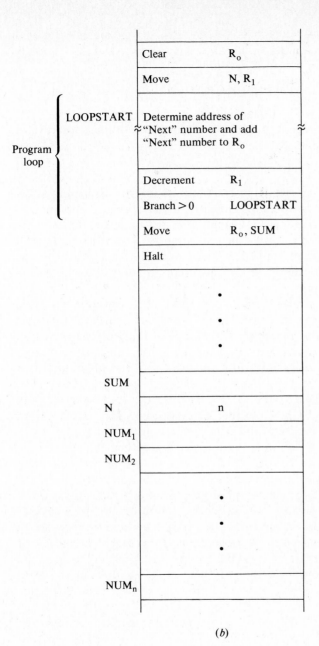

(b)

obviously depends on the problem, must be controlled by means of additional instructions. In the above example, register R_1 is used as a counter. It is initially loaded with the value n from memory location N. The instruction

Decrement R_1

decrements the contents of R_1 by 1 each time through the loop.

We now introduce the concept of a branch instruction. To cause a return to the first instruction of the loop, the conditional branch instruction

Branch>0   LOOPSTART

is used. The effect of executing such an instruction is as follows. Branching takes place to the instruction at the location indicated if the specified condition is fulfilled; otherwise, straight-line sequencing of instructions continues. The mechanics of causing a branch during the execution of a conditional branch instruction are simple. If it is determined that branching is to take place, the PC is loaded with the address named in the instruction; otherwise, the PC is incremented in the usual way.

Branch conditions are usually related to the result of an arithmetic or logic operation. In our example, the desired condition is that the result of the most recent arithmetic operation is greater than 0. Since the Decrement instruction immediately precedes the conditional branch instruction, this means that a branch to LOOPSTART occurs as long as the contents of R_1 remain greater than 0. After the loop has been executed n times, R_1 will have been decremented to 0, and the branch to LOOPSTART will not occur. Instead, the next instruction moves the final result from R_0 into the memory location SUM, and program execution stops with the execution of the Halt instruction.

The capability for testing conditions, and subsequently choosing one of a set of alternative ways to continue computation, has many more applications than just loop control. This capability is reflected in the instruction sets of all computers and is fundamental to the programming of most nontrivial tasks.

Until now, we have considered only instructions where operand addresses are explicitly given within the instruction. This simple addressing mechanism means that the address field of the Add instruction in the unspecified block of instructions in Figure 2.4b must be modified in successive passes through the loop. It is possible to do this by adding 1 to the address field of the Add instruction. This is required if a single Add instruction must reference successive entries in the list of numbers. The approach of directly modifying address fields of instructions is a bad programming practice. It leads to difficulties in program debugging and initialization. The problem is resolved through the introduction of different schemes for specifying addresses of operands. These schemes are called *addressing modes*. They are intended to provide more flexibility in the way in which operand addresses are specified. With some of these schemes, it is possible to enable a given instruction to refer to different operands when it is executed a number of times. The instruction itself is not changed. The next section will examine some of the important possibilities in detail.

2.4 ADDRESSING MODES

In Section 2.3, we used only one mode for addressing operands, namely, the absolute mode. Let us define this mode as:

> **Absolute mode** The address of the location of the operand is given explicitly as a part of the instruction.

We have actually used two versions of this mode in our examples. These are memory absolute mode, where the operand is in a main memory location, and register mode, where the operand is in one of the CPU registers. We should mention that the term "direct" is often used as an alternative to absolute.

Next, we will consider other important addressing modes, and indicate how they can be used in the loop program of Figure 2.4b.

> **Immediate mode** The operand is given explicitly in the instruction.

This mode is particularly useful in specifying address and data constants in programs. For example, the instruction

$$\text{Move} \quad 200 \text{ (immediate)}, \text{ } R_0$$

places the value 200 in register R_0.

In this section, we will use subscript words to specify all addressing modes other than the absolute mode. The absolute mode will continue to be indicated by stating the address of the location of the operand. Of course, at the instruction encoding level, the addressing mode information will need to be specified by some bit positions in the instruction. An example of how this can be done will be described in Section 2.5.

In the definition of the next two modes, and in subsequent discussions, we will refer to the address of the location of the operand as its *effective address*.

> **Indirect mode** The effective address of the operand is in the register or main memory location whose address appears in the instruction.

Figure 2.5 gives examples of indirect addressing. The execution of the Add instruction in Figure 2.5a starts by fetching the contents of location A from the main memory. This value, B, is the effective address, which is then used to fetch the desired operand from the memory. Finally, the operand is added to the contents of register R_0. Similarly, in Figure 2.5b the operand is accessed indirectly through register R_j.

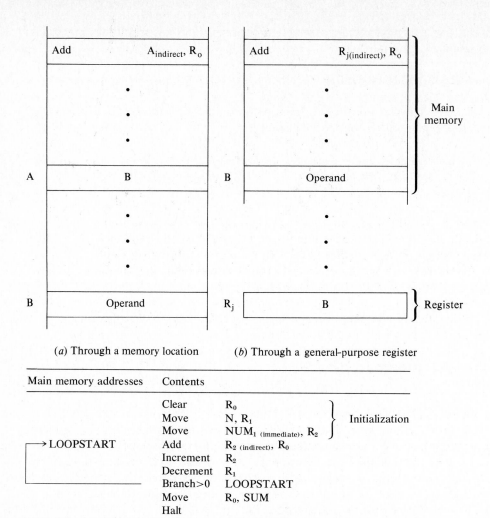

(a) Through a memory location   *(b)* Through a general-purpose register

Main memory addresses	Contents		
	Clear	R_0	⎫
	Move	N, R_1	Initialization
	Move	NUM_1 (immediate), R_2	⎭
→LOOPSTART	Add	R_2 (indirect), R_0	
	Increment	R_2	
	Decrement	R_1	
	Branch>0	LOOPSTART	
	Move	R_0, SUM	
	Halt		

(c) The use of indirect addressing in the program of Figure 2.4*b*

Figure 2.5 Indirect addressing.

Let us now return to the loop program in Figure 2.4*b*. The indirect addressing mode can be used in accessing successive numbers in the list, which are used as operands in the addition operation, resulting in the program shown in Figure 2.5*c*. Register R_2 is used as a *pointer* to numbers in the list; that is, the operands are accessed indirectly through R_2. The first two instructions in the loop implement the unspecified instruction block starting at LOOPSTART in Figure 2.4*b*. The initialization section of the program clears R_0 to 0, moves the counter value *n* into R_1, and places the address value NUM_1 into R_2, using the immediate addressing mode. The first time through the loop, the Add instruction fetches the operand at location NUM_1 into the CPU and adds it to R_0. The Increment instruction then adds 1 to the contents of the pointer R_2, so that it will contain the address value NUM_2 when the Add instruction is executed in the second pass through the loop. It is easily seen that R_2 is incremented so that it contains the address values NUM_3, NUM_4, etc., when the Add instruction is executed in successive passes through the loop.

The next addressing mode that we will discuss can also provide the addressing flexibility required in the addition loop example.

Index mode The effective address of the operand is generated by adding an *index* value to the address given in the instruction.

The index value, or simply the index, is usually contained in a CPU register. In some computers, one register is dedicated solely to this purpose. It is called the *index register* and is involved implicitly when the index mode is specified. Figure 2.6a illustrates the generation of an effective address by the index mode. In many computers, any one of the general-purpose CPU registers can contain the index value. In such a case, the register must be named explicitly in the instruction. In the process of generating the effective address, neither the index value nor the address in the instruction is changed.

Figure 2.6b illustrates the use of indexed addressing in our addition loop example. Register R_2 is used as the index register and is initially set to 0. It is incremented by 1 after the Add instruction each time through the loop. Therefore, the first time through the loop, the effective address generated by the Add instruction is NUM_1. In subsequent passes, the effective address will be $NUM_1 + 1$, $NUM_1 + 2$, . . . , etc., since R_2 is incremented by 1 each time through the loop. The power of indexed addressing, in general, is that the index can be changed arbitrarily, not just incremented by 1 as in our example here.

The addressing modes defined in this section have been illustrated by simple examples. This has allowed us to introduce the basic concepts without a need to discuss the details of their implementation in a particular computer. The various possible instruction formats, and straight-line and loop sequencing, have also been discussed in earlier sections without reference to any specific computer.

At this point, it is useful to examine the implementation of instructions and addressing modes in a specific computer. We will use the PDP-11 minicomputer for this purpose. However, it should be emphasized that the concepts discussed in the remainder of this chapter are general in nature.

2.5 THE PDP-11 ADDRESSING MODES AND INSTRUCTIONS

The PDP-11 is a 16-bit word-length minicomputer with eight CPU registers. The names R_0, R_1, . . . , R_7, will be used for these registers. Each of them contains 16 bits. Only registers R_0 through R_5 are used as truly general-purpose registers; R_7 is the PC, and the use of register R_6 will be explained later.

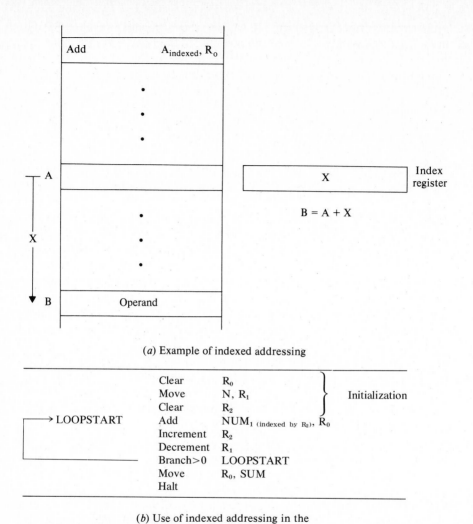

(a) Example of indexed addressing

Clear	R_0	
Move	N, R_1	Initialization
Clear	R_2	
→ LOOPSTART Add	NUM$_1$ (indexed by R_2), R_0	
Increment	R_2	
Decrement	R_1	
Branch>0	LOOPSTART	
Move	R_0, SUM	
Halt		

(b) Use of indexed addressing in the
program of Figure 2.4b

Figure 2.6 Indexed addressing.

The main memory is organized in 16-bit words. Each word can be interpreted as two separate 8-bit *bytes*. To facilitate referencing of individual bytes, each byte location is assigned a distinct address, as shown in Figure 2.7. Successive words are given the even-address values 0, 2, 4, etc. The word at an even-numbered address i consists of the bytes at addresses i and $i + 1$. The low-order byte of a word occupies the location with the even address i, and the high-order byte occupies location $i + 1$. Addresses are 16 bits long, so that up to $65,536 (= 2^{16})$ bytes or $32,768 (= 2^{15})$ words can be addressed. Instructions in the PDP-11 can deal with operands that consist of either one byte or one word. The operation field of an instruction specifies the operand length.

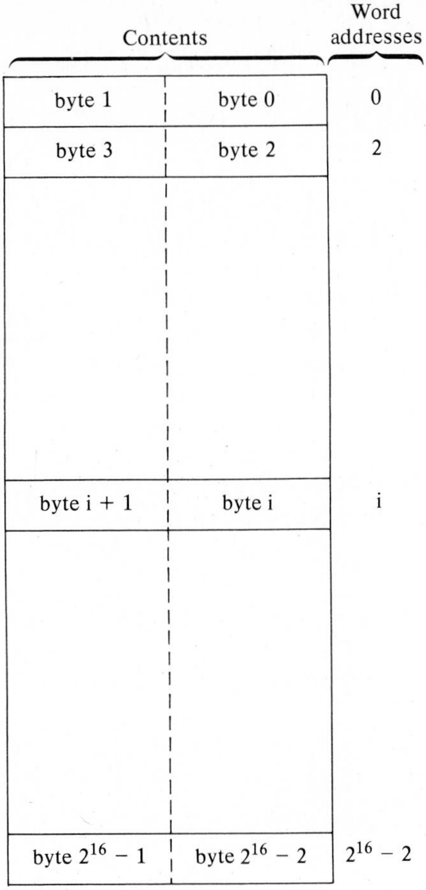

Word
Contents   addresses

Contents		Word addresses
byte 1	byte 0	0
byte 3	byte 2	2
byte i + 1	byte i	i
byte $2^{16} - 1$	byte $2^{16} - 2$	$2^{16} - 2$

Figure 2.7 Map of addressable locations in the PDP-11.

2.5.1 Addressing

The PDP-11 has a number of addressing modes, including those described in Section 2.4. There are both one- and two-operand instruction formats. We will begin our discussion of addressing in the context of the one-operand format, shown in Figure 2.8a. The instruction is divided into two fields. Bits b_6 to b_{15} specify the operation to be performed and are hence called the OP-code field. Bits b_0 to b_5 constitute the address field. This short 6-bit field obviously cannot contain a full 16-bit address. The way that this field is interpreted to generate a 16-bit address will be discussed in the remainder of this section.

The detailed interpretation of the 6-bit address field is shown in Figure 2.8b. The rightmost 3-bit field names one of the eight registers R_0 through R_7. We will refer to this register as R_n. The other 3-bit field specifies the addressing mode. Thus there are eight possible modes. They are summarized in Table 2.1. The table is organized into five columns, indicating the 3-bit code, its decimal equivalent as a convenient abbreviation, the name of the mode, the PDP-11 assembler syntax, and the operational meaning for each mode. The assembler

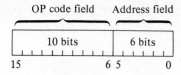

(a) One-operand instruction format

Indirect bit

(b) Address field   **Figure 2.8** The 6-bit address field in PDP-11 instructions.

syntax column indicates the way in which the addressing mode is represented by a sequence of alphanumeric characters in the assembly language of the PDP-11. We will discuss this computer language later when we introduce example programs. In the last column, the square-brackets notation, [L], means the contents of the location whose address is L. The address L can be that of a main memory location or a register.

The organization of Table 2.1 indicates that bits b_5 and b_4 specify four fundamental addressing modes. Determination of the effective address of an

Table 2.1 PDP-11 addressing modes

$b_5b_4b_3$	Decimal equivalent	Name	Assembler syntax	Meaning
0 0 0	0	Register	Rn	$A_{effective} = R_n$ (that is, Operand = $[R_n]$)
0 1 0	2	Autoincrement	(Rn)+	$A_{effective} = [R_n]$; Increment R_n
1 0 0	4	Autodecrement	−(Rn)	Decrement R_n; $A_{effective} = [R_n]$
1 1 0	6	Index	X(Rn)	Fetch X; Increment PC; $A_{effective} = X + [R_n]$
0 0 1	1	Register indirect	@Rn	$A_{effective} = [R_n]$
0 1 1	3	Autoincrement indirect	@(Rn)+	$A_{effective} = [[R_n]]$; Increment R_n
1 0 1	5	Autodecrement indirect	@−(Rn)	Decrement R_n; $A_{effective} = [[R_n]]$
1 1 1	7	Index indirect	@X(Rn)	Fetch X; Increment PC; $A_{effective} = [X + [R_n]]$

operand can be viewed as follows. The bit pattern in b_5 and b_4 specifies how to obtain an address value. If bit $b_3 = 0$, this value is the effective address of the operand, denoted $A_{\text{effective}}$ in the table; but if $b_3 = 1$, the value obtained is the address of a location that contains the effective address. Thus bit b_3 is used to designate indirect addressing. Let us now consider the four fundamental addressing modes in detail.

Register mode. When $b_3 = 0$, the operand is the contents of register R_n. In the indirect version of this mode, that is, when $b_3 = 1$, the register R_n contains the effective address of the operand.

Autoincrement mode. The effective address is in R_n. After the contents of R_n have been used to fetch the operand, the register is automatically incremented. If the operand is a byte, as specified in the OP-code field of the instruction, register R_n is incremented by 1. If the operand is a word, R_n is incremented by 2. In the indirect case, the effective address is contained in the memory location pointed at by R_n before incrementing is performed, and R_n is always incremented by 2.

Autodecrement mode. The contents of R_n are decremented and then used as the effective address. For byte operands, R_n is decremented by 1; for word operands, R_n is decremented by 2. In the indirect version, the effective address is contained in the memory location pointed at by R_n after it has been decremented, and R_n is always decremented by 2.

Index mode. The effective address is generated by adding the contents of R_n to the value X which is contained in the word immediately following the OP-code word. If indirection is specified, it is performed after indexing.

The autoincrement and autodecrement addressing modes provide a simple mechanism for referencing a list of data items in successive word or byte locations in the memory on successive passes through a program loop. For example, we can eliminate the Increment instruction in the program in Figure 2.6*b* by using the autoincrement mode in the Add instruction. A complete PDP-11 program for this task will be given in a later section. These modes are also useful in implementing the stack data structure, which will be discussed in Section 2.7. The autoincrement indirect mode can be used to reference a list of addresses of data items instead of the data items themselves. An example of this is shown in Section 2.8 where a list of addresses is passed to a subroutine as parameters from a main program. The autodecrement indirect mode does not seem to have any obvious, important uses. Indeed, an extensive study [2.1] has found that it is seldom, if ever, used in practice. As we shall see in Chapter 3, this addressing mode is not included in the VAX-11 addressing modes, which were designed based upon the experience gained from the use of the PDP-11.

An example of a one-operand instruction using the index mode is shown in Figure 2.9. Note that the instruction occupies two consecutive memory word locations. Before the instruction is fetched into the CPU, the PC points at the first word of the instruction. After this word is fetched into the IR, the PC is

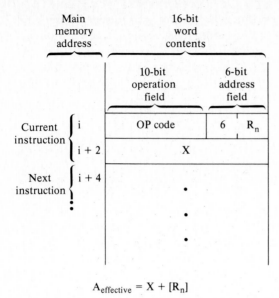

$$A_{\text{effective}} = X + [R_n]$$

Figure 2.9 Indexed addressing in the PDP-11.

incremented by 2 to point at the second word, which contains the value X. Similarly, after fetching X, the PC is incremented again to point at the first word of the next instruction. Upon completion of this step, the contents of register R_n are added to the value X to generate the effective address of the operand. If X is interpreted as the starting address of a list of data items, then the index mode can be used to access an individual item by arranging for R_n to contain its displacement from the starting address. Another important use for the index mode is where the program counter is used as the index register. This will be described in the next section. As in the case of the autoincrement indirect mode, the index indirect mode can be used for accessing individual operands via a list of their addresses.

2.5.2 The Role of the Program Counter in Addressing

The PC is actually register R_7 in the PDP-11 computer. When it is specified as the register R_n in the address field, some interesting and useful addressing actions result. Since we have already discussed all eight possible addressing modes, this section does not introduce anything that cannot be deduced from Table 2.1. We are merely highlighting the features that result when $R_n = PC$. Of course, these features are not accidental; they represent a central idea in the implementation of the addressing modes in the PDP-11.

Immediate mode results from the autoincrement mode with $R_n = PC$. After the first word of an instruction has been fetched, the PC points at the following word. Since the contents of the specified register, in this case the PC, are used as the address of the operand in the autoincrement mode, the second word of the instruction is the immediate operand. The PC is again increment by 2, so that it points at the next word after the immediate operand. The PC is incremented by 2 whether the immediate operand is a word or a byte.

Absolute mode results from the autoincrement indirect mode with R_n = PC. By adding a further level of indirection to the immediate mode, the second word of the instruction is interpreted as the effective address of the operand. This implements absolute addressing as defined earlier.

Relative mode results from the index mode with R_n = PC. The effective address of the operand is the sum of the value X and the contents of the PC. This means that X represents the displacement in bytes from the word immediately following X to the location of the operand. In other words, the memory address of the operand is given relative to the instruction. Figure 2.10 shows a specific example of this addressing mode. Note that X can be negative as well as positive. Therefore, operands with addresses lower than that of the instruction, as well as those with higher addresses, can be specified.

Relative indirect mode results from the index indirect mode with R_n = PC. The memory location containing the address of the operand is specified relative to the instruction.

Table 2.2 summarizes these four addressing modes. Note that special assembly language syntax is used for them. The use of the PC as R_n in the

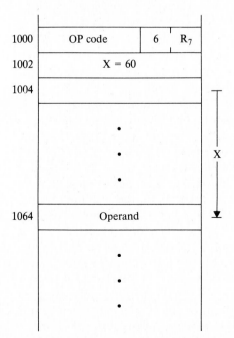

Figure 2.10 An example of relative addressing in the PDP-11.

Table 2.2 PDP–11 addressing modes with R_n = PC

$b_5b_4b_3$	Decimal equivalent	Name	Assembler syntax	Meaning
0 1 0	2	Immediate (autoincrement)	#n	$A_{effective}$ = [PC]; Increment PC (that is, operand n follows instruction)
0 1 1	3	Absolute (autoincrement indirect)	@#A	$A_{effective}$ = [[PC]]; Increment PC (that is, $A_{effective}$, which is A, follows instruction)
1 1 0	6	Relative (index)	A	Fetch X; Increment PC; $A_{effective}$ = X + [PC] (that is, $A_{effective}$ is A. It is specified relative to [PC] by displacement X in word following instruction)
1 1 1	7	Relative indirect (index indirect)	@A	Fetch X; Increment PC; $A_{effective}$ = [X + [PC]] (that is, the address A of location containing $A_{effective}$ is specified relative to [PC] by displacement X in word following instruction)

register and register indirect modes is of limited usefulness. Neither version of the autodecrement mode should ever be used with R_n = PC.

In terms of our earlier general discussion of indexed addressing, the value X involved in the PDP-11 index mode is "the address given in the instruction" and R_n contains the "index value." This is the correct viewpoint when R_n is one of the registers R_0 through R_5, and its contents are used to index into a list of operands whose first item is stored in memory location X. However, when R_n is specified as R_7, it is more natural to take the viewpoint that X is an index or displacement value. It gives the location of an operand relative to the location of the instruction. Because of the frequent use of this addressing mode in PDP-11 programs, most of the written material on the PDP-11 refers to the value X in the index mode as the index value. Of course, the mechanics of generating the effective address of an operand are the same, regardless of the viewpoint taken. Strictly speaking, the contents of R_n should always be considered as the index value because they can be changed. The value X is fixed at the time the program is written, and does not change during execution. We will take the informal approach in this chapter and use the viewpoint that is most natural in the context at hand.

2.5.3 Some PDP-11 Instructions and a Simple Program

This section, and following sections, will discuss some basic aspects of the PDP-11 instruction set. We will introduce instructions and their formats through simple examples. Some aspects of the PDP-11 assembly language will also be described. A complete listing of the PDP-11 instruction set is given in Appendix B.

Let us start by introducing the two-operand instructions that have the format shown in Figure 2.11*a*. The abbreviation src is used to denote the effective address of the first operand, called the *source* operand. Correspondingly, dst is used to denote the effective address of the second operand, called the *destination* operand. The values of src and dst are generated by using the information in the corresponding 6-bit fields of the instruction, as indicated in Figure 2.8*b* and Tables 2.1 and 2.2.

Figure 2.11*b* shows an example of the Add instruction. It has the OP code ADD and performs the action

$$\text{dst} \leftarrow [\text{src}] + [\text{dst}]$$

The source operand, 17, is contained in the word immediately after the OP-code word and is accessed by the immediate addressing mode; that is, the autoincrement mode, with $R_n = PC$, is specified by the src field. The destination operand is contained in register R_3, accessed by the register mode with $R_n = R_3$, as shown in the dst field.

The same format is used to provide a Subtract instruction, which has the OP code SUB and performs the action

$$\text{dst} \leftarrow [\text{dst}] - [\text{src}]$$

Another useful instruction in the two-operand format is the Move instruction that performs the action

$$\text{dst} \leftarrow [\text{src}]$$

The OP code for this instruction is denoted as MOV.

If we now specify a Halt instruction, denoted by HALT (a zero-address format), we can write a PDP-11 program for the task $C \leftarrow A + B$ that was discussed in Section 2.3.1. Figure 2.3 showed that the three-instruction sequence

$$\text{Move} \quad A, R_0$$

$$\text{Add} \quad B, R_0$$

$$\text{Move} \quad R_0, C$$

can be used to perform the task in a machine with a two-address instruction format.

A PDP-11 program for this task is given in Figure 2.12. In this program, operands A, B, and C are addressed using the relative mode. The first Move

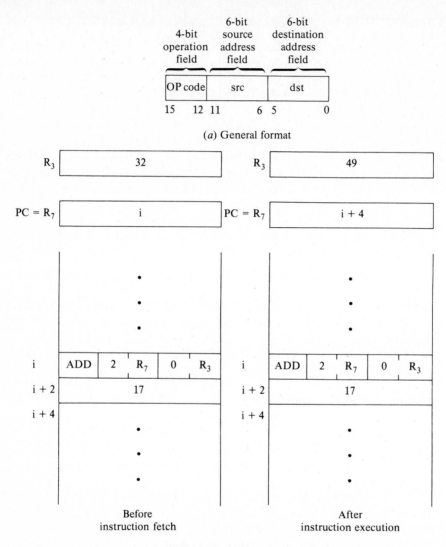

(a) General format

(b) Example of the Add instruction

Figure 2.11 The two-operand instruction format in the PDP-11.

instruction occupies two words, because the generation of the source address requires a relative displacement value. At the time that the source address is calculated, the PC contains 1204. Therefore, the displacement value must be -54, so that the operand address value will be $1204 - 54 = 1150$.

The Add instruction and the second Move instruction both use the same addressing modes as the first Move instruction. The reader is encouraged to check that the displacement values -56 and 988 are correct.

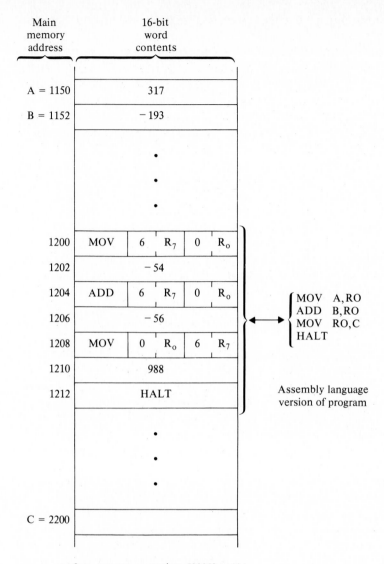

After program execution, [2200] = 124

Figure 2.12 A PDP-11 program for $C \leftarrow A + B$.

2.5.4 The PDP-11 Assembly Language

Machine instructions in computers are represented by patterns of 0s and 1s. Such patterns are awkward to deal with when discussing or preparing programs. Therefore we use symbols to represent the patterns. For example, in the case of the Move and Add instructions, we use the symbolic names MOV and ADD to represent the corresponding OP-code patterns. Similarly, we use the notation Rn instead of a 3-bit pattern when specifying the general-purpose register R_n in a program. A complete set of such symbolic names together with some rules for their use constitutes a programming language, generally referred to as an *assembly language*. The symbolic names are called *mnemonics*. The set of rules for using the mnemonics in the specification of complete instructions and programs is called the *syntax* of the language.

Let us return to the program in Figure 2.12. The first move instruction is written in assembly language form as

MOV   A,RO

The mnemonic MOV represents the 4-bit OP code. It must be followed by at least one blank space. Then the information that specifies the address of the source operand is given. The assembly language formats for specifying the different addressing modes are included in Tables 2.1 and 2.2. The source address is followed by a comma. The information that determines the address of the destination operand then directly follows the comma. The figure gives the assembly language statements for all four instructions of the example program.

Programs written in an assembly language can be automatically translated into a sequence of machine instructions by a special program called an *assembler*. The assembler is similar to any other program in that it is stored as a sequence of machine instructions in the main memory of the computer. A user program is usually entered via a terminal and stored either in the main memory or on a magnetic disk or tape. At this point, the user program is simply a set of lines of alphanumeric characters, in ASCII or EBCDIC coding. When the assembler program is executed, it reads the user program, analyzes it, then generates the desired machine language program. We will not give any further discussion of how the assembler program does this but instead will present a few more aspects of the assembly language itself.

The four assembly language statements in Figure 2.12 do not contain enough information to generate the corresponding machine language program. A complete assembly language program usually provides information regarding the desired location in memory of the machine language program and its data. Figure 2.13 shows a complete program for our example. In addition to the four statements that correspond to the machine instructions, there are six *assembler commands*. They provide the necessary information about the memory locations to be used for storing the program and its data. The first of these associates the constant 2200 with the symbol C. The next assembler command, . =, specifies the starting memory address 1150. The following .WORD command performs two functions. It associates the label A with the address 1150 and specifies that an initial value of 317 is to be placed in that word location. The next command associates the label B with the address of the succeeding word location, 1152, and gives its initial value as −193. The fifth command in this block declares a new starting address, 1200. Therefore the succeeding block of four instructions is assembled beginning at memory word location 1200. Finally, the .END command indicates the end of the program.

Until now in this chapter, we have used the decimal number representation for convenience when referring to numerical quantities. However, several other number representations are used in programming. In addition to binary, two other frequently used representations are octal and hexadecimal, which will be described later. It is necessary for the programmer to specify the representation used. In the example of Figure 2.13, and in the PDP-11 assembly language in general, decimal numbers are indicated by a "." following the number.

We should emphasize that when using the relative adressing mode, the value of the displacement, for example, -54 in the first instruction of our example, need not be explicitly specified in the assembly language program. Such displacements are computed by the assembler program based on its knowledge of the location of the instruction and the address of the operand involved.

In the assembly language program examples that are used in the remainder of this book, we will not always include the assembler command statements unless they are essential for an understanding of the points being illustrated. The reader should be aware that they are required if the programs are to be assembled and executed.

2.5.5 Branch Instructions and Condition Codes

We introduced the program loop idea in Section 2.3.2. The conditional branch instruction was found to be an essential part of loop control. In general, conditional branches are used in any programming situation in which one of two possible paths for continuing the computation must be chosen. This choice is usually based on an arithmetic or logic property, or condition, of the result of a recently performed operation.

	Memory address label	Operation	Addressing or data information
Assembler commands		C=	2200.
		.=	1150.
	A:	.WORD	317.
	B:	.WORD	−193.
		.=	1200.
Statements that generate machine instructions		MOV	A,RO
		ADD	B,RO
		MOV	RO,C
		HALT	
Assembler command		.END	

Figure 2.13 A complete assembly language program for the program of Figure 2.12.

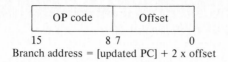

15   8 7   0

Branch address = [updated PC] + 2 x offset

(a) General format and branch address determination

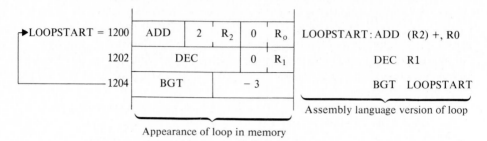

Appearance of loop in memory

[PC] = 1206 when a branch address is computed

Branch address = 1206 + 2 × (− 3) = 1200 = LOOPSTART

(b) Example of using a branch instruction in the loop
program of Figure 2.5c

Figure 2.14 PDP-11 branch instructions.

The format of PDP-11 branch instructions is shown in Figure 2.14a. The 8-bit OP-code field specifies the branch condition to be tested. If the condition is true, or satisfied, a branch takes place. The branch address, that is, the address to be loaded into the PC, is computed by adding two times the value in the offset field to the current contents of the PC. When this addition is performed, the PC has already been updated to point at the word following the branch instruction. Therefore the offset is the distance, in words, between that word and the branch address. The 8-bit offset value is interpreted as a signed number in 2's-complement representation. This number representation will be discussed in detail in Chapter 7. The offset can have any value in the range −128 through 127.

As an example of the use of a branch instruction, consider the program segment shown in Figure 2.14b. The three instructions correspond to the addition loop in Figure 2.5c. The PDP-11 autoincrement addressing mode, applied to the pointer register R_2 in the Add instruction, removes the need for the Increment instruction that was used in the program in Figure 2.5c. The Decrement instruction, with the OP code DEC, has the one-operand format shown in Figure 2.8a. The branch instruction BGT specifies that a branch is to take place if the result of the most recent operation was greater than 0. Since the immediately preceding operation was performed by the DEC instruction, the branch will take place if the decremented value is greater than 0. Observe that the operations that influence the branch conditions are performed before the branch instruction is fetched into the CPU. Hence it is necessary to temporarily store the status of such test conditions. A number of bit-storage elements, referred to as the *condition code* bits or flags, are used for this purpose.

In the PDP-11 there are four condition code flags:

N (negative)	Set to 1 if the result is negative; otherwise, cleared to 0.
Z (zero)	Set to 1 if the result is 0; otherwise, cleared to 0.
V (overflow)	Set to 1 if arithmetic overflow occurs; otherwise, cleared to 0.
C (carry)	Set to 1 if a carry-out results from the operation; otherwise, cleared to 0.

The usefulness of the V and C flags will become apparent in the discussion of arithmetic in Chapter 7. Most of the one- and two-operand instructions affect the setting of the condition codes. The detailed effects for all instructions are given in Appendix B. The branch instructions themselves do not affect the condition codes. They only inspect them to determine whether or not branching takes place.

A PDP-11 program for the full program of Figure 2.5c is given in Figure 2.15. The first instruction is a one-operand instruction that clears register R_0. The second instruction uses the relative addressing mode to load counter R_1 with the value n in memory location N. The next instruction loads the address value NUM into the pointer register R_2 by using the immediate addressing mode. We have already discussed the loop portion of the program in the explanation of the

	CLR	RO	R_0 is used to accumulate the sum.
	MOV	N,R1	N contains n, the number of numbers to be added, and R_1 acts as a counter register in determining how many times to execute the loop.
	MOV	#NUM,R2	R_2 is a pointer register, and it is initialized to contain the address, NUM, of the location containing the first number of the list of numbers.
LOOPSTART:	ADD	(R2)+,RO	Successive numbers are added in R_0.
	DEC	R1	The counter register R_1 is decremented.
	BGT	LOOPSTART	If [R_1] have not reached 0, that is, if the loop has not been executed n times, branch back and execute the loop again.
	MOV	RO,SUM	Store the sum in SUM.
	HALT		Stop program execution.

Figure 2.15 A PDP-11 assembly language program for the addition program in Figure 2.5c.

PDP-11 branch instructions. The last Move instruction places the sum into memory location SUM. Note that comments have been added to each instruction to make the program self-explanatory. When such comments are included in a program, they must be separated from the instruction by semicolons. Comments are ignored by the assembler program.

2.5.6 Byte Operands

The operands of the PDP-11 ADD, SUB, MOV, CLR, and DEC instructions that we have introduced are 16-bit words. With the major exception of the Add and Subtract instructions, most one- and two-operand instructions can also be applied to byte operands. The leftmost bit of the OP code is set to 0 to specify word operands, and it is set to 1 to specify byte operands. The assembler mnemonics for the OP codes, as we have used them until now, have been the word operand versions. The letter B is appended to the OP codes to signify byte operands. As an example.

$$\text{MOVB} \quad \text{LOC1, LOC2}$$

moves the byte from memory byte location LOC1 into memory byte location LOC2. If a CPU register R_i is the source or destination location for a byte operand, the low-order 8 bits of the register are involved.

In many computer applications, it is convenient to use byte-sized operands. A specific example is the text manipulation performed by "language processors" such as assemblers. In such tasks, the data is in the form of characters, which are usually represented by 8-bit codes.

To introduce further features of the PDP-11 instruction set and to discuss character manipulation in general, we will use an example program that sorts a list of bytes. Each byte encodes a character from the set of letters A through Z. It is desired to sort them into alphabetic order. Assume that either the ASCII or EBCDIC code is used for encoding individual characters. Appendix D shows the details of these codes. It is also pointed out there that the letter sequence A, B, C, . . . , Z is represented by a sequence of binary code patterns that have increasing value when interpreted as positive integers. We can therefore regard the list as a set of positive integers that are to be sorted into increasing numerical order. The list has N bytes, not necessarily distinct, and it is stored at consecutive byte locations LIST through LIST $+ \text{ N } - 1$. The sorted list is to occupy the same memory locations as the original list. If necessary, it is permissible to use a few additional temporary storage locations in performing the required operations. This is called an "in-place" sort.

The specific algorithm that we will use is called the "straight selection sort." The main idea is as follows. Find the smallest number first and place it in the first position of the list (location LIST), leaving the remaining numbers in the sublist consisting of the last $N - 1$ positions. Then, find the next smallest number and place it in location LIST $+ 1$, leaving the remaining numbers in the sublist consisting of the last $N - 2$ positions. This procedure is repeated until the list is sorted.

A Pascal-like program for the sorting algorithm is given in Figure 2.16a. In this program, the list elements are referenced as the one-dimensional array LIST(0), LIST(1), . . . , LIST(N−1). The loop variable J in the outer for-loop specifies the first subscript of the sublist being searched. During the pass through a sublist LIST(J) to LIST(N−1), the current value of element LIST(J) is compared to successive elements of the sublist. The subscripts of these elements are specified by the loop variable K in the inner for-loop. Whenever a smaller element is encountered, it is interchanged with element LIST(J).

A PDP-11 assembly language program for the sorting algorithm is shown in Figure 2.16b. This program is written in a straightforward manner to correspond

```
for   J := 0 to N−2 do
    begin
    for   K := J+1 to N−1 do
        begin
        if LIST(J) > LIST(K) then
            begin
            TEMP   := LIST(J) ;
            LIST(J)  := LIST(K) ;
            LIST(K) := TEMP
            end
        end
    end
```

(a) Pascal-like program for sorting.

	CLR	R1	Initialize outer loop control variable J to 0 in R_1.
OUTER:	MOV	R1,R2	Initialize inner loop control
	INC	R2	variable K to J +1 in R_2.
INNER:	CMPB	LIST (R1),LIST (R2)	Compare LIST (J) to
	BLOS	ENDINNER	LIST (K) and interchange
	MOVB	LIST (R1),R3	if LIST(J)>LIST(K).
	MOVB	LIST (R2),LIST (R1)	
	MOVB	R3,LIST (R2)	
ENDINNER:	INC	R2	Increment R_2 to contain
	CMP	R2,#N−1	next K value and
	BLOS	INNER	check for end of inner loop.
	INC	R1	Increment R_1 to contain
	CMP	R1,#N−2	next J value and
	BLOS	OUTER	check for end of sort.
	HALT		

(b) PDP-11 program implementation.

Figure 2.16 A byte-sorting program.

directly to the program in part (*a*) of the figure. Registers R_1 and R_2 are used to hold the loop variables J and K. Register R_3 is used as a temporary storage location during the interchange operation. The index addressing mode in the form LIST(R1) and LIST(R2) is used to access individual bytes in the list.

The assembler commands needed to define the values of N and LIST should be added to the program. This can be done in a style similar to that shown in Figure 2.13.

The use of the expressions $N - 1$ and $N - 2$ in the immediate addressing modes toward the end of the program illustrates a common assembler feature. The values of these expressions are computed at assembly time and then used as the immediate data.

The reader should note that this program is not very general because the values LIST and N are constants that are fixed at assembly time. In a more general sorting routine, these parameters would be programmed as variables whose values are determined at execution time. (See Problem 2.21.)

In the sort program given in Figure 2.16*b*, the Compare instruction is used on both word operands and byte operands, represented by the OP codes CMP and CMPB, respectively. It performs the operation

$$[src] - [dst]$$

and manipulates the condition code bits as follows:

N   Set to 1 if result < 0; cleared to 0 otherwise.
Z   Set to 1 if result $= 0$; cleared to 0 otherwise.
V   Set to 1 if arithmetic overflow occurs; cleared to 0 otherwise.
C   Set to 1 if no carry occurs from the most significant bit of the result; cleared to 0 otherwise.

This instruction does not affect either of the operands; it affects only the condition code bits. It is normally followed by a branch instruction, as it is in the sort program. The Compare, Branch sequence is used to make a branching decision based on the relative order of the values of the two operands of the Compare instruction. For example, the instructions

CMP   R2,#N−1

BLOS   INNER   (Branch if Lower Or Same)

in lines 10 and 11 of the program cause a branch to the instruction in memory location INNER if $[R2] \leq N - 1$. The instructions

CMPB   LIST(R1),LIST(R2)

BLOS   ENDINNER

in lines 4 and 5 cause a branch to the instruction in memory location ENDINNER if the first operand byte is smaller than or equal to the second operand byte.

The only other new instruction introduced in this program is the Increment instruction INC. It is a one-operand instruction that adds 1 to the operand.

In the above examples, we have used two conditional branch instructions, BGT and BLOS. The way in which these and other conditional branch instructions use the four condition code flags is specified in detail in Appendix B. The use of these flags is obvious for some conditional branch instructions. For example, in executing the instruction BMI (Branch if MInus), the branch is taken if the result of the previous operation was negative; that is, if the N flag is equal to 1. For other branch instructions, the tests performed on the condition code flags are more complicated. These tests depend on the details of how arithmetic is performed on signed numbers. We will return to this topic in Chapter 7 in Section 7.5.

2.5.7 Logic Instructions

Until now, we have performed only arithmetic operations or comparisons on word and byte data. In many applications, it is necessary to manipulate some of the individual bit positions of byte or word data. Most computers have a few instructions, called logic instructions, that perform standard logic operations on the operands.

Let us consider some specific examples. The PDP-11 has three logic instructions in the two-operand instruction format. They are

$$\text{Bit-clear (BIC, BICB):} \quad \text{dst} \leftarrow \overline{[\text{src}]} \wedge [\text{dst}]$$

$$\text{Bit-set (BIS, BISB):} \quad \text{dst} \leftarrow [\text{src}] \vee [\text{dst}]$$

$$\text{Bit-test (BIT, BITB):} \quad [\text{src}] \wedge [\text{dst}]$$

Each of these instructions manipulates the condition code bits as follows:

N Set to 1 if the most significant bit of the result is 1.
Z Set to 1 if the result is 0.
V Set to 0.
C Not affected.

The AND ($\wedge$) and OR ($\vee$) logic operations in these instructions are applied to corresponding bit positions in the source and destination operands. For example, let

$$[\text{src}] = A = a_{15} \cdots a_1 a_0$$

and

$$[\text{dst}] = B = b_{15} \cdots b_1 b_0$$

Then, the Bit-clear operation

$$\text{dst} \leftarrow \overline{[\text{src}]} \wedge [\text{dst}]$$

means

$$\text{dst}_{15} \leftarrow \overline{a_{15}} \wedge b_{15}$$

$$\cdots \cdots \cdots \cdots$$

$$\text{dst}_1 \leftarrow \overline{a_1} \wedge b_1$$

and

$$\text{dst}_0 \leftarrow \overline{a_0} \wedge b_0$$

In words, the Bit-clear instruction results in clearing the bits in the destination at each position where there is a 1 in the corresponding bit of the source operand. The destination bits that correspond to 0 bits in the source operand remain unchanged. The Bit-set instruction sets destination bits to 1 wherever there are 1s in the source operand. The Bit-test instruction does not change either operand. It manipulates the condition code bits as specified above, based on the result of performing an AND operation on the two operands.

Consider a data processing problem that uses decimal digits, encoded in the binary-coded decimal (BCD) code, described in Appendix D. Assume that four digits are packed into the 16-bit word at location DIGITS in the main memory. It is required to set the digit in bit positions $b_7 b_6 b_5 b_4$ to the value $9_{10} = 1001_2$, where the subscripts on these two numbers denote decimal (base 10) and binary (base 2) representations, respectively. A simple way of doing this is to first clear the desired bits with a Bit-clear instruction, and then insert the required pattern using a Bit-set instruction. Both instructions can include the required binary source operand patterns as immediate operands. These patterns, often called masks in this context, are shown in Figure 2.17. The masks are also given in octal (base 8) notation, which is commonly used to concisely specify bit patterns. The

	Decimal digits					
[DIGITS] initially	$b_{15}b_{14}b_{13}b_{12}b_{11}b_{10}b_9b_8b_7b_6b_5b_4b_3b_2b_1b_0$					
Binary mask for BIC instruction	0 0 0 0	0 0 0 0	1 1	1 1 0	0 0 0	
Octal notation	0	0	0	3	6	0
[DIGITS] after execution of BIC instruction	$b_{15}b_{14}b_{13}b_{12}b_{11}b_{10}b_9b_8$ 0 0 0 0 $b_3b_2b_1b_0$					
Binary mask for BIS instruction	0 0 0 0	0 0 0 0	1 0	0 1 0	0 0 0	
Octal notation	0	0	0	2	2	0
[DIGITS] after execution of BIS instruction	$b_{15}b_{14}b_{13}b_{12}b_{11}b_{10}b_9b_8$ 1 0 0 1 $b_3b_2b_1b_0$					
	Inserted digit 9_{10}					

Figure 2.17 An example of digit insertion using logic operations.

octal version of a binary number is derived by grouping the bits in threes from the least significant end of the binary number. The octal digit corresponding to each group of 3 bits is simply the value represented by that group.

The two instructions required to perform the above task are

$$\text{BIC} \quad \text{\#000360,DIGITS}$$

$$\text{BIS} \quad \text{\#000220,DIGITS}$$

The immediate operands are expressed in octal notation. In the PDP-11 assembly language, numerical quantities are considered to be in octal notation unless they are followed by a decimal point, in which case they are taken to be decimal numbers. Leading zeros need not be shown explicitly. In our example, they are included only to emphasize the correspondence with Figure 2.17. The figure also shows the effect of executing the two instructions on the location DIGITS.

The third logic instruction mentioned above, Bit-test, serves a similar purpose as the Compare instruction. It is useful in testing the status of one or more bits in a byte or a word in order to set the condition code flags for use by a subsequent conditional branch instruction. For example, if a branch is to take place to PROCEED when bit b_2 of memory location STATUS is equal to 1, the following two instructions can be used:

$$\text{BIT} \quad \text{\#4,STATUS}$$

$$\text{BNE} \quad \text{PROCEED}$$

The OP-code mnemonic BNE denotes the Branch if Not Equal to 0 conditional branch instruction. If two or more bits of the test pattern are set to 1, branching will take place if any one of the corresponding bits of the destination operand is equal to 1.

2.6 SIMPLE INPUT-OUTPUT PROGRAMMING

In this section, the instructions needed to transfer data between the CPU and peripheral devices will be discussed. Consider the general situation of programming a task that requires character input from the keyboard of a teletypewriter unit and produces character output that is to be printed on the teleprinter of the same unit. We will discuss only the part of the program that directly controls the I/O activity, using the method known as *program-controlled I/O*. The teletypewriter device, consisting of a keyboard unit and a printer unit, is a simple I/O device. The word *teletypewriter* is used in this book to refer to any hard-copy computer terminal that prints one character at a time, essentially in a typewriter-like manner. The operation of such a device is easily understood and is familiar to most people. It can be conveniently used to illustrate the basic principles of program-controlled I/O. Another device, the CRT terminal, is extensively used for I/O purposes. It consists of a keyboard and a CRT display.

CRT displays will be discussed in detail in Chapter 9. At this point, it is sufficient to note that a CRT terminal uses essentially the same control and data transfer operations as are used in a teletypewriter. Therefore, our discussion applies to CRT terminals as well as to teletypewriters.

A basic problem is to synchronize the operation of a fast CPU with that of a relatively slow I/O device. The speed discrepancy is best illustrated by an example. A teleprinter can print 30 characters per second, but a CPU can execute instructions at a rate of about one every 2 μs. Now suppose that a line of 50 characters is to be printed. The CPU could send these to the teleprinter by executing 50 instructions, requiring about 100 μs. This is considerably less than the time needed to print one character. A solution to this problem is as follows. The CPU sends the first character, then waits for a signal from the teleprinter that the character has been printed. It then sends the second character, and so on. An analogous situation exists with input from the keyboard. The CPU must wait for a signal indicating that a character key has been struck and that its code is available for transmission to the CPU.

We have described the keyboard and teleprinter as separate devices inside the teletypewriter unit. This means that when the teletypewriter is operating under computer control, the action of striking a key on the keyboard does not mechanically cause the corresponding character to be printed on the teleprinter. In most applications, when a key is struck to send a character code to the computer, it is natural that this character should also be printed on the teleprinter. The way in which this actually happens is that one block of instructions in the I/O program transfers the character into the CPU, and another associated block of instructions causes the character to be printed. This process of sending the received character to the teleprinter for printing is called *echoback*. It allows a form of error checking in that if the operator does not see the correct character printed, it is immediately apparent that something has gone wrong in the process of transmitting the character to or from the computer.

Let us now consider the problem of moving a character code from the keyboard to the CPU. Striking a key stores the corresponding character code in an 8-bit buffer register associated with the keyboard. We will call this register TTYIN. To inform the CPU that a valid character is in TTYIN, a synchronization control flag, CIN, is set to 1. The CPU can monitor the flag CIN, so that when CIN = 1, the CPU can read the contents of TTYIN. When the character is transferred to the CPU, CIN is cleared to 0. If a second character is entered at the keyboard, CIN is again set to 1, and the process repeats.

An analogous synchronization process takes place when transferring characters from the CPU to the teleprinter. For this purpose, an 8-bit buffer register, TTYOUT, and a synchronization control flag, COUT, are provided. When COUT = 1, the teleprinter is ready to print a character. The CPU can thus monitor COUT, and when COUT is set to 1, the CPU can transfer a character code to TTYOUT. The transfer of a character into TTYOUT clears COUT to 0, and when the character has been printed, COUT is set to 1 and the process can be repeated.

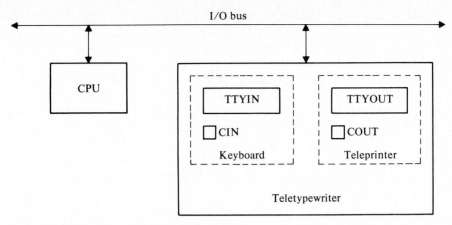

Figure 2.18 Connection of a teletypewriter to a CPU.

Peripheral devices such as teletypewriters are usually connected to the CPU by an I/O bus as indicated in Figure 2.18. The computer has a set of I/O instructions that is used to transfer data and flag status between the CPU and specific devices across the bus. The general format of these instructions is similar to those we have already discussed for moving data between the CPU and the main memory. For example, the CPU can monitor the keyboard control flag CIN and transfer a character from TTYIN to register R_1 by the following sequence of operations:

READWAIT: Branch to READWAIT if CIN = 0

Input from TTYIN to R_i

The Branch operation is usually implemented by two machine instructions, the first of which typically tests the control flag and the second performs the branch. The details vary considerably from computer to computer. The main idea is that the CPU monitors the control flag by executing a short "wait loop," proceeding to the actual input data transfer operation when CIN is set to 1. As well as transferring the character from TTYIN to R_1, the above Input operation resets CIN to 0.

An analogous sequence of operations is used for output to the teleprinter, for example,

WRITEWAIT: Branch to WRITEWAIT if COUT = 0

Output from R_1 to TTYOUT

Again the Branch operation will normally be implemented by two machine instructions. The control flag COUT is set to 1 by the teleprinter when it is free to print a character. The Output operation clears COUT to 0 when it transfers a character from R_1 to TTYOUT to be printed.

The above discussion assumes that the initial state of CIN is 0 and the initial state of COUT is 1. This initialization is normally performed by the device control circuits when the devices are placed under computer control before program execution begins.

It is helpful to see how the above general types of I/O operations are implemented in the case of a specific computer such as the PDP-11. The PDP-11 has a single bus (called the UNIBUS by DEC) that is used for CPU–main memory transfers as well as for CPU–peripheral device transfers.

Until now, we have assumed that the 16-bit addresses issued by the CPU to access instructions and operands always refer to main memory locations. In fact, some of the address values are used to refer to peripheral device buffer registers such as TTYIN and TTYOUT. This means that the PDP-11 does not need to have specific I/O instructions. Data and status information can be transferred to and from peripheral devices by the two-operand Move instruction that we have already discussed. In particular, the 8-bit contents of the keyboard character buffer TTYIN can be transferred to the CPU register R_1 by the instruction

$$\text{MOVB} \quad \text{TTYIN,R1}$$

Similarly, an 8-bit character code can be transferred from the low-order 8 bits of register R_1 to the teleprinter buffer TTYOUT by the instruction

$$\text{MOVB} \quad \text{R1,TTYOUT}$$

The control flags CIN and COUT are automatically cleared when the buffer registers TTYIN and TTYOUT are referenced. These two instructions directly implement the general Input and Output operations discussed above.

The implementation of the CIN and COUT synchronization flags in the PDP-11 will now be discussed, after which we will be ready to give a complete, simple I/O program. The keyboard flag CIN is represented by the leftmost bit position (the sign bit) of an 8-bit status register which we will call KBSTATUS. Some of the other positions of this register are used for different functions that we will not need to discuss here. The short wait loop required to monitor CIN can be implemented by the two-instruction sequence

$$\text{READ:} \quad \text{TSTB} \quad \text{KBSTATUS}$$
$$\text{BPL} \quad \text{READ}$$

The one-operand Test instruction with the OP code TST or TSTB is used to set the condition codes N and Z in accordance with the arithmetic property of the operand tested. The Test instruction also clears the condition code bits V and C to 0. It does not change the operand in any way. Since CIN is the sign bit of KBSTATUS, the test instruction sets N to 1 if CIN is equal to 1; otherwise, N is set to 0. The Branch on PLus instruction (BPL) causes a branch to READ if N = 0. Therefore execution of the two-instruction wait loop continues until CIN is set to 1.

The synchronization flag COUT, associated with the teleprinter, is handled in a similar manner. COUT is the sign-bit position of an 8-bit status register PRSTATUS. The two-instruction loop

WRITE: TSTB   PRSTATUS

            BPL   WRITE

can therefore be used to wait until the teleprinter is ready to print another character.

Let us now consider a program for reading a line of characters entered at a teletypewriter keyboard and transferring this data into the main memory. We assume that the line is terminated when the "carriage return" key is struck. The program must check each character as it is read to see whether or not it is the "carriage return" code. Each character is to be echoed back to the teleprinter as soon as it is read. Also, the string of character codes is to be placed in successive memory byte locations beginning with location LOC. A program for this task is shown in Figure 2.19.

The program illustrates an interesting aspect of program-controlled I/O. Let us assume that both the keyboard and teleprinter handle characters at the rate of 30 per second and that the computer executes instructions at 500,000 per second. For every character read and printed by the teletypewriter, enough time has elapsed for 17,000 instructions to be executed. Almost all the 17,000 instruction

	MOV	#LOC,RO	Initialize pointer register R_0 to contain the address of the first location of the area in main memory where the characters are to be loaded.
READ:	TSTB BPL	KBSTATUS READ	Wait for a character to be entered into the keyboard buffer register TTYIN.
	MOVB	TTYIN,@RO	Transfer the character from TTYIN into the main memory (this clears CIN to 0).
ECHOBACK:	TSTB BPL	PRSTATUS ECHOBACK	Wait for the teleprinter to become ready.
	MOVB	@RO,TTYOUT	Move the character just read to the teleprinter buffer register TTYOUT for printing (this clears COUT to 0).
	CMPB BNE HALT	(RO)+,#CR READ	Check to see if the character just read is "carriage return" (CR). If it is not CR, branch back and read another character; otherwise stop. The pointer register R_0 is incremented, anticipating that another character will be read.

Figure 2.19 A program for reading a line of characters from a teletypewriter into main memory.

executions are accounted for in the two wait loops, while the CPU is waiting for a character to be struck or for the teleprinter to become available.

In some situations, particularly where larger machines are involved, it is desirable to avoid "wasting" the CPU time in this way. Other I/O techniques, based on the use of interrupts and I/O channels, may be employed to improve the utilization of the CPU. Such techniques will be discussed in Chapter 6.

2.7 PUSHDOWN STACKS

We will now introduce the topic of *pushdown stacks*. They constitute an important data structure that is used in a variety of programming situations.

A pushdown stack is a list of data elements, usually words or bytes, with the accessing restriction that elements can be added or removed at one end of the list only. This end is usually called the top of the stack, with the other end being called the bottom. The term pushdown is motivated by the analogy with a pile of trays in a cafeteria. Customers pick up new trays from the top of the pile, and clean trays are added to the pile by pushing them onto the top of the pile. Another descriptive phrase, "last-in first-out," is also used to describe this type of storage mechanism, leading to the abbreviation LIFO stack. Clearly, the last item placed on the stack is the first one removed when retrieval begins. In what follows we will use the term stack to mean pushdown stack. The terms "push" and "pop" are often used to describe placing a new item on a stack, and removing the top item from the stack, respectively.

A stack can be stored in the main memory of a computer, with successive elements in the stack occupying successive memory locations. Assume that the first element placed in the stack occupies memory location BOTTOM and that successive items are placed in lower-address locations. There is no reason why we could not have assumed that the stack grows in the direction of increasing memory addresses (which in fact will be the case in Section 3.6). However, the addressing modes in the PDP-11 make it more convenient to use the above assumed possibility. This is our choice in this chapter because we are using PDP-11 programming examples.

Figure 2.20 shows a stack as it might be implemented in the main memory of a computer. For convenience, we will assume that the stack contains numerical values, with 43 on the bottom and -28 on the top in the example. Register R_i is used as the *stack pointer*; that is, R_i contains the address of the current top element of the stack. The two basic operations of push and pop can be implemented easily, using the PDP-11 instructions

$$\text{MOV} \quad \text{NEWITEM}, -(R1) \quad \text{(push)}$$

and $\qquad \text{MOV} \quad (R1)+, \text{TOPITEM} \quad \text{(pop)}$

when register R_1 is used as the stack pointer. The first instruction moves (pushes) the word from the memory location NEWITEM onto the top of the stack, decrementing the pointer register before the move. The second instruc-

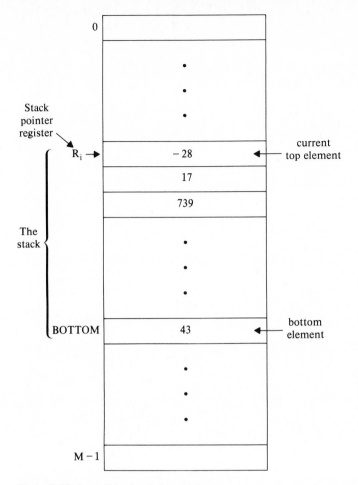

Figure 2.20 A stack in the main memory.

tion moves (pops) the top value from the stack into memory location TOPITEM and increments the pointer register so that it points to the new top element. Figure 2.21 shows the effect of these two operations on the stack of Figure 2.20.

One of the uses of the stack data structure is in holding operands and intermediate computations in a sequence of arithmetic operations. A standard arithmetic operation on stacks is one which pops the two top values from the stack, adds (subtracts, multiples, etc.) them, and then pushes the result onto the stack. The addressing modes of the PDP-11 allow an Add operation of this type to be performed by the single instruction

$$\text{ADD} \quad (R1)+,@R1$$

Its effect is shown in Figure 2.21*d*. The reader should carefully step through the execution of this instruction to see that it indeed achieves the desired action. This example assumes that address calculations and operand fetches proceed

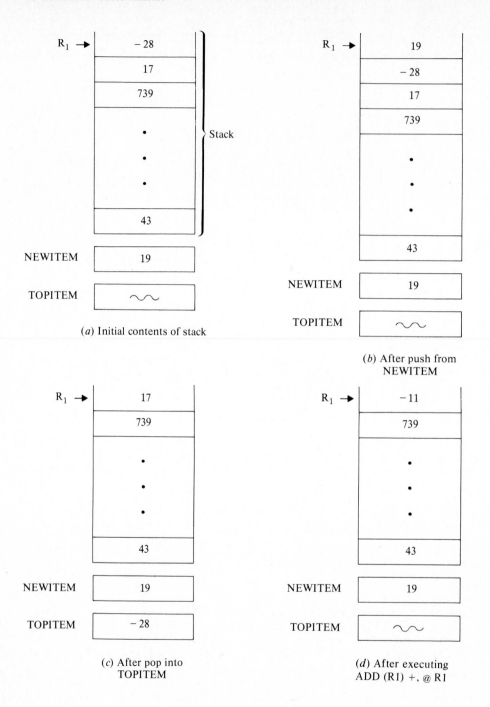

(a) Initial contents of stack

(b) After push from NEWITEM

(c) After pop into TOPITEM

(d) After executing ADD (R1) +, @ R1

Figure 2.21 Examples of stack operations.

strictly left to right in two-operand instructions. All steps required in the source address determination and operand fetch, including the autodecrementing and autoincrementing operations, are completed before destination operand addressing or fetching is begun.

In many cases where stacks are used in programming, it is necessary to carefully avoid popping an item from an empty stack or pushing an item onto a full stack. In this discussion we assume that the stack is allocated some fixed amount of main memory. Suppose that a stack runs from location 2000 (BOTTOM) down no farther than location 1500. If R_1 is the stack pointer, and the stack is initially empty, then R_1 is loaded initially with the address value 2002. To prevent making either of the errors mentioned above, we replace the simple one-instruction push and pop operations by the instruction sequences shown in Figure 2.22.

This completes our brief introduction to stacks. A further and more important example of their use will be given in the next section, and a discussion of how they may affect computer design itself will be presented in Chapter 3.

2.8 SUBROUTINES

The last topic to be discussed in this chapter is the special form of instruction sequencing needed to implement the *subroutine* concept. In a given program, it

		(a) Routine for a safe pop operation	
SAFEPOP:	CMP BGT	R1,#2000 EMPTYERROR	Check to see if the pointer register R_1 contains an address value greater than 2000. If it does, the stack is empty. Branch to the routine EMPTYERROR for appropriate action.
	MOV	(R1)+,TOPITEM	Otherwise, pop the top of the stack into memory location TOPITEM.
		(b) Routine for a safe push operation	
SAFEPUSH:	CMP BLE	R1,#1500 FULLERROR	Check to see if the pointer register R_1 contains an address value equal to or less than 1500. If it does, the stack is full. Branch to the routine FULLERROR for appropriate action.
	MOV	NEWITEM,−(R1)	Otherwise, push the element in memory location NEWITEM onto the stack.

Figure 2.22 Checking for empty and full errors in pop and push operations on a stack.

is often necessary to perform a particular task a number of times on different data values. Such a task is normally implemented as a subroutine. Examples of this include a subroutine to evaluate the *sine* function or a subroutine to sort a list of values into increasing or decreasing order.

It is possible to include the block of instructions that constitute a subroutine at every place where it is needed in any program. However, this is wasteful of memory space. It is better to place only one copy of this block of machine instructions in the main memory. Any program that requires the use of the subroutine branches to its starting location. This is usually termed *calling* the subroutine. After the subroutine has been executed, it is necessary to return to the program that called it. Since the subroutine is intended to be called from different locations in a calling program, provision must be made for branching back, or *returning*, to the appropriate location. In each case, this location contains the instruction immediately following the one that called the subroutine. The way in which any particular computer makes it possible to call and return from subroutines is referred to as its *subroutine linkage* method.

2.8.1 Subroutine Linkage and Parameter-Passing Methods

It is obvious that the contents of the PC at the time a subroutine is called must be preserved to enable the return to the appropriate place. This is necessary since there is only one PC in the CPU, and it must be used to control sequencing through the subroutine. The simplest linkage method is to preserve the contents of the PC in a specific location, for example, memory location LINK. The return to the calling program can be achieved by branching indirectly through memory location LINK, as illustrated in Figure 2.23a. This simple method has the problem that a subroutine cannot call another subroutine. If it did, the return address for the first call, which is stored in location LINK, would be destroyed when the second call places a new return address in LINK. Since it is a very reasonable and practical programming technique to allow one subroutine to call another, we will discard this possibility for subroutine linkage as being unsuitable.

The situation where one subroutine calls a second subroutine can clearly be extended to the case where the second subroutine calls a third subroutine, and so on. This process, called *subroutine nesting*, can be carried out to any depth. Eventually, the last subroutine called completes its computations and returns to the subroutine that called it. Note that the return address involved in this first return operation is the last one that was generated in the nested call sequence. In other words, the return addresses are stored and recalled in a last-in first-out order. We are thus naturally led to suggest that the return addresses associated with subroutine calls should be pushed onto a stack. This mechanism is indicated in Figure 2.23b. Execution of the Call-subroutine instruction consists of two steps. First, the return address, which is 201 in the example in the figure, is pushed onto the return address stack. Second, the address of the first instruction of the subroutine, symbolically given as SUB in the example, is loaded into the

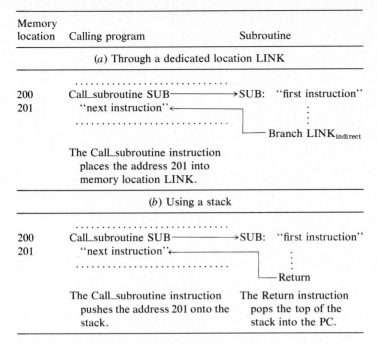

Memory location	Calling program	Subroutine
	(a) Through a dedicated location LINK	

200   Call_subroutine SUB ——————→ SUB: "first instruction"
201   "next instruction" ←

                                       Branch LINK$_{indirect}$

The Call_subroutine instruction places the address 201 into memory location LINK.

(b) Using a stack

200   Call_subroutine SUB ——————→ SUB: "first instruction"
201   "next instruction" ←

                                    Return

The Call_subroutine instruction pushes the address 201 onto the stack.

The Return instruction pops the top of the stack into the PC.

Figure 2.23 Subroutine linkage possibilities.

PC. This enables a branch to the subroutine. Now, suppose that this subroutine runs to completion without calling any other subroutines. Execution of the Return instruction pops the top of the stack into the PC. Therefore, the return address 201 will be placed into the PC, effecting the branch back to the proper location in the calling program. On the other hand, if the first subroutine calls another subroutine, etc., the return addresses associated with the nested call sequence will be pushed onto the stack. The ordering of these addresses is correct, because they should be accessed in a last-in first-out order by the Return instructions. The returns, then, proceed in reverse order to the calls, with the final return being to the original calling program.

As well as preserving the PC value, that is, the return address, it is usually necessary to provide a means for sending operands or their addresses to the subroutine and for returning results from the subroutine to the calling program. This is referred to as the *parameter-passing* function. In a multiregister machine it is possible to pass the parameters via some of the registers. Alternatively, the parameters can be passed through memory locations.

Let us consider the subroutine linkage and parameter-passing protocols that are used in the PDP-11. As pointed out in Section 2.7, stacks can be easily implemented in the PDP-11 through the use of the autoincrementing and autodecrementing address modes. While any CPU register can be used by the programmer as a stack pointer, register R_6 is used by the processor as a pointer to the "processor stack." This stack is used as part of the subroutine linkage mechanism. It is also used in connection with interrupt-controlled I/O, as will be discussed in Chapter 6.

The instruction

$$\text{JSR} \quad R_L,\text{dst}$$

implements the call operation by branching to the location specified by the 6-bit dst field. This location is the starting point of the subroutine program. The value in the PC, which has been incremented to point at the instruction after the JSR instruction, is preserved in the CPU register R_L which is called the *linkage register*. The previous contents of R_L are pushed onto the processor stack. The format of the JSR instruction is shown in Figure 2.24a. This instruction may seem to be overly complicated. All that we require, based on our previous discussion, is that the contents of the PC be pushed onto a stack. The reason for introducing R_L is to facilitate the passing of parameters, as will be explained shortly.

The return from a subroutine to the calling program is achieved by the instruction

$$\text{RTS} \quad R_L$$

whose format is shown in Figure 2.24b. This instruction moves the saved PC value from R_L into the PC and pops the top of the processor stack into register R_L. The computation then continues at the instruction following the JSR instruction, with the original contents of R_L restored.

Passing parameters from the calling program to a subroutine can be implemented conveniently in two ways in the PDP-11. If there are only a few operands or results to be exchanged between the calling program and the subroutine, it may be convenient to pass them via the CPU registers R_0 through

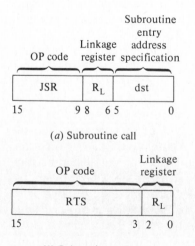

(a) Subroutine call

(b) Subroutine return

Figure 2.24 PDP-11 subroutine Call and Return instructions.

R_5. As an alternative, the two programs can be written so that the addresses of the memory locations containing the operands and results occupy a sequence of memory locations immediately following the JSR instruction. The PC value that is saved in register R_L when the JSR instruction is executed is the address of the first of these locations. The subroutine can then access these locations by using the autoincrement addressing mode, $(R_L)+$. This allows a straightforward way of accessing the parameter address list. After the last parameter address has been accessed, the contents of R_L point to the "next instruction" to be executed in the calling program. This is exactly what is required to implement the return via the RTS instruction. We should emphasize that we have chosen to use parameter addresses, as opposed to the parameters themselves, in the list that follows the JSR instruction. This avoids the need for the calling program to "write" the actual parameters into its own program area at execution time. Modification of program areas at execution time is not a good programming practice. In fact, in some machines, it is possible to prevent any Write operations in the memory areas containing program instructions. This enables protection of these programs against accidental changes resulting from programming errors.

Let us discuss an example of programming with subroutines. Suppose we reprogram the addition algorithm, presented earlier in Figure 2.15, as a subroutine. The address parameters N and NUM will be passed to the subroutine by listing them immediately after the JSR instruction, as discussed above. The sum of the n numbers, beginning at NUM, will be passed back to the calling program through register R_0.

A subroutine for this task, along with an appropriate calling program, is shown in Figure 2.25. After the subroutine has been called by the JSR instruction, the linkage register R_5 points to the memory location containing the

Calling program	JSR	R5,ADDNUM	Call the subroutine ADDNUM
	.WORD	N	using R_5 as the
	.WORD	NUM	linkage register.
	MOV	R0,SUM	After return from the
	HALT		subroutine store the
			sum in SUM.
Subroutine			
ADDNUM:	CLR	R0	
	MOV	@(R5)+,R1	Initialize register R_1 to
			contain n (=[N]).
	MOV	(R5)+,R2	Initialize register R_2 to
			contain the address
			NUM.
LOOPSTART:	ADD	(R2)+,R0	Accumulate sum in R_0.
	DEC	R1	
	BGT	LOOPSTART	
	RTS	R5	Return from subroutine
			with sum in R_0.

Figure 2.25 A subroutine example.

address N. The contents of location N are moved into register R_1 by the second instruction of the subroutine. The third instruction moves the address NUM into register R_2. At this time, R_5 has been incremented to point to the MOV instruction in the calling program. This permits a return to the correct location by the RTS instruction when the subroutine has finished its computation. Upon returning to the calling program, the MOV instruction places the sum of the n numbers into main memory location SUM, the sum having been passed from the subroutine to the calling program through register R_0.

Note that the addition subroutine uses CPU registers R_1 and R_2 for its own computation. In this particular example, we have assumed that the calling program is not using any of these registers for holding valid data of its own at the time it calls the addition subroutine. Should this not be the case, it is the responsibility of the subroutine to first save the contents of any CPU registers that it uses. Just before returning to the calling program, the original CPU register contents must be restored. It is convenient to use the processor stack for the required temporary storage, as will be described in the next subsection.

We have seen that the use of any one of the registers R_0 through R_5 as the linkage register in a subroutine call facilitates passing parameters to the subroutine through main memory locations. However, if parameters are passed through CPU registers, it is more appropriate to use R_7, the PC, as the linkage register. This eliminates the need for using one of the registers R_0 through R_5 as the linkage register. The net effect of the instruction

$$JSR \quad R7,dst$$

is to push the updated contents of the PC onto the processor stack and load the subroutine address (specified by the dst field) into the PC. The return instruction

$$RTS \quad R7$$

pops the top of the processor stack into the PC, thus implementing a proper return to the calling program.

We should note that register R_6 must always contain an even number. This is necessary because R_6 is used as the processor stack pointer. It must always be available for pushing and popping addresses associated with subroutine call and return operations. The CPU hardware is organized such that when register R_6 is used in either the autoincrement or autodecrement mode, it is always incremented or decremented by 2, even for byte instructions. For obvious reasons, register R_7 is treated in the same manner.

2.8.2 Examples of Nested Subroutines

Figure 2.25 shows the basic way that subroutine entry and exit are achieved by the JSR and RTS instructions in the PDP-11. The use of the linkage register in passing parameter addresses through memory is also illustrated. Let us now consider an example where one subroutine calls another subroutine.

Figure 2.26 shows a part of a main program that calls subroutine SUB1, which in turn calls subroutine SUB2. Subroutine SUB2 returns to SUB1, which

	Memory location		Instructions		Comments
			. . . .		
Main	2000		JSR	R5,SUB1	Call SUB1, passing
program	2004		.WORD	PARAM	addresses PARAM
	2006		.WORD	ANSWER	and ANSWER
	2008		"next	instruction"	through memory lo-
			. . . .		cations.
Subroutine	2200	SUB1:	MOV	R0,−(R6)	Save $[R_0]_{main}$ and
SUB1			MOV	R1,−(R6)	$[R_1]_{main}$ on the pro-
					cessor stack.
			MOV	(R5)+,R0	Load PARAM into R_0.
			. . . .		
	2250		JSR	R7,SUB2	
	2254		"next	instruction"	
			. . . .		
			MOV	RESULT,@(R5)+	Send [RESULT] as a
					"result" into loca-
					tion ANSWER in
					the main program.
			MOV	(R6)+,R1	Restore original con-
			MOV	(R6)+,R0	tents of registers R_0
			RTS	R5	and R_1.
Subroutine	3000	SUB2:	MOV	R0,−(R6)	Save $[R_0]_{sub1}$ on the
SUB2					processor stack.
			. . . .		
			MOV	R0,R1	Send $[R_0]$ as a "re-
					sult" to SUB1
					through R_1.
			MOV	(R6)+,R0	Restore R_0.
			RTS	R7	

Figure 2.26 Nested subroutine calls.

eventually returns to the main program. The contents of the processor stack are shown in Figure 2.27 at a number of different points during the execution of the two subroutines.

A few comments are in order about this nested call sequence. It is assumed that subroutine SUB1 uses registers R_0 and R_1 in its calculations. Since these registers may contain meaningful data for the main program, it is necessary to save these values when SUB1 is entered and restore them just before returning to the main program. This is accomplished through the use of the processor stack. The first two MOV instructions of SUB1 push the contents of R_0 and R_1 onto the processor stack, and the last two MOV instructions restore them.

Parameter addresses PARAM and ANSWER are accessed through the linkage register R_5. Subroutine SUB1 performs the first part of its calculations and calls subroutine SUB2. Parameter passing between subroutines SUB1 and SUB2 takes place through register R_1. Furthermore, it is assumed that subrou-

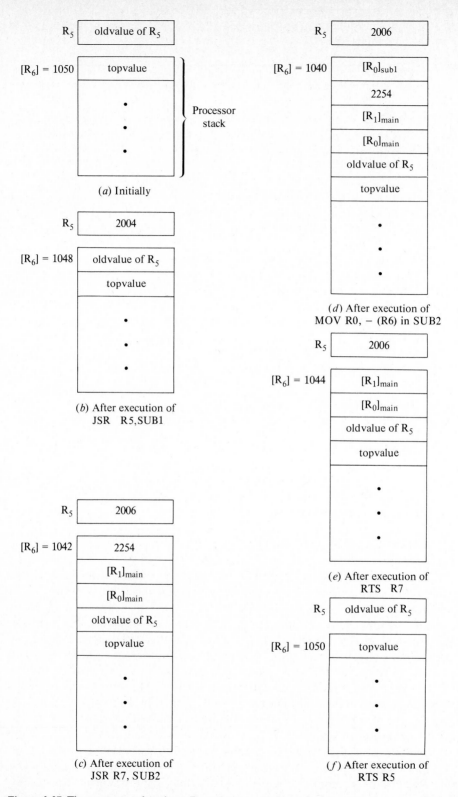

Figure 2.27 The contents of register R_5 and the processor stack as execution proceeds in the programs of Figure 2.26.

tine SUB2 uses R_0 in its internal calculations. Hence, the contents of R_0 are saved on the processor stack. Note that the program counter, R_7, is used as the linkage register in calling SUB2, since parameter passing is done via a register.

After control is passed back to SUB1 from SUB2, subroutine SUB1 completes its calculations and stores the result into location ANSWER. The MOV instruction that stores this result also autoincrements the linkage register R_5 for the second time in SUB1. As a result, R_5 contains the correct return address, 2008, when control is passed back to the main program by the RTS instruction. The return is executed after the contents of registers R_0 and R_1 have been restored from the processor stack. The reader is encouraged to study the contents of the processor stack, as shown in Figure 2.27, as the execution of these programs proceeds.

In this section, we have presented some schemes for subroutine linkage and parameter passing. There are other possibilities. In particular, the subroutine linkage mechanism in some machines is organized to facilitate parameter passing via the same stack that is used for storing return addresses. The VAX-11 computer, discussed in Chapter 3, Section 3.4.3, uses such a mechanism.

2.9 CONCLUDING REMARKS

This chapter introduced the representation and execution of instructions and programs at the machine language level as seen by the programmer. The emphasis was on the basic principles of addressing techniques and instruction sequencing. To illustrate these fundamental notions, we used the PDP-11 instructions in our examples.

The ease and flexibility of programming at the machine instruction level is strongly influenced by the addressing modes in a given computer. A significant part of the chapter was devoted to a discussion of addressing methods in general, followed by a complete and detailed description of those used in the PDP-11. Other computer manufacturers have used different techniques for addressing instructions and operands. Some of these will be discussed in Chapter 3.

The programming examples included in this chapter were chosen to illustrate the basic types of operations that must be implemented by the instruction set of any computer. Moving instructions and operands to and from the main memory was discussed first, followed by a discussion of program branching. The elements of simple I/O operations were discussed with respect to transferring characters between a teletypewriter device and the CPU. The subroutine concept and the instructions needed to implement it were also discussed. Subroutine linkage methods provided an example of the application of the stack data structure, which is also important in other situations. Indeed, it will be seen in Chapter 3 that stacks have been incorporated into the design of some computers in a basic way.

We should emphasize that this chapter is by no means complete in the sense of introducing the full range of instructions that are needed in an instruction set. Representative instructions of each of the major operational types were presented. However, there has been no mention of one important class of instructions that are found in most computers. These are the "shift" and "rotate" instructions which are used to shift the binary pattern in a byte or a word either to the right or left by some specified number of positions. The main applications for these instructions arise in implementing arithmetic routines, which will be discussed in Chapter 7. Appendix B contains a summary of the full instruction set of the PDP-11.

The remainder of the book, with the exception of Chapter 10 on software, is concerned with computer design. Major subsystems, namely, the CPU, the main memory, I/O device interfaces and controllers, and peripheral devices will be described.

2.10 PROBLEMS

2.1 Assume that

$$\text{Multiply} \quad A, R_i$$

is a Multiply instruction in a computer that has a 1½-address format for instructions that need to reference two operands. The execution of this instruction is similar to that of the instruction

$$\text{Add} \quad A, R_i$$

Also assume that the computer has a few general-purpose CPU registers, and that it has other instructions and addressing modes like those described in Sections 2.3 and 2.4 and used in the programs of Figures 2.3 to 2.6.

A program on this computer is required for the computation

$$C \leftarrow A_1 \times B_1 + A_2 \times B_2 + A_3 \times B_3$$

on the contents of main memory locations C, A_1, B_1, A_2, B_2, A_3, and B_3. None of the contents of the locations A_i or B_i are to be destroyed.

(a) Write a straight-line program for this task on the above-described computer.

(b) Write a loop program for the same task on the same computer.

(c) Calculate the number of main memory accesses (Read or Write operations) required for each of the programs in (a) and (b). Include all accesses required for fetching and executing the instructions. For example, the instruction

$$\text{Load} \quad A, R_i$$

requires two memory accesses: one for reading the instruction from the main memory into the CPU and one for reading the operand from main memory location A into the CPU.

2.2 A program is required for the task

$$C \leftarrow \sum_{i=1}^{n} A_i \times B_i$$

(a) Write a loop program for this task on the computer described in Problem 2.1. Assume that all the variables C, A_i, and B_i, are located in the main memory, and that the value n is stored in main memory location N. The contents of N, A_i, and B_i, are not to be destroyed by executing the program.

(b) Would the two-address instruction format have been any better than the assumed 1½-address format for the above program or for either of the programs in Problem 2.1?

(c) Calculate the values of the constants k_1 and k_2 in the expression $k_1 + k_2 n$, which represents the number of main memory accesses required to execute your program for part *(a)* of this problem.

2.3 Write a program for evaluating the polynomial

$$P(x) = a_n x^n + a_{n-1} x^{n-1} + \cdots + a_1 x + a_0$$

on the computer defined in Problem 2.1. The coefficients a_i, the argument x, and the value n are all stored in the main memory. The computed value $P(x)$ is to be stored in main memory location P, and none of the other operand values are to be destroyed by execution of the program.

Hint: Consider the alternative formula $P(x) = ((\cdots(a_n x + a_{n-1}) x + \cdots + a_2)x + a_1)x + a_0$ for polynomial evaluation.

2.4 Consider the following state of the PDP-11:

Register R_1 contains 1000
Register R_2 contains 2000
Memory location 1000 contains 2000
Memory location 2000 contains 3000
Memory location 3000 contains 1000

All numbers are in octal (base 8) notation.

For the following three instructions, each executed from the above initial state, what is the effect of executing each instruction? How many words does each instruction occupy? How many memory accesses does the fetching and execution of each instruction require?

(a) ADD   R1,@R2
(b) ADD   1000(R1),@R2
(c) ADD   #20000,@R2

2.5 A *program trace* is a tabular listing of the contents of certain registers and memory locations at different times during the execution of the program.

(a)   Using the tabular format outlined below, complete the trace for the PDP-11 program of Figure 2.15, assuming the following initial decimal values:

$[R_0] = \cdots$	$[SUM] = \cdots$
$[R_1] = \cdots$	$[1000] = 17$
$[R_2] = \cdots$	$[1002] = -723$
$[N] = 4$	$[1004] = -519$
NUM $= 1000$	$[1006] = 184$

Time	Contents of locations					
	R_0	R_1	R_2	N	NUM	SUM
After first execution of ADD						
After second execution of ADD						
After third execution of ADD						
After fourth execution of ADD						
After execution of HALT						

(b) Using a tabular format similar to that used in part (a) of this problem, construct a trace for the sorting program of Figure 2.16b. Assume that a list of 5 bytes is to be sorted. The address, LIST, of the first byte of the list is 1000, and the decimal values of the bytes in the list are

$$[1000] = 200$$

$$[1001] = 213$$

$$[1002] = 196$$

$$[1003] = 227$$

$$[1004] = 213$$

The trace should show the contents of all list positions and the CPU registers R_1, R_2, and R_3 immediately after each execution of the instruction BLOS OUTER.

2.6 Consider the following two PDP-11 programs:

Program 1			Program 2		
	CLR	R0		CLR	R0
	MOV	M,R1		MOV	#X,R1
	SUB	#2,R1		MOV	N,R2
LOOP:	ADD	X(R1),R0	LOOP:	ADD	(R1)+,R0
	SUB	#2,R1		DEC	R2
	BGE	LOOP		BGT	LOOP
	MOV	R0,RESULT		MOV	R0,RESULT
	HALT			HALT	

The labels X, N, M, and RESULT refer to main memory locations. Memory locations N and M contain the values n and $2n$, respectively.

(a) Do the programs accomplish the same task?
(b) What task(s) do they accomplish?
(c) Which program executes faster? why?
(d) How many 16-bit words are required to represent each program in the main memory?

2.7 Consider the following PDP-11 program:

	MOV	N,R0
	MOV	#1000.,R1
	MOV	#2000.,R2
	MOV	#3000.,R3
	JSR	R7, ROUTINE
	HALT	
ROUTINE:	MOV	(R1)+,R4
	ADD	−(R2),R4
	MOV	R4,(R3)+
	INC	R0
	BLT	ROUTINE
	RTS	R7
N:	.WORD	−25.

(a) What does this program do?
(b) How many 16-bit words do the instructions require for their representation in the main memory?
(c) How many main memory cycles are required to fetch and execute the first five instructions?

2.8 Consider the following PDP-11 program:

	CLR	SUM
	MOV	N,R0
	MOV	#X,R1
	MOV	#Y,R2
LOOP:	MOV	(R1)+,R3
	MOV	(R2)+,R4
	JSR	R7,SUB
	ADD	R4,SUM
	DEC	R0
	BGT	LOOP
	HALT	
SUB:	CMP	R3,R4
	BEQ	EXCEPTION
	RTS	R7
EXCEPTION:	CLR	R4
	RTS	R7

(a) What does this program do?

(b) How many 16-bit words do the instructions require for their representation in the main memory?

(c) Give an expression for the execution time of the whole program in terms of the number of main memory accesses required. The expression should be of the form $T = a + bn$, where $[N] = n$. Use the "worst case" path through the subroutine in calculating the constants in the expression.

2.9 Each of the following four PDP-11 assembly language program segments will cause errors at either the assembly or execution stages. What are the errors?

(a)

MOV	#1000,R1
MOVB	(R1)+,R0
MOV	@R1,R2

(b)

	JSR	R7,READ
	HALT	
	. . . .	
READ:	TSTB	KBSTATUS
	BPL	READ
	MOVB	TTYIN,−(R6)
	RTS	R7

(c)

	.=	1000
	MOV	#1000,R5
	MOV	#7,R0
A:	MOV	R0,(R5)+
	DEC	R0
	BNE	A

(d)

	.=	1000.
	BR	A
	.=	1500.
A:	HALT	

2.10 Describe what happens when the instruction

$$\text{JSR} \quad \text{R7,@(R6)+}$$

is executed. Assume that the instruction is stored at main memory location 2050, and that before it is executed, [R6] = 950 and memory location 950 contains 3000. What happens if the same instruction is executed by the subroutine?

2.11 Write PDP-11 programs for the tasks in Problems 2.1 to 2.3. Assume that only single-length products are required in all these programs.

2.12 Write a PDP-11 subroutine that compares corresponding bytes of two lists of bytes and places the larger byte in a third list. The two lists start at byte locations X and Y, and the "larger byte" list starts at LARGER. The length of the lists is stored in main memory location N.

2.13 Write a PDP-11 subroutine that reads n characters from the teletypewriter keyboard and echoes them back to the teleprinter. The characters must be pushed onto a stack as they are read. Use R_0 as the stack pointer.

2.14 A PDP-11 program is required for the following character manipulation task. A string of n characters is stored in the main memory in consecutive byte locations beginning at location STRING. Another shorter string of m characters is stored in consecutive byte locations beginning at location SUBSTRING. The program must search the string stored beginning at STRING to determine whether or not it contains a contiguous substring identical to the string stored beginning at SUBSTRING. The length parameters n and m $(n > m)$ are stored in main memory locations N and M, respectively. The result of the search is to be stored in register R_0 as follows: If a matching substring is found, the address of its first byte is to be stored in register R_0; otherwise, the contents of R_0 are to be cleared to 0. The program does not need to determine multiple occurrences of the substring. The address of the first matching substring only is required.

2.15 Write a PDP-11 program to accept three decimal digits from a teletypewriter. Each digit is represented in the ASCII code. Assuming that these three digits represent a decimal integer in the range 0 to 999, convert the integer into a binary number representation. The high-order digit is received first. To aid in this conversion, there are two tables of words stored in the main memory. Each table has 10 entries. The first table, starting at word location TENS, contains the binary representations for the decimal values 0, 10, 20, . . . , 90. The second table starts at word location HUNDREDS and contains the decimal values 0, 100, 200, . . . , 900 in binary representation.

2.16 The implementation of last-in first-out (LIFO) stacks in the PDP-11 was discussed in Section 2.7. The purpose of this question is to investigate the implementation of first-in first-out (FIFO) queues in the PDP-11. These types of data structures can serve as data buffers during input or output operations.

A FIFO queue of bytes is to be implemented in the main memory, occupying a fixed region of k bytes. You will need two pointers, an IN pointer and an OUT pointer. The IN pointer keeps track of the location where the next byte is to be appended to the queue; and the OUT pointer keeps track of the location containing the next byte to be removed from the queue. The state of the queue, which can be full, empty, or partly filled, also needs to be known in order to correctly perform the append and remove operations.

Write APPEND and REMOVE subroutines, being careful to inspect and update the state of the queue and the pointers each time an operation is attempted and performed.

2.17 In some computers, subroutine linkage is implemented in the following way. The Call-subroutine instruction stores the return address (that is, the address of the "next instruction" in the calling program) into the first location of the subroutine, and then branches to the second location, where execution of the subroutine begins.

(a) Define a suitable instruction for returning from the subroutine.

(b) How would you pass parameters between the calling program and the subroutine?

(c) Would the above linkage method support subroutine nesting?

(d) Consider the nested call sequence Main program, SUB1, SUB2, . . . , SUBi, SUB1. This type of nesting, where a subroutine "calls itself," is referred to as *recursion*. Would the above linkage method support recursive calls?

(e) Would the stack linkage method discussed in Section 2.8.1 support recursive calls?

2.18 In Section 2.8.2, it was pointed out that the subroutine linkage mechanism in some computers is organized such that parameters may be passed via the same stack that is used for storing return addresses. Suggest an approach for implementing this.

2.19 Show how one could use PDP-11 instructions to implement the scheme you have devised for Problem 2.18.

Hint: Do not try to use the JSR instruction.

2.20 *(a)* Formulate the decimal to binary conversion program of Problem 2.15 as two nested subroutines. Any calling program that invokes the first subroutine passes two parameter addresses to it through main memory locations following the JSR instruction. The first of these is the address of a 3-byte main memory buffer area that the subroutines are to use for storing the input decimal digit characters. The second address is the location for the converted binary value.

The task of the first subroutine is to read in the three decimal digit characters from the teletypewriter. It then calls a second subroutine to perform the actual conversion. The necessary parameters are passed to this subroutine via CPU registers.

Both subroutines must save the contents of any CPU registers that they use, on the processor stack.

(b) Give the contents of the processor stack and the linkage register immediately after the execution of the JSR instruction that calls the second subroutine. Do this in the format of Figure 2.27.

2.21 *(a)* In the byte-sorting program shown in Figure 2.16*b*, the address value LIST and the value N are fixed in the program code at assembly time. Rewrite the program as a PDP-11 subroutine under the assumption that the values LIST and N are contained in main memory locations whose addresses are placed immediately after the JSR instruction in a calling program.

(b) The execution-time efficiency of the byte-sorting subroutine of part *(a)* can be improved by keeping track of the address of the smallest byte of a sublist LIST(J) to LIST(N−1) and performing, at most, one swap at the end of the sublist search. Rewrite the part *(a)* subroutine to achieve this efficiency, and estimate the improvement. What happens to code space requirements when time efficiency is improved?

2.22 Consider the following PDP-11 program

```
            MOV    N,R0
            MOV    R0,R2
            MOV    #2000.,R1
LOOP:       JSR    R7,ROUTINE
            DEC    R0
            DEC    R0
            BGT    LOOP
            HALT
ROUTINE:    MOVB   @R1,R4
            MOVB   2000.(R2),(R1)+
            MOVB   R4,2000.(R2)
            DEC    R2
            RTS    R7
```

(a) What does this program do?
(b) For each of the instructions indicate the following.
   (1) How many 16-bit words are required to represent the instruction in main memory?
   (2) How many main memory accesses are required to fetch and execute the instruction?
   (3) Give an expression for the execution time, as in Problem 2.8, part *(c)*.

2.23 The following PDP-11 program transfers a sequence of bytes from the main memory to an output device:

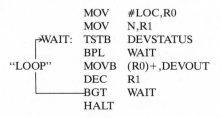

```
            MOV    #LOC,R0
            MOV    N,R1
WAIT:       TSTB   DEVSTATUS
            BPL    WAIT
"LOOP"      MOVB   (R0)+,DEVOUT
            DEC    R1
            BGT    WAIT
            HALT
```

(a) If a main memory access takes 0.5 μs, and if the device is ready, how long does it take to execute the "LOOP" once?

(b) If the device can only accept bytes at the rate of one every millisecond, approximately how many times is the BPL WAIT instruction executed for every byte transferred?

2.24 (a) Draw a series of 10 "pictures" showing the complete contents of the processor stack after *each* of the instructions of the following PDP-11 program is executed. The initial register contents are

$$[R0] = 7$$
$$[R1] = -11$$
$$[R5] = 721 \quad \text{All values are in decimal notation.}$$
$$[R6] = 2000$$
$$[R7] = 100$$

	JSR	R5, SUBR
	HALT	
SUBR:	MOV	R0, −(R6)
	MOV	R1, −(R6)
	MOV	#3, −(R6)
	MOV	#12, −(R6)
	ADD	(R6)+, @R6
	MOV	(R6)+, R4
	MOV	(R6)+, R1
	MOV	(R6)+, R0
	RTS	R5
	MOV	#12, −(R6)
	ADD	(R6)+, @R6
	MOV	(R6)+, R4
	MOV	(R6)+, R1
	MOV	(R6)+, R0
	RTS	R5

The initial "picture," before JSR is executed, is

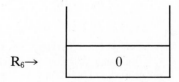

(b) Write down the sequence of distinct values that exist in registers R5 and R6 over the course of executing the program.

(c) List the number of main memory words needed to represent each instruction of the program, along with the number of main memory accesses needed to fetch and execute each instruction.

2.25 (a) For the following PDP-11 program, record the number of 16-bit words needed to represent each of the instructions in the main memory; and also record the number of main memory accesses needed to fetch and execute each instruction.

```
              CLR    R0
              MOV    #XLIST,R1
              MOV    #YLIST,R2
              MOV    N,R3
      LOOP:   MOV    @R1,R4
              MOV    @R2,R5
              ADD    R4,R5
              ADD    R5,R0
              ADD    #2,R1
              ADD    #2,R2
              DEC    R3
              BNE    LOOP
              MOV    R0,SUM
              HALT
```

(b) Calculate the values a and b in the expression $T = a + bn$, where T is the number of main memory accesses required to execute the program. The value n is the positive integer stored at location N.

(c) Rewrite the program using as few instructions and registers as you can while still performing the same overall computation, that is, ending with the same answer in location SUM, without changing the values in any other main memory locations.

(d) Recalculate a and b in the T expression for your new program.

2.11 REFERENCES

2.1 Bell, C. G., J. C. Mudge, and J. E. McNamara: "Computer Engineering: A DEC View of Hardware Systems Design," Digital Press, Bedford, Mass., 1978.

THREE

INSTRUCTION SETS

Chapter 2 dealt with basic programming ideas. A number of simple examples of typical programs were presented. They illustrated the need for various machine instructions and different addressing modes. The instruction set of the PDP-11 minicomputers was introduced to give the examples in the context of a real computer.

In this chapter we will discuss some important features of instruction sets found on machines that are larger and more powerful than the PDP-11. First we will complete our discussion of the PDP-11 instruction set; then we will point out some of its limitations, which are attributable to the relatively short 16-bit word length. The ways in which these limitations are removed by 32-bit computers will follow, using the VAX-11[1] and the IBM 370[2] family of computers as examples. Next we will examine some aspects of machines that have a stack as their dominant feature, using the HP3000[3] as a specific example.

Having observed that a typical computation, or digital processing in general, involves a number of functionally different steps to be performed, it is reasonable to assume that a corresponding number of different classes of instructions should be available. In the previous chapter, it was stated that these classes involve data transfers between the main memory and the CPU registers,

[1]Manufactured by Digital Equipment Corporation.
[2]Manufactured by International Business Machines Corporation.
[3]Manufactured by Hewlett-Packard Company.

arithmetic and logic operations on data, program-sequencing control, input-output transfers, and machine control functions. Another important aspect of instruction sets is the way in which they support high-level language features.

A large instruction set makes it easier to write programs. However, there obviously are practical limits to the number of instructions that can be provided. Implementation of a large instruction set involves more complicated control and possibly, higher cost. Cost is only one of the factors influencing the size of the instruction set. There are others related to the memory organization and the number of bits in a word. These factors will be considered in our discussion.

The properties of instruction sets found in microprocessors are treated in greater detail in Chapter 11.

3.1 THE PDP-11

The basic operating principles follow the same general pattern for all computers, large and small alike. Many design features are independent of the size of the machine, but there are some that are strongly influenced by it. The instruction set of a given computer reflects the effects of the word length, the maximum size of the main memory, and the desired versatility of the operations that can be performed.

PDP-11 minicomputers offer a good example of a sophisticated design. Some machine instructions and the addressing modes used in these computers were introduced in Chapter 2 in the programming examples. That discussion, in conjunction with the complete detailed listing of the instruction set in Appendix B, is sufficient to give the reader an adequate picture of the number, structure, meaning, and usefulness of the available instructions. At this point, we will extend the discussion of the PDP-11 instruction set in an attempt to identify some of the constraints imposed by a 16-bit word length. Some implementation details will be given to supplement the material presented in Chapter 2.

Word length is a basic constraint in the design of instruction sets. The number of available bits determines the maximum size of the addressable space, as well as the number of available codes that can be used to encode instructions. We saw that the problem of realizing a sufficiently large addressable space was solved by making use of the contents of general-purpose registers and/or using more than one word per instruction. Thus, 16-bit addresses are generated, permitting access to 64K memory byte locations. The specification of addressing information through additional words means that many instructions can vary in length from one to three words.

Instructions are encoded as bit patterns within the provided "bit space." This obviously limits the number of instructions that can be encoded. Most instructions consist of an OP code and some addressing data, usually formatted in separate fields. However, an instruction consisting of a particular OP code and specific addressing data is really just one of the many possible (2^{16}) codes. It is not an essential requirement that OP codes and addressing data be represented in nicely partitioned fields. They could be encoded in a random fashion as long as the control circuits are able to decode them properly.

Partitioning of instructions into well-defined fields is found in the PDP-11, and many other machines, because it simplifies the interpretation of the encoded information. For example, in a 6-bit field that specifies the address of an operand, bit position 3 is used to indicate indirect addressing. If indirect addressing is wanted, b_3 is set to 1, otherwise $b_3 = 0$. This is the case in all addressing modes. It is easy to see that dedicating 1 bit to such a specific purpose simplifies the encoding and decoding tasks. But, it may also result in wasting a part of the available bit space. Two modes created by the use of a separate bit for specifying indirection are seldom found in real programs. These are the index indirect and the autodecrement indirect modes. Consider, for example, the autodecrement indirect mode (see Table 2.1). The operand address is $A_{effective} = [[R_n]]$, where R_n was first decremented. This mode would be useful if one wanted to go through a list of operand addresses in the "backward" direction, that is, from high to low memory addresses. Such a requirement is not likely to arise very often, so that it could be argued that the mode is really a waste of bit space. This mode can be specified in conjunction with any of the registers R_0 through R_7. Thus it uses eight of the available 2^6 codes. Extending this argument to two-operand instructions, it is apparent that 64 codes are not likely to be utilized in programs. We may also recall that the autodecrement mode makes no sense at all when $R_n = PC$, hence its indirect version is equally useless. This example illustrates the trade-off between full utilization of the bit space, which is likely to result in some codes being assigned in "random" fashion, and partitioning of instruction words into easily interpretable fields, which is potentially wasteful of the bit space.

The OP-code field in two-operand instructions consists of 4 bits (see Figure 3.1). This allows 16 distinct valuations. However, it is obviously not possible to assign all these codes to two-operand instructions. At least one of them must be used to denote the remaining instructions. It is interesting to see how this

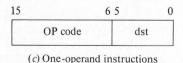

```
15    12 11      6 5        0
┌────────┬────────┬──────────┐
│OP code │  src   │   dst    │
└────────┴────────┴──────────┘
```
(*a*) General two-operand instructions

```
15        9 8   6 5        0
┌──────────┬─────┬──────────┐
│ OP code  │ reg │   dst    │
└──────────┴─────┴──────────┘
```
(*b*) Two-operand instructions with restricted source operand

```
15              6 5        0
┌────────────────┬──────────┐
│    OP code     │   dst    │
└────────────────┴──────────┘
```
(*c*) One-operand instructions

Figure 3.1 Formats for PDP-11 instructions that access memory operands.

problem is resolved in the PDP-11. Five two-operand instructions have both word and byte versions. These are MOV(B), CMP(B), BIT(B), BIS(B), and BIC(B). This accounts for 10 of the 16 available codes. The ADD and SUB instructions are provided only in the word version, needing another two codes. There are other two-operand instructions that can be useful, for example, XOR (Exclusive-OR), MUL (Multiply), and DIV (Divide). The problem is that if they were assigned distinct 4-bit OP codes, this would leave insufficient bit space to accommodate the rest of the instruction set. A compromise solution is to limit the scope of less important two-operand instructions by allowing the full addressing range for one operand (destination) and restricting it for the other operand (source). If the latter is only allowed to be in one of the CPU registers, then 3 bits are needed to specify the particular register, while the three address mode bits are no longer required. Thus, one code for bits b_{15} to b_{12} can be used to implement instructions such as XOR, MUL, and DIV. The particular code used is $b_{15}b_{14}b_{13}b_{12} = 0111$. The format of these instructions is given in Figure 3.1b.

The above two-operand instructions utilize 13 valuations of bits b_{15} to b_{12}. There is a large group of instructions that require one operand only. These present significantly less demanding requirements on the available bit space, because only 6 bits are taken by the operand address. Thus, if we take one valuation of bits b_{15} to b_{12} that is not used by the two-operand instructions and combine it with the remaining 6 bits, it becomes possible to provide as many as 64 one-operand instructions in the format shown in Figure 3.1c. The easiest instructions to accommodate are those that do not require any operands. These are instructions of a purely control nature, such as HALT, WAIT, RESET, etc. Since no operands are needed, all 16 bits of the instruction can be used as an OP code.

Control and one-operand instructions use two codes in bits b_{15} to b_{12}. When the 13 codes needed for two-operand instructions are added, this leaves only one code unaccounted for. But, until now we have considered an instruction set intended primarily for operation on data represented in *integer* format, where the operand is interpreted as a signed integer with the most significant bit being the sign. Chapter 7 will discuss another useful method for representing data where each operand consists of a sign, an exponent, and a fraction. This is the *floating-point* representation. Such data should have a longer word length, but preferably some multiple of the integer word length. To process this data efficiently, a set of floating-point instructions is desirable. We should note that these instructions are not essential in a general-purpose computer as the desired functions can always be implemented with extensive software routines. Thus, many small computers do not incorporate any floating-point instructions. In larger models of the PDP-11 minicomputer series, it is possible to include a floating-point processor as an optional arithmetic processor that performs all floating-point operations and converts data between integer and floating-point formats. It contains six 64-bit floating-point registers. A distinct set of floating-point instructions is provided by making use of the code $b_{15} \ldots b_{12} = 1111$ to designate the entire set. The instructions use essentially the same addressing modes as those discussed in Section 2.5.1, with the restriction that a full addressing range is not permitted for both operands in two-operand instructions.

3.1.1 Program Status Control

Individual processing steps carried out by separate instructions are seldom unrelated. During the discussion of branch instructions in Chapter 2, it was pointed out that branching often depends upon the status of the condition codes. Obviously, it must be possible to store the condition codes temporarily within the CPU, as they form a part of the vital "processor status" information.

Execution of a given program may be interrupted by requests for service from peripheral devices. It should be possible to accommodate such requests. This may be done by stopping the execution of the current program, saving the necessary processor status information in temporary storage, and then allowing the CPU to handle the interrupt by executing an appropriate interrupt service routine. Upon completion of this routine, it is necessary to resume processing of the original program, which clearly requires the ability to restore the processor status information. Interrupt-handling techniques will be discussed in detail in Chapter 6. Here, we are only motivating the need for a simple representation of the processor status information.

In many computers there exists a special register that contains the *processor status word* (PSW). Its format in the PDP-11 is shown in Figure 3.2. In addition to the condition codes, it contains other status information. Bits b_7 to b_5 indicate the CPU interrupt priority, which will be discussed in Chapter 6. The trap bit (T) is an indicator that causes a processor trap (interrupt) at the end of execution of an instruction. This is a useful aid in program debugging. Bits b_{15} to b_{12} show the current and previous operational modes of the processor. In larger models of PDP-11 minicomputers there are two basic operational modes for the processor, called kernel and user. In the kernel mode all functions of the machine are under complete control of the program. On the other hand, the user mode does not permit execution of certain instructions and may restrict direct access to peripherals. This feature may be used to provide protection in a multiuser environment, so that each program is protected against undesirable interference by other user programs. Furthermore, it prevents any user program from causing a failure of the entire system.

The PSW, in conjunction with the PC, contains all the status information needed in interrupt handling, as will be explained in Chapter 6.

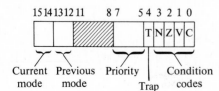

Figure 3.2 Processor status word in PDP-11.

3.2 LIMITATIONS OF SHORT WORD-LENGTH MACHINES

Let us summarize the limitations imposed by the 16-bit word length of the PDP-11 that were discussed in the previous section. An address length of 16 bits allows a total of only 64K addressable locations in the main memory space. The size of this space has proved to be very restrictive for many large application programs. Such programs must be broken down into a number of segments. The programmer must arrange for these segments to be repeatedly moved into the main memory from secondary disk storage as they are required for execution. The extra complication of programming these transfers, along with the time delays involved, are an annoyance to the user. Some modifications to the instruction sets of short word-length machines have been developed which extend their main memory addresses by a few bits. However, this only alleviates the problem in a minor way, since the programmer needs to manipulate the extended address bits with special instructions in order to access the expanded main memory space.

A second limitation is that 16-bit data paths inside the CPU and between the CPU and the main memory place constraints on the computational throughput that can be achieved. Two factors are involved in this limitation. First, the small number of bits that can be allotted to OP codes and addressing modes results in small instruction sets and limited addressing capabilities. Therefore, many instructions are required to implement relatively simple program tasks. Second, the range of numbers that can be represented in a single word is too small for many applications. Both of these problems can be eliminated by using multiple words to represent an expanded instruction set and larger number ranges. However, there is an obvious performance loss in this approach because several main memory cycles are required to fetch an instruction or move a data item between the CPU and the main memory.

As we will see later, in the case of VAX-11 and IBM 370 computers, longer word lengths can largely remove these limitations.

3.3 HIGH-LEVEL LANGUAGE CONSIDERATIONS

Most programs are written in high-level languages, independent of the size or power of the computer used. A difficulty with many minicomputers and microcomputers is that a large number of instructions are needed to implement computing tasks that have quite short expressions in high-level languages. This is a direct consequence of the fact that only simple instructions are usually provided on such machines.

Consider, for example, the problem of matrix multiplication. Two $n \times n$ matrices, A and B, are to be multiplied, and the product is to be stored in matrix C. A program for this calculation, written in Pascal-like notation, is shown in Figure 3.3.

```
for      I := 0 to N−1 do

    begin

    for      J := 0 to N−1 do

        begin

        C(I,J) := 0 ;

        for      K := 0 to N−1 do

            C(I,J):=C(I,J)+A(I,K)*B(K,J)

        end

    end
```

Figure 3.3 A matrix multiplication program.

Let us consider a PDP-11 program for this task. In order to keep the program simple, the size of the numbers will be restricted. All three of the arrays are assumed to consist of 16-bit integers and all products and sums involved in the calculation are assumed to fit into 16-bit words. Array subscripts run from $(0, 0)$ to $(n − 1, n − 1)$, and the value n is assumed to be stored in main memory location N. The elements of each array are stored in consecutive word locations beginning with element $(0, 0)$ and continuing in column order. That is, element $A(0, 0)$ is stored in the main memory at byte address A, element $A(1, 0)$ is stored at byte address $A + 2$, and so on.

A possible PDP-11 program for this task is given in Figure 3.4. This program is organized in a straightforward manner to follow the sequence of operations given in Figure 3.3. First, consider the implementation of the for-loop structure. The loop control variables I, J, and K are initialized to 0 and stored in registers R_0, R_2, and R_4, respectively. The outer loop is controlled by the value of I in R_0. Register R_0 is incremented and tested by the INC and CMP instructions immediately preceding the HALT instruction. If I is less than n, the loop is repeated; otherwise, the program halts. Three machine instructions (INC, CMP, BLT) are required to implement loop termination control for each loop.

Next, consider the way in which array elements are addressed. Recall that the arrays are stored in the main memory in column order. The byte address of element (I, J) of an array, relative to the address of the first element, is given by the expression $2(n * J + I)$, where the factor of 2 is required because each word element consists of 2 bytes. For example, suppose $n = 10$. Then element $C(5, 3)$ is stored at main memory location $C + 2(10 \times 3 + 5) = C + 70$. In the first part of the program, four instructions compute the address of C(I, J) relative to C. Note that an arithmetic left-shift instruction is used to perform multiplication by 2. Similar four-instruction sequences are used to compute the addresses of A(I, K) and B(K, J).

Some general observations can now be made about the PDP-11 implementation of the matrix multiplication operation. Loop termination control consists of the following functions. The loop control variable is incremented. Then, its new

	CLR	R0	I loop control variable in R_0.
LOOPI:	CLR	R2	J loop control variable in R_2.
LOOPJ:	MOV	R2,R1	Compute relative address of
	MUL	N,R1	C(I,J) in R_1.
	ADD	R0,R1	
	ASL	R1	
	CLR	C(R1)	Clear C(I,J).
	CLR	R4	K loop control variable in R_4.
LOOPK:	MOV	R4,R3	Compute relative address of
	MUL	N,R3	A(I,K) in R_3.
	ADD	R0,R3	
	ASL	R3	
	MOV	A(R3),R3	Move A(I,K) to R_3.
	MOV	R2,R5	Compute relative address of
	MUL	N,R5	B(K,J) in R_5.
	ADD	R4,R5	
	ASL	R5	
	MUL	B(R5),R3	$R_3 \leftarrow$ A(I,K)*B(K,J).
	ADD	R3,C(R1)	C(I,J) $\leftarrow$ C(I,J)+[R_3].
	INC	R4	Termination of K loop.
	CMP	R4,N	
	BLT	LOOPK	
	INC	R2	Termination of J loop.
	CMP	R2,N	
	BLT	LOOPJ	
	INC	R0	Termination of I loop.
	CMP	R0,N	
	BLT	LOOPI	
	HALT		

Figure 3.4 Matrix multiplication in a PDP-11.

value is compared to the upper limit. If the upper limit has not been exceeded, a branch back to the beginning of the loop is taken; otherwise, the loop has been completed, and execution of the next part of the program proceeds. Note that individual instructions are used for each of these functions in the program of Figure 3.4. Also, the calculation of the address of an array element from its two subscripts is done by a sequence of four instructions. Clearly, it would be useful if the instruction set allowed a more concise implementation for such tasks.

In the above example, the array elements were assumed to be 16-bit numbers. Suppose we wish to solve the same problem with larger integers. The program would become much more complex. Multiple words are needed to represent the larger numbers. A sequence of instructions is required to generate partial products and handle the associated carries so that multiple-word products can be accumulated. An analogous task involving floating-point numbers is even more difficult.

This discussion of the implementation of matrix multiplication on a short word-length minicomputer suggests three requirements that instruction sets of larger computers should satisfy if they are to facilitate the implementation of high-level language programs.

The first and most obvious requirement is to provide support for a number of *data types*. By data types we mean integers, floating-point numbers, and character strings for the representation of names and text. In addition to the usual binary number representation schemes, it is also very useful in business applications to have a direct representation for decimal numbers. Two important aspects of numeric data types must be considered. First, the size of numbers that can be handled must encompass the range of values encountered in scientific and business calculations. Secondly, the instruction set must include instructions for each of the basic arithmetic operations on each number type. In the case of character strings, the instruction set should facilitate common operations such as translation between different character representations.

The second requirement is to include addressing modes, and possibly even some specialized instructions, to handle arrays. In this respect, a basic task is the calculation of main memory addresses of multidimensional array elements from their subscripts.

Finally, it would be convenient to have the three operations involved in loop termination control, that is, loop-control variable manipulation, testing, and branching, provided in a single instruction.

We have considered only a few specific examples of the way in which machine instruction sets can support high-level languages. A number of other features are also highly useful, for example:

- Efficient procedure (subroutine) call instructions, including parameter passing and register save and restore operations
- Efficient representation and manipulation of stacks for the support of nested procedure calls
- Implementation of common tasks in single instructions, such as searching for a given pattern in a string of characters

Machines discussed in this chapter provide examples of support for such features.

3.4 THE VAX-11

The VAX-11 is a 32-bit computer. All addresses and data paths are 32 bits wide. The main memory space is byte-addressable. Therefore, a 32-bit address reaches a total of 2^{32} bytes (4 gigabytes). This address space is more than adequate for most programming tasks; indeed, the physical main memory provided in most implementations of the VAX-11 is usually only up to a few megabytes. The mechanisms for mapping from the large programmer space provided by 32-bit addresses to the smaller physical memory space will be discussed in Chapter 8.

There are sixteen 32-bit CPU registers, named R_0 through R_{15}. Registers R_0 through R_{11} are general-purpose registers that can be used to hold data or addresses. Register R_{14} is the stack pointer (SP) and R_{15} is the program counter

(PC). Registers R_{12} and R_{13} have special roles in conjunction with handling procedure calls and parameter passing. Their use will be discussed later.

The VAX-11 supports many different data types. Signed integers in byte, word (2 bytes), long-word (4 bytes), and quad-word (8 bytes) sizes are handled by the instruction set. Floating-point numbers in both long-word and quad-word sizes are also included. All of these numeric data types can be stored in the main memory beginning at an arbitrary byte address; that is, there are no word, long-word, or quad-word boundary restrictions on the location of the multiple-byte types. Some typical examples are shown in Figure 3.5. Note that the least significant byte of multiple-byte integers is stored in the lowest address location.

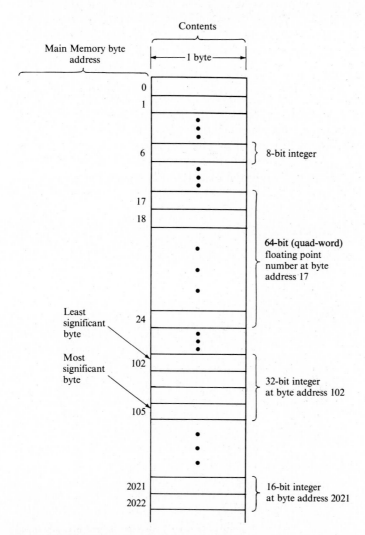

Figure 3.5 Examples of numeric data types in the VAX-11.

In addition to these, specific formats are provided for representing binary-coded decimal (BCD) numbers, character strings, and bit strings.

The instruction set in the VAX-11 is very extensive in comparison to the PDP-11. A large number of instructions are provided for operating directly on the various data types. In addition to the basic instructions, which include arithmetic and logic operations, tests, branches, and subroutine calls, there are a number of more complex machine instructions which facilitate the implementation of high-level language constructs. Some specific examples, including those related to the matrix multiplication task of Figure 3.3, will be discussed in Section 3.4.3.

The addressing modes provided in the VAX-11 include the PDP-11 modes. Other modes are provided for efficient access to data arrays and compact representation for short immediate data.

3.4.1 Instruction Formats

Instructions in the VAX-11 consist of a variable number of bytes and can begin at any byte address. The operation code (OP code) is contained in the first byte of an instruction. Addressing information needed to access operands is then placed in the bytes that follow. The term *operand specifier* is used to refer to the addressing information for an individual operand.

The general format of a single-operand instruction is shown in Figure 3.6a.

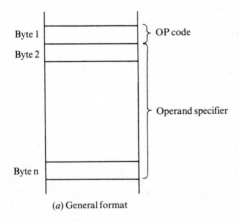

(a) General format

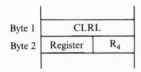

(b) Example instruction: CLRL   R4

Figure 3.6 VAX-11 one-operand instruction format.

The operand specifier consists of 1 or more bytes. Although most specifiers require 1 to 5 bytes, up to 10 bytes may be needed. A simple example of a one-operand instruction which requires only 1 byte for the operand specifier is a Clear Long-word instruction that clears the contents of register R_4. It is written in assembler notation as

CLRL   R4

The representation of this instruction in the main memory is shown in Figure 3.6*b*. Note that the instruction details are given as a vertical listing of its individual byte contents. This style is particularly convenient when two or more operand specifiers are involved. Full details on the format of an operand specifier, including the addressing modes available, are given in the next subsection.

The general multiple-operand instruction format is shown in Figure 3.7. Instructions with up to six operands are included in the VAX-11 instruction set. Consider an example of a three-operand instruction that adds the words (2 bytes each) at main memory locations LOC1 and LOC2 and places their sum in the low-order half of register R_0. It is written in assembler notation as

ADDW3   LOC1,LOC2,R0

The fact that this is a three-operand operation involving 16-bit words is specified in the OP code by the descriptors 3 and W. As we shall see later in the discussion

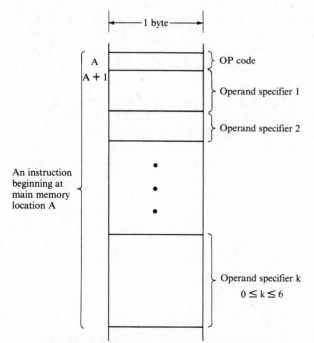

Figure 3.7 VAX-11 general instruction format.

of addressing modes, each of the first two operand specifiers in this instruction requires several bytes for its representation.

3.4.2 Addressing Modes

We will now discuss the addressing modes used in the VAX-11. A 32-bit address is needed to specify the location of a main memory operand. Such an address may be contained in a CPU register or in the instruction itself. Operands may also be held in CPU registers or included as immediate data directly in an instruction. In addition to these basic modes, the VAX-11 includes a very flexible index mode. It facilitates access to elements of data arrays in a way that is compatible with the use of subscripts in high-level languages.

Each operand specifier in an instruction begins with a mode byte whose bit format is shown in Figure 3.8. The high-order half, bits b_7 through b_4, specifies the mode. A CPU register is usually involved in the generation of the address of the operand. The register, one of R_1 through R_{15}, is specified in the low-order 4 bits of the mode byte.

A complete listing of the VAX-11 addressing modes is given in Tables 3.1 and 3.2. Modes 5 through 9, including the cases where R_n = PC in modes 8 and 9, are the same as the modes with the corresponding names in the PDP-11 (see Tables 2.1 and 2.2 in Chapter 2). Two examples of the use of these modes are given in Figure 3.9.

The first example uses the autoincrement mode. The register that contains the address of the operand is R_9. In this case, no further bytes are needed in the operand specifier. The instruction clears the long word at the memory location specified in R_9. After the use of its contents, R_9 is incremented by 4, because the operand is 4 bytes long. The second example, shown in Figure 3.9b, involves a Move-byte (MOVB) instruction that uses the immediate mode to specify the first operand and the register mode to specify the second operand. This instruction moves the value 53, which is stored in the byte immediately following the mode byte in the first operand specifier, into register R_2. The symbol I↑, that precedes the immediate data specification, #53, is an example of a general prefix that consists of a single letter followed by ↑. The letter is used to describe the length of the immediate operand or address displacement (described below) that is contained in the operand specifier.

The displacement and displacement indirect modes (numbered 10 through 15) are functionally the same as the index and index indirect modes in the PDP-11. The 16-bit index value X in the PDP-11 modes (see Table 2.1) is replaced by a displacement D. The value D may be a byte, word, or long word, denoted by the prefixes B↑, W↑, or L↑, respectively. When R_n = PC in the

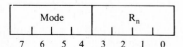

Figure 3.8 Operand specifier mode byte in the VAX-11.

Table 3.1 VAX-11 addressing modes

$b_7b_6b_5b_4$	Decimal equivalent	Name	Assembler syntax	Meaning
0 0 X X	"0"	Literal	S ↑ #Value	Bits b_{5-0} of mode byte specify operand
0 1 0 0	4	Index	$\left\{\begin{array}{c}\text{Indexable} \\ \text{mode}\end{array}\right\}[Ri]^\dagger$	$A_{effective} = A + k\,[R_i]$, where A is generated by the indexable mode, and k is determined by the operand length in bytes
0 1 0 1	5	Register	Rn	$A_{effective} = R_n$
0 1 1 0	6	Register indirect	(Rn)	$A_{effective} = [R_n]$
0 1 1 1	7	Autodecrement	−(Rn)	Decrement R_n; $A_{effective} = [R_n]$
1 0 0 0	8	Autoincrement	(Rn)+	$A_{effective} = [R_n]$; Increment R_n
1 0 0 1	9	Autoincrement indirect	@(Rn)+	$A_{effective} = [[R_n]]$; Increment R_n
1 0 1 0 1 1 0 0 1 1 1 0	10 12 14	Displacement	$\left\{\begin{array}{c}B\uparrow \\ W\uparrow \\ L\uparrow\end{array}\right\}D(Rn)$	$A_{effective} = D + [R_n]$
1 0 1 1 1 1 0 1 1 1 1 1	11 13 15	Displacement indirect	$@\left\{\begin{array}{c}B\uparrow \\ W\uparrow \\ L\uparrow\end{array}\right\}D(Rn)$	$A_{effective} = [D + [R_n]]$

†The indexable modes are modes 6 through 15.
R_i = R0, R1, . . ., R14.

Table 3.2 VAX-11 addressing modes with $R_n = PC$ (R_{15})

$b_7b_6b_5b_4$	Decimal equivalent	Name	Assembler syntax	Meaning
1 0 0 0	8	Immediate (autoincrement)	I ↑ #Value	$A_{effective} = [PC]$; Increment PC
1 0 0 1	9	Absolute (autoincrement indirect)	@#A	$A_{effective} = [[PC]] = A$; $PC \leftarrow [PC] + 4$
1 0 1 0 1 1 0 0 1 1 1 0	10 12 14	Relative (displacement)	$\left\{\begin{array}{c}B\uparrow \\ W\uparrow \\ L\uparrow\end{array}\right\}A$	$A_{effective} = D + [PC] = A$
1 0 1 1 1 1 0 1 1 1 1 1	11 13 15	Relative indirect (displacement indirect)	$@\left\{\begin{array}{c}B\uparrow \\ W\uparrow \\ L\uparrow\end{array}\right\}A$	$A_{effective} = [D + [PC]]$ $= [A]$

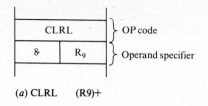

(*a*) CLRL   (R9)+

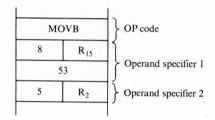

(*b*) MOVB   I↑#53, R2   **Figure 3.9** VAX-11 addressing mode examples.

displacement modes, the resulting relative modes are the same as the relative modes in the PDP-11. Examples of the use of displacement and relative indirect modes are shown in Figure 3.10. The byte displacement mode is used in the Clear-word (CLRW) instruction in part (*a*) of the figure. In part (*b*), the relative indirect mode in the Move Long-word (MOVL) instruction generates the effective address 200. The 4 bytes starting at this location are moved into register R_0. In the example depicted in the figure, the value of this long word is -327. The instruction begins at byte address 1000. The PC has been incremented to contain the value 1004 at the time that the displacement value 1146 is added to it to generate the address 2150. This is the address POINTER. The effective address, $A_{\text{effective}}$, is the 32-bit value 200 stored at location POINTER. Note that the name POINTER is used in the instruction. The assembler program computes the displacement value 1146 at assembly time. The instruction

$$\text{MOVL} \quad @W↑1146(R15),R0$$

is equivalent to the instruction shown in the figure.

It should now be apparent that the functional capability of the PDP-11 addressing modes is included in the corresponding modes of the VAX-11. The one exception is that the VAX-11 does not have the autodecrement indirect mode. Experience with PDP-11 programs has shown that this is not a very useful mode.[2.1] The two VAX-11 modes that remain to be described are the literal and index modes. Both of them are motivated by high-level language considerations.

The literal mode provides for a short, 6-bit, unsigned integer to be included as an immediate data operand directly in the mode byte itself. Many studies have indicated that small constants appear quite often in a wide variety of application programs. Therefore, their inclusion in a 1-byte operand specifier should lead to reduced program storage space and improved execution time. Longer constants

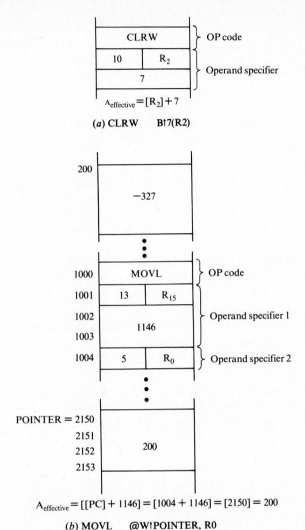

$A_{\text{effective}} = [R_2] + 7$

(a) CLRW   B↑7(R2)

$A_{\text{effective}} = [[PC] + 1146] = [1004 + 1146] = [2150] = 200$

(b) MOVL   @W↑POINTER, R0

Figure 3.10 VAX-11 displacement addressing mode examples.

can be specified by the immediate mode discussed earlier. The literal mode is indicated by setting the left-most 2 mode field bits of the mode byte to 0. The next 2 bits of the mode field, b_5 and b_4, along with bits b_3 through b_0, are used to specify the 6-bit immediate value. No register is involved in this mode. The decimal equivalent of the 4-bit mode field value thus varies from 0 to 3 in the literal mode, depending upon the high-order 2 bits of the constant being represented. We have simply shown the decimal equivalent of this mode as "0" in Table 3.1. The constant is represented by "Value" in the table, preceded by the # sign. The prefix S↑ indicates that short immediate data is to be used (the literal mode) to distinguish it from the immediate mode, indicated by the I↑ prefix, which is used for longer immediate data.

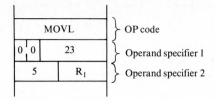

MOVL   S†#23, R1   **Figure 3.11** VAX-11 literal mode example.

   Figure 3.11 shows the use of the literal mode in loading the value 23 into register R_1. Since a Move Long-word instruction is used, the 6-bit operand is padded out with zeroes to the left to form a 32-bit value which is then loaded into R_1. It should be noted that short, floating-point constants can also be represented in the 6-bit data field of the literal mode. The OP code determines how the field is to be interpreted.
   The VAX-11 index mode is intended to be used for accessing individual elements in an array of fixed-length data elements. Suppose an array of integers is stored in consecutive main memory locations beginning at location ARRAY. In a high-level language program, the array elements may be referenced as ARRAY(0), ARRAY(1), etc. In machine instructions that refer to these elements, it is convenient if the starting address ARRAY can be specified in any of the usual addressing modes. Then, some simple way is needed to specify the subscript. A CPU register R_i can be used for this purpose. If the OP code specifies the length of an array element, then the actual address of the desired element can be computed during instruction execution. For example, if the elements are 4-byte integers in a byte-addressable machine, then the address of ARRAY(J) is computed as ARRAY + $[R_i]*4$, where $[R_i]$ = J. This is how the VAX-11 index mode is used.
   The VAX-11 index mode is named in the first byte of an operand specifier. This byte also specifies a register R_i, $0 \le i \le 14$, to be used as the index register. The index mode is always used in conjunction with another addressing mode, which can be any of the modes 6 through 15, and it is named in the second byte of the operand specifier. Suppose that this mode specifies the main memory address LOC. Then, if the instruction OP code indicates that the operand length is n bytes, the address generated by the complete operand specifier is

$$A_{\text{effective}} = \text{LOC} + [R_i]*n$$

   An example using the index mode is shown in Figure 3.12. A Clear-word instruction is used to clear the fourth element of a one-dimensional array whose first element is stored at main memory location ARRAY. The subscript defining the element to be cleared is stored in register R_6. The index mode is indicated by the code 4 in the first byte of the operand specifier, which also names R_6 as the index register. The address ARRAY = 1050 is generated by the relative mode with a byte displacement of 46 added to the current PC value of 1004. The subscript value 3 (specifying the fourth element) in register R_6 is multiplied by 2

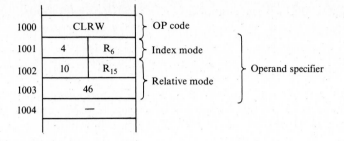

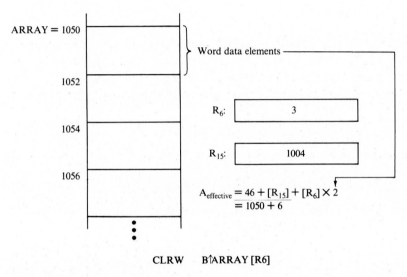

CLRW   B↑ARRAY [R6]

Figure 3.12 VAX-11 index mode example.

because the OP code specifies that word data is involved. The value 1056 is thus generated as the address of the word to be cleared.

As a further example of the usefulness of the VAX-11 index mode, let us suppose that the address 200 in location POINTER in Figure 3.10*b* is the starting address of an array of long-word integers. If register R_0 is used to hold an index into this array, then the address specification @POINTER[R0] can be used to access individual array elements. This is an example of an addressing mode in which indexing is applied after indirection. Such a technique is useful in accessing an array whose starting address (200 in our example) is stored in the main memory. This is the case if one routine passes the starting address of an array to other routines as a parameter through a designated memory location (POINTER in our example). Note that this style of addressing is not available in the PDP-11, where indirection is applied after indexing in the index indirect mode.

3.4.3 Instructions

The general format of VAX-11 instructions has already been discussed in Section 3.4.1. The instruction set is large, using most of the available 256 codes provided by the 8-bit OP code in the first byte of each instruction. In addition to the usual operations found in most computers, such as arithmetic and logic operations, data transfers, tests, and branches, the VAX-11 instruction set contains a number of more complex instructions. These instructions are intended to facilitate implementation of basic constructs that are common in high-level languages. This section will discuss examples of complex instructions, as well as the usual, simpler instructions.

Arithmetic and logic The operations of addition, subtraction, multiplication, and division are available for byte, word, and long-word integers, and for long-word and quad-word floating-point numbers. Each operation is provided in both two- and three-operand formats. An example of the two-operand format is the instruction

$$\text{ADDW2} \quad \text{op1,op2}$$

This instruction performs the operation

$$\text{op2} \leftarrow [\text{op1}] + [\text{op2}]$$

The three-operand format implements the three-address instructions discussed in Section 2.3. For example, the instruction

$$\text{ADDW3} \quad \text{op1,op2,op3}$$

performs the operation

$$\text{op3} \leftarrow [\text{op1}] + [\text{op2}]$$

Note that the combination of the 4 basic arithmetic operations, 5 data types, and 2 formats uses 40 of the 256 available OP codes.

In addition to providing for the standard operations on integer and floating-point numbers in binary representations, the VAX-11 instruction set includes the arithmetic operations on signed integers in packed decimal representation, which are useful in business applications. In this representation, decimal digits are represented in consecutive 4-bit fields, two per byte, with high-order digits first. An instruction referring to such a number must specify the address of the high-order byte and the length (in digits) of the number.

A full range of logical operations in both two- and three-operand formats is available.

Data transfers and conversions Move instructions are used to transfer operands between CPU registers and the main memory or from one area of the main memory to another. In any computer that supports a large number of data types, it is convenient, if not essential, to support conversions between the data types directly in the instruction set. The VAX-11 does this. For example, conversions from integer to floating-point format, and vice versa, are implemented.

Tests and branches Comparisons between two operands, and tests on individual operands, are used to set condition codes so that data-dependent branching can be done. A full set of conditional branches is included in the instruction set. An 8-bit signed offset value follows the OP code byte in the simplest form of a conditional branch instruction. Since such instructions allow branching only within a limited range, they are supplemented by a jump instruction which enables branching to any location in the address space. Some specialized instructions combine counter manipulation, testing, and branching operations. These instructions are convenient for loop termination control, as will be illustrated below.

More powerful instructions The VAX-11 has a number of instructions that are considerably more powerful than the types of instructions found on PDP-11 computers. These instructions implement sequences of simple machine operations that occur as common high-level language operations. Typical examples are calculations involving array subscripts and procedure calls that pass parameters on a stack. We will discuss a few such instructions because they are representative of instruction sets in modern computers that have been designed with high-level languages in mind.

Loop termination The VAX-11 has a three-operand instruction AOBLEQ (Add One and Branch on Less than or EQual) which is useful for loop-termination control. It increments the loop-control variable, compares it to a specified upper limit, and branches to the beginning of the loop if the limit has not been exceeded. The first operand specifies the upper limit, the second names the loop-control variable, and the third operand is the branch offset. Versions of this instruction which allow options such as decrementing the loop-control variable and using different termination conditions are also available.

Case structure A number of programming languages use a Case structure. It consists of a number of blocks of instructions. The first statement in the structure is the Case statement, which names a Case variable. The value of the Case variable determines which block is to be executed.

In the VAX-11, a three-operand instruction with the OP code CASE is provided. The operands specify the Case variable and its range. Address displacements to the beginning of the blocks are placed immediately after the

CASE instruction. Execution of this instruction causes a branch to the beginning of the block selected by the Case variable.

Array indexing Multidimensional arrays are a commonly used data structure. A specific element in a two-dimensional array might be referenced as ARRAY(I,J). Suppose the array is placed in the main memory in column order, with the first element, ARRAY(0, 0), in memory location ARRAY. Then, the element ARRAY(I, J) is found at memory location

$$ARRAY + J*m + I$$

where m is the number of rows (that is, the number of elements in each column). The index expression added to ARRAY is called an address polynomial. Generalizing to three dimensions with the use of a third subscript, K, we have the address polynomial

$$K*n*m + J*m + I$$

where n is the number of columns.

A more convenient computational form for the three-dimensional array address polynomial is

$$((K*n) + J)m + I$$

This form leads to an iterative calculation in which each individual step is: "add next subscript to the incoming accumulated index value and multiply by size." A VAX-11 instruction, with the OP code INDEX, is provided for this basic step. It has six operands:

Operand 1	subscript
Operand 2	low limit
Operand 3	high limit
Operand 4	size
Operand 5	incoming accumulated index value
Operand 6	outgoing accumulated index value

The operation of this instruction is as follows. The subscript value is checked to verify that it is in the range defined by the low and high limits. If it is not in this range, an error condition is indicated. Otherwise, the subscript value is added to the incoming accumulated index value and multiplied by the size operand. The result is placed in the outgoing accumulated index value location.

Consider a three-dimensional array ARRAY(I, J, K), where each element is a word and the subscripts range from 0 to $m-1$, $n-1$, and $p-1$, respectively. Let R_0 be used to accumulate the index value. The operation ARRAY (I, J, K) $\leftarrow$ 250 can be implemented by the instruction sequence

$$INDEX \quad K,\#0,\#p-1,\#n,\#0,R0$$

$$INDEX \quad J,\#0,\#n-1,\#m,R0,R0$$

INDEX   I,#0,#m−1,#1,R0,R0

MOVW   #250,ARRAY[R0]

It is easy to use the INDEX instruction in cases where the lower and upper limits are more general.

Procedure calls The efficiency of executing procedure calls is an important factor in evaluating the instruction set of a computer. The reason is that modern programming style emphasizes the use of procedures in organizing large programs into smaller, more manageable units that can be easily understood.

Two important aspects of executing procedure calls are: (*a*) the way in which parameters are passed from the calling program to the called procedure, and (*b*) the way in which CPU register contents are saved on entry to the called procedure and restored on return to the calling program. The VAX-11 allows two methods for handling procedure calls. They differ in the way in which parameters are passed. In the first method, parameters are placed in a main memory block, and a pointer to this block is named in the Procedure-call instruction. In the second method, parameters are passed via the processor stack. We will describe this second method in more detail.

The sequence of operations in calling a procedure is as follows. First, the parameters are pushed onto the stack. Then the Procedure-call instruction is executed. This instruction saves the contents of the CPU registers used by the procedure on the stack. Then, the old PC and PSW values are pushed onto the stack, and a branch is executed to the first instruction of the procedure. When execution of the procedure is completed, the Return instruction reverses the above sequence of steps by restoring the saved state of the CPU and then eliminating the parameters from the stack. The saved state consists of all CPU registers saved on the stack.

A number of details have been omitted from the above general description of the VAX-11 Procedure-call and Return instructions. In order to describe the complete process, it is necessary to introduce the use of registers R_{12} and R_{13} into the discussion. Register R_{12} is the argument pointer (AP) and R_{13} is the frame pointer (FP). The AP register is used as a pointer to the parameter list, and the FP register is used as a pointer to the saved state, called a frame in the VAX-11 literature. The parameter list and the saved state are blocks of long words stored on the stack. The AP and FP registers are set as part of the execution of the Procedure-call instruction. Since the old contents of these two registers are a part of the saved state, nesting of procedure calls is possible.

The Procedure-call instruction CALLS has two operands. The first operand, *n*, specifies the number of long-word parameters that were previously pushed onto the stack. The second operand is the address of the called procedure. After execution of the instruction

CALLS   #n,PROC

the stack contents are as shown in Figure 3.13. The AP and FP registers have

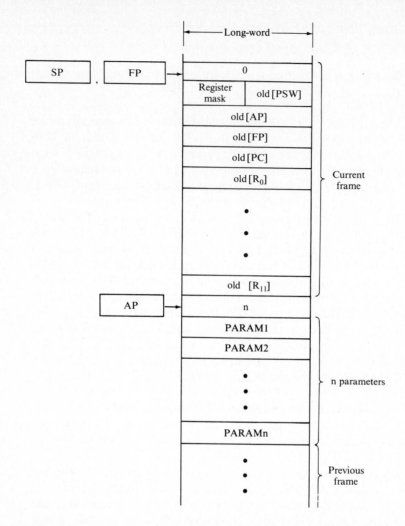

Figure 3.13 VAX-11 stack after execution of CALLS #n,PROC.

been loaded with the addresses of the beginning of the parameter list and frame, respectively. The value n has been placed at the beginning of the parameter list. It is used during the execution of the Return instruction in eliminating the parameters from the stack. The long word 0 at the beginning of the frame is a reserved space used under some special conditions.

The first word of the called procedure is a register mask which specifies the CPU registers to be used by the procedure. If bit b_i of the mask is 1, then register R_i will be used, and its old contents are saved on the stack. This mask is pushed onto the stack so that, during execution of the Return instruction, the CPU can determine which registers should be restored from the stack.

During execution of the called procedure, the n parameters on the stack will be accessed and used according to the calculation to be performed by the procedure. In order to further illustrate the flexibility of the VAX-11 addressing modes, we will briefly consider how parameters are accessed by the called procedure through the argument pointer (AP) register, which is R_{12}. Suppose the second parameter, PARAM2 in the list shown in Figure 3.13, is an operand that is to be moved into register R_0. Since each parameter is a long word, the displacement of the address of PARAM2 from the address in AP is 8. Thus, the instruction

$$\text{MOVL}\quad 8(\text{AP}),\text{R0}$$

will achieve the desired operation. If PARAM2 is the address of the operand, the operand can be accessed using the addressing mode @8(AP). Finally, if PARAM2 is the starting address of an array, the ith item of this array can be addressed by @8(AP)[RJ]. In this case, the offset i is the contents of index register R_j. This last possibility illustrates the usefulness of an addressing mode that involves two registers (AP and R_j) and also shows the motivation for performing indexing after indirection.

When execution of the called procedure is completed, the frame information on the stack is used to restore the contents of the CPU registers. Note that restoring AP and FP returns the CPU to the previous procedure.

3.4.4 Programming Examples

This section discusses two VAX-11 programs. They illustrate the instructions and the addressing modes in the context of two simple tasks: sorting and matrix multiplication.

Byte sorting A byte-sorting routine for the PDP-11 was discussed in Section 2.5.6. A list of unsigned byte integers is stored in the main memory, beginning at location LIST. The number of bytes in the list is N, and the bytes are to be sorted in increasing numerical order.

A VAX-11 program for this task that corresponds to the PDP-11 program in Figure 2.16 is shown in Figure 3.14. The first two instructions of the VAX-11 program initialize the J and K loop-control variables stored in registers R_1 and R_2. The next five instructions perform the basic sorting step of comparing two entries and interchanging them if necessary. Note that the Compare and Move instructions use the index mode in selecting list elements. In each case, the other mode used to generate the address LIST is the relative mode. Finally, a single instruction (AOBLEQ) is used to terminate each loop. This is in contrast to the Increment, Compare, and Branch instruction sequence used in the PDP-11 program.

Matrix multiplication A Pascal-like program for multiplication of two $n \times n$ matrices A and B was given in Figure 3.3, with a PDP-11 implementation in Figure 3.4. Recall that the array entries are assumed to consist of 16-bit integers.

	CLRL	R1	Initialize outer loop-control variable J to 0 in R_1.
OUTER:	ADDL3	S↑#1,R1,R2	Initialize inner loop-control variable K to J+1 in R_2.
INNER:	CMPB	LIST[R1],LIST[R2]	Compare LIST(J) to LIST(K) and interchange if LIST(J)>LIST(K).
	BLEQU	ENDINNER	
	MOVB	LIST[R1],R3	
	MOVB	LIST[R2],LIST[R1]	
	MOVB	R3,LIST[R2]	
ENDINNER:	AOBLEQ	#N−1,R2,INNER	Increment K and branch back if K≤N−1.
	AOBLEQ	#N−2,R1,OUTER	Increment J and branch back if J≤N−2.
	HALT		

Figure 3.14 VAX-11 byte-sorting program.

A VAX-11 program for the same task, under the same conditions, is shown in Figure 3.15. This program has the same structure as the PDP-11 program. The use of registers R_0 through R_5 is the same in both programs. The main observation to be made is that the availability of the INDEX and AOBLSS instructions reduces the number of machine instructions required. For example, a pair of INDEX instructions replaces four PDP-11 instructions in the calculation of each array index.

An obvious advantage of the availability of powerful instructions is that they simplify the implementation of common programming constructs.

	MOVL	N,R6	Load high limit of array
	DECL	R6	subscripts into R_6.
	CLRL	R0	I and J loop-control variables
LOOPI:	CLRL	R2	initialized to 0 in R_0 and R_2.
LOOPJ:	INDEX	R2,#0,R6,N,#0,R1	Compute relative address of
	INDEX	R0,#0,R6,#1,R1,R1	C(I,J) in R_1.
	CLRW	C[R1]	Clear C(I,J).
	CLRL	R4	K loop variable set to 0 in R_4.
LOOPK:	INDEX	R4,#0,R6,N,#0,R3	Compute relative address of
	INDEX	R0,#0,R6,#1,R3,R3	A(I,K) in R_3.
	MOVW	A[R3],R3	Move A(I,K) into R_3.
	INDEX	R2,#0,R6,N,#0,R5	Compute relative address of
	INDEX	R4,#0,R6,#1,R5,R5	B(K,J) in R_5.
	MULW2	B[R5],R3	$R_3 \leftarrow$ A(I,K)∗B(K,J).
	ADDW2	R3,C[R1]	C(I,J) $\leftarrow$ C(I,J) + [R_3].
	AOBLSS	N,R4,LOOPK	Termination of K loop.
	AOBLSS	N,R2,LOOPJ	Termination of J loop.
	AOBLSS	N,R0,LOOPI	Termination of I loop.
	HALT		

Figure 3.15 Matrix multiplication in a VAX-11.

3.5 THE IBM 370

Mid-size computers like the VAX-11 and large computers like the upper end of the IBM 370 line are characterized by a large main memory space, an extensive repertoire of instructions, fast operation, and considerable cost. All these characteristics are closely linked to the fundamental design decisions that determine the word length. In the last section we discussed the VAX-11, a 32-bit computer, in some detail. In this section we will briefly discuss some of the instruction set and addressing mode aspects of the IBM 370 family of computers, which also has a 32-bit word length.

Let us start by considering the generation of addresses for operands in the main memory. Similar to the scheme in the VAX-11, a common starting point is the contents of some register. The IBM 370 computers have sixteen 32-bit general-purpose registers that may be used for this function. Consider first a general form of indexed addressing. It is provided by making use of a *base register* R_b, an *index register* R_x, and an offset which in this case is called a *displacement* D. The effective address of the operand then becomes

$$A_{effective} = [R_b] + D + [R_x]$$

Registers R_b and R_x can be any two of the general-purpose registers other than register 0. A zero specification for a base or index register indicates that no base or index register is involved, respectively. The value $[R_b] + D$ may be regarded as the address of the first location of an array. The contents of index register R_x represent the distance between this location and the location of the operand that is being addressed. This is similar to one of the index modes in the VAX-11.

An additional degree of freedom is introduced through inclusion of the base register R_b. It, in effect, serves as a second index register whose main purpose is to allow *relocatability* of programs. In a large computer, it is common to have several programs residing in the main memory at the same time. In this environment it is desirable that a program and its associated data can be moved into any available space in the memory. An effective way of doing this is to specify a base register as part of each instruction that refers to storage operands. Then, a complete program can be located anywhere in the memory and executed correctly, simply by loading an appropriate address value into the base register. The contents of the base register remain unaltered during the computation of addresses. Thus, the value of R_b needs to be set only once at the start of each program. This means that R_b must not be used by the program as a general-purpose register in a way that changes its contents.

The requirement for relocating programs implies that the base register should be involved in all addressing modes for operands in the main memory. There are situations where this may not be true. In particular, an assembly language program can be written in such a way that absolute addresses, called *address constants*, are generated at assembly and initial load time. For example, one of the ways in which a subroutine call can be implemented involves loading the absolute address of the subroutine entry point into a register. Then a Branch instruction is executed which takes the contents of that register as the destination of the branch. In this case, the program will be executed correctly only if it is loaded in the main memory area for which it was originally assembled and loaded. If the program is loaded in a different position with a different value in the base register R_b, all references to main memory that are relative to R_b will operate correctly. But absolute references, such as the subroutine entry point mentioned above, will not be handled correctly because they are not specified relative to R_b. It is possible to explicitly manipulate such absolute references in the program to take into account the contents of R_b. However, this is not a desirable programming style.

A possible solution to the above problem involving address constants is to make all memory references relative to the contents of the base register. All programs in a computer that uses this approach will be relocatable. In this case, the programmer has no need to access the contents of the base register. In fact, it should not be permissible to include user instructions which access that register. Many computers incorporate mechanisms to enforce such restrictions. This provides protection against a user either accidentally or intentionally causing damage to other users' programs.

Another possibility for handling address constants is to adjust their values every time the program is loaded into a new position in the main memory. This is usually implemented by means of a program called a relocating loader, which will be discussed in Chapter 10. A more elegant solution to the relocatability problem is provided in computer systems that have a virtual memory feature. This topic will be treated in detail in Chapter 8.

Let us now return to our discussion of addressing modes in the IBM 370. An effective address is computed to involve 24 bits, which permits access to 2^{24} locations. This corresponds to approximately 16 million addressable units, which in this case are bytes. Since a 32-bit word contains 4 bytes, it follows that about 4 million words may be accessed.

The above discussion indicates that 8 bits are needed to specify R_b and R_x. The displacement D is allocated 12 bits. Another design decision resulted in a fixed OP-code field of 8 bits in all instructions, so that a total of 256 ($= 2^8$) distinct functions can be indicated. This means that in a two-operand instruction where one operand is to be specified in the indexed address mode, a total of 28 bits must be dedicated to this operand and the OP code. Therefore, if the instruction is to fit within a 32-bit word, the second operand must be in one of the registers. This corresponds to the RX (register and indexed storage) format in Figure 3.16.

Accepting the base register as a desirable part of all memory reference address modes, it follows that the simplest and most direct access mode would involve R_b and D, where $A_{effective} = [R_b] + D$. This requires a total of 16 bits. Since an 8-bit OP code is also part of each instruction, there are 8 bits left which can be used for specification of a second operand, or perhaps some control information. Figure 3.16 shows two ways of assigning these bits. In the SI (immediate data and storage) format they are used as immediate data. We

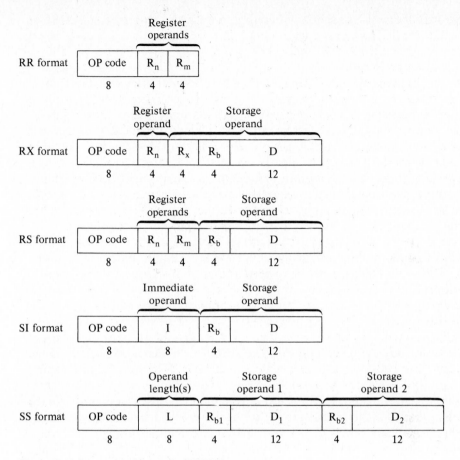

Figure 3.16 Instruction formats in IBM 370 computers.

should reemphasize that immediate data must be an integral part of the instruction. Having only 8 bits for the immediate operands is not a significant drawback, because in most cases such operands tend to be either characters or small number constants, which can fit in the available 8-bit space. The RS (register and storage) format makes use of the same field to specify two of the general-purpose registers. These registers, R_n and R_m, indicate the range of the registers to be affected by the instruction. For example, in the case of a Load Multiple instruction, a number of registers are loaded from the main memory location given by the storage operand field. The registers are loaded in ascending order starting with the register specified in the R_n field and ending with the register specified as R_m. This illustrates the most general application of the RS format, but we should point out that instructions in this group are rather diverse in nature.

Having presented the instruction formats that use 32-bit words, we should consider possible departures from this number. For example, it is quite common to have two-operand instructions where both operands are in registers. Such an instruction can be specified using an 8-bit OP code and 4 bits for each of the registers, as shown in the RR (register to register) format in Figure 3.16. Thus, a 16-bit instruction is defined.

At the other extreme, it is desirable to have two-operand instructions where both operands are in the main memory. This implies the existence of two address fields, each consisting of a base register and a displacement field. Thus, including the OP code, at least 40 bits must be available. Clearly, instructions of this type cannot fit into a single word. A good solution is to extend the instruction as indicated by the SS (storage to storage) format in Figure 3.16. The L field is introduced to allow specification of the length of either one or both operands. For example, an instruction of this type may be used to move character strings of up to 256 bytes in length from the memory location specified as the second operand to the location specified as the first operand.

The above five formats constitute the full set of instruction formats used in IBM 370 computers. The instructions have variable length, requiring 2, 4, or 6 bytes. The 8-bit OP-code field provides sufficient bit space to implement a versatile set of instructions including a full set of floating-point and decimal operations. The latter are particularly useful in business data processing applications.

Comparing the IBM 370 instruction set to that of the PDP-11, we can observe some interesting differences. The IBM 370 set benefits from the longer word length, so that the instructions, except for the SS format, fit into a single 32-bit word. This means that fewer words have to be fetched from the main memory in the execution of comparable programs. The instruction set is very extensive, and, like the instruction set in the VAX-11, includes many powerful instructions that have no PDP-11 counterparts. For example, a single instruction can move a string of characters from one memory area to another. Perhaps the most significant advantage lies in the simple mechanism for relocatability, which permits efficient implementations of multiprogram systems. However, some of the interesting features of the PDP-11 are completely absent in the IBM 370 machines. Indirect addressing does not exist. This is not necessarily a drawback, since indexed addressing can normally be substituted in tasks that might use the indirect mode. There is no equivalent to autoincrement and autodecrement address modes. As a result, there is no simple processor stack manipulation facility, and subroutine linkage is somewhat cumbersome.

Finally we should note that the IBM 370 computers were designed for multiuser environments. The addressable main memory space is sufficiently large to accommodate a number of sizable programs. In contrast, the 16-bit word length of the PDP-11 minicomputers limits their addressable space to 64K locations. Often, it is desirable to have a considerably larger memory. Some of the bigger models of the PDP-11 line contain a hardware unit that allows extension of the addressable space up to the equivalent of a 22-bit address. However, while the physical addresses are extended, the programs can still generate only 16-bit addresses. The extension of addresses to 22 bits is achieved by means of additional information that is kept in special registers. Data in these registers is manipulated by means of special machine instructions that we will not consider here.

3.6 THE HP3000

Section 2.7 introduced the concept of stacks as a useful data structure for digital processing. It showed how a stack may be implemented in the main memory and accessed by means of autoincrement and autodecrement addressing modes. This is the mechanism employed in the PDP-11 minicomputers. Many other computers allow similar implementations of stacks. A commonly used technique is to dedicate one hardware register to serve as a stack pointer (SP) that contains the memory address of the top word in the stack. In addition, two "stack instructions" PUSH and POP are provided. The PUSH instruction causes data to be pushed onto the top of the stack. It specifies the address of this data, or perhaps the data itself. Conversely, the POP instruction transfers the top element on the stack into the location specified in the instruction. Of course, both PUSH and POP instructions update the contents of the SP automatically.

The capability of realizing a stack data structure in the main memory has become a common feature in modern computers. It is equally important in large and small machines. However, despite its importance, it is usually not the dominant characteristic of a typical computer. This leads to an interesting question. Is it worthwhile to design computers that are stack-oriented to a greater extent? Indeed, might it be advantageous to have a machine in which the stack structure is its dominant feature? A simple answer to these questions cannot be given, since expert opinions lack consensus. There are a number of computational tasks where the stack data structure naturally leads to an efficient implementation. Indeed, a number of commercially successful "stack computers" have been developed. The best known examples are the Burroughs Corporation's line of computers: B5500, B6500, and B6700. These are large general-purpose computers. A notable example of a smaller stack machine is the Hewlett-Packard Company's HP3000 minicomputer.

Let us explore some possibilities for the organization of a stack computer. Its key component is the stack. We already know that the stack can reside in the main memory. An alternative may be to implement a stack using a set of registers. Let us assume that a stack capable of storing n-bit words is needed. Furthermore, let the required capacity of the stack be k words. Figure 3.17a shows a configuration where k registers, of n bits each, realize the desired stack. The registers are connected so that a Push signal transfers the contents of all registers downward by one position; that is, the contents of register i are transferred into register $i + 1$. The n-bit word is pushed onto the stack by loading it into register 0. Similarly, a Pop signal transfers the contents of all registers upward by one position. Thus the contents of register i are transferred into register $i - 1$. The original contents of register 0 are the n-bit word popped off the stack.

Another possibility is to use n shift registers, each of which has a capacity of

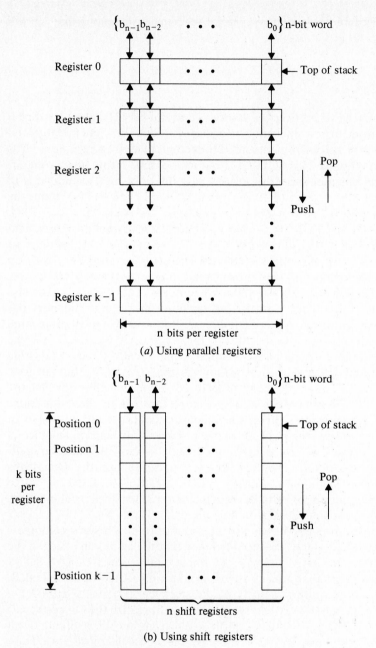

(a) Using parallel registers

(b) Using shift registers

Figure 3.17 Register implementation of a stack.

k bits, as indicated in Figure 3.17b. The shift registers must have the capability of shifting their contents in either direction, one bit position at a time. Under a Push signal the ith word in the stack, which occupies the ith bit position in all n registers, is shifted into the $(i + 1)$st position. Bit position 0 is loaded with the n-bit word that is being pushed onto the stack. A similar operation is performed under the Pop signal. In this case, the contents in bit position 0 are shifted out of the registers as the n-bit word is popped off the stack.

The main disadvantage of these schemes is the cost of the needed hardware. The stack depth k may be large ($k > 1000$), which implies the usage of either many relatively short n-bit registers, or considerably fewer long shift registers.

In practice, neither of the above schemes has found much favor. The alternative of using the main memory to implement the stack remains the most cost-effective approach that is used in commercial stack computers. Such machines rely heavily upon a set of hardware registers, used as pointers to the stack in the memory. On the other hand, they do not normally contain general-purpose registers of the type found in conventional computers. To give the reader an idea of how a stack computer may be organized, we will consider a few of the features of the HP3000 minicomputer.

3.6.1 Stack Structure of the HP3000 Computer

The HP3000 is a 16-bit minicomputer that exhibits a number of features more usually found in larger machines. However, since the aim of this section is to consider the stack mechanism, the discussion will concentrate only on the features that characterize the stack organization of this computer.

The main memory of the HP3000 contains the program instructions and the required data in separate domains. Instructions and data cannot be intermixed except for immediate data that may be used in the programs. Hardware registers are used as pointers to the program and data segments as shown in Figure 3.18.

Three registers define the program segment. The program base (PB) and the program limit (PL) registers indicate the memory area occupied by the program. The program counter (PC) has the usual function of pointing at the current instruction. Each of these registers contains the appropriate 16-bit address.

The data segment is divided into two parts: the stack and the data area. Five 16-bit pointers are used to delineate and access these memory locations. The contents of the data base (DB) register denote the starting location of the stack. The stack grows in the higher-address direction. Thus, if the top element of the stack is at location i, then the next element, when pushed onto the stack, will be at location $i + 1$. This is in contrast to the PDP-11 stack that expands in the direction of decreasing addresses, as explained in Section 2.7. The location of the top element in the stack, also called the top of stack (TOS), is stored in the 16-bit stack pointer (SP). The SP is not a single hardware register, as will be explained shortly, but it can be thought of as being such. It is incremented or decremented when data elements are pushed onto or popped off the stack, respectively. From the user's point of view, it functions as any other 16-bit

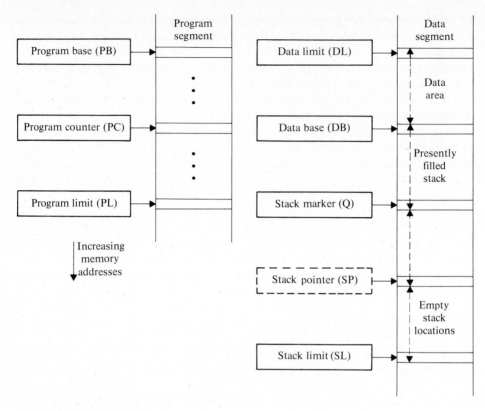

Figure 3.18 Program and data segment organization in the HP3000.

pointer register. The upper limit of the stack is defined by the contents of the stack limit (SL) register. Therefore, the stack is allowed to grow until [SP] = [SL]. Any attempt to extend the stack past the limits defined by DB and SL is automatically checked by the hardware. The data area extends from the location immediately preceding the location pointed at by the DB register to the limit specified in the data limit (DL) register.

The above pointer registers specify the existing size, the maximum size, and the location in memory of the stack. Thus the stack is a dynamic structure that can be easily changed. Figure 3.18 shows one other pointer that has not yet been discussed: the stack marker (Q) register. It is used to denote the starting point for the data of the current routine or "procedure." Actually, it points to the fourth word of a four-word entry in the stack, named the stack marker, which facilitates passing of control between procedures. When processing of the current procedure has to be suspended and a new procedure (for example, an interrupt-handling routine) is to be initiated, it is necessary to temporarily store the information required to allow proper return to the suspended procedure. This information is placed onto the stack in the form of the stack marker. The first word stores the current contents of an index register. The second word contains the return address. This information is actually stored as the difference between the value of the PC (pointing at the next instruction that is to be executed in the current procedure) and the contents of the PB register. Note that storing this difference, instead of the absolute value of the PC, allows programs to be moved out of the memory and later to be returned to a different place in the memory. Thus programs can be dynamically relocated by changing the value of the PB register. The third word saves the status information contained in the status register. In the fourth word, the distance (that is, the number of locations) between this stack marker and the one immediately preceding it is stored. Figure 3.19 shows two stack markers, one corresponding to the current procedure (Procedure$_k$) and another that is placed onto the stack when a new procedure

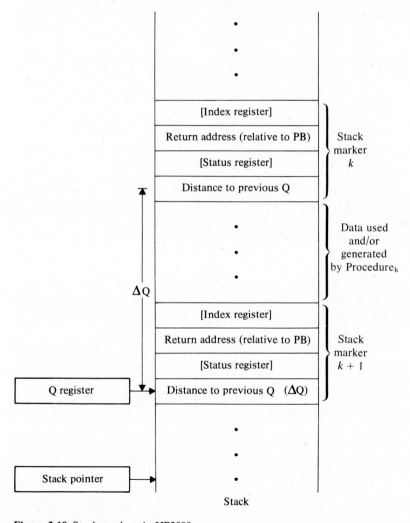

Figure 3.19 Stack markers in HP3000.

(Procedure$_{k+1}$) is initiated. Upon completion of the new procedure, control is transferred to the previous procedure by means of the data in the stack marker $k + 1$. At that time, the Q register must be set to point at the fourth word of the stack marker k. This is readily accomplished, since the distance between the stack markers is stored as a part of each marker. Also, the SP is set to point at the location immediately preceding the stack marker $k + 1$. Thus, the SP points at the top of the stack used by Procedure$_k$. This restores the situation that existed at the time when Procedure$_{k+1}$ was invoked. The technique described above can be used to nest any number of procedures. Note that we have simplified our discussion by leaving out the parameter-passing protocols, which also make use of the stack.

In addition to the pointer registers, the HP3000 computers have many other hardware registers. They are used to facilitate the internal organization of the machine. Only two of these are "visible" to the programmer, namely, the index and the status registers. Their function is essentially the same as that of equivalently named registers in most other computers. We should note that there are no general-purpose registers available to the programmer. Instead, data is manipulated using the stack as temporary storage, as will be shown in an example in the next section.

3.6.2 Stack Instructions in the HP3000

The basic strategy in stack computers is to perform most operations on the data that is in the top few locations of the stack. This implies that many instructions will use operands that are already in these locations. Furthermore, the results generated are left on the stack. Of course this assumes the existence of instructions that can move data between the stack and other main memory locations.

The HP3000 instructions are 16 bits in length. There is a considerable variety of instructions provided. Most of them involve the stack in some way. Typically, either the operands, operand addresses, or other relevant parameters reside in the stack. This allows great flexibility in making use of the 16-bit code space of the instructions.

There are 13 major classes of instructions. Instead of a full description of the HP3000 instruction set, we will restrict our attention to only a few classes, which illustrate the stack organization of the machine. Let us first consider the "Memory Address" instructions, whose format is shown in Figure 3.20. Eleven valuations of the 4-bit OP-code field are used to specify this class of instructions, which include:

LOAD Push a specific memory word onto the stack.

STOR Pop the top word of the stack (TOS) into a specified memory location.

ADDM Add a specified memory word to TOS and replace the TOS operand with the resultant sum.

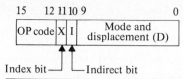

Mode		Bit pattern b_9 b_8 b_7 b_6 b_5 b_4 b_3 b_2 b_1 b_0	Effective memory address
PC+	relative	0 0 ←————— D —————→	$[PC] + D$
PC−	relative	0 1 ←————— D —————→	$[PC] - D$
DB+	relative	1 0 ←————— D —————→	$[DB] + D$
Q+	relative	1 1 0 ←——— D ———→	$[Q] + D$
Q−	relative	1 1 1 0 ←—— D ——→	$[Q] - D$
SP−	relative	1 1 1 1 ←—— D ——→	$[SP] - D$

Figure 3.20 "Memory Address" instruction format in HP3000.

MPYM   Multiply a specified memory word with TOS and replace the TOS operand with the least significant word of the product.

INCM   Increment a specified memory word.

These instructions specify the memory operand in the relative address mode, where the addresses are given relative to the contents of the PC, DB, Q, or SP registers. The 10-bit mode and displacement field indicates the mode and the magnitude of the displacement as shown in the figure. Note that the range of the displacement is not the same in all modes, since the displacement field varies from 6 to 8 bits. Index and indirect bits are used to denote that indexed and/or indirect addressing is to be performed. We should mention that these are the only addressing modes that can be used to address operands in the data area of Figure 3.18.

The second class of instructions that reference either one or two memory operands are the "Move" instructions. These are instructions that can move a number of words or bytes of data from one memory location to another, compare two strings of bytes in the memory, scan a byte string until a particular byte is found, etc. Again, in this class of instructions, the memory addresses are computed in the relative mode. However, the displacement is not given explicitly within the instruction. Instead, it is included as data in the stack. Moreover, the relative addresses can be specified only with respect to the program or data bases, that is, the contents of the PB or DB registers, respectively. A good example of this class of instructions is the basic MOVE instruction, which transfers k words from the source memory locations into the destination memory locations, where

- k is specified by the first stack element (TOS).
- The address of the first source memory location is given by the contents of the second stack element, relative to either PB or DB.

• The address of the first destination memory location is given by the contents of the third stack element, relative to DB.

The only reason that this instruction can be represented within a 16-bit code space is the fact that most of the addressing data as well as the length parameter are defined in stack locations that are implicitly specified. Of course, such data must be loaded onto the stack, before instructions of the above type can be executed.

Next, we will consider the "Stack" instructions, whose format is shown in Figure 3.21. This class of instructions is identified by four 0s in the high-order bit positions. The remaining 12 bits are available to specify particular instructions. They are split into two 6-bit fields, each of which may be used to specify a distinct operation. Since 6 bits allow 64 distinct valuations, it follows that up to 64 distinct stack operations may be defined in this manner. This number is large enough to accommodate a variety of stack operations. As a result of this structure, an instruction specifying one stack operation uses 10 bits (main OP code plus the stack OP code A), while the remaining 6 bits are not used. However, the remaining 6 bits may be used to specify a second stack operation (stack OP code B) that will be performed after the completion of the first operation. In this way, two stack operations may be packed within a single instruction. We should reemphasize that such efficient utilization of the instruction code space is possible only because addressing data and/or operands are not included explicitly as part of an instruction.

Some examples of "Stack" instructions are:

ADD Add the contents of the top two words on the stack, delete these words from the stack, and push the sum onto the stack.

CMP Compare the contents of the top two words on the stack, set the condition codes accordingly, and delete both words from the stack.

DIV Divide the integer in the second word of the stack by the integer in TOS. Replace the second word with the quotient and the word in TOS with the remainder.

DEL Delete the top word of the stack.

Many instructions of this type are provided. Some of the instructions are more complicated. For example, a Divide Long instruction, DIVL, divides a double-word integer in the second and third elements of the stack by the integer in the first element. These three words are then deleted, while the quotient and the

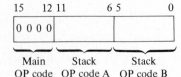

Main   Stack   Stack
OP code OP code A OP code B   **Figure 3.21** Format for "Stack" instructions in HP3000.

remainder are pushd onto the stack, becoming the second and the first elements, respectively. In this paragraph, we have used the term instruction somewhat loosely. It would have been more rigorous to refer to Add and Divide operations, since two such operations can be specified within a single instruction. However, it is more customary to speak in terms of instructions when describing such actions. Indeed, it is appropriate to describe the above technique as packing two instructions into one.

The OP-code field B for specifying a second stack operation can be used to advantage only when two consecutive stack operations are to be performed. In other cases this part of the instruction remains unused. So far we have emphasized only one advantage of compressing instructions, namely, the low code-space requirements. Another advantage stems from the reduced number of memory accesses, since effectively two instructions are fetched as part of one 16-bit word. Of course, we must remember that during the execution of a stack instruction it is necessary to access operands in the stack, which implies memory accesses if the stack resides in the main memory.

We will not discuss the remaining classes of instructions in the HP3000. Let us only note that they make good use of the available bit space by means of implicit specification of operands on the stack.

To illustrate the role of the stack as temporary storage for intermediate results in arithmetic processing, it is useful to consider a simple example. Figure 3.22 shows an arithmetic expression that is to be evaluated. We will assume that the values of the variables A, B, . . . , and H are not available at the top of the stack. They are stored in memory locations with addresses A, B, . . . , and H. Thus, they may be accessed using the addressing mechanism given in Figure 3.20. Furthermore, let all operands be integers whose range is such that only single-length products need to be considered. The figure shows 13 processing steps that must be performed. The required operations follow the order obtained when the expression is scanned from left to right. In our notation the top element of the stack (TOS) is denoted as S. Thus, the operation $S \leftarrow [S] + [B]$ means that the contents of TOS and the operand B are added, and the sum replaces the value in TOS. Similarly, the operation $S \leftarrow [S-1]/[S]$ indicates that the contents of the second element in the stack are divided by the contents of TOS. The two operands are deleted from the stack and the resultant quotient is pushed onto the stack. The HP3000 machine instructions needed to perform the necessary computation are also shown in the figure. Their functional description was given earlier in this section. Most steps can be implemented with a single instruction. The only exception is the division operation. The DIV instruction replaces the dividend and the divisor with the quotient and the remainder, respectively. Since we are interested only in the quotient, it is necessary to delete the remainder from TOS, which can be accomplished with the DEL instruction. Note that whenever two consecutive Stack instructions are encountered, they can be combined into one 16-bit instruction as explained previously. All intermediate results are stored on the stack. Figure 3.22b shows the top elements of the stack after the completion of step 9.

$$W = (A + B)/\{C/D + (EF)/(G + H)\}$$

(*a*) Operations to be performed and the necessary machine instructions

Step	Operation performed	Machine instruction	
1	$S \leftarrow [A]$	LOAD	A
2	$S \leftarrow [S] + [B]$	ADDM	B
3	$S \leftarrow [C]$	LOAD	C
4	$S \leftarrow [D]$	LOAD	D
5	$S \leftarrow [S-1]/[S]$	DIV, DEL	combined
6	$S \leftarrow [E]$	LOAD	E
7	$S \leftarrow [S] * [F]$	MPYM	F
8	$S \leftarrow [G]$	LOAD	G
9	$S \leftarrow [S] + [H]$	ADDM	H
10	$S \leftarrow [S-1]/[S]$	DIV, DEL	combined
11	$S \leftarrow [S-1] + [S]$	ADD	
12	$S \leftarrow [S-1]/[S]$	DIV, DEL	combined
13	$W \leftarrow [S]$	STOR	W

(*b*) Temporary results stored in the stack after step 9

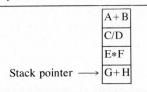

Stack pointer $\longrightarrow$

Figure 3.22 An example of stack usage in arithmetic processing.

3.6.3 Hardware Registers in the Stack

Accessing of main memory locations is one of the most critical time constraints in a computer. The time needed to read (write) an operand from (into) the main memory tends to be long in comparison with the time required to transfer data or perform operations within the CPU. This is the main argument for inclusion of general-purpose registers in the CPU. In the case of stack computers, the temporary storage function of the general-purpose registers is provided through the stack mechanism. If the stack is implemented strictly in the main memory, it will be necessary to make frequent memory accesses, as all temporary storage locations are a part of the stack. In view of the time that has to be spent on such accesses, it is unlikely that a stack machine of this type will compare favorably with a standard computer that has a set of hardware registers for general-purpose use.

In Section 3.6.1 we considered the possibility of implementing the entire stack with hardware registers. It was suggested that this is an expensive and somewhat inflexible approach. But, there is a possible compromise between the all-register and all-memory implementations of the stack. Let us suppose that most of the stack resides in the main memory but that its top few elements are held in hardware registers in the CPU. It would then be possible to shorten the time for most accesses to the stack, since they most frequently involve only the top few elements and such accesses would only require register transfers within the CPU. How many registers should be provided as part of the stack? The number should clearly be small. In the HP3000 computer there are four such registers that contain the top four elements of the stack.

Inclusion of hardware registers in the stack implies that the true top of the stack (TOS) will often be in one of the registers. This means that the SP does not necessarily point at a memory location. To keep track of the actual situation at any given time the SP function is implemented by two registers. A 16-bit stack in memory (SM) register contains the address of the highest memory address presently occupied by the stack. A 3-bit register SR is used to indicate whether zero, one, two, three, or four top elements of the stack are presently contained in the hardware registers. Thus, the value [SP] is, in effect,

$$[SP] = [SM] + [SR]$$

The value [SP] is equal to the address in the main memory where the top of the stack would be if all elements of the stack were in the main memory. This structure is illustrated in Figure 3.23.

The programmer does not have to be aware of the inclusion of hardware registers in the stack. For the programmer's purpose, there is only one relevant pointer, namely, the stack pointer, which appears as if it is indeed an actual

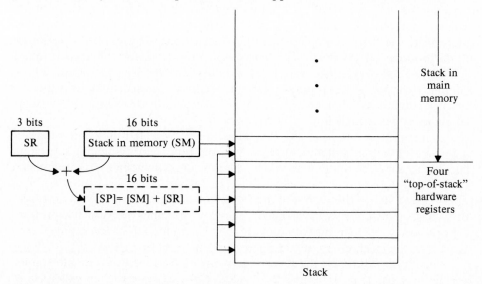

Figure 3.23 Top-of-stack structure in the HP3000.

pointer register. The existence of hardware stack registers merely reduces the number of memory references required and in doing so speeds up the operation of the computer.

3.7 CONCLUDING REMARKS

One of the main objectives of this chapter was to impress upon the reader the fact that there exist considerable differences between various computers. The fundamental principles of operations of digital machines that execute programs stored in a main memory are essentially the same for all computers. However, the more detailed characteristics vary from machine to machine, as they are dependent upon the size and structure of the machine. The differences between various computers are readily understood when one understands the common basic principles.

Let us summarize some of the ideas discussed in this chapter. A key feature of any computer is its mechanism for addressing operands in the main memory. The addressing scheme is inevitably dependent upon the word length of a given machine. The longer the word length the more bits can be dedicated for addressing purposes. Thus a larger number of memory locations can be addressed, and the addressing mechanism may be simplified. Maximum size of the main memory is a very important factor in many applications. In a 16-bit minicomputer, such as the PDP-11, it is not easy to provide more memory than the "natural" maximum of 64K bytes. In larger word-length machines such as the VAX-11 or the IBM 370, there is no difficulty in providing sufficient memory space.

Instruction sets are also heavily dependent upon the word length. The number and the variety of instructions that can be provided depend upon the utilization of the bit space within each instruction. It is often necessary to use more than one word to implement some instructions. This effect is, obviously, more pronounced in short word-length machines (minicomputers and microcomputers). However, we should also note that the basic structure of the computer can be such that many operands are implicitly specified, as is the case in stack computers. Then, a wide variety of instructions can be provided using a single word per instruction.

In a multiuser environment, it is important to be able to relocate programs anywhere in the main memory. Moreover, the process of relocating a program should be easy to implement. Computers where all memory references are computed relative to the contents of some registers are best suited for such applications. In our discussion of the IBM 370 computers, we saw that inclusion of a base register in addressing of memory operands serves this purpose. Relocatability of programs is also easily achieved in the HP3000 computer, since all memory references are made relative to the pointer registers.

Finally, we discussed the issue of how instruction sets can provide support for high-level languages. Using the VAX-11 instruction set as an example, we illustrated a few of the ways that specialized, complex instructions can be used to implement certain constructs that commonly occur in high-level languages.

3.8 PROBLEMS

3.1 A given computer has 16-bit instructions. Operand addresses are specified using 6-bit fields. There are K two-operand instructions (for example, Compare) and L zero-operand instructions (for example, Halt) required. What is the maximum number of one-operand instructions that can be provided in this computer?

3.2 It is desirable to add a new instruction to the PDP-11 instruction set. This instruction, called INSERT, is supposed to achieve the combined effect of the instructions BIC and BIS as used in the example of Figure 2.17. Assume that an arbitrary pattern of bits can be inserted into a destination operand that may be specified in any of the eight address modes. The instruction INSERT may affect an arbitrary number of bit positions of the destination operand, while the remaining bit positions are not affected.

(*a*) Show how this instruction may be implemented using the format of Figure 3.1*b*.

(*b*) How could the instruction be implemented using the format of Figure 3.1*c*?

(*c*) How do execution time (in terms of memory accesses required) and memory space requirements of this instruction compare with the BIC, BIS sequence that implements the same function?

3.3 Show how an instruction INSERT similar to that of Problem 3.2 may be implemented for the IBM 370 computers. In this case, the instruction can insert one or more BCD (binary-coded decimal) digits into any of the eight 4-bit fields of a 32-bit destination operand. Which of the formats of Figure 3.16 are suitable for implementation of this instruction?

3.4 Discuss the relative merits of addressing modes in the PDP-11, VAX-11, and IBM 370 computers. In particular, discuss how the addressing modes in each machine facilitate the following: relocatability, implementation of a stack, accessing an operand list, and manipulating character strings.

3.5 IBM 370 computers do not have indirect addressing. Assume that an address of an operand is stored in the main memory. How would you access this operand?

3.6 Discuss the facility for relocating programs in the PDP-11, VAX-11, IBM 370, and HP3000 computers. How would you rank these computers with respect to this facility?

3.7 Write a PDP-11 program to evaluate the arithmetic expression in Figure 3.22. How does your program compare with the one given in the figure with respect to the number of memory locations and memory accesses required?

3.8 Show how the expression

$$W = A\{(BC + DE) + FG/HI\}$$

can be evaluated in an HP3000 computer. How many memory words are needed for the program?

3.9 In an HP3000 computer, Procedure$_i$ generates eight words of data DI$_1$, . . . , DI$_8$, which are stored in the stack. After these words are placed in the stack, but before the completion of Procedure$_i$ a new Procedure$_j$ is called. It generates 10 words of data DJ$_1$, . . . , DJ$_{10}$, which are also stored in the stack. Then, another Procedure$_k$ is called, which places three words of data in the stack.

Show the contents of the top words of the stack at this time.

3.10 (*a*) In the byte-sorting program shown in Figure 3.14, the address value LIST and the value N are fixed in the program code at assembly time. Rewrite the program as a VAX-11 procedure under the assumption that addresses of memory locations containing these values are passed on the stack from a calling program. See Figure 3.13 for the stack format.

(*b*) The execution-time efficiency of the byte-sorting procedure of part (*a*) can be improved by keeping track of the address of the smallest byte of a sublist LIST(J) to LIST(N−1) and performing, at most, one swap at the end of the sublist search. Rewrite the part (*a*) procedure to achieve this efficiency, and estimate the improvement. What happens to code-space requirements when time efficiency is improved?

3.11 Using the VAX-11 INDEX instruction, and other instructions as necessary, give a program segment that clears the word at array location A(I, J, K) in the case where the subscript ranges are

$$I: \quad IF, IF + 1, \cdots, IL$$

$$J: \quad JF, JF + 1, \cdots, JL$$

$$K: \quad KF, KF + 1, \cdots, KL$$

3.12 Show how the expression

$$W = (A + B)(C + D) + D*E$$

can best be evaluated on both the HP3000 and the PDP-11. The values of variables W, A, B, C, D, and E are stored in memory locations and the following assumptions are made. The addresses do not reference successive locations. Direct memory addressing in the DB+ relative mode is used in the HP3000. Absolute memory addressing is used in the PDP-11. All products are single length and the PDP-11 has a MULT instruction in the double-operand class with the restriction that the destination operand must be in a CPU register.

3.13 Although there are fewer instructions in Figure 3.15 than in Figure 3.4, what about total number of bytes needed to represent each program? Also, how many main memory accesses are needed to execute each program. Assume that the PDP-11 reads or writes 16 bits (a word) per access, and the VAX-11 can access up to 32 bits (a long word) at a time. (Assume that when fetching instructions, the VAX-11 always fetches 32 bits at a time.)

3.14 Repeat Problem 3.13 for the programs in Figures 2.16 and 3.14.

THE PROCESSING UNIT

In the previous chapters, the reader was introduced to a reasonably detailed picture of the computer as seen by the programmer. We shall now turn our attention to the organization and operation of the different building blocks that comprise a computer system.

In its simplest form, a computer system has one unit that executes program instructions. This unit communicates with, and often controls the operation of, other subsystems within the computer. Because of the central role of such a unit, it is known as a central processing unit, or CPU. In many computers, a subsystem within the computer, such as an input unit or a mass storage device, may incorporate a processing unit of its own. Such a processing unit, while being central to its own subsystem, is clearly not "central" to the computer system as a whole. However, the principles involved in the design and operation of a CPU are independent of its position in a computer system. In this chapter we will deal with the organization of the hardware which enables a CPU to perform its main function: to fetch and execute instructions.

The solution algorithm for any problem consists of a number of steps that should be carried out in a specific sequence. To implement such an algorithm on a computer, these steps are broken down into a number of smaller steps, where each of the smaller steps represents one machine instruction. The resulting sequence of instructions is a machine language program representing the algorithm in question. The same general approach is used to enable the computer to perform the functions specified by individual machine instructions. That is, each of these instructions is executed by carrying out a sequence of more rudimentary operations. These operations, and the means by which they are generated, will be the main topic of discussion in this chapter.

117

4.1 SOME FUNDAMENTAL CONCEPTS

The instructions constituting a program to be executed by a computer are loaded in sequential locations in its main memory. To execute this program, the CPU fetches one instruction at a time and performs the functions specified. Instructions are fetched from successive memory locations until the execution of a branch or a jump instruction. As discussed in previous chapters, the CPU keeps track of the address of the memory location where the next instruction is located through the use of a dedicated CPU register, referred to as the program counter (PC). After fetching an instruction, the contents of the PC are updated to point at the next instruction in sequence.

Let us assume, for simplicity, that each instruction occupies one memory word. Therefore, execution of one instruction requires the following three steps to be performed by the CPU:

1. Fetch the contents of the memory location pointed at by the PC. The contents of this location are interpreted as an instruction to be executed. Hence, they are stored in the instruction register (IR). Symbolically, this can be written as

$$IR \leftarrow [[PC]]$$

2. Increment the contents of the PC by 1.

$$PC \leftarrow [PC] + 1$$

3. Carry out the actions specified by the instruction stored in the IR.

Note that in cases where an instruction occupies more than one word, steps 1 and 2 can be repeated as many times as necessary to fetch the complete instruction. These two steps are usually referred to as the *fetch phase*, while step 3 constitutes the *execution phase*.

Before proceeding to study the above operations in detail, we shall pause briefly to examine the structure of the main data paths inside the CPU. Most of the building blocks of the CPU were introduced in Figure 1.8. These blocks can be organized and interconnected in a variety of ways. One such organization is shown in Figure 4.1. In this case, the arithmetic and logic unit (ALU) and all CPU registers are connected via a single common bus. This bus, of course, is internal to the CPU, and should not be confused with the external bus, or buses, connecting the CPU to the memory and I/O devices. The external memory bus is shown in Figure 4.1 connected to the CPU via the memory data and address registers MDR and MAR. The number and function of registers R0 to R(n − 1) vary considerably from one machine to another. They may be provided for general-purpose use by the programmer. Alternatively, some of them may be dedicated as special-purpose registers, such as index registers or stack pointers.

Two registers in Figure 4.1, namely, registers Y and Z, have not been mentioned before. These registers are transparent to the programmer. That is, the programmer need not be concerned with their existence, since they are never

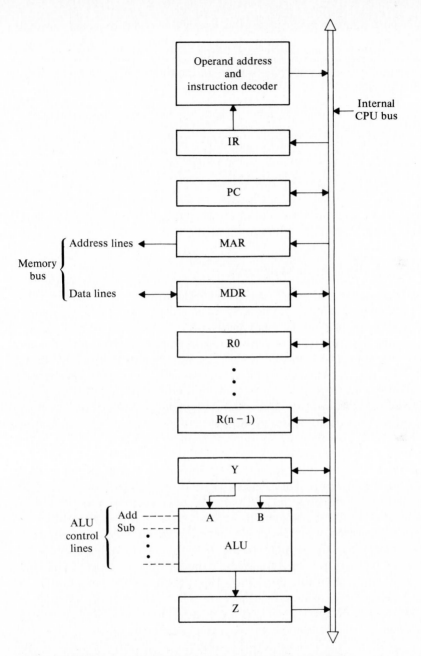

Figure 4.1 Single-bus organization of the data paths inside the CPU.

referenced directly by any instruction. They are used only by the CPU for temporary storage during execution of some instructions. However, they are never used for storing data generated by one instruction for later use by another instruction. The means by which registers Y and Z, as well as other components in Figure 4.1, participate in instruction execution will become apparent from the ensuing discussion.

With few exceptions, most of the operations in steps 1 to 3 mentioned earlier can be carried out by performing one or more of the following functions in some prespecified sequence:

1. Fetch the contents of a given memory location and load them into a CPU register.
2. Store a word of data from a CPU register into a given memory location.
3. Transfer a word of data from one CPU register to another or to the ALU.
4. Perform an arithmetic or logic operation, and store the result in a CPU register.

Let us now consider in some detail the way in which each of the above functions is implemented in a typical computer.

4.1.1 Fetching a Word from Memory

In a random-access memory, information is stored in locations identified by their addresses. To fetch a word of information from memory, the CPU has to specify the address of the memory location where this information is stored and request a Read operation. This applies whether the information to be fetched represents a new instruction in a program or a word of data (operand) specified by an instruction. Thus, to perform a memory fetch, the CPU transfers the address of the required information word to the memory address register (MAR). As shown in Figure 4.1, the MAR is connected to the address lines of the memory bus. Hence the address of the required word is transferred to the main memory. Meanwhile, the CPU uses the control lines of the memory bus to indicate that a Read operation is required. Normally, after issuing this request the CPU waits until it receives an answer from the memory, informing it that the requested function has been completed. This is accomplished through the use of another control signal on the memory bus, which will be referred to as Memory-Function-completed (MFC). The memory sets this signal to 1 to indicate that the contents of the specified location in the memory have been read and are available on the data lines of the memory bus. We will assume that as soon as the MFC signal is set to 1, the information on the data lines is loaded into MDR and is thus available for use inside the CPU. This completes the memory fetch operation. As an example, assume that the address of the memory location to be accessed is in register R1 and that the memory data is to be loaded into register R2. This is achieved by the following sequence of operations:

1. MAR ← [R1]
2. Read
3. Wait for the MFC signal
4. R2 ← [MDR]

The duration of step 3 depends upon the speed of the memory used. Usually, the time required to read a word from the memory is longer than the time required to perform any single operation within the CPU. Therefore, the overall execution time of an instruction can be decreased if the sequence of operations is organized such that a useful function is performed within the CPU while waiting for the memory to respond. Obviously, only functions that do not require the use of MDR or MAR can be carried out during this time. Such a situation arises during the fetch phase. As we will see shortly, the PC can be incremented while waiting for the Read operation to be completed.

In the above discussion, we have presented an example of the way in which data transfer can take place between two devices, namely, the CPU and the main memory. The transfer mechanism where one device initiates the transfer (Read request) and waits until the other device responds (MFC signal) is referred to as an *asynchronous* transfer. It can be easily seen that this mechanism enables transfer of data between two independent devices that have different speeds of operation. An alternative scheme found in some computers uses *synchronous* transfers. In this case, one of the control lines of the bus carries pulses from a continuously running clock of a fixed frequency. These pulses provide common timing signals to the CPU and the main memory. A memory operation is completed during every clock period. Furthermore, the instants at which the address is placed on the address lines and the data is loaded into MDR are fixed relative to the clock pulses. The synchronous bus scheme leads to a simpler implementation. However, it cannot accommodate devices of widely varying speed, except by reducing the speed of all devices to that of the slowest one. In the remainder of the discussion of the operation of the CPU, we will assume that an asynchronous memory bus is used.

4.1.2 Storing a Word into Memory

The procedure for writing a word into a given memory location is similar to that for reading from the memory. The only exception is that the data word to be written is loaded into the MDR before the Write command is issued. If we assume that the data word to be stored in the memory is in R2 and that the memory address is in R1, the Write operation requires the following sequence:

1. MAR ← [R1]
2. MDR ← [R2]
3. Write
4. Wait for MFC

It is interesting to note that steps 1 and 2 are independent. Therefore they can be carried out in any order. In fact, steps 1 and 2 can be carried out simultaneously, if this is allowed by the architecture, that is, if the two transfers do not use the same data path. Of course, this would not be possible in the single-bus organization of Figure 4.1. Note also that, as in the case of the Read operation, the wait period in step 4 may be overlapped with other operations, provided that such operations do not involve registers MDR or MAR.

4.1.3 Register Transfers

To enable data transfer between various blocks connected to the common bus in Figure 4.1, input and output gating must be provided. This is represented symbolically in Figure 4.2. The input and output gates for register Ri are controlled by the signals Ri_{in} and Ri_{out}, respectively. Thus, when Ri_{in} is set to 1, the data available on the common bus is loaded into Ri. Similarly, when Ri_{out} is set to 1, the contents of register Ri are placed on the bus. While Ri_{out} is equal to 0, the bus can be used for transferring data from other registers. The details of implementation of input and output gating will be discussed in Section 4.1.5.

Let us now consider data transfer between two registers. For example, to transfer the contents of register R1 to register R4, the following actions are needed:

- Enable the output gate of register R1 by setting $R1_{out}$ to 1. This places the contents of R1 on the CPU bus.
- Enable the input gate of register R4 by setting $R4_{in}$ to 1. This loads data from the CPU bus into register R4.

This data transfer can be represented symbolically as

$$R1_{out}, R4_{in}$$

4.1.4 Performing an Arithmetic or Logic Operation

When performing an arithmetic or logic operation, it should be remembered that the ALU itself is a combinational circuit that has no internal storage. Therefore, to perform an addition, for example, the two numbers to be added should be made available at the two inputs of the ALU simultaneously. Register Y, in Figure 4.1, is provided for this purpose. It is used to hold one of the two numbers while the other number is gated to the bus. The result is stored temporarily in register Z. Therefore, the sequence of operations to add the contents of register R1 to register R2 and store the result in register R3 should be as follows:

Step	Action
1	$R1_{out}, Y_{in}$
2	$R2_{out}, Add, Z_{in}$
3	$Z_{out}, R3_{in}$

In step 2 of this sequence the contents of register R2 are gated to the bus, hence to input B of the ALU which is connected directly to the bus. The contents of register Y are always available at input A. The function performed by the ALU depends upon the signals applied to the ALU control lines. In this case, the Add line is set to 1, causing the output of the ALU to be the sum of the two numbers

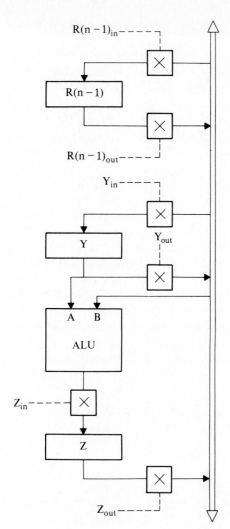

Figure 4.2 Input and output gating for the registers in Figure 4.1.

at A and B. This sum is loaded into register Z, since its input gate is enabled (Z_{in}). In step 3, the contents of register Z are transferred to the destination register R3. Obviously, this last transfer cannot be carried out during step 2, since only one register output can be meaningfully connected to the bus at any given time.

4.1.5 Register Gating and Timing of Data Transfers

Before proceeding to discuss the execution of machine instructions, we shall pause briefly to present some of the implementation details required for gating data to and from the common bus in Figure 4.1. We shall also present a brief overview of the required timing for the control signals involved in transferring data between registers.

Let us consider the case where each bit of the registers in Figures 4.1 and 4.2 consists of the simple latch shown in Figure 4.3 (see also Appendix A). The storage element shown is assumed to be one of the bits of register Z. While the control input Z_{in} is equal to 1, the state of the latch changes to correspond to the data on the bus. Following a 1 to 0 transition at the Z_{in} input, the data stored in the latch immediately before this transition is locked in until Z_{in} is again set to 1. Thus the two input gates of the latch implement the function of the input control switch in Figure 4.2.

Inspection of the output switches in Figure 4.2 shows that, ideally, they should be mechanical ON/OFF switches. When a given switch is in the ON state, it transfers the contents of its corresponding register to the bus. When it is in the OFF state, it is electrically disconnected from the bus. That is, it does not put the bus in any specific state, thus allowing another register to place data on the bus. Hence the output of the register-switch combination can be in one of the three states 1, 0, or open-circuit.

In actual implementations, mechanical switches are incompatible, in terms of speed of operation and other characteristics, with the electronic technology used in a computer. Instead, the output gate of a register, which transfers the contents of that register to the common bus, is designed to behave in the same manner as a mechanical switch. That is, it is capable of being electrically disconnected from the bus. It is also able to place either a 0 or a 1 on the bus

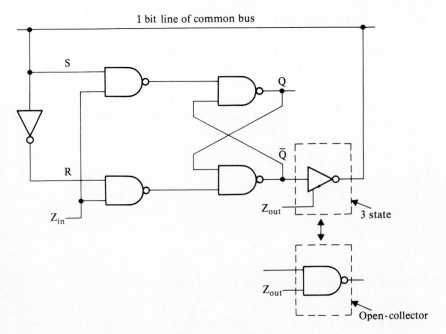

Figure 4.3 Input and output gating for one register bit.

when needed. Because it supports these three possibilities, such a gate is said to have a *three-state* output. A separate control input is used to either enable the gate output or to put it in a high-impedance (electrically disconnected) state. The latter corresponds to the open-circuit state of a mechanical switch.

We should note that neither the TTL nor the CMOS logic gate circuits given in Appendix A are suitable for direct connection to a bus. Connecting the outputs of two such circuits in parallel constitutes a short circuit, which will lead to improper operation, or even damage the gates involved. These circuits may be modified for three-state operation by arranging for a control input to turn off all transistors of the output stage in Figures A.16 and A.18.

An alternative design for the common bus of Figure 4.2 that does not require the output switches shown makes use of open-collector (for bipolar) or open-drain (for MOS) gates. The output of such a gate is equivalent to a switch to ground. The switch is open when the gate output is in the 1 state and closed when it is in the 0 state. The structure of an open-collector bus is represented symbolically in Figure 4.4. When idle, the bus is maintained in the 1 state by the "pull-up" resistor shown. Thus, as long as all gate output switches are open, that is, all outputs are in the 1 state, the bus remains in the 1 state. If any gate output changes to the 0 state, the corresponding output switch is closed, and the bus is "pulled down" to the 0 state. In other words, the bus performs an AND function on all gate outputs connected to it. Sometimes, this is referred to as a "wired-AND" connection. If this gating arrangement is used, the three-state output gate of Figure 4.3 may be replaced by an open-collector NAND gate, as shown. When Z_{out} is high (1), the bit stored in the latch is fed to the bus. When Z_{out} is low (0), the bus is left in the 1, or idle, state, allowing data from another register to be transferred to the bus.

In general, the three-state design enables faster data transfers in comparison with the open-collector, or open-drain, approach. For this reason, it is much more commonly used in bus design. The main distinguishing feature of an open-collector bus is its wired-AND capability. Hence, the open-collector arrangement is used primarily for bus lines where this capability is needed. For example, it is often used for interrupt request lines, as will be discussed in Section 6.4.2.

Let us now discuss some aspects of the timing of data transfers inside the

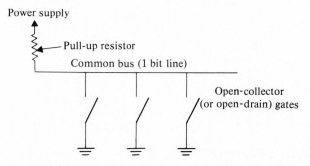

Figure 4.4 Open-collector bus structure.

CPU. Consider, for example, the addition operation in step 2 in Section 4.1.4. From the time the signal $R2_{out}$ is set to 1, a finite delay is encountered for the gate to open and then for the data to travel along the bus to the input of the ALU. Further delay is introduced by the ALU adder circuits. For the result to be properly stored in register Z, data should be maintained on the bus for an additional period of time equal to the setup and hold times for this register (see Appendix A). This situation is depicted in the timing diagram given in Figure 4.5. The sum of the five delay times shown defines the minimum duration of the signal $R2_{out}$.

4.1.6 Multiple-Bus Organization

The single-bus organization of Figure 4.1 represents only one of the possibilities for interconnecting different building blocks of the CPU. An alternative arrangement is the two-bus structure shown in Figure 4.6. All register outputs are connected to bus A, and all register inputs are connected to bus B. The two buses are connected through the bus tie G, which, when enabled, transfers the data on bus A to bus B. When G is disabled, the two buses are electrically isolated. Note that the temporary storage register Z in Figure 4.1 is not required

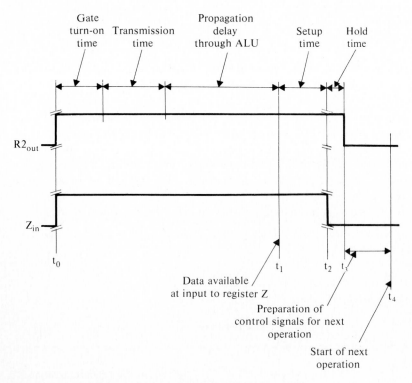

Figure 4.5 Timing of the control signals during the Add step.

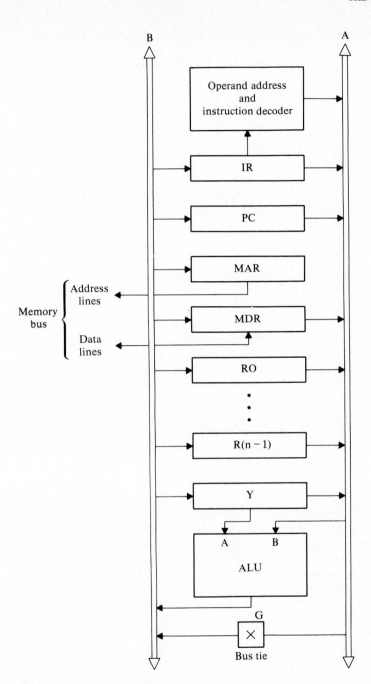

Figure 4.6 Two-bus structure.

in this organization because, with the bus tie disabled, the output of the ALU can be transferred directly to the destination register. For example, the addition operation discussed earlier (R3 ← [R1] + [R2]) can now be performed as follows:

Step	Action
1	$R1_{out}$, G_{enable}, Y_{in}
2	$R2_{out}$, Add, ALU_{out}, $R3_{in}$

It is important to note that if the registers are simple latches as in Figure 4.3, the destination register in the above sequence should be different from R2, because the two operations $R2_{in}$ and $R2_{out}$ cannot be performed at the same time. This is because the ALU is a combinational network. Hence it has no internal storage. The operation R2 ← [R1] + [R2] can still be performed, however, by interchanging $R1_{out}$ and $R2_{out}$ and replacing $R3_{in}$ by $R2_{in}$ in step 2. The restriction that $R2_{out}$ and $R2_{in}$ cannot be performed in the same step may be relaxed through the use of edge-triggered flip-flops (see Appendix A). Assuming that edge-triggered flip-flops are used, the timing of a register transfer involving R2 remains essentially the same as that of Figure 4.5, with Z_{in} replaced by $R2_{in}$. In this case, $R2_{in}$ represents the clock input to the register, which is assumed to be negative edge-triggered. The output of R2 remains unchanged until t_2, at which time the data available on the input bus is loaded into R2.

Let us consider one more example of a CPU organization. Figure 4.7 illustrates a three-bus architecture, with each bus connected to only one output and a number of inputs. The elimination of the need for connecting more than one output to the same bus leads to faster bus transfers and simpler control. A multiplexer is provided at the input to each of the two work registers A and B, which allows them to be loaded from either the input data bus or the register data bus.

The general-purpose registers of the CPU in Figure 4.7 are shown as a single block. They are assumed to be implemented using a random-access memory unit (RAM). The internal organization of a RAM will be discussed in Chapter 8. We should emphasize that in this context the term RAM simply refers to the type of hardware used to implement the registers and should not be confused with the RAM that constitutes the main memory of the computer. The latter is connected to the external bus.

4.2 EXECUTION OF A COMPLETE INSTRUCTION

Let us now try to put together the sequence of elementary operations required to execute one instruction. Consider the instruction "Add contents of memory location NUM to register R1." Let us assume, for simplicity, that the address NUM is given explicitly in the address field of the instruction. That is, location

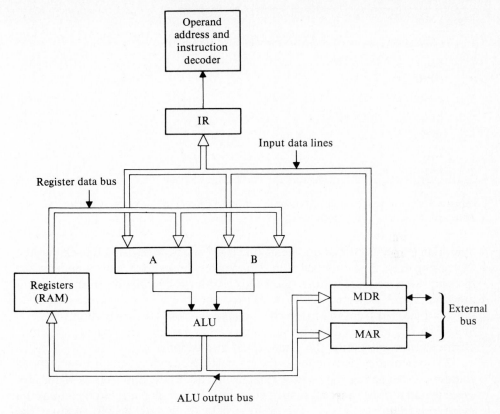

Figure 4.7 Three-bus structure.

NUM is specified in the memory direct mode. Executing this instruction requires the following actions:

1. Fetch instruction.
2. Fetch first operand (contents of memory location pointed at by the address field of the instruction).
3. Perform addition.
4. Load result into R1.

Figure 4.8 gives the sequence of control steps required to implement the above operations for the single-bus architecture of Figure 4.1. Thus, instruction execution proceeds as follows. In step 1, the instruction fetch operation is initiated by loading the contents of the PC into the MAR and sending a Read request to the memory. At the same time the PC is incremented by 1 through the use of the ALU. This is accomplished by setting one of the inputs to the ALU (register Y) to 0 and by setting the other input (CPU bus) to the current value in the PC. At the same time the carry-in to the ALU is set to 1 and an Add

Step	Action
1	PC_{out}, MAR_{in}, Read, Clear Y, Set carry-in to ALU, Add, Z_{in}
2	Z_{out}, PC_{in}, Wait for MFC
3	MDR_{out}, IR_{in}
4	Address_field_of_IR_{out}, MAR_{in}, Read
5	$R1_{out}$, Y_{in}, Wait for MFC
6	MDR_{out}, Add, Z_{in}
7	Z_{out}, $R1_{in}$
8	End

Figure 4.8 Control sequence for execution of the instruction "Add contents of memory location addressed in memory direct mode to register R1".

operation is specified. The updated value is moved from register Z back into the PC during step 2. Note that step 2 is started immediately after issuing the memory Read request without the need to wait for completion of the memory function. Step 3, however, has to be delayed until the MFC is received. In step 3, the word fetched from the memory is loaded into the IR (instruction register). Steps 1 through 3 constitute the instruction fetch phase of the control sequence. Of course, this portion is the same for all instructions.

As soon as the IR is loaded, the instruction decoding circuit interprets its contents. This enables the control circuitry to choose the appropriate signals for the remainder of the control sequence, steps 4 to 8, which are referred to as the execution phase. In step 4, the address field of the IR, which contains the address NUM, is gated to the MAR, and a memory Read operation is initiated. Then the contents of R1 are transferred to register Y. When the Read operation is completed, the memory operand is available in register MDR. The addition operation is performed in step 6, and the result is transferred to R1 in step 7. The End signal, step 8, indicates completion of execution of the current instruction and causes a new fetch cycle to be started by going back to step 1.

4.2.1 Branching

As described in Chapter 2, branching is accomplished by replacing the current contents of the PC by the branch address, that is, the address of the instruction to which branching is required. The branch address is usually obtained by adding an offset X, which is given in the address field of the branch instruction, to the current value of the PC. Figure 4.9 gives a control sequence that enables execution of an unconditional branch using the single-bus organization of Figure 4.1. Execution starts as usual with the fetch phase, ending with the instruction being loaded into the IR in step 3. To execute the branch instruction, the contents of the PC are transferred to register Y in step 4. Then, the offset X is

Step	Action
1	PC_{out}, MAR_{in}, Read, Clear Y, Set Carry-in to ALU, Add, Z_{in}
2	Z_{out}, PC_{in}, Wait for MFC
3	MDR_{out}, IR_{in}
4	PC_{out}, Y_{in}
5	Address_field_of_IR_{out}, Add, Z_{in}
6	Z_{out}, PC_{in}
7	End

Figure 4.9 Control sequence for an unconditional branch instruction.

gated to the bus, and the addition operation is performed. The result, which represents the branch address, is loaded into the PC in step 6.

It is important to note that in this example the PC is incremented during the fetch phase irrespective of the type of instruction being executed. Thus, at the time the offset X is added to the contents of the PC, steps 4 and 5 in Figure 4.9, these contents have already been updated to point at the instruction following the Branch instruction in the program. Therefore, the offset X should be the difference between the branch address and the address immediately following the Branch instruction. For example, if the Branch instruction is at location 1000, and it is required to branch to location 1050, the value of X should be set to 49.

Consider now the case of a conditional instead of an unconditional branch. The only difference between this case and that of Figure 4.9 is the need to check the status of the condition codes between steps 3 and 4. For example, if the instruction decoding circuitry interprets the contents of the IR as a Branch on Negative (BRN) instruction, the control unit proceeds as follows. First, the condition code register is checked. If bit N (negative) is equal to 1, the control unit proceeds with steps 4 through 7 as in Figure 4.9. If, on the other hand, N is equal to 0, an End signal is issued. This, in effect, terminates execution of the Branch instruction and causes the instruction immediately following in the program to be fetched when a new Fetch operation is performed. Therefore, the control sequence for the conditional branch instruction BRN can be obtained from that of Figure 4.9 by replacing step 4 by

$$4 \quad \text{If } \overline{N} \text{ then End}$$

$$\text{If } N \text{ then } PC_{out}, Y_{in}$$

4.3 SEQUENCING OF CONTROL SIGNALS

To execute instructions, the CPU must have some means of generating the control signals discussed above in the proper sequence. Computer designers have used a wide variety of techniques to solve this problem. Most of these techniques, however, fall into one of two categories:

1. Hardwired control
2. Microprogrammed control

Hardwired control is discussed in this section, followed by a brief introduction to microprogrammed control. The latter will be discussed in detail in Chapter 5.

4.3.1 Hardwired Controllers

Consider the sequence of control signals given in Figure 4.8. It is obvious that eight nonoverlapping time slots are required for proper execution of the instruction represented by this sequence. Each time slot must be at least long enough for the functions specified in the corresponding step to be completed. Let us assume, for the moment, that all time slots are equal in duration. Therefore the required controller may be implemented based upon the use of a counter driven by a clock, as shown in Figure 4.10. Each state, or count, of this counter corresponds to one of the steps in Figures 4.8 and 4.9. Hence the required control signals are uniquely determined by the following information:

- Contents of the control counter
- Contents of the instruction register
- Contents of the condition code and other status flags

By status flags we mean the signals representing the state of the various sections of the CPU and various control lines connected to it, such as the MFC status signal in Figure 4.8.

In order to gain some insight into the structure of the control unit we will start by giving a simplified view of the hardware involved. The actual hardware that might be used in a modern computer will be discussed later.

The decoder-encoder block in Figure 4.10 is simply a combinational circuit that generates the required control outputs, depending upon the state of all its inputs. By separating the decoding and encoding functions we obtain the more detailed block diagram of Figure 4.11. The step decoder provides a separate signal line for each step, or time slot, in the control sequence. Similarly, the output of the instruction decoder consists of a separate line for each machine instruction. That is, for any instruction loaded in the IR, one of the output lines INS_1 to INS_m is set to 1 and all other lines are set to 0. For design details of such decoders, refer to Appendix A.

All input signals to the encoder block in Figure 4.11 should be combined to generate the individual control signals Y_{in}, PC_{out}, Add, End, etc. The structure of the encoder is exemplified by the circuit given in Figure 4.12. This circuit is an implementation of the logic function

$$Z_{in} = T_1 + T_6 \cdot ADD + T_5 \cdot BR + \cdots$$

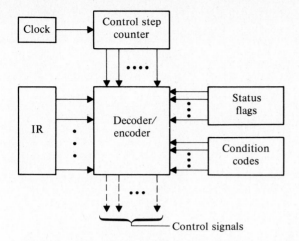

Figure 4.10 Control unit organization.

That is, the control signal Z_{in}, which enables the input to register Z, is turned ON during time slot T_1 regardless of the instruction, during T_6 for an ADD instruction, and so on. This part of the Z_{in} function has been compiled from the control sequences in Figures 4.8 and 4.9. The term T_1 is common to all instructions since it occurs during the fetch phase. Similarly, the End control signal, Figure 4.13, is generated from the logic function

$$\text{End} = T_8 \cdot \text{ADD} + T_7 \cdot \text{BR} + (T_7 \cdot N + T_4 \cdot \overline{N}) \cdot \text{BRN} + \cdots \quad (4.1)$$

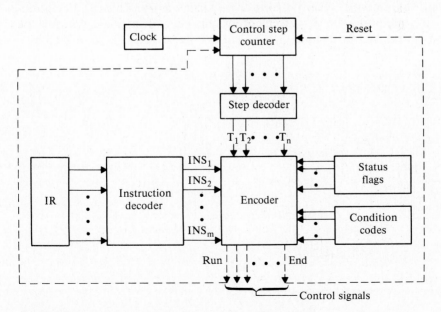

Figure 4.11 Separation of the decoding and encoding functions.

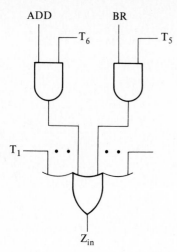

Figure 4.12 Generation of the Z_{in} control signal.

Figure 4.11 shows how the End signal can be used to start a new instruction fetch cycle by resetting the control step counter to its starting value.

The signals MFC and WMFC (Wait for MFC) require some special considerations. The WMFC signal itself can be generated in the same way as the other control signals, using the logic equation

$$WMFC = T_2 + T_5 \cdot ADD + \cdots$$

The desired effect of this signal is to delay the initiation of the next control step until the MFC signal is received from the main memory. This can be accomplished by inhibiting the advancement of the control step counter for the required period. Let us assume that the control step counter is controlled by a

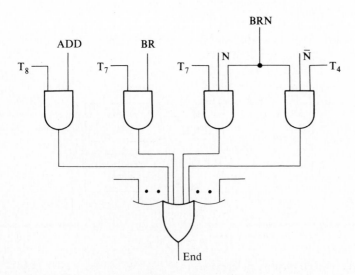

Figure 4.13 Generation of the End control signal.

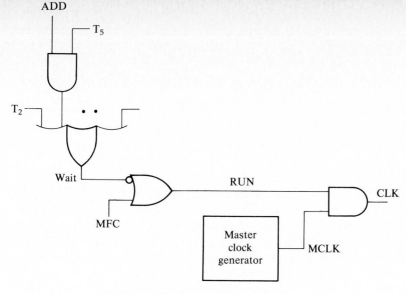

(a) Generation of the RUN signal

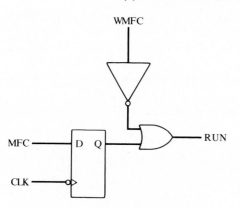

(b) Synchronization of the MFC signal

Figure 4.14 Control of the CPU timing.

signal called RUN. The counter is advanced one step for every clock pulse only if the RUN signal is equal to 1. The circuit of Figure 4.14a will achieve the desired control. As soon as the WMFC signal is generated, RUN becomes equal to 0. Thus, counting is inhibited, and no further signal changes take place. The CPU remains in this wait state until the MFC signal is activated and the control step counter is again enabled. The next clock pulse increments the counter, which results in resetting the WMFC signal to 0.

The simple circuit of Figure 4.14a gives rise to an important problem. The MFC signal is generated by the main memory whose operation is independent of the CPU clock. Hence MFC is an asynchronous signal that may arrive at any time relative to that clock. However, proper functioning of the CPU circuitry, including the control step counter, requires that all control signals have known setup and hold times relative to the clock, as was illustrated in Figure 4.5. Therefore, the MFC signal must be synchronized with the CPU clock before being used to produce the RUN signal. A flip-flop may be used for this purpose,

135

as shown in Figure 4.14*b*. The output of this flip-flop, which is assumed to be negative edge-triggered, changes on the falling edge of CLK. This allows enough time for the RUN signal to settle before the following rising edge of CLK which advances the counter. A timing diagram for an instruction fetch operation is given in Figure 4.15. In this figure, we have assumed that the main memory keeps the MFC signal high until the Read signal is dropped, indicating that the CPU has received the data.

The above discussion has presented a simplified view of the way in which the sequence of control signals needed to fetch and execute instructions may be generated. The overall organization depicted in Figures 4.10 and 4.11, together with the circuit diagrams of Figures 4.12 through 4.14, represent an approach which enables the implementation of an arbitrary instruction set. We shall now consider some practical aspects of realizing such circuitry.

By necessity, the approach used in the design of a digital system must take into account the capabilities and limitations of the chosen implementation technology. The circuits of Figures 4.12 and 4.13 are easy to understand and to design. However, it can be readily appreciated that the number of logic gates needed and the complexity of the wiring make this direct approach impractical. The implementation of modern computers is based on the use of VLSI technology. In VLSI, structures that involve regular interconnection patterns are much easier to implement than the random connections used in the above circuits. One such structure is a programmable logic array (PLA). As described in Appendix A, a PLA consists of an array of AND gates followed by an array of OR gates. It can be used for implementing combinational logic functions of several variables. The entire decoder-encoder block of Figure 4.10 can be

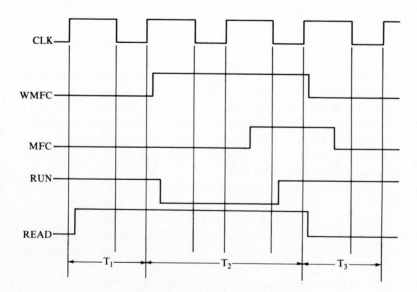

Figure 4.15 Timing of control signals during instruction fetch.

PLA

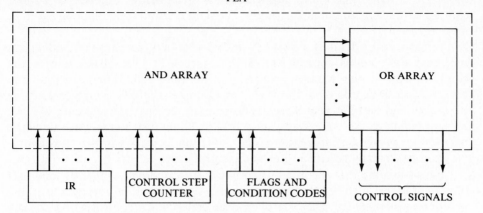

Figure 4.16 Implementation of a sequence controller on a VLSI chip.

implemented in the form of a single PLA. Thus, the control section of a CPU, or for that matter, of any digital system, may be organized as shown in Figure 4.16.

Before concluding the discussion on hardwired controllers, a few comments are in order. So far, we have assumed that all control steps occupy equal time slots. This leads to an implementation consisting of a state counter driven by a clock. It can be readily appreciated that this approach is not very efficient with regard to the utilization of the CPU, since not all operations require the same amount of time. For example, a simple register transfer is usually much faster than an operation involving addition or subtraction. It is possible, at least in theory, to build a completely asynchronous control unit. In this case, the clock would be replaced by a circuit that advances the step counter as soon as the current step is completed. The main problem in such an approach is the incorporation of some reliable means to detect the completion of various operations. As it turns out, propagation delay in many cases is a function not only of the gates used but also of the particular data being processed. Some of the difficulties involved can be appreciated by studying the analysis of propagation delay in arithmetic circuits given in Chapter 7.

Some compromises are possible, however. For example, a maximum delay can be established for each operation, and the timing signals can be derived on that basis. It is also possible to use separate clocks for individual subsections of a circuit. Communication among various subsections can then be done asynchronously, in much the same way as data transfers between the CPU and the main memory.

4.3.2 Microprogrammed Control

In Section 4.3.1, we saw how all the control signals required inside the CPU can be generated using a state counter and a PLA circuit. In the remainder of this chapter we shall discuss an alternative approach which is widely used in computer design. Only a brief introduction is given below, followed by a more comprehensive treatment in Chapter 5. We shall first introduce some frequently used terms.

Let us start by defining a *control word* (CW) as a word whose individual bits represent the various control signals in Figure 4.11. Therefore each of the control steps in the control sequence of an instruction defines a unique combination of 1s and 0s in the CW. For example, the CWs corresponding to steps 5, 6, and 7 of Figure 4.8 are as shown in Figure 4.17. A sequence of CWs corresponding to the control sequence of a machine instruction constitutes the *microprogram* for that instruction. The individual control words in this micro-program are usually referred to as *microinstructions*.

Let us assume that the microprograms corresponding to the instruction set of a computer are stored in a special memory which will be referred to as the *microprogram memory*. The control unit can generate the control signals for any instruction by sequentially reading the CWs of the corresponding microprogram from the microprogram memory. This suggests organizing the control unit as shown in Figure 4.18. To read the control words sequentially from the microprogram memory a *microprogram counter* (μPC) is used. The block labeled "starting address generator" is responsible for loading the starting address of the microprogram into the μPC every time a new instruction is loaded into the IR. The μPC is then automatically incremented by the clock, causing successive microinstructions to be read from the memory. Hence the control signals will be delivered to various parts of the CPU in the correct sequence.

So far one important function of the control unit has not been discussed and, in fact, cannot be implemented by the simple organization of Figure 4.18. This is the situation that arises when the control unit is required to check the status of the condition codes or status flags in order to choose between alternative courses of action. We have seen that in the case of hardwired control this situation is handled by including an appropriate logic function, as in Equation (4.1), in the encoder circuitry. An alternative approach which is frequently used with microprogrammed control is based on the introduction of the concept of conditional branching in the microprogram. This can be accomplished by expanding the microinstruction set to include some conditional branch microin-structions. In addition to the branch address, these microinstructions can specify

Step	$R1_{in}$	$R1_{out}$	Y_{in}	Y_{out}	Z_{in}	Z_{out}	MDR_{in}	MDR_{out}	ADD
5	0	1	1	0	0	0	0	0	0
6	0	0	0	0	1	0	0	1	1
7	1	0	0	0	0	1	0	0	0

Figure 4.17 Example of microinstructions for Figure 4.8.

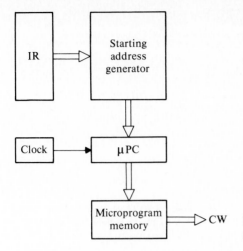

Figure 4.18 Basic organization of a microprogrammed control unit.

which of the status flags, condition codes, or, possibly, bits of the instruction register should be checked as a condition for branching to take place. The instruction Branch on Negative may now be implemented by a microprogram such as that shown in Figure 4.19. It is assumed that the microprogram for this instruction starts at location 25. Therefore, a Branch microinstruction at the end of the instruction fetch portion of the microprogram transfers control to location 25. It should be noted that the branch address of this Branch microinstruction is, in fact, the output of the "starting address generator" block. At location 25, a conditional branch microinstruction tests the N bit of the condition codes and causes a branch to End if this bit is equal to 0.

To support microprogram branching, the organization of the control unit

Address	Microinstruction
0	PC_{out}, MAR_{in}, Read, Clear Y, Set carry-in to ALU, Add, Z_{in}
1	Z_{out}, PC_{in}, Wait for MFC
2	MDR_{out}, IR_{in}
3	Branch to starting address of appropriate microprogram.
....	....
25	If $\overline{N}$ then branch to 29
26	PC_{out}, Y_{in}
27	Address_field_of_IR_{out}, Add, Z_{in}
28	Z_{out}, PC_{in}
29	End

Figure 4.19 Microprogram for the instruction Branch on Negative.

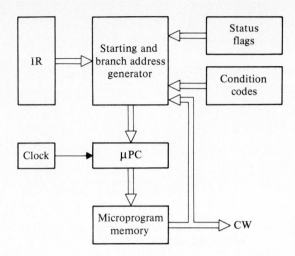

Figure 4.20 Organization of the control unit to enable conditional branching in the microprogram.

should be modified as shown in Figure 4.20. The bits of the microinstruction word which specify the branch conditions and address are fed to the "starting and branch address generator" block. This block performs the function of loading a new address into the μPC when instructed to do so by a microinstruction. To enable the implementation of a conditional branch, inputs to this block consist of the status flags and condition codes as well as the contents of the instruction register. Therefore, the μPC is always incremented every time a new microinstruction is fetched from the microprogram memory, except in the following situations:

1. When an End microinstruction is encountered, the μPC is loaded with the address of the first CW in the microprogram for the instruction fetch cycle (address = 0 in Figure 4.19).
2. When a new instruction is loaded into the IR, the μPC is loaded with the starting address of the microprogram for that instruction.
3. When a Branch microinstruction is encountered, and the branch condition is satisfied, the μPC is loaded with the branch address.

Organizations similar to that of Figure 4.20 have been implemented in many machines. However, some alternative approaches have also been developed and implemented in practice. These approaches and the situations in which they become advantageous will be discussed in Chapter 5.

In conclusion, a few important points should be noted regarding microprogrammed machines, namely:

1. Microprograms define the instruction set of the computer. Hence it is possible to change the instruction set simply by changing the contents of the microprogram memory. This offers considerable flexibility to both the designer and user of the computer.

2. Since the contents of the microprogram memory are changed very infrequently, if at all, a read-only type memory (ROM) is usually used for that purpose.
3. Execution of any machine instruction involves a number of fetches from the microprogram memory. Therefore the speed of this memory plays a major role in determining the overall speed of the computer.

So far we have covered the basic features of microprogrammed machines. Various design alternatives and trade-offs are discussed in more detail in Chapter 5.

4.4 CONCLUDING REMARKS

In this chapter, we presented an overview of the organization of the central processing unit of a computer. Many variations of the organizations presented here are encountered in commercially available machines. The choice of a particular organization involves trade-offs between speed of execution and cost of implementation. It is also influenced by a number of other factors, such as the technology used, flexibility for modification, or the desire to provide some special capabilities in the instruction set of the computer.

Two approaches were presented regarding the implementation of the control unit of a CPU: hardwired control and microprogrammed control. Microprogrammed control provides considerable flexibility in the implementation of instruction sets. It also facilitates the addition of new instructions to existing machines.

When microprogrammed control was first introduced, it was much slower than hardwired control because of the slow speed of ROM storage. However, advances in ROM technology have reduced the speed differences. As a result, microprogrammed control is now much more commonly used because of its flexibility.

4.5 PROBLEMS

4.1 Assume that propagation delay along the bus and through the ALU of Figure 4.1 are 20 and 100 ns, respectively. The setup time for the registers is 10 ns, and the hold time is 0. What is the minimum time that must be allowed for performing each of the following operations:

• Transferring data from one register to another
• Incrementing the program counter

4.2 Write the sequence of control steps required for the bus structure of Figure 4.1 for each of the following three instructions:

(a) Add the number NUM to register R1.
(b) Add contents of memory location NUM to register R1.
(c) Add contents of the memory location whose address is at memory location NUM to register R1.

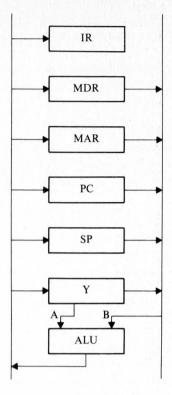

Figure P4.1 Internal organization of the CPU of Problem 4.4.

Assume that the instruction consists of two words. The first word specifies the operation and the addressing mode, and the second word contains the number NUM.

4.3 Consider a 16-bit byte-addressable machine that has the organization of Figure 4.1. Show a suitable gating scheme for connecting register MDR to the memory bus and to the internal CPU bus to enable byte transfers to take place. Note that when a byte is being handled, it should always be in the low-order byte position inside the CPU.

4.4 Figure P4.1 gives a part of the internal organization of the CPU of a computer. All data transfers between the two buses go through the arithmetic and logic unit (ALU). Among other things, the ALU is capable of performing the following functions:

$$F = A \qquad F = B$$

$$F = A + 1 \qquad F = B + 1$$

$$F = A - 1 \qquad F = B - 1$$

where A and B are the ALU inputs and F is the ALU output. Write the sequence of control steps required to fetch and execute the instruction Jump to Subroutine (JSR). In this machine, the JSR instruction occupies two words. The first word is the OP code, and the second word contains the starting address of the subroutine. The return address is saved in a memory stack. A stack pointer (SP) is used to point at the top of this stack at all times.

4.5 Consider the Add instruction which has the control sequence given in Figure 4.8. The CPU is driven by a continuously running clock, such that each control step is 200 ns in duration. How long will the CPU have to wait in steps 2 and 5, assuming that a memory Read operation takes 0.5 μs to complete? Estimate, on the average, the percentage of time that the CPU is idle.

4.6 In a 16-bit byte-addressable machine, the PC should be incremented by 2 after fetching an instruction word from memory. Suggest some modification to Figure 4.1 to simplify this operation.

4.7 Figure 4.6 gives the internal organization of the CPU of a computer. It is required to use this CPU to emulate the operation of a PDP-11 computer. Give the control sequences required to fetch and execute the following instructions

      (*a*) CMP (R1)+,X(R7) (Compare)
      (*b*) RTS R2   (Return from subroutine)

Recall that R7 is the PC and that register R6 is used as a pointer to the memory stack. Assume that a temporary storage register (TEMP) is available. It is connected to the two buses in the same way as registers R0 to R7.

4.8 Why can't the five-step sequence

    1. temp ← dst
    2. SP   ← [SP] − 2
    3. [SP] ← [reg]
    4. reg   ← [PC]
    5. PC   ← [temp]

be replaced by the sequence

    1. SP   ← [SP] − 2
    2. [SP] ← [reg]
    3. reg ← [PC]
    4. PC ← dst

in implementing the instruction:

JSR   reg,dst

4.9 It is required to implement the instructions Arithmetic Shift Left/Right R,n in a computer. This instruction results in shifting the contents of register R to the left or to the right n times, where $0 < n \leq 4$. Show how to replace the bus tie G with multiplexers in the organization of Figure 4.6 to implement these instructions, and give the sequence of control steps for their execution.

4.10 A computer uses the shift register shown in Figure P4.2 to perform shift and rotate operations. Inputs to the control logic for this register consist of

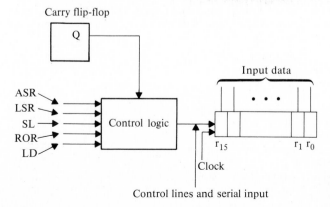

Figure P4.2 Organization of shift-register control for Problem 4.10.

ASR   Arithmetic Shift Right
LSR   Logic Shift Right
SL   Shift Left
ROR   Rotate Right
LD   Parallel Load

All shift and load operations are controlled by one clock input. The shift register is implemented by using D flip-flops. Give a complete logic diagram for the control logic and for bits r_0, r_1, and r_{15} of the shift register.

4.11 A digital controller, Figure P4.3, has three outputs, X, Y, and Z, and two inputs, A and B. It is externally driven by a clock. The controller is continuously going through the following sequence of events. At the beginning of the first clock period, line X is set to 1. At the beginning of the second clock period, either line Y or Z is set to 1, depending on whether line A is equal to 1 or 0, respectively. The controller then waits until line B is set to 1. On the following positive edge of the clock, the controller sets output Z to 1 for the duration of one clock period, then resets all output signals to 0 for one clock period. The sequence is repeated starting at the next positive edge of the clock. Give a suitable logic design for this controller.

4.12 Refer to the decoder and encoder blocks in Figure 4.11. Whenever the step counter is incremented, false signals may appear on the control lines while the gates within the decoder and encoder blocks settle to their new states. This may cause errors. Assume that some control signals are to be disabled for a short period after incrementing the control step counter. Give a design for the CPU clock, using a high-frequency oscillator, and show how a gating signal may be generated for a period equal to one-eighth $(\frac{1}{8})$ of the clock period.

4.13 To take advantage of the differences in the times required to perform various operations in the CPU, it is necessary to have the facility to prolong some time slots to accommodate slow operations. Assume that one of the control signals generated by the encoder block of Figure 4.11 is called SHORT/LONG. When this line is equal to 1, the control step counter is advanced at successive positive edges of the clock. When the SHORT/LONG line is equal to 0, the length of the corresponding time slot is doubled. Give a suitable design for the clock gating circuitry to implement this feature.

4.14 The three control step sequences in Problem 4.2 have common control steps. However, these control steps occur at different counts of the control step counter. Show two different alternatives that exploit these common steps in reducing the complexity of the encoder block of Figure 4.11.

4.15 A simple oscillator can be designed by feeding the output of an inverting gate back to its input, through a delay element. Use this arrangement to design a clock generator which can be started and stopped under control of an input RUN. No partial pulses should be produced at the output under any contition.

4.16 The output of a shift register is inverted and fed back to its input. This arrangement is known as a Johnson counter.

    (a) What is the count sequence of a 4-bit Johnson counter, starting with the state 0000.

    (b) Show how you can use a Johnson counter to generate the timing signals T_1, T_2, etc., in Figure 4.11, assuming there is a maximum of 10 timing intervals.

4.17 Assume that the latches shown in Figure 4.3 are used to form the registers in Figure 4.6. What

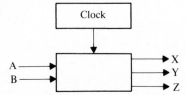

Figure P4.3 A digital controller.

happens if the operation R2 ← [R1] + [R2] is attempted? Suggest a simple modification to the data path that enables this operation to be performed.

4.18 The ALU of a computer is implemented in the form of a PLA (see Appendix A). It accepts two 2-bit numbers A and B, a carry input C_{in}, and a 2-bit function input F. The output of the ALU consists of a 2-bit result Y and a carry output C_{out}. The operation performed by the ALU is determined by the function inputs according to the following table:

F_1	F_0	Operation	C_{out}
0	0	A + B	Carry output
0	1	A $\vee$ B	1
1	0	A $\wedge$ B	0
1	1	A $\vee$ $\overline{B}$	0

Design the required PLA by defining its product and sum terms. You should attempt to use as few product terms as possible.

4.19 The three-bus organization of Figure 4.7 allows a number of transfers to be carried out simultaneously (e.g., A ← [MDR] and B ← [R_i]). Give a sequence of steps for implementing the PDP-11 instruction

$$\text{ADD} \qquad \text{@R3, X(R4)}$$

to take advantage of these possibilities. Assume that any constants needed in the implementation are stored in the register file. Also, register B can, if desired, be operated in a transparent mode, transferring data from its input to its output without storing it.

4.20 In order to speed up instruction execution, it is sometimes possible to start the fetch operation for the next instruction before completion of execution of the current instruction. Examine the following PDP-11 instructions and suggest suitable points during their execution where a fetch operation can be safely started for the next instruction:

$$\text{INC, TST, MOV, BR}$$

For each instruction, consider both register and memory operands.

4.21 Give a control step sequence for implementing the scheme suggested in Problem 4.19 in the instruction: CMP #N,(R3)+. Assume that the CPU has the internal organization shown in Figure 4.7.

4.22 Refer to the timing diagram in Figure 4.15. Consider a control sequence which involves two successive Memory Read operations. Can MAR_{in} for the second operation be issued in the same control step as WMFC for the first operation? Explain the conditions under which this might be possible.

4.23 Repeat Problem 4.22 for MDR_{in} and MDR_{out}.

FIVE

MICROPROGRAMMED CONTROL

Chapter 4 introduced the possibility of generating control signals in the CPU by software means, known as microprogrammed control. It dealt briefly with the general approach and some relative merits of such designs. In this chapter we will pursue this alternative to hardwired circuits in greater detail.

Let us start with the basic premise that microprogramming is a software approach and therefore can be handled by using hardware structures akin to those used for sequencing of ordinary programs. Assuming that microinstructions are going to be executed in sequential order from consecutive locations in the microprogram memory (also called the *control store*), it is natural to use a microprogram counter (μPC) to keep track of addresses. The μPC is incremented by 1 in order to fetch the next microinstruction. Since each machine instruction is executed by a corresponding microroutine, it follows that a starting address for the microroutine must be specified as a function of the contents of the instruction register (IR). The structure of Figure 4.20 fits these comments rather well. In addition to incremental sequencing achieved by the μPC, a branch address generator is included to provide the means for branching within the microprogram. Unconditional or conditional branching is possible, the latter as a result of tests on status flags and condition codes. This organization is remarkably similar to the basic sequencing hardware in the CPU, where the PC is used to fetch instructions from the main memory. In normal operation, the PC is incremented to point at the next instruction unless branching is indicated.

5.1 MICROINSTRUCTIONS

Having looked at a possible scheme for sequencing microinstructions, we should take a closer look at the format of individual microinstructions. As suggested in

146

Chapter 4, a straightforward method of structuring microinstructions is to have one bit position assigned to each control signal required in the CPU. A simple example was shown in Figure 4.17. To assess the usefulness of this approach, we will consider fully the example in Figure 4.8. There are 17 distinct control signals involved in it. We could assign one microinstruction bit per signal as indicated in Figure 5.1. Each bit is set to 1 if the corresponding control signal must be turned ON.

Eight timing steps are required in this example, suggesting the need for eight microinstructions. However, it is obviously wasteful to have a separate microinstruction generating the End signal, when the same effect can be achieved by setting the End bit in the preceding microinstruction. Thus a single microword can cover steps 7 and 8.

A different problem arises with the Wait for Memory-function-completed (WMFC) signal. The signal was used in Chapter 4 to synchronize the fast hardwired-controlled CPU circuits with the slower main memory. In microprogrammed control the need for such signals is less obvious. Microinstructions are fetched from the control store and are available at a rate determined by the access time of the store. If the control store had the same access time as the main memory, it may be argued that there would be no need for the WMFC signaling mechanism. However, control stores are usually relatively small, so that it is feasible to speed up their cycle times through costly circuitry. This is often not an economical proposition with the main memories which are normally considerably larger. Hence main memory cycle times tend to be longer than those of the control store. As a result, to ensure that data read out of the main memory is valid, it is essential to wait for a signal from the memory that verifies the validity of the data in the MDR. This can be accomplished by a microinstruction test loop, similar to the instruction loops in Figure 2.19 used to test the status of

Microinstruction	...	PC_{in}	PC_{out}	MAR_{in}	Read	MDR_{out}	IR_{in}	$Address_{out}$	Y_{in}	Clear Y	Carry-in	Add	Z_{in}	Z_{out}	RI_{out}	RI_{in}	WMFC	End	...
1		0	1	1	1	0	0	0	0	1	1	1	1	0	0	0	0	0	
2		1	0	0	0	0	0	0	0	0	0	0	0	1	0	0	1	0	
3		0	0	0	0	1	1	0	0	0	0	0	0	0	0	0	0	0	
4		0	0	1	1	0	0	1	0	0	0	0	0	0	0	0	0	0	
5		0	0	0	0	0	0	0	1	0	0	0	0	0	1	0	1	0	
6		0	0	0	0	1	0	0	0	0	0	1	1	0	0	0	0	0	
7		0	0	0	0	0	0	0	0	0	0	0	0	1	0	1	0	1	

Figure 5.1 An example of bit patterns for a microprogram corresponding to Figure 4.8.

ready flags in I/O devices. However, the method is wasteful of space in the control store. An alternative scheme is to modify the hardware slightly, so that execution of the next microinstruction is not started until the Memory-function-completed (MFC) signal arrives. Of course, this should only be done when indicated by the WMFC bit in a microinstruction. Figure 4.8 shows the required WMFC delay as part of steps 2 and 5. It is possible to achieve the desired effect by setting the WMFC bit in the corresponding microinstructions. The presence of the WMFC bit need not delay the fetching of the next microinstruction. It should merely inhibit its execution until the MFC signal is received. A simple way of implementing this inhibiting function is to provide a flip-flop that is set by the WMFC bit and reset by the MFC signal.

5.2 GROUPING OF CONTROL SIGNALS

The above scheme for microprogrammed control has one serious drawback. Assigning individual bits to each control signal is certain to lead to long microinstructions, since the number of required signals is normally fairly large. Moreover, only a few bits are set to 1 (and therefore used for active gating) in any given microinstruction, which obviously results in poor utilization of the available bit space. Consider the CPU block diagram in Figure 4.1. Assume that it contains four general-purpose registers R0, R1, R2, and R3. In addition, let there be three other registers called SOURCE, DESTIN, and TEMP. These are used for temporary storage within the CPU but are completely transparent to the programmer. Most computers have such registers, as their inclusion tends to simplify internal sequencing structure and control. The augmented block diagram is shown in Figure 5.2, indicating the control signals necessary to provide the transfers within the CPU. Note that some connections are permanent, for example, the output of IR to the decoding circuits and both inputs to the ALU. There is a total of 24 gating signals on the diagram. In addition, a number of other control signals are needed, as seen in the previous example. These include the Read, Write, Clear Y, Set Carry-in, WMFC, and End signals. Finally, it is necessary to specify the function to be performed by the ALU. Let us assume that, in our example, there are 16 functions provided, including Add, Subtract, AND, XOR, etc. These functions depend upon the particular ALU used and do not necessarily show a one-to-one correspondence with the OP codes in machine instructions.

The above discussion indicates that 46 distinct signals are required, which would imply the existence of at least 46 bits in each microinstruction. Such poor utilization of bits can be rather unattractive from the design point of view. Fortunately, the scheme can be improved easily. Observe that most signals are not needed simultaneously. Furthermore, many signals are mutually exclusive. For example, only one function of the ALU can be activated at a time. A source for data transfers must be unique, which means that it should not be possible to gate the contents of two different registers onto the bus at the same time. Read and Write signals to the memory cannot be active simultaneously. This suggests

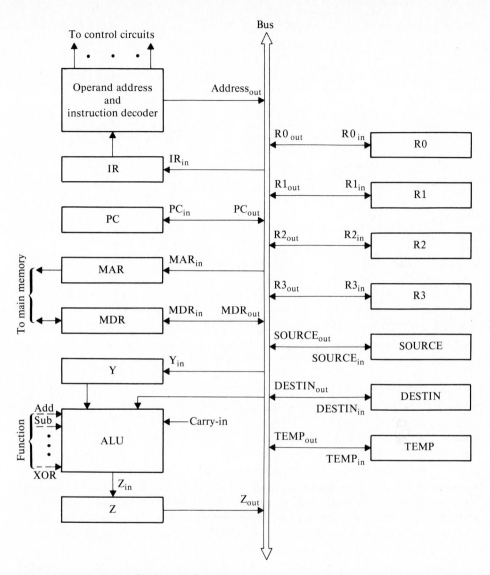

Figure 5.2 A single-bus CPU block diagram.

the possibility of grouping the signals so that all signals that are mutually exclusive are placed in the same group. Thus a group can specify one *microoperation* at a time. Then it is possible to use a binary coding scheme to represent given signals within a group. In the case of ALU functions, it is apparent that 4 bits suffice for representation of the 16 available functions. Register output control signals can be placed in a group consisting of PC_{out}, MDR_{out}, Z_{out}, $Address_{out}$, RO_{out}, $R1_{out}$, $R2_{out}$, $R3_{out}$, $SOURCE_{out}$, $DESTIN_{out}$, and $TEMP_{out}$. Any one of them can be selected by a unique 4-bit code.

Further natural groupings can be made for the remaining signals. Figure 5.3

Microinstruction

...	F1	F2	F3	F4	F5	

F1 (4 bits)	F2 (3 bits)	F3 (2 bits)	F4 (2 bits)	F5 (4 bits)	
0000: No transfer	000: No transfer	00: No transfer	00: No transfer	0000: Add ⎫	
0001: PC_{out}	001: PC_{in}	01: MAR_{in}	01: Y_{in}	0001: Sub ⎬ 16 ALU functions	
0010: MDR_{out}	010: IR_{in}	10: MDR_{in}	10: $SOURCE_{in}$	....	
0011: Z_{out}	011: Z_{in}	11: $TEMP_{in}$	11: $DESTIN_{in}$	1111: XOR ⎭	
0100: $R0_{out}$	100: $R0_{in}$				
0101: $R1_{out}$	101: $R1_{in}$				
0110: $R2_{out}$	110: $R2_{in}$				
0111: $R3_{out}$	111: $R3_{in}$				
1000: $SOURCE_{out}$					
1001: $DESTIN_{out}$					
1010: $TEMP_{out}$					
1011: $Address_{out}$					

F6	F7	F8	F9	F10	...

F6 (2 bits)	F7 (1 bit)	F8 (1 bit)	F9 (1 bit)	F10 (1 bit)
00: No action	0: No action	0: Carry-in = 0	0: No action	0: Continue
01: Read	1: Clear Y	1: Carry-in = 1	1: WMFC	1: End
10: Write				

Figure 5.3 An example of a partial format for field-encoded microinstructions.

shows a possible partial format for the microinstructions, where each group occupies a field large enough to contain the required codes. Most fields must include one inactive code for the cases where no action is required. This is not necessarily a requirement for all fields. For example, F5 contains 4 bits that specify one of the 16 operations performed in the ALU. Since no spare code is included, the ALU will be active during execution of every microinstruction. However, its activity is monitored by the rest of the machine through register Z, which is loaded only when the Z_{in} signal is present.

Grouping of control signals into fields results in a relatively small increase in the required hardware, as it becomes necessary to use decoding circuits to translate the bit patterns of each field into actual control signals. The cost of additional hardware is more than offset by the reduced number of bits in microinstructions, which will result in a smaller control store. Note that in Figure 5.3 only 21 bits are needed to store the patterns for the 46 desired signals.

So far we have considered one level of grouping and encoding of the control signals. It is possible to extend this idea further by attempting to enumerate the required signals at all possible instances. Then, each combination of signals can be assigned a distinct code that would be stored in microinstructions. Such full encoding is likely to result in further reduction in the length of microwords. However, this will also increase the complexity of the required decoder circuits.

Highly encoded schemes, where compact codes are used to specify only a small number of control functions in each microinstruction, are often referred to as the *vertical* organization. On the other hand, the minimally encoded scheme of Figure 5.1, where a large number of resources can be controlled with a single microinstruction, is called the *horizontal* organization. The latter approach is desirable when the operating speed of a computer is the critical factor and where the machine structure allows parallel usage of a number of resources. The vertical approach results in considerably slower operating speeds, as more microinstructions are needed to perform the desired control functions. However, fewer bits are required for each microinstruction. This obviously does not imply that the total number of bits in the control store is smaller. The significant factor is the reduced requirement for parallel hardware needed to handle the execution of microinstructions.

Horizontal and vertical organizations represent the two organizational extremes in microprogrammed control. Many intermediate schemes are also possible, where the degree of encoding is a design parameter. The layout of Figure 5.3 is in this category. It is closer to the horizontal organization because of the effort to group only mutually exclusive microoperations in the same fields, which results in a considerable number of fields per microinstruction. Such *mixed* organizations are found in most practical computers, although it is a common practice to describe their control structures as being basically either horizontal or vertical.

The example used in this chapter is based on the structure of Figure 5.2, which shows only the basic components. It is apparent that a number of details are not included in it, since they are not essential for understanding the principles of operation. We considered only a subset of the control signals needed in a typical machine, although this subset is quite representative of actual requirements.

The number of bits in microinstructions depends upon the size and complexity of the computer. An average minicomputer can be designed conveniently and efficiently with 30 to 60 bits per microinstruction. Of course, this number is determined solely by the design decisions, which are influenced by a number of factors such as the desired speed of the machine, size of the control store, and complexity of the bus structure.

5.3 MICROPROGRAM SEQUENCING

The simple example of a microprogram in Figure 5.1 requires only straightforward sequential execution of microinstructions, without any need for branching capability. If each machine instruction can be implemented by a microroutine of this kind, it is possible to make effective use of the microcontrol structure suggested in Figure 4.20, where a μPC governs the sequencing. Each microroutine can be accessed initially by decoding the machine instruction into the starting address to be loaded into the μPC. Some branching capability within the microprogram may be introduced through special "branch microinstructions," which can specify the branch address in a similar way as the corresponding machine branch instructions do.

It was suggested at the beginning of this chapter that the above approach is natural in that it follows general patterns of computer organization and operation. Writing of microprograms is likely to be fairly simple, since good use can be made of standard software techniques. However, these advantages are counterbalanced by two major disadvantages. Having a separate microroutine for each machine instruction can result in a large number of microinstructions and hence a large control store. Noting that most machine instructions can operate in several addressing modes, it is apparent that having a separate microroutine for each instruction in every address mode is not an appealing proposition, as many microroutines would show considerable duplication in parts. Therefore it is more reasonable to organize the microprogram so that as many common parts as possible are shared by the microroutines. This results in a considerable number of branch microinstructions being needed to transfer control among various parts. Hence a second disadvantage arises, where execution time is lengthened by the time necessary to carry out the required branches.

Let us consider a more complicated example of a complete machine instruction. In Chapter 2 we used the PDP-11 instruction set to illustrate some basic programming concepts. A typical two-operand instruction in that set is

$$\text{ADD} \quad \text{src,dst}$$

which adds the contents of the source (src) and destination (dst) and places the sum into the destination location. Operand locations (both src and dst) can be specified in any of the eight allowable address modes. We will use this instruction in conjunction with the CPU structure described in Figure 5.2 to demonstrate a possible microprogrammed implementation. It is important to keep in mind that Figure 5.2 is a simplified block diagram, which does not represent exactly any particular machine, although it is quite representative of the structure used in many commercially available machines.

A suitable microprogram is shown in Figure 5.4. It is presented in a flowchart form for easier understanding. Each box corresponds to a microinstruction that controls the transfers and operations indicated within the box. The microinstruction is assumed to be located at the address indicated by the octal number above the upper right-hand corner of the box. Most of the flowchart is self-explanatory, although some details warrant elaboration.

The microprogram in the figure is arranged in such a way that each microinstruction controls transfers that can be performed simultaneously. It is possible to have a more compact microprogram if some of the microinstructions are combined. For example, following the initiation of the instruction fetch, it is necessary to update (that is, increment) the contents of the PC. Assuming that the main memory is organized on a word-addressable basis, the PC must be incremented by 1. (In a 16-bit, byte-addressable machine, the PC would be incremented by 2.) This is indicated as

$$Z \leftarrow [PC] + 1$$

$$PC \leftarrow [Z]$$

The required action is to gate the contents of the PC onto the bus, set the carry-in signal, clear register Y, perform the addition, and gate the result into register Z. As the next step, the updated value must be transferred from Z to the PC. It is obvious that both steps cannot be carried out at the same time, as only one register can be meaningfully gated onto the bus at any given time. However, it is not essential that the actions to be performed in these steps be specified in two separate microinstructions.

Consider the alternative of using a single microinstruction and a two-phase clock to sequence gating onto the bus in the above two steps. During clock phase 1, the first step can be performed, at the end of which the updated contents of the PC are available in the Z register. Then, phase 2 can be used to transfer these contents into the PC, as required in the second step.

Other microinstructions can be combined in the same fashion. For example, single microinstructions can be used in place of the pairs of microinstructions at the following addresses: (121, 122), (141, 142), (161, 162), (164, 165), (221, 222), (241, 242), (261, 262), and (264, 265). In each pair the transfers indicated in the first microinstruction can be performed during phase 1, while those in the second microinstruction can be carried out during phase 2.

The obvious advantages of controlling gating by means of a two-phase clock are the accompanying reduction in the size of the control store and faster execution because fewer microinstructions need to be fetched. On the disadvantage side, we should note that some extra hardware is needed and the flexibility in assigning codes for representation of control signals in microinstructions is somewhat diminished. The latter point may be illustrated by the Z_{out} signal. When the contents of the PC are being updated, the Z_{out} signal must be asserted

ADD src,dst

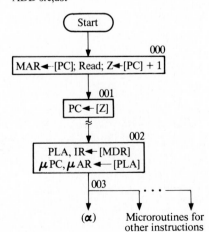

Figure 5.4 Flowchart of a microprogram for the ADD src,dst instruction.

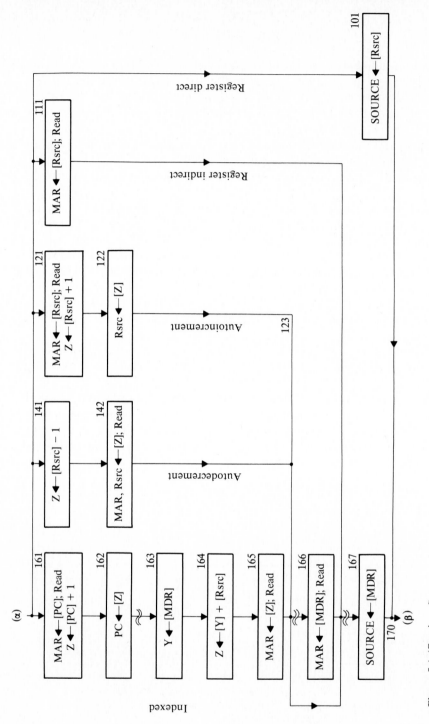

Figure 5.4 (Continued)

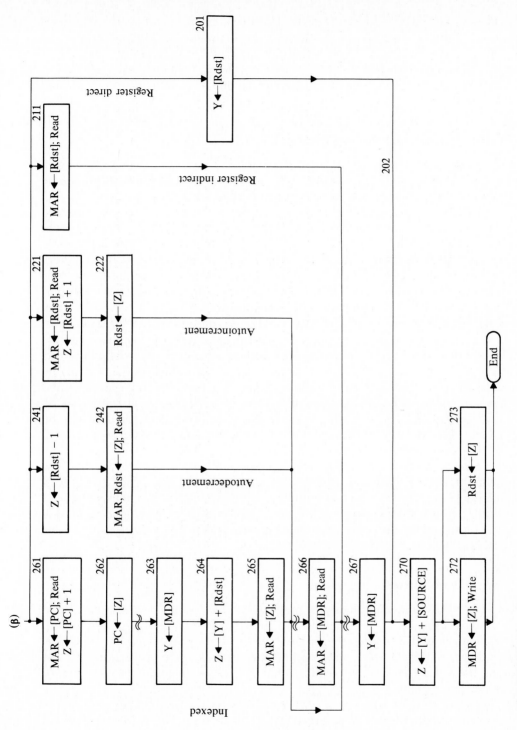

Figure 5.4 (Continued)

only during phase 2 (P2) of the clock. However, in the case of microinstructions in locations 272 and 273, it is not necessary to wait until P2, and Z_{out} can be asserted during phase 1 (P1), which would result in a somewhat faster operation. If speed is of extreme importance, such cases could be handled by assigning two codes to Z_{out} (in the microinstruction field F1), one corresponding to $Z_{out} \cdot$ P1 and the other to $Z_{out} \cdot$ P2.

5.3.1 Branch Address Modification

The microprogram in Figure 5.4 shows that branches are not always made to a single branch address. This is a direct consequence of trying to combine simple microroutines through sharing of common parts. Consider the point labeled β in Figure 5.4. At this point, it is necessary to derive the destination (dst) operand address and fetch the operand. The figure shows five possible branches which, from left to right, correspond to indexed, autodecrement, autoincrement, register indirect, and register address modes. A straightforward and very inefficient way of generating the proper branch address would be to use four consecutive two-way conditional branch microinstructions. Alternatively, it is possible to include several fields within the branch microinstruction, where each field is used to generate a particular branch address. Actual generation of addresses may be done in a variety of ways. A good technique is to arrange the microinstructions so that the five branch addresses differ in a few designated bits only (at least three in this case). Then, a single branch microinstruction can be used to specify the other bits, leaving the designated bits equal to zero, and instruct the control circuitry to modify them on the basis of the address mode held in the IR. The necessary modification can be accomplished simply by ORing of the desired bits from the IR, or some decoded version of them, as will be illustrated in the example that follows.

Similar modification is required when computing the source address (point α in the flowchart), but it is a part of an even wider branch. Note that branch microinstructions are not shown explicitly in Figure 5.4, since their presence is implicit in the structure of the flowchart. However, addresses of some branch microinstructions are shown for the convenience of interpretation of a later example.

5.3.2 Wide-Branch Addressing

The above technique of modifying branch addresses results in increasingly more complex circuitry as the number of branches becomes larger. One of the complex cases arises when the machine instruction fetch is completed and it is necessary to decide which microroutine corresponds to the instruction. It is not unusual to have 30 or more possible branches, depending upon organization of the microprogram.

A simple and inexpensive way of generating the required branch addresses is to use a programmable logic array (PLA). A description of PLA integrated circuits is given in Appendix A. In the case of the above wide-branch addressing, it is necessary to translate the OP code of a machine instruction into the starting address of the corresponding microroutine. This may be done by connecting the OP-code bits of the instruction register as inputs to the PLA that acts as a decoder. Then, the output of the PLA is the address of the desired microroutine. This approach is particularly attractive when the OP-code field is variable in length, since a considerable number of input variables (to the decoder) are needed to produce relatively few output addresses.

5.3.3 Detailed Example

Let us examine one path of the flowchart in Figure 5.4 in more detail. Before proceeding, recall that each microinstruction is assigned an address in the control store, indicated by the octal number above the upper right-hand corner. It is assumed that all microinstructions require the same amount of time to be fetched from the control store, and that this time is shorter than the access time for the main memory. Therefore, in some instances, it is necessary to wait for completion of a main memory cycle. These situations are indicated in the figure by breaks in the flow lines.

As a particular example, consider a specific version of the general ADD instruction, where the source involves autoincrement mode and the destination is in register mode. That is, we will look at the path (microroutine) needed to execute

$$\text{ADD} \quad (\text{Rsrc})+,\text{Rdst}$$

where Rsrc and Rdst are general registers in the machine. Figure 5.5 shows the detailed signals that are specified by the microinstructions in this path. Actual signals are shown, instead of encoded bit patterns, for ease of understanding. The corresponding codes may be as given in Figure 5.3. One additional class of register transfer signals is required. Allowing specification of any general-purpose register as part of the address modes implies that gating functions involving a particular register cannot be indicated in the microinstructions. Instead, it is necessary to resort to a more general indication of src and dst registers. Thus microinstructions should contain codes for Rsrc_{out}, Rsrc_{in}, Rdst_{out}, Rdst_{in}. These microinstruction-generated signals must then be translated into specific register transfer signals by the decoding circuitry, which is connected to the src and dst address field of the IR. Note that this involves a two-level decoding process. First, microinstruction fields must be decoded to determine that an Rsrc or Rdst register is involved. The output of this decoder can, then, be used to gate the contents of the src or dst fields in the IR into a second decoder, which produces the gating signals for the actual registers R0 to R3.

The microprogram in Figure 5.4 is derived by combining a number of separate microroutines to save space in the control store, resulting in a structure that necessitates many branch points. In our example of Figure 5.5, there are five

Contents of IR:	0	1	1	0	0	1	0	Rsrc	0	0	0	Rdst
	15			12	11		9	8 6	5		3	2 0

Address (octal)	Microinstruction
000	PC_{out}, MAR_{in}, Read, Clear Y, Set carry-in, Add, Z_{in}
001	Z_{out}, PC_{in}, WMFC
002	MDR_{out}, IR_{in}
003	μBranch $\{\mu PC \leftarrow [PLA] \}$
121	$Rsrc_{out}$, MAR_{in}, Read, Clear Y, Set carry-in, Add, Z_{in}
122	Z_{out}, $Rsrc_{in}$
123	μBranch $\{\mu PC \leftarrow 166; \mu PC_0 \leftarrow \overline{[IR_9]} \}$, WMFC
166	MDR_{out}, MAR_{in}, Read, WMFC
167	MDR_{out}, $SOURCE_{in}$
170	μBranch $\{\mu PC \leftarrow 201; \mu PC_{5,4} \leftarrow [IR_{5,4}]; \mu PC_3 \leftarrow \overline{[IR_5]} \cdot \overline{[IR_4]} \cdot [IR_3] \}$
201	$Rdst_{out}$, Y_{in}
202	μBranch $\{\mu PC \leftarrow 270\}$
270	$SOURCE_{out}$, Add, Z_{in}
271	μBranch $\{\mu PC \leftarrow 272; \mu PC_0 \leftarrow \overline{[IR_5]} \cdot \overline{[IR_4]} \cdot \overline{[IR_3]} \}$
273	Z_{out}, $Rdst_{in}$, End

Figure 5.5 Microroutine for ADD (Rsrc)+,Rdst. *Note:* Microinstruction at location 166 is not executed in this specific example.

branch points, and hence five branch microinstructions are required. In each case, the expression in brackets indicates the branch address that is to be loaded into the μPC. It also shows how this address is modified according to the bit-ORing scheme discussed in Section 5.3.1. As an illustration, consider the microinstruction in location 123. The action of its unmodified version is to cause a branch to the microinstruction in 166, which causes another fetch from the main memory, corresponding to an indirect address mode. When a direct address mode appears, this fetch must be bypassed by branching directly to location 167. This is accomplished simply by ORing the inverse of the "indirect" bit in the src address field (that is, bit 9 in the IR) with the 0 bit position of the μPC.

An example of a multiple branch is presented by the microinstruction in location 170. In this case, the five different branch addresses differ in the middle octal digit only. Therefore, the octal pattern 201 is loaded into the μPC, while the 3 bits to be ORed with the middle octal digit are supplied by the decoding circuitry connected to the dst address mode field, that is, bits 3, 4, and 5 of the IR. Note that microinstruction addresses have been chosen so that this modification is easy to implement. Bits 4 and 5 of the μPC are set directly from the corresponding bits in the IR. This suffices to select the appropriate microinstruction for all dst address modes except register indirect. The latter is covered by setting bit 3 of the μPC to 1 through the AND gate $\overline{[IR_5]} \cdot \overline{[IR_4]} \cdot [IR_3]$.

5.4 MICROINSTRUCTIONS WITH NEXT-ADDRESS FIELD

One of the most striking features of the microroutine in Figure 5.5 is the existence of a relatively large number of branch microinstructions. They constitute one-third of the total, presenting a serious constraint on the operating speed of the computer. The situation can become significantly worse when other microroutines are considered. One factor contributing to the increase in branch microinstructions stems from the limitations in the ability to assign successive addresses to all microinstructions that are generally executed in consecutive order. For example, in cases of wide branching with address modification, some addresses have to be assigned in a rather inflexible fashion, frequently leaving address spaces that are difficult to use efficiently.

This situation prompts a reevaluation of the sequencing technique built around an incrementable μPC. As an alternative, we may consider a scheme where each microinstruction includes some branching capability. The simplest approach is to include an address field as a part of every microinstruction to indicate the location of the next microinstruction to be fetched. This means, in effect, that every microinstruction becomes a branch microinstruction, in addition to its other functions.

The major disadvantage of this approach is the need for additional bits for the address field. Its severity can be assessed by considering the relevant quantitative aspects. In a typical computer, it is possible to design an adequate microprogram that governs most control functions, with fewer than 4K microinstructions, employing perhaps 50 to 80 bits per microinstruction. This implies that an address field of 12 bits is required. Therefore, approximately one-sixth of the control store capacity must be devoted to addressing purposes. Even if more extensive microprograms are needed, the address field is going to become only slightly larger.

The most obvious advantage of the approach is the virtual elimination of separate branch microinstructions. Furthermore, there are few limitations in assignment of addresses to microinstructions. These advantages more than offset the negative attributes, making the scheme attractive from the practical point of view. In fact, some versions of this approach are adopted in most commercially available computers that use microprogrammed control. It is no longer necessary to have an incrementable μPC, but instead a simple *microinstruction address register* (μAR) may be used to hold the address of the microinstruction to be fetched. A new control structure is desired, and one possible organization is given in Figure 5.6. Note that the next-address bits are fed through the OR gates to the μAR. The address may be modified on the basis of the data in the IR, status flags, and condition codes. The decoding circuits include a PLA decoder that is used to generate the starting address of a given microroutine on the basis of the OP code in the IR.

Let us now reconsider the example of Figure 5.5 to see how a microroutine for the ADD (Rsrc)+,Rdst machine instruction may be arranged in light of the

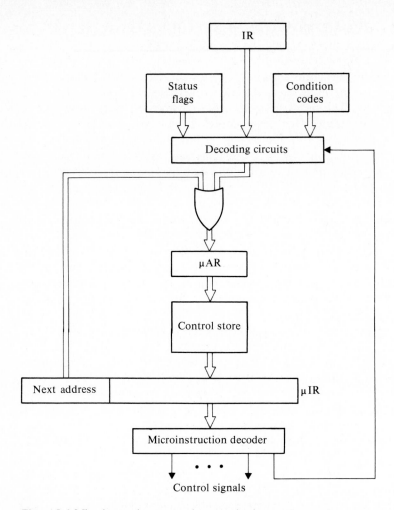

Figure 5.6 Microinstruction-sequencing organization.

ideas introduced in this section. Let us assume that the CPU to be used has eight general-purpose registers. Otherwise, it is structured essentially the same as the block diagram of Figure 5.2. Furthermore, let its microprogrammed control follow the pattern of Figure 5.6.

A number of control signals that were not included in Figure 5.3 will be needed. Instead of referring to registers R0 to R7 explicitly, we will make use of the Rsrc and Rdst names, which can be decoded into the actual control signals with the aid of the data in the src and dst fields of the IR. Branching by means of the bit-ORing technique will necessitate inclusion of the appropriate commands in the microinstructions. Let the bit ORing needed in microinstructions 123, 170, 271 of Figure 5.5 be denoted by the signals OR_{indsrc}, OR_{dst}, and OR_{result}, respectively. For completeness, we will also include OR_{inddst}, which indicates indirect addressing for the destination operand. These signals will be encoded in a 3-bit field in the microinstructions. Assuming that a PLA is used for initial decoding of the instruction OP codes, 1 bit in a microinstruction will be used to indicate when the output of the PLA is to be gated into the μAR. Finally, each microinstruction will contain an 8-bit field that contains the address of the next microinstruction. Figure 5.7 shows a complete format of the assumed microin-

F0	F1	F2	F3

F0 (8 bits)	F1 (4 bits)	F2 (3 bits)	F3 (2 bits)
Address of next microinstruction	0000: No transfer 0001: PC_{out} 0010: MDR_{out} 0011: Z_{out} 0100: $Rsrc_{out}$ 0101: $Rdst_{out}$ 1000: $SOURCE_{out}$ 1001: $DESTIN_{out}$ 1010: $TEMP_{out}$	000: No transfer 001: PC_{in} 010: IR_{in} 011: Z_{in} 100: $Rsrc_{in}$ 101: $Rdst_{in}$	00: No transfer 01: MAR_{in} 10: MDR_{in} 11: $TEMP_{in}$

F4	F5	F6	F7

F4 (2 bits)	F5 (4 bits)	F6 (2 bits)	F7 (1 bit)
00: No transfer 01: Y_{in} 10: $SOURCE_{in}$ 11: $DESTIN_{in}$	0000: Add 0001: Sub .... 1111: XOR	00: No action 01: Read 10: Write	0: No action 1: Clear Y

F8	F9	F10	F11

F8 (1 bit)	F9 (1 bit)	F10 (3 bits)	F11 (1 bit)
0: Carry-in = 0 1: Carry-in = 1	0: No action 1: WMFC	000: No action 001: OR_{dst} 010: OR_{indsrc} 011: OR_{inddst} 100: OR_{result}	0: No action 1: PLA_{out}

Figure 5.7 Format for microinstructions in the example of Section 5.4.

Octal address	F0	F1	F2	F3	F4	F5	F6	F7	F8	F9	F10	F11
0 0 0	0 0 0 0 0 0 0 1	0 0 0 1	0 1 1	0 1	0 0	0 0 0 0	0 1	1	1	0	0 0 0	0
0 0 1	0 0 0 0 0 0 1 0	0 0 1 1	0 0 1	0 0	0 0	0 0 0 0	0 0	0	0	1	0 0 0	0
0 0 2	0 0 0 0 0 0 0 0	0 0 1 0	0 1 0	0 0	0 0	0 0 0 0	0 0	0	0	0	0 0 0	1
1 2 1	0 1 0 1 0 0 1 0	0 1 0 0	0 1 1	0 1	0 0	0 0 0 0	0 1	1	1	0	0 0 0	0
1 2 2	0 1 1 1 0 1 1 0	0 0 1 1	1 0 0	0 0	0 0	0 0 0 0	0 0	0	0	1	0 1 0	0
1 6 6	0 1 1 1 0 1 1 1	0 0 1 0	0 0 0	0 1	0 0	0 0 0 0	0 1	0	0	1	0 0 0	0
1 6 7	1 0 0 0 0 0 0 1	0 0 1 0	0 0 0	0 0	1 0	0 0 0 0	0 0	0	0	0	0 0 1	0
2 0 1	1 0 1 1 1 0 0 0	0 1 0 1	0 0 0	0 0	0 1	0 0 0 0	0 0	0	0	0	0 0 0	0
2 7 0	1 0 1 1 1 0 1 0	1 0 0 0	0 1 1	0 0	0 0	0 0 0 0	0 0	0	0	0	1 0 0	0
2 7 3	0 0 0 0 0 0 0 0	0 0 1 1	1 0 1	0 0	0 0	0 0 0 0	0 0	0	0	0	0 0 0	0

Figure 5.8 Implementation of the microroutine of Figure 5.5, using a next-microinstruction address field (see Figure 5.7 for the encoded signals).

structions. Note that it is essentially an expanded version of the format in Figure 5.3.

Using such microinstructions we can implement the microroutine of Figure 5.5 as shown in Figure 5.8. In this case, fewer microinstructions are needed, since the branch microinstructions are no longer required. The reader should note that this microroutine does not terminate by producing the End signal. When sequencing of microinstructions is controlled by a μPC, then the End signal is used to reset the μPC to point at the starting address of the microinstruction that will fetch the next machine instruction to be executed. In our example this starting address is 000_8. However, in an organization corresponding to Figure 5.8 the starting address is not specified through a resetting mechanism triggered by the End signal. Instead, it is specified explicitly in the F0 field.

A more detailed diagram of the control structure of Figure 5.6 is given in Figure 5.9. It shows how control signals can be decoded from the microinstruction fields and used to control the sequencing. Detailed circuits for bit-ORing are shown in Figure 5.10.

5.5 PREFETCHING OF MICROINSTRUCTIONS

The major drawback of microprogrammed control is the inherently slower operating speed of the resulting computer. Fetching a microinstruction from the control store takes considerably longer than the time needed to generate equivalent control signals using hardwired circuits. It is obvious that microprogrammed machines will never be able to match the speed of hardwired ones.

Having made a fundamental decision to use microprogramming, the designer may still desire to produce as fast a machine as possible. To this end, the designer is likely to choose the fastest available control store, and make use of long microinstructions in order to simultaneously generate as many control

Figure 5.9 (Opposite) Some details of the control-signal-generating circuitry.

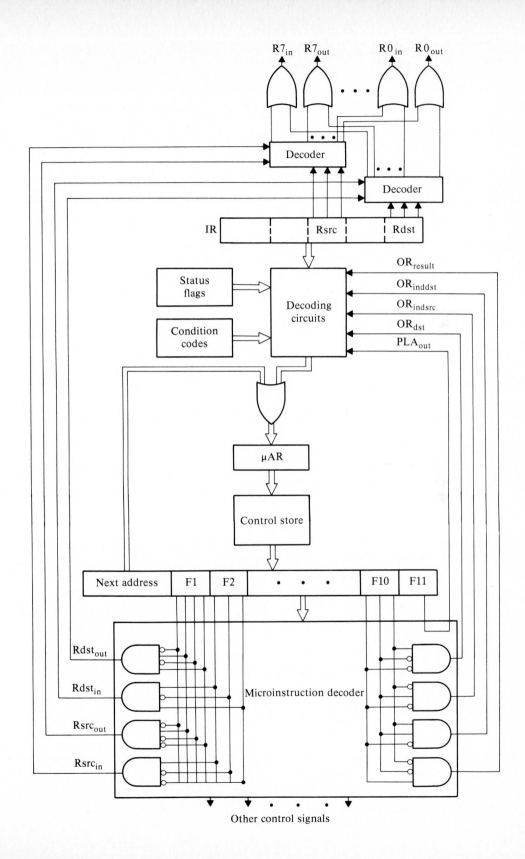

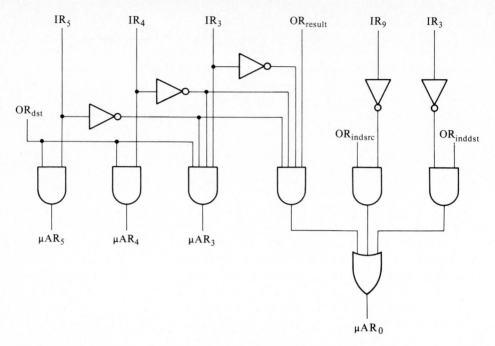

Figure 5.10 Control circuitry for bit-ORing (part of decoding circuits in Figure 5.9).

signals as possible. But, there is another option available. Instead of following the natural sequence of fetching a microinstruction, executing it, and then fetching the next one, it is possible to save time by prefetching the next microinstruction while the current one is being executed. In this way most of the execution time can be overlapped with the fetch time. Thus the overall machine speed is essentially dependent upon the fetch times. Such techniques of overlapping as many operations as possible to keep the hardware units as busy as possible are often referred to as "pipelining."

Prefetching of microinstructions presents some organizational difficulties. Sometimes it is necessary to use the status flags and the results of the currently executed microinstruction to determine the address of the next microinstruction. Thus straightforward prefetching will, occasionally, prefetch a wrong micro-instruction. In such cases it is necessary to repeat the fetch with the correct address. This implies somewhat more complex hardware. However, the disadvantages are minor and the prefetching technique is often found in practice.

5.6 EMULATION

The main function of microprogrammed control, as discussed above, is to provide a means for simple, flexible, and relatively inexpensive control of a computer. However, it offers other interesting possibilities. Its flexibility in handling of resources within a machine allows implementation of diverse classes of instructions. Given a computer with a certain instruction set, as a result of a given architecture, it is possible to define other additional machine instructions and implement them with extra microroutines. Thus users can be given the option of defining some instructions that may be particularly useful to them, and adding these instructions to the basic machine instruction set. Of course, this is not a routine job, and, in practice, only a very small number of users can advantageously undertake such modifications.

An extension of the above idea leads to an even more attractive possibility. Suppose that we add to the instruction repertoire of a given computer M_1 an entirely new set of instructions that is in fact the instruction set of a different computer M_2. In this way, we could run programs written in the machine language of M_2 on computer M_1. Indeed, from the point of view of the users, machine M_1 would look no different from machine M_2, and we would say that M_1 *emulates* M_2. This is a very useful concept as it can enable replacement of obsolete equipment with more up-to-date machines, without forcing the users to rewrite the bulk of their software. If the replacement computer fully emulates the original one, then no software changes have to be made to run the existing programs. This is an important consideration for the users, since rewriting of such software is usually a costly and time-consuming proposition. Thus emulation facilitates transitions into new systems with a minimum of disruption.

Emulation is easier when the machines involved have similar architectures. However, there have also been many successes in emulating computers using machines with totally different architectures.

Finally, we should note the possibility of designing a computer with a highly flexible structure that is controlled by a microprogram in RAM storage. Let us assume that the structure is flexible enough to permit easy reconfiguration of the machine through simple replacement of the microprogram. Then we may use different microprograms for execution of different tasks. If a program written for a given class of machines, say, IBM S/370, is to be executed, the computer would be configured to emulate "IBM S/370" machines by loading the corresponding microprogram into the control store. Another microprogram could be used to emulate the PDP-11 architecture, etc. Thus a single computer could be made to exhibit the characteristics of a number of distinct machines.

We have considered emulation by means of special microprograms added to a given computer. Similar effects can be attained with additional hardware and software. Therefore, in general, it is reasonable to define an *emulator* as hardware, microprograms, and software added to a computer M_1, so that it can execute programs written for a different computer M_2. It is customary to assume that emulation always involves either additional hardware or microprograms, or both. If only software means are employed, the process is usually referred to as simulation.

5.7 BIT SLICES

The flexibility attainable through microprogramming makes it possible to design the data path section of a processor, that is, the ALU, registers, and internal connections, independently of its instruction set. Moreover, it is possible to design general-purpose microinstruction sequencing hardware that can be used in conjunction with a wide range of data path configurations and instruction sets. In other words, we can define building blocks which can be easily assembled into a computer that meets the needs of a given application. The capabilities and the instruction set of such a computer are determined by the particular building blocks chosen, by the way they are interconnected, and of course by the microprogram.

The flexibility of this building block approach can be enhanced considerably if the blocks can be used to build processors of arbitrary word lengths. This is the basis of the bit-slice idea. A *bit slice* is a "slice" through the data path of a typical processor. It contains all circuits necessary to provide ALU functions, register transfers, and control functions for a few bits only, typically 2, 4, or 8. The connection patterns for the circuits on the slice are under microprogram control. The necessary control signals are provided by other building blocks.

A 4-bit slice provides the functions of an ALU and a number of registers for 4 bits of data. It also provides the signals necessary for interconnection of a number of such slices side by side to form a wider data path. Thus, it is possible to use four slices to form the basis of a 16-bit processor, or eight slices for a 32-bit processor.

The bit-slice building block is highly compatible with VLSI technology. Individual blocks are produced in the form of single chips. In order to illustrate the structure and use of bit slices, we will use the AMD 2900* family of chips. Two of the building blocks in this family are a 4-bit ALU chip (AMD 2903) and a microprogram control sequencer chip (AMD 2910). A computer implemented with these chips has a number of 2903s for its data path and uses a 2910 to generate the control store addresses.

The internal structure of the ALU chip is given in Figure 5.11. It consists of a 4-bit ALU, two 4-bit shifters, and a number of 4-bit registers. The ALU provides a full set of arithmetic and logic functions, and the shifters perform shift and rotate operations. The registers consist of 16 general-purpose registers and one register, called the Q register, which can be used for temporary storage of operands. The general-purpose registers are implemented in the form of a *two-port memory*. This is a random-access memory in which all addressing circuits are duplicated. Hence, two registers can be accessed at the same time, using the two address inputs AA and AB. The contents of these two registers are available at the data outputs A and B, respectively. Data fed to the DATA IN input of the register file is stored in the register pointed to by the AB address. The outputs A and B are fed to the ALU via two multiplexers. Data may also be fed to the inputs of the ALU from sources external to the chip. This allows additional registers to be used when implementing a processor with more than 16 registers. Of course, these inputs can also be used for connecting the ALU chip to the main memory bus.

Several ALU chips may be concatenated to form a wider data path, as illustrated in Figure 5.12. The address inputs to the register file are connected in

*Manufactured by Advanced Micro Devices, Inc., Sunnyvale, California.

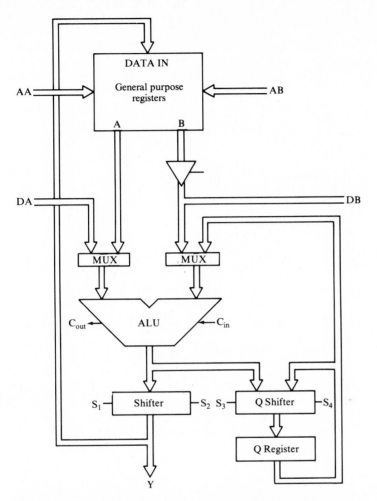

Figure 5.11 Internal organization of the AMD 2903 processing element.

parallel so that the corresponding registers are selected on all chips. The serial input-output terminals of the shifter are connected to implement a 16-bit shifter. The carry inputs and outputs of the arithmetic and logic units are connected in a similar manner. Various aspects of dealing with carry signals will be discussed in Chapter 7.

The organization of the AMD 2910 microprogram control sequencer is illustrated in Figure 5.13. A control store address is generated at the output of the sequencer from one of four sources. A microprogram counter is used for sequential addresses. At any time, the output of this counter can be pushed onto a stack to allow subroutine calls within the microprogram. Branching is implemented by supplying a branch address to the input of the sequencer chip. A register/loop counter is also provided for storing temporary addresses and for simplifying the implementation of loops in the microprogram.

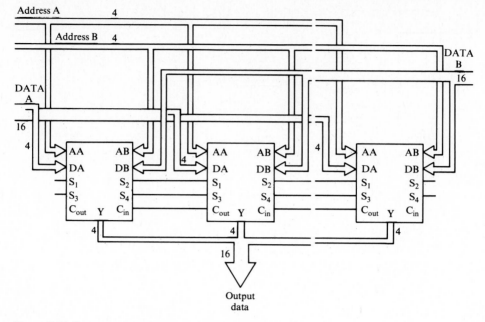

Figure 5.12 Concatenation of 4-bit slices to form a 16-bit data path.

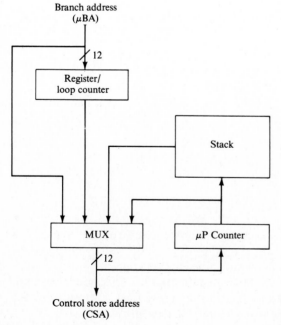

Figure 5.13 Organization of the AMD 2910 microprogram control sequencer.

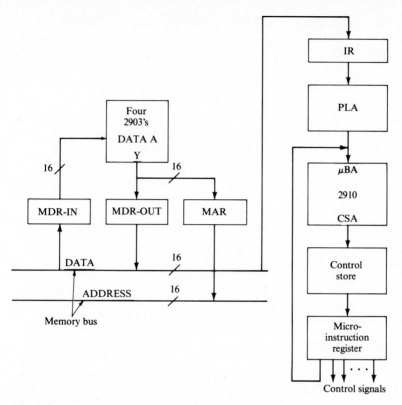

Figure 5.14 A 16-bit processor based on the AMD 2903 bit slice.

A simple, 16-bit processor that uses four AMD 2903 chips and one AMD 2910 chip is shown in Figure 5.14. The bit slices are connected to the memory data and address buses via the MDR and MAR registers, respectively. Two MDR registers are used, one for each direction of transfer. The control section of the processor is organized in a manner similar to the scheme of Figure 5.6. The μBA input of the sequencer is connected to the output of a PLA which provides the starting microprogram address for each machine instruction. It is also connected to one of the fields in the microinstruction register to allow branching in the microprogram.

The above example illustrates how bit slices can be used to implement a processor unit. It is apparent that this approach enables the design of a processor with arbitrary word length which is also fully microprogrammable. Hence, it can be tailored to meet the requirements of any special task.

5.8 CONCLUDING REMARKS

Microprogrammed control is a powerful concept. It provides simple and efficient means for replacing hardwired control logic, not only in computers but also in the most general class of digital control circuits.

Preparation of microprograms can be an arduous task. Optimization of microcode is often difficult to achieve. Consequently, there is great need for tools to help cope with these difficulties. Much work has been done in the development of high-level languages for microprogramming. Considerable progress has also been made in development of techniques for microcode optimization.

Microprogrammed processors are having significant impact on many special-purpose applications, mostly as a result of advances in VLSI technology. The bit-slice approach is of particular significance in this area.

5.9 PROBLEMS

5.1 Write a microroutine (such as the one shown in Figure 5.5) for the instruction

$$\text{MOV} \quad \text{X(Rsrc)}, -\text{(Rdst)}$$

where the source and destination operands are specified in indexed and autodecrement addressing modes, respectively.

5.2 Suppose that the two-operand instructions of the PDP-11 minicomputer are to be implemented by using microprogrammed control patterned after Figure 5.4. Estimate the size of the control store that would be required to implement the following instructions (defined in Appendix B): MOVB, CMPB, BITB, ADD, SUB, and XOR.

5.3 A BGT (Branch if > 0) machine instruction has the expression $Z + (N \oplus V) = 0$ as its branch condition, where Z, N, and V are the zero, negative, and overflow condition flags, respectively. Write a microroutine that can implement this instruction. Show the circuitry needed to appropriately test the condition codes.

5.4 Write a combined microroutine that can implement the BGT, BPL (Branch if Plus), and BR (Branch Unconditionally) instructions. What is the total number of microinstructions required? How many microinstructions would be needed if a separate microroutine was used for each machine instruction?

5.5 Figure 5.5 shows an example of a microroutine where bit ORing is used to accomplish the modification of microinstruction addresses. Write an equivalent routine, without the use of bit ORing, where conditional branch microinstructions are used instead. How many additional microinstructions are needed? Assume that the conditional branch microinstructions can test some of the bits in the IR.

5.6 In the example of Figure 5.5, bit ORing is used in conjunction with branch microinstructions. Can the same approach be used for the instruction

$$\text{ADD} \quad \text{X(Rsrc),Rdst}$$

using the details given in Figure 5.4? What modification, if any, may be needed in the suggested approach?

5.7 Write a microroutine for the instruction ASH (Arithmetic Shift), defined in Appendix B. Assume that the ALU can shift the data word on one of its input terminals one bit position to the right, under the control of the shift right signal. In this operation the most significant bit position remains unchanged while the least significant bit becomes the carry-out. Note that the required shifting to the left can be accomplished by adding the given data word to itself (that is, multiplying it by 2). Is any additional hardware desirable in the implementation of this instruction?

5.8 Assuming similar conditions to those specified in Problem 5.7, write a microroutine for the instruction ASHC (Arithmetic Shift Combined), defined in Appendix B.

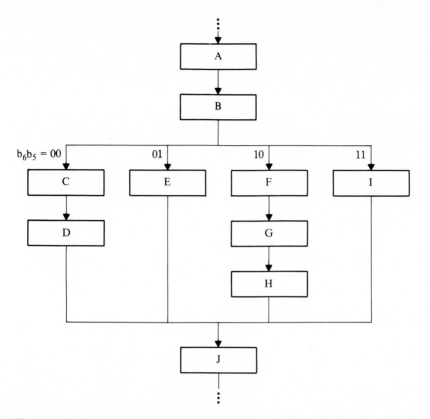

Figure P5.1 A microinstruction-sequence pattern.

5.9 Figure P5.1 gives a part of the microinstruction sequence corresponding to one of the machine instructions of a microprogrammed computer. Microinstruction B is followed by either C, E, F, or I, depending upon bits b_6 and b_5 of the machine instruction register. It is required to compare the three possible implementations described below.

(a) Microinstruction sequencing is accomplished by means of a microprogram counter. Branching is achieved by microinstructions of the form

If b_6b_5 branch to X

where b_6b_5 is the branch condition and X is the branch address.

(b) Same as (a) except that the branch microinstruction has the form

Branch to X

where X is a base branch address, to be modified by bit ORing of bits b_5 and b_6 with the appropriate bits within X.

(c) A field in each microinstruction specifies the address of the next microinstruction, with bit-ORing capability.

Assign suitable addresses for all microinstructions in Figure P5.1 in each of the above implementations. Note that you may need to insert branch instructions in some cases. You may choose arbitrary addresses, as long as they are consistent with the method of sequencing used. For example, in case (a):

Address	Microinstruction
00010	A
00011	B
00100	If $b_6 b_5 = 00$ branch to XXXXX
....	....
XXXXX	C

5.10 It is desired to reduce the number of bits needed to encode the control signals in Figure 5.3. Show a possible format for encoding these signals that requires not more than 18 bits, instead of the 21 in the figure. No two signals may be in the same field if they are likely to be specified in any one microinstruction.

5.11 Could the control signals in Figure 5.3 be encoded using only 12 bits in a microinstruction? If so, what will be the effect of such encoding on microroutines corresponding to the ADD and BR machine instructions in Figures 4.8 and 4.9, respectively?

5.12 What are the relative merits of horizontal and vertical microinstruction formats? Relate your answer to the answers found in Problems 5.10 and 5.11.

5.13 What are the advantages and disadvantages of hardwired and microprogrammed control? Why is microprogrammed control becoming increasingly more popular?

5.14 Consider the possibility of using the AMD 2903 bit slices to implement the PDP-11 instruction set.

    (a) Is the arrangement of Figure 5.14 suitable for this objective?

    (b) How would you implement the program counter and PSW registers?

    (c) How would the JSR instruction be implemented? Show a sequence of microinstruction steps needed to execute the instruction

$$\text{JSR} \qquad \text{R5,@\#2000}$$

5.15 Show how one could use the AMD 2903 bit slices to implement a Multiply operation. The operation is to multiply two unsigned 16-bit numbers in registers R1 and R2, and leave the 32-bit result in registers R0 and R1. Make any necessary assumptions about the control signals needed to gate the data within a bit-slice element.

5.16 The 16 general-purpose registers in the AMD 2903 bit slice (see Figure 5.11) are addressed by means of the AA and the AB address lines.

    (a) Indicate the circuitry needed to generate the signals on these lines, if a PDP-11 instruction set is to be implemented with these bit slices. In particular, consider the effects of the instruction fetching process, two- and one-operand instructions, and subroutine calls.

    (b) Can your circuit support the execution of the MUL instruction, defined in Appendix B? If not, what modifications are required?

INPUT-OUTPUT ORGANIZATION

One of the basic features of a computer is its ability to send and receive data to and from other devices. This *communication* capability enables a human operator, for example, to enter a program and its associated data via the keyboard of a CRT terminal and receive results on a printer. There is a variety of equipment with which a computer may be required to communicate. It includes teletypewriters, CRT terminals, and plotters, as well as magnetic disk and tape drives. In addition to these standard I/O devices, a computer may be connected to other types of equipment. For example, in industrial control applications, input to a computer may be the digital output of a voltmeter, a temperature sensor, or a fire alarm. Similarly, the output of a computer may be a digitally coded command to change the speed of a motor, open a valve, or cause a digital voltmeter to take the next reading. In short, a general-purpose computer should have the ability to deal with a wide range of device characteristics in varying environments.

Let us start by identifying the functions that need to be performed by a computer to handle I/O operations. Obviously, it is necessary to have some means for:

1. Addressing or selection of individual I/O devices for a given transfer operation
2. Transferring data to and from the selected device

Another requirement arises from the fact that operation of external devices is, to a considerable degree, independent of the CPU. Therefore a third function that should be performed by the computer is:

3. Synchronization, or coordination, of the timing of input and output operations

In this chapter we shall consider in detail the various ways in which the above functions can be implemented. First, we will consider the problem from the point of view of the programmer. Then, we will present some of the hardware details associated with bus and I/O interfaces. The discussion in Sections 6.1 through 6.6 applies directly to small- and medium-sized computers. Larger machines use special-purpose units, usually referred to as channels, to handle I/O operatons. I/O channels can be regarded as small computers. In that sense, the concepts discussed apply to all machines, large and small. The functional characteristics of channels, as well as some of their hardware and software aspects, will be treated in Section 6.7.

6.1 ADDRESSING OF I/O DEVICES

Since more than one device is usually connected to a computer, some means have to be provided by which only one of these devices can be selected to participate in a given I/O operation. This can be accomplished through the use of an I/O bus arrangement, as shown in Figure 6.1. This bus, to which all I/O devices are connected, consists of three sets of lines used for transmission of address, data, and control signals. Therefore if each device is assigned an identifying code, or address, the CPU can select a device by placing its address on the address lines. Only the device that recognizes its address responds to the CPU commands issued on the control lines.

In the case of single-bus machines, for example, the PDP-11 and most microcomputers, the same bus serves both as a memory bus and as an I/O bus. Thus I/O devices may be identified by assigning them unique codes within the memory address space of the computer. Using this arrangement, it is possible to access the I/O devices in the same way as any other memory location, providing considerable flexibility in handling I/O operations. This is known as *memory-mapped I/O*. We should emphasize that it is necessary to assign a unique address code to each device. It may be convenient, although not necessary, to dedicate a

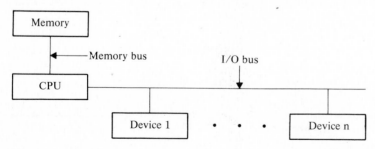

Figure 6.1 Use of I/O bus.

contiguous block of addresses to I/O devices, and this is often done in practice. In PDP-11 computers the address range 765008_8 to 777570_8 is reserved for peripheral devices. System software for these computers, provided by the manufacturer, allocates specific addresses to the commonly used devices. For example, a teletypewriter connected to the PDP-11 bus has four status and data registers, as discussed in Section 2.6. The addresses assigned to these registers are as follows:

Keyboard status register (KBSTATUS)	777560
Keyboard data buffer (TTYIN)	777562
Printer status register (PRSTATUS)	777564
Printer data buffer (TTYOUT)	777566

Of course, users who are willing to write their own system software do not have to use these assignments.

6.2 DATA TRANSFER

In the previous section we saw how a particular device can be selected by the CPU to participate in an I/O operation. We shall now discuss the means by which data can be moved from the device buffers to the main memory or to CPU registers, and vice versa. Usually, this is accomplished by executing special IN and OUT instructions. In machines where data registers of external devices are treated as memory locations, a Move instruction can be used to perform I/O operations. Thus, as we have seen in Chapter 2 in the case of the PDP-11, the instruction

MOVB @#TTYIN,LOC

moves the contents of the keyboard data buffer to location LOC in the memory.

Figure 6.2 illustrates the arrangement required to connect any device to the I/O bus of a computer. The address decoder enables the device to recognize its address when this address is placed on the address bus by the CPU. The data register is used to hold data to be transferred to the CPU from an input device or to receive data from the CPU for transfer to an output device. In some machines, as in the PDP-11 computer, status registers are also connected to the data bus. The address decoder, the data and status registers, and the control circuits required to coordinate I/O transfers constitute the device *interface*.

The above method of implementing I/O transfers is usually referred to as *program-controlled I/O*. With this method, the execution of one I/O instruction causes the transfer of one word of data. In the case of I/O devices which can handle only one character at a time, such as a teletypewriter, only one character is transferred by an I/O instruction.

When large blocks of data need to be transferred at high speed to or from an external device, an alternative approach may be used. A special control circuit

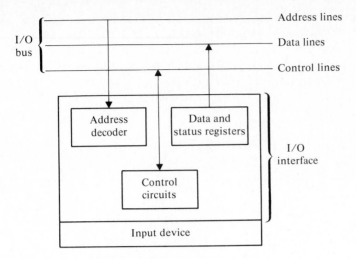

Figure 6.2 I/O interface for an input device.

may be provided to enable transfer of a block of data directly between the device and the main memory. The control circuit transfers data, one word at a time, at a speed consistent with the characteristics of the external device. This approach is generally referred to as *direct memory access*, or DMA.

6.2.1 Direct Memory Access

Let us consider the case of a high-speed peripheral device that needs to transfer large blocks of data in and out of the main memory. The use of program-controlled I/O with such a device is, at best, very inefficient, if not outright impossible. The reasons for this are twofold:

1. In program-controlled I/O, considerable overhead is incurred because several program instructions have to be executed for each data word transferred between the external device and the main memory.
2. Many high-speed, peripheral devices have a synchronous mode of operation. That is, data transfers are controlled by a clock of fixed frequency, independent of the CPU.

The overhead incurred in program-controlled I/O is illustrated by the example given in Figure 6.3. This program transfers 80 characters from memory, starting at location LOC, to a line printer. Register R0 is used as a pointer to data characters in the memory, while register R1 keeps track of the character count. The status and buffer registers of the printer are represented by the names LPRSTATUS and LPROUT, respectively. The column "memory cycles" gives the number of memory references required to execute each instruction. For example, the instruction

WAIT: TSTB   @#LPRSTATUS

			Memory cycles	
	MOV	#LOC,R0	2	
	MOV	#−80..R1	2	
WAIT:	TSTB	@LPRSTATUS	3	
	BP	WAIT	1	
	MOVB	(R0)+,@LPROUT	4	Character transfer loop
	INC	R1	1	
	BNE	WAIT	1	
	HALT		1	

Figure 6.3 An example of program-controlled I/O. LPRSTATUS is the printer status register. LPROUT is the printer data register. Register R0 contains the address of data in the main memory. Register R1 keeps track of the word count.

requires three memory references. Two of these are required to fetch the instruction and the addressing data for the operand. The third memory cycle is required to fetch the operand itself, that is, the contents of the status register, in order to perform the test.

Inspection of the character transfer loop reveals that there are at least five instructions executed, requiring a total of 10 memory cycles, for each character transferred to the printer. This represents an overhead of 9 to 1.

The requirement for synchronous data transfers is, in many cases, dictated by the physical characteristics of the peripheral device. For example, a high-speed magnetic tape drive cannot be stopped after each character. Data transfer from such a drive takes place at rates approaching, and sometimes exceeding, 1 million characters per second. This is of the same order of magnitude as the speed at which main memory fetches can be executed. The combination of the high speed and the requirement for synchronism makes operation of these devices incompatible with program-controlled data transfer as given in Figure 6.3.

The problems encountered in operating high-speed devices can be overcome by incorporating all functions performed by the program of Figure 6.3 in a hardwired controller. This controller enables direct data transfer between the device and the main memory without involvement of the CPU. Inspection of Figure 6.3 suggests that such a DMA controller can be implemented through the use of two counter registers, one for generating the memory address and the other for keeping track of the word count. A third register is needed to store the CPU command specifying the function to be performed, and a fourth register is normally used as a data buffer between the main memory and the I/O device. In the case of more complex devices, such as tape and disk drives, other registers may also be required. The controller registers must be accessible for initialization by the CPU under program control. Therefore, the DMA controller should be connected to the bus in the normal fashion, as in the case of any other I/O device interface.

Figure 6.4 shows two schemes for connecting DMA controllers and I/O devices to the bus. Part (*a*) depicts a single-bus structure, where an I/O device is

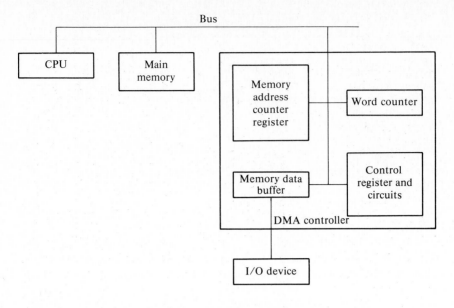

(*a*) Single-bus structure

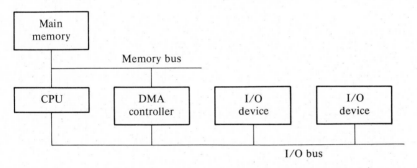

(*b*) Two-bus structure with a "floating" DMA controller

Figure 6.4 Bus organization for direct memory access.

connected to the bus through a DMA interface. The I/O device is handled by a dedicated DMA controller. Part (*b*) depicts a two-bus structure. Here, the CPU communicates with the DMA controller via the I/O bus. The controller is also connected to the memory bus, to allow data transfers between the I/O devices and the main memory, via the DMA interface. In this case the DMA controller can be used to handle more than one I/O device. Such controllers are often referred to as "floating" DMA controllers.

To start an I/O operation using DMA, it is necessary to execute a program that performs the following functions:

• Load memory address counter
• Load word count

• Load function to be performed (Read, Write)
• Issue a GO command

Upon receiving the GO command, the DMA controller proceeds independently to implement the function specified in its function register. Meanwhile, the CPU may start executing another part of the program that issued the I/O request or a different program altogether.

   Note that a conflict situation may now arise when both the CPU and a DMA controller are trying to access the main memory. To resolve this conflict, a special circuit should be provided to coordinate the activities of all devices requesting a memory transfer. This *memory bus controller* implements a priority system, as will be described later. Memory accesses by the CPU and peripheral devices are interwoven, with top priority given to synchronous, high-speed peripherals such as disk and tape drives. Considering that in most cases the CPU originates the majority of memory access cycles, the DMA controller can be regarded as "stealing" memory cycles from the CPU. Hence, this technique is usually referred to as *cycle stealing*.

6.3 SYNCHRONIZATION

A computer should have some means of coordinating its activities with those of the external devices connected to it. For example, when accepting characters from a teletypewriter, it needs to know when a new character has been entered on the keyboard and is ready for transfer. Similarly, during an output operation, the computer cannot send a character to the printer until printing of the previous character has been completed. Some examples of the means by which this can be accomplished have been discussed in connection with the programs of Figures 2.19 and 6.3. A more detailed discussion of different aspects of this problem will be presented in this section.

   In general, there are two commonly used techniques to achieve the required coordination: *polling*, or status checking, and *interrupts*.

6.3.1 Polling or Status Checking

Two examples of the use of this technique have been presented in Figures 2.19 and 6.3. The current status of each input or output device connected to a computer is indicated by one or more bits of information. The most important of these bits, usually referred to as the "Ready" bit, is set whenever the device is ready to participate in a new character transfer. To perform an I/O operation on a given device, the program should first poll this device by testing its status bits. When the Ready bit is set, an I/O instruction may be issued to perform the required transfer. This immediately clears the Ready bit, which remains equal to 0 until the device is ready for another transfer. In simple devices, such as teletypewriters, the Ready bit is all that is needed. In a more complex device, for example a high-speed printer, more status bits are used to indicate conditions such as whether the paper is jammed or whether the printer is out of paper.

The way in which the I/O device status is presented to the computer varies from one machine to another. In some machines, as in the case of the PDP-11 computers, the status bits are assembled in a status register associated with each I/O device. The contents of this register can be accessed by the CPU over the data lines. Thus they can be tested as regular data. In some other machines, for example, the Nova* minicomputer or 8085 microcomputer⁺, the Ready bit is connected to one of the control lines. Special instructions are provided to test the state of this line to determine whether the external device is ready for data transfer.

6.3.2 Interrupts

An alternative means for coordinating the activities of the CPU with those of I/O devices is the use of interrupts. Instead of executing the waiting loop in Figure 2.19, the CPU may temporarily suspend the execution of instructions. The processor stays in this state until the external device is ready for data transfer. At this point, the device alerts the CPU by activating one of the control lines which we shall refer to as the *interrupt-request* (INTR) line. This signals the CPU to proceed with the execution of the data transfer instruction.

The use of interrupts extends much beyond the simple illustrative example described above. Since the computer is no longer required to continuously check the status of external devices, the waiting period can be utilized to perform other useful functions. Indeed, by using interrupts, such waiting periods can ideally be eliminated.

> **Example** Consider a task which requires some computations to be performed and the results to be printed on a line printer. This is followed by more computations and output, and so on. Let the program consist of two routines, COMPUTE and PRINT. Assume that COMPUTE produces n lines of output. These are printed by the PRINT routine.
>
> The required task may be performed by repeatedly executing the COMPUTE routine, then the PRINT routine. The printer accepts one line of text at a time. Hence, the PRINT routine must send one line of text, wait for it to be printed, then send the next line, until all the results have been printed. The disadvantage of this simple approach is that the CPU spends a considerable amount of time waiting for the printer to become ready. It is possible to overlap the printing and computation processes, that is, to execute the COMPUTE routine while printing is in progress, resulting in a higher overall speed of execution. This may be achieved as follows. First, the COMPUTE routine is executed to produce the first n lines of output. Then,

---

*Manufactured by Data General Corporation.
⁺Manufactured by Intel Corporation.

the PRINT routine is executed to send the first line of text to the printer. At this point, instead of waiting for this line to be printed, the PRINT routine may be temporarily suspended. This makes it possible to continue execution of the COMPUTE routine. Whenever the printer becomes ready, it alerts the CPU by sending an interrupt-request signal. This causes the CPU to interrupt the execution of the COMPUTE routine and transfer control to the PRINT routine. The PRINT routine sends the second line to the printer. Then, it returns control to the interrupted COMPUTE routine, which resumes execution at the point of interruption. This process continues until all n lines have been printed.

The PRINT routine will be restarted whenever the next set of n lines are available for printing. If COMPUTE takes about the same amount of time to generate n lines as the time required to print them, then it is likely that the next set of n lines will be available immediately.

The above example is intended to introduce the concept of interrupts. The routine which is executed in response to an interrupt request is called the *interrupt-service routine*. In the above case, this is the PRINT routine. Interrupt servicing bears considerable resemblance to subroutine calls. Assume that the interrupt arrives during execution of instruction i in Figure 6.5. The CPU first completes execution of instruction i. It should then load the program counter (PC) with the address of the first instruction of the interrupt-service routine. Let us assume, for the time being, that this address is hardwired in the CPU. After execution of the interrupt-service routine, the CPU should come back to instruction $i + 1$. Therefore, when an interrupt is received, the current contents of the PC, which point at instruction $i + 1$ in the case of Figure 6.5, should be put in temporary storage. A Return-from-interrupt instruction at the end of the interrupt-service routine causes the CPU to reload the PC from that temporary storage location. Thus, execution resumes at instruction $i + 1$. In most computers, the return address is saved on the processor stack.

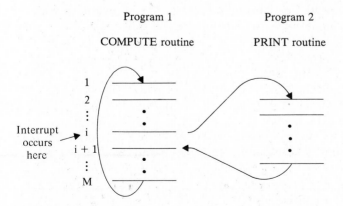

Figure 6.5 Transfer of control through the use of interrupts.

We should note that as part of handling interrupts, the CPU must inform the device that its request has been recognized, so that it may remove its interrupt-request signal. This may be accomplished by means of a special control signal on the bus. An *interrupt-acknowledge* signal, used in some of the interrupt schemes to be discussed later, may serve this function. A common alternative is to have the transfer of data between the CPU and the I/O device interface accomplish the same purpose. The execution of an instruction in the interrupt-service routine that either reads from or writes into the data register in the device interface implicitly informs the device that its interrupt request has been recognized. A detailed example of an interface that operates in this manner will be given in Chapter 11, Section 11.4.2.

So far, treatment of an interrupt-service routine is very similar to that of a subroutine. An important departure from this similarity should be noted at this point. A subroutine performs a function required by the main program by which it is called. However, the interrupt-service routine may not have anything in common with the program being executed at the time the interrupt is received. In fact, the two programs often belong to two different users. Therefore, before starting execution of the interrupt-service routine, the CPU should save, along with the contents of the PC, any information that may affect execution after return to the original program. Namely, the CPU should save the *status word* which includes the condition codes and any other status indicators at the time of interruption. Upon return from the interrupt-service routine, the CPU reloads the status word from its temporary storage location. This enables the original program to resume execution without being affected in any way by the occurrence of the interrupt, except, of course, for the time delay.

The contents of CPU registers, other than the program counter and the processor status register, may or may not be saved automatically by the interrupt-handling mechanism. Obviously, if the CPU saves register contents before entering the interrupt-service routine, it must also restore them before returning to the interrupted program. The process of saving and restoring registers involves a number of memory transfers. These transfers represent a time overhead that is associated with every interrupt accepted by the CPU. In a computer which does not automatically save all register contents following an interrupt, the interrupt-service routine should save the contents of any CPU register that it needs to use. The saved data should be restored to their respective registers before returning to the interrupted program. In order to minimize the interrupt overhead, some computers provide two types of interrupts. One saves all register contents, and the other does not. A particular I/O device may use either type, depending upon its response time requirements. An example of this approach is found in the Motorola M6809 microprocessor, which will be described in Chapter 11. Another interesting approach is to provide duplicate sets of CPU registers. Then a different set of registers can be used in servicing interrupt requests. This approach is found in the Z80 microprocessor* and IBM Series 1 minicomputers.

*Manufactured by Zilog Corporation

The above discussion shows that an interrupt is more than a simple mechanism for coordinating I/O transfers. In a general sense, interrupts enable transfer of control from one program to another to be initiated by an event external to the computer. Execution of the interrupted program resumes after completion of execution of the interrupt-service routine. As such, the concept of interrupts is useful in operating systems and in many control applications where processing of certain routines has to be accurately timed relative to external events. The latter application is generally referred to as *real-time* processing.

6.4 INTERRUPT HANDLING

The facilities available in a computer should be sufficient to enable the programmer to have complete control over the events that take place during program execution. The arrival of an interrupt request from an external device causes the CPU to suspend the execution of one program and start the execution of another. Since interrupts can arrive at any time, they may alter the sequence of events envisaged by the programmer. Hence, they should be carefully controlled. A fundamental facility found in all computers is the ability to enable and disable the occurrence of program interruptions as desired. We will examine this in some detail below. Since proper handling of interrupts requires close cooperation between the software and the hardware, no attempt will be made to separate these two aspects in the discussion.

6.4.1 Enabling and Disabling Interrupts

There are many situations in which the CPU should ignore interrupt requests. For example, in the case of the COMPUTE-PRINT program of Figure 6.5, an interrupt request from the printer should be accepted only if there are output lines to be printed. After printing the last line of a set of n lines, interrupts should be disabled until another set becomes available for printing. In another case, it may be necessary to guarantee that a particular sequence of instructions is executed to the end without interruption, since the interrupt-service routine may change some of the data used by the instructions in question. For these reasons, some means for enabling and disabling interrupts must be made available to the programmer. A simple way is to provide machine instructions, such as Interrupt-enable and Interrupt-disable, which perform these functions.

Let us consider in some detail the specific case of a single interrupt request from one device. When a device activates the interrupt-request signal, it keeps this signal activated until it learns that the CPU has accepted its request. This means that the interrupt-request signal will be active during execution of the interrupt-service routine, perhaps until an instruction is reached which accesses the device in question. It is essential to ensure that this active request signal does not cause a second interruption during this period. An erroneous interpretation of a single interrupt as multiple requests would cause the system to enter an infinite loop from which it could not recover. Several mechanisms are available to alleviate this problem. We will describe three simple possibilities here. Other schemes that involve more than one interrupting device will be presented later.

The first possibility is to have the CPU hardware ignore the interrupt-request line until the execution of the first instruction of the interrupt-service routine has been completed. Thus, using an Interrupt-disable instruction as the first instruction in the interrupt-service routine, the programmer can ensure that no further interruptions will occur until an Interrupt-enable instruction is executed. Typically, this will be the last instruction in the interrupt-service routine before the Return-from-interrupt instruction. Again the CPU must guarantee that execution of the Return-from-interrupt instruction is completed before further interruption can occur.

Another option, commonly encountered in practice, is to have the CPU automatically disable interrupts before starting the execution of the interrupt-service routine. That is, after saving the contents of the PC and the processor status (PS) on the stack, the CPU automatically performs the equivalent of executing an Interrupt-disable instruction. It is often the case that one bit in the PS register indicates whether interrupts are enabled or disabled. The CPU sets this bit to disable interrupts. Then it starts execution of the interrupt-service routine. Similarly, the CPU may automatically enable interrupts when a Return-from-interrupt instruction is executed. This is one of the results of the restoration of the contents of the PS register from the stack.

The third approach that can be used is to arrange the interrupt-handling circuit in the CPU so that it responds only to the leading edge of the interrupt-request signal. Obviously, only one such transition will be seen by the CPU for every request generated by the device.

A proper understanding of the sequence of events involved in servicing interrupts is essential, both for the hardware designer and for the programmer. Before proceeding to study more complex aspects of interrupts, let us summarize the sequence of events involved in handling an interrupt request from a single device:

1. The device raises an interrupt request.
2. The CPU interrupts the program being executed at the time.
3. Interrupts are disabled.
4. The device is informed that its request has been recognized, and in response, it deactivates the interrupt-request signal.
5. The action requested by the interrupt is performed.
6. Interrupts are enabled.
7. Execution of the interrupted program is resumed.

Let us now consider the situation where a number of devices capable of initiating interrupts are connected to the CPU. Since these devices are operationally independent, there is no definite order in which they will generate interrupts. For example, device X may request an interrupt while an interrupt caused by device Y is being serviced, or all devices may request interrupts at exactly the same time. This gives rise to a number of questions:

1. How can the CPU recognize the device requesting an interrupt?
2. Since different devices are likely to require different interrupt-service routines, how can the CPU obtain the starting address of the appropriate routine in each case?
3. Should any device be allowed to interrupt the CPU while another interrupt is being serviced?
4. How can the situation be handled when two or more interrupt requests occur simultaneously?

The means by which the above problems are resolved vary considerably from one machine to another. The approach taken in any machine is an important consideration in determining its suitability for a given application. We shall discuss some of the more commonly used techniques in the remainder of this section.

6.4.2 Device Identification

In the simple I/O bus configuration of Figure 6.1, external devices are identified by their addresses. The same address lines can be used to identify interrupting devices. This can be accomplished through a simple polling arrangement. An external device requests an interrupt by activating an interrupt-request line which is common to all devices. The interrupt-service routine starts by polling all devices in order, that is, by testing the Ready bit of each device, to establish the identity of the device that initiated the interrupt. The device interface is usually arranged such that the interrupt-request signal is removed as soon as the device is addressed by the CPU.

A single interrupt-request line may be used to serve several devices by means of the open-collector organization depicted in Figure 6.6. Each of n devices are attached to a common line via an open-collector gate. As was mentioned in Chapter 4, an open-collector gate is equivalent to a switch to ground, which is closed when the gate is activated. Thus, if all interrupt-request signals $INTR_1$ to $INTR_n$ are inactive, that is, are in the 0 state, the interrupt-request line will be maintained in the 1 state by resistor R. When a

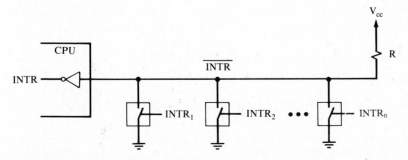

Figure 6.6 An equivalent circuit for an open=collector bus used to implement a common interrupt=request line.

device requests an interrupt, the corresponding switch is closed, which forces the line to the 0 state. The signal on the interrupt-request line is inverted in the CPU, so that the interrupt-request INTR is

$$\text{INTR} = \text{INTR}_1 + \cdots + \text{INTR}_n$$

It is customary to use the complemented form $\overline{\text{INTR}}$ to name the interrupt-request signal on the common line, since this signal is low when active.

The polling scheme described above is very simple. Its main disadvantage, however, is the time spent to interrogate the status bits of all the devices that may not be requesting any service. An alternative approach is to provide hardware means which enable the interrupting device to send an identifying code to the CPU. This is usually referred to as *vectored interrupts*.

6.4.3 Vectored Interrupts

In order to reduce the overhead involved in the polling process, a device requesting an interrupt may identify itself directly to the CPU. Then, the CPU can immediately start executing the required interrupt-service routine. The term *vectored interrupts* refers to all interrupt-handling schemes based on this approach.

In a computer which has multiple interrupt-request lines, vectored interrupts may be implemented by simply associating a unique starting address with each line. Alternatively, a device requesting an interrupt may identify itself by sending a special code to the CPU over the I/O bus. This is a more powerful technique, since it enables identification of individual devices that may share a single interrupt-request line. The code supplied by the device may then be chosen to represent the starting address of the interrupt-service routine for that device. In some cases, especially in smaller machines, only a few bits of the address are supplied, with the remainder of the address being fixed. This minimizes the number of bits that need to be transmitted by the I/O device, thus simplifying the design of its interface. Note, however, that it limits the number of devices that can be automatically identified by the CPU. For example, if 4 bits are supplied by the device, only 16 distinct codes, representing 16 different devices, can be recognized by the CPU. It is possible to assign each code to a group of devices. When a given code is received, the CPU can identify the device causing the interrupt by polling the members of the group represented by that code.

The above arrangement implies that the interrupt-service routine for a given device must always start at the same location. The programmer may gain some flexibility by storing in this location an instruction which causes a jump or a branch to the appropriate routine. In some machines, this is done automatically by the interrupt-handling mechanism. The CPU uses the code received from the interrupting device as an indirect specification of the starting address of the interrupt-service routine. That is, this code is interpreted as an address of a memory location which contains the required starting address. The contents of this location, which comprise a new value for the PC, are referred to as the *interrupt vector*. In many machines, the interrupt vector also includes a new value for the processor status register. For example, in the case of the PDP-11 computer, the CPU receives a 16-bit address from the device requesting an interrupt at the time the request is accepted. This is the address of a two-word interrupt vector associated with the device. After saving the current contents of the PC and the PS on the processor stack, the CPU loads the first word of this vector into the PC and the second word into the PS. The ability to change the contents of the PS at the time the interrupt-service routine is entered provides the programmer with considerable flexibility in changing the priority of the CPU or disabling further interrupts, as will be explained later. In general, this is a useful facility, found in many computers.

Some modifications to the hardware are required to support the vectored-interrupt feature. The key modification follows from the realization that the CPU may not respond immediately when it receives an interrupt request. The minimum delay in the CPU response is dictated by the requirement to complete execution of the current instruction. Further delays may occur because of an earlier execution of an Interrupt-disable instruction or because the interrupt in question has lower priority than that of the program currently being executed. Since the CPU may require the use of the I/O bus during this delay, the interrupting device should not be allowed to put data on the I/O bus until the CPU is ready to receive it. The necessary coordination can be achieved through the use of another control signal that may be termed *interrupt acknowledge* (INTA). As soon as the CPU is ready to service the interrupt, it sets the INTA line to on. This, in turn, causes the device interface to place the interrupt-vector address on the data lines, and to turn off the INTR signal. The CPU uses the addresses supplied by the device interface to determine the new values of the PC and the PS and, hence, to start executing the appropriate interrupt-service routine.

6.4.4 Interrupt Nesting

It was suggested in Section 6.4.1 that interrupts should be disabled during the execution of an interrupt-service routine. This ensures that an interrupt request from one device will not cause more than one interruption. The same arrangement is often used when several devices are involved, in which case execution of a given interrupt-service routine, once started, will always continue to completion before a second interrupt request is accepted by the CPU. Interrupt-service routines are typically short, and a possible delay in responding to the second request is acceptable for most simple devices.

For some devices, a long delay in responding to an interrupt request may lead to erroneous operation. Consider, for example, a computer which keeps track of the time of day. This can be implemented by using an I/O device, usually called a real-time clock, which sends interrupt requests to the CPU at regular intervals. For each of these requests, the CPU executes a short interrupt-service routine which increments a set of counters in the memory to obtain time in seconds, minutes, etc. Proper operation of this subsystem requires that the delay in responding to an interrupt request from the real-time clock be small in comparison with the interval between two successive requests. In order to ensure that this requirement is satisfied in the presence of other interrupting devices, it may be necessary that an interrupt request from the real-time clock be accepted by the CPU during the execution of an interrupt-service routine for another device.

The example of the real-time clock suggests that I/O devices should be organized in a hierarchical priority structure. An interrupt request from a high-priority device should be accepted even while the CPU is servicing another request from a lower-priority device.

A multiple-level priority organization means that during execution of an interrupt-service routine, interrupt requests will be accepted from some devices but not from others, depending upon the device priority. In order to facilitate implementation of this scheme, it is useful to assign a priority level to the CPU which can be changed under program control. The priority level of the CPU is in fact the priority of the program that is currently being executed. The CPU will accept interrupts only from devices having priorities higher than itself. At the time the execution of an interrupt-service routine for some device is started, the priority of the CPU should be set to correspond to that of the device. This, in effect, disables interrupts from devices at the same level of priority or lower. However, interrupt requests from higher-priority devices will continue to be accepted. The CPU priority is usually incorporated as a part of the processor status word, thus making it program controlled.

From the hardware point of view, a multiple-priority scheme can be implemented easily by using separate interrupt-request and interrupt-acknowledge lines for each device. Such an arrangement is shown in Figure 6.7. Each of the interrupt-request lines is assigned a different priority level. Interrupt requests received over these lines are arbitrated by a priority circuit in the CPU. A request is accepted only if it has a higher priority level than that currently assigned to the CPU.

6.4.5 Simultaneous Requests

Let us now consider the problem of simultaneous arrivals of interrupt requests from two or more devices. The CPU should have some means of arbitration by which only one request is serviced and the others are either delayed or ignored. In the presence of a priority scheme such as that of Figure 6.7 the solution to this problem is straightforward. The CPU simply accepts the request having the highest priority. However when several devices share the use of one interrupt-request line, some other mechanism has to be implemented to assign relative priority to these devices.

In the polling scheme, priority is automatically implemented by the order in which devices are polled. Therefore, no special treatment is required to accommodate situations where simultaneous interrupt requests may occur.

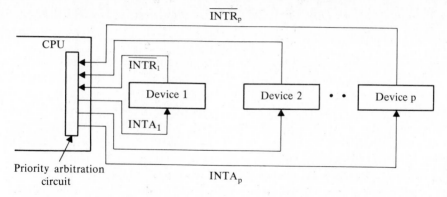

Figure 6.7 Implementation of interrupt priority using individual interrupt=request and acknowledge lines.

In the case of vectored interrupts, the priority of any device is usually determined by the way in which it is connected to the CPU. The most common method is the *daisy-chain* arrangement shown in Figure 6.8*a*. The interrupt-request line ($\overline{\text{INTR}}$) is common to all devices. However, the interrupt-acknowledge line (INTA) is connected in a daisy-chain fashion as shown. When one or more devices issue an interrupt request, the $\overline{\text{INTR}}$ line is activated. The CPU responds, after some delay, by setting the INTA line to 1. This signal is received by device 1. Device 1 passes the signal on to the next device only if it does not require any service. If device 1 has a pending request for interrupt, it blocks the acknowledgment signal INTA and proceeds to put its interrupt vector

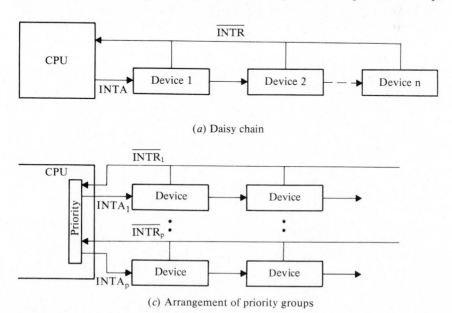

(*a*) Daisy chain

(*c*) Arrangement of priority groups

Figure 6.8 Interrupt priority schemes.

on the data lines. Therefore, the daisy-chain arrangement results in the device that is electrically closest to the CPU having the highest priority. The second device along the chain has second highest priority, and so on.

The scheme of Figure 6.8*a* has the advantage that it requires considerably fewer wires than the individual connections of Figure 6.7. The main advantage of the latter scheme is that it makes it possible for the CPU to accept interrupt requests from some devices, but not from others, depending upon their priorities. The two schemes may be combined to produce the more general structure of Figure 6.8*b*. This organization is used in many computer systems, including the PDP-11, which will be described in Section 6.5.4.

We should note that the general organization of Figure 6.8*b* makes it possible for a device to be connected to several priority levels. Thus, at any given time, it can request an interrupt at the priority level consistent with the urgency of the function being performed. This approach offers additional flexibility. However, it requires complex control circuitry in the device interface.

6.4.6 Selective Interrupt Masking

In most machines, a selective interrupt enable-disable facility that is independent of the device priority is provided. This is accomplished through the use of an "interrupt-enable" flip-flop associated with each device or group of devices. When set to 1 by the CPU, this flip-flop allows an interrupt request issued by the corresponding device to reach the CPU. Otherwise the interrupt is masked and does not reach the CPU until the flip-flop is set to 1. Physically, the interrupt-enable flip-flop may be incorporated in the device interface, usually as one of the bits in the status register. In machines using the organization of Figure 6.8*b*, an interrupt-enable flip-flop may also be provided for each $\overline{\text{INTR}}$ line. The collection of these flip-flops forms an *interrupt mask*. It precedes the priority arbitration circuit, as shown in Figure 6.9. In this case, the interrupt mask constitutes an internal CPU register. Its contents can be easily changed at any time under program control.

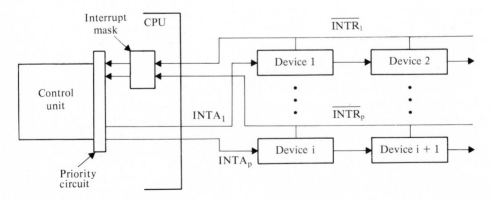

Figure 6.9 Interrupt masking.

6.4.7 The PDP-11 Interrupt Structure

We have discussed the organizational aspects of interrupts in considerable detail. In order to illustrate the use of interrupts and some of the implementation details, we will describe the interrupt-handling mechanism of the PDP-11 computers. Software considerations will be discussed in the following section.

The PDP-11 uses vectored interrupts, with I/O devices organized in eight priority groups. Only the top four of these are in actual use in most existing systems. Within each group, daisy-chain priority may be used, as in Figure 6.8b. A two-word interrupt vector is associated with each device, as was described in Section 6.4.3. The CPU priority is determined by 3 bits in the processor status register PS (see Section 3.1.1). When an I/O device with a priority higher than that of the CPU generates an interrupt request, the following sequence of actions takes place:

1. The CPU completes execution of the current instruction.
2. The CPU sends an interrupt-acknowledge signal to the highest priority device requesting an interrupt.
3. The device responds by turning off its interrupt request and sending the address of its interrupt vector to the CPU.
4. The CPU pushes the current contents of the PS and the PC registers on the processor stack.
5. The CPU reads the first word of the interrupt vector at the address obtained from the device and loads it into the PC. It loads the second word of the interrupt vector into the PS.
6. The CPU resumes instruction execution.

In step 6 the CPU starts executing the interrupt-service routine at the location given in the first word of the interrupt vector. The second word of the interrupt vector includes the 3 bits which determine the new priority of the CPU. The interrupt-service routine ends with a Return-from-interrupt (RTI) instruction. This causes the return address and the old contents of the PS, which were stored in step 4, to be popped off the stack and loaded into the PC and the PS registers, respectively. The restoration of these registers sets the CPU priority back to its value prior to interruption and causes execution of the interrupted program to be resumed.

6.4.8 An Example of an Interrupt Program

Let us now consider a simple example of an interrupt-service routine. Assume that at some point in a program MAIN it is necessary to read an input line from a keyboard terminal. The input characters are to be stored in a buffer area in the main memory, starting at location LOC.

We have already encountered the use of status registers in device interfaces in PDP-11 computers (see Section 2.6). In particular, the Ready bit b_7 of the keyboard status register KBSTATUS, is used to indicate that a character is available in the data buffer TTYIN. It is set when a key is pressed, and cleared when the data in TTYIN is read. Another bit, usually b_6, is used for enabling and disabling interrupts. We will refer to this as the Interrupt-enable bit. While it is set, an interrupt request is generated by the interface whenever the Ready bit is set, that is, whenever a key is pressed causing an input character to be deposited in the TTYIN register. The format of the KBSTATUS register is shown in Figure 6.10.

Assume that the interrupt vector for the keyboard is in main memory locations 60 and 62. Thus, it will be necessary to load these locations with the starting address of the interrupt-service routine and the desired program status word, respectively. This must be done by program MAIN before enabling interrupts. Figure 6.11 gives a possible program. The interrupt-service routine starts at the address READ. Program MAIN places this value in location 60 and the value 200 in location 62. Following an interrupt, this value will be loaded into the PS, and as a result, the CPU priority level will be set to 4. The choice of this priority level is based on the assumption that the keyboard interface operates at priority level 4. By raising the CPU priority to 4, further interrupts from the keyboard are ignored during the execution of the interrupt-service routine.

In addition to setting the interrupt vector, program MAIN loads the value LOC into location PNTR in the main memory. The interrupt-service routine uses this location as a pointer for storing input characters in the memory buffer. Just before enabling interrupts from the keyboard, the PS is cleared, thus setting the CPU priority to 0. This ensures that keyboard interrupts, which arrive at priority level 4, will be accepted. Finally, keyboard interrupts are enabled by setting b_6 of KBSTATUS to 1.

Program MAIN may now proceed to perform other tasks. However, it should not change the contents of PNTR or use the contents of the main memory data buffer at LOC until a complete input line has been read. Whenever a key is pressed on the keyboard, program MAIN will be interrupted and the service routine READ will be executed. The input character will be

Bit position	Function
7	Set when data is available in TTYIN. Cleared by a program reference to TTYIN
6	Enables interrupts when set. Interrupt is raised when $b_6 = b_7 = 1$.

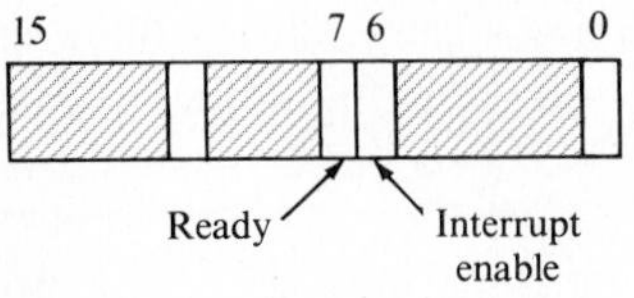

Figure 6.10 Status bits in the keyboard status register KBSTATUS.

```
        LOC60  = 60                          Interrupt Vector address
        LOC62  = 62
        PR4    = 200                         Value of PS to set
                                               priority to 4
        INTEN  = 100                         Keyboard interrupt enable
        INTDIS = 0                             and disable masks
        CR     = 15                          ASCII code for carriage
                                               return
MAIN:   MOV    #READ,@#LOC60                 Set interrupt vector
        MOV    #PR4,@#LOC62
        MOV    #LOC,PNTR                     Initialize buffer pointer
        CLR    PS                            Set CPU priority to 0
        MOV    #INTEN,@#KBSTATUS             Enable keyboard interrupts
          .
          .
          .

        main program
          .
          .
          .

READ:   MOVB   @#TTYIN,@PNTR                 Store input character
        CMPB   #CR,@PNTR                     Check if carriage return
        BNE    DONE
        MOV    #INTDIS,@#KBSTATUS            Disable keyboard interrupts
        JSR    LINE                          Process input line
DONE:   INC    PNTR
        RTI
PNTR:   .WORD 0
```

Figure 6.11 Example of an interrupt-service routine.

transferred to the memory buffer. Unless the character is Carriage Return (CR), a Return-from-interrupt instruction is executed. This causes the PC and the PS to be restored from the stack. When a CR character is encountered, keyboard interrupts are disabled and routine LINE is called to process the input line in the memory data buffer. Of course, this routine may enable interrupts once more in order to cause another line of input to be received.

6.4.9 High-Level Language View of Interrupts

The above discussion has presented details of interrupt mechanisms in modern computers. We have concentrated on describing interrupt handling at the machine level, using assembly language programs as examples.

It is illustrative at this point to consider how interrupts are handled in an environment where user programs are written in a high-level language. The way in which such programs are executed will be discussed in Chapter 10. For purposes of the present discussion, it is sufficient to observe that in such an environment all activities within a computer are coordinated by a control program known as the "operating system." Among other things, the operating system incorporates interrupt-service routines for all devices connected to the computer.

When a high-level language program requests an I/O operation, the operating system performs all the necessary steps. Namely, it looks after setting up interrupt vectors, enabling and disabling interrupts, etc. When the requested operation has been completed, the operating system transfers control back to the user's program. Thus, a high-level language user need not be as familiar with details of interrupt handling as a user writing programs in assembly language. However, we should note that a good understanding of these details is conducive to writing programs that will be executed efficiently. This is particularly important when dealing with real-time applications.

6.5 I/O INTERFACES

The function of an I/O interface is to coordinate the transfer of data between the CPU and an external device. From the discussions in earlier sections in this chapter, such an interface should perform the following functions:

1. Store the device status for presentation to the computer when required. A "device status register" is used for this purpose.
2. Provide storage space for at least one data character, or perhaps one word, to be used when transferring data to or from the computer. Let this be called the "data buffer register."
3. Recognize the device address when this address appears on the I/O address lines.
4. Provide appropriate timing and gating signals to accomplish the transfer of data or status information as required.

To illustrate the means by which these functions are implemented, we shall discuss a specific interface example. Although details may differ from one computer to another, the basic ideas are applicable to most interface designs. We shall start by studying the *protocols* used for data transfer on a bus.

6.5.1 Control of Data Transfer

A typical I/O bus consists of three sets of lines: data lines, address lines, and control lines. A few control lines are required to coordinate data transfers over the bus, and hence they are used by all devices connected to the bus. Other control lines are needed for handling requests for interrupts and direct memory access (DMA) operations. These lines are used only by devices that have such capabilities. The remaining control lines may carry information related to detection of power failures, initialization of the system, etc. In what follows, we will discuss the operation of the bus in the context of a computer with a single-bus organization. That is, we will assume that the CPU, the main memory, and all peripherals exchange data via a single common bus (see Figure 1.11).

Let us first consider the lines that are required for transferring data between the CPU and one of the I/O devices. The control signals involved in such transfers should be capable of specifying two types of information, namely, the nature of the transfer and its timing. The first of these, which we will refer to as the mode of the transfer, involves the specification of whether a Read or a Write operation is to be performed. When both word and byte transfers are possible, the required size of data should also be indicated. Hence two lines are needed for the mode information. A Read/$\overline{\text{Write}}$ line specifies Read when set to 1 and Write when set to 0. Similarly, a Word/$\overline{\text{Byte}}$ line specifies a word transfer when set to 1 and a single-byte transfer when set to 0.

The second component of the bus control signals carries the timing information. This relates to the specification of the instants at which the CPU and the I/O devices may place data on the bus or receive data from the bus. A variety of schemes have been devised for the timing of data transfers over a bus. As mentioned in Chapter 4, they may be broadly classified as either synchronous or asynchronous schemes. In the case of a synchronous bus, all devices derive the timing information from a common clock line. Equally spaced pulses on this line define equal time intervals. Each of these intervals constitutes a "bus cycle," during which one data transfer may take place. Such a scheme is illustrated in Figure 6.12.

Let us consider the sequence of events during an input operation. At time t_0, the CPU places the device address on the address lines and sets the mode control lines to indicate an input operation. This information travels over the bus at a speed determined by its physical and electrical characteristics. The clock pulse

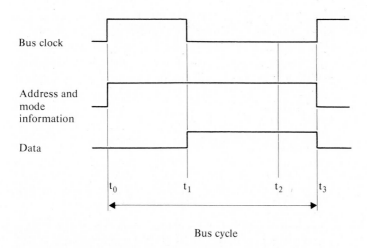

Bus cycle

Figure 6.12 Timing of an input transfer on a synchronous bus.

width $t_1 - t_0$ should be chosen such that it is greater than the maximum propagation delay between the CPU and any of the devices connected to the bus. It should also be wide enough to allow all devices to decode the address and control signals so that the addressed device can be ready to respond at time t_1. The addressed device, recognizing that an input operation is requested, places its input data on the data lines at time t_1. After some further delay, $t_2 - t_1$, the CPU strobes the data lines and loads the data into its input buffer (MDR in Figure 4.1). As before, this delay should be greater than the maximum bus propagation time plus the setup time for the input buffer of the CPU. After t_2, all the bus lines are cleared in preparation for a new bus cycle.

The procedure for an output operation is similar to the above sequence. The CPU places the output data on the data lines at the same time it transmits the address and mode information. At time t_1, the addressed device strobes the data into its data buffer.

The synchronous bus scheme described above is very simple, and it results in simple designs for the device interface. As can be easily appreciated, the clock speed has to be chosen such that it accommodates the longest delays on the bus and the slowest interface. Furthermore, the CPU has no way of determining whether the addressed device has actually responded. It simply assumes that at t_2 the output data has been received or that the input data is available on the data lines. If as a result of a malfunction the device does not respond, the error will not be detected.

An alternative scheme for controlling data transfers on the bus is based on the use of a "handshake" between the CPU and the device being addressed. The common clock is eliminated, and hence the resulting bus operation is asynchronous. The clock line is replaced by two timing control lines, which we will refer to as "Ready" and "Accept." In principle, a data transfer controlled by a handshake protocol proceeds as follows. The CPU places the address and mode information on the bus. Then, it indicates to all devices that it has done so by sending a pulse on the Ready line. When the addressed device receives the Ready signal, it performs the required operation, then transmits a pulse on the Accept line. The CPU waits for the Accept signal before it clears the bus and before it strobes the data into its input buffer in the case of an input operation.

An example of the timing of a data transfer using the handshake scheme described above is given in Figure 6.13. The delays involved in this input operation are similar to those in the synchronous transfer, with a few exceptions. The sequence of events in Figure 6.13 is described below.

t_0: The CPU places the address and mode information on the bus.

t_1: The CPU sets the Ready line to 1 to inform the I/O devices that the address and mode information is ready. The delay $t_1 - t_0$ is intended to allow for any "skew" that may occur on the bus. Skew refers to the situation where two signals transmitted from one source at the same time arrive at the destination at different times. It arises from differences in the propagation speed on different lines of the bus. Thus, to guarantee that the Ready signal will not

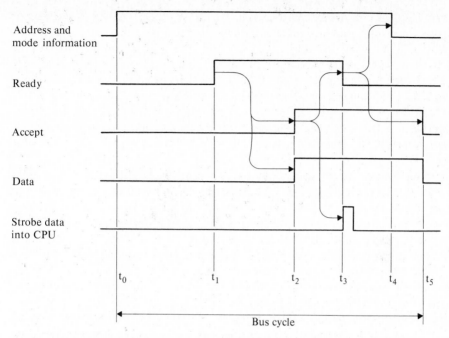

Figure 6.13 Handshake control of data transfer during an input operation.

arrive at any device ahead of the address and mode information, the delay $t_1 - t_0$ should be larger than the maximum possible bus skew. (We should note that in the synchronous case bus skew is accounted for as a part of the maximum propagation delay.) When the address information arrives at any device, it is decoded by the interface circuitry. The Ready signal is used by the addressed device to gate its input data on the bus. Therefore, sufficient time should be allowed for the interface circuitry to decode the address before the Ready signal is received. We will assume that this delay is also included in the period $t_1 - t_0$.

t_2: The interface of the addressed device receives the Ready signal, and having already decoded the address and mode information, it recognizes that it should perform an input operation. Hence it gates the data from its internal buffer to the data lines. At the same time it sets the Accept signal to 1. If extra delays are introduced by the interface circuitry before placing the data on the bus, it must delay the Accept signal accordingly. The period $t_2 - t_1$ is dependent upon the distance between the CPU and the device interface. It is also a function of the delays introduced by the interface circuitry. It is this variability that gives the bus its asynchronous nature.

t_3: The Accept signal arrives at the CPU, indicating that the input data is available. However, since it was assumed that the device interface transmits the Accept signal at the same time it places the data on the bus, the CPU should allow for bus skew. After a delay equivalent to the maximum bus skew, the CPU strobes the data into its input buffer. At the same time it drops the Ready signal, indicating that it has received the data.

t_4: The CPU removes the address and mode information from the bus. The delay between t_3 and t_4 is again intended to allow for bus skew. Erroneous addressing may take place if the address, as seen by some device on the bus, starts to change while the Ready signal is still equal to 1.

t_5: When the 1 to 0 transition of the Ready signal is received by the device interface, it removes the data and the Accept signal from the bus. This completes the input transfer.

The timing for an output operation is essentially the same as for an input operation. It is illustrated in Figure 6.14. In this case, the CPU places the output data on the data lines at the same time it transmits the address and mode information. The addressed device strobes the data into its output buffer when it receives the Ready signal. It indicates that it has done so by setting the Accept signal to 1. The remainder of the cycle is identical to the input operation.

In the timing diagrams of Figures 6.13 and 6.14 it is assumed that the compensation for bus-related delays, namely, bus skew and address decoding, is performed by the CPU. This simplifies the I/O interface at the device end, since it can use the Ready signal directly to gate other signals to or from the bus.

The asynchronous scheme described above is often used in practice. An

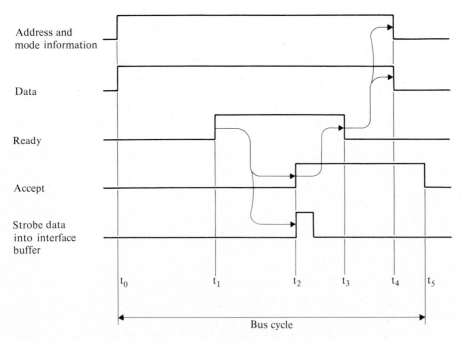

Figure 6.14 Handshake control of data transfer during an output operation.

almost identical set of signals can be found on the Unibus of the PDP-11 computer. Many alternatives that represent a compromise between the fully synchronous case of Figure 6.12 and the fully asynchronous case of Figures 6.13 and 6.14 are also possible. For example, a fixed pulse width may be used for the Ready and Accept signals. The choice of a given design involves a trade-off between many factors. Some of the important considerations are:

- Simplicity of the device interface
- Ability to accommodate device interfaces that introduce differing amounts of delay
- Total time required for a bus transfer
- Ability to detect errors resulting from addressing a nonexistent device or from an interface malfunction

The fully asynchronous scheme provides the highest degree of flexibility and reliability at the expense of complexity of the interface. The error-detection capability is provided by the interlocking of the Ready and Accept signals. If the Accept signal is not received within a fixed time-out period after setting Ready to 1, the CPU assumes that an error has occurred. This may be used to cause an interrupt and hence to execute a routine that alerts the operator to the malfunction, or to take some other appropriate action.

6.5.2 Interface Design Example

The I/O interface consists of the circuitry required to transfer data between the I/O bus of a computer and an I/O device. Therefore, on one side of the interface we have the bus signals: address, data, and control. On the other side we have a data path, with its associated controls, that enables transfer of data between the interface and the I/O device. This side is obviously device-dependent. However, it may be broadly classified as either a parallel or a serial interface. A parallel interface transfers data in the form of one or more bytes in parallel to or from the device. On the other hand, a serial interface transmits and receives data one bit at a time; communication with the I/O bus remains the same as in the case of a parallel interface. The conversion from the parallel to the serial format, and vice versa, takes place inside the interface.

Before discussing a specific example, let us recall the functions of an I/O interface. According to the discussion in the previous section, an I/O interface performs the following functions:

1. Provides a storage buffer for one word of data (or 1 byte in the case of byte-oriented devices).
2. Contains status flags that can be accessed by the computer to determine whether the buffer is full (for input) or empty (for output).
3. Contains address decoding circuitry to determine when it is being addressed by the computer.

4. Generates the appropriate timing signals as required by the bus control scheme used.

5. Performs any format conversion that may be necessary to transfer data between the I/O bus and the I/O device (for example, parallel-serial).

Parallel interface We will present first an example for a parallel interface. A 16-bit byte-addressable computer is assumed, where program-controlled I/O takes place in essentially the same manner as in the case of the PDP-11. The I/O bus is the fully asynchronous type, and timing of bus transfers is the same as in Figures 6.13 and 6.14. We will further assume that the interface contains separate data buffers (DIN and DOUT) for input and output, and that there is one status register associated with each buffer (SIN and SOUT). The two buffers and the two status registers are assigned four adjacent word addresses. These addresses differ only in the least significant 3 bits. Since only one status flag is required for each data buffer, only 1 bit of SIN and SOUT need to be implemented. This is chosen to be bit 7 for consistency with the example programs in Chapter 2 and Figure 6.3. A logic diagram for the required interface is shown in Figure 6.15.

The operation of the interface can be described as follows. For an input operation, one word (or 1 byte) of data is transferred from the input device to register DIN, and flip-flop SIN is set to 1. The data and control lines required for this transfer are not shown in the figure, as this circuitry is internal to the device and not a part of the interface. The interface circuitry shown is responsible for transferring the contents of either SIN or DIN to the CPU whenever a Read request is received specifying these locations. The high-order 13 bits of the address lines, A_3 to A_{15}, are decoded by the address decoder block. Whenever these lines carry the address assigned to this interface, point P goes to the logic 1 state. Then, as soon as the Ready signal is received, the Enable line is set to 1. At the same time, bits A_0 to A_2 together with the mode control lines Read/$\overline{\text{Write}}$ and Word/$\overline{\text{Byte}}$ select one of the six gates E_1 to E_6. This results in enabling the output gates corresponding to the addressed byte or word, hence placing its contents on the data lines. While the Enable line is in the 1 state, the output signal Accept is also set to 1. This constitutes the response of the interface to the Read request issued by the CPU. As soon as the Ready signal drops to 0, the Accept signal is removed, and all the bus driver gates are disabled. The reader should verify that this sequence will result in bus signals that are consistent with the timing diagram of Figure 6.13. Note that when the DIN buffer is addressed, the input status flag SIN is reset to 0. This is essential in order to guarantee that each item of input data is read by the computer only once.

An output operation proceeds in essentially the same way as above. When the Enable signal is set to 1, while DOUT is selected, the clock input to the output buffer is set. This results in loading the buffer, which is assumed to be positive edge-triggered, with the data on the data lines. At the same time SOUT is reset to 0. When the data in DOUT is transferred to the output device, SOUT is set to 1 to indicate that the interface is ready to accept a new output transfer.

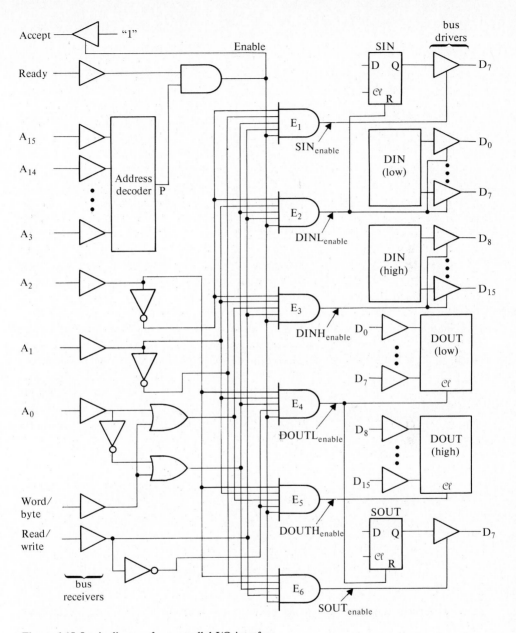

Figure 6.15 Logic diagram for a parallel I/O interface.

Serial interface A serial interface contains the same addressing and control circuitry as the parallel interface of Figure 6.15. In addition, some controls are needed to transfer data serially between registers DIN or DOUT and the I/O device. For example, the data and status registers in Figure 6.15 may be replaced

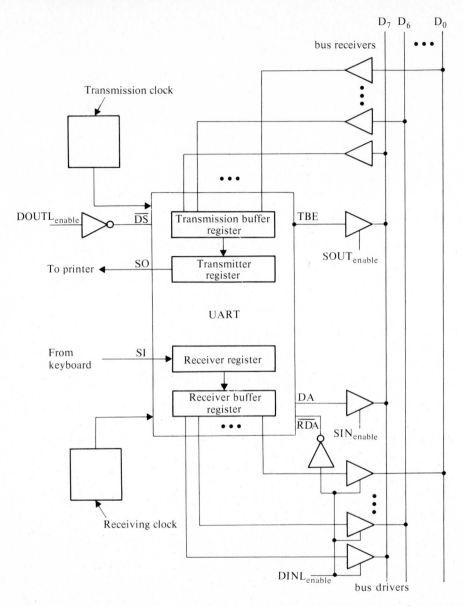

Figure 6.16 Serial to parallel conversion using a universal asynchronous receiver transmitter (UART).

by the circuit given in Figure 6.16. This circuit enables transmission in the asynchronous start-stop format, which is commonly used with low-speed serial devices such as CRT terminals. A discussion of this transmission format will be given in Chapter 9.

The example of Figure 6.16 is based on the use of a UART (universal asynchronous receiver transmitter) chip. This is an integrated circuit chip that contains all the logic circuitry for the required parallel-serial conversion. The two registers DIN and DOUT and the status flags SIN and SOUT are included on the chip. Thus they can be used to replace the corresponding registers in Figure 6.15. However, all address decoding and control circuitry in the parallel interface remain unchanged. Note that in this case, only 1 byte is transferred at a time. Therefore, only the low-order bytes of DIN and DOUT are implemented.

In order to illustrate the operation of the UART let us consider a UART connected to a CRT terminal. Input and output transfers can be described briefly as follows:

Input. When a character is depressed on the keyboard, the corresponding 8-bit code is transmitted serially to the serial input (SI) pin of the UART and shifted into the receiver register. At the end of transmission, the character is transferred to the receiver buffer register, and the output DA (data available) is set to 1. Hence, DA can be used as the status flag SIN. It is, therefore, gated to line D_7 of the data bus under control of the SIN_{enable} signal. Similarly, the contents of the receiver buffer register are gated to the low-order byte of the data bus under control of $DINL_{enable}$. The $DINL_{enable}$ signal is also inverted and connected to the $\overline{RDA}$ (reset data available) pin of the UART. When $\overline{RDA}$ is set to 0, it resets the DA output to 0. Thus, when a character is transferred from the receiver buffer register to the bus, the keyboard Ready flag is simultaneously reset to 0, to be set to 1 again when a new character is entered at the keyboard.

Output. Serial transmission of one character to the CRT is accomplished by serially shifting data out of the transmitter register in the UART to the SO (serial output) pin. The transmission buffer register can hold a second character waiting for transmission. Output data is loaded into the transmission buffer register when a 0 is applied to the $\overline{DS}$ (data strobe) pin. When transmission of the character in the transmitter register is completed, the contents of the transmission buffer register are transferred to it and their transmission is started immediately. At the same time, the output TBE (transmitter buffer empty) is set to 1. Hence, the transmission buffer register can be used as the output data buffer DOUT; and TBE constitutes the output status flag SOUT, as shown.

The above interface example is suitable, with minor modifications, for a variety of devices that use the asynchronous serial-transmission format. In particular, it can be used for connection of a *modem* (MODulator dEModulator) for transmission of data over telephone lines. Data transmission over telephone lines will be treated in more detail in Chapter 12.

6.5.3 Bus Scheduling

The discussion in the previous two subsections concentrated on the data transfer operations between the CPU and the I/O devices. The transfers were initiated by the CPU, which was implicitly assumed to be the only device with the capability to drive the address and the mode lines. However, an I/O bus is usually required to carry other types of data transfer. For example, in computers that have a vectored-interrupt capability, the interrupting device transfers an identifying code to the CPU, as was discussed in Section 6.4.3. The interrupt sequence that includes this transfer is initiated by the I/O device. Also, a device with DMA capability transfers data directly to and from the main memory without involvement of the CPU.

Transfers such as those taking place during interrupts and DMA operations may use the same data paths and control lines as those used by the CPU. Therefore, some means have to be introduced to coordinate the use of these lines to prevent two devices from initiating two transfers at the same time. A bus controller, which may be part of the CPU, is usually used to perform the required scheduling function. During the discussion of interrupts, it was pointed out that simultaneous requests can be handled by means of a variety of priority structures. This requires the use of control lines such as interrupt-request and interrupt-acknowledge. An almost identical approach can be used to schedule the use of the bus. The control signals required for this purpose may be referred to as Bus Request and Bus Grant. Priorities for use of the bus may be established in the same way as for acknowledging interrupts.

When a Bus Grant signal is received from the bus controller, the device gains the right to initiate one or more bus transfers. Now, it can use the address, control, and data lines to transfer data to or from the main memory or any other device. While one device is performing data transfers, other devices may request the use of the bus. One of them is chosen by the bus controller as next in line and is so informed via a Bus Grant signal. When the current device completes its transfers, the next-in-line device gains control, and so on. A Bus Busy signal may be set to 1 by any user of the bus to prevent the next-in-line device from starting transmission prematurely.

The above discussion is only intended to point out some of the problems in the design of a bus. Further details will not be given, since the principles involved are essentially the same as in the handling of interrupt requests discussed earlier in this chapter.

6.5.4 Bus Example: The Unibus

Having discussed the main features encountered in the design of a computer bus, we will now present the complete set of bus signals in a typical machine. The example is intended to give the reader an appreciation of the range of functions that a computer bus is expected to support. We will examine briefly the signals of the Unibus. This is the bus used in the PDP-11 family of computers. It is also used as an I/O bus for the VAX computers.

The Unibus consists of a total of 72 lines, which may be divided into four functional groups: data, address, control, and power supply, as indicated in Table 6.1. All data transfers are initiated by the device controlling the bus, which

Table 6.1 Unibus signals

Function	Name	Description	Number
Data	D0 to D15	8- or 16-bit data	16
Address	A0 to A17	Byte address	18
Control			22
Data transfer	C0, C1	Mode	
	MSYN, SSYN	Handshake	
	PA, PB	Error indication	
Scheduling	BR4, ..., BR7, NPR	Bus request	
	BG4, ..., BG7, NPG	Bus grant	
	BBSY	Bus busy	
	SACK	Selection acknowledge	
Interrupt	INTR	Interrupt request	
Misc.	DC LO, AC LO	Power failure	
	INIT	Initialization	
Power supply	+5,GND		16
		Total	72

is known as the *bus master*. The other device involved in a transfer is known as the *slave*.

Most of the time the CPU acts as the bus master. However, during DMA operations, a DMA controller becomes a bus master. The transfer of bus mastership from one device to another is accomplished by means of a set of Bus Request and Bus Grant signals, using an organization similar to that of Figure 6.8b. Priority arbitration is performed by a bus controller circuit known as the *bus arbiter* or *bus arbitrator*.

The control signals involved in data transfer are the mode signals C0 and C1 and the timing signals MSYN and SSYN. C0 and C1 specify the type of a transfer, that is, read or write, and whether 1 or 2 bytes are involved. The timing signals MSYN (Master Synchronization) and SSYN (Slave Synchronization) perform the same functions as the Ready and Accept signals in Figure 6.13. Two lines, PA and PB are provided for error-handling purposes. If a slave device detects an error in the data, it can inform the bus master of this condition by transmitting a 2-bit code on these two lines.

Bus scheduling and interrupts are implemented in essentially the same manner as discussed earlier. The details are somewhat complicated. Since the PDP-11 uses vectored interrupts, a device interface requesting an interrupt must be able to transfer a vector address to the CPU. Hence, before requesting an interrupt, the device interface first acquires control of the bus, that is, it becomes the bus master. It does this by asserting one of the Bus Request signals BR4 to BR7. Then it waits for the corresponding Bus Grant (BGi). Priority arbitration during this step takes place according to the scheme depicted in Figure 6.8*b*, where BRi and BGi replace INTR$_i$ and INTA$_i$, respectively.

When the device requesting the bus receives the grant signal, it waits for Bus Busy (BBSY) to be deactivated by the current bus master, at which point the requesting device becomes the bus master. It may now request an interrupt by placing its vector address on the data lines, then asserting the interrupt-request (INTR) line. During this transfer, the INTR signal performs a dual role. It informs the CPU that a device is requesting an interrupt, and it replaces the handshake signal MSYN in providing timing information. The CPU responds, using SSYN in the normal manner.

The NPR (Nonprocessor Request) and NPG (Nonprocessor Grant) signals perform the same functions as BRi and BGi, respectively. The difference is that the NPR and NPG signals are intended for devices which require the use of the bus but do not intend to interrupt the CPU. NPR requests are given the highest priority since they are typically issued by the interface of a time-critical device, such as a disk drive, during a DMA transfer. Furthermore, a BGi signal is asserted by the CPU only at the end of an instruction, since this is the only time when the CPU can respond to an interrupt request. On the other hand, NPG may be issued at any time.

A Selection Acknowledge (SACK) signal plays a minor role in the process of transferring bus mastership from one device to another. When an interface receives a bus grant, either BGi or NPG, and while it is waiting for BBSY to become 0, it asserts SACK. By doing this, it acknowledges the fact that it is next in line for bus mastership. When the bus controller receives SACK, it deactivates the grant signal. This sequence of events is illustrated in Figure 6.17. Note that because of the existence of the BBSY and SACK signals, the entire sequence in the figure can take place while the current bus master is using the bus to transfer data. When a device becomes "next-in-line," it starts using the bus as soon as the current bus master is finished. It removes the SACK signal sometime before it

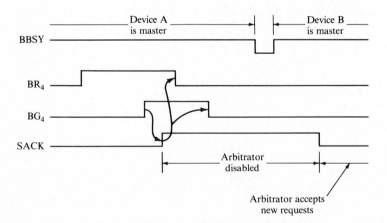

Figure 6.17 Sequence of events during transfer of bus mastership on Unibus.

relinquishes bus mastership. This allows the bus arbitrator to select another device as next-in-line. As a result, no time is wasted in transferring bus mastership from one device to another.

Consider next the power supply status signals DC LO and AC LO. The power supply of a computer accepts AC voltage from the power utility line and generates DC voltages according to the requirements of the computer circuitry. The signals DC LO and AC LO are asserted by the power supply whenever its DC output or the AC utility line voltage, respectively, drop below their specified values. The two signals enable an orderly power-down, even in cases of unexpected power interruption. This typically involves the saving of critical data in the main memory by transferring it to a nonvolatile device such as a disk.

When power is first applied, the DC output of the power supply rises slowly from 0. During this period both AC LO and DC LO are asserted. Since logic circuitry may produce erroneous outputs when the power supply voltage is below its rated value, all devices should ignore the bus while DC LO is equal to 1. When the DC voltage reaches its full value, DC LO becomes 0, and after some delay AC LO is also deactivated by the power supply. Changes in the state of AC LO cause a processor trap. A trap is equivalent to an interrupt, except that it is generated inside the CPU instead of being caused by an external device. The vector address associated with a trap is fixed in the CPU circuitry. The trap caused by changes in the state of AC LO is known as a power fail trap.

When AC power is interrupted, the AC LO line is asserted immediately by the power supply. However, DC power continues to be available for several tens of milliseconds, maintaining the DC LO line in the 0 state. The assertion of the AC LO line causes a power fail trap, which the programmer can use to force the execution of a short power-down routine. This routine may be used to save critical data by transferring it to the disk. The power supply asserts DC LO before the DC power supply voltage drops below its minimum acceptable value. All device interfaces must be designed so that no activity takes place while this line is asserted.

The INIT signal is used to reset all I/O devices, that is, to put them in a known initial state. It is asserted by the CPU whenever a RESET instruction is executed and as a part of the power-up sequence. It is prudent to use a RESET instruction at the beginning of a program. This guarantees a known starting point, independent of any actions that may have been taken by other programs which were executed before on the same computer.

The function of the power supply lines is obvious: they deliver power to the circuit boards connected to the bus. The large number of +5 and GND lines serves two purposes. It provides parallel paths for the power supply current, thus reducing the voltage drop over the bus. These lines also provide isolation between other bus lines to reduce the amount of electrical coupling between them. Hence, they reduce the electric noise resulting from "cross-talk" between signals on adjacent lines.

A modified Unibus design, referred to as the Q-bus, is used in several low-cost versions of the PDP-11 computers. The main distinguishing feature of the Q-bus is that it uses fewer lines. This has been accomplished by *time multiplexing* address and data information on the same lines. In a given bus cycle, the address is transmitted first; then, after a device has been selected, data transfer takes place. Appropriate control signals are used to coordinate this process. Time multiplexing of address and data information leads to a reduction in the total number of bus lines at the cost of a somewhat longer bus cycle.

6.6 STANDARD I/O INTERFACES

In the previous sections, it was pointed out that there are a number of alternatives for the design of the I/O bus of a computer. In fact, the possible variations are rather numerous. This leads to a difficult situation. I/O devices that are fitted with an interface suitable for one computer may not be usable with other computers. A different interface may have to be designed for every I/O device-computer combination. This is likely to result in a need for a large number of different interfaces. A better alternative is to attempt to standardize the interface functions.

It is difficult to define a uniform standard for the main I/O bus of a computer. The structure of this bus is closely related to the architecture of the computer. Therefore, it can be expected to change from one computer to another. It is equally difficult to develop a standard that covers all computer peripherals because of the extremely wide range of transfer speeds and other requirements. A workable alternative is to define standards for certain classes of interconnection which are suitable for both computers and peripherals.

Figure 6.18 illustrates the way in which some commonly used standards may be incorporated in a computer system. The CPU is connected through its processor bus to the memory and I/O interfaces. The properties of this bus are determined by the structure of the computer in question, and more specifically, by the CPU signal lines. In fact, different computer models made by the same manufacturer often have different bus structures. For example, the Unibus serves as the main bus in PDP-11 computers. However, VAX computers, also made by Digital Equipment Corporation, use a different bus, known as SBI (Synchronous Backplane Interconnect). Since the processor bus itself cannot be made to conform to any particular standard, interface circuits are used in order to adapt the connection lines and signals to the requirements of a given standard. Three examples of this approach are shown in Figure 6.18. Two of these standards, namely, Multibus and IEEE-488, allow the interconnection of several devices via a bus. The third example involves the RS-232-C standard, which defines an interface for connecting a single device.

The word "interface" refers to the boundary between two circuits or devices. A standard for this interface comprises a set of specifications for the functional, electrical, and mechanical characteristics of all signal and power lines that cross that boundary. This means that it defines a standard connector and the signals it carries. The reader should be warned that an interface circuit is often referred to simply as an interface in the literature, and particularly so in the

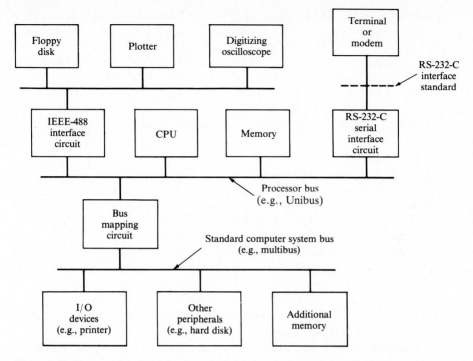

Figure 6.18 An example of a computer system showing different interface standards.

commercial literature. However, in the context of a standard, the word "interface" is used only in the more precise sense defined above. It is the role of the designer of a computer system to design a circuit that meets the requirements of a given interface standard.

Perhaps the most commonly used interface standard is RS-232-C, also known as CCITT Recommendation V.24. It is intended for the interconnection of devices that use serial transmission, either synchronous or asynchronous, and it is widely available with computer peripherals such as CRT terminals and modems. This standard will be discussed in Chapter 12.

A number of bus standards have evolved. Some of these, such as Multibus and S-100, implement a full complement of the functions normally supported by a computer bus. Hence, they can be used as an extension of a computer bus, as shown in Figure 6.18. They serve to provide a standard interface for connecting additional main memory modules, secondary storage units, or I/O devices. The existence of a standard bus connected in this manner is transparent to the CPU, and hence to the programmer. The function of the bus-mapping circuit shown in Figure 6.18 is to translate one set of bus signals into the other, and to provide any temporary buffering that may be needed because of differences in the timing of data transfers.

Another interface standard, IEEE-488, is intended for connecting laboratory instruments, plotters, floppy disks, and other low- to medium-speed peripherals. However, the manner in which data transfers are controlled on this bus and the speed of these transfers do not make it suitable for use as a computer bus in the same manner as the Multibus. Moreover, the interface circuit shown in the figure between the processor bus and the IEEE-488 bus cannot be designed so that it is transparent to the CPU. This circuit contains data and control registers which must be accessed explicitly by the software.

In what follows we discuss briefly the Multibus, the S-100 bus, and the IEEE-488 bus.

6.6.1 The Multibus

The Multibus was originally developed for use in Intel's Microcomputer Development System (MDS). It has now evolved into a recommended IEEE Standard No. 796.[6.1] This standard gives a full functional, electrical, and mechanical specification for a "backplane" bus through which a number of circuit boards may be interconnected. A full range of devices may be involved, including computers, memory boards, I/O devices, and other peripherals.

The Multibus consists of the 86 signals given in Table 6.2. We will discuss some of the distinguishing features of this bus. For full details, interested readers are referred to the Standard document.

Data transfers are initiated by the bus master, and they are controlled by an asynchronous handshake similar to that of Figures 6.13 and 6.14. The main difference is that the two signals, Read/$\overline{\text{Write}}$ and Ready, are replaced by MRDC* (Memory Read Command) and MWTC* (Memory Write Command). In the nomenclature of this Standard, a signal whose name ends with a * is active when low. During a memory read operation, the MRDC* signal is activated, while for a write operation the MWTC* signal is used instead, as shown in Figure 6.19. The slave uses the XACK* (Transfer Acknowledge) signal to indicate that it has accepted the command. Note that the address and data lines in this and subsequent figures are shown as high and low at the same time. This is intended to indicate that some lines are high and some low, depending upon the particular address or data pattern being transmitted. The crossing points indicate the time at which these patterns change. When a signal line is in an indeterminate or high impedance state, this is represented by an intermediate level half-way between the low and high signal levels.

In computer systems that use memory-mapped I/O, the MRDC* and MWTC* signals suffice for all data transfers. When used in conjunction with a computer that has separate I/O instructions, such as Intel microprocessors, these two commands are replaced by IORC* and IOWC* during I/O transfers.

The Multibus supports both 8-bit and 16-bit data transfers. It also allows an 8-bit computer to exchange data with a 16-bit computer, 1 byte at a time. The HBEN* (High Byte Enable) signal is used during these transfers to indicate whether the high-order data lines D8 to D15 carry valid data.

Another interesting facility is provided by the Inhibit lines INH1* and INH2*. In order to illustrate the use of these lines, let us consider a typical

Table 6.2 IEEE 796 bus (multibus) signals

Function	Name	Description	Number
Data	D0* to D15*	8- or 16-bit data	16
Address	A0* to A19*	Byte address	20
Control:			25
Data transfer	MRDC*	Memory read cmd.	
	MWTC*	Memory write cmd.	
	IORC*	I/O read cmd.	
	IOWC*	I/O write cmd.	
	XACK*	Transfer acknowledge	
	BHEN*	Byte high enable	
	INH1*, INH2*	Inhibit	
Scheduling	CBRQ*	Common bus request	
	BREQ*	Bus request	
	BPRN*	Bus priority in	
	BPRO*	Bus priority out	
	BUSY*	Bus busy	
	BCLK*	Bus clock	
Interrupts	INT0* to INT7*	Interrupt requests	
	INTA*	Interrupt acknowledge	
Misc.	CCLK*	Constant clock	
	INIT*	Initialize	
Power supply	+5,±12,GND		20
Reserved		For future use	5
		Total	86

example. Most of the address space of a computer is filled with RAM locations. However, small portions of this space are occupied by memory-mapped I/O devices and by ROM. The latter may be needed, for example, to store a short power-up routine. This arrangement of the address space may be implemented

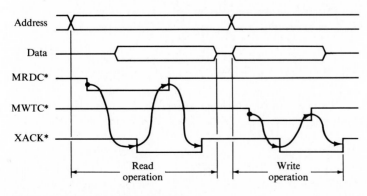

Figure 6.19 Multibus handshake signals.

by designing the address decoder of the RAM in such a way that it responds to memory read and write commands only when they are outside the regions occupied by the ROM or the I/O devices. The Inhibit lines offer an alternative approach. When the interface for the ROM or for one of the I/O devices recognizes its address, it asserts one of the Inhibit lines. At the same time, the RAM interface responds to all addresses, provided that neither of the two Inhibit lines is asserted. Whenever one of the Inhibit lines is active, the RAM interface turns off all its bus drivers and does not participate in the bus operation.

Figure 6.20 shows the sequence of events for a memory read cycle involving the use of the inhibit feature. At the beginning of the cycle, the bus master places a new address on the bus and asserts MRDC*. This may result in two devices being selected, a RAM and a ROM. As soon as the ROM interface is selected, it activates the INH1* line, which forces the RAM interface to be deselected. After a short delay to allow for propagation delays, the ROM interface enables its output drivers to place its data on the bus, and it asserts XACK*. The remainder of the cycle proceeds in the normal manner.

The existence of two Inhibit lines makes it possible to implement a two-level hierarchy among three classes of devices, A, B, and C. Addressing device B inhibits the operation of device A, while addressing device C inhibits both A and B.

The use of the Inhibit lines offers considerable flexibility in the allocation of the memory address space to different devices. In particular, it makes it possible to assemble independently designed circuit boards into a single system. For example, all RAM circuit boards for the system of Figure 6.18 can be designed without any knowledge of the addresses to be allocated to the ROM and the I/O devices. On the other hand, devices that use the Inhibit facility cannot operate at

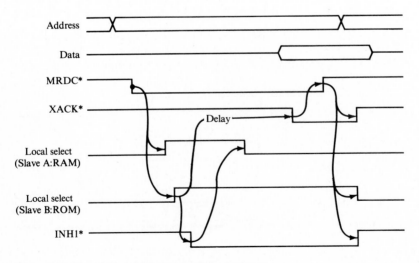

Figure 6.20 Use of the Inhibit signals of the Multibus.

the maximum speed of the bus. Sufficient time must be allowed for a device to recognize its address and then inhibit other devices at a lower level in the addressing hierarchy. As a result, the use of the Inhibit feature in a device slows down all data transfers involving that device.

Scheduling Six signals are used for scheduling the use of the bus (see Table 6.2). They allow either parallel or daisy-chain priority or both. The Bus Clock signal BCLK* provides a timing reference for the operation of all bus scheduling circuitry. Interested readers are referred to the Standard document for details.

Interrupts The interrupt-request lines INT0* to INT7* provide eight levels of priority, with INT0* having the highest priority. Each of these lines is an open-collector line to which several devices may be connected. If polling is used to identify the device requesting an interrupt, these eight lines are all that is needed. In order to support computer systems in which the interrupting device sends an interrupt-vector address to the CPU, an interrupt-acknowledge line INTA* is provided.

While there are eight interrupt-request lines, there is only one INTA* line. When several INTi* lines are active, it is necessary to identify which of these requests is being acknowledged. The address lines are used for this purpose. Figure 6.21 illustrates the sequence of events leading to the transfer of an interrupt-vector address from the highest priority device requesting an interrupt to the CPU. Following the arrival of an interrupt request, the CPU activates the INTA* line for a short period. This is interpreted by all devices on the bus as a command to freeze the state of the interrupt-request logic. That is, no device is allowed to change the state of its interrupt-request line after receiving this pulse. The CPU uses this quiet period to select the highest priority line among those that may be simultaneously active. Then, it places the number of this line on the address bus and activates the INTA* line a second time. The combination of

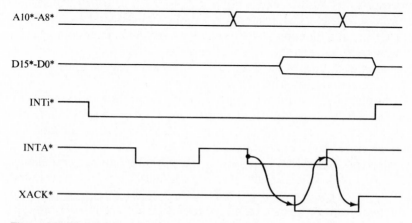

Figure 6.21 Timing for a vectored interrupt operation.

the INTA* line and the priority level information on the address lines has exactly the same effect as the multiple INTA lines in Figure 6.8b. The highest priority device responds to the second activation of the INTA* line by placing its interrupt-vector address on the data lines and activating XACK* in the same manner as for a Read operation.

The Multibus is used in many 8- and 16-bit microprocessor systems. The specifications in the IEEE Standard document cover electrical and mechanical details, including the shape and dimensions of interface boards, connectors, etc. Another useful feature in the Standard specifications is the definition of a number of subsets of the bus functions and a corresponding nomenclature for identification. For example, a Multibus interface board identified as "Slave D8, M20, V0" is a slave device, that is, it cannot become a temporary bus master, which uses 8 bits of data, 20 bits of address, and has no vectored interrupt capability. Careful attention to such details in the documentation of a standard is very important. It makes it possible for a designer to obtain subsystem components from different suppliers and integrate them into one system with ease.

6.6.2 The S-100 Bus

The S-100 bus is intended for use as a computer system bus in the same manner as the Multibus. It too has been adopted as a recommended IEEE Standard, No. 696.[6.2] It has evolved from the buses used in some early microcomputer systems based on Intel microprocessors, and it was intended primarily for the hobbyist market. In those systems, the conceptual simplicity of structure was a major objective, which was achieved by using a large number of bus lines. When IEEE 696 was defined, many modifications were introduced to overcome the problems that existed in the early designs.

The S-100 bus consists of a total of 100 lines. It supports both 8- and 16-bit data transfers, and 24-bit addresses. It has two interrupt-request lines and allows vectored interrupts. One of the devices connected to the bus, usually a CPU, is assumed to be a permanent bus master. Up to 16 other devices, either DMA controllers or CPUs, can function as temporary bus masters. They compete for the use of the bus, using a set of priority arbitration lines.

The large number of lines in the S-100 bus is a result of using dedicated lines for such functions as transmitting status information and interrupt-vector addresses. Eight bits of status are transmitted during every bus cycle to specify the type of transaction taking place, for example, memory read, OP-code fetch, I/O write, and vector-address transfer. The availability of this information simplifies the design of interface circuits.

Priority arbitration for DMA requests on the S-100 bus uses an interesting scheme, which we will describe briefly. Arbitration takes place in a distributed manner. That is, no central arbiter is needed to select the highest-priority device requesting the bus. Instead, parts of the arbitration circuit are incorporated in each device interface circuit.

Contention for the use of the bus takes place over six lines: four priority lines, a Bus Request line, and a Bus Grant line. In S-100 nomenclature, the priority lines are called DMA0* to DMA3*, the Bus Request line is called HOLD*, and the Bus Grant line is called pHLDA. Names ending with a * indicate that the corresponding lines are active when low.

Each device which is capable of becoming a temporary bus master, for example, a DMA controller, is assigned a unique priority. When it requires the use of the bus, it sends a request to the permanent master by asserting HOLD*. This is an open-collector line; hence, several devices can activate it at the same time. When the permanent master is ready to release the bus, it activates pHLDA. Meanwhile, a priority code appears on the DMAi* lines in a manner described in the next paragraph. This causes one device to be selected. It becomes a temporary bus master and may start using the bus.

In contrast to the bus control scheme of the Multibus, the code on the DMAi* lines is not transmitted by a single controlling device. Rather, it is the result of the interaction between the signals transmitted by all devices requesting the use of the bus at any given time. The net outcome of this interaction is that the code on the four priority lines represents the request having the highest priority. We will illustrate the means by which this is accomplished using a simple example. Consider two devices A and B that are requesting the use of the bus. Let their priorities be 5 and 6, respectively. Each device is connected to the priority lines as shown in Figure 6.22. A device requesting the bus attempts to place a 4-bit code representing its own priority on the priority lines. Thus, device A transmits the pattern 0101, and device B the pattern 0110. The priority lines are active when low. Furthermore, they are of the open-collector type. Thus, the priority pattern seen by either of the two devices will be 0111. Each device

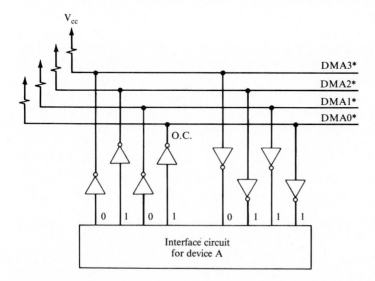

Figure 6.22 Connection of device interface circuit to priority arbitration lines.

continually compares this pattern to its own priority, starting from the most significant bit. If it detects a difference at any bit position, it disables its bus drivers for the corresponding line and for all lower-order lines. In the case of our example, device A detects a difference on line DMA1*. Hence, it disables its drivers for lines DMA1* and DMA0*. This causes the pattern seen by device B to change to 0110, which means that B will become the temporary bus master. Note that since for a short period the code on the priority lines is 0111, device B may temporarily disable its driver for line DMA0*. However, it will enable it again once device A has disabled its drivers. The timing specification for the bus allows sufficient delay to guarantee that the signals on the priority lines have settled before any device assumes bus mastership.

Despite the large number of lines and the technical difficulties encountered in some of the early versions of the S-100 bus, it has gained widespread popularity in microcomputer systems. A large number of S-100 compatible peripherals are available from different suppliers.

6.6.3 The IEEE-488 bus

As pointed out earlier, this bus is intended for laboratory instrumentation. It may be used, for example, for connecting a number of measuring devices, a digital oscilloscope, a plotter, and a printer to a desktop computer.

The standard[6.3] defines a bus that enables interconnection of up to 15 devices. Data transfer takes place in a bit-parallel byte-serial format. The interface allows transfer rates of up to 250,000 bytes/s over a distance of 20 m. A transfer rate of 1 Mbyte/s is possible over shorter distances. The bus consists of eight data lines and eight control lines, as shown in Figure 6.23. The eight data lines may be used to carry either data or commands to the device interfaces. The eight control lines are used to carry timing and other control information.

The interface of any device connected to the bus has the capability to assume one or more of three modes of operation; namely, it may be a listener, a talker, or a controller. The operations that a device interface can perform in each of these modes are as follows:

Listener. When the interface is in this mode, it can receive data from the bus. Hence this is the mode required for the interface of an output device or for an instrument that receives data from other devices.
Talker. A talker interface transfers data from an input device to the bus.
Controller. This is the interface of the device that controls the bus. It has the ability to place any device interface in either the listener or the talker mode.

To illustrate the operation of the instrumentation bus, let us consider the following situation. A computer acts as the controller for the bus and is about to start reading data from one of the instruments connected to it. To read data from the instrument, the computer has to place the instrument interface in the talker mode. This is accomplished by sending a command addressed to this interface.

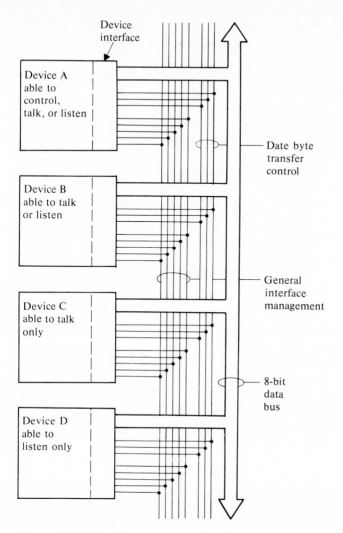

Figure 6.23 IEEE standard instrumentation bus. [6.3]

As soon as the device interface assumes the talker mode, it starts data transmission. The controller assumes the listener mode in order to receive the data transmitted by the talker. Before proceeding to consider this process in more detail, let us first examine the mechanism by which a byte of data is transferred over the bus.

Data transfer over the bus is controlled by an asynchronous handshake protocol. The main difference between this protocol and the scheme of Figures 6.13 and 6.14 is that three control signals are used instead of the two signals Ready and Accept. The protocol also allows one "source" to transfer data to a number of "acceptors" simultaneously. The byte-transfer control signals used are Data Valid (DAV), Ready for Data (RFD), and Data Accepted (DAC). The functions of the DAV and DAC signals are identical to the Ready and Accept signals, respectively, of Figure 6.13. The RFD signal is used to inform the source of data when the acceptor is ready to receive a new byte of data.

Transfer of data takes place as shown in Figure 6.24a. Let us consider first the case of one acceptor. The source starts by placing a data byte on the data lines (t_0), then waits until the data lines settle (t_1). If at time t_1 the RFD signal is

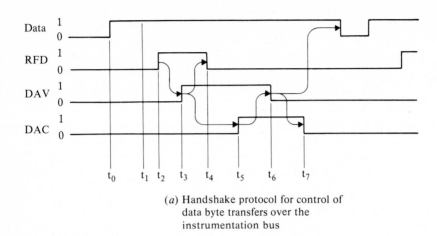

(a) Handshake protocol for control of data byte transfers over the instrumentation bus

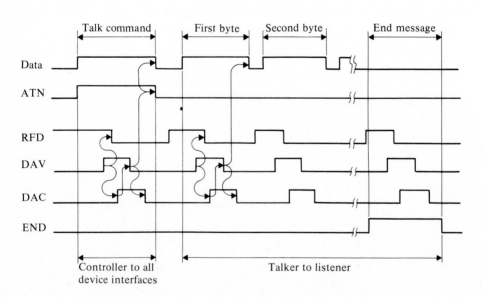

(b) A multibyte transfer over the instrumentation bus

Figure 6.24 Timing of data transfer over the instrumentation bus.

equal to 0, indicating that the acceptor is not ready to receive data, the source waits until RFD changes to 1 (t_2). Then it sets DAV to 1 (t_3). When this is received by the acceptor, it immediately drops RFD to 0 (t_4), strobes the data in, then sets DAC to 1 (t_5). The source responds by removing the DAV signal (t_6). Then, after some delay to allow for bus skew, it starts changing the data to place a new byte on the data lines. When DAV = 0 is detected by the acceptor, it resets DAC to 0 (t_7). The acceptor interface does not set RFD to 1 until it is ready to accept a new byte of data.

Let us now consider the case where there is more than one acceptor on the bus. The instrumentation bus is of the open-collector type (see Section 4.1.5). Recall that the state of an open-collector bus is the logical AND function of all outputs connected to it. Therefore, the RFD line will be in the 1 state only when all acceptors on the bus are ready for receiving data. Similarly, the DAC line goes to the 1 state when all acceptors have accepted the data. This means that the handshake protocol of Figure 6.24a enables proper transfer of data, irrespective of the number of acceptors receiving the data. Because of electrical limitations, no more than 15 devices should be connected to the instrumentation bus, out of which up to 14 devices may be accepting data simultaneously.

The eight data lines of the bus are used to carry commands to the device interfaces (for example, to place an interface in the talker or listener mode) and for transferring data which is to be passed by the interface to the I/O device. Some means have to be provided for identifying these two types of information. One of the interface management lines, which is referred to as the attention line (ATN), is provided for this purpose. Whenever ATN = 1, all interfaces connected to the bus monitor the data lines, and interpret the 8-bit byte on the data lines as a command. A command addressed to a particular device carries a 5-bit address. The command is ignored by all devices other than the one being addressed.

Let us now return to the input operation discussed earlier. The sequence of signals for this operation is shown in Figure 6.24b. To place the input device interface in the talker mode, the controller starts by placing a command on the data lines and sets ATN to 1. The command contains the device address and specifies that the device should be set in the talker mode. This information is transferred to the device interface under control of the DAV, RFD, and DAC lines, as described above. As soon as ATN drops to 0, the device interface assumes the talker mode and begins transmitting data. Transmission of each byte is under control of the handshake protocol between the talker and the listener. When all data bytes have been transferred, the talker indicates this by sending an END message. This is accomplished by setting the END control line (one of the control lines for interface management) to 1 and transferring this information to the listener, using the handshake protocol.

In the above example, it was assumed that the controller was also a listener. The controller may, if required, assign the listener mode to one or more other devices, either in addition to or instead of itself. In such a case, the talker command of Figure 6.24b should be preceded by a listener command (or commands) addressed to the desired device interfaces. Such a procedure allows the computer to read data from an instrument, for example, and at the same time to have this data transferred to a printer or a plotter.

The instrumentation bus provides a high degree of flexibility. It offers many capabilities in addition to the simple transfers described above. For example, a device may request the attention of the controller at any time. The controller may simultaneously check the status of a number of devices. A full description of these capabilities is beyond the scope of this text. The interested reader should refer to the documentation on the IEEE or ANSI standards.[6.3]

6.7 I/O CHANNELS

So far, we have seen two methods for implementing I/O data transfers, namely, program-controlled I/O and direct memory access. The main features of these two approaches can be summarized as follows:

1. Program-controlled I/O requires continuous involvement of the CPU. However, only a minimal amount of external hardware is needed to connect peripheral devices to the computer.
2. Direct memory access relieves the CPU of all I/O functions except for the initialization of the transfer parameters. An external controller is required for each device that makes use of the DMA facility.

The above two mechanisms are adequate for fulfilling all I/O requirements of most small- and medium-sized machines. Program-controlled I/O is normally used with low-speed devices, while high-speed devices are usually connected through a DMA facility. The economics of operating large computers, however, give rise to slightly different requirements. The size of the system and the cost of the CPU justify the expenditure of considerable effort to optimize the utilization of the CPU time. The overhead incurred with program-controlled I/O makes this approach highly undesirable with large machines. Therefore some sort of DMA arrangement should be used for all I/O operations. Furthermore, since it is uneconomical to provide a separate DMA controller for each device, some means should be provided to share the DMA controller among a number of devices. This gives rise to the concept of I/O *channels*. A channel, in its simplest form, is a small processor that acts as a shared DMA facility for a number of devices. For example, Figure 6.25 gives a possible organization of a computer using two I/O channels. A memory controller serves to coordinate access to the main memory by the CPU and the two channels. This enables the implementation of the cycle-stealing feature which is necessary to perform direct memory access. Each I/O device is connected to a channel via a control unit. The function of the control unit is to communicate with the channel and issue the appropriate control signals to the device. One control unit may be used for a number of similar devices, provided only one of these devices is active at any given time. The control unit is equivalent to the interface block in Figure 6.2.

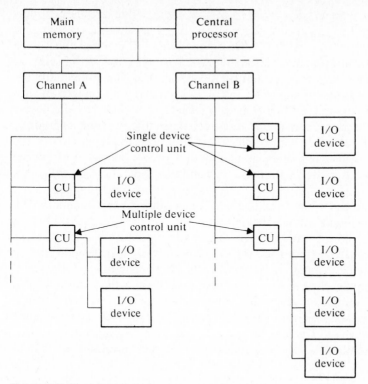

Figure 6.25 Use of channels for performing I/O operations.

I/O channels are peripheral processors, which are computers in their own right, but their instruction sets are limited to I/O operations. The name "channel" has been used to describe such processors, largely because this is the name associated with the corresponding I/O units in the IBM 370 series of computers. Other manufacturers do not necessarily use the word "channel" to describe their equipment of similar type.

Three types of channels are usually found in large computers:

1. Multiplexer channels
2. Selector channels
3. Block multiplexer channels

Multiplexer channels A multiplexer channel is used for connecting a number of slow- and medium-speed devices. The channel to memory link is capable of transferring data at rates much faster than that of the individual devices connected to the channel. Therefore it is possible to operate a number of I/O devices simultaneously.

Operation of the multiplexer channel can take place in either of two modes, namely, the *byte-interleave* and the *burst* modes. In the byte-interleave mode, channel operation is divided into short segments of time. During each of these time segments the channel services one of the devices that are currently in operation. Information transferred during this time may consist of a byte of data, control, or status information. The device is logically connected to the channel only for the duration of this transfer, which is typically less than 100 μs. If the transfer of information requested by the device takes more than 100 μs, the channel switches to the burst mode. In this case, the logical connection with an I/O device is maintained until all character transfers requested by the device are completed. The channel uses a time-out mechanism to determine its mode of operation with any device. If data transfer requests from the device cause the logical connection to be maintained longer than a preset period, the channel switches to the burst mode. Otherwise it continues operation in the byte-interleave mode.

Figure 6.26 indicates the organization of a multiplexer channel. The multiplexing arrangement allows the channel to handle a large number of devices at the same time. Parameters relating to the operation of each of these devices, for example, byte count and memory data addresses, are usually kept in fixed locations in the main memory. Whenever the channel addresses a device, it fetches the appropriate parameters from memory. At the time the device is disconnected, the updated values are placed back in the same locations. However, the channel still requires some hardware that can be dedicated to each I/O operation in progress. This part of the channel hardware is referred to as a *subchannel*. The number of subchannels determines the maximum number of

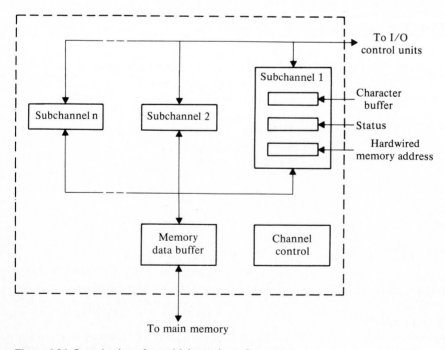

Figure 6.26 Organization of a multiplexer channel.

I/O operations that can be maintained at any given time. The subchannel must have sufficient storage capacity for at least 1 byte of information plus a few status flags. A fixed address in memory is associated with each subchannel for storing the relevant data transfer parameters.

Selector channels High-speed devices, such as magnetic disks, require sufficiently high data transfer rates that they cannot be easily multiplexed with other devices by means of a multiplexer channel. Instead, it is necessary to use a separate channel to handle such devices one at a time. A selector channel serves this purpose. Its operation is similar to that of a multiplexer channel that operates in a burst mode, except that higher speed of operation is required.

Organization of a selector channel is shown in Figure 6.27. It contains hardware registers that hold the parameters needed in I/O transfers. These include the address of the next main memory location to or from which the data is to be transferred, and the byte count, which is the number of bytes that remain to be transferred as part of a particular I/O operation. Transfers between the selector channel and the main memory usually involve 16, 32, or 64 bits in parallel. Since most I/O devices are byte-oriented, the channel includes the circuitry necessary to assemble serially received bytes into larger words for parallel transfer to the memory, and vice versa.

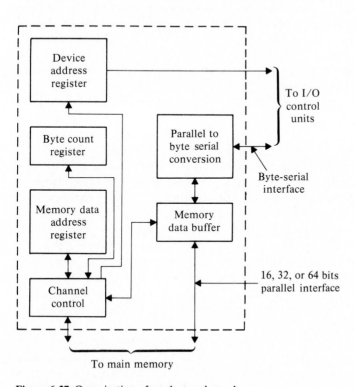

Figure 6.27 Organization of a selector channel.

When an I/O operation is initiated by means of a selector channel, the channel remains dedicated to that task for the duration of the entire operation. It cannot be used for another I/O operation until the current one is completed.

Block multiplexer channels This type of channel combines the features of both the multiplexer and selector channels. It allows multiplexing of a number of high-speed I/O operations on a block by block basis. Thus it corresponds to a high-speed multiplexer channel that operates only in the burst mode. The advantages gained from the use of block multiplexer channels in comparison with selector channels stem from the nature of operation of I/O devices such as magnetic disks and tapes. A typical transaction with a disk drive may require the following sequence of commands (see Chapter 9):

- Seek (Move Read/Write head to a given track).
- Search for a particular record.
- Start reading the data in the record.

Because of the considerable mechanical delay involved in the first two operations, it is not appropriate to tie up the entire channel throughout this sequence, which would be the case with a selector channel. A block multiplexer channel can send the Seek command to the disk drive and then disconnect so it can service other I/O devices. When the Seek operation is completed, the channel reconnects, sends the Search command, and disconnects once more. Upon completion of the Search, the channel begins the transfer of the desired record and stays connected until the I/O operation is terminated. Using a block multiplexer channel in this way results in substantially improved throughput in comparison with selector channels.

6.7.1 Channel Program

In the simple DMA controller discussed in Section 6.2.1, the parameters relating to any data transfer are loaded in the appropriate registers using I/O instructions. In large machines that use I/O channels, this is replaced by the concept of a *channel program*. As mentioned earlier, the channel is a small processor that has access to the main memory on a cycle-stealing basis. It is capable of executing a limited set of instructions, referred to as *channel commands*. These commands specify the parameters needed by the channel to control the I/O devices and perform data transfer operations. A channel program is a sequence of these commands stored in the main memory. The CPU initiates an I/O operation by issuing a special command to the channel. This causes the channel to start fetching and executing the commands that constitute the channel program.

To examine channel operation in more detail, let us consider the sequence of events that takes place during an I/O operation in IBM System 370. The channel program consists of *channel command words* (CCWs), whose format is given in Figure 6.28. A CCW contains a 24-bit address of the data in the main memory

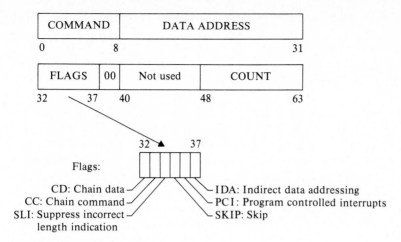

Figure 6.28 Channel command word (CCW).

and a 16-bit byte count which indicates how many bytes of data are involved in the transfer. Thus transfers of up to 64K bytes can be specified in a single CCW. The CCW also contains command and flag fields which are interpreted as explained below.

Command field This field corresponds to the OP-code field in machine instructions. It specifies the operation to be performed. There are six basic types of commands:

Read. This command instructs the channel to read the number of characters specified in the count field from the device. The channel deposits the characters into the main memory in ascending order of addresses, starting at the address specified in the address field.

Write. The Write command causes the channel to transfer data from the main memory to the device. Characters are transferred in the same order as with the Read command.

Read Backward. In the case of magnetic tapes, this has the same effect as the Read command except that tape motion is in the reverse direction. Data bytes are stored in the main memory in descending order of addresses, starting at the address specified in the address field.

Sense. This is a command to the channel to sense the status of the selected device and store it in the channel status word (see Section 6.7.2). The Sense command enables the CPU to get detailed information, for example, about the error conditions in an I/O device.

Control. The CPU can use this command to send specific instructions to the I/O device, such as rewinding and unloading a magnetic tape reel. It may also be used to specify a main memory location that contains further control information, for example, the address of a record on a disk file.

Transfer in Channel. This command performs the function of a Jump instruction in the channel program. Normally, the channel fetches CCWs from consecutive memory locations. When a Transfer in Channel command is encountered, the data address field is used to determine the address of the next CCW.

It is apparent that it is not necessary to have as many as 8 bits to specify the above basic types of operation. The command field includes some "modifier" bits that are interpreted as device-dependent operations. This enables specification of such operations as rewinding a magnetic tape, writing a file mark on a tape, moving the head to a particular track on a disk, etc. The modifier bits can also be used to designate which of a number of I/O devices that are connected to the same control unit is to take part in a given operation.

The command field is sent to the control unit of the device. The control unit decodes the command and modifier bits and sends the appropriate control signals to the device.

Flag field The six bits of this field are defined in Figure 6.28. Their interpretation is as follows:

Chain command (CC). When this bit is set, it indicates to the channel that the next CCW specifies a new I/O operation to be performed with the same device. The channel first proceeds with the I/O operation specified in the CCW that has the CC flag set. When this is completed, the logical connection with the device is discontinued. The channel then fetches the next CCW, restores the connection with the I/O device, and starts performing the new command. From the device end, the two operations resulting from execution of the first and second CCWs appear as two separate I/O commands.

Chain data (CD). A CCW with the CD bit set indicates to the channel that the following CCW contains a new address and a new byte count. These are to be used for transferring a second block of data to or from the I/O device using the command specified by the current CCW. When the channel completes transferring the data specified in the CCW with the CD bit set, it does not drop the connection with the I/O device. Instead, it continues the transfer using the memory address and byte count in the next CCW. With data chaining, the data transferred by the first and second CCWs appears as one block to the I/O device. This facilitates transfers between a device and noncontiguous locations in the main memory.

To illustrate the difference between command and data chaining let us consider the transfer of two blocks of data from the main memory to magnetic tape. If command chaining is used, the two blocks would be written on the tape separated by a record gap (see Chapter 9), which is automatically inserted by the tape drive at the end of an I/O operation specified by a CCW where CD = 0. On the other hand, data chaining causes the two blocks to be merged into one record on the magnetic tape, with a record gap inserted only at the end of the second block. A CCW with neither CD nor CC flags set constitutes the end of the particular channel program.

Suppress incorrect length indication (SLI). When an I/O operation is terminated before the byte count reaches zero, this condition is reported to the CPU as a part of the channel status information (see Section 6.7.2). However, the condition is ignored if the SLI flag is set.

Skip. This bit, when set, causes the channel to skip the number of bytes specified in the count field. When used with the Read command, this flag results in data being read from the device without being transferred to the main memory.

Program-controlled interrupt (PCI). The channel raises an interrupt when a CCW with the PCI flag set is fetched. If this CCW is preceded by other CCWs, connected by command chaining, the interrupt is requested only after all previously specified data transfers are completed. Thus the programmer can use the PCI flag to check the progress of I/O operations.

Indirect data addressing (IDA). This flag, used in conjunction with the address translation mechanism in System 370, will not be discussed here.

The channel fetches the CCWs from the main memory (MM) and executes them in the same way as the CPU executes machine instructions. Complex I/O operations can be performed by means of channel programs that consist of a number of CCWs. Figure 6.29 shows an example of a program that transfers three blocks of data from the MM to a magnetic tape. The first CCW results in reading 70 bytes from the MM starting at location 2000, and writing them on the tape. The Write operation and the particular tape drive that is to be used are specified by the command field. Since the CD bit is set, the second CCW must be interpreted as a continuation of the first one. Thus the same I/O operation, that is, a Write on the same device, is performed, using the data specified in the second CCW. Note that the command bits are ignored in this case. This transfers 100 bytes from the MM beginning at location 2200 to the tape as a continuation of the previously started record. In the second CCW the CC bit is set, which means that another CCW follows, but it is not necessarily related to the current one. Therefore, upon completion of the second CCW, a record gap is inserted on the tape. The third CCW again specifies a Write on the same tape. It results in a transfer of 50 bytes from MM location 2500 to the tape. Since both the CD and CC flags are zero, the end of the channel program is indicated.

Figure 6.30 gives a channel program that illustrates the use of the skip flag. The first CCW transfers 80 bytes from tape drive #n (specified in the command field) to the MM starting at location 4500. Since CD = 1, the second CCW is interpreted as implying the same operation. However, in the second CCW the skip flag is set, which means that the channel will not transmit the next 30 bytes read from the tape. Since CD is still set, the same Read operation continues with

Command		Address	Flags C C S S P I D C L K C D I I I A P						Count
CCW1	Write (tape drive *n*)	2000	1	0	0	0	0	0	70
CCW2	ignored	2200	0	1	0	0	0	0	100
CCW3	Write (tape drive *n*)	2500	0	0	0	0	0	0	50

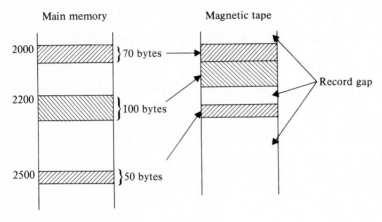

Figure 6.29 A channel program illustrating the use of command and data chaining during a Write operation.

the third CCW, causing the transfer of the following 50 bytes to the MM, starting at location 4700. Therefore, the program transfers two blocks of data to the main memory from one record on the tape, skipping 30 bytes in the middle of the record. It should be noted that if the record is longer than the 160 bytes specified in this program, the tape drive will continue the Read operation, independent of the channel, until the end of the record is reached. This is necessary to enable the tape drive to respond properly to a subsequent Read command, since it is not possible to start a Read operation in the middle of a record.

6.7.2 Initiation and Control of Channel Operations

In the previous section we discussed the manner in which channel programs are used to perform I/O operations. These programs reside in the main memory of the computer, and they are fetched by the channel for execution. Now we should consider the question of how I/O operations are set into action and supervised by the CPU. In IBM System 370 there are four machine instructions that the

Command		Address	Flags C D I	C C L I	S S K I	S P C P	P I C A D	I	Count
CCW1	Read (tape drive n)	4500	1	0	0	0	0	0	80
CCW2	ignored	ignored	1	0	0	1	0	0	30
CCW3	ignored	4700	0	0	0	0	0	0	50

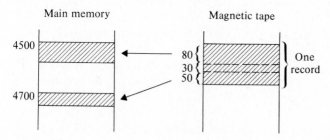

Figure 6.30 A channel program illustrating the use of the Skip flag during a Read operation.

CPU may use for I/O purposes. These instructions have the SI format that was described in Section 3.5. They are:

START I/O — Causes an I/O operation to begin. The instruction address field is used to specify the channel and the I/O device that are to be used.

HALT I/O — Terminates the channel operation.

TEST CHANNEL — Tests the state of the addressed channel.

TEST I/O — Tests the state of the addressed channel, sub-channel, and I/O device.

An I/O operation is initiated through the START I/O instruction. The address field of this instruction is used to specify which channel and I/O device are to be involved in the operation. The next parameter that must be determined is the location of the channel program in the main memory. This is accomplished by means of a *channel address word* (CAW), which is always stored in location 72 of the main memory. Figure 6.31 shows the format of the CAW. The 24-bit address specifies the location of the first CCW that is to be executed. A 4-bit memory protection key is included in the CAW. It is used to prevent unauthorized access by one user to another user's data or program in the main memory. Access to a particular segment of the memory is allowed if its key matches that of the I/O task that requests the access.

The required CAW must be loaded into location 72 prior to the execution of

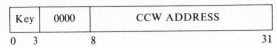

0   3   8   31   **Figure 6.31** Channel address word.

the START I/O instruction. After fetching the CAW, the channel proceeds to address the I/O device named in the START I/O instruction. The device indicates its readiness to participate in an I/O operation by returning its address to the channel. From this moment on, the device remains logically connected to the channel, through its control unit, until the I/O operation is completed. Having established the availability of the I/O device, the channel signals the CPU accordingly. This constitutes the end of the START I/O instruction, and the CPU need no longer be concerned with this particular I/O task. Upon completion of the START I/O instruction, the channel proceeds to execute the channel program which specifies the particular I/O operations to be performed.

When the channel completes an I/O operation, it communicates its status to the CPU via the *channel status word* (CSW) given in Figure 6.32. Bits 8 to 31 contain the address of the last CCW executed by the channel, while bits 48 to 63 store the residual character count. If the I/O transfer is completed successfully, the residual count should be zero. Any other status information, such as error conditions for the channel or the control unit, can be found in bits 32 to 47.

The CPU can terminate the channel operation at any time by executing the HALT I/O operation. It can test the status of the I/O system by means of the TEST CHANNEL and TEST I/O instructions.

Since the channel has the capability to execute channel programs without constant supervision by the CPU, it is necessary to provide it with the ability to interrupt the CPU. An interrupt occurs when an I/O operation is completed, when an error is detected, when an I/O device requests an interrupt, or when the channel starts executing a CCW that has the PCI flag set to 1.

6.8 CONCLUDING REMARKS

In this chapter we discussed three basic approaches to the handling of I/O transfers. The simplest technique is to make use of programmed I/O, where the CPU performs all the necessary control functions. When speed becomes a problem, one may turn to the DMA approach, which requires additional hardware. In large computers it is reasonable to dedicate a separate peripheral processor to I/O tasks.

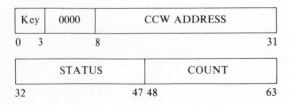

32   47 48   63   **Figure 6.32** Channel status word.

A key concept presented in the chapter is that of interrupts. In many computer applications it is essential to be able to interrupt the normal execution of programs in order to service higher-priority requests that require urgent attention. Most computers, both large and small, have a mechanism for dealing with such situations. However, the complexity and sophistication of interrupt-handling schemes vary from computer to computer.

6.9 PROBLEMS

6.1 Assume a machine with a vectored-interrupt capability, where an I/O device supplies the starting address of the interrupt-service routine at the time the interrupt is acknowledged. The processor status is saved on a memory stack. Describe, in point form, the sequence of events from the time the device requests an interrupt, until execution of the interrupt-service routine is started. If machine instructions require one to five memory cycles to execute, estimate the maximum number of memory cycles that may occur before execution of the interrupt-service routine is started.

6.2 *(a)* Specify the sequence of steps that takes place when an interrupt is received by the CPU of the PDP-11 computer. Give the number of bus transfers required during each of these steps (do not give details of bus signals or microprogram).

(b) Estimate the maximum possible number of memory cycles to fetch and execute an instruction in the PDP-11. Name the data read from or written into the main memory in each cycle.

(c) Estimate the maximum number of bus transfers that may occur from the instant a device requests an interrupt until the first instruction of the interrupt-service routine is fetched for execution.

6.3 The CPU of a computer has the internal structure given in Figure 4.1. The CPU inspects the interrupt lines at the end of the execution phase of each instruction. If an I/O device is requesting an interrupt, the CPU performs all the functions related to accepting the interrupt vector address, storing the processor status in a memory stack, and branching to the interrupt-service routine. Assume the sequence of events to be identical to that in the PDP-11. Give the control steps (as in Figure 4.8) required for this function. Make any necessary additions to Figure 4.1.

6.4 Some of the I/O devices connected to a PDP-11 computer are two magnetic disk units, a real-time clock, and a number of teletypewriters. All devices are serviced via interrupts. The real-time clock interrupts the CPU at regular time intervals (for example, every $\frac{1}{60}$ s) for time-keeping purposes. The disk interrupts the CPU when it has completed an operation and is ready to receive a new command. Servicing of disk interrupts should take priority over teletypewriter interrupts, with the real-time clock having the highest priority.

Suggest suitable numerical values for the priorities of the above devices, and specify the interrupt vector associated with each (refer to Figure 3.2 for details of the PS word).

6.5 A logic circuit is needed for implementation of the priority network shown in Figure 6.8*b*. The network handles three interrupt request lines. When a request is received on line $INTR_i$, the network generates an acknowledgment on line $INTA_i$. If more than one request is received, only the request that has the highest priority is acknowledged, where the ordering of priorities is as follows:

$$\text{Priority of } INTR_1 > \text{priority of } INTR_2 > \text{priority of } INTR_3$$

(a) Give a truth table for each of the outputs $INTA_1$, $INTA_2$, and $INTA_3$.

(b) Give a logic circuit for implementing this priority network.

(c) Can your design be easily extended for more interrupt-request lines?

(d) By adding two inputs DECIDE and RESET, modify your design such that $INTA_i$ is set to 1 when a pulse is received on the input DECIDE and is reset to 0 when a pulse is received on the input RESET.

6.6 A PDP-11 computer is required to accept characters from 20 teletypewriters. The four status and data buffers associated with TTY 1 occupy the four word addresses 172000_8 to 172006_8. The next four words are used for TTY 2, and so on. Memory location 64 is used to store the interrupt vector for all teletypewriters. The main memory area to be used for storing data for each TTY is pointed at by a pointer $PNTR_n$ (n = 1 to 20). The 20 pointers are stored in memory locations 5000_8 to 5046_8.

It is required to collect input data from the teletypewriters while another program PROG is being executed. This may be accomplished in one of two ways:

(a) Every T seconds, the program PROG calls a subroutine DEVSUB. This subroutine checks the status of each of the 20 TTYs in sequence and transfers any input characters to the memory. Then it returns to PROG.

(b) Whenever a character is ready in any of the interface buffers of the TTYs, an interrupt is generated. This causes the interrupt routine DEVINT to be executed. After polling the status registers, it transfers the input character, then returns to PROG.

Write the routines DEVSUB and DEVINT, assuming that registers R_4 and R_5 are not used by PROG.

In order not to lose any input characters, the period T in method *(a)* should be less than the minimum time between the reception of two successive characters. As an approximation, assume that the maximum character rate for any of the teletypewriters is $1/T$ characters per second. The average rate, however, is equal to r/T, where $r \le 1$. Estimate, on the average, the percentage of time spent in servicing the terminals for methods *(a)* and *(b)* for $T = 10$ ms and $r = 0.01, 0.1, 0.5$, and 1. Assume that each bus transfer requires 1 µs.

6.7 Successive data blocks of N bytes each are to be read from a teletypewriter to the main memory. A program PROG is to perform some computation on each block of data. Prepare a control program, CNTRL, for the PDP-11, which will perform the following functions:

(a) Read data block 1.

(b) Activate PROG and point it to the location of block 1 in the main memory, and, meanwhile, start reading block 2.

(c) Start PROG on block 2, and, meanwhile, start reading block 3, and so on.

Parallel execution of PROG and the loading of a data block can be accomplished by using the interrupt capability of the computer to interrupt execution of PROG every time a new character is typed.

Note that CNTRL must maintain correct buffer pointers, keep track of the character count, and transfer control correctly to PROG, whether PROG takes more or less time than block input.

6.8 A 32-bit computer has two selector channels and one multiplexer channel. Each selector channel supports two magnetic disk and two magnetic tape units. The multiplexer channel has two line printers, two card readers, and 10 CRT terminals connected to it. Assume that the transfer rates for these peripherals are as follows:

Disk drive	800K bytes/s
Magnetic tape drive	200K bytes/s
Line printer	6.6K bytes/s
Card reader	1.2K bytes/s
CRT terminal	1K bytes/s

Estimate the maximum aggregate I/O transfer rate in this system.

6.9 In most computers, interrupts are not acknowledged until the end of execution of the current machine instruction. Consider the possibility of suspending operation of the CPU in the middle of execution of an instruction in order to acknowledge an interrupt. Discuss the difficulties that may arise.

6.10 Figure P6.1 shows a possible arrangement of the Bus Request (BR) and Bus Grant (BG) signals in a decentralized bus assignment scheme. Describe how device i should generate BR_i, interpret BG_i, and generate BG_{i+1}. Specify the timing for the rising and falling edges of each signal and the priority of each device.

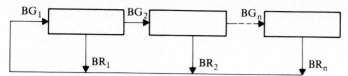

Figure P6.1 A decentralized bus assignment scheme.

What happens in your scheme when one or more devices request the use of the bus while another device is actively using the bus?

6.11 Design the logic circuitry required in each device interface to implement the bus assignment scheme you have devised in Problem 6.10.

6.12 "It is not possible to transfer data to a computer unless the computer is expecting arrival of such data." Comment on the validity of this statement by considering the following three possibilities for input operations:

(a) Status checking
(b) Interrupts
(c) Direct memory access

6.13 It is required to reformat a 200-byte record stored on a magnetic tape into two separate records. The first record should contain the first 80 bytes, and the second record should contain the remaining 120 bytes. The first record should start at the same point on tape as the original 200-byte record.

Write a channel program similar to that of Figure 6.29 to accomplish the above task, assuming that a scratch-pad area is available in the main memory starting at location 6400. Also assume that the command Backspace One Record can be issued in the same way as the Read and Write commands.

6.14 (This problem is suitable for use as a laboratory experiment.) Given a PDP-11 computer and a teletypewriter, or a CRT terminal, write the following two programs to demonstrate the multilevel interrupt mechanism of the computer.

(a) A programmed I/O routine which prints letters in alphabetical order. It prints two lines as follows:

$$ABC \cdots YZ$$

$$ABC \cdots YZ$$

then executes a HALT instruction.

(b) A programmed I/O routine which prints the numeric characters 0 to 9 in increasing order three times. Its output should have the following format:

$$012 \cdots 9012 \cdots 9012 \cdots 9$$

Use program (a) as the main program, and program (b) as an interrupt-service routine whose execution is initiated by entering any character at the keyboard. Execution of program (b) may also be interrupted by entering another character at the keyboard. Upon completion of program (b), execution of the most recently interrupted program should be resumed from the point of interruption. Thus the printed output may appear as follows:

$$ABC$$

$$012 \cdots 901$$

$$012 \cdots 9012 \cdots 9012 \cdots 9$$

$$2 \cdots 9012 \cdots 9$$

$$DE \cdots YZ$$

Show how you can use the processor priority to either enable or inhibit interrupt nesting.

6.15 Write a program (c) in addition to programs (a) and (b) of Problem 6.14. Program (c) should perform the carriage control functions required to put the printed output in the following format:

ABC

012 · · · 901

012 · · · 9012 · · · 9012 · · · 9

2 · · · 9012 · · · 9

DE · · · YZ

6.16 (This problem is suitable for use as a laboratory experiment.)

(a) Given a PDP-11 computer, a CRT terminal, and a stopwatch, devise a scheme to measure the execution time for the following instructions:

CMP   R0,R1

CMPB   R0,R1

CMP   @R0,R1

CMP   R0,@R1

(b) Prepare a program to measure the time between two external events in the form of interrupts from the CRT terminal. Estimate the maximum uncertainty in this measurement, and suggest some means for reducing this uncertainty as much as possible.

(c) Show how the SOB instruction may be used to implement a program loop for timing purposes.

6.17 An industrial plant uses a number of limit sensors for monitoring temperature, pressure, etc. The output of each sensor consists of an ON/OFF switch. It is required to connect eight such sensors to the bus of a small computer. Design an appropriate interface so that the state of all eight switches can be read simultaneously as a single byte at address 177020_8. Assume a synchronous bus that has a Read/Write control line and uses the timing sequence of Figure 6.12

6.18 Repeat Problem 6.17 using Multibus signals.

6.19 Design an appropriate interface for connecting a seven-segment display as an output device on the Unibus, at address 177100_8 (see Section A.10 for a description of a seven-segment display).

6.20 Consider the interface of Figure 6.15. Assume that the propagation delay through each gate varies between 5 and 15 ns, and that the address decoder is equivalent to three gate delays. Flip-flops require a minimum setup and hold times of 20 and 3 ns, respectively. Three-state gates require a maximum of 30 ns to change from the high impedance state to the enabled state. Assume also that propagation over the bus, including delays through the bus drives and receivers in the CPU, is in the range of 5 to 25 ns.

(a) What is the maximum bus skew?

(b) Suggest suitable values for the fixed delays introduced by the bus master in the timing diagrams of Figures 6.13 and 6.14.

(c) Estimate the durations of a Read operation and a Write operation.

6.21 Estimate the bus cycle time for a synchronous bus using the timing diagram of Figure 6.12. Modify Figure 6.15 as appropriate, and assume the same delay parameters as in Problem 6.20.

6.22 It is required to add an interrupt-request line to the interface of Figure 6.16. An interrupt request should be generated whenever an input character is available, or when the transmission buffer is empty. Bit b_6 of the input and output status registers of this interface should enable interrupts when set to 1 under program control. Suggest a suitable circuit.

6.23 Three devices A, B, and C are connected to the bus of computer. I/O transfers for all three devices use interrupt control. Interrupt nesting for devices A and B is not allowed, but interrupt requests from C are to be accepted while A or B are being serviced. Suggest different ways in which this can be accomplished in each of the following cases:

(a) The computer has one interrupt-request line and no vectored-interrupt capability.

(b) Two interrupt-request lines $INTR_1$ and $INTR_2$ are available, with $INTR_1$ having higher priority, Specify when and how interrupts are enabled and disabled in each case.

6.24 Bus extenders are sometimes used to increase the number of devices that can be connected to a bus. A bidirectional bus driver, consisting of two 3-state or open-collector gates connected in opposite directions, may be used for this purpose. Consider the following signals of the Unibus: Address, Data, $C_{0,1}$, MSYN, SSYN, BBSY, NPR, and NPG. In which direction should the bidirectional buffers point

(a) during Read and Write operations initiated by the CPU?

(b) during DMA transfers initiated by a device on the extension section of the bus?

Assume that all the main memory is on the main section of the bus.

6.25 Design a logic circuit to control the extender gates for the address and data lines in Problem 6.24.

6.26 Consider the section of a bus interface circuit which handles the daisy-chain signals for device i, in Figure 6.8a. This circuit receives an Interrupt Acknowledge signal, $INTA_i$, from the interface of device i − 1 and generates $INTA_{i+1}$ for device i + 1. Let REQUEST and READY be a pair of handshake signals that are used for communication between device i and the daisy-chain circuit in its bus interface. When the device requires service it asserts REQUEST. The daisy-chain circuit activates the INTR line, and when it receives $INTA_i$, it asserts READY.

Show how you can use an edge-triggered D flip-flop and some logic gates to implement the daisy-chain circuit.

6.27 The daisy-chain circuit of Problem 6.26 can be designed as an asynchronous sequential machine. Give a state diagram representing the operation of this circuit and derive the smallest number of states needed. Use asynchronous circuit design techniques to obtain a suitable implementation.

The implementation in Problem 6.26 uses one flip-flop. Compare this to the number of states obtained above, and comment.

6.28 Consider the output operation performed by the program of Figure 6.3. Write a suitable program for the same task, using interrupts. Write another program to initiate a DMA transfer, assuming that the DMA interface is organized as described in Section 6.2.1.

Determine the total number of memory transfers needed in each case, and compare this total to the number needed by the program of Figure 6.3.

6.29 A number of Multibus compatible peripherals are to be connected to a PDP-11 computer. A design for the bus-mapping circuit of Figure 6.18 is required. Give a suitable implementation for the part of the mapping circuit needed to enable Read and Write operations initiated by the CPU.

6.30 Repeat Problem 6.29 for the interrupt control signals. (Remember that, on the Unibus, a device must first become a bust master before transferring its interrupt vector.)

6.31 In some computers, the CPU responds only to the leading edge of the interrupt-request signal on one of its interrupt-request lines. What happens if two independent devices are connected to this line?

6.32 Consider the priority circuit on the S-100 bus, described in Section 6.6.2. A device requiring use of the bus asserts the HOLD* signal. When it receives pHLDA, it begins the priority arbitration sequence. Design a suitable circuit for this purpose, assuming that the priority of a device is defined by four ON/OFF switches.

6.33 Draw a timing diagram that illustrates the sequence of events during priority arbitration in the example described in Section 6.6.2. Assume that the two devices, A and B, are at opposite ends of the bus.

6.10 REFERENCES

6.1 Boberg, R.W.: Proposed Microcomputer System 796 Bus Standard, *Computer*, vol. 13, no. 10, pp. 89–105, Oct. 1980.
6.2 Kells, A.E., H. Fullmer, D.B. Gustavson, and G. Morrow: Standard Specification for S-100 Bus Interface Devices, *Computer*, vol. 12, no. 7, pp. 28–52, July 1979.
6.3 IEEE Standard Digital Interface for Programmable Instrumentation, *ANSI/IEEE* Standard 488, 1978.

CHAPTER SEVEN

ARITHMETIC

A basic operation in all digital computers is the addition or subtraction of two numbers. Such operations are provided at the machine instruction level. They are implemented, along with basic logic functions such as AND, OR, NOT, and EXCLUSIVE-OR, in the arithmetic and logic unit (ALU) subsystem of the CPU as mentioned in Chapters 1 and 4. These functions are normally performed by combinational logic circuitry. The operands are presented to the ALU as the outputs of two CPU registers, possibly via a bus. A typical arrangement was shown in Figure 4.1. The result is usually routed to another CPU register after an amount of time that permits the combinational logic to complete the computations. Modern integrated circuits permit these operations to be executed within the time allotted for a basic step in a hardwired CPU control sequencer or within the execution time of a microinstruction in a CPU implemented with microprogrammed control. Usually, an ALU operation is faster than a memory access operation. This means that an instruction that involves an ALU operation on operands that must be brought from memory does not require much more execution time than an instruction that only moves the contents of one memory location to another memory location.

Multiply and divide operations are comparatively more complex than either addition or subtraction. These operations are usually included in the basic instruction set. However, their execution times may be significantly slower than other instructions such as Add, Move, etc. This is because they are implemented as a sequence of addition and subtraction steps through the ALU, controlled by a microprogram. In high-performance computers, hardware multipliers and dividers are often used to increase the speed of arithmetic operations. Of course, as long as Add and Subtract are available as machine instructions, both multiply and divide operations can be supplied as software routines. These routines basically implement multiplication as a sequence of adds and shifts, and division as a sequence of subtracts and shifts, as will be explained.

Compared with arithmetic operations, logic operations are simple from the combinational circuit viewpoint. They require only independent boolean operations on individual bit positions of the operands, whereas carry-borrow lateral signals are required in arithmetic operations.

Before discussing details of the implementation of computer arithmetic, we will first need to discuss number-representation schemes. We start by presenting the representation for integers. In a later section of the chapter, the need for floating-point arithmetic in addition to the basic integer or fixed-point arithmetic will be explained. The implementation of multiply and divide operations on either fixed- or floating-point operands will also provide an excellent example of hardware-software trade-off issues.

7.1 NUMBER REPRESENTATIONS

The binary number system is the most conventional internal representation for numbers in digital computers. Consider an n-bit vector

$$B = b_{n-1} \cdots b_1 b_0$$

where $b_i = 0$ or 1 for $0 \leq i \leq n - 1$. This vector can represent positive integer values V in the range 0 to $2^n - 1$, where

$$V(B) = b_{n-1} \times 2^{n-1} + \cdots + b_1 \times 2^1 + b_0 \times 2^0$$

There are three widely used techniques for representing both positive and negative numbers:

- Sign and magnitude
- 1's complement
- 2's complement

In all three techniques, a bit b_n is added at the left end of the B vector. Bit b_n is 0 for positive numbers and 1 for negative numbers. Figure 7.1 illustrates all three of these signed-number representation systems. Note that the positive values have identical representations in all systems, while variations occur in the representation of negative values. In the sign and magnitude case, negative values are represented by changing b_3 to 1 in the B vector of the corresponding positive value. For example, $+5$ is represented by the B vector 0101, and -5 is represented by the B vector 1101. In the 1's-complement representation system, negative values are obtained by complementing each bit of the representation of the corresponding positive value. Therefore, the value -3 is obtained by bit complementing the vector 0011 to obtain 1100. Finally, in the 2's-complement system, a negative value is obtained by subtracting the corresponding positive value from 2^{n+1}. The same result is achieved by adding 1 to the 1's-complement

B		Values represented	
$b_3b_2b_1b_0$	Sign and magnitude	1's complement	2's complement
0 1 1 1	+7	+7	+7
0 1 1 0	+6	+6	+6
0 1 0 1	+5	+5	+5
0 1 0 0	+4	+4	+4
0 0 1 1	+3	+3	+3
0 0 1 0	+2	+2	+2
0 0 0 1	+1	+1	+1
0 0 0 0	+0	+0	+0
1 0 0 0	−0	−7	−8
1 0 0 1	−1	−6	−7
1 0 1 0	−2	−5	−6
1 0 1 1	−3	−4	−5
1 1 0 0	−4	−3	−4
1 1 0 1	−5	−2	−3
1 1 1 0	−6	−1	−2
1 1 1 1	−7	−0	−1

Figure 7.1 Binary, signed-integer representations.

representation of the desired negative value. In other words, to form a particular negative value in the 2's-complement system, we take the representation of the corresponding positive value, bit complement this value, and add 1. This assumes we know how to perform binary addition. We will explain the details in the next section.

Some final comments are pertinent before we proceed to show how to perform addition or subtraction in these representations. Note that there are distinct +0 and −0 representations in both the sign and magnitude and 1's-complement system, while there is only a +0 representation in the 2's-complement system. The value −8 is representable in the 2's-complement system, and it is not in the other systems. The sign and magnitude technique seems the most natural since we deal with sign and magnitude decimal values in hand computations. The 1's-complement system is easily related to this system, and the 2's-complement system seems unnatural. However, we will soon see that the 2's-complement system is the best choice (and the one most often used in computers) from the standpoint of the ease of implementation of both the add and subtract operations in logic circuitry.

7.2 ADDITION OF POSITIVE NUMBERS

In this section, and in the next section, we will be concerned only with positive numbers; hence, we will drop the sign-bit position from most of our discussions. Such numbers are called *unsigned* numbers. Consider adding two 1-bit numbers.

$$
\begin{array}{cccc}
0 & 1 & 0 & 1 \\
+\,0 & +\,0 & +\,1 & +\,1 \\
\hline
0 & 1 & 1 & \\
\end{array}
$$

Carry-out ⟋ 10   **Figure 7.2** Addition of 1-bit numbers.

The results are shown in Figure 7.2. The sum of 1 and 1 requires the 2-bit vector 10 to represent the value 2. We say that the *sum* is 0 and the *carry-out* is 1. These examples extend to the addition of multibit vectors in an obvious way. The operation is analogous to the usual hand computation with decimal numbers. We add bit pairs starting from the low-order (right) end of the bit vectors, propagating carries toward the high-order (left) end. The truth table for the sum and carry-out functions for adding two equally weighted bits x_i and y_i in vectors X and Y is shown in Figure 7.3. The figure also gives two-level AND-OR logic expressions for these functions, along with an example of addition. Note that each stage of the addition algorithm must be able to accommodate a *carry-in* bit. We shall use c_i to represent the carry-in to the ith stage and the carry-out from the $(i-1)$st stage.

A combinational logic implementation of the truth table for addition is shown in Figure 7.4a along with a convenient symbol to be used in the subsequent discussion. Other logic circuits can be used to realize these functions; for example, either NAND or NOR gates can be used. A cascaded connection of n ADDER blocks, as shown in Figure 7.4b, can be used to add two n-bit numbers. Since the carries propagate, or ripple, through this cascade, the configuration is called an *n-bit ripple-carry adder*. When the carry-out c_n from the *most significant bit* (MSB) position is equal to 1, there is an *overflow* from the

x_i	y_i	Carry-in c_i	Sum s_i	Carry-out c_{i+1}
0	0	0	0	0
0	0	1	1	0
0	1	0	1	0
0	1	1	0	1
1	0	0	1	0
1	0	1	0	1
1	1	0	0	1
1	1	1	1	1

$$
s_i = \bar{x}_i \bar{y}_i c_i + \bar{x}_i y_i \bar{c}_i + x_i \bar{y}_i \bar{c}_i + x_i y_i c_i
$$
$$
c_{i+1} = y_i c_i + x_i c_i + x_i y_i
$$

Example:

$$
\begin{array}{rcl}
X = & 7 = & 0\ 1\ 1\ 1 \\
+\,Y = & +\,6 = & +0\ 0\ 1\ 1 \quad 1\ 1\ 0\ 0\ 0 \\
\hline
Z = & 13 = & 1\ 1\ 0\ 1 \\
\end{array}
$$

Legend for stage i

x_i

y_i

Carry-out c_{i+1} s_i Carry-in c_i

Figure 7.3 Logic specification for a stage of binary addition.

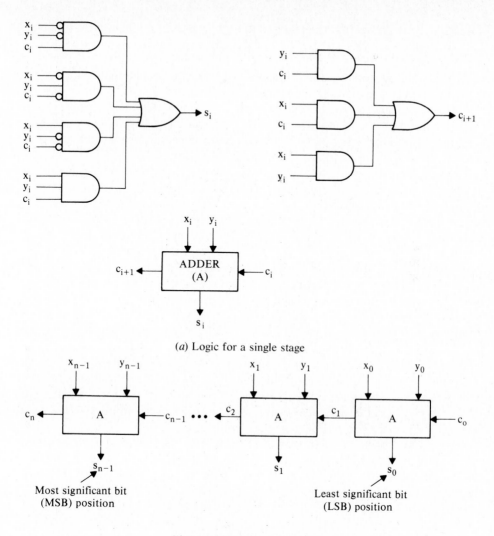

(a) Logic for a single stage

(b) An n-bit ripple-carry adder

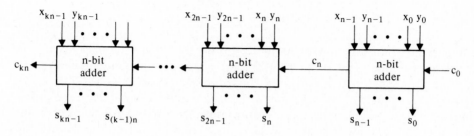

(c) Cascade of k n-bit adders

Figure 7.4 Logic for addition of binary vectors.

operation. This means that the result cannot be represented in an n-bit number. The carry-in c_0 into the *least significant bit* (LSB) position is 0 for the addition of two positive numbers but may be 0 or 1 in more general situations. For instance, in the previous section we stated that forming the 2's complement of a number involves adding 1 to the bit complement of the number. The input c_0 can be conveniently used to perform the +1 part of the operation. This allows complementation to be combined with addition. The convenience of that combination will become clearer in a later section on addition and subtraction of signed numbers in the 2's-complement representation.

Figure 7.4c shows k n-bit adders cascaded to form an adder capable of handling input vectors of length kn bits. This schematic is representative of a number of different addition situations. In some instances, k logic hardware adders are involved. However, the figure is also representative of the use of one n-bit hardware adder that is serially reused by software means to perform k n-bit additions. The simplest case is that of full hardware addition of two kn-bit words in the ALU of a CPU. If $n = k = 4$, the picture could represent a 16-bit adder implemented by a cascade of four 4-bit MSI adder chips. For $n = 32$, the picture could represent a multiple-precision addition operation in a 32-bit word-length computer using a 32-bit hardware adder. The parameter k, then, determines the precision. If $k = 1$, it is normal to say that a single-precision operation is being performed; if $k = 2$, double precision is being implemented. In this particular case, a single n-bit adder is used in a time sequence of k n-bit additions performed by software. The carry-out signal from each n-bit addition is stored in a flip-flop to be used as the carry-in signal to the next n-bit addition. This storage of the carry-out signal will also occur when implementing multiplication as a series of additions. We will present the details later.

This rather extended discussion of Figure 7.4c is intended to indicate that an n-bit adder with both carry-in (c_0) and carry-out (c_n) signals is an important building block in all arithmetic operations. With this motivation, we will devote the next section to a discussion of the logic design of fast n-bit adders.

7.3 LOGIC DESIGN FOR FAST ADDERS

The n-bit ripple-carry adder shown in Figure 7.4b may have too much delay in developing its outputs $c_n, s_{n-1}, \ldots, s_1$, and s_0. Whether the delay associated with any particular implementation technology is acceptable can be decided only in the context of the speed of other CPU components and the main memory cycle time. Delay through a network of logic gates is clearly dependent on the electronic technology (see Appendix A) used in fabricating the basic gates and the number of gates in the paths from inputs to outputs. After a particular technology (often called a logic family) is specified, the delay associated with any combinational logic network constructed from gates in that technology can be determined by adding up the number of logic-gate delays along the longest path through the network. In the case of the ripple-carry adder, the longest signal propagation is clearly from the inputs x_0, y_0, c_0 at the LSB-position stage along the cascade toward the left to the outputs c_n and s_{n-1} at the MSB-position stage.

In the introductory remarks of this chapter, it was suggested that addition can be performed within the execution time of a microinstruction. This time might typically be 50 to 100 ns in a 16-bit word-length computer. Now consider the delay of the n-bit ripple-carry adder of Figure 7.4b. Suppose that the delay from c_i to c_{i+1} of any ADDER block is 10 ns. An n-bit addition can be performed in the time it takes the carry signal to reach the c_{n-1} position, followed by the delay in developing s_{n-1}. Assuming this last delay is 15 ns, a 16-bit addition takes $15 \times 10 + 15 = 165$ ns.

There are two approaches that can be taken to reduce this 165-ns delay to the desired 50- to 100-ns range. The first approach, which is suggested by our earlier discussion, is to use faster electronic circuit technology in implementing the same ripple-carry logic design of Figure 7.4b. The second approach to reducing the n-bit adder delay is to use a logic network structure different from that shown in Figure 7.4b.

Logic structures for fast adder design must address the problem of speeding up the formation of the carry signals. Obviously, it is important to reduce the time required to form the c_i inputs toward the MSB end of the adder. The usual two-level logic expressions for s_i (sum) and c_{i+1} (carry-out) from Figure 7.3 are

$$s_i = \bar{x}_i \bar{y}_i c_i + \bar{x}_i y_i \bar{c}_i + x_i \bar{y}_i \bar{c}_i + x_i y_i c_i$$

$$\text{and } c_{i+1} = y_i c_i + x_i c_i + x_i y_i$$

Factoring the second of these into

$$c_{i+1} = x_i y_i + (x_i + y_i) c_i$$

and defining a *generate* function

$$G_i = x_i y_i$$

and a *propagate* function

$$P_i = x_i + y_i$$

we can write

$$c_{i+1} = G_i + P_i c_i$$

Note that all the G_i and P_i functions for $0 \le i \le n - 1$ can be formed independently and in parallel in one logic-gate delay after the X and Y vectors are available as parallel inputs to the n-bit adder. Expanding c_i in terms of $i - 1$ subscripted variables and substituting into the c_{i+1} equation, we obtain

$$c_{i+1} = G_i + P_i G_{i-1} + P_i P_{i-1} c_{i-1}$$

Continuing with this type of expansion, the final expression for any carry variable is

$$c_{i+1} = G_i + P_i G_{i-1} + P_i P_{i-1} G_{i-2} + \cdots + P_i P_{i-1} \cdots P_1 G_0 + P_i P_{i-1} \cdots P_0 c_0$$

Thus all carries can be obtained three logic-gate delays after the input operands X, Y, and c_0 are available, because one gate delay is needed to develop all P_i and G_i signals, followed by two gate delays in the AND-OR circuit for c_{i+1}. After another three gate delays (one delay to invert the c_i's and two delays to form s_i as shown earlier), all sum bits are available. Therefore, independent of n, the n-bit addition process requires only six levels of logic.

A practical problem with this approach is that of gate fan-in constraints. The expression for c_{i+1} requires $i + 2$ inputs to the largest AND term and $i + 2$ inputs to the OR term. Due to electronic circuit considerations, logic gate fan-in is usually restricted to eight or less. Let us then consider the design of a 4-bit adder as a basic unit. The function

$$c_4 = G_3 + P_3G_2 + P_3P_2G_1 + P_3P_2P_1G_0 + P_3P_2P_1P_0c_0$$

requires a fan-in of five for the basic gates, and needs two gate delays after the G_i and P_i functions are available. Using four of these connected as in Figure 7.4c (with $n = 4$), a 16-bit adder is obtained that requires an amount of time equal to 12 gate delays. This total is composed of one delay for G_i and P_i formation, plus two each for c_4, c_8, c_{12}, and c_{15} and a final three for s_{15}. All other sum bits and c_{16} are available at or before the time for s_{15}. In our earlier discussion that involved absolute time values, an implied gate delay of 5 ns was used because we let a two-level logic function (c_{i+1} for an ADDER function) have a delay of 10 ns. In those terms, this latest 16-bit adder requires 60 ns to develop all outputs as compared to the 165 ns required by the original Figure 7.4b design. This is well within the previously stated 50- to 100-ns objective for the addition operation. Fast adders that form carry functions as in this simple example are called *carry lookahead adders*. Note that in the above 16-bit adder example, we have assumed that the carries inside of each block are formed by lookahead circuits. However, they still ripple between blocks.

For longer word lengths and in higher-performance computers, it is necessary to speed up the addition operation even further. This may be done by applying the lookahead technique to the carry signals between blocks. Thus a second level of lookahead is employed. We will illustrate this procedure by redesigning the above 16-bit adder. Suppose that each of the 4-bit adder blocks provides two new output functions defined as G_k^I and P_k^I, where $k = 0$ for the first 4-bit block, $k = 1$ for the second 4-bit block, etc. In the first block,

$$P_0^I = P_3P_2P_1P_0$$

and
$$G_0^I = G_3 + P_3G_2 + P_3P_2G_1 + P_3P_2P_1G_0$$

In words, if we say that G_i and P_i determine whether or not bit stage i generates or propagates a carry, then G_k^I and P_k^I determine whether or not block k generates or propagates a carry. With these new functions available, it is not necessary to wait for carries to ripple through blocks. For example, c_{16} can be formed as

$$c_{16} = G_3^I + P_3^IG_2^I + P_3^IP_2^IG_1^I + P_3^IP_2^IP_1^IG_0^I + P_3^IP_2^IP_1^IP_0^Ic_0$$

using gates with a fan-in of five. The delay in developing c_{16} is two gate delays more than the time needed to develop the G_k^l and P_k^l functions. The latter require two and one gate delays, respectively, after the generation of G_i and P_i. Therefore c_{16} is available five gate delays after X, Y, and c_0 are applied as inputs. Earlier, using only G_i and P_i functions, c_{16} required nine gate delays.

Now consider that longer adders are constructed by cascading 16-bit basic blocks built using G_k^l and P_k^l functions as well as G_i and P_i functions. Then the total adder delay will be about half what it would have been if the longer adders had been built by cascading 4-bit basic blocks, using only G_i and P_i functions.

7.4 ADDITION AND SUBTRACTION OF POSITIVE AND NEGATIVE NUMBERS

In Section 7.1 we discussed three methods for representing positive and negative numbers, hereafter simply called *signed* numbers. These methods differ only in the way in which they represent negative values. Their relative merits from the standpoint of ease of implementation of arithmetic operations can be determined by means of a few simple examples. The conclusions that can be drawn are as follows. The sign and magnitude method is the simplest representation but also the most awkward for addition and subtraction operations. The 1's-complement method is somewhat better. However, the 2's-complement system, which seems rather unnatural from a representation standpoint, is actually the best method in terms of implementation of addition and subtraction operations.

Let us discuss why the 2's-complement representation is a good choice. First, consider addition modulo N (mod N). A helpful graphical device for the description of addition mod N of positive integers is a circle with the N values 0 through $N - 1$ marked along its perimeter, as shown in Figure 7.5a. To treat some specific examples, we will choose $N = 16$. The operation $(7 + 4)$ mod 16 yields the value 11. To perform this operation graphically, locate 7 mod 16 = 7 on the circle and then step off 4 units in the clockwise direction to arrive at the answer 11. As a second example, consider $(9 + 14)$ mod 16 = 7, which is modeled on the circle by locating 9 mod 16 = 9 and stepping off 14 units in the clockwise direction to arrive at the answer 7. This graphical technique works for the computation of $(a + b)$ mod 16 for any positive numbers a and b; that is, locate a mod 16 and step off b units in the clockwise direction to arrive at $(a + b)$ mod 16.

The n-bit positive-value adders of the previous two sections compute $S = (X + Y)$ mod 2^n, where X and Y are in the range 0, 1, 2, . . . , $2^n - 1$. The overflow value c_n is 1 if $X + Y \geq 2^n$.

Now consider a different interpretation of the mod 16 circle. Let the values 0 through 15 be represented by the 4-bit binary vectors 0000, 0001, . . . , 1111, according to the binary number system, and then reinterpret these binary vectors to represent signed numbers in the range -8 through $+7$ in the 2's-complement method (see Figure 7.1), as shown in Figure 7.5b.

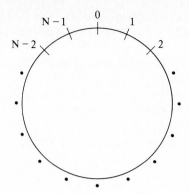

(*a*) Circle representation of integers mod N

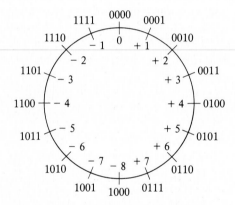

(*b*) Mod 16 system for 2's-complement numbers

Figure 7.5 Modular number systems and the 2's complement system.

Let us apply the mod 16 addition technique discussed above to the simple example of adding $+7$ to -3. The 2's-complement representation for these numbers is 0111 and 1101, respectively. To add these numbers, locate 0111 on the circle of Figure 7.5*b*. Then step off 1101 (13) steps in the clockwise direction to arrive at 0100, which corresponds to $+4$. Alternatively, if we use one of the adder circuits for positive numbers, discussed earlier, we obtain

$$
\begin{array}{ccccc}
 & 0 & 1 & 1 & 1 \\
+ & 1 & 1 & 0 & 1 \\
\hline
\text{Carry-out} \longrightarrow 1 & 0 & 1 & 0 & 0 \\
\end{array}
$$

Note that if we ignore the carry-out from the fourth bit position in this addition, we obtain the correct answer. In fact, this is always the case.

We now state the rules governing addition and subtraction of n-bit signed numbers using the 2's-complement representation system.

1. To perform *addition* of two numbers, add their representations in an n-bit adder, ignoring the carry-out signal from the MSB position. The sum will be the algebraically correct value in the 2's-complement representation as long as the answer is in the range -2^{n-1} through $+2^{n-1} - 1$.

2. To perform *subtraction* of two numbers X and Y, that is, to perform $X - Y$, form the 2's complement of Y and then add it to X as in rule 1. Again, if the answer is in the range -2^{n-1} through $+2^{n-1} - 1$, the result will be the algebraically correct value in the 2's-complement representation system.

Figure 7.6 shows some examples of addition and subtraction. In all these 4-bit examples the answers fall into the representable range of -8 through $+7$. When answers do not fall within the representable range, we say that an *arithmetic overflow* has occurred. Section 7.4.2 will deal with such situations. The four addition operations (*a*) through (*d*) in Figure 7.6 follow rule 1 above, and the six subtraction operations (*e*) through (*j*) follow rule 2. Note that the subtraction operation requires the subtrahend (bottom) value to be 2's complemented before the addition is performed. In the logic circuit implementa-

(*a*)		0 0 1 0	(+2)		(*b*)			0 1 0 0	(+4)					
	+	0 0 1 1	(+3)			+	1 0 1 0	(−6)						
		0 1 0 1	(+5)				1 1 1 0	(−2)						

(*c*)		1 0 1 1	(−5)		(*d*)		0 1 1 1	(+7)						
	+	1 1 1 0	(−2)			+	1 1 0 1	(−3)						
		1 0 0 1	(−7)				0 1 0 0	(+4)						

(*e*) 1 1 0 1 (−3) − 1 0 0 1 (−7) => 1 1 0 1 + 0 1 1 1 = 0 1 0 0 (+4)

(*f*) 0 0 1 0 (+2) − 0 1 0 0 (+4) => 0 0 1 0 + 1 1 0 0 = 1 1 1 0 (−2)

(*g*) 0 1 1 0 (+6) − 0 0 1 1 (+3) => 0 1 1 0 + 1 1 0 1 = 0 0 1 1 (+3)

(*h*) 1 0 0 1 (−7) − 1 0 1 1 (−5) => 1 0 0 1 + 0 1 0 1 = 1 1 1 0 (−2)

(*i*) 1 0 0 1 (−7) − 0 0 0 1 (+1) => 1 0 0 1 + 1 1 1 1 = 1 0 0 0 (−8)

(*j*) 0 0 1 0 (+2) − 1 1 0 1 (−3) => 0 0 1 0 + 0 0 1 1 = 0 1 0 1 (+5)

Figure 7.6 2's-complement ADD and SUBTRACT operations.

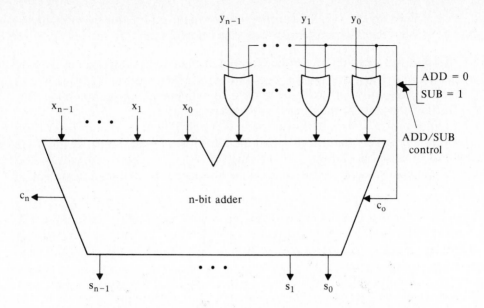

(a) An n-bit binary adder with 2's-complement ADD/SUBTRACT control

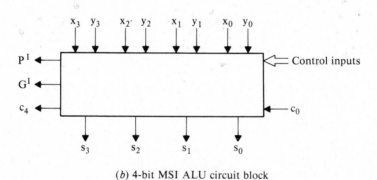

(b) 4-bit MSI ALU circuit block

Figure 7.7 Binary addition-subtraction logic networks.

tion of subtraction, this complementation can be combined with the addition operation as shown in Figure 7.7a. The ADD/SUB control wire is set to 0 for addition. This allows the Y vector to be applied unchanged to one of the adder inputs along with a carry-in signal c_0 of 0. When the ADD/SUB control wire is set to 1, signifying subtraction, the Y vector is 1's complemented (that is, bit complemented) by the EX-OR gates, and c_0 is set to 1 to complete the 2's complementation of Y. Note that 2's complementing a negative value, as in Figure 7.6e, is done in exactly the same manner as 2's complementing a positive value.

The logical simplicity and speed of performing either addition or subtraction of signed numbers in 2's-complement representation is the reason why this number representation is used in the ALU subsystems of most modern computers. It might seem that the 1's-complement representation would be just as good as the 2's-complement system for use in a combined addition-subtraction logic network. However, although complementation is easy, the result obtained after the add operation is not always correct. In fact, the carry-out c_n cannot be ignored. If $c_n = 1$, then 1 must be added to the result to make it correct; otherwise, if $c_n = 0$, the result as obtained is correct. The requirement for this "correction cycle," which is conditional upon the carry-out from the add operation, means that addition and subtraction cannot be implemented as conveniently in the 1's-complement system as in the 2's-complement system.

7.4.1 A 4-Bit MSI ALU Circuit

We have now discussed carry lookahead logic design for fast binary adders and the way in which such adders can be controlled to perform either addition or subtraction on signed n-bit numbers. Since these operations are basic to all computers, a number of MSI circuits are commercially available as building blocks for ALU design. The input and output variables for a typical 4-bit circuit are shown in Figure 7.7b. The three internal carries c_1, c_2, and c_3, as well as the carry-out c_4, are generated by lookahead logic. A number of these circuits can be cascaded as shown in Figure 7.4c to form adders of any desired length. If the carries c_8, c_{12}, etc., in such a cascade are not generated fast enough for some application, then the use of a second level of lookahead is facilitated by the provision of block propagate and generate variables P^I and G^I. External logic, using these variables, can directly generate the carries c_8, c_{12}, etc., faster than if they simply ripple between the blocks as in the cascade connection. The control inputs determine which function is performed on the input vectors X and Y to generate the output vector S. The versatility of these circuits as ALU building blocks is enhanced by inclusion of the operations AND, OR, EX-OR, etc., as well as addition and subtraction.

7.4.2 Overflow in Integer Arithmetic

When adding unsigned numbers, the carry-out c_n serves as the overflow indicator. However, the case of signed numbers is slightly more involved. If we try to add the numbers $+7$ and $+4$ in the mod 16 adder of the previous section, the output vector S will be 1011, which is the code for -5, an obviously wrong result. The carry-out signal from the MSB position will be 0. Similarly, if we try to add -4 and -6, we get $S = +6$, another obvious error, and in this case the carry-out signal is 1. The addition of numbers with different signs clearly cannot cause overflow errors. The above discussion leads to the following conclusions:

1. The carry-out signal from the sign-bit position is not a sufficient indicator of overflow in the case of signed-number addition.
2. The only possibility for overflow is when both operands have the same sign.

It is readily seen that an overflow has occurred whenever the sign of S does not agree with the signs of X and Y when the signs of X and Y are the same. In an n-bit adder, we can define an overflow signal Overflow by the logical expression

$$\text{Overflow} = x_{n-1}y_{n-1}\overline{s_{n-1}} + \overline{x_{n-1}}\,\overline{y_{n-1}}s_{n-1}$$

For the case of a combined addition-subtraction unit, such as that of Figure 7.7a, the variable y_{n-1} in the Overflow expression should be taken from the output of the leftmost EX-OR gate. This will lead to the correct indication of overflow from either addition or subtraction.

Occurrence of an overflow is an important condition to detect in any computation. It is customary to dedicate a condition code flag as its indicator. It is possible to have this flag cause an interrupt when an add or subtract instruction results in an overflow. It is then the programmer's responsibility to decide on subsequent action.

7.5 ARITHMETIC AND BRANCHING CONDITIONS

We have now discussed addition of unsigned numbers, as well as addition and subtraction of signed numbers, in the 2's-complement representation. At this point it is useful to return to the discussion of condition codes and conditional branches presented in Chapter 2 (Section 2.5.6).

That discussion was based on the PDP-11 example. Its four condition code flags are set and cleared by arithmetic operations as follows:

N   Set to 1 if the result is negative; otherwise, cleared to 0.
Z   Set to 1 if the result is 0; otherwise, cleared to 0.
V   Set to 1 if arithmetic overflow occurs; otherwise, cleared to 0.
C   For an add operation, C is set to 1 if a carry-out results; otherwise, it is cleared to 0. For a subtract operation, C is set to 1 if no carry-out results; otherwise, it is set to 0.

For purposes of this discussion, it can be assumed that addition and subtraction are performed as indicated by the logic unit of Figure 7.7a. The carry-out signal referred to in the definition of the C flag is synonymous with the signal c_n in that figure. The V flag is set according to the Overflow expression given in Section 7.4.2.

Let us now consider how conditional branch instructions make use of the condition code flags. In some of these instructions, the branch condition is determined by the value of a single flag. For example, the instructions BNE

(Branch if Not Equal to 0) and BEQ (Branch if EQual to 0) test the Z flag in an obvious way.

Other instructions involve the testing of two or more flags. Consider the BLOS (Branch if LOwer or Same) instruction. It is normally used after a Compare instruction, which compares two unsigned integers. The branch is taken if the first operand is smaller than or equal to the second. The comparison is done by subtracting the second operand from the first. The C flag is set to 1 if no carry occurs. By trying a few examples, it is easy to see that no carry occurs when the second operand is larger than the first, and a carry occurs when the second operand is smaller. When both operands are the same, a carry occurs, but then the Z flag is set to 1 because the result is 0. Therefore, the required branch condition is $C + Z = 1$.

Consider now a similar comparison dealing with signed numbers. In this case, the BLE (Branch if Less than or Equal) instruction should be used instead of BLOS. The result of the comparison will be negative if the first operand is less than the second. This is one of the conditions for which the branch should occur. Therefore, it would seem that $N + Z = 1$ is the branch condition for the BLE instruction. This is sufficient if arithmetic overflow does not occur when the subtraction is performed. However, if overflow occurs when comparing a large positive number to a large negative number, then the sign of the result will be opposite to what it should be. To obtain the proper branch condition in this case, the complement of the N flag should be tested. Therefore, the complete branch condition for the BLE instruction is $(N \oplus V) + Z = 1$.

Another important aspect of condition code flags is the role of the C flag in performing multiple-precision arithmetic. Consider a typical task of adding two operands, each occupying several words in memory. The required addition can be done by a program loop which adds individual words in successive iterations. The C flag must be preserved from one iteration to the next in order to propagate the carries through the complete addition operation. A problem would arise if the C flag were altered by instructions other than the Add instruction in the loop. For example, either an Increment or a Decrement instruction might be used to manipulate a loop counter variable at the end of each iteration. Therefore, these instructions should not modify the C flag.

Finally, we should note that the way in which condition code flags are affected and tested by various instructions may differ from one computer to another. A complete listing for the PDP-11 machine is given in Appendix B.

7.6 MULTIPLICATION OF POSITIVE NUMBERS

The usual "paper-and-pencil" algorithm for multiplication of integers represented in any positional number system is illustrated in Figure 7.8a for the binary system, assuming positive 4-bit operands. The product of two n-digit numbers can be accommodated in $2n$ digits, so the product in this example fits into 8 bits,

```
      1 1 0 1        (13) Multiplicand M
    × 1 0 1 1        (11) Multiplier Q
      1 1 0 1
    1 1 0 1
  0 0 0 0
1 1 0 1
1 0 0 0 1 1 1 1      (143) Product P
```

(*a*) "Paper-and-pencil" multiplication algorithm

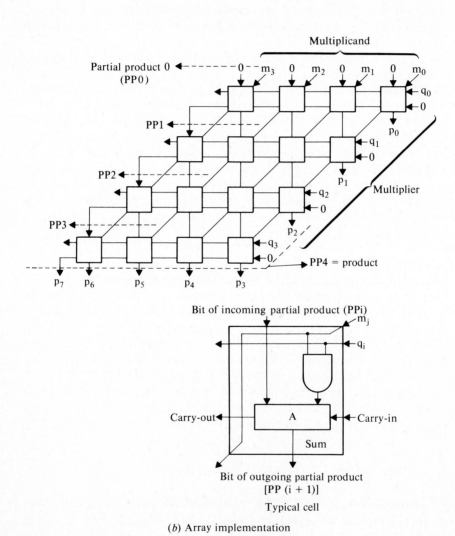

(*b*) Array implementation

Figure 7.8 Array multiplication of positive binary operands.

as shown. In the binary system, multiplication of the multiplicand by 1 bit of the multiplier is easy. If the multiplier bit is 1, the multiplicand is entered in the appropriately shifted position to be added with other shifted multiplicands to form the product. If the multiplier bit is 0, then 0s are entered as in the third row of the example. It is possible to implement positive operand binary multiplication in a purely combinational two-dimensional logic array, as shown in Figure 7.8b. The main component in each cell is an Adder circuit. The AND gate in any cell determines whether or not a multiplicand bit m_j is added to the incoming partial-product bit, based on the value of the multiplier bit q_i. Each row i, $0 \leq i \leq 3$, of this array adds the multiplicand (appropriately shifted) to the incoming partial product PPi to generate the outgoing partial product PP$(i + 1)$ if $q_i = 1$. If $q_i = 0$, PPi is passed vertically downward unchanged. PP0 is obviously all 0s, and PP4 is the desired product. The multiplicand is shifted left one position per row by the diagonal signal path.

Although the above combinational multiplier is quite easy to understand, it is usually impractical to use in computers because it uses a large number of gates and performs only one function. Many computers that provide multiplication in the basic machine instruction set implement it by a sequence of operations, as shown in Figure 7.9. The block diagram in part (a) of the figure describes a suitable hardware arrangement. This circuit performs multiplication by using the single adder n times to implement the addition being performed spatially by the n rows of ripple-carry adders of Figure 7.8b. The combination of registers A and Q holds PPi during the time that multiplier bit q_i is generating the signal ADD/NOADD. This signal controls the addition of the multiplicand M to PPi to generate PP$(i + 1)$. There are n cycles needed to compute the product. The partial product grows in length by 1 bit per cycle from the initial vector (PP0) of n 0s in register A. The carry-out from the adder is stored in flip-flop C shown at the left end of register A. At the start, the multiplier is loaded into register Q, the multiplicand into register M, and C and A are set to 0. At the end of each cycle, C, A, and Q are shifted right one bit position to allow for growth of the partial product as the multiplier is shifted out of register Q. Because of this shifting, multiplier bit q_i appears at the LSB position of Q to generate the ADD/NOADD signal at the correct time, starting with q_0 during the first cycle, q_1 during the second, etc. After use, the multiplier bits can be discarded. This is accomplished by the right-shift operation. Note that the carry-out from the adder is the leftmost bit of PP$(i + 1)$, and it must be held in the C flip-flop to be shifted right with the contents of A and Q. After n cycles, the high-order half of the product is held in register A and the low-order half is in register Q. The multiplication example of Figure 7.8a is shown in Figure 7.9b as it would be performed by the above hardware arrangement.

We can now relate the components of Figure 7.9a to Figure 4.1. Assume that the multiply sequence is to be hardwired as a machine instruction. Furthermore, assume that the multiplier and multiplicand are in R2 and R3, respectively, and that the two-word product is to be left in R1 and R2. First, the multiplicand is moved into register Y. Thus register Y corresponds to M, and R1 and R2

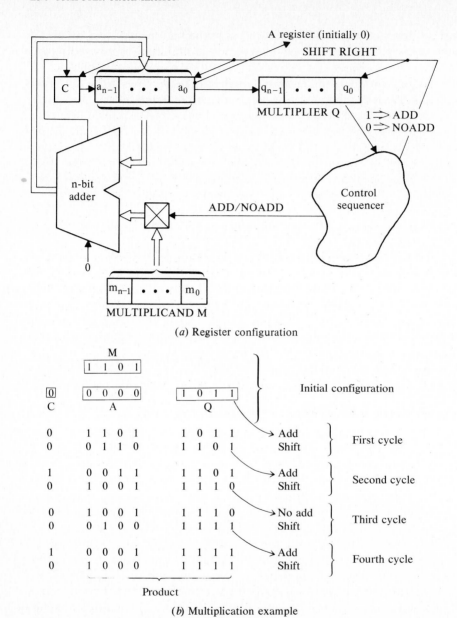

(a) Register configuration

(b) Multiplication example

Figure 7.9 Sequential circuit binary multiplier.

correspond to A and Q in Figure 7.9a. Connections must be made so that R1 and R2 can be right-shifted as a two-word combination. A transfer from Z to R1 is made after each cycle. The C bit in Figure 7.9a is actually the carry flag in the condition codes (for example, see Figure 3.2). It must be connectable to R1 for shifting operations as in Figure 7.9a. We will not give the register transfer sequencing for multiplication at the level used in Chapter 4, since it should now be reasonably clear how it can be done.

Since we assumed at the start of this discussion that the multiply operation is hardwired, the component called Control sequencer is implemented by the general instruction execution sequencer as shown in Chapter 4. This results in a relatively complicated single machine instruction. If the adder has a delay of about 50 ns, and the control settings and shift operations associated with each cycle take another 50 ns, then a hardwired multiply operation in a 16-bit word-length computer might take 1.5 to 2 μs. Since 250- to 500-ns memory cycle times for instruction and operand fetch and store are common, this multiply instruction time is not unreasonable.

Even though most computers include multiplication and division operations in the machine instruction set, it is instructive to see how multiplication can be programmed using the more basic Add and Shift instructions. Therefore, we will give a program for the PDP-11 that performs multiplication. This example serves two purposes. First, we will be able to develop a software speed value to compare to the 1.5- to 2-μs hardware speed given above, and second, we will illustrate the use of shift operations and the associated C-bit manipulation. Although we are using the specific instruction set of the PDP-11, the same general type of instruction capability exists in any computer. It is convenient to program the multiply function in the PDP-11 by inspecting the high-order bits of the multiplier first and accumulating partial products in the reverse order to that discussed previously. This shows that the order of accumulating partial products is unimportant. The register arrangement and shifting directions are shown in Figure 7.10. Let R1 (multiplier) and R2 (multiplicand) contain the two operands

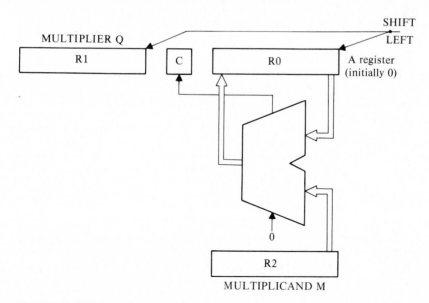

Figure 7.10 PDP-11 register arrangement for software multiply.

at the start. Registers R0 and R3 are also used in the operation. R0 is initially 0 and will finally contain the low-order end of the product, while R3 is used as a counter. The high-order end of the product will be in register R1 at the end of the multiplication operation and the original multiplier will have been destroyed. The complete program for multiplication is shown in Figure 7.11, along with enough comments to make it self-explanatory.

Assuming, as a very rough estimate, that each instruction of the seven-instruction loop takes 1 μs (including instruction fetch) and that half the multiplier bits are 1, the program takes approximately $6 \times 1 \times 16 = 96$ μs for execution. This is much more than the 1.5 to 2 μs estimated earlier for execution of the hardwired multiply instruction.

We have considered both hardwired and software implementations of multiplication. Such operations can also be conveniently implemented using microprogrammed control, which was discussed in Chapter 5. A micropro-grammed implementation of multiplication would closely resemble the organization of the program in Figure 7.11. This approach leads to a significant gain in

	CLR	R0	Clear register R_0 and load register R_3 with −16 so that it can act as the cycle counter.
	MOV	#-16.,R3	
MLOOP:	ASL	R0	The ASL (Arithmetic Shift Left) instruction shifts the contents of R_0 (low-order half of partial product) left one bit position and shifts the MSB of R_0 into the C bit. The LSB of R_0 is set to 0. the ROL (Rotate Left) instruction rotates the contents of R_1 and the C bit by one bit position. The old contents of C are moved into the LSB of R_1, and the old contents of the MSB of R_1 are moved into C. The combination of ASL and ROL have thus shifted the (R_1, R_0) pair left one position, placing the old MSB of R_1 into C.
	ROL	R1	
	BCC	NOADD	The multiplier bit to be checked (first q_{n-1}, then q_{n-2}, etc.) is now in C, and the instruction BCC causes a branch around the add operation if C is O.
	ADD	R2,R0	If C = 1, the multiplicand in R_2 is added into the low-order end of the partial product in R_0. Any carry-out that goes into C must be added to the high-order half of the partial product. This is done by the ADC instruction which adds the contents of C to the LSB position of R_1. Note that this process will never damage the unused portion of the multiplier in R_1 because the very first time that (R_1,R_0) is shifted left, a 0 is placed in the LSB position of R_1, and this creates enough space for any later encroachment by the partial product.
	ADC	R1	
NOADD:	INC	R3	The counter is incremented, and when 16 cycles are completed, the BNE (Branch if Not Equal to 0) instruction does not cause a branch back to MLOOP and the program terminates.
	BNE	MLOOP	
	HALT		

Figure 7.11 PDP-11 program for 16-bit positive-number multiplication.

speed with little increase in the required hardware. It is commonly used in modern computers.

7.7 SIGNED-OPERAND MULTIPLICATION

Multiplication of signed operands generating a double-length product in the 2's-complement number system requires a few further remarks about that representation. We will not discuss multiplication in the other representations because it reduces to the multiplication of positive operands already discussed. The accumulation of partial products by adding versions of the multiplicand as selected by the multiplier bits is still the general strategy.

Let us first consider the case of a positive multiplier and a negative multiplicand. When we add a negative multiplicand to a partial product, we must extend the sign-bit value of the multiplicand to the left as far as the extent of the eventual product. Consider the example shown in Figure 7.12, where the 5-bit signed operand −13 (multiplicand) is multiplied by +11 (multiplier) to get the 10-bit product −143. The sign extension of the multiplicand is shown underlined. To see why this sign-extension operation is correct, consider the following argument. The extension of a positive number is obviously achieved by the addition of zeros at the left end. For the case of negative numbers, consider Figure 7.5. It is easily seen by scanning around the mod 16 circle in the counterclockwise direction from the code for 0 that if 5-bit, 6-bit, 7-bit, etc., negative numbers were written out, they would be derived correctly by extending the given 4-bit codes by 1s to the left. This sign extension must be done by any hardware or software implementation of the multiply operation.

We will now consider the case of negative multipliers. A straightforward solution is to form the 2's complement of both the multiplier and the multiplicand and proceed as in the case of a positive multiplier. This is possible, of course, since complementation of both operands does not change the value or the sign of the product. Another technique that works correctly for negative numbers in the 2's-complement representation is to proceed as follows. Add shifted versions of the multiplicand, properly sign-extended, just as in the case of positive multipliers, for all 1 bits of the multiplier to the right of the sign bit. Then add −1 × multiplicand, properly shifted, as the contribution to the product determined by the 1 in the sign-bit position of the multiplier. The sign position is thus viewed as the same as the other positions, except that it has a

```
                    1  0  0  1  1   (−13)
                 ×  0  1  0  1  1   (+11)
      1  1  1  1  1  1  0  0  1  1
      1  1  1  1  1  0  0  1  1
      0  0  0  0  0  0  0  0
      1  1  1  0  0  1  1
      0  0  0  0  0  0
      ─────────────────────────────
      1  1  0  1  1  1  0  0  0  1   (−143)
```

Figure 7.12 Sign extension of negative multiplicand.

negative weight. The justification for this procedure will be discussed more fully later in this section.

A powerful direct algorithm for signed-number multiplication is the Booth algorithm. It generates a $2n$-bit product and treats both positive and negative numbers uniformly. Consider a multiplication operation in which a positive multiplier has a single block of 1s with at least one 0 at each end, for example, 0011110. To derive the product, we could add four appropriately shifted versions of the multiplicand as in the standard procedure. However, the number of required operations can be reduced by observing that a multiplier in this form can be regarded as the difference of two numbers as follows:

$$
\begin{array}{ll}
0\ 1\ 0\ 0\ 0\ 0\ 0 & (32) \\
-\ 0\ 0\ 0\ 0\ 0\ 1\ 0 & (2) \\
\hline
0\ 0\ 1\ 1\ 1\ 1\ 0 & (30)
\end{array}
$$

This suggests generating the product by one addition and one subtraction operation. In particular, in the above case, adding $2^5 \times$ multiplicand and subtracting $2^1 \times$ multiplicand gives the desired result.

For convenience in later discussions, we will represent the standard scheme by writing the multiplier as $0 \quad 0 +1 +1 +1 +1 \quad 0$, and the new recoding scheme by writing the multiplier as $0 +1 \quad 0 \quad 0 \quad 0 -1 \quad 0$. Note that in the new scheme $-1 \times$ (shifted multiplicand) is selected at $0 \to 1$ boundaries and $+1 \times$ (shifted multiplicand) is selected at $1 \to 0$ boundaries as the multiplier is scanned from right to left. Figure 7.13 illustrates the two schemes. This clearly extends to any number of blocks of 1s in a multiplier including the situation where a single 1 is considered a block. See Figure 7.14 for another example.

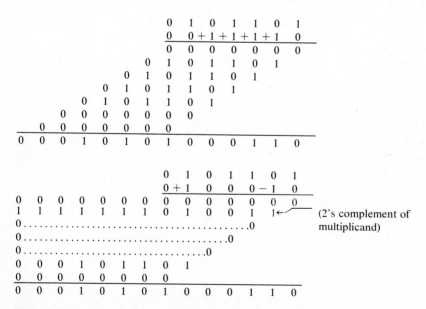

Figure 7.13 Normal and Booth multiplication schemes.

0	0	1	0	1	1	0	0	1	1	1	0	1	0	1	1	0	0
0	+1	−1	+1	0	−1	0	+1	0	0	−1	+1	−1	+1	0	−1	0	0

Figure 7.14 Booth recoding of a multiplier.

Until now we have shown positive multipliers. Since there is at least one 0 at the left end of any multiplier, a $+1$ operation can be matched to the left of every -1 operation to preserve the correctness of the operation. It is also true that if we apply the method to a negative multiplier, we get the correct answer. An example is given in Figure 7.15. To show the correctness of this technique we need to introduce a property of the negative-number representation in the 2's-complement system. If

$$X = 1\ x_{n-2}x_{n-3} \cdots x_1 x_0$$

is an n-bit negative number, its value is given by

$$V(X) = -2^{n-1} + x_{n-2} \times 2^{n-2} + x_{n-3} \times 2^{n-3} + \cdots + x_1 \times 2^1 + x_0 \times 2^0$$

This can be checked by applying it to some of the codes in Figure 7.1; for example,

$$V(1011) = -2^3 + 0 + 2^1 + 2^0 = -5$$

$$V(1110) = -2^3 + 2^2 + 2^1 + 0 = -2$$

and so forth. Consider that X is a multiplier. If X has no zeros, then $X = 11 \cdots 11$, and $V(X) = -1$. Applying the above Booth scheme for recoding the multiplier, we interpret X as $00 \cdots 0\ -1$. Then the product is computed as $-1 \times$ multiplicand, which is correct. On the other hand, if X has at least one 0, let the leftmost 0 be in the x_k position. The form of X is then $X = 11 \cdots 10x_{k-1}x_{k-2} \cdots x_0$. After the recoded version of the rightmost $k + 1$ bits of X has been applied to the selection of appropriately shifted versions of the multiplicand, and these summands have been added together, the partial product (PP) at that point is correct. In other words, PP $= (0x_{k-1}x_{k-2} \cdots x_0) \times$ multiplicand has been correctly computed according to our interpretation of the computation of the value of X. It remains to compute the $(1_{n-1}1_{n-2} \cdots 1_{k+1}) \times$ multiplicand portion of the multiplication, call it PP',

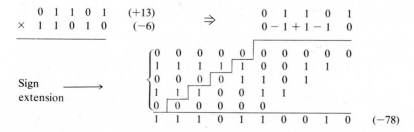

Figure 7.15 Booth multiplication with a negative multiplier.

Multiplier		Version of multiplicand
Bit i	Bit i-1	selected by bit i
0	0	$0 \times M$
0	1	$+1 \times M$
1	0	$-1 \times M$
1	1	$0 \times M$

Figure 7.16 Booth multiplier recoding table.

and add it to PP to derive the product. Algebraically, this means we should compute $PP' = (-2^{n-1} + 2^{n-2} + \cdots + 2^{k+1}) \times$ multiplicand. But, as shown above, this group of 1s can be interpreted as $00 \cdots 0-1$, yielding $PP' = -2^{k+1} \times$ multiplicand.

A simple way of demonstrating that $-2^{n-1} + 2^{n-2} + \cdots + 2^{k+1}$ is equal to -2^{k+1} is as follows. Add -2^{k+1} to both sides to obtain $-2^{n-1} + 2^{n-2} + \cdots + 2^{k+2} = -2^{k+2}$, and then add -2^{k+2} to both sides to obtain $-2^{n-1} + 2^{n-2} + \cdots + 2^{k+3} = -2^{k+3}$. This iteration eventually leads to $-2^{n-1} + 2^{n-2} = -2^{n-2}$. Now the addition of -2^{n-2} to both sides yields a true equality. Therefore the original equality is correct.

The Booth technique for recoding or reinterpreting multipliers is summarized in Figure 7.16.

7.8 FAST MULTIPLICATION

The basic transformation $011 \cdots 110 \Rightarrow + 100 \cdots 0-10$ that is fundamental to the Booth algorithm has been called the "skipping over 1s" technique. The motivation for this term is that in cases where the multiplier has its 1s grouped into a few contiguous blocks, only a few versions of the multiplicand (summands) need to be added to generate the product. If only a few summands need to be added, the multiplication operation can potentially be speeded up. However, in the worst case, that of alternating 1s and 0s in the multiplier, each bit of the multiplier selects a summand. In fact, this results in more summands than if the Booth algorithm is not used. A 16-bit "worst-case" multiplier, a more "normal" multiplier, and a "good" multiplier are shown in Figure 7.17.

The Booth algorithm thus actually achieves two purposes. First, it uniformly transforms both positive and negative n-bit multipliers into a form that selects appropriate versions of n-bit multiplicands which are added to generate correctly signed $2n$-bit products in the 2's-complement number representation system. Second, it achieves some efficiency in the number of summands generated when the multiplier has a few large blocks of 1s. The speed gain possible by skipping over 1s is clearly data-dependent.

We will now describe a multiplication speedup technique which guarantees that an n-bit multiplier will generate at most $n/2$ summands and which uniformly handles the signed-operand case. This represents a multiplication speedup by a factor of 2 over the worst-case Booth algorithm situation.

```
0  1  0  1  0  1  0  1  0  1  0  1  0  1  0  1   ⟹
1  1  0  0  0  1  0  1  1  0  1  1  1  1  0  0   ⟹
0  0  0  0  1  1  1  1  1  0  0  0  0  1  1  1   ⟹
```

$$+1 - 1 + 1 - 1 + 1 - 1 + 1 - 1 + 1 - 1 + 1 - 1 + 1 - 1 + 1 - 1$$
$$ 0 - 1 \quad 0 \quad 0 + 1 - 1 + 1 \quad 0 - 1 + 1 \quad 0 \quad 0 \quad 0 - 1 \quad 0 \quad 0$$
$$ 0 \quad 0 \quad 0 + 1 \quad 0 \quad 0 \quad 0 \quad 0 - 1 \quad 0 \quad 0 \quad 0 + 1 \quad 0 \quad 0 - 1$$

Figure 7.17 Booth-recoded multipliers.

The new technique can be derived from the Booth technique. Recall that in the Booth technique multiplier bit q_i selects a summand as a function of the bit q_{i-1} on its right. The summand selected is shifted i binary positions to the left of the LSB position of the product before the summand is added. Let us call this "summand position i" (SPi). The basic idea of the speedup technique is that bits $i + 1$ and i select one summand, as a function of bit $i - 1$, to be added at SPi. To be practical, this summand must be easily derivable from the multiplicand. The $n/2$ summands are thus selected by bit pairs (x_1, x_0), (x_3, x_2), (x_5, x_4), etc. The technique is called the bit-pair recoding method. Consider the multiplier of Figure 7.15, repeated in Figure 7.18a. Grouping the Booth-recoded selectors in pairs, we obtain a single, appropriately shifted summand for each pair as shown. The rightmost Booth pair $(-1, 0)$ is equivalent to $-2 \times$ (multiplicand M) at SP0. The next pair, $(-1, +1)$, is equivalent to $-1 \times$ M at SP2; finally, the leftmost pair of zeros is equivalent to $0 \times$ M at SP4. Restating these selections in terms of the original multiplier bits, we have the cases $(1, 0)$ with 0 on the right selects

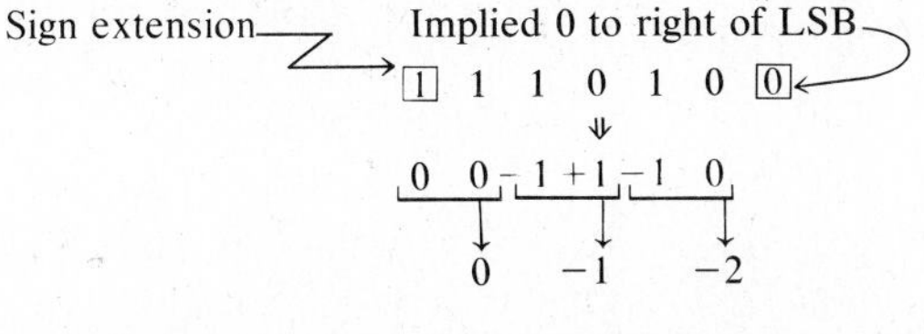

```
Sign extension⟶        Implied 0 to right of LSB⟍
                  ⬚1  1  1  0  1  0  ⬚0↩
                         ⇓
             0  0 ⌐1 +1⌐-1  0⌐
             ↓       ↓      ↓
             0      -1     -2
```

(a) Example of bit-pair recoding derived from Booth recoding

Multiplier bit-pair		Multiplier bit on the right	Multiplicand
$i+1$	i	$i-1$	selected at SPi
0	0	0	$0 \times M$
0	0	1	$+1 \times M$
0	1	0	$+1 \times M$
0	1	1	$+2 \times M$
1	0	0	$-2 \times M$
1	0	1	$-1 \times M$
1	1	0	$-1 \times M$
1	1	1	$0 \times M$

(b) Table of multiplicand selection decisions

Figure 7.18 Multiplier bit-pair recoding.

$$
\begin{array}{r}
0\ 1\ 1\ 0\ 1 \quad (+13)\\
\times\ 1\ 1\ 0\ 1\ 0 \quad (-6)\\
\end{array}
$$

(−78)

Figure 7.19 Multiplication requiring only $n/2$ summands.

$-2 \times M$, $(1, 0)$ with 1 on the right selects $-1 \times M$, and $(1, 1)$ with 1 on the right selects $0 \times M$. The complete set of eight cases is shown in Figure 7.18*b*, and the multiplication example of Figure 7.15 is shown again in Figure 7.19 as it would be computed using the bit-pair recoding method.

It is possible to extend the sequential hardware multiplication circuit of Figure 7.9 to implement both the signed-operand (Booth) algorithm and the bit-pair recoding speedup technique. Instead of a sequential circuit, we will describe an MSI circuit, copies of which can be interconnected in a planar array to implement signed-number multiplication combinationally. The circuit is based on the bit-pair recoding technique and uses carry lookahead to achieve high-speed addition of a summand and a partial product. Consider the multiplication of two 16-bit signed numbers, producing a 32-bit signed product. Figure 7.20 shows the arrangement of 2×4 multiplier circuits with the input operands applied. Each row of four circuits takes the partial-product (PP) input at its row level and adds the summand determined by its multiplier pair inputs to generate the PP output for the next row. Since eight rows are needed in the case shown, a 16×16 multiplication can be implemented with thirty-two 2×4 circuits. The name 2×4 is derived from the fact that each circuit inspects 2 bits of the multiplier and operates on a 4-bit slice of the partial product.

There are a number of details that have not been covered in the above overall description. Figure 7.21 shows a 2×4 circuit with its inputs and outputs labeled to indicate that its position is in the row corresponding to multiplier bits q_i and q_{i+1}. One of its input vectors from the top is the 4-bit slice p'_{k+3}, p'_{k+2},

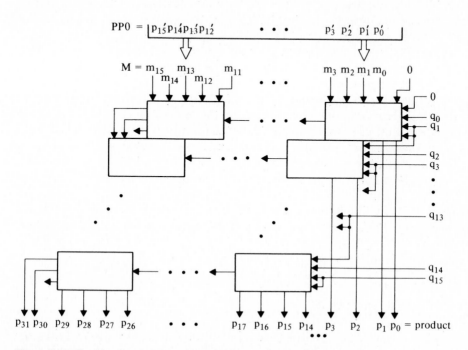

Figure 7.20 Combinational signed multiplication using MSI circuits.

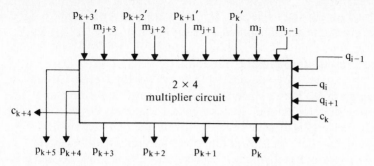

Figure 7.21 MSI 2×4 multiplier circuit.

p'_{k+1}, p'_k of the incoming partial product. The other input vector from the top is the 4-bit slice m_{j+3}, m_{j+2}, m_{j+1}, m_j of the appropriately shifted multiplicand. A fifth bit, m_{j-1}, from the multiplicand is also provided. This bit is needed if $\pm 2 \times M$ is to be applied at this row level. This chip generates the 4-bit slice p_{k+3}, p_{k+2}, p_{k+1}, p_k of the outgoing partial product. Although carries are determined internally in each 2×4 circuit by carry lookahead techniques, the carries c_k, c_{k+4}, etc., ripple laterally between circuits in performing the required addition. Finally, since signed numbers are being handled, the left-end 2×4 circuit of any row must implement a partial-product extension operation (with correct sign extension). This is necessary to provide the left pair of partial-product inputs to the 2×4 circuit directly below it in the next row. In Figure 7.21, output bits P_{k+5} and P_{k+4} are the extension bits. These outputs are used only in the 2×4 circuits at the left end of each row. In the last row, they constitute bits p_{31} and p_{30} of the 32-bit product in the example of Figure 7.20.

Figure 7.22 shows the input and output variables of each of the six 2×4 multiplier circuits of an array implementation of the multiplication example shown on the right side of Figure 7.19. Note that although the example is a 5×5 multiplication, this array can handle up to an 8×6 case. The first partial product in Figure 7.22 corresponds to the first summand on the right side of Figure 7.19. It can easily be checked that the second partial product is the sum of the first and second summands. Since the third summand is 0, this second partial product is the final answer (the product).

Although this discussion has been rather sketchy, it is intended to give the reader some grasp of the algorithms that have been used in commercially available MSI circuits that are intended for high-performance signed-integer multiplication. These and similar circuits can be used in both general-purpose computers and special-purpose digital processors where arithmetic operation speeds are critical.

7.9 INTEGER DIVISION

In Section 7.6 we discussed positive-number multiplication by relating the way in which the multiplication operation can be done on paper to the way a logic

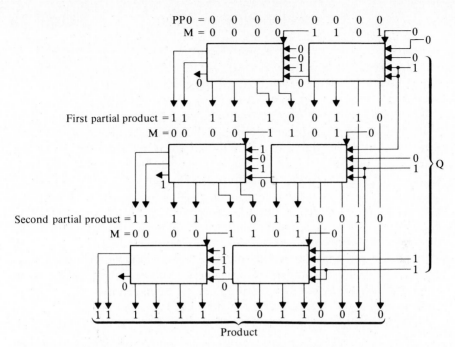

Figure 7.22 The multiplication example of Figure 7.19 performed by an array of 2 × 4 multiplier circuits.

circuit can do it. It is instructive to follow the same strategy here. We will only discuss positive-number division in detail. Some general comments on the signed-operand case will be made later.

Figure 7.23 shows an example of decimal division along with the binary-coded division of the same values. Consider the decimal version. The 2 in the quotient is determined by the following reasoning. We first "try" 13 divided into 2 and it "doesn't go." Next we "try" 13 divided into 27. We go through the trial exercise of multiplying 13 by 2 to get 26, and knowing that $27 - 26 = 1$ is less than 13, we finally enter 2 as the quotient and perform the required subtraction. The next digit of the dividend, 4, is "brought down" and we finish by deciding that 13 goes into 14 once, with the remainder being determined as 1. A similar discussion can be given for the binary case, with the simplification that the only possibilities for the quotient bits are 0 and 1.

The important point to conclude from the above division "algorithm" is that

Figure 7.23 "Longhand" division examples.

the process of trial determination of the quotient digits is more difficult to automate in a logic circuit than the selection and addition of summands in the multiplication case. The simplest circuit that implements binary division must methodically position the divisor with respect to the dividend and perform a subtraction. If the remainder is zero or positive, a quotient bit of 1 is determined, the remainder is extended by another bit of the dividend, the divisor is repositioned, and another subtraction is performed. On the other hand, if the remainder is negative, a quotient bit of 0 is determined, the dividend is restored by adding back the divisor, and the divisor is repositioned for another subtraction.

Figure 7.24 shows a logic circuit arrangement that implements the above *restoring-division* technique. Note its similarity to the structure for multiplication that was shown in Figure 7.9. An n-bit positive divisor is loaded into register M and an n-bit positive dividend is loaded into register Q at the start of the operation. Register A is set to 0. After the division is complete, the n-bit quotient will be in register Q with the remainder in A. The required subtractions are facilitated by using 2's-complement arithmetic. The extra bit position at the left end of both A and M is for the sign bit for the subtractions.

The following algorithm performs the division:

S1: DO n times

Shift A and Q left one binary position.

Subtract M from A, placing the answer back in A.

If the sign of A is 1, set q_0 to 0 and add M back to A (restore A); otherwise, set q_0 to 1.

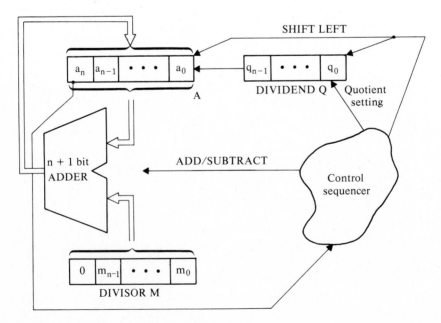

Figure 7.24 Circuit arrangement for binary division.

$$\frac{10}{11\,\overline{)\,1000}}$$
$$\frac{11}{10}$$

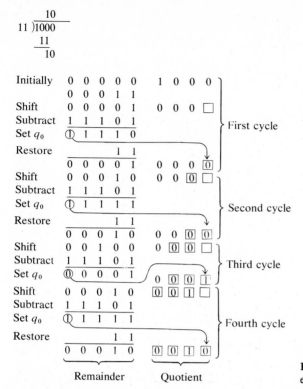

Figure 7.25 shows a 4-bit example as it would be processed by the circuit in Figure 7.24.

It is possible to improve on this algorithm by avoiding the need for restoring A after an unsuccessful subtraction. (We define a subtraction to be unsuccessful if the result is negative.) Consider the sequence of operations that takes place after the subtraction operation in the above algorithm. If A is positive, we shift it left and subtract M; that is, we perform $2A - M$. If A is negative, we restore it by performing $A + M$, and then we shift it left and subtract M. This is equivalent to performing $2A + M$. The q_0 bit is appropriately set to 0 or 1 after the correct operation has been performed. We can summarize this into the following *nonrestoring-division* algorithm:

S1: Do n times
   If the sign of A is 0, shift A and Q left one binary position and subtract M
      from A; otherwise, shift A and Q left and add M to A.
   If the sign of A is 0, set q_0 to 1; otherwise, set q_0 to 0.
S2: If the sign of A is 1, add M to A.

The S2 step is needed to leave the proper positive remainder in A at the end of n cycles. It is clear that the logic circuitry of Figure 7.24 can also be used to perform this algorithm as well as the original one. Note that the restore operations are not used and exactly one add or subtract operation is performed

```
Initially    0  0  0  0  0    1  0  0  0 ⎤
             0  0  0  1  1                 ⎥
Shift        0  0  0  0  1    0  0  0 □  ⎬ First cycle
Subtract     1  1  1  0  1                 ⎥
Set q₀       ① 1  1  1  0    0  0  0 ⓪ ⎦
Shift        1  1  1  0  0    0  0 ⓪ □ ⎤
Add          0  0  0  1  1                 ⎥
Set q₀       ① 1  1  1  1    0  0 ⓪ ⓪ ⎬ Second cycle
Shift        1  1  1  1  0    0 ⓪ ⓪ □ ⎤
Add          0  0  0  1  1                 ⎥
Set q₀       ⓪ 0  0  0  1    0 ⓪ ⓪ ①  ⎬ Third cycle
Shift        0  0  0  1  0   ⓪ ⓪ ① □ ⎤
Subtract     1  1  1  0  1                 ⎥
Set q₀       ① 1  1  1  1   ⓪ ⓪ ① ⓪ ⎦ Fourth cycle
```

Quotient

```
Add          1  1  1  1  1 ⎤
             0  0  0  1  1  ⎬ Restore remainder
             0  0  0  1  0 ⎦
```

Remainder

$F(B) = -b_0 \times 2^0 + b_{-1} \times 2^{-1} + b_{-2} \times 2^{-2} + \cdots + b_{-(n-1)} \times 2^{-(n-1)}$

Figure 7.26 A nonrestoring-division example.

per cycle. Figure 7.26 shows how the division example of Figure 7.25 is executed by the nonrestoring-division algorithm.

There are no simple algorithms for performing signed division that are comparable to the multiplication situation. In division, preprocessing of the operands and/or postprocessing of the results are usually required. These extra operations depend on the sign of the operands in conjunction with the desired signs of the results, and complementation of one or more numbers is usually involved. We will not discuss any of the possibilities in detail. It is useful, however, to note that we can always transform the operands to positive values, use one of the algorithms discussed above, and transform the results to the correct signed values as necessary.

7.10 FLOATING-POINT NUMBERS AND OPERATIONS

Until now in this chapter we have been exclusively concerned with signed, fixed-point numbers. It has been convenient to consider them as integers, that is, with an implied binary point at the right end of each number. It would have been just as easy to consider that the binary point is at the left end, thus dealing with fractions. In the 2's-complement system, the signed value F, represented by the n-bit binary fraction

$$B = b_0 . b_{-1}b_{-2} \cdots b_{-(n-1)}$$

is given by

$$F(B) = -b_0 \times 2^0 + b_{-1} \times 2^{-1} + b_{-2} \times 2^{-2} + \cdots + b_{-(n-1)} \times 2^{-(n-1)}$$

where the range of F is

$$-1 \le F \le -2^{-(n-1)} \qquad F = 0 \qquad \text{or} \qquad 2^{-(n-1)} \le F \le 1 - 2^{-(n-1)}$$

Consider the range of values representable in these fixed-point formats. Let us assume 16-bit signed values. Interpreted as integers, the value range is $-32,768 (= -2^{15})$ to $+32,767 (= +2^{15} - 1)$. If we consider them to be fractions, the range is approximately $\pm 3 \times 10^{-5} (\approx \pm 2^{-15})$ to ± 1. Neither of these ranges is sufficient for scientific calculations which might involve parameters like Avogadro's number (6.0247×10^{23} mole^{-1}) or Planck's constant (6.6254×10^{-27} erg · s). Hence, there is a need to easily accommodate very large integers and very small fractions. This means that a facility should be provided for both representing numbers and operating on numbers in such a way that the position of the binary point is variable and is automatically adjusted as computation proceeds. In such a case, the binary point is said to float, and the numbers are called *floating-point numbers*. This distinguishes them from fixed-point numbers, whose binary point is always in the same position.

Because the position of the binary point in a floating-point number is variable, it must be given explicitly in the floating-point representation. For example, in the familiar decimal scientific notation, numbers may be written as 6.0247×10^{23}, 6.6254×10^{-27}, -1.0341×10^2, -7.3000×10^{-14}, etc. These numbers are said to be given to five *significant digits*. The *scale factors* (10^{23}, 10^{-27}, etc.) indicate the true position of the decimal point with respect to the significant digits. By convention, a decimal point is placed to the right of the first (nonzero) significant digit, and the number is said to be *normalized*. Note that the base 10 in the scale factor is fixed and does not need to appear explicitly in the machine representation of a floating-point number. The sign, the significant digits, and the exponent in the scale factor comprise the representation. We are thus motivated to define a floating-point number representation as one in which a number is represented by its sign, followed by a string of significant digits, commonly called a *mantissa*, and an *exponent* to an implied base. Let us state a general form for such numbers in the decimal system and then relate the form to a comparable binary representation. A widely used form is

$$\pm X_1.X_2X_3X_4X_5X_6X_7 \times 10^{\pm Y_1Y_2}$$

where X_i and Y_i are decimal digits. This is sufficient for a wide range of scientific calculations. As we shall see, it is possible to approximate this range and mantissa precision in a binary representation that occupies 32 bits. A 24-bit number can approximately represent a seven-digit decimal number. Therefore, 24 bits are assigned to represent the mantissa in the binary representation. One bit is needed for the sign of the number, leaving 7 bits for a signed exponent.

A specific binary format for floating-point numbers is shown in Figure 7.27a. Let us first assume that the implied base is 2 and that the 7-bit signed exponent is expressed as a 2's-complement integer. The 24-bit mantissa is considered to be a fraction with the binary point at its left end and the sign of the number is given in the leftmost bit of the format. To retain as many significant bits as possible, the fractional mantissa is kept in a normalized form in which, for nonzero values, its leftmost bit is always 1. Thus the magnitude of the mantissa M is either 0 or lies in the range of $\frac{1}{2} \leq M < 1$. A number that is not in this form can always be put in normalized form by shifting the fraction and adjusting the exponent, assuming

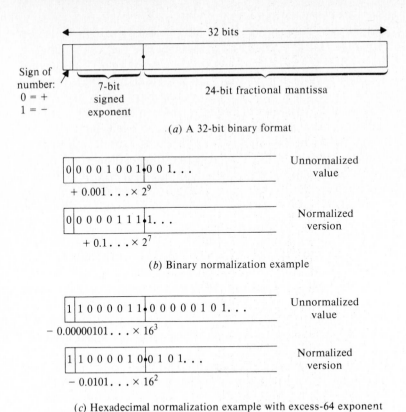

(a) A 32-bit binary format

(b) Binary normalization example

(c) Hexadecimal normalization example with excess-64 exponent

Figure 7.27 Floating-point format.

that exponent overflow/underflow does not occur. Figure 7.27b shows an unnormalized value $0.001 \cdots \times 2^9$ and its normalized version $0.1 \cdots \times 2^7$. A 7-bit, 2's-complement exponent has a range of -64 to $+64$, which means that the scale factor has a range of 2^{-64} to 2^{63}, not large enough to represent the desired scale factor range of 10^{-99} to 10^{99}. If we reduce the size of the mantissa to allocate more bits to the exponent, then we will not be able to approximate the desired seven-decimal-digit accuracy. The solution that has been used in a number of computers is to change the value of the implied base in the scale factor. The base should be of the form 2^q so that a right or left shift of the mantissa by q binary positions with respect to its binary point corresponds to a decrease or increase of 1 in the exponent of the scale factor, respectively. If we let the implied base be 16, then the range of the scale factor becomes 16^{-64} to 16^{63}, which corresponds approximately to the decimal range 10^{-76} to 10^{76}. This representation for floating-point numbers has both a reasonable range and number of bits in the mantissa. (However, as we shall see later, a floating-point standard has been developed in which a significantly larger range and mantissa accuracy is provided.) Since the base is now 16, shifting of the mantissa to perform normalization must take place in steps of 4-bit shifts. This corresponds to the smallest changes (±1) in the exponent. A representation is now considered to be normalized if any of the leading 4 bits of its mantissa is 1. This is often called *hexadecimal normalization.*

It should be pointed out that the gain in range achieved by using a base of 16 in the scale factor may result in a lower precision mantissa. Even though 24 bits are still used for the mantissa, the fact that hexadecimal normalization is used means that the leading 3 bits of a mantissa might be 0s. Thus, in some cases, only 21 significant bits are retained in the mantissa. This is in contrast with the use of the base 2 in the scale factor, where 24 bits of precision are always maintained.

Another change in the format of a floating-point number is useful. Instead of representing the exponent in a signed 2's-complement integer format, we represent it in *excess-64* format. In this format, an exponent having the signed value E is represented by the value $E' = E + 64$. Since the desired range for E is $-64 \leq E \leq 63$, the excess-64 value E' will be in the range $0 \leq E' \leq 127$. The smallest scale factor, 16^{-64}, is then represented by seven 0s, and the largest scale factor, 16^{+63}, is represented by seven 1s. This change facilitates the use of simple circuitry for determining the relative size of two floating-point numbers. An unnormalized value and its corresponding normalized version in the excess-64, base-16 scale factor scheme are shown in Figure 7.27c. The value 0 is represented by all zeros. As computations proceed, a number that does not fall in the representable range may be generated. This means that its normalized representation requires an exponent less than -64 or greater than $+63$. In the first case, we say that *underflow* has occurred, and in the second case, we say that *overflow* has occurred. Events like this are generally called arithmetic *exceptions.* A uniform way to handle exceptions in a computer system is to raise an interrupt when they occur. The interrupt-service routine can then take action as specified by the user or by a system convention. For example, on underflow the decision might be to set the value to 0 and proceed. A further discussion of exception handling is beyond the scope of our presentation here.

The above format for floating-point numbers is the one used in the IBM 370 computers, which have a 32-bit word length. Identical or very similar formats have been used by other computer manufacturers. The format is convenient for use in 16-bit word-length minicomputers, where two words can be used to represent a floating-point number. To see the gain in range that has been achieved by using the floating-point representation, we should note the range provided by fixed-point 32-bit formats. A 2's-complement 32-bit integer format has a range of approximately -2.15×10^9 to 2.15×10^9, and a corresponding fractional range of $\pm 4.66 \times 10^{-10}$ to ± 1. Of course, the gain in range has been traded for a loss of significant bits. A large number range is a significant feature of a floating-point system. However, the user convenience provided by automatic handling of the variable position of the binary point with respect to the significant bits is the most important feature of such systems.

7.10.1 Arithmetic Operations on Floating-Point Numbers

In this section we will discuss the general procedures for addition, subtraction, multiplication, and division of floating-point numbers. The rules we give below apply to hexadecimal-normalized 24-bit fraction mantissas and scale factors that have an implied base of 16 and an explicit 7-bit signed exponent in excess-64 format. This format was discussed in the previous section, and an example is shown in Figure 7.27c. The rules are only intended to specify the major steps needed in performing the four operations. The possibility that overflow or underflow might occur is not handled. Furthermore, intermediate results for both mantissas and exponents might require more than 24 and 7 bits, respectively, for their representation. Both of these aspects of the operations need to be carefully considered when designing an arithmetic processor. While we do not provide that level of detail in specifying the rules, some consideration will be given to these implementation aspects, including rounding, in later sections.

Addition and subtraction require the mantissas to be shifted with respect to each other before they are added or subtracted when their exponents differ. Let us consider a decimal example in which we wish to add 2.9400×10^2 to 4.3100×10^4. We rewrite 2.9400×10^2 as 0.0294×10^4 and then perform addition of the mantissas to get 4.3394×10^4. A general rule for addition and subtraction may be stated as follows.

ADD/SUBTRACT Rule

1. Choose the number with the smaller exponent and shift its mantissa right (in 4-bit steps) a number of steps equal to the difference in exponents.
2. Set the exponent of the result equal to the larger exponent.
3. Perform addition-subtraction on the mantissas and determine the sign of the result.
4. Normalize the resulting value if necessary, and then use the first 24 bits after the binary point (truncated, as discussed later) as the mantissa of the result.

Multiplication and division are somewhat easier than addition and subtraction in that no alignment of mantissas is needed.

MULTIPLY Rule

1. Add exponents and subtract 64.
2. Multiply mantissas and determine the sign of the result.
3. Normalize the resulting value if necessary, and then use the first 24 bits after the binary point (truncated) as the mantissa of the result.

DIVIDE Rule

1. Subtract exponents and add 64.
2. Divide mantissas and determine the sign of the result.
3. Normalize the resulting value if necessary, and then use the first 24 bits after the binary point (truncated) as the mantissa of the result.

The addition or subtraction of 64 in the above two rules is a result of using the excess-64 notation for exponents.

7.10.2 Guard Bits and Rounding

Before discussing the implementation of floating-point operations, we should consider some details associated with the steps in the above algorithms. Although the mantissas of initial operands and final results are limited to 24 bits, it is important to retain extra bits, often called *guard* bits, during the intermediate steps. This enables retaining maximum accuracy in the results.

The operation of removing guard bits in generating final results raises an important issue. The problem is that a binary fraction must be *truncated* to give a shorter fraction that is an approximation to the longer value. This problem also arises in other situations, for instance, in the conversion from decimal to binary fractions.

There are a number of ways that truncation can be done. The simplest way is to remove the guard bits and make no changes in the retained bits. This is called *chopping*. Suppose we wish to truncate a 6-bit fraction to a 3-bit fraction by this method. All fractions in the range $0.b_{-1}b_{-2}b_{-3}000$ to $0.b_{-1}b_{-2}b_{-3}111$ will be truncated to $0.b_{-1}b_{-2}b_{-3}$. The error in the 3-bit result obviously ranges from 0 to 0.000111. It is more convenient to say that, in general, the error in chopping ranges from 0 to almost 1 in the least significant position of the retained bits. In our example, this is the b_{-3} position. The result of chopping is called a *biased* approximation because the error range is not symmetrical about 0.

The next simplest method of truncation is *Von Neumann rounding*. If the bits to be removed are all zeroes, they are simply dropped, with no changes to the retained bits. However, if any of the bits to be removed are 1, the least significant bit of the retained bits is set to 1. In our 6-bit to 3-bit truncation example, all 6-bit fractions with $b_{-4}b_{-5}b_{-6}$ not equal to 000 will be truncated to $0.b_{-1}b_{-2}1$. It is easy to see that the error in this truncation method ranges between -1 and $+1$ in the LSB position of the retained bits. Although the range of error is larger with this technique than it is with chopping, the maximum magnitude is the same, and the approximation is *unbiased* because the error range is symmetrical about 0.

It is advantageous to use unbiased approximations if a large number of operands and operations are involved in generating a few results and if it can be assumed that the individual errors are approximately symmetrically distributed over the error range. Positive errors should tend to offset negative errors as the computation proceeds. From a statistical standpoint, we might then expect the results to have a high probability of being very accurate.

The third truncation method is a *rounding* procedure. It achieves the closest approximation to the number being truncated, and it is an unbiased technique. The procedure is as follows. A 1 is added to the LSB position of the bits to be retained if there is a 1 in the MSB position of the bits being removed. Thus, $0.b_{-1}b_{-2}b_{-3}1 \cdots$ rounds to $0.b_{-1}b_{-2}b_{-3} + 0.001$, and $0.b_{-1}b_{-2}b_{-3}0 \cdots$ rounds to $0.b_{-1}b_{-2}b_{-3}$. This provides the desired approximation except for the case where the bits to be removed are $10 \cdots 0$. This is a tie situation. The longer value is half way between the two closest truncated representations. In order to break the tie in an unbiased way, one possibility is to choose the retained bits to be the nearest even number. In terms of our 6-bit example, the value $0.b_{-1}b_{-2}0100$ is truncated to the value $0.b_{y_{41}}b_{-2}0$, and $0.b_{-1}b_{-2}1100$ is truncated to $0.b_{-1}b_{-2}1 + 0.001$. The descriptive phrase "round to the nearest number, or nearest even number in case of a tie" is sometimes used to refer to this truncation technique. The error range is approximately $-\frac{1}{2}$ to $+\frac{1}{2}$ in the LSB position of the retained bits. Clearly, this is the best method. However, it is also the most costly to implement because it requires an addition operation and a possible renormalization. This rounding technique is used in the IEEE floating-point standard which is described in Section 7.10.4.

The above discussion of errors that are introduced when guard bits are removed by truncation treats the case of only a single truncation operation. When a long series of calculations involving floating-point numbers is performed, the analysis that determines error ranges or bounds for the final results can be a quite complicated study. We will not dwell further on this aspect of numerical computation.

7.10.3 Implementation of Floating-Point Operations

The provision of floating-point arithmetic in both large and small computers is a tremendous convenience for many users. Aside from any consideration of the expanded range of values, the flexibility in location of the binary point is an important aspect. The user (programmer) does not need to worry about manipulating scale factors, aligning binary points, etc. Fractions and mixed numbers can be used as easily as integers at the programming level.

The implementation of floating-point operations involves considerable circuitry. These operations may also be implemented by software routines. In either case, provision must be made for input and output conversion to and from the user's decimal representation of numbers. In many computers, floating-point operations are available at the basic machine instruction level. Hardware implementations range from serial through highly parallel forms, analogous to the range of hardware multipliers discussed earlier.

As an example of the implementation of floating-point operations, let us consider the block diagram for a hardware implementation of addition and subtraction on 32-bit floating-point operands that have the format shown in Figure 7.27c. Let the signs, exponents, and mantissas of operands A and B be represented by S_A, E_A, M_A and S_B, E_B, M_B, respectively. Following the ADD/SUBTRACT rule given in Section 7.10.1, we see that the first step is to compare exponents to determine how far to shift the mantissa of the number with the smaller exponent. This shift-count value, n, is determined by the 7-bit subtractor circuit in the upper left corner of Figure 7.28. The magnitude of the difference $E_A - E_B$, which is n, is sent to the SHIFTER unit. The range of n is restricted to $0, 1, \ldots, 7$, where $n = 7$ if $|E_A - E_B| \geq 7$; otherwise, $n = |E_A - E_B|$. If $n = 7$, it is possible to determine the result immediately as being equal to the larger operand (or its negative). However, this option is not explicitly shown in Figure 7.28. The sign of the difference resulting from the exponent comparison determines which mantissa is to be shifted. Therefore, the sign is sent to the

32-bit operands $\left\{ \begin{array}{l} A: S_A, E_A, M_A \\ B: S_B, E_B, M_B \end{array} \right\}$

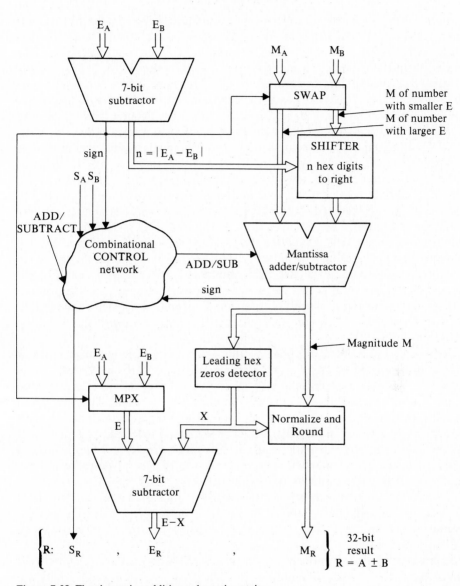

Figure 7.28 Floating-point addition-subtraction unit.

SWAP network in the upper right corner of the figure. If the sign is 0, then $E_A \geq E_B$, and the mantissas M_A and M_B are sent straight through the SWAP network. This results in M_B being sent to the SHIFTER, to be shifted n hex positions to the right. The other mantissa, M_A, is sent directly to the Mantissa adder-subtractor. If the sign is 1, then $E_A < E_B$, and the mantissas are swapped before being sent to the SHIFTER. This completes step 1 of the ADD/SUBTRACT rule.

Step 2 is performed by the two-way multiplexer, MPX, in the bottom left corner of the figure. The exponent of the result, E, is tentatively determined as E_A if $E_A \geq E_B$, or E_B if $E_A < E_B$. This is determined by the sign of the difference resulting from the exponent comparison operation in step 1.

Step 3 involves the major component, the Mantissa adder-subtractor in the middle of the figure. The CONTROL logic determines whether the mantissas are to be added or subtracted. This is decided by the signs of the operands, S_A and S_B, and the operation, Add or Subtract, that is to be performed on the operands. The CONTROL logic also determines the sign of the result S_R. For example, if A is negative ($S_A = 1$), B is positive ($S_B = 0$), and the operation is $A - B$, then the mantissas are added and the sign of the result is negative ($S_R = 1$). On the other hand, if A and B are both positive and the operation is $A - B$, then the mantissas are subtracted. The sign of the result S_R now depends on the mantissa subtraction operation. For instance, if $E_A > E_B$, then $M_A - $ shifted M_B will be positive and the result will be positive. But if $E_B > E_A$, then $M_B - $ shifted M_A will be positive and the result will be negative. This example shows that the sign from the exponent comparison is also required as an input to the CONTROL network. When $E_A = E_B$ and the mantissas are subtracted, the sign of the Mantissa adder-subtractor output is crucial in determining the sign of the result. The reader should now be able to construct the complete truth table for the CONTROL network.

Step 4 of the ADD/SUBTRACT rule is the normalization of the result mantissa M produced by step 3. The number of leading zeros in M determines the number X of hex digit shifts to be applied to M. Then, the normalized value is truncated to generate the 24-bit mantissa, M_R, of the result. The value X is also subtracted from the tentative result exponent E to generate the true result exponent E_R. We should note that it is possible that a single hex digit right shift might be needed to normalize the result. This would be the case if two mantissas of the form 0.1xx . . . are added. The vector M would then have the form 1.xxx . . . . This would correspond to an X value of -1 in the figure.

We have not given any details on the guard bits that need to be carried along with intermediate mantissa values. In general, only a few bits are needed, depending upon the truncation technique used to generate the 24-bit normalized mantissa of the result.

A few comments are in order about the actual hardware that might be used to implement the blocks in Figure 7.28. The two 7-bit subtractors and the Mantissa adder-subtractor can be implemented by combinational logic as discussed earlier in this chapter. Since their outputs are required in sign and magnitude form, some modifications to our earlier discussions need to be made. A combination of 1's-complement arithmetic and sign and magnitude representation is often used. There is considerable flexibility in the implementation of the SHIFTER and the output normalization operation. To make these parts inexpensive, they should be constructed as shift registers. However, if speed of execution is important, they can be built in a more combinational manner. Figure 7.28 is organized along the lines of part of the floating-point hardware used in some IBM computers.

A modern approach is to implement floating-point operations in a VLSI chip that can be used as a peripheral device with general-purpose processors. Several such chips are commercially available. Typical examples are the Intel 8231[7.1] and the AMD 9511.[7.2] As well as performing the four basic floating-point operations of add, subtract, multiply, and divide, they are capable of computing square roots, and trigonometric, logarithmic, and exponential functions. Both of these chips use a 32-bit, floating-point format with a 24-bit, binary-normalized mantissa. A processor usually communicates with these chips through a parallel I/O port. A string of bytes consisting of operands and an encoded operation are sent to the arithmetic chip. The processor either enters a polling loop (or awaits an interrupt) until the chip completes the operation. A string of bytes representing the result is then returned to the processor or the main memory.

One of the best-known floating-point chips is Intel's 8087.[7.3] It is intended for use with the Intel 8086 microprocessor. It does not operate as a peripheral device, as is the case with the two chips just described. The 8087 is closely synchronized with the 8086 CPU chip. It executes the floating-point instructions directly as they are fetched from the main memory. It has a register file for operands and the required arithmetic circuitry. The data formats used in the 8087 conform to the IEEE standard that will be discussed in Section 7.10.4. The 8087 evaluates trigonometric, logarithmic, and exponential functions, in addition to performing the four basic floating-point operations.

7.10.4 The IEEE Floating-Point Standard

The IEEE Computer Society has developed a standard for binary floating-point arithmetic.[7.4] The main motivation for such a standard stems from an interest in facilitating the portability of numerically oriented programs from one computer system to another and encouraging the development of high-quality numerical software. This is particularly important in the microprocessor and small machine environment, where individual manufacturers are not likely to develop extensive, generally usable numerical routines.

The standard consists of three aspects: the format of the data types, the arithmetic operations, and exception handling when errors occur (overflow/underflow, divide by 0, etc.). We will only discuss the first of these in detail.

The basic format sizes are 32 bits (single precision) and 64 bits (double precision). These sizes are easily addressable in 8-, 16-, or 32-bit word-length computers. The main criterion used in formulating the 32-bit single precision format is to provide as much precision (significant bits) as possible in the mantissa, while maintaining a sufficiently large range (determined by the number of bits in the exponent). This leads to a choice of binary normalization (as opposed to octal or hexadecimal) for the mantissa and an implied base of 2

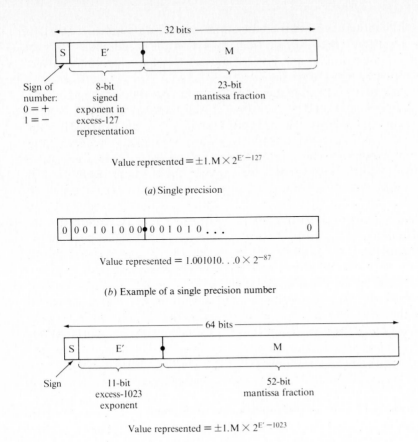

Value represented $= \pm 1.\text{M} \times 2^{\text{E}'-127}$

(*a*) Single precision

Value represented $= 1.001010\ldots 0 \times 2^{-87}$

(*b*) Example of a single precision number

Value represented $= \pm 1.\text{M} \times 2^{\text{E}'-1023}$

(*c*) Double precision

Figure 7.29 IEEE standard floating-point formats.

for the exponent. In order to provide as many bits as possible for the mantissa, the exponent must be kept as small as possible. A field of 8 bits is assigned to the exponent. The complete format is shown in Figure 7.29*a*. The exponent, denoted as E′ in the figure, is represented in the excess-127 representation. The end values of E′, namely 0 and 255, are used to indicate special values such as exact 0 and infinity. Thus the range of E′ for normal values is $0 < \text{E}' < 255$. This means that the actual exponent E is in the range $-126 \le \text{E} \le 127$. Since binary normalization is used, the most significant bit of the mantissa is always equal to 1. This bit is not explicitly represented. It is assumed to be to the immediate left of the binary point. The 23 bits stored in the M field represent the fractional part of the mantissa, that is, the bits to the right of the binary point. An example of a single precision floating-point number is shown in Figure 7.29*b*.

Comparing the single precision format of the IEEE standard to the format given earlier in Figure 7.27*c*, we observe that both formats use 24 bits of significance. Note that the bit position saved by using the implicit mantissa bit, as described above, has been added to the exponent field in the standard. The scale factor in the standard has the range 2^{-126} to 2^{127} (approximately $10^{\pm 38}$). This should be compared to the larger scale factor range of 16^{-64} to 16^{63} (approximately $10^{\pm 76}$), of the earlier format. On the other hand, the standard provides more precision because it uses binary normalization.

The double precision format has increased exponent and mantissa ranges. This 64-bit format is shown in Figure 7.29c. The excess-1023 exponent E' is in the range $0 < E' < 2047$ for normal values, with 0 and 2047 being used to indicate special values, as before. Thus, the actual exponent E is in the range $-1022 \leq E \leq 1023$, providing scale factors of 2^{-1022} to 2^{1023} (approximately $10^{\pm 308}$).

An implementation must provide at least single precision to conform to the standard. The provision of double precision is optional. The standard also specifies certain optional extended forms of both of these formats. The extended formats are intended to provide increased precision and increased exponent range in the representation of intermediate values in a sequence of calculations. For example, the dot product of two vectors of numbers can be computed by accumulating the sum of products in extended precision. The inputs are given in a standard precision (single or double) and the answer is truncated to the same precision. The use of extended formats helps to reduce the size of the accumulated round-off error in a sequence of calculations. The accuracy of evaluation of elementary functions (sin, cos, etc.) is also enhanced by use of the extended formats.

In addition to the four basic arithmetic operations, the standard requires that the operations of remainder, square root, and conversion between binary and decimal representations be provided. Results of single operations must be computed to be accurate within half a unit in the LSB position. In general, this requires that rounding be used as the truncation method, as described in Section 7.10.2. The implementation of this rounding scheme requires only 3 guard bits to be carried along during the intermediate steps in performing the above operations. The first 2 of these bits are just the 2 most significant bits of the section of the mantissa to be removed. The third bit is the logical OR of all bits beyond the above mentioned 2 bits in the full representation of the mantissa. This bit is relatively easy to maintain during the intermediate steps of the operations to be performed. It should be initialized to 0. If a 1 is shifted through this position, the bit becomes 1 and retains that value. Hence, it is usually called the *sticky bit*.

A few brief comments on exceptions will complete our discussion. The standard specifies the action to be taken when operations produce results outside the range of normalized floating-point numbers. In general, these exceptions should cause a trap (software interrupt) whose action is under user control. Five exceptions are to be detected: invalid operation, division by 0, overflow, underflow, and inexact. A simple example of an invalid operation is an attempt to take the square root of a negative number. A division by 0 exception is signalled when the divisor is 0 and the numerator is a finite, nonzero number.

The result is infinity, which has a representation as mentioned earlier. The handling of overflow and underflow exceptions, and the results produced, are given in the standard. It is beyond the scope of this discussion to give the details. One interesting aspect of the standard in this area is that it defines a class of *denormalized* numbers: nonzero numbers whose magnitude is smaller than the magnitude of the smallest normalized number. These numbers may be used in the handling of underflow. Finally, an inexact exception is signalled if the rounded result of an operation is not exact.

7.11 CONCLUDING REMARKS

There is a great deal known about computer arithmetic. This subject has been the source of a number of interesting logic design problems. The main theme in this chapter has been to discuss some of the design techniques which have been developed to solve the problems. We have emphasized basic ideas which have proven to be useful in the design of integrated circuits that can be used to construct binary arithmetic units. Carry lookahead techniques have been discussed as the major idea involved in high-performance adder design. In the design of fast multipliers, the method of bit pairing in the multiplier leads to a reduction of the number of summands that need to be added to generate the product.

The floating-point number representation system has been described, including a set of rules for performing the four standard operations. Hardware implementation of floating-point units can be expensive. To provide an appreciation for the circuit complexity required in such an implementation, we have sketched the block diagram of an addition-subtraction unit. The IEEE floating-point standard has been outlined. The adoption of this standard by manufacturers will greatly enhance the portability and quality of numerical software.

7.12 PROBLEMS

7.1 Represent each of the decimal values 26, -37, 497, and -123 as signed 10-bit numbers in the following binary formats:
   (a) Sign and magnitude.
   (b) 1's complement.
   (c) 2's complement.
(See Appendix D for decimal to binary integer conversion.)

7.2 Binary fractions were discussed briefly in Section 7.10.
   (a) Express the decimal values 0.5, -0.123, -0.75, and -0.1 as signed 6-bit numbers in the binary formats of Problem 7.1 (See Appendix D for decimal to binary fraction conversion.)
   (b) What is the maximum representation error e involved in using only 5 significant bits after the binary point?
   (c) Calculate the number of bits needed after the binary point so that (1) $e < \frac{1}{10}$, (2) $e < \frac{1}{100}$, (3) $e < \frac{1}{1000}$, and (4) $e < 1/10^6$.

7.3 The 1's-complement and 2's-complement binary representation methods are special cases of the $(b - 1)$'s-complement and b's-complement representation techniques in base b number systems. For example, consider the decimal system. The sign and magnitude values $+527$ and -382 have four-digit signed-number representations in each of the complement systems as shown in Table P7.1. The 9's complement is formed by taking the complement of each digit position with respect to 9. The 10's complement is formed by adding 1 to the 9's complement. In each of the latter two representations, the leftmost digit is 0 for a positive number and 9 for a negative number.

Table P7.1 Signed numbers in base 10

Representation	Two examples	
Sign and magnitude	+527	−382
9's complement	0527	9617
10's complement	0527	9618

Now consider the base 3 (ternary) system, where the positive five-digit number $t_4t_3t_2t_1t_0$ has the value $t_4 \times 3^4 + t_3 \times 3^3 + t_2 \times 3^2 + t_1 \times 3^1 + t_0 \times 3^0$, with $0 \le t_i \le 2$. Express the ternary sign and magnitude numbers $+2120$, -1212, $+10$, and -201 as five-digit signed ternary numbers in both the 2's-complement and 3's-complement systems.

7.4 Consider the binary numbers in the following add and subtract problems to be signed 6-bit values in the 2's-complement representation. Perform the operations indicated, specify the cases where overflow occurs and where no overflow occurs, and check your answers by converting operands and results to decimal sign and magnitude representation.

$$
\begin{array}{ccc}
010110 & 101011 & 111111 \\
+\ 001001 & +\ 100101 & +\ 000111 \\
\end{array}
$$

$$
\begin{array}{ccc}
011001 & 110111 & 010101 \\
+\ 010000 & +\ 111001 & +\ 101011 \\
\end{array}
$$

$$
\begin{array}{ccc}
010110 & 111110 & 100001 \\
-\ 011111 & -\ 100101 & -\ 011101 \\
\end{array}
$$

$$
\begin{array}{ccc}
111111 & 000111 & 011010 \\
-\ 000111 & -\ 111000 & -\ 100010 \\
\end{array}
$$

7.5 Using the "paper-and-pencil" methods, perform the operations $A \times B$ and $A \div B$ on the 5-bit positive numbers

$$A = 10101 \quad \text{and} \quad B = 00101$$

7.6 Show how the multiplication and division operations in Problem 7.5 would be performed by the hardware in Figures 7.9a and 7.24, respectively, by constructing the equivalent of Figures 7.9b and 7.26 for the above A and B operands.

7.7 Multiply the signed 6-bit numbers

$$A = 010111 \quad \text{(multiplicand)}$$

and

$$B = 110110 \quad \text{(multiplier)}$$

using the Booth algorithm.

7.8 Repeat Problem 7.7 using bit pairing of the multiplier.

7.9 Construct the equivalent of Figure 7.22 for the multiplication operation in Problem 7.7.

7.10 Derive logic equations that specify the ADD/SUB and S_R outputs of the combinational CONTROL network in Figure 7.28.

7.11 Show a microroutine that can implement the MUL (Multiply) instruction defined in Appendix B. Assume that the basic structure of Figure 5.2 is used, with eight general-purpose registers. What other hardware would be useful to have (if any)?

7.12 Write two PDP-11 programs for integer division, one based on the restoring-division algorithm and the other based on the nonrestoring-division algorithm. Assume both operands are positive; that is, $b_{15} = 0$ for both dividend and divisor.

Which of these programs is better from the standpoint of execution speed?

7.13 In Section 7.10.1, we used a practical size 32-bit format for floating-point numbers. In this problem, we will use a shortened format that retains all the pertinent concepts but is manageable for working through numerical exercises.

Consider that floating-point numbers are represented in a 12-bit format as follows:

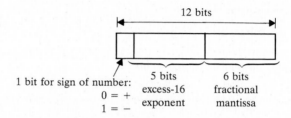

The scale factor has an implied base of 4, and a 5-bit, excess-16 exponent. The 6-bit mantissa is normalized.

(a) What does "normalized" mean in the context of this format?

(b) Represent the numbers +1.7, −0.012, +19, and ⅛ in this format.

(c) What is the range representable in this format?

(d) How does the range calculated in (c) compare to 12-bit integer or fraction ranges?

(e) Perform Add, Subtract, Multiply, and Divide operations on the operands.

$$A = \boxed{0\ |\ 1\ 0\ 0\ 0\ 1\ |\ 0\ 1\ 1\ 0\ 1\ 1}$$

$$B = \boxed{1\ |\ 0\ 1\ 1\ 1\ 1\ |\ 1\ 0\ 1\ 0\ 1\ 0}$$

7.14 The IBM 370 32-bit floating-point format is described in Section 7.10.

(a) Represent the following decimal numbers in this format.

(1) 0	(6) 3.92×10^2
(2) −1	(7) −0.000125
(3) 0.5	(8) 500
(4) 10	(9) -1.0×10^5
(5) 4096	(10) 1.1×10^{-4}

(b) What problems do you encounter when trying to convert the following decimal numbers into this format?

(1) 7.1239×10^{51}

(2) -1.4325×10^{-27}

(c) Propose some solution to the problem encountered in part (b). Your solution should be programmable on a machine that has the four arithmetic operations on the 32-bit internal format that you must convert into. You may also use the machine's 32-bit integer facilities if it helps your conversion.

7.15 Consider the representation of the decimal number 0.1 as a signed 8-bit binary fraction in the representation discussed at the beginning of Section 7.10. If this number does not convert exactly in this 8-bit format, give the approximations to it that are developed by all three of the truncation methods discussed in Section 7.10.2

7.16 Write a program for the PDP-11 computer to transform a 16-bit positive binary number into a five-digit decimal number, where each digit of this number is coded in the binary-coded decimal (BCD) code and occupies the low-order 4 bits of five successive byte locations in the main memory. Use the conversion technique based on successive division by 10, which is analogous to successive division by 2 when converting decimal to binary as discussed in Appendix D. Consult Appendix B for the format and operation of the PDP-11 Divide instruction.

7.17 It is required to build a modulo 10 adder for adding BCD digits. Modulo 10 addition of two numbers $A = A_3A_2A_1A_0$ and $B = B_3B_2B_1B_0$ can be achieved in two stages:

1. Add A to B (binary addition).
2. If the result is an illegal code that is greater than or equal to 10_{10}, add 6_{10}; otherwise, add 0. Ignore overflow from this stage of the adder.

    (a) Show that the above algorithm will give correct results for:
        (1) A = 0101   B = 0110
        (2) A = 0011   B = 0100
    (b) Design a BCD digit adder using logic gates and the 4-bit MSI chip described in Section 7.4.1. The inputs are $A_3A_2A_1A_0$, $B_3B_2B_1B_0$, and a carry-in. The outputs are the sum digit $S_3S_2S_1S_0$ and the carry-out. A cascade of such blocks can form a ripple-carry BCD adder.

7.18 If gate fan-in is limited to four, how can the hex digit SHIFTER in Figure 7.28 be implemented combinationally?

7.19 *(a)* Sketch a logic-gate network that implements the multiplexer MPX in Figure 7.28.
    (b) Relate the structure of the SWAP network in Figure 7.28 to your solution to part *(a)*.

7.20 How can the "leading hex zeros detector" of Figure 7.28 be implemented combinationally?

7.21 The Mantissa adder-subtractor in Figure 7.28 operates on positive, unsigned binary fractions and must produce a sign and magnitude result. In the discussion accompanying Figure 7.28, we stated that 1's-complement arithmetic is convenient because of the required format for input and output operands. When adding two signed numbers in 1's-complement notation, the carry-out from the sign position must be added to the result to obtain the correct signed answer. This is called "end-around carry" correction. Consider the following examples of addition using signed 4-bit encodings of operands and results in the 1's-complement system:

$$
\begin{array}{rcrc}
(3) & 0\ 0\ 1\ 1 & (6) & 0\ 1\ 1\ 0 \\
+(-5) & +\ \boxed{0}\ \ 1_00_11_00_0 & +(-3) & +\ \boxed{1}\ \ 1_11_00_00_0 \\
\hline
-2 & \phantom{+\ \boxed{0}}\begin{array}{|l}1\ 1\ 0\ 1\\ {\longrightarrow}0\end{array} & 3 & \phantom{+\ \boxed{1}}\begin{array}{|l}0\ 0\ 1\ 0\\ {\longrightarrow}1\end{array} \\
\hline
& 1\ 1\ 0\ 1 & & 0\ 0\ 1\ 1 \\
\end{array}
$$

1's-complement arithmetic is convenient when a sign and magnitude result is to be generated because a negative number in 1's-complement notation can be converted to sign and magnitude by complementing the bits to the right of the sign-bit position. Using 2's-complement arithmetic, addition of +1 is needed for conversion of a negative value into sign and magnitude notation.

    If a carry lookahead adder is used, it is possible to incorporate the end-around carry operation required by 1's-complement arithmetic into the lookahead logic.

    With the above discussion as a guideline, give the complete design of the 1's-complement adder-subtractor required in Figure 7.28.

7.22 Give the complete design of the 4-bit ALU circuit block shown in Figure 7.7b. Omit the control inputs and assume that the circuit performs only 4-bit addition. Carry lookahead logic is to be used for all the internal carries c_1, c_2, and c_3 as well as for the block output c_4.

Your answer can be in the form of a sketch of the logic-gate network required or a listing of logic equations that describe the network.

7.23 Four 4-bit adder circuits shown in Figure 7.7b can be cascaded to form a 16-bit adder. In this cascade, the output c_4 from the low-order circuit is connected as the carry-in to the next circuit. Its carry-out, c_8, is connected as the carry-in to the third circuit, etc.

(a) A faster adder can be constructed by using external logic to generate the carry-in variables for the three high-order circuits. Give the logic design for an integrated circuit "carry lookahead" chip that has outputs c_4, c_8, and c_{12}. Its inputs are c_0, P_0^I, G_0^I, P_1^I, G_1^I, P_2^I, and G_2^I. Estimate the increase in adder speed achievable by using this circuit in conjunction with the four 4-bit adder circuits, as opposed to using a cascade of the adder circuits, in building a 16-bit adder.

(b) Extend your part (a) design by assuming that the carry lookahead chip has P_3^I and G_3^I as additional inputs and provides additional outputs P_0^{II} and G_0^{II}. These higher-level propagate and generate functions are defined by

$$P_0^{II} = P_3^I P_2^I P_1^I P_0^I$$

$$G_0^{II} = G_3^I + P_3^I G_2^I + P_3^I P_2^I G_1^I + P_3^I P_2^I P_1^I G_0^I$$

Note that this extended circuit requires 16 external pin connections, consisting of 14 for input and output variables and 2 for power connections, so that it can be accommodated in a standard 16-pin IC package.

(c) Design a 64-bit adder that uses sixteen 4-bit adder circuits, some carry lookahead circuits defined by the design from part (b), and some additional logic to generate c_{16}, c_{32}, and c_{48} from c_0 and the P_i^{II} and G_i^{II} variables generated by the lookahead circuits. What is the relationship of the additional logic to the logic inside each lookahead circuit?

7.24 Figure P7.1 shows a two-dimensional array of combinational logic cells for 3×3 positive-number multiplication. Analyze the typical cells and the data flow to verify that it computes products properly.

(a) Compare the total delay in developing the product in this type of array with that of Figure 7.8 as a function of the input operand length n.

(b) Which of the cells in Figure P7.1 and its $n \times (n + 1)$ extension perform no useful function? This cellular logic arrangement is the basis for some of the VLSI multiplier chips that are commercially available.

7.25 The array described in Problem 7.24 is an example of the application of the principle of *carry-save addition*. This principle can be applied in any situation where a number of summands need to be added to generate a sum.

The simplest example is in the case of adding three numbers W, X, and Y. The straightforward way to do this is to add W to X and then add the resulting sum to Y to generate the answer. An alternative, using carry-save addition, is to combine the three operands with n full adders to generate two numbers, S (sum bits) and C (carry bits), which are then added in a ripple-carry adder to generate the desired sum. This process is shown in Figure P7.2.

(a) Apply this idea to the multiplication of two n-bit positive numbers. Start by considering the problem as one of adding n summands, appropriately shifted, as in the paper-and-pencil method. Reduce these n summands to $\frac{2}{3} n$ numbers by performing carry-save additions on them in parallel in groups of three. Then reduce the results, etc., until only two numbers remain. They are finally added to generate the desired product. This principle is used in many high-performance computers.

(b) Compare the speed and cost of this type of multiplier with that of Problem 7.24 or Figure 7.8.

(c) Can bit grouping of the multiplier be combined with carry-save addition to configure a faster and/or cheaper multiplier?

7.26 Write a PDP-11 program to implement the Booth algorithm for signed-number multiplication.

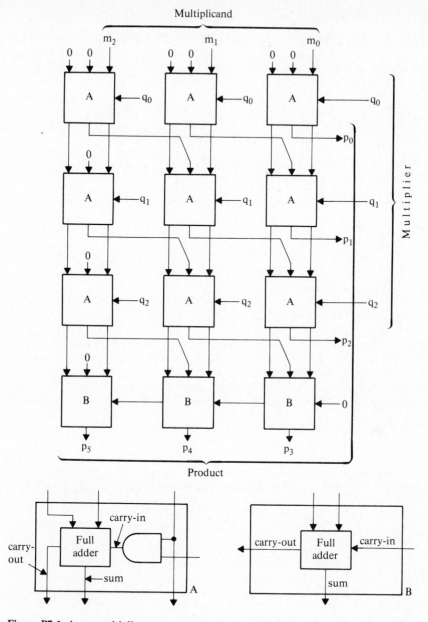

Figure P7.1 Array multiplier.

7.27 The following PDP-11 routine multiplies the binary number in register R_1 by the value 10.

```
ASL   R1
MOV   R1,R0
ASL   R1
ASL   R1
ADD   R0,R1
```

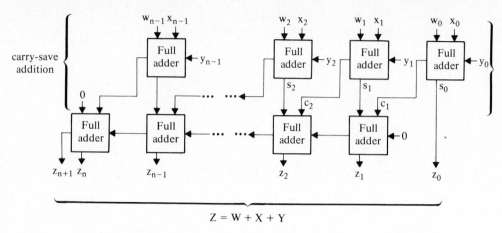

$$Z = W + X + Y$$

Figure P7.2 Carry-save addition principle.

Assume that four BCD digits, representing a decimal integer in the range 0 to 9999, are packed into the 16-bit word at main memory location DECIMAL.

Write a PDP-11 subroutine to convert the decimal integer stored at DECIMAL into binary representation and store it in main memory location BINARY.

7.28 In the discussion of rounding in Section 7.10.4 in association with the IEEE floating-point standard, it was claimed that 3 guard bits are sufficient to implement rounding as defined in Section 7.10.2. Construct an example that shows that all 3 guard bits are needed to produce the correct answer. (*Hint*: Consider the subtraction of two positive numbers.)

7.29 Repeat Problem 7.14 for the IEEE standard single precision floating-point format.

7.30 *(a)* Multiply the signed 2's-complement 8-bit numbers

$$A = 00011010 \quad \text{(Multiplicand)}$$

and $$B = 11000111 \quad \text{(Multiplier)}$$

using the Booth algorithm and generating a 16-bit product.

(b) Compute the sign and magnitude decimal representations of A, B, and the product from part *(a)*.

7.31 Repeat Problem 7.30 *(a)* using bit pairing of the multiplier.

7.32 Consider a 16-bit floating-point number in a format similar to that of Problem 7.13 with a 6-bit exponent and a 9-bit normalized fractional mantissa. The base of the scale factor is 8 and the exponent is represented in excess-32 format.

(a) Add the numbers

$$A = 0\ 100001\ 111111110$$

and $$B = 0\ 011111\ 101010101$$

which are expressed in the above format, giving the answer in normalized form. Use rounding as the truncation method when producing the final normalized 9-bit mantissa.

(b) Using decimal numbers w, x, y, and z, express the magnitude of the largest and smallest (nonzero) values representable in the above normalized floating-point format, in the form

$$\text{Largest} = w \times 8^x$$

$$\text{Smallest} = y \times 8^{-z}$$

7.33 Show how to modify the circuit diagram of Figure 7.9 to implement multiplication of signed, 2's-complement, n-bit numbers using the Booth algorithm.

7.13 REFERENCES

7.1 "The Intel 8231 Arithmetic Processing Unit," Intel Corporation, Santa Clara, Calif., January 1980.

7.2 "The Advanced Micro Devices Am9511 Floating-Point Processor," Advanced Micro Devices, Inc., Sunnyvale, Calif., 1979.

7.3 "The Intel 8087 Numeric Data Processor," Intel Corporation, Santa Clara, Calif., May 1980

7.4 A Proposed Standard for Floating-Point Arithmetic, *Computer,* vol. 14, no. 3, pp. 51-62, March 1981.

EIGHT

THE MAIN MEMORY

Programs and the data they operate on are assumed to be held in the main memory (MM) of the computer during execution. In this chapter, we will discuss the way in which this vital part of the computer operates. By now, the reader appreciates the fact that the speed of execution of instructions is highly dependent upon the speed with which data can be transferred to or from the MM. Thus it is not surprising that memory design has been, and continues to be, an important topic in computer development.

In most modern computer systems, the physical MM is not as large as the address space spanned by an address issued by the CPU. When a program does not totally fit into the MM, parts of it not currently being executed are stored on secondary storage devices such as magnetic disks. Of course, all parts of a program which are eventually executed must first be brought into the MM. When a new segment of a program is to be moved into a full MM, it must replace another segment already in the MM. The programmer should not need to be concerned with the details of the transfers. Modern computers have automatic means for managing such operations. These memory management techniques will be discussed in this chapter.

8.1 SOME BASIC CONCEPTS

The maximum size of the MM that can be used in any computer is determined by the addressing scheme. For example, a 16-bit computer that generates 16-bit addresses is capable of addressing up to 2^{16} (= 64K) memory locations. Similarly, a machine whose instructions generate 24-bit addresses can utilize an MM that contains up to 2^{24} (= 16×10^6) memory locations. This number represents the size of the address space of the computer.

In some computers, the smallest addressable unit of information is a memory word. Successive memory addresses refer to successive memory words, and the machine is called *word-addressable*. Alternatively, individual memory bytes may be assigned distinct addresses, thus yielding a *byte-addressable* computer. In such a case, a memory word contains one or more memory bytes which can be addressed individually. For example, in a byte-addressable 32-bit computer, each memory word contains 4 bytes. A possible way of address assignment in this case is shown in Figure 8.1. The address of a word is that of its high-order byte. Thus word addresses are always integer multiples of 4. It should be noted that in some machines, including the PDP-11, byte-address assignment within a word is opposite to that in Figure 8.1 (see Figure 2.7).

The MM is usually designed to store and retrieve data in word-length quantities. In fact, the number of bits actually stored or retrieved in one MM access is the most usual way of defining the word length of a computer. Consider, for example, a byte-addressable computer with the addressing structure of Figure 8.1, whose instructions generate 24-bit addresses. When a 24-bit address is sent from the CPU to the MM unit, the high-order 22 bits determine which word will be accessed. If a byte quantity is specified, the low-order 2 bits of the address specify which byte location is involved. In the case of a Read operation, other bytes may be fetched from the MM, but they are ignored by the CPU. However, if the byte operation is a Write, the control circuitry of the MM must ensure that the contents of other bytes of the same word are not changed.

From the system standpoint, we can view the MM unit as a "black box." Data transfer between the MM and the CPU takes place through the use of the two CPU registers MAR (memory address register) and MDR (memory data register). Let MAR be k bits long and MDR n bits long. Thus the MM unit may contain up to 2^k addressable locations. During a "memory cycle," n bits of data are transferred between the MM and the CPU. This transfer takes place over the *memory bus*, which consists of k address lines and n data lines. It also includes the control lines Read, Write, and Memory Function Completed (MFC) for coordinating data transfers. In the case of byte-addressable computers, another control line may be added to indicate when only a byte, rather than a full word of n bits, is to be transferred. The connection between the CPU and the MM is shown schematically in Figure 8.2. As described in Chapter 4, the CPU initiates a memory operation by loading the appropriate data into registers MDR and MAR, then setting either the Read or Write memory control line to 1. When the required operation is completed, the memory control circuitry indicates this to the CPU by setting MFC to 1. The details of operation of the bus have been presented in Chapter 6.

Word address   Byte address

0	1	2	3
4	5	6	7
8	9	10	11

Word address: 0, 4, 8

Figure 8.1 Organization of the main memory in a 32-bit byte-addressable computer.

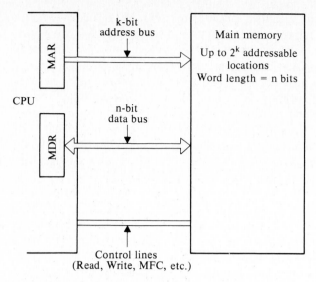

Figure 8.2 Connection of the main memory to the CPU.

A useful measure of the speed of memory units is the time that elapses between the initiation of an operation and the completion of that operation (for example, the time between Read and MFC). This is referred to as the *memory access time*. Another important measure is the *memory cycle time*. This is the minimum time delay required between the initiation of two independent memory operations (for example, two successive Read operations). The cycle time is usually slightly longer than the access time. The difference is highly dependent upon the implementation details of a particular MM unit.

Recall that a memory unit is called a *random-access memory* (RAM) if any location can be accessed for a Read or Write operation in some fixed amount of time that is independent of its position or address. Main memory units are of this type. This distinguishes them from serial, or partly serial, access storage devices such as magnetic tapes, drums, and disks. Access times on the latter devices depend upon the address or position of the data. Such devices will be discussed in Chapter 9.

The basic technology for the implementation of main memories uses semiconductor integrated circuits. The sections that follow will present some basic facts about the internal structure and operation of such memories. We will then discuss two significant problems associated with MM units, namely, speed and size.

The speed problem arises because the CPU can usually process instructions and data faster than they can be fetched from compatibly priced conventional MM units. That is, the MM cycle time is the bottleneck in the system. In many cases, high-speed performance is required. This may be achieved in a number of ways. One possibility is the use of a *cache memory*—a small and fast memory that is inserted between the larger and slower MM and the CPU. It serves to hold the currently active segments of a program and its data. Another technique is to divide the system into a number of memory modules. Addressing is arranged so that successive words in the address space are in different modules. If requests for memory access tend to involve consecutive addresses, such as in executing straight-line program segments, then the accesses will be to different modules. Since parallel access to these modules is possible, the average rate of fetching words from the MM to the CPU can be increased. The technique is called *memory interleaving*. This brief discussion of solutions to the speed problem will be expanded later.

Before discussing the problem of MM size, let us introduce the notion of *virtual memory*, which is an important concept related to memory organization. So far, it has been assumed that the addresses generated by the CPU directly specify physical locations in the MM. This may not always be the case. For reasons that will become apparent later, data may be stored in physical memory locations that have addresses different from those specified by the program. The memory control circuitry translates the address specified by the program into an address that can be used for accessing the physical memory. In such a case, an address generated by the CPU is referred to as a *virtual address*. The virtual address space, which is used by the program, is mapped onto the physical memory where data is actually stored. The mapping function is implemented by memory control circuitry often called the *memory management unit*. This mapping function may be changed dynamically during program execution according to system requirements.

The concept of virtual memory can be used to deal with the problem of size of the MM. Almost every computer reaches a point in its existence where programmers require more memory than is available. It is often more economical to use magnetic disks or drums to increase the available memory space before the maximum possible size (2^k in the above discussion) of MM is reached. The programmer would like to address data stored on the bulk storage devices as if it were in the MM. It is at this point that the concept of virtual memory can be utilized. Data is addressed in a virtual address space that can be as large as the addressing capability of the CPU. At any given time, only the active portion of this space is mapped onto the physical MM. The remaining virtual addresses are mapped onto the bulk storage devices used. As the active portion of the virtual address space changes during program execution, the memory management unit changes the mapping function and transfers data between the bulk storage and the MM as required. Thus, during every memory cycle, an address-processing mechanism (hardware and/or software) determines whether or not the address generated by the CPU is in the physical MM unit. If it is, then the proper word is accessed and execution proceeds. If it is not, a contiguous block of words containing the desired word is transferred from the bulk storage to the MM, displacing some block in the MM that is currently inactive. Because of the time required for movement of blocks between the bulk storage and the MM, there is a speed degradation in this type of a system. However, by a suitable choice of block replacement methods, it is possible to have reasonably long periods during which the probability is high that the words accessed by the CPU are in the physical MM unit. It should be noted that block movement can be achieved by DMA cycle-stealing techniques. Therefore, other active programs that are resident in the MM can be executed while a block transfer is taking place for a particular program.

This introductory section has attempted to introduce a number of nontrivial ideas. They have been developed to solve the problems of trying to provide a computer system with as large and as fast an MM component as can be afforded in relation to the overall cost of the system. We do not expect the reader to have grasped all the ideas or their implications. More detail will be given later. The reason for introducing these terms together is to establish the notion that they are related. A study of their interrelationships is as important as a detailed study of their individual features.

8.2 SEMICONDUCTOR RAM MEMORIES

Semiconductor memories are available in a wide range of speeds. Their cycle times range from a few hundred nanoseconds to a few tens of nanoseconds. When first introduced in the late 1960s, they were much more expensive than magnetic-core memories that they replaced. Because of the advances in VLSI (very large-scale integration) technology, the cost of semiconductor memories has dropped dramatically. As a result, they are now used almost exclusively in the implementation of main memories.

Semiconductor memories may be divided into bipolar and MOS (metal-oxide semiconductor) types. In what follows, we will present a configuration for a storage cell in each of these technologies. However, we should note that these are by no means the only possibilities. There are many cell configurations that represent various design trade-offs. The purpose of this discussion is to point out the major characteristics of semiconductor memories and their impact on the performance of the MM unit of a computer. We will start by introducing the way in which a number of memory cells are organized inside a chip.

8.2.1 Internal Organization of Memory Chips

A memory cell is capable of storing 1 bit of information. A number of cells are usually organized in the form of an array. One such organization is shown in Figure 8.3. Each row of cells constitutes a memory word, and all cells of a row are connected to a common line referred to as the *word line*. The word lines are driven by the address decoder on the chip. The cells in each column are connected by two lines, known as *bit lines*, to a Sense/Write circuit. The Sense/Write circuits are, in turn, connected to the data input-output lines of the chip. During a Read operation, the Sense/Write circuits sense, or read, the information stored in the cells selected by a word line and transmit this

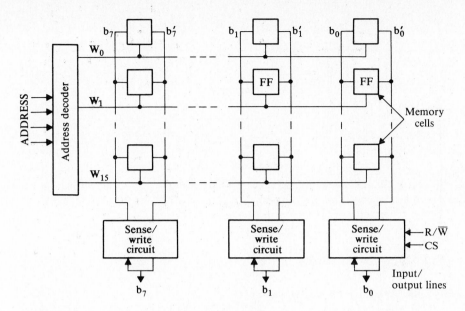

Figure 8.3 Organization of bit cells in a memory chip.

information to the output data lines. During a Write operation, they receive input information and store it in the cells of the selected word.

Figure 8.3 shows a memory chip consisting of 16 words of 8 bits each, usually referred to as a 16×8 organization. The data input and the data output of each Sense/Write circuit are connected to a single bidirectional data line in order to reduce the number of pins required. In addition to address and data lines, two control lines, $R/\overline{W}$ and CS, are provided. The $R/\overline{W}$ (Read/$\overline{Write}$) input is used to specify the required operation. The CS (Chip Select) input is needed to select a given chip in a multichip memory system, as will be discussed in Section 8.3.

The memory circuit of Figure 8.3 has 128 bits and a total of 14 pins. Thus, it can be manufactured in the form of a 16-pin chip, allowing 2 pins for power supply and ground connections. Consider now a slightly larger memory circuit, one that has 1K (1024) memory cells. This can be organized as a 128×8 memory chip, requiring a total of 19 external connections. A 20-pin chip may be used, leaving 1 pin unused. Alternatively, the circuit can be organized into a $1K \times 1$ format. This makes it possible to use a 16-pin chip even if separate pins are provided for the data input and data output lines. Figure 8.4 shows such an organization. The required 10-bit address is divided into two groups of 5 bits each to form the row and column addresses for the cell array. A row address selects a row of 32 cells, all of which are accessed in parallel. However, according to the column address, only one of these cells is connected to the external data lines via the input and output multiplexers.

We should note that commercially available chips contain a much larger

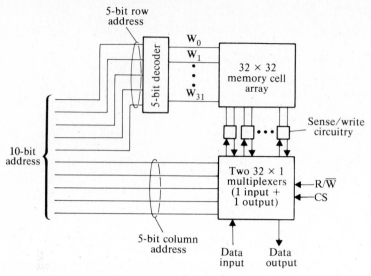

Figure 8.4 Organization of a 1K × 1 memory chip.

number of cells than those shown in Figures 8.3 and 8.4. In order to make these figures simple and easy to understand, we have chosen to use small-size chips as examples. Larger chips have essentially the same organization as that shown in Figure 8.4.

8.2.2 Bipolar Memory Cell

A typical bipolar storage cell is shown in Figure 8.5. Two transistor inverters (see Appendix A) are connected to implement a basic flip-flop. The cell is connected to one word line and two bit lines as shown. Normally, the bit lines are kept at about 1.6 V, while the word line is kept at a slightly higher voltage, about 2.5 V. Under these conditions the two diodes D_1 and D_2 are reverse-biased. Thus, since no current flows through the diodes, the cell is isolated from the bit lines.

Read operation Let us assume that a 1 is stored in the cell when Q_1 is conducting and Q_2 is Off, and a 0 is stored when Q_2 is conducting and Q_1 is Off. To read the contents of a given cell, the voltage on the corresponding word line is reduced from 2.5 V to approximately 0.3 V. This causes one of the two diodes D_1 or D_2 to become forward-biased, depending on whether transistor Q_1 or Q_2 is conducting. As a result, current flows from bit line b when the cell is in the 1 state and from bit line b' when the cell is in the 0 state. The Sense/Write circuit at the end of each pair of bit lines monitors the current on lines b and b' and sets the output bit lines accordingly.

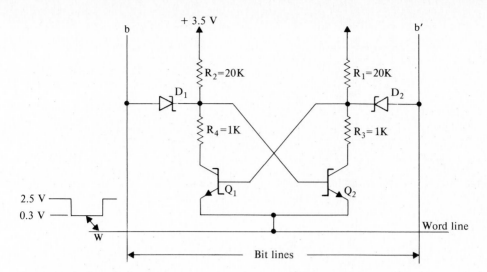

Figure 8.5 A bipolar memory cell.

Write operation While a given row of bits is selected, that is, while the voltage on the corresponding word line is 0.3 V, the cells can be forced individually to either the 1 state by applying a positive voltage (≈ 3 V) to line b' or to the 0 state by driving line b. This function is performed by the Sense/Write circuit.

8.2.3 MOS Memories

MOS technology is used extensively in MM units. Two important advantages of MOS devices, in comparison with bipolar devices, are that they allow higher bit densities on integrated circuit chips and they are fundamentally easier to manufacture. Moreover, MOS transistors are higher-impedance devices, thus leading to lower power dissipation. Their main disadvantage is their relatively slow speed of operation.

As in the case of bipolar memories, many MOS cell configurations are possible. The simplest of these is the flip-flop circuit of Figure 8.6. Operation of the circuit is similar to its bipolar counterpart. Transistors T_3 and T_4 perform the same function as resistors R_1 and R_2 in Figure 8.5. Transistors T_5 and T_6 correspond to the two diodes D_1 and D_2. They act as switches that can be opened or closed under control of the word line. When these two switches are closed, the contents of the cell are transferred to the bit lines. As in the case of the bipolar memory, when a given cell is selected, its contents can be overwritten by applying appropriate voltages on the bit lines.

Both the bipolar cell of Figure 8.5 and its MOS counterpart of Figure 8.6 require a continuous flow of current from the power supply through one of the two branches of the flip-flop. They are capable of storing information indefinite-

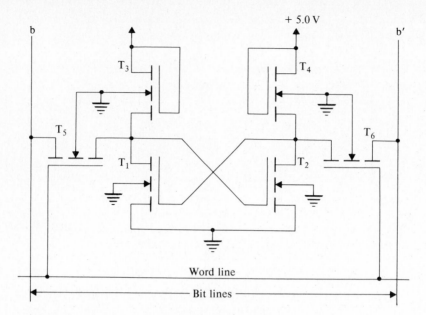

Figure 8.6 An example of an n-channel MOS memory cell.

ly, provided that this current flow is maintained. Hence they are referred to as static memories.

The high impedance attainable in the MOS technology allows construction of a different type of memory known as dynamic memory (DRAM). A dynamic memory is based on simple cells, which allow higher bit density and lower power consumption relative to static configurations.

Dynamic memories The basic idea of a dynamic memory is very simple. Information is stored in the form of a charge on a capacitor. If the capacitor discharges very slowly, the stored information will be retained for some time. Such memories are capable of storing information only for periods of time of the order of a few milliseconds. If it is required to store the information for a longer time, the contents of each memory cell must be periodically refreshed by restoring the capacitor charge to its full value.

An example of a dynamic memory cell is shown in Figure 8.7. It consists of a capacitor C and a transistor T. In order to store information in this cell, transistor T is turned On and an appropriate voltage V is applied to the bit line. This causes a known amount of charge to be stored on the capacitor.

After the transistor is turned Off, the capacitor discharges slowly. This is due to the capacitor's own leakage resistance and the fact that the transistor conducts a small amount of current, of the order of picoamperes, even when it is turned Off. Hence, the information stored in the cell can be retrieved correctly only if it is read before the charge on the capacitor drops below some threshold

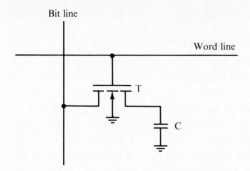

Figure 8.7 A single-transistor dynamic memory cell.

value. During a Read operation, the bit line is placed in a high-impedance state, and the transistor is turned On. A sense circuit connected to the bit line is used to determine whether the charge on the capacitor is above or below the threshold value. Because this charge is small, the Read operation is quite involved. The details are beyond the scope of this text. However, we should note one important feature. During the process of reading the contents of the cell, the charge on the capacitor is restored to its original value. That is, a memory cell is *refreshed* every time its contents are read.

A typical organization of a 64K $\times$ 1 dynamic memory chip is shown in Figure 8.8. The cells are organized in the form of a square array, where the high- and low-order 8 bits of the 16-bit address constitute the row and column

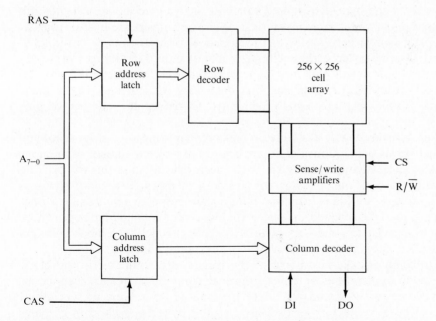

Figure 8.8 Internal organization of a 64K $\times$ 1 dynamic memory IC.

addresses of a given cell, respectively. In order to reduce the number of pins needed for external connections, the row and column addresses are multiplexed on eight pins. During a Read or a Write operation, the row address is applied first. In response to a signal pulse on the Row Address Strobe (RAS) input of the chip, this part of the address is loaded into the row address latch, and a Read operation is initiated on the corresponding row. All cells on this line are read and refreshed. Shortly after the row address is latched, the column address is applied to the address pins. It is loaded into the column address latch under control of the Column Address Strobe (CAS) signal. The information in this latch is decoded and the appropriate Sense/Write circuit is selected. If the $R/\overline{W}$ control signal indicates a Read operation, the output of the selected circuit is transferred to the data output, DO. For a Write operation, the information at the data input DI is transferred to the selected circuit. This information is then used to overwrite the contents of the cell in the corresponding column.

It is important to emphasize that the application of a row address causes all cells on the corresponding row to be read and refreshed. This takes place during both Read and Write operations. In order to ensure that the contents of a dynamic memory are maintained, each row of cells must be addressed periodically, typically once every 2 ms. This function is usually performed automatically by a *Refresh circuit*. Some dynamic memory chips incorporate a Refresh facility within the chip itself. In this case, the dynamic nature of the memory is almost completely transparent to the user. Such memory chips are often referred to as pseudostatic.

Because of the high density and low cost of dynamic memories, they are widely used in computer main memories. Available chips range in size from 1K to 256K, with even larger chips being developed. In order to provide flexibility in designing memory systems, these chips are manufactured in different organizations. For example, a 64K chip may be organized as $64K \times 1$ or as $16K \times 4$. The latter differs from Figure 8.8 in that four data lines are provided. In this case, input and output lines are usually combined to reduce the number of pins needed.

A useful feature that is available on many dynamic memory chips should be mentioned at this point. Consider an application in which a number of memory locations at successive addresses are to be accessed. Assume further that the cells involved are all on the same row inside a memory chip. Since row and column addresses are loaded separately into their respective latches, it is only necessary to load the row address once. Then different column addresses can be loaded during successive memory cycles. The rate at which such block transfers can be carried out is typically double that for random access.

It is difficult to take advantage of the higher rate attainable in the block transfer mode in memories of general-purpose computers. In such computers, successive accesses to memory tend to be random. However, in specialized machines, where memory accesses follow regular patterns, such as in graphics terminals, this feature can be exploited.

8.3 MEMORY SYSTEM CONSIDERATIONS

The choice of a RAM chip for a given application depends on several factors. Foremost among these are the speed, power dissipation, and size of the chip. In certain situations, other features, such as the availability of block transfers, may be important.

Bipolar memories are generally used whenever very fast operation is the primary requirement. For example, this is usually the case in microprogram memories and cache memories. High power dissipation in bipolar circuits makes it difficult to achieve high densities. Hence, a memory implemented with bipolar memory chips requires a relatively large number of chips.

Dynamic MOS memory is the predominant technology used in computer main memories. The high densities achievable in this technology make the implementation of large memories economically attractive.

Static MOS memory chips have higher densities and slightly longer access times than bipolar chips. They have lower densities than dynamic memories. They are also easier to use because they do not require refreshing. A static memory is particularly well suited to applications in which the occasional increase in access delay caused by Refresh cycles cannot be tolerated.

We will now discuss the design of memory subsystems using static and dynamic chips. Consider first a small memory consisting of 64K (65,536) words of 16 bits each. An example of the organization of this memory using 16K × 1 static memory chips is given in Figure 8.9. A set of four chips is required to implement each bit position. The set corresponds to one column in the figure. Sixteen such sets provide the required 64K × 16 memory. Each chip has a control input called Chip Select. A chip can be enabled to accept data input or to place data on the output bus by setting its Chip Select input to 1. The data output for each chip is of the three-state type (see Section 4.1.5). Only the selected chip places data on the output line, while all other outputs are in the high-impedance state. The address bus for this 64K memory is 16 bits wide. The high-order 2 bits of the address are decoded to obtain the four Chip Select control signals. The remaining 14 address bits are connected to all the chips. They are used to access a specific bit location inside each chip of the selected row. The R/$\overline{\text{W}}$ inputs of all chips are also tied together to provide a common Read/$\overline{\text{Write}}$ control (not shown).

Next let us consider a large, dynamic memory. The organization of such a memory is essentially the same as that in Figure 8.9. However, the control circuitry differs in three respects. First, the row and column parts of the address for each chip usually have to be multiplexed. Secondly, a Refresh circuit is needed. Finally, the timing of various steps of a memory cycle must be carefully controlled.

An example of a dynamic memory unit is given in Figure 8.10. The figure depicts an array of 64 dynamic memory chips and the required control circuitry. The memory chips are assumed to be arranged in a 4 × 16 array, in exactly the

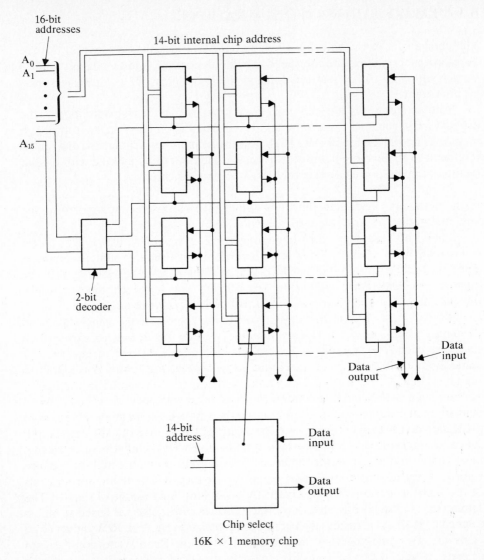

Figure 8.9 Organization of a 64K × 16 memory using 16K × 1 static memory chips.

same way as in Figure 8.9. Thus, if individual chips have a 64K × 1 organization, the array has a total storage capacity of 256K words of 16 bits each. The control circuitry provides the multiplexed address and Chip Select inputs, as well as the Row and Column Address Strobe signals (RAS and CAS) to the memory chip array. It is also responsible for generating Refresh cycles as needed. The memory unit is assumed to be connected to an asynchronous memory bus which has 18 address lines, $ADRS_{17-0}$; 16 data lines, $DATA_{15-0}$; two handshake signals,

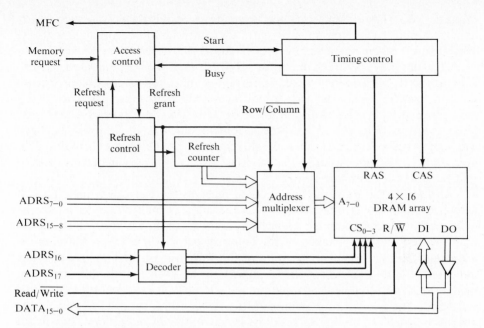

Figure 8.10 A block diagram of a 256K × 16 dynamic memory unit.

Memory Request and Memory Function Completed (MFC); and a Read/$\overline{\text{Write}}$
line to indicate the type of memory cycle requested.

   In order to understand the operation of the control circuitry in Figure 8.10,
let us start by examining a normal memory read cycle. The cycle begins by the
CPU asserting the address, the Read/$\overline{\text{Write}}$ and the Memory Request lines. Such
a request is recognized by the access control block when the Memory Request
signal becomes active, and as a result, the Start signal is set to 1. The timing
control block responds immediately by activating the Busy signal, in order to
prevent new requests from being accepted by the access control block, until the
cycle ends. Then it loads the row and column addresses into the memory chips
by activating the RAS and CAS lines, respectively. During this time, it uses the
Row/$\overline{\text{Column}}$ line to select first the row address, $ADRS_{15-8}$, followed by the
column address, $ADRS_{7-0}$. The decoder block performs exactly the same
function as the decoder in Figure 8.9. It decodes the 2 most significant bits of the
address, $ADRS_{17,16}$, and activates one of the Chip Select lines, CS_{0-3}.

   Having obtained the row and column parts of the address, the selected
memory chips place the contents of the requested bit cells on their data outputs.
This information is transferred to the data lines of the memory bus via
appropriate drivers. The timing control block allows for delays in the circuitry
involved; then it activates the MFC line, indicating that the requested data is
now available on the memory bus. At the end of the memory cycle, the timing
block deactivates the Busy signal. The access unit is now free to accept new

requests. We should note that the exact time at which various signals are activated and deactivated must be carefully controlled in accordance with the specifications of the particular type of memory chips used.

Consider now a Refresh operation. Refresh requests are generated periodically by the Refresh control block. In response, the access control block starts a memory cycle in the normal way. It indicates to the Refresh control block that it may proceed with a Refresh operation by activating the Refresh Grant line. Note that the function of the access control block is to arbitrate between Memory Access requests and Refresh requests. In the case of simultaneous arrivals, Refresh requests are given priority. This is necessary in order to ensure that no stored information is lost.

As soon as the Refresh control block receives the Refresh Grant signal, it activates the Refresh line. This causes the address multiplexer to select the output of the Refresh counter. Hence, the contents of the counter will be loaded into the row address latches of all memory chips when the RAS signal is activated. During this time, the state of the $R/\overline{W}$ line of the memory bus may indicate a Write operation. It is important to ensure that this does not inadvertently result in new information being loaded into some of the cells being refreshed. The needed protection can be provided in several ways. A possible approach is that, while the Refresh line is active, the decoder block deactivates all CS lines. This prevents any memory chip from responding to the $R/\overline{W}$ line. The remainder of the Refresh cycle is the same as in a normal cycle. At the end, the Refresh control block increments the Refresh counter in preparation for the next Refresh cycle.

We should note that the Refresh counter is only 7 bits wide, although an 8-bit row address is needed. This choice is related to the way in which cells are organized inside the memory chips. The 256×256 array in Figure 8.8 in fact consists of two 128×256 arrays, each having its own set of Sense/Write circuits. One row in each of the two arrays is accessed during any memory cycle, depending upon the low-order 7 bits of the row address. The most significant bit of the row address is used only in a normal Read/Write cycle. It selects one of two groups of 256 columns. Because of this organization, the frequency of Refresh operations can be reduced to one-half of what would be needed had the memory cells been organized in a single 256×256 array.

The main purpose of the Refresh circuit is to maintain the integrity of the stored information. Ideally, its existence should be transparent to the remainder of the computer system. That is, other parts of the system, such as the CPU, should not be affected by the operation of the Refresh circuit. However, the CPU and the Refresh circuit, in effect, compete for access to the memory. In order to ensure that no information is lost, the Refresh circuit must be given priority. Thus, the response of the memory to a request from the CPU, or from a DMA device, may have to be delayed if a Refresh operation is in progress. The amount of delay caused by Refresh cycles depends upon the mode of operation of the Refresh circuit. During a Refresh operation, all memory rows may be refreshed in succession, before the memory is returned to normal use. A more common scheme is to interleave Refresh operations on successive rows with accesses from the memory bus. This results in Refresh periods which are shorter in duration but more frequent. In either case, the total number of memory cycles lost to Refresh operations is typically in the range 3 to 5 percent. Thus, the time penalty caused by the need for refreshing is small.

It is instructive at this point to recall the discussion of synchronous and asynchronous buses in Chapter 6. There is an apparent increase in the access time of the memory when a request arrives while a Refresh operation is in progress. The resulting variability in access time is naturally accommodated on an asynchronous bus. However, it is important that the maximum access time not exceed the time-out period that usually exists in such systems. This constraint is easily met when the interleaved Refresh scheme is used.

In the case of a synchronous bus, it may be possible to hide a Refresh cycle within the early part of a bus cycle. This can be done if sufficient time remains after a Refresh cycle to carry out a Read or a Write access. Alternatively, the Refresh circuit may request bus cycles in the same manner as any device having a DMA capability. In this case, it may be desirable to use non-interleaved refresh to avoid the overhead that may result from frequent DMA requests.

8.4 SEMICONDUCTOR ROM MEMORIES

Chapter 5 discussed the use of read-only memory (ROM) units as the control store component in a microprogrammed CPU. Semiconductor ROMs are well suited for this application. They can also be used for implementing a part of the MM of a computer which contains fixed programs or data that are not to be changed. This use of ROMs is particularly common in microprocessor systems, as will be discussed in Chapter 11.

Figure 8.11 shows a possible configuration for a ROM cell. The word line is normally held at a low voltage. If a word is to be selected, the voltage on the corresponding word line is momentarily raised, causing all transistors whose emitters are connected to their corresponding bit lines to be turned on. The

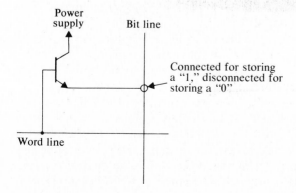

Figure 8.11 A storage cell for a bipolar read-only memory.

current that flows from the voltage supply to the bit line can be detected by a sense circuit as in Figure 8.3. The bit positions where current is detected are read as 1s, and the remaining bits are read as 0s. Therefore the contents of a given word are determined by the pattern of emitter to bit-line connections. Similar configurations are possible in MOS technology.

Data is written into a ROM at the time of manufacture. However, some ROM designs allow the data to be loaded by the user, thus providing a programmable ROM (PROM). This may be achieved by connecting a fuse between the emitter and the bit line in Figure 8.11. Thus prior to programming, the memory contains all 1s. The user can insert 0s at the required locations by burning out the fuses at these locations, using high-current pulses. Of course, this process is irreversible.

PROMs provide flexibility and convenience not available with ROMs. The latter are economically attractive for storing fixed programs and data where high production volumes are involved. However, the cost of preparing the masks needed for storing a particular information pattern in ROMs makes them very expensive when only a small number is required. In such a case, PROMs provide a faster and considerably less expensive approach, since they can be programmed directly by the user.

Another type of ROM chip allows the stored data to be erased and new data to be loaded. Such a chip is an erasable, reprogrammable ROM, usually called an EPROM. It provides considerable flexibility during the development phase of digital systems. Since EPROMs are capable of retaining stored information for long periods, they can be used in place of ROMs while software is being developed. In this way, changes and updates can be easily implemented.

An EPROM cell bears considerable resemblance to the dynamic memory cell discussed in Section 8.2.3. As in the case of dynamic memory, information is stored in the form of a charge on a capacitor. The main difference is that the capacitor in an EPROM cell is very well insulated. Its rate of discharge is so low that it retains the stored information for over a year. However, the need for high insulation makes the process of writing new information into a cell more difficult than in other types of memories. A Write operation usually involves the application of a voltage higher than normal operating voltages in MOS circuitry. The high voltage is used to cause a temporary breakdown in insulation, and thus allow charge to be stored on the capacitor.

The contents of EPROM cells can be erased by increasing the discharge rate of the storage capacitors by several orders of magnitude. This can be accomplished by exposing the chip to ultraviolet light or by the application of a high voltage similar to that used in a Write operation. If ultraviolet light is used, all cells in the chip are erased at the same time. However, when electrical erasure is used, the process can be made selective. An electrically erasable EPROM, often referred to as an E^2PROM, offers another potential advantage. It need not be physically removed for reprogramming. This convenience is offset by the need to provide the high voltages required during the Write and Erase operations. For this reason, many manufacturers incorporate the circuitry for generating these voltages on the E^2PROM chip itself.

8.5 MULTIPLE-MODULE MEMORIES AND INTERLEAVING

If main memory is structured as a collection of physically separate modules, each with its own address buffer register (ABR) and data buffer register (DBR), it is possible for more than one module to be performing Read or Write operations at any given time. The average rate of transmission of words to and from the total MM system can thus be increased. Extra controls will be required, but since the MM speed is often the bottleneck in computation speeds, the expense involved is usually justified in large computers.

The way in which individual addresses are distributed over the modules is a critical factor in determining the average number of modules that can be kept busy as computations proceed. Two methods of address layout are indicated in Figure 8.12. In the first case, the MM address generated by the CPU is decoded as shown in Figure 8.12a. The high-order k bits of the address name one of n modules, and the low-order m bits name a particular word in that module. If the CPU issues Read requests to consecutive locations, as it does when fetching instructions of a straight-line program, then only one module is kept busy by the

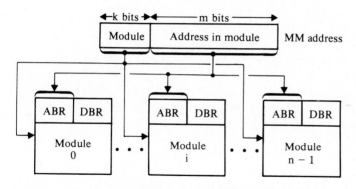

(*a*) Consecutive words in a module

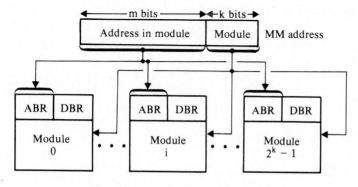

(*b*) Consecutive words in consecutive modules

Figure 8.12 Addressing multiple-module memory systems.

CPU. However, devices with direct memory access (DMA) ability may be operating in other memory modules.

The second and more effective way of addressing the modules is shown in Figure 8.12*b*. It is called *memory interleaving*. A module is selected by the low-order k bits of the MM address, and the high-order m bits name a location within that module. Therefore, consecutive addresses are located in successive modules. Thus, any component of the system, for example, the CPU or a DMA device, that generates requests for access to consecutive MM locations can keep a number of modules busy at any one time. This results in a higher average utilization of the memory system as a whole.

In the system of Figure 8.12*b*, there must be 2^k modules; otherwise, there will be gaps of nonexistent locations in the MM address space. This raises a practical issue. The first system described, Figure 8.12*a*, is more flexible than the second in that any number of modules up to 2^k can be used. The modules are normally assigned consecutive MM addresses from 0 up. Hence, an existing system can be expanded by simply adding one or more modules as required. The second system must always have the full set of 2^k modules, and a failure in any module affects all areas of the address space. A failed module in the first system affects only a localized area of the address space.

To take advantage of an interleaved MM unit, the CPU should be able to issue the requests for memory words before these words are actually needed for execution. Obviously, this "lookahead" process is useful only for words in a straight-line program segment. Addressing of operands normally results in out-of-sequence requests to memory and therefore decreases the average rate of memory transfers. Furthermore, when a branch takes place, the words that have been prefetched from memory at the time of execution of the branch instruction have to be discarded. Thus, in summary, memory operands and program branching have a randomizing effect on the sequence of memory addresses generated by the CPU.

Consider a memory consisting of r modules. The effective cycle time of this memory is inversely proportional to the number of modules that can be kept busy at any given time. If all r modules are busy continuously, the effective memory cycle time is decreased by a factor of r relative to that of individual modules. In practical implementations of interleaved memories, the value of the improvement factor is dependent upon the particular algorithm used to control access to individual memory modules. It is also affected by the randomizing effect of operand fetching. This factor is usually in the range $\sqrt{r}$ to r. The number of modules in practical systems may be in the range of 16 to 32, which leads to a reduction in the effective memory cycle time by a factor of at least 4 to 6.

8.6 CACHE MEMORIES

Analysis of a large number of typical programs has shown that most of their execution time is spent in a few main routines. When execution is localized within these routines, a number of instructions are executed repeatedly. This may be in the form of a simple loop, nested loops, or a few procedures that repeatedly call each other. The actual detailed pattern of instruction sequencing is not important. The main observation is that many instructions in each of a few localized areas of the program are repeatedly executed, while the remainder of the program is accessed relatively infrequently. This phenomenon is referred to as *locality of reference*.

Now, if it can be arranged to have the active segments of a program in a fast memory, then the total execution time can be significantly reduced. Such a memory is referred to as a *cache* (or *buffer*) memory. It is inserted between the CPU and the MM, as shown in Figure 8.13. To make this arrangement effective, the cache must be considerably faster than the MM. Their relative access times usually differ by a factor of 5 to 10. This approach is more economical than the use of fast memory devices to implement the entire MM.

Conceptually, operation of a cache memory is very simple. The memory control circuitry is designed to take advantage of the property of locality of reference. When a Read request is received from the CPU, the contents of a block of memory words containing the location specified are transferred into the cache one word at a time. When any of the locations in this block is referenced by the program, its contents are read directly from the cache. Usually, the cache memory can store a number of such blocks at any given time. The correspondence between the MM blocks and those in the cache is specified by means of a *mapping function*. When the cache is full and a memory word (instruction or data) is referenced that is not in the cache, a decision must be made as to which block should be removed to create space for the new block that contains the referenced word. The collection of rules for making this decision constitute the *replacement algorithm*.

In each of the cache techniques that we will describe, there are some basic assumptions and operations that are independent of the particular mapping function and replacement algorithm used. It is best to describe them first. The CPU does not need to know explicitly about the existence of the cache. The CPU simply makes Read and Write requests as described previously. The addresses generated by the CPU always refer to locations in the MM. The memory-access control circuitry shown in Figure 8.13 determines whether or not

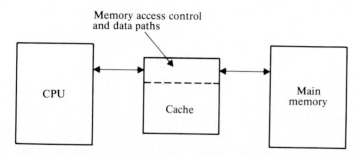

Figure 8.13 Use of cache memory between the CPU and the main memory.

the requested word currently exists in the cache. If it does, the Read or Write operation is performed on the appropriate cache location. When the operation is a Read, the main memory is not involved. However, if the·operation is a Write, there are two ways that the system can proceed. In the first case, the cache location and the MM location are updated simultaneously. This is called the *store-through* method. The alternative is to update the cache location only and to mark it as such through the use of an associated flag bit. Later, when the block containing this marked word is to be removed from the cache to make way for a new block, the permanent MM location of the word is updated. The store-through method is clearly simpler, but it results in unnecessary Write operations in the MM when a given cache word is updated a number of times during its cache residency period.

Next, consider the case where the addressed word is not in the cache and the operation is a Read. If this happens, the block of words in the MM that contains the requested word is brought into the cache, and then the particular word requested is forwarded to the CPU. There is an opportunity for some time saving here if the word is forwarded to the CPU as soon as it is available from the MM instead of waiting for the whole block to be loaded into the cache. This is called *load-through*.

During a Write operation, if the addressed word is not in the cache, the information is written directly into the MM. In this case, there is little advantage in transferring the block containing the addressed word to the cache. A Write operation normally refers to a location in one of the data areas of a program rather than to the memory area containing the program instructions. The property of locality of reference is not as pronounced in accessing data when Write operations are involved.

Finally, we should recall that in the case of an interleaved memory, contiguous block transfers are very efficient. Thus, transferring data in blocks from the MM to the cache enables an interleaved MM unit to operate at its maximum possible speed.

8.6.1 Mapping Functions

In order to discuss possible methods for specifying where MM blocks are placed in the cache, it is helpful to use a specific example. Consider a cache of 2048 (2K) words with a block size of 16 words. This means that the cache is organized as 128 blocks. Let the MM have 64K words, addressable by a 16-bit address. For mapping purposes, the memory will be considered as composed of 4K blocks of 16 words each.

The simplest way of associating MM blocks with cache blocks is the *direct-mapping* technique. In this technique, block k of the MM maps onto block k modulo 128 of the cache. This is depicted in Figure 8.14. Since more than one MM block is mapped onto a given cache block position, contention may arise for that position. This situation occurs even when the cache is not full. Contention is resolved by allowing the new block to overwrite the currently resident block.

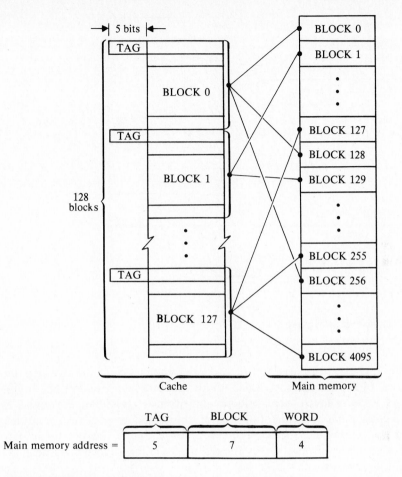

Figure 8.14 Direct-mapping cache.

Thus the replacement algorithm is trivial. The detailed operation of the direct-mapping technique is as follows. Let an MM address consist of three fields, as shown in Figure 8.14. When a new block is first brought into the cache, the high-order 5 bits of its MM address are stored in five tag bits associated with its location in the cache. When the CPU generates a memory request, the 7-bit block address determines the corresponding cache block. The tag field of that block is compared to the tag field of the address. If they match, the desired word (specified by the low-order 4 bits of the address) is in that block of the cache. If there is no match, the required word must be accessed in the MM. The direct-mapping technique is easy to implement, but it is not very flexible.

Figure 8.15 shows a much more flexible mapping method, whereby an MM block can potentially reside in any cache block position. This is called the *associative-mapping* technique. In this case, 12 tag bits are required to identify an MM block when it is resident in the cache. The tag bits of an address received

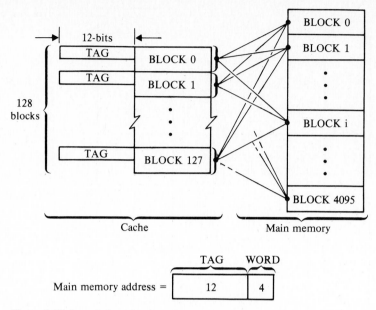

Figure 8.15 Associative-mapping cache.

from the CPU must be compared to the tag bits of each block of the cache to see if the desired block is present. Since there is complete freedom in block positioning, a wide range of replacement algorithms is possible. However, it might not be practical to make full use of this freedom, because complex replacement algorithms may be too difficult to implement. The cost of implementation is also adversely affected by the requirement for a 128-way associative search of 12-bit patterns.

The final mapping method to be discussed is the most practical. It is intermediate to the above two techniques. Blocks of the cache are grouped into sets, and the mapping allows a block of MM to reside in any block of a specific set. Hence the contention problem of the direct method is eased by having a few choices for block placement. At the same time, the hardware cost is reduced by decreasing the size of the associative search. An example of this *block-set-associative-mapping* technique is given in Figure 8.16 for the case of two blocks per set. The 6-bit set field of the address determines which set of the cache might contain the desired block, as in the direct-mapping method. The tag field of the address must then be associatively compared to the tags of the two blocks of the set to see if a match occurs signifying block presence. This two-way associative search is not difficult to implement.

It is clear that four blocks per set would be accommodated by a 5-bit set field, eight blocks per set by a 4-bit set field, etc. The extreme condition of 128 blocks per set requires no set bits and corresponds to the fully associative

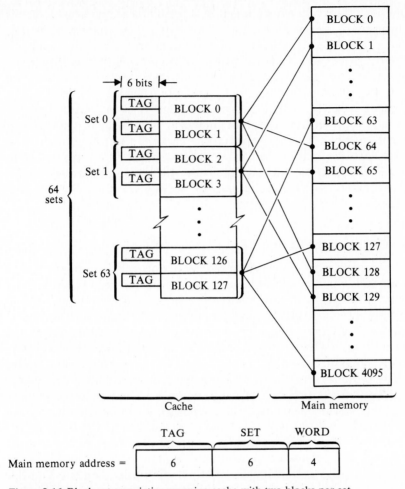

Figure 8.16 Block-set-associative-mapping cache with two blocks per set.

technique with 12 tag bits. The other extreme of one block per set is the direct-mapping method.

There has been a tacit assumption that both tags and data are in the cache memory. But it is quite reasonable to have the few tag bits in a separate, even faster memory, especially when associative searches are required. The result of accessing or searching this faster *tag directory* determines whether or not the desired block is in the cache. If it is, the block is in the cache position that directly corresponds to the directory tag position where the match is found.

Another technical detail that should be mentioned, that is in fact independent of the mapping function, is that it is usually necessary to have a *Valid bit* associated with each block. This bit indicates whether or not the block contains valid data. It does not serve the same function as the bit mentioned earlier that is needed to distinguish whether or not the cache contains an updated version of the MM block. The Valid bits are all set to 0 when power is initially applied to the system or when the MM is loaded with new programs and data from mass storage devices. These latter transfers normally bypass the cache and are achieved by an I/O channel or some simpler DMA mechanism. The Valid bit of a particular cache block is set to 1 the first time this block is loaded from the MM. Once set, a Valid bit stays equal to 1 unless an MM block is updated by a source, other than the CPU, that bypasses the cache. In this case, a check is made if the block is currently in the cache. If it is, the Valid bit is set to 0. The introduction of the Valid bit also means that a slight modification should be made to our earlier discussion of cache accesses. As well as tag matching being a condition, accessing should only proceed if the Valid bit is equal to 1.

8.6.2 Replacement Algorithms

When a new block must be brought into the cache and all the positions that it may occupy are full, a decision must be made as to which of the old blocks is to be overwritten. This problem has generated a great deal of interest among computer scientists, because the decision can potentially be a strong determining factor in system performance. In general, a strategy is required to keep blocks in the cache when they are likely to be referenced in the near future. However, it is not easy to determine directly which of the blocks in the cache are about to be referenced. The property of locality of reference in programs gives a clue to a reasonable strategy. Since programs usually stay in localized areas for reasonable periods of time, it can be assumed that there is a high probability that blocks which have been referenced recently will also be referenced in the near future. Therefore, when a block is to be overwritten, a sensible decision is to overwrite the one that has gone the longest time without being referenced. This is defined as the least recently used (LRU) block, and this type of decision is called the *LRU algorithm*. Keeping track of the LRU block must be done as computation proceeds.

As a specific example, suppose it is required to track the LRU block of a four-block set. A 2-bit counter may be used for each block. When a hit occurs, that is, when a read request is received for a word that is in the cache, the counter of the block that is referenced is set to 0. All counters with values originally lower than the referenced one are incremented by 1, while all others remain unchanged. When a miss occurs and the set is not full, the counter associated with the new block loaded from the main memory is set to 0, and the values of all other counters are increased by 1. When a miss occurs and the set is full, the block with the counter value 3 is removed, the new block is put in its place, and its counter is set to 0. The other three block counters are incremented by 1. It can be easily verified that the counter values of occupied blocks are always distinct.

Other algorithms that require less overhead are possible. An intuitively reasonable rule would be to remove the "oldest" block from a full set when a new block must be brought in. Using this technique, no updating is needed when hits occur. However, since the algorithm does not track the most active blocks when hits occur, it is not as good as the LRU algorithm in choosing the best blocks to remove. The simplest algorithm is to choose the block to be overwritten at random. Interestingly enough, this simple algorithm has been found to be very effective in practice.

8.6.3 Examples

Finally, let us discuss some typical cache parameter values that are found in commercially available computers. In general, cache memory access times of 50 to 100 ns are available in high-speed caches. This is to be contrasted with 200- to 500-ns access times in MOS main memory modules. The percentage of memory accesses that result in the desired information being found in the cache ranges from 90 percent to over 99 percent. This parameter is usually called the *hit ratio* and depends mainly on the total size of the cache, as well as on the type of program being executed.

Caches are usually organized in the block-set-associative manner, with two to eight blocks per set. The number of bytes per block typically ranges from 4 to 64, and the total cache size ranges from 2K to 64K bytes. Naturally, the larger numbers apply to expensive, high-performance computers. For example, the IBM 3033 has a 64K-byte cache. It has 64 sets with 16 blocks per set, and there are 64 bytes per block. The medium-sized VAX 11/780 has an 8K-byte cache with 512 sets. Each set has two blocks, and there are 8 bytes per block.

8.7 VIRTUAL MEMORIES

In any computer system in which the currently active programs and data do not fit into the physical MM space, secondary storage devices such as magnetic drums, disks, or tapes are used to hold the overflow. This space problem was first solved by requiring programmers to explicitly move programs or parts of programs from secondary storage to MM when they are to be executed. However, the problem of management of the available MM space is a machine-dependent problem that should not need to be solved by the programmer.

The general techniques of automatically moving the required program and data blocks into the physical MM for execution are called virtual-memory techniques. Programs, and hence the CPU, reference an instruction and data space that is independent of the physical MM space. The binary addresses that the CPU issues for either instructions or data are called virtual or logical addresses. The mechanism that operates on these virtual addresses and translates them into actual locations in the physical hierarchy is usually implemented by a combination of hardware and software components. If the result of translating (or mapping) a specific virtual address is a physical MM location, the contents of that location are used immediately as required. On the other hand, if the location is not in the MM its contents must be brought into a suitable location in the MM and then used.

The simplest form of translation method is based on the assumption that all programs and data are composed of fixed-length pages. These pages are basic units of word blocks that must always occupy contiguous locations, whether they are resident in the MM or in secondary storage. Pages are commonly 512 or 1024 words long. They constitute the basic unit of information that is moved back and forth between the MM and secondary storage whenever the translation mechanism determines that a move is required. This discussion clearly parallels many of the ideas that were introduced in the cache memory section. The cache concept is intended to bridge the speed gap between the CPU and the MM. Hence the cache control is implemented in the hardware. The virtual-memory idea is primarily meant to bridge the size gap between the MM and secondary storage. It is usually implemented in part by software techniques. Conceptually, cache techniques and virtual-memory techniques involve very similar ideas. They differ mainly in the details of their implementation.

An address translation method based on the concept of fixed-length pages is shown schematically in Figure 8.17. Each virtual address generated by the CPU, whether it is for an instruction fetch or an operand fetch/store operation, is interpreted as a page number (high-order bits) followed by a word number (low-order bits). A page table in the MM specifies the location of the pages that are currently in the MM. The starting address of the page table is kept in the page table base register. By adding the page number to the contents of this register, the address of the corresponding entry in the page table is obtained. The contents of this location name the block of the MM where the requested page currently resides; or if the page is not in the MM, the page table entry points to where the page is in the secondary storage. The control bits indicate whether or not the page is present in the MM. They also may contain some past usage information, etc., for purposes of implementing the page replacement algorithm.

If the page table is stored in the MM unit, as assumed above, then two MM accesses need to be made for every MM access requested by a program. This degradation in execution speed by a factor of 2 is the price that is paid for the programming convenience of a wider addressable memory space. It is not necessary that the page table be implemented in the MM unit. The system can operate faster if the page table is stored in a small fast memory.

When a new page is to be brought from secondary storage to the MM, the page table may provide the details of where this data can be found on a magnetic disk. On the other hand, it may provide an address pointer to a block of words in the MM where this detailed information is stored. In either case, a long delay is now incurred while the page transfer into the MM takes place. This is usually

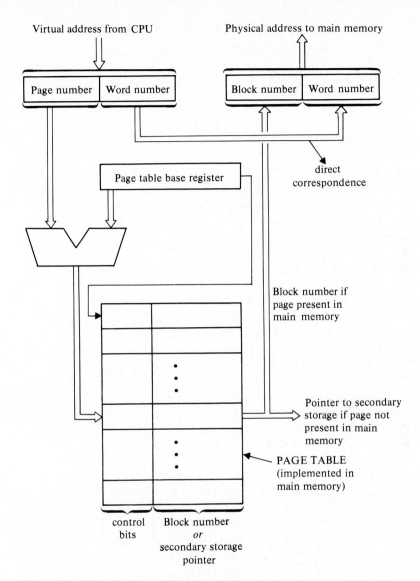

Virtual address from CPU

Physical address to main memory

Page number	Word number

Block number	Word number

Page table base register

direct
correspondence

Block number if
page present in
main memory

Pointer to secondary
storage if page not
present in main
memory

PAGE TABLE
(implemented in
main memory)

control
bits

Block number
or
secondary storage
pointer

Figure 8.17 Virtual-memory address translation.

done by an I/O channel or a DMA operation. At this point, the CPU may be used to execute another task whose pages are in the MM.

The general problem of deciding which page is to be removed from a full MM, when a new page is to be brought in, is just as critical here as in the cache situation. The notion that programs tend to spend most of their time in a few localized areas is also equally applicable. Since MMs are considerably larger than cache memories, it should be possible to keep relatively larger portions of a program in the MM. This will reduce the frequency of transfers to and from secondary storage. Concepts like the LRU replacement algorithm can be applied to page replacement. The data that determines the LRU page or set of pages can be kept in the page table control bits. The need to update the LRU information on every MM reference is another reason why the page table should be implemented in a high-speed memory.

8.8 MEMORY MANAGEMENT REQUIREMENTS

In the discussion of virtual-memory concepts, we have tacitly assumed that only one large program is being executed. If all of it does not fit into the available physical MM, parts of it (pages) are moved from secondary storage into the MM when they are to be executed, displacing pages that have become idle. Although we have alluded to software routines that are needed to manage this movement of program segments, we have not been very specific about the details. Of course, these management routines must also reside in the MM when they are executed.

The management routines are part of a collection of programs that constitute the *operating system* of the computer. It is convenient to assemble the operating system routines into a virtual address space, called the *system space*, that is separate from the virtual space in which user application programs reside. The latter space is called the *user space*. In fact, there may be a number of user spaces, one for each user. At any one point in time, the physical MM is shared by the active pages of the system space and each of the user spaces. One of the operating system routines, called the *scheduler*, determines how the CPU execution time is shared among all active programs. The task of scheduling, and other aspects of operating system software, will be discussed in Chapter 10.

In any computer system in which independent user programs coexist in the MM along with operating system programs, the notion of *protection* must be addressed. The protection requirement is that no program should be allowed to destroy either data or instructions of other programs in the MM. There are a number of implementation techniques used to enforce the protection rules. Let us first consider the most basic form of protection. We have already introduced the notion of the state of the CPU in Chapter 3. In the simplest case there are two states, the *supervisor state* and the *user state*. As the name suggests, the CPU is usually placed in the supervisor state when operating system routines are being executed. The CPU is placed in the user state for execution of user programs. In the user state, some machine instructions cannot be executed. These *privileged instructions* can only be executed while the CPU is in the supervisor state. They include operations such as modification of the page table base register(s). Therefore, a user program is prevented from accessing the page tables of the other user spaces or the system space.

A second type of protection is used in controlling access by one user to the data area of another user. Suppose a page of data is to be shared by placing it in two or more user spaces. One user controls the updating of this shared page, while the others may only read it. A convenient way to implement page access rules such as these is to indicate access privileges in the control bits in the page table entry (see Figure 8.17). The user program responsible for updating the shared page has Read and Write access privileges to the shared page. The other users have Read Only access to this page.

Finally, we should comment on one other important consideration in the management of a virtual-memory system. It concerns the movement of pages back and forth between the MM and the secondary storage as execution of a particular program proceeds. Suppose the information on a page is not changed during its MM residency. Then, when it must be removed to make space for a new page, it does not need to be written back to secondary storage. The original copy in the secondary storage is correct. However, if changes have been made, the altered page must be written back. It is therefore useful to record, in the page table control bits, whether or not a page has been changed while it is in the MM.

8.9 THE VAX-11 VIRTUAL-MEMORY SYSTEM

The discussion of virtual-memory techniques in Section 8.7 is quite simplified. In order to appreciate the complexity of current practical designs, it is instructive to examine a commercial example. The VAX-11 system is described in this section.

The organization of the VAX-11 virtual-memory system follows the general scheme outlined in Figure 8.17. A virtual address in the VAX-11 is 32 bits long. It is interpreted as shown in Figure 8.18. The high-order bit b_{31} differentiates between user space and system space. User space is further divided into

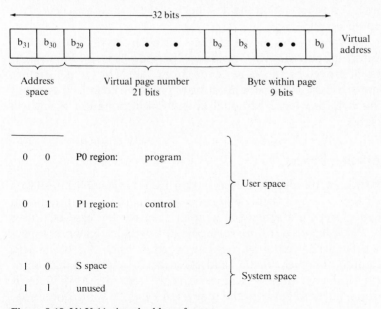

Figure 8.18 VAX-11 virtual-address format.

program and control regions, as determined by bit b_{30}. The user program region contains both programs and data. The user control region contains the user stack and some of the operating system data structures pertinent to a particular user. The system space contains operating system procedures (memory management software, user program scheduling, etc.) common to all users. It also contains the page tables for all spaces. The remaining 30 bits of a virtual address specify a 21-bit virtual page number and a 9-bit address of a byte within that page.

A page consists of 512 bytes. The address of a byte within a page is given in the low-order 9 bits of a virtual address. During the address translation process, this component of a virtual address is taken directly as the low-order 9 bits of the corresponding physical address. The page is the basic unit that is transferred from secondary storage to the physical MM when successive parts of a program become active. The 21-bit virtual page number is used as an offset into a page table as shown in Figure 8.19. The address of the page table is held in a page table base register in the CPU. Each page table entry is 32 bits long. It contains a 21-bit physical page frame number that is used to construct a 30-bit physical address, as shown in the figure. The remaining 11 bits in the page table entry provide access control information for the referenced page.

The detailed format of a page table entry is shown in Figure 8.20. There are four fields in the access control section:

Valid (1 bit). This bit is 1 if the virtual page number names a page that is currently resident in the MM. If this is the case, translation continues. If this bit is 0, the page is not in the MM, and a *page fault* is said to have occurred. The whole page must then be brought into the MM before access can proceed.

Protection (4 bits). The protection field specifies the access privileges for programs that access the page.

Modified (1 bit). The value of this bit is 1 if there has been a Write operation to the page during its current MM residency period. This information is necessary when a page is to be removed from the MM. It determines whether or not the page must be written back into the secondary storage.

Own (5 bits). This field provides additional protection information which will not be discussed.

8.9.1 The Translation Process

It is instructive to follow the details of translation from a virtual address to a physical address in the VAX-11 system. When the virtual address is in the system space, the translation steps are somewhat simpler than for the case of a user space translation. We will consider both cases. First, however, a general aspect of the translation process shown in Figure 8.19 is worth noting. Two accesses to the MM are required for each virtual address access. A page table entry containing the physical page frame number is read from the MM. This is followed by a second access to perform the requested Read or Write operation.

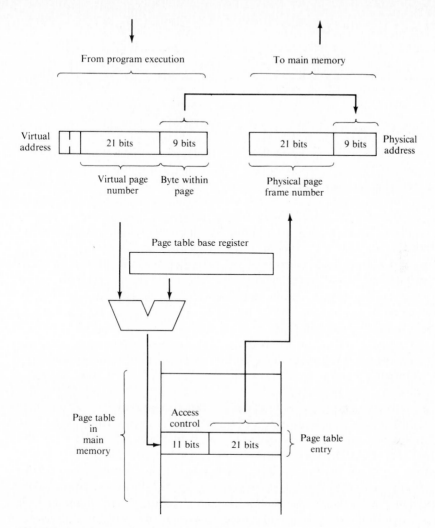

Figure 8.19 VAX-11 general address translation.

This is a severe execution time penalty to pay for the flexibility of a virtual-memory system.

Considering that consecutive instruction fetches will usually reference the same physical page, it would be helpful if a hardware mechanism were available to detect such occurrences. The page table entry Read operation could then be avoided. The VAX-11 contains a small cache memory which holds the most recently used page table entries for this purpose. This address translation cache is distinct from an MM cache, as described in Section 8.6, which is also used in the VAX-11. A discussion of the translation cache will be given later. Let us now return to the translation process itself.

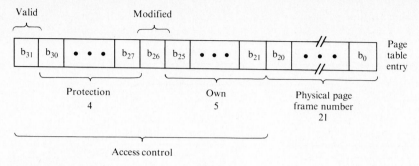

Figure 8.20 VAX-11 page table entry format.

System space translation A pictorial display of the required sequence of steps is given in Figure 8.21. There are two million possible virtual pages in each of the system and the user spaces. However, only a small fraction of these is in actual use in most applications. The number of virtual pages in use in the system space is recorded in the system length register (SLR). Programs prepared for execution on a virtual-memory system always start at address 0 and occupy contiguous addresses. Therefore, the number in the SLR is one larger than the highest virtual page number in the program.

When a system virtual address is generated by the CPU, the virtual page number is compared to the contents of the SLR. If it is smaller, then the translation process continues. Otherwise, an interrupt indicating an error occurs.

A valid virtual page number is added to the contents of the system base register (SBR) to generate the physical address of the appropriate page table entry. This entry is then fetched from the main memory. If the Valid bit in the access control field is 1, and the protection bits indicate that the requested access may proceed, then a physical address is generated. The requested Read or Write access is then performed. If the Valid bit is 0, a page fault has occurred, and a procedure must be invoked to load the requested page into the main memory. If the access protection check fails, that is, the requested access is not authorized, an interrupt is raised.

User space translation The translation of user space virtual addresses is essentially the same as for system space virtual addresses. The main difference is that user page tables are maintained at virtual addresses in the system space. Hence, they may not always be in the physical main memory. This is in contrast to the system page tables which are always in the physical main memory.

Translation of an address in the program region of a user space is shown in Figure 8.22. After a length check, the virtual page number is added to the base address of the corresponding page table. The result is a virtual address in the system space. This address is translated using the complete process of Figure 8.21 to yield the physical address of the page table entry. Then this entry is fetched from the main memory. The remainder of the translation process is the

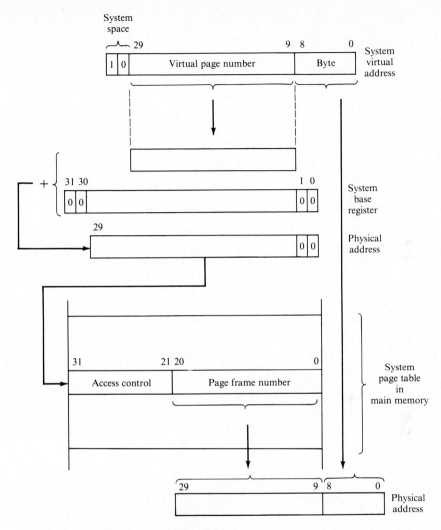

Figure 8.21 Translation of a system address.

same as described above for the system space. It should be noted that user space address translation requires two main memory accesses. First, the address of the page table entry is fetched. Then, the entry itself is fetched. A third main memory access is finally needed to access the actual operand.

8.9.2 Translation Speedup Techniques

If every Read or Write operation in user space actually required three main memory accesses, as described above, the flexibility of the virtual-memory system would be overshadowed by the threefold increase in program execution

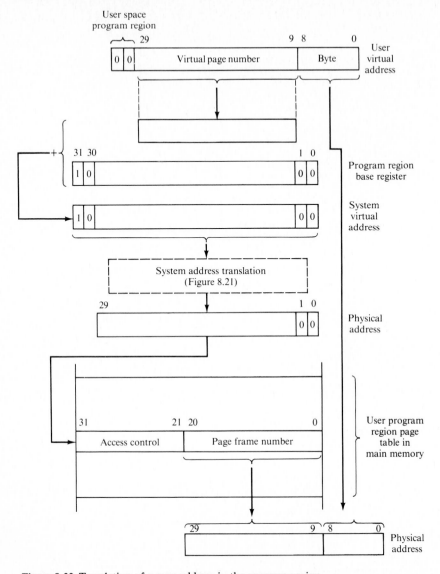

Figure 8.22 Translation of a user address in the program region.

time. Most commercial virtual-memory systems incorporate a mechanism whereby the bulk of the main memory accesses called for by the virtual-to-physical address translation process are avoided. This may be done by the use of a cache memory, called a *translation buffer*, which retains recent translations.

In the VAX-11/780, the translation buffer is a block-set-associative cache with 64 sets and 2 blocks per set, for a total of 128 address translation entries. It is divided into two halves: one half for user space translations and the other half

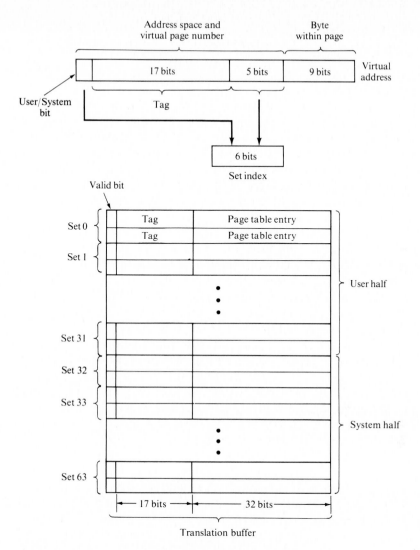

Figure 8.23 Address translation buffer in the VAX-11/780.

for system space translations. Figure 8.23 shows the organization of the translation buffer. The operation of this cache is the same as that given for block-set-associative caches in Section 8.6. A random replacement rule is used when an entry must be displaced from a set.

Another address translation speedup technique is used during instruction fetches in the VAX-11. The number of the physical page frame containing the current instruction stream is maintained in the CPU. Consider the usual case where the virtual address of the next instruction is obtained by incrementing the address of the previous instruction, and a page boundary is not crossed. Then the physical address of the new instruction can be obtained simply by concatenating the current physical page frame number with the low-order 9 bits from the program counter. This technique is called *pretranslation* of instruction stream addresses because neither the translation buffer nor the main memory page tables are used in the process.

The combined use of pretranslation and the translation buffer has a significant impact on execution time. A simulation study[8.1] has shown that about two-thirds of all translation requests from the CPU can be avoided by pretranslation. Furthermore, of all translation requests actually issued to the translation buffer, only about 1 percent result in misses, where a miss means that the main memory page tables need to be accessed to perform the translation.

8.9.3 Paging

The above discussion has outlined the address translation mechanism and its associated hardware in the VAX-11 virtual-memory system. We have given details only in the case where the requested item, either an instruction or a data element, is actually currently resident in the main memory. When it is not, the page containing the item must be transferred into the main memory before execution of the program can continue. A great deal of the design effort in realizing virtual-memory systems is concerned with determining how and when user program pages are to be moved between the main memory and secondary storage. Many issues are involved. A large computer system is usually operated in a manner that maintains sections of a number of different user programs in the main memory simultaneously. The CPU is time-shared among these programs in a way that will be discussed in Chapter 10. In such a setting, virtual-memory software routines determine the number of pages that each user program should occupy in the main memory. The overall strategy is to supply the CPU with a steady work load while minimizing the shuffling of pages back and forth between the main memory and the secondary storage. A detailed study of these topics is beyond the scope of this book. Interested readers may consult Reference 8.2 for a discussion of the techniques used in the VAX-11 system.

8.10 MEMORY MANAGEMENT HARDWARE

The implementation of memory management features requires considerable hardware support. This may include associative memories, address translation hardware, and high-speed memories for storing page tables. Such facilities are available for many computer systems.

For microcomputer systems, memory management hardware is typically provided in the form of a single chip which is directly compatible with the microprocessor used. Such a chip accepts a logical address from the microprocessor and generates the corresponding physical address using its internal tables. Separate tables may be provided for user spaces and the system space.

The contents of these tables, which may also contain protection and access restriction information, are loaded by the microprocessor. The microprocessor informs the memory management chip when it should switch from one user space to another or from a user space to the system space. We should note that most 16- and 32-bit microprocessors are supported by memory management chips.

8.11 CONCLUDING REMARKS

The main memory is one of the major components in any computer. Its characteristics in terms of size and speed play an important role in determining the capabilities of a given computer. In this chapter, we have presented some of the technological and organizational details of the MM.

Developments in technology have led to a considerable reduction in the cost of semiconductor memories. Bipolar memories are particularly useful in the implementation of cache memories because of their high-speed capabilities. On the other hand, MOS memories are used in the MM because of their relatively low cost.

Virtual-memory systems are rapidly increasing in numbers. Many new computer designs, including high-performance microcomputer systems, have virtual-memory capability as a part of their basic hardware and operating software. Others are designed in such a way as to facilitate its implementation.

8.12 PROBLEMS

8.1 The address decoder in Figure 8.3 has 4 input lines and 16 output lines. Exactly one output line is selected (that is, set to 1) for each possible 4-bit input pattern (address). A decoder with the same general form as given in Figure A.32 can be used. It consists of 16 four-input AND gates. It is called a *single-level decoder*.

For large numbers of inputs, a different form of decoder is more economical. Consider the three-input to eight-output configuration shown in Figure P8.1. It is called a *tree decoder*.

(a) Sketch the form of a 4-input to 16-output tree decoder.

(b) If decoder cost is determined by the total number of gates plus gate inputs, the cost of a three-input single-level decoder is 32, while the cost of a three-input tree decoder is 36. What are the costs for four-input and eight-input single-level and tree decoders?

8.2 It is possible to improve on the tree-decoder scheme introduced in Problem 8.1. Consider the block diagram in Figure P8.2. The decoders shown are called *dual-tree* or *matrix decoders*. In Figure P8.2a, the four inputs are decoded in pairs in two-input decoders. The outputs of these decoders are combined pairwise in all possible ways by 16 AND gates in the final block to generate the required 16 outputs. The extension of this scheme to the eight-input case is shown in Figure P8.2b.

Compute the cost (gates plus gate inputs) of four-input and eight-input dual-tree decoders and compare your results with the cost figures developed in Problem 8.1.

8.3 Show how to construct a 10-input decoder from resistors and diodes in a configuration similar to the AND array of the programmable logic array shown in Figure A.38. Which of the decoder forms from Problems 8.1 and 8.2 corresponds to this configuration?

8.4 Suppose an "Enable" input is added to an integrated circuit that performs the decoding

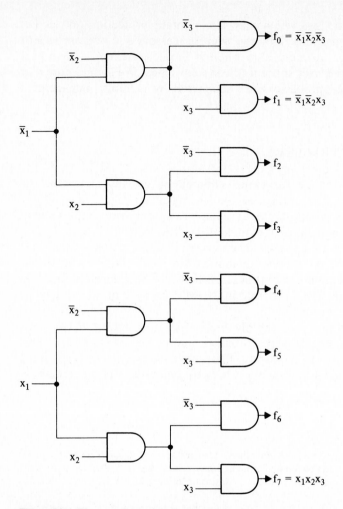

Figure P8.1 Three-variable tree decoder.

function. When Enable = 0, all the outputs are held at 0; when Enable = 1, the circuit performs the decode function. This can be implemented internally by adding Enable as an input to each of the AND gates that generate the decoder outputs.

Show how to use two-input decoders that have Enable inputs to implement a single four-input decoder.

8.5 Give a block diagram, similar to Figure 8.9, for a 256K × 16 memory using 64K × 1 memory chips.

8.6 Consider the dynamic memory cell of Figure 8.7. Assume that $C = 5$ pF and that leakage current through the transistor is about 2 nA. The voltage across the capacitor when it is fully charged is equal to 4.5 V. The cell must be refreshed before this voltage drops below 3 V. Estimate the minimum Refresh rate.

8.7 A dynamic memory is connected to a synchronous bus. Data transfers take place according to

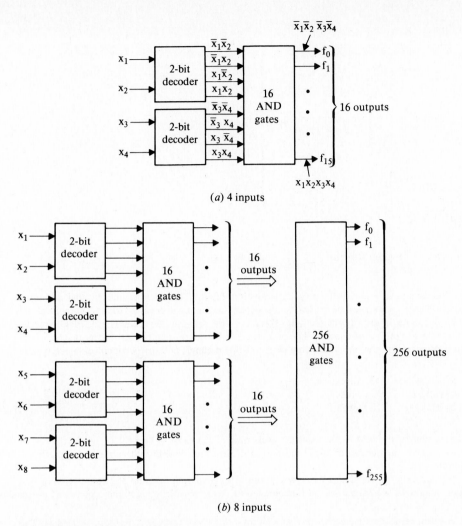

(*a*) 4 inputs

(*b*) 8 inputs

Figure P8.2 Dual tree decoders.

the timing diagram of Figure 6.12. What changes should you make to the circuit of Figure 8.10 in this case? Give a suitable design for the Refresh Control and Access Control blocks of this circuit.

8.8 It was pointed out in Section 8.3 that the cell array of Figure 8.8 is usually implemented as two 128×256 arrays. Redraw Figure 8.8 to illustrate this. What would the refresh overhead be if all memory cells are organized as a single 256×256 array? Assume that the cells used in a 256K-bit memory IC have the same refresh requirements as the 64K chip. Suggest a suitable organization in this case.

8.9 (*a*) Estimate the potential speedup in executing the program in Figure 2.5*c* if the MM is configured as in Figure 8.12*b* with $k = 2$.

(*b*) Repeat (*a*) for the program in Figure 2.16*b*.

8.10 A certain program consists of two nested DO loops, a small inner loop, and a much larger outer

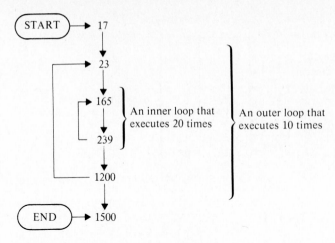

Figure P8.3 A program structure.

loop. The general structure of the program is given in Figure P8.3. The decimal memory addresses shown delineate the location of the two loops and the beginning and end of the total program. All memory locations in the various sections, 17–22, 23–164, 165–239, etc., contain instructions to be executed in straight-line sequencing. The program is to be run on a computer that has a cache. The cache is organized in the direct-mapping (Figure 8.14) manner, and the pertinent parameters are:

MM size	64K words
Cache size	1K words
Block size	128 words

The cycle time of the MM is 10τ s and the cycle time of the cache is 1τ s.

(a) Specify the number of bits in the TAG, BLOCK, and WORD fields in the interpretation of MM addresses.

(b) Ignoring the Read and Write operations associated with operand and result fetching and storing, compute the total amount of time needed for instruction fetching in the program of Figure P8.3.

8.11 A block-set-associative cache consists of a total of 64 blocks divided into four-block sets. The MM contains 4096 blocks. Each block consists of 128 words.

(a) How many bits are there in an MM address?

(b) How many bits are there in each of the TAG, SET, and WORD fields?

8.12 A computer system has an MM consisting of 32K 16-bit words. It also has a 4K-word cache organized in the block-set-associative manner with four blocks per set and 64 words per block.

(a) Calculate the number of bits in each of the TAG, SET, and WORD fields of the MM address format.

(b) Assume that the cache is initially empty. Suppose that the CPU fetches 4352 words from locations 0, 1, 2, . . . , 4351, in order. It then repeats this fetch sequence nine more times. The cache is 10 times faster than the MM. Estimate the improvement factor resulting from the use of the cache. Assume that the LRU algorithm is used for block replacement.

8.13 Repeat Problem 8.12, assuming that whenever a block is to be brought from the MM and the corresponding set in the cache is full, it replaces the most recently used block of this set.

8.14 In Section 8.9.1, it was pointed out that user page tables are located at virtual addresses in the system space. Why is this done? In other words, what is the advantage of having the user page tables pageable?

8.15 For a set of user programs that share the main memory in a virtual-memory system, suggest a strategy for allotting the available total set of physical main memory pages among the users. (*Hint*: Consider the distinct pages accessed by each user program over its last T memory accesses.)

8.16 Suggest reasons why the page size in a virtual-memory system should be neither very small nor very large.

8.17 When a channel or DMA block transfer is done between a disk and the main memory in a computer system that has a main memory cache, there are two ways to proceed. The transfer can go through the cache or it can bypass the cache. Give the advantages and disadvantages of each choice. (See Section 8.6.1.)

8.18 How might the value of k in the memory system of Figure 8.12b influence block size in the design of a cache memory to be used with the system?

8.19 In a certain large, high-performance computer system there are a number of independent CPUs and a number of memory modules. A communication network interconnects the CPUs with the memory modules in such a way that many CPUs can simultaneously access different memory modules. The main memory cache technique is to be used to increase computation rates. Should caches be associated with processors or with memory modules? Give advantages and disadvantages associated with each choice. In answering this question the following facts are relevant: (1) The communication network has a delay that is almost as long as a memory module access time; (2) the address space spanned by each processor runs over all memory modules; (3) programs running in different processors may access the same memory locations.

8.20 In a computer with a virtual-memory system, what features are needed to allow a multiple-word instruction to start at the end of one virtual page and end in the beginning of the next virtual page, or to allow an instruction to access data on a different page?

8.21 If memory interleaving is used as in Figure 8.12b, what properties must the memory bus and CPU have if the speedup gains due to simultaneous multiple-module accesses are to be realized?

8.22 Suppose that the program discussed in Problem 8.10 is to be run on a VAX-11 computer with a virtual-memory system. (See Section 8.9.) Ignore the cache in the problem and interpret all addresses as virtual. Assume that all addresses in this program are byte addresses. Furthermore, assume that, on average, an instruction occupies 4 bytes and 4 bytes can be fetched from the memory in one memory access. A translation buffer and the pretranslation technique (as described in Section 8.9.2) are both used to increase speed. Assuming that the complete program is resident in the main memory, and that the translation buffer is initially empty, estimate the total number of virtual-memory accesses (4 bytes per access,) requested by the CPU during execution of the program. What percentage of these accesses is handled by pretranslation and what percentage results in a hit in the translation buffer? What is the total number of translation buffer misses in this problem? problem?

8.13 REFERENCES

8.1 Satyanarayanan, M., and D. Bhandarkov: Design Tradeoffs in VAX-11 Translation Buffer Organization, *Computer*, vol. 14, no. 12, pp. 103–111, December 1981.

8.2 Levy, H. M., and P. H. Lipman: Virtual Memory Management in the VAX/VMS Operating System, *Computer*, vol. 15, no. 3, pp. 35–41, March 1982.

COMPUTER PERIPHERALS AND WORK STATIONS

In previous chapters we discussed hardware and software features of the central processing unit (CPU) and the main memory of a computer. We also discussed the means by which a computer communicates with any external devices connected to it, including the hardware and software facilities provided for supporting program-controlled I/O, direct memory access, and interrupts. This chapter is devoted to the presentation of the characteristics of commonly used computer peripherals.

The word "peripheral" is used to refer to any external device connected to a computer. In this context, the computer consists of the CPU, the main memory, and the I/O channels, if any. Functionally, computer peripherals can be divided into two categories. The first category contains devices that are intended to perform input and output operations. Such devices are keyboards, printers, CRT terminals, etc. The second category contains devices that are intended primarily for secondary storage of data, with primary storage being in the main memory of the computer. These are usually mass storage devices, such as magnetic tape and magnetic disk units, that are capable of storing large amounts of data. Their main use is as an extension or backup for the main memory of the computer. In this case, the devices are used *on-line*. Another important use is for *off-line* storage of programs and data files. An example of this is data stored on tape reels and disk packs that can be removed from the drive units when not in use.

In addition to the above two basic types of peripherals, other types of equipment can be incorporated into a computer system. Such equipment may be intelligent terminals capable of performing considerable computing tasks. It may be machines capable of more substantial stand-alone operation, as exemplified by personal computers. It may also be sizeable computers intended for dedicated tasks, as in the case of engineering work stations. Discussion of equipment of this type is included in the material of this chapter.

9.1 I/O DEVICES

A wide range of devices may be used in conjunction with a computer for I/O purposes. Some of the commonly used devices are:

- CRT terminals
- Graphic displays
- Printers
- Plotters
- Card readers and card punches

We will discuss the main features of these devices in the subsequent sections.

9.1.1 CRT Terminals

CRT (cathode-ray tube) terminals are the most commonly used I/O devices. They are also often referred to as video display terminals (VDT). They consist of a keyboard as the input device and a video screen as the output device.

A CRT terminal is usually found in a computer system whenever direct human interaction with the computer is required. It is used for entering and modifying programs, and receiving results, in an interactive environment. It may also be used by an operator for monitoring and controlling the progress of programs.

Early CRT terminals were relatively simple in their functional capability, being able only to perform primitive I/O operations. Such terminals are sometimes called *dumb* terminals. The development of VLSI technology and the availability of microprocessors has had a great impact on the evolution of terminals. Inclusion of powerful microprocessors in CRT terminals permits incorporation of considerable processing capability into these devices, resulting in *smart* terminals. Such terminals often possess sophisticated graphics and text manipulation facilities.

We will discuss the display aspects of CRT terminals in subsequent sections. However, first we will consider how such terminals can be connected into a computer system. A terminal may be physically located in the immediate proximity of the computer, or it may be a considerable distance away. Any interconnection scheme can be used in the former case, while the latter possibility favors an interconnection scheme that is inexpensive and easy to implement. Since terminals are used for interaction with human operators, very high rates of data transmission are not necessary. Therefore, a simple serial link, suitable for transmission of characters one bit at a time, is normally used for connection of terminals. There exists a standard format for transmitting such data, which we will describe next.

Serial transmission of data can be achieved only if both the transmitting and the receiving devices use the same timing information for interpretation of individual bits. This implies the use of a clock signal that indicates when each data bit occurs. There are two basic ways of realizing serial transmission. In a *synchronous* scheme, the same clock is used by the transmitter and the receiver. Thus, some mechanism must be provided to enable the receiver to obtain the clock information. This may involve using a separate clock line. Alternatively, an *asynchronous* scheme may be used, where the sender and the receiver generate their own clock signals. In this case, the clock line is not needed, but it is necessary to ensure that the two clocks have reasonably close frequencies and that the start of a sampling period for each unit of data can be identified.

The asynchronous serial transmission scheme that is commonly used for connection of terminals is known as the *start-stop* scheme. It is used for transmission of alphanumeric characters, usually encoded in 8-bit codes. Its format is shown in Figure 9.1. Ten or eleven bits are transmitted for each character. The line connecting the transmitter and the receiver is normally in the 1 state when idle. Transmission of a character is preceded by a 0 bit, referred to as the Start bit, followed by 8 bits of data and 1 or 2 Stop bits (each with logic value 1). The Start bit alerts the receiver that data transmission is about to begin. The leading edge of the Start bit is also used to synchronize the receiver clock with that of the transmitter. The Stop bits at the end serve to isolate consecutive characters in the case of continuous transmission. If only one character is being transmitted, the line remains in the 1 state after the end of the Stop bits. During an input operation, it is the responsibility of the interface connecting the terminal to the I/O bus of the computer to remove the Start and Stop bits. The interface also assembles the 8 serially transmitted data bits in its input data register in preparation for later parallel transmission to the computer when an input instruction is executed. The reverse sequence takes place for an output operation. An example of an interface of this type was given in Figure 6.16.

In order to ensure proper synchronization of the receiving end, the frequency of the local clock should be substantially higher than the transmission rate. Usually, the clock frequency is chosen to be 16 times the rate of transmission. This means that 16 clock pulses occur during each data bit interval. The receiver clock is used to increment a modulo-16 counter. This counter is reset to 0 when the leading edge of a Start bit is detected. Then, when the count reaches 8, in the middle of the Start bit, the value of the Start bit is sampled as a further check, and the counter is again reset to 0. From this point onward, the

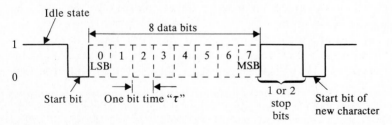

Figure 9.1 Asynchronous serial character transmission.

incoming data signal is sampled whenever the count reaches 16, which should be close to the middle of each bit transmitted. Therefore, as long as the relative positioning of bits within a transmitted character is not in error by more than eight clock cycles, the receiver will correctly interpret the bits of the encoded character.

A range of standard transmission rates is found in practical applications. The most common rates are 300 Hz, 600 Hz, 1200 Hz, 2400 Hz, 4800 Hz, 9600 Hz, and 19,200 Hz. A typical commercially available terminal is likely to be able to operate throughout this range. The actual rate chosen is usually dependent upon the characteristics of the computer system and the transmission link, as well as upon the nature of the application. The rate is the signalling frequency at which the bits are transmitted. A 300-Hz rate implies that 300 bits are transmitted per second. The rate of transmission is often referred to as the *baud* rate.[1] For example, a terminal may operate at 300 baud, 9600 baud, etc.

The transmitted characters are represented by the 7-bit ASCII code (see Appendix D) occupying bits 0 to 6 in Figure 9.1. The MSB, bit 7, is usually set to 0. The character set consists of capital letters, numbers, and special symbols, such as $, +, and >. A number of nonprinting characters are also provided, for example, EOT (end of transmission) and CR (carriage return). These characters may be used by the programmer to request specific actions, particularly when transmitting or receiving messages to or from a remote computer.

The start-stop scheme defines the format which is universally used for transmission of character data. However, there are several techniques for establishing the physical connection. Particularly popular standards that define the electric connections required are the RS-232-C and the 20-mA current loop. These standards and other aspects of communicating with terminals will be discussed in detail in Chapter 12.

9.1.2 CRT Displays

A video display based on a CRT unit is an integral part of any CRT terminal. However, the usage of CRT displays is much wider. They are used wherever visual representation of output information from a computer is needed, but where a hard copy of this information is not required. Moreover, although the CRT is basically an output device, it can perform limited input functions when used in conjunction with a light pen, as will be discussed later. In this section we shall present a brief description of the commonly used CRT displays. Our intention is to give the reader an appreciation of the complexity of the digital hardware involved in each case. Detailed technological and engineering aspects of the design of the CRT display itself are beyond the scope of this book.

---

[1] A baud is a unit of signalling speed, which refers to the number of times the state of a signal changes per second. For binary signals, the baud rate is the same as the bit rate. However, there exist more complicated signalling schemes where the baud rate is not the same as the bit rate. See Problem 9.2 for an example.

Let us start by describing how a CRT picture is formed. A focused beam of electrons strikes a fluorescent screen, causing emission of light that can be seen as a bright spot against a dark background. The dot thus formed disappears when the beam is turned off or moved to another spot. Thus, in general, there are three independent variables that need to be specified at all times, namely, the position of the beam, which can be specified in terms of its X and Y coordinates, and whether the beam is turned on, which is usually referred to as the Z-axis control. The size of the spot formed on the screen by the electron beam determines the total number of points that can be resolved on the screen, that is, distinguished by the eye. This is usually in the range of 300 to 1000 points along each of the X and Y coordinates. The amount of information required to define the status of all these points is very large. We shall not attempt to quantify this parameter until we have defined the format in which the data is presented to the display. Usually, a considerable amount of hardware is provided in the display to convert data from the format generated by the computer to that required to drive the CRT.

There are basically two types of CRT displays: (1) alphanumeric and (2) graphic.

Alphanumeric displays Alphanumeric displays are capable of displaying a character set such as that provided in the ASCII code. Because of the need to continuously refresh the display on the CRT screen, the characters received from the computer should be stored in a local memory. An example of the organization of such a display terminal is shown in Figure 9.2. The four counters, COLUMN COUNTER, X COUNTER, ROW COUNTER, and Y COUNTER, in conjunction with the clock, generate a raster scan of the CRT screen. Each character is represented by a dot matrix. The two counters ROW COUNTER and COLUMN COUNTER keep track of the row and column positions, respectively, within the dot matrix of any given character. Character positions on the screen are defined by the contents of X COUNTER and Y COUNTER. In the case of Figure 9.2, a 6×8 dot character pattern is assumed, and the screen has a capacity of 25 lines with 40 characters each.

A read-only memory (ROM) is used to store the dot pattern for each character and is thus called the *character generator*. The dot pattern for a given row of any character can be obtained by using the character code and the row number to address this memory. The multiplexer MPX 1 connects successive bits of this pattern to the Z-axis control, as the beam scans across the screen. The character to be displayed at a given position on the screen is stored in the corresponding location of the random-access memory (RAM). Thus, as the values of the address counters change, the corresponding character codes are read from the RAM and sent to the character generator, which, in turn, provides the appropriate row pattern for the Z-axis control.

Because of the need to refresh the display, the scanning process runs at a rate of about 60 full screen scans per second, providing a flicker-free display. In our example this requires a clock rate of approximately $60 \times (40 \times 6) \times (25 \times$

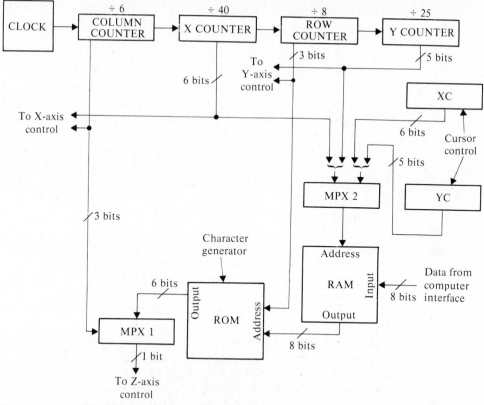

Figure 9.2 Control logic for an alphanumeric CRT display.

8)$\approx$ 3 MHz. The RAM is being addressed at one-sixth of this rate, or once every 2 μs.

To write new information on the screen, the contents of the RAM must be updated. The memory location where a new character can be written is defined by the two counters XC and YC. The multiplexer MPX 2 allows these two counters to replace X COUNTER and Y COUNTER in providing the memory address during writing. The location thus defined is referred to as the *cursor* position. Counter XC is incremented by 1 every time a new character is entered. A carriage-return character causes XC to be reset to 0, while a line-feed character causes YC to be incremented by 1. Various controls may be provided to enable moving the cursor on the screen by changing the contents of the two counters XC and YC. This may be done either manually or under computer control.

The example of Figure 9.2 illustrates the basic principles involved in most alphanumeric CRT displays. The total number of points and the order in which they are scanned vary from one model to another.

In some displays, the need for continuous refreshing is eliminated by using a *storage tube*. Outwardly, this tube behaves like a CRT with a very long persistence (up to an hour) phosphor. The basic principle is that the beam of electrons does not write the picture directly on the phosphor in a continuous refresh mode. It writes the picture once, electrostatically, on a fine-mesh wire storage grid coated with a dielectric and mounted just inside the tube face. A continuous flood of electrons from a separate source is then accelerated onto the phosphor to the points defined by the storage grid pattern, projecting this pattern on the face of the tube. Since it is very difficult to selectively erase the pattern on the storage grid, the display can be changed only by erasing and rewriting the whole screen. However, adding information to the display can be done at any time. The erasure process is accompanied by a flash of light across the entire screen. This fact, coupled with the need for a complete rewrite, even for small changes in the displayed pattern, makes the storage tube unsuitable for the display of patterns that need to be changed often.

Graphic displays In many applications the output of a computer is best presented in the form of a graphical plot. One important example is in computer-aided design applications. The computer may be required to present to the designer a drawing representing the layout of an integrated circuit, a circuit diagram, or the outline of a structural member to be analyzed or modified. Another important example can be found in real-time control applications. From a human factor point of view, it is very convenient to represent the state of the switchgear in a power generating station or the valves in a chemical plant by familiar graphical symbols. In this way, operators can assess the overall state of the system much faster than if they have to interpret the corresponding alphanumeric descriptions. Graphic displays are also used in applications such as game playing, computer animation, and many others.

Graphical pictures can be constructed by using a raster scan technique similar to that used in the alphanumeric display described above. CRTs used in such displays are similar to those found in standard television sets. A continuously scanning beam gets modulated by the information stored in a display memory. In this case, however, 1 memory bit should be provided for each dot position on the screen. Hence a screen with a 240×200 dot matrix requires a total of 48,000 memory bits. To refresh the display at the rate of 60 times/s, the data rate is 3×10^6 bits/s. The memory and data rate requirements make the raster scan scheme very attractive for low-resolution screens. As the number of points increases, this scheme requires much more extensive circuitry. An alternative approach is to move the electron beam on a curvilinear path in such a way as to plot the required graph directly. This means that the beam needs to scan only those points of the screen defined by the graph. Such displays are known as random scan or dedicated beam displays.

The random scan approach results in a considerable saving in time as well as in the required size of memory. It also simplifies the job of defining the points of the graph. However, it requires a much higher degree of sophistication in the design of the control circuitry associated with the CRT. This control circuitry is sometimes referred to as a *display processor*. The display processor accepts and executes commands of the type "Move the beam from its present position at point A to point B," where point B is specified by providing its absolute X and Y coordinates. Alternatively, point B can be specified relative to the current position of the beam. That is, only ΔX and ΔY, which are the X and Y coordinates of the vector AB, need be supplied. Each command should also indicate whether the beam should be turned on or off during its movement along the straight-line segment AB. In some displays, it is possible to specify the intensity of the beam when it is turned on. It may also be possible to define the type of line to be drawn, for example, solid or dashed. A sequence of such commands can be used to describe an arbitrary curve as a collection of straight-line segments.

Let us consider a very simple problem in which a rectangle is to be drawn on a graphic display. Suppose the viewing area of the screen consists of 1024 addressable points along each of the X and Y axes. Furthermore, assume that the display processor communicates with the remainder of the computing system through a controller in a manner similar to the way that an I/O device communicates through a DMA controller or a channel, as described in Chapter 6. Figure 9.3 shows a block diagram of the overall system. The block of commands that instructs the display processor to draw the rectangle is assembled in an area of the main memory by a CPU program. The CPU program sends the starting address of this block of commands to the controller over the I/O bus, accompanied by a Start signal. The controller then fetches the commands, one by one, from the main memory using cycle-stealing while the CPU is allowed to continue with other tasks.

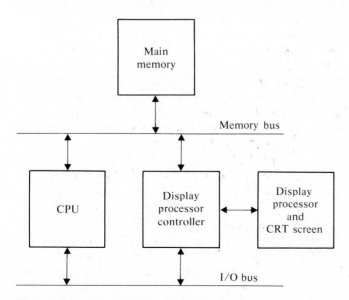

Figure 9.3 Graphic display in a computer system.

Command number	Block of commands in the main memory	Comments
1	Position beam to (300, 400), beam off	Get beam positioned at bottom left corner of rectangle
2	Move incrementally (0, 150), beam on	Draw left side
3	Move incrementally (400, 0), beam on	Draw top side
4	Move incrementally (0, −150), beam on	Draw right side
5	Move incrementally (−400, 0), beam on	Draw bottom side
6	Branch to command number 1	Go back to beginning of block and begin refresh cycle

Figure 9.4 Block of commands for drawing a rectangle on a graphic display.

An outline of the block of commands that could be used to draw a rectangle of size 400 × 150 points is given in Figure 9.4. The long side of the rectangle is parallel to the X axis, and its lower left corner is at the point (300, 400). The rectangle is drawn by proceeding clockwise from this corner. In this simple example, the display processor continually traces out the rectangle until it is halted by the CPU. Another possibility would be to replace command number 6 with a "Stop" command. The Stop command results in an interrupt request being sent to the CPU. The CPU can then update the commands, if desired, and restart execution. Frequent and orderly transfer of control to the main CPU facilitates the implementation of such effects as "animation."

In the above discussion, we have introduced the basic ideas involved in raster scan and random scan displays. Both types of displays have found widespread use. Both can be used as alphanumeric or graphic displays. Random scan displays tend to have greater resolution than raster scan displays. They are particularly suitable for drawing wire frame models. However, the complexity of the picture has an effect on the displayed image. If a large number of line segments are involved in a given picture, the image will start flickering if the display processor cannot keep up with the required rate for refreshing the screen.

Raster scan displays have a fixed scanning rate, hence a fixed refresh rate. Their main drawback is that high resolution in the displayed image is not easy to achieve. High resolution is contingent upon the existence of a large memory and considerable circuitry needed to prepare the large number of points that must be presented to the CRT at the fixed scanning rate. On the positive side, raster scan displays are flicker-free, regardless of the complexity of the displayed picture. They lend themselves to color applications. They are particularly suitable for solid modelling, where picture surfaces may be painted with different colors. We will present further aspects of CRT displays in the discussion of graphic display stations in Section 9.1.5.

9.1.3 Flat Panel Displays

While CRT displays have dominated the display applications, there has been considerable research effort aimed at developing other display technologies. An interesting class of alternative devices are known as flat panel displays. Such displays offer some potential advantages over CRT displays. They are thinner, hence attractive for environments where the depth of the display device is of importance. The voltage needed to drive them is much lower than for CRTs. They provide better linearity and possibly even higher resolution. However, their cost is still relatively high.

Several different types of flat panel displays have been developed. They include:

• Plasma panels
• Liquid crystal panels
• Electroluminescent panels

Plasma panels consist of two glass plates, separated by a thin gap filled with a gas such as neon. Each plate has a number of parallel electrodes running across it. The electrodes on the two plates run at right angles to each other. A voltage pulse on one electrode on each plate causes a small segment of gas at the intersection of the two electrodes to start glowing. The glow of gas segments turned on in this way is maintained by a lower voltage that is continuously applied to all electrodes. A similar pulsing arrangement can be used to selectively turn points off.

Liquid crystal panels may be constructed by sandwiching a thin layer of liquid crystal (that is, a liquid that exhibits crystalline properties) between two electrically conducting plates. The top plate has transparent electrodes in it, and the back plate is a mirror that reflects light. By applying proper electric signals across the plates, various segments of the liquid crystal can be activated, whereby their light diffusing or polarizing properties are changed. These segments either transmit or block the light. The image is produced by the light passing through the selected segments of the liquid crystal, then reflecting back from the mirror to the viewer. Liquid crystal displays have found extensive use in calculators, watches, and other devices where small-size displays are needed. Their applicability in larger computer systems will depend upon further technological improvements that may allow construction of more sizeable displays.

Electroluminescent panels use a thin layer of phosphor between two electrically conducting plates. The image is created by applying electric signals to the plates, which make the phosphor glow.

The viability of flat panel displays is closely linked to developments in the competing CRT display technology. CRTs provide a good combination of price, performance, and availability. Moreover, they permit easy implementation of color displays. Extensive use of flat panels is contingent on their attractiveness vis-à-vis CRT displays.

9.1.4 Graphic Input Devices

Video displays are basically output devices. However, when they are used in terminals, it is important to have adequate means for creating and changing a displayed image. In commonly used CRT terminals, a keyboard is used as the basic input device. It is used to enter both control commands and characters to be displayed. An operator can determine the position on the screen where the next input character will be displayed by cursor control. This may be done with simple commands such as Space, Backspace, Carriage Return, Line Feed, and Tab. They are activated through the keys on the keyboard.

In addition to such primitive cursor control, it is often desirable to have more powerful means of specifying locations on the screen. Two relatively simple input devices, the light pen and the joystick, can be used for this purpose. The *light pen* consists of a pen with a light sensor mounted at its tip. When placed in proximity with the CRT screen, the light sensor produces an output pulse whenever the electron beam illuminates a spot on the screen that is in the immediate vicinity of the sensor. This event is referred to as a "hit." A hit can be used to cause an interrupt request to be sent to the controlling processor. The X and Y coordinates of the beam at the moment the hit occurred are available for reference by the processor. This facility enables the programmer to use the light pen as an input device for defining points on the display screen.

The *joystick* is a short pivoted stick that can be moved by hand to define a point in two dimensions. The position of the stick, hence the coordinates of that point, can be sensed by a suitable linear or angular position transducer. For example, the potentiometer arrangement of Figure 9.5 can be used for this purpose. The voltage outputs of the X and Y potentiometers are fed to two analog-to-digital (A/D) converters. The output of the A/D converters can be connected to the input bus of a computer, thus enabling the computer to sense the position of the joystick at any time. Another input device of a similar type is the *trackball*. It can be rotated in any direction to move the cursor on the screen.

A different type of graphic input device not necessarily associated with a CRT display is the *graphics tablet*. It emulates the most natural way in which we record graphical information, namely, using pencil and paper. The device consists of a special writing pen that can be used in conjunction with a writing tablet of suitable size. The tablet is equipped with special sensors for determining the X and Y coordinates of the pen when it is placed close to, or in contact with, its surface. In one such system the tip of the pen emits short ultrasonic pulses that travel through the air. Ultrasonic detectors mounted at the edges of the tablet enable the propagation delay to be measured and, hence, the X and Y coordinates to be determined. The main disadvantage of these tablets is that their operation is hampered by foreign objects placed on the tablet.

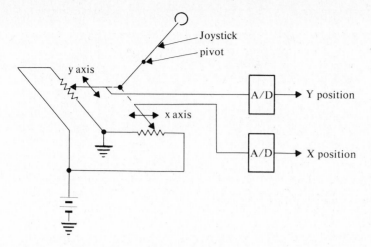

Figure 9.5 Joystick, using potentiometers as position transducers.

An alternative graphic tablet design is based on measurement of the delay of magnetostrictive waves. A suitable transducer launches a continuous stream of magnetostrictive pulses along an array of fine magnetic wires on the surface of the tablet. The tip of the writing pen causes these pulses to be reflected backward toward the source at the edge of the tablet. Thus the delay between transmitted and received pulses is a measure of the distance between the tip of the pen and the edge of the tablet. Since the magnetostrictive waves are constrained to the wires, this system is less sensitive to interference by extraneous objects.

9.1.5 Graphic Display Stations

In previous sections we considered some basic aspects of video displays and their applicability to graphics tasks. The diminishing cost of hardware has given impetus to the development of powerful systems for graphics applications. Such systems do not rely on one CPU to do all computing and graphics functions. Instead, many of the graphics functions are performed by a separate unit that may be referred to as a graphic display station. Such a station is connected to a host computer which supplies the information needed to draw an image. The station performs all functions associated with displaying the image.

A block diagram of a simple station using a raster scan CRT is shown in Figure 9.6. It consists of four major parts: the CRT, an image display unit, a memory that serves as a refresh buffer, and an image update processor. The CRT may be of the type used in standard color television sets. It is a raster scanning device, where the electron beam sweeps across the screen, displaying points along one horizontal line at a time. The number of points along each line and the number of lines on the screen define the resolution of the display. As pointed out in Section 9.1.2, the entire picture must be scanned approximately 60 times per second, in order to produce a flicker-free image.

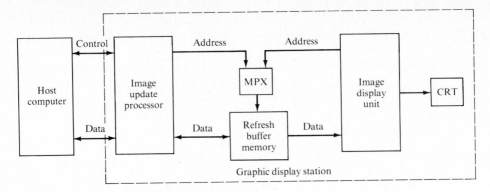

Figure 9.6 A simple raster scan graphic display system.

For each point on the screen, there must exist a unit of data that defines the nature of a picture element to be displayed. A picture element is called a *pixel*. The data associated with each pixel specifies the way in which the pixel is illuminated. A single bit of information can specify whether or not a given pixel is illuminated. However, in color displays each pixel must also specify the desired color, which means that several bits are needed per pixel. High-quality displays may use 8 bits per pixel, which allow encoded specification of up to 256 different color shades.

The data for each pixel for an image that is displayed is held in the refresh buffer, sometimes also called a *bit map*. This buffer may be a costly item because of its potential size and required speed. High-resolution displays may involve of the order of 1000×1000 pixels. If each pixel requires 8 bits of data, then a 1-Mbyte memory is needed. Fortunately, the cost of semiconductor memories has fallen to the point where this size of memory can be used in display stations.

Perhaps the most difficult problem to cope with in raster scan displays is to provide the output data to the CRT at the required scanning rate. The higher the resolution of the display, the more difficult this problem becomes. The function of the image display unit is to fetch the data from the refresh buffer and convert it into analog signals that drive the CRT. This is a complex unit. It includes X and Y counters for keeping track of the position on the screen, timing circuits for maintaining synchronization with the CRT, and a look-up table for translating the encoded pixel information into actual video signals for the CRT.

Displaying an image from the refresh buffer is just one function that requires sophisticated circuitry. Another aspect is the need to update the information in the buffer in a way that results in smooth transitions in the displayed picture. An image in the refresh buffer is created and updated by the image update processor. It is a processing unit capable of performing a number of basic graphics operations, such as drawing various geometric shapes (lines, circles, rectangles) and alphanumeric character fonts. A powerful image update processor simplifies the interaction between the display station and the host computer. The host can define a picture at a relatively high level. The image update processor then generates the details at the pixel level.

Design of graphic display stations has been enhanced by the availability of a number of VLSI chips intended for use in the image update processor and the image display unit. These chips are in fact special-purpose microprocessors. Their development has had a significant impact on lowering the cost of display stations.

In addition to providing a means for displaying a high-quality picture, most display stations provide the user with numerous aids that simplify image specification and manipulation. These include capabilities to:

- Zoom on a part of an image
- Pan across an image
- Scroll the picture vertically
- Divide the screen into several viewports for displaying independent pictures

Graphic display stations are actually special-purpose computers. But, they are normally used in conjunction with another computer, the host. Thus, it is not unreasonable to think of them as being sophisticated peripheral devices.

9.1.6 Printers

Printers are used to produce hard copy of output data or text. There exists a variety of printing devices suitable for use in computer systems. They range from simple mechanisms that print one character at a time to sophisticated units that print one page at a time. Between these extremes are the line printers, which print one line at a time.

Printers are usually classified as being of impact or nonimpact type, depending upon the nature of the printing mechanism used. Impact printers use mechanical printing mechanisms, while nonimpact printers rely on electrostatic, thermal, or optical techniques. Mechanical printers are limited in speed by the motion of mechanical parts. Yet, speeds upward of 1000 lines per minute are attainable. Considerably higher speeds can be achieved with nonimpact printers, where printing several thousand lines per minute is possible.

We will consider two representative examples of mechanical printers: drum and chain printers. Consider a drum line printer first. If a line contains n characters (132 characters is a popular choice), then the drum is divided into n tracks, each track consisting of a complete set of characters. A set of n print hammers (one per track) is used to press the printing paper and the ink ribbon against the characters on the drum. The line to be printed is held in a buffer, which is loaded by the output circuits of the computer. As the drum rotates, the characters on the drum are compared with those in the buffer. When a desired character passes in front of the hammer, the hammer is activated, which results in the printing of this character. Thus a complete line is printed within one revolution of the drum.

Chain printers employ a belt that contains a set of characters. As the belt rotates along the line, past the print hammers, each hammer is activated when a desired character passes in front of it. A complete line is printed within one revolution of the belt. Faster printing operation can be achieved if duplicate copies of the character set are used on the belt. For example, if five full sets of characters are used, a complete line can be printed within one-fifth of one revolution of the belt.

Nonimpact printers use fewer mechanical parts and can be operated at higher speeds. A number of different techniques are used in printers of this type. Photocopying technology has been used in laser printers, which print one page at a time. In this scheme a drum coated with positively charged photoconductive material is exposed to a laser beam. The positive charges that are illuminated by the beam are dissipated. Then, a negatively charged toner powder is spread over the drum. It adheres to the positive charges, thus creating an image which is then transferred to the paper. As the last step the drum is cleaned of any excess toner material to prepare it for printing the next page.

An electrostatic printing mechanism can be used effectively in character and line printers. Characters are formed by charging the printing paper with character patterns under the control of electrodes. In this case, special paper containing electrically conductive material is used.

Other types of nonimpact printers include those using thermal and ink-jet principles. In a thermal printer, a heating element in the print head is used to develop the character image on special heat-sensitive paper. In an ink-jet printer, electrically charged droplets of ink are fired from a nozzle. They are deflected by an electric field to trace out the desired character patterns on the paper they strike. Several nozzles with different color inks can be used to generate color output.

Printers are often referred to as either solid character or dot matrix printers. In the former, each character is represented by a solid outline of the character. In dot matrix printers, characters are formed by printing dots in matrices that typically involve 7×5 or 7×9 dot positions. These printers are becoming increasingly popular because they can easily accommodate a variety of fonts and they can also be used for printing graphical images. A possible problem with dot matrix printers is poor definition of character outlines. This can be overcome by overlapping the dots and increasing their number.

Development of printers has been characterized by intense activity. A variety of different techniques have been developed and successfully applied in practice. While this has resulted in lower costs, the cost of high-quality printers is still high relative to the cost of other units in a computer system, particularly in the case of microcomputer systems.

9.1.7 Card Readers and Card Punches

A *card reader* is an electromechanical device that reads computer input information in the form of patterns of small holes punched on heavy paper cards. The cards measure approximately 8.3×18.4 cm, and the hole patterns are organized into 80 columns spread across the long dimension of the card. Each column consists of a line of 12 row positions equally spaced across the short dimension of the card. At each row position, a hole may or may not be punched, where a hole represents a 1 and no hole represents a 0. This results in a 12-bit code for representing characters. The code most commonly used with punched cards is the Hollerith code. It includes the alphabet letters A through Z, the decimal digits 0 through 9, punctuation marks, etc.

The card reader must be interfaced to the computer. A standard arrangement is to have the card reader connected to a direct memory access (DMA) controller or a multiplexer channel. The CPU can initiate reading a card by sending a main memory buffer address and a length count, say, 80 bytes. When the CPU issues the start I/O command, the controller signals the card reader to access the next card in the card hopper and begin translating the hole patterns into electric signals corresponding to 0s and 1s. This process can be done in parallel for all 80 columns, or serially by column. We will describe the serial scheme first. The card reader moves the card column by column past the card-reader read station. For high-speed operation, the holes are read by passing light through them onto a photoelectric device. As each 12-bit column of the card is read, it is passed to the interface circuitry and sent to the controller. The controller may translate the 12-bit pattern, representing a character, into a standard internal computer code, such as the 8-bit EBCDIC code described in Appendix D. An alternative is to compress each 12-bit pattern into some other code (≤ 8 bits), which can be translated later to a standard internal code by software. The controller packs successive bytes (characters) together until it forms a word. A word of characters is then transmitted to the main memory by cycle stealing. The buffer address and count values are updated and the next word of characters is gathered from the card reader interface and sent to the controller, etc. It is not necessary to restrict the buffer to 80 characters or less. If the controller is instructed to read more than 80 characters from cards, it will automatically proceed to access enough cards to acquire the requested number of characters.

As mentioned earlier, it is possible to read the hole patterns on a card in parallel, instead of serially by column. If the patterns are read in parallel, they must be temporarily stored in an 80-character buffer either in the interface or the controller. The contents of this buffer can then be transmitted, word by word, to the main memory under control of the DMA controller or multiplexer channel.

Using the photoelectric hole-reading scheme, cards can be read at speeds in excess of 1000 cards per minute. This is fast by mechanical standards but slow relative to the electronic speeds in the remainder of the computer system. Let us estimate the rate at which memory cycles are stolen by the controller when it is transferring characters from a 1200 cards per minute card reader into the main memory. Assume that the memory has a 32-bit word length and a cycle time of 1 μs. The card reader interface transmits characters to the controller at the rate of $1200 \times 80 \times 1/60 = 1600$ per second. These are packed four characters per word for transmission to the memory, so that a rate of 400 words per second is directed into the memory by cycle stealing. The maximum rate of transferring words into the memory in this example is 10^6 words per second. Therefore less than 0.05 percent of the available memory cycles are stolen by transfers from the card reader.

Computer programmers prepare program input for the computer by punching program statements on cards at off-line keypunch stations. The cards are assembled into decks and fed into the computer, as described above, through the on-line card reader. In some cases, it is useful to have the capability for the computer system to punch information onto cards. This is true, for instance, in the case where a machine language program is to be stored off-line on cards. The program words can be punched byte by byte onto cards by a device called a *card punch*. When the program is to be run later, it is simply read into the main memory through the card reader and is directly executable. This avoids the need to translate the program again from its original source language form. Since punching holes in paper cards is a slower process than reading the cards photoelectrically, card punches operate at slower speeds than card readers.

9.2 ON-LINE STORAGE

In many computer systems a storage space much larger than the available main memory is required. However, expansion of the main memory is limited by economic considerations. In small computer systems, it may also be limited by the addressing capability of the CPU. The required extra storage space can be provided by magnetic disks and tapes.

9.2.1 Magnetic-Disk Systems

As the name implies, the storage medium in a magnetic-disk system consists of one or more disks (platters) stacked on top of each other. A thin magnetic film is deposited on each disk, usually on both sides. The disks are mounted on a rotary drive such that the magnetized surfaces move in close proximity to a series of Read/Write heads, as shown in Figure 9.7a. The disks are rotated at a uniform speed and are not started or stopped during access operations. Each head consists of a magnetic yoke and a magnetizing coil, as in Figure 9.7b. Digital information can be stored on the magnetic film by applying current pulses of suitable polarity to the magnetizing coil. This causes the magnetization of the film in the area immediately underneath the head to be switched into a direction parallel to the applied field. The same head can be used for reading the stored information. In this case, changes in the magnetic field in the vicinty of the head resulting from the movement of the film relative to the yoke cause an induced voltage in the coil, which now serves as a sense coil. The polarity of this voltage is monitored by the control circuitry to determine the state of magnetization of the film. It should be noted that only changes in the magnetic field under the head can be sensed during the Read operation. Therefore, if the binary states 0 and 1 are represented by two opposite states of magnetization, a voltage is induced in the head only at 0 to 1 and 1 to 0 transitions in the bit stream. A long

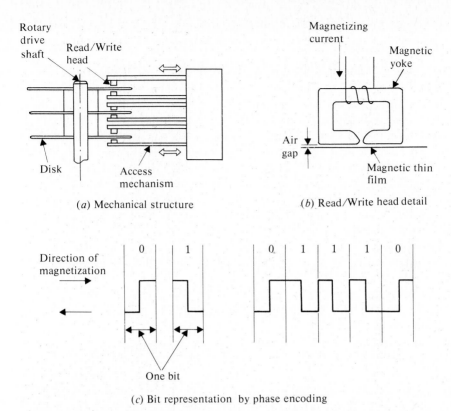

(a) Mechanical structure

(b) Read/Write head detail

(c) Bit representation by phase encoding

Figure 9.7 Magnetic-disk principles.

string of 0s or 1s will cause an induced voltage only at the beginning and end of the string. In order to determine the number of consecutive 0s or 1s stored, it is necessary to provide information for synchronization, or a *clock*. The clock can be recorded on a separate track, where a change in magnetization is forced for each bit period. Then, a simple memory circuit that remembers the direction of the last change in magnetization on the data track, plus the clock signal, will allow correct reading of the stored data. Many commercial disk units are based on the scheme of storing the clock information on a separate track.

A number of different techniques for encoding data on magnetic disks have been developed. As an alternative to storing the clock on a separate track, the clocking information can be combined with the data. One popular scheme is depicted in Figure 9.7c. It is known as *phase encoding* or *Manchester code*. In this scheme, a change in magnetization is forced for each data bit, as shown in the figure. This change occurs at the midpoint of each bit period. Thus, it can also be used as clocking information. With this type of encoding, it is not necessary to provide a separate track for clocking purposes, as the clock is easily extracted from the encoded data. The drawback of Manchester code is its poor bit-storage density. Other, more compact codes based on similar principles can be used. They require more complex control circuitry, but provide better storage density. The details of such codes are beyond the scope of this book.

Organization and accessing of data on a disk The organization of data on a disk is illustrated in Figure 9.8a. Each surface is divided into concentric *tracks*, and each track is divided into *sectors*. Data bits are stored serially on each track. Addressing of data on disks is accomplished by specifying the surface number, the track number, and the sector number. The set of corresponding tracks on all surfaces of a stack of disks is said to form a *cylinder*. In some cases, it is possible to specify an individual word within an addressed sector. However, in most disk systems, Read and Write operations always start at sector boundaries. If the number of words to be written is smaller than that required to fill a sector, the disk controller repeats the last bit of data for the remainder of the sector.

The Read/Write heads of a disk system are either fixed or movable. In the former case, a separate head is provided for each track of each surface. In the latter case, there is one head per surface. All heads are mounted on a comb-like arm that can move radially across the stack of disks to provide access to individual tracks, as shown in Figure 9.7a. In many moving-head disk systems, the stack of disks can be removed for off-line storage and is usually called a *disk pack*.

The fixed-head organization results in faster access to a sector location, because in the moving-head case the arm holding the Read/Write heads must first be positioned to the correct track. There are many other factors that should be taken into account in comparing fixed-head systems with moving-head systems. For instance, there is more electronic circuitry involved in the head per

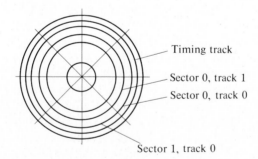

Timing track

Sector 0, track 1

Sector 0, track 0

Sector 1, track 0

(*a*) Organization of one surface of a disk

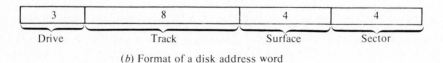

3	8	4	4
Drive	Track	Surface	Sector

(*b*) Format of a disk address word

Figure 9.8 Addressing of data on magnetic disks.

track scheme than in the movable-head disk system. On the other hand, there is more mechanical complexity in the moving-arm mechanism of the other organization. As we will see later, the tracks are spaced very close together, so the servomechanism that performs track positioning is a nontrivial electromechanical system.

It is common to have one or more permanently written tracks to provide timing pulses. The pulses, in conjunction with counters in the disk control circuits, can be used to determine sector and track origin positions on the data tracks. Figure 9.8a indicates a timing track at the outer edge of the surface. This is a feasible arrangement in fixed-head systems. The heads that operate on the timing tracks provide positional addressing information for the remainder of the tracks. In multiple-surface moving-head systems, one of the surfaces may be dedicated to providing timing-pulse information that can be used in addressing data on the remainder of the surfaces. In addition to these methods of deriving positional information from timing tracks, there are a number of ways in which additional timing information may be included in the data-encoding scheme.

Read/Write heads must be maintained at a very small distance away from the moving disk surfaces in order to achieve high bit densities and reliable Read/Write operations. When the disks are moving at their steady rate, air pressure develops between the surface and the head and forces the head away from the surface. This force can be counteracted by a spring-loaded mounting arrangement for the head that allows it to be pressed toward the surface. The flexible spring connection between the head and its arm mounting permits the head to "fly" at the desired distance away from the surface in spite of any small variations in the flatness of the surface.

Let us consider an example of how a disk might be organized, using specific values for the various parameters. Suppose that the disk system has 16 data recording surfaces with 256 tracks per surface. Tracks are divided into 16 sectors, and each sector of a track contains 512 bytes (or characters) of data, recorded bit-serially. The total capacity of the disk is $16 \times 256 \times 16 \times 512 \approx 30$ million bytes. Assume that the diameter of the inner cylinder is 10 in and that of the outer cylinder is 14 in. Since the bit capacity of all tracks is the same, the maximum bit density occurs along the inner tracks, where it is $(16 \times 512 \times 8)/10\pi \approx 2000$ bits/in. Since there are 256 tracks per surface, the track density is $256/2 = 128$ tracks per inch.

The data transfer rate for this disk is calculated as follows. Assuming a rotational speed of 3600 revolutions per minute, a complete track can be read or written in $60/3600 \approx 0.016$ s. This corresponds to a byte transfer rate of $(16 \times 512)/0.016 = 512,000$ bytes/s.

In the case of a moving-head system, there are two time components involved in the delay between receiving an address at the disk controller and the beginning of the actual data transfer. The first, called the *seek time*, is the time required to move the Read/Write head to the proper track. This obviously depends on the initial position of the head relative to the track specified in the address. Average values in the 30-ms range are typical. The second component is the *rotational delay*, also called *latency time*. This is the amount of time that elapses after the head is positioned over the correct track until the starting position of the addressed sector comes under the Read/Write head. On the average, this is the time for half a rotation of the disk, that is, $0.5(60/3600) = 8.3$ ms in the above example. The sum of these two delays is usually called the disk *access time*. We should note that if only a few sectors of data are moved in a single operation, the access time is about an order of magnitude longer than the actual data transfer period. Also, since the major component of the access time is the seek time, it is clear that fixed-head systems, which require no seek time, have a distinct time advantage over moving-head systems.

Communication between a disk and the main memory is done through either DMA or channel control. The operation of these I/O access mechanisms has been described in Chapter 6. Here, we will concentrate on the logical requirements and will not be concerned with the method of implementation. The information that must be exchanged between the CPU and the disk controller in order to specify a transfer includes:

Main memory address. The address of the first main memory location of the block of words involved in the transfer.
Disk address. The location of the sector containing the beginning of the desired block of words.
Word count. The number of words in the block to be transferred.

We can assume, for convenience, that these three quantities are placed in registers in the disk controller.

The disk address format for our typical disk example is shown in Figure 9.8*b*. The lengths of the track, surface, and sector fields are consistent with the parameters we have used in the above example. The fourth field, named the drive field, specifies which of eight disk drives is involved. This applies to the case in which a number of disk drives are controlled by one controller. Normally, only one disk can be actively performing an access or transfer operation at any point in time.

The word count may correspond to fewer or more bytes than is contained in a sector. The padding out of the unused part of a sector has been mentioned earlier. An interesting aspect of the disk-address word format of Figure 9.8*b* should be noted. Let us consider a data block that is longer than 16 sectors. The disk address register is incremented as successive sectors are read or written. When the sector count goes from 15 to 0, the surface count increases by 1. Thus long data blocks are laid out on cylinder surfaces as opposed to being laid out on successive tracks of a physical disk surface. This is efficient for the case of moving-head systems. It means that successive 16-sector areas of data storage on the disk can be accessed by electrically switching from one Read/Write head to the next as opposed to mechanically moving the arm from track to track. The track-to-track move will need to be made only at cylinder-to-cylinder boundaries.

The disk controller must be able to accept commands to initiate various functions in the disk drives, as well as handling the addressing and block-length information. The major functions are:

Seek. In the case of a moving-head system, the disk drive specified in the disk address register moves the Read/Write head arm from its current position to the track specified; in the case of a fixed-head system, the appropriate Read/Write head is selected electronically.

Read. Initiates a Read operation starting at the address specified in the disk address register. Data read serially from the disk is assembled into words and transferred to the main memory, starting at the location specified in the memory address register. The number of words transferred to memory is determined by the word count register. The word count is decremented after each word transfer and the memory address is incremented. The disk address is incremented at the end of each sector.

Write. Transfers data from the main memory to the disk. Data transfers are controlled in a way similar to that given for the Read command.

Write Check. Can be used after a Write operation to ensure that no errors have been introduced during the transfer. The controller starts a Read operation on the disk and compares the contents of the addressed sector with the data read from the corresponding locations in the main memory. If a mismatch is detected, an error message is returned to the CPU via the interrupt system.

To sequence these commands properly from the CPU, the disk system may be arranged to raise an interrupt at the completion of a Seek operation in a moving-head disk. Interrupts will also normally be used to signal the completion of a Read, Write, or Write Check operation. A "lookahead" register is provided in many disk systems. This register contains the address of the sector currently passing underneath the Read/Write head. This enables the programmer to check the disk position at any time for purposes of scheduling input or output operations.

Winchester disks So far we have discussed the most general aspects of disk storage mechanisms. We have assumed that a disk is a multisurface structure, with either movable or fixed Read/Write heads used to access the data. But, there are several different ways of implementing disk units that are encountered in practice. In some units the disk packs are removable and therefore interchangeable. In other units the disk pack cannot be removed. Some advantages can be derived if the disk pack and the Read/Write heads are placed in a sealed, air filtered enclosure. This approach is known as *Winchester technology*. In such units the Read/Write heads can be placed closer to the magnetized track surfaces because no difficulties are encountered with dust particles that are a problem in unsealed assemblies. The closer the heads are to a track surface, the more densely data can be packed along the track. Moreover, the tracks can be narrower. Thus, Winchester disks exhibit greater density and have larger capacity for a given physical size. This ultimately results in lower-cost units.

Another advantage of Winchester technology is that data integrity tends to be greater in sealed units where the storage medium is not exposed to contaminating elements. The main drawback of Winchester disks is that disk modules are not cost effective for off-line storage because they are considerably more expensive than standard disk packs.

Floppy disks The devices discussed above are known as hard or rigid disk units. Another class of smaller, simpler, and cheaper disk units can be constructed by using a flexible plastic diskette coated with magnetic material. Such devices are called *floppy disks*. The diskette is enclosed in a cardboard or plastic jacket. It is usually referred to as a cartridge. The jacket has an opening where the Read/Write head comes in contact with the diskette. A hole in the center of the cartridge allows a spindle mechanism in the disk drive to position and rotate the diskette.

Information is recorded on floppy disks by combining the clock and data information along each track. One of the simplest schemes used is essentially the same as phase encoding, mentioned earlier. Disks encoded in this way are known as having *single density*. A more complicated variant of this scheme, called *double density*, is frequently used. It increases the storage density by a factor of 2, but it also requires more complex circuits in the disk controller.

The main attractiveness of floppy disks is their low cost. For this reason they are the dominant secondary storage devices used in microprocessor systems. They have small storage capacities compared to hard disks. Floppy disks that can store 1 MByte of data are in common use, but units capable of storing up to 10 MBytes have been developed. While such capacities are adequate for most microcomputer applications, they are insufficient for larger installations. With the rapid growth of microcomputers, the use of floppy disks has increased greatly. One should also not overlook their suitability for transporting information off-line. A floppy disk cartridge is inexpensive, small, and easily shipped by mail.

Disk technology has been characterized by rapid development. We have discussed the main features of the commonly used disk types. We have not emphasized the details of specific units. In order to give the reader some feeling for the quantitative parameters of typical disk units available in the early 1980s, we have summarized such parameters for several disks in Table 9.1.

9.2.2 Magnetic-Drum Systems

Magnetic drums are similar to magnetic disks in their principle of operation. The main difference is that the storage medium, that is, the magnetic film, is deposited on the surface of a drum instead of a disk. Tracks are organized around the surface of the drum as shown in Figure 9.9.

The storage capacity of a drum varies considerably from one system to another. It starts at around 2×10^6 characters and goes as high as 9×10^9 characters. Small drum systems are similar in performance to disk drives. Large

Table 9.1 Characteristics of some commercial magnetic-disk systems

Model	Type	Capacity per drive, char. $\times 10^6$	Transfer rate, (char./s) $\times 10^3$	Average access time, ms	Speed of rotation, rpm
DEC:					
RA60	Standard	205	1980	50	3600
RA81	Winchester	456	1200	36.3	3600
RX02	Floppy	0.5	61	262	360
IBM:					
3330		100	806	38.4	3600
3350		317	1198	33.4	3600
3380		630	3000	24.3	3600
CDC:*					
9760	Standard	40	1200	38.3	3600
9766	Standard	300	1200	38.3	3600
9775	Winchester	675	1200	33.3	3600
Shugart:					
SA4008	Winchester	24.8	889	75.1	2964
SA851	Floppy	1.2	62.5	174	360
Fujitsu:					
M2351A/AF	Winchester	475	1859	25.5	3960

*Control Data Corp.

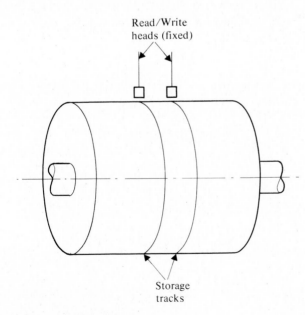

Figure 9.9 Magnetic drum.

Table 9.2 Characteristics of two commercial magnetic-drum systems

Model	Capacity, char. $\times 10^6$	Organization, no. of tracks $\times$ char./track	Average access time, ms	Transfer rate, (char./s) $\times 10^3$
IBM 2301	4.1	800×5120	8.6	1200
Univac FH-880	320	$62{,}500 \times 5120$	16.7	300

drum systems, however, are capable of storing a much larger amount of information compared with currently available disk drives. The parameters of two commercially available drum systems are given in Table 9.2.

In many drum systems, a set of Read/Write heads is used to access the bits of a given character in parallel. With few exceptions, only one Read/Write head is enabled in a disk drive at any given time.

9.2.3 Magnetic-Tape Systems

Magnetic tapes are particularly suited for off-line storage of large amounts of data and are also used extensively for transferring information between two machines when a direct communication facility is not available. Magnetic-tape recording uses the same principle as in recording data on disks. The main difference is that the magnetic film is deposited on a very thin ½-in-wide plastic tape. Seven or nine bits (corresponding to one character) are recorded in parallel across the width of the tape, perpendicular to the direction of motion. A separate Read/Write head is provided for each bit position on the tape. Hence data transfer takes place parallel by bit and serial by character. One of the character bits is used as a parity bit.

Data on the tape is organized in the form of records separated by gaps, as shown in Figure 9.10. Tape motion is stopped only when a record gap is underneath the Read/Write heads. The length of the gap is such that when the tape starts moving again it can attain its normal speed before the beginning of

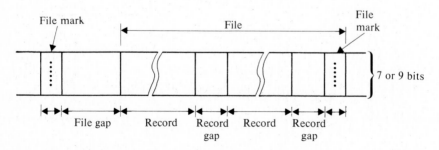

Figure 9.10 Organization of data on magnetic tape.

the next record is reached. If a coding scheme such as that of Figure 9.7c is used for recording data on the tape, record gaps are identified as areas where there is no change in magnetization. This allows record gaps to be detected independently of the recorded data. To help programmers organize their data, a group of records are considered to form a *file*. The beginning of a file is identified by a *file mark*, as shown in Figure 9.10. The file mark is a special single- or multi-character record, usually preceded by a gap longer than the interrecord gap. The first record following a file mark may be used as a *header* or *identifier* for this file. This enables a tape containing a large number of files to be searched for a particular file.

The controller of a magnetic tape drive enables the execution of a number of commands relating to the operation of the drive. Typical commands accepted by such a controller are Read, Write, Read Backward, Sense, and Control. The functions associated with these commands have been discussed in conjunction with channel operation in Chapter 6. The Control command may further specify one of the following operations:

Rewind Tape
Rewind and Unload Tape
Erase Tape
Write Tape Mark
Forward Space One Record
Backspace One Record
Forward Space One File
Backspace One File

The tape mark referred to in the operation Write Tape Mark is similar to a file mark except that it is used for identifying the beginning of the tape. The end of the tape is sometimes identified by the EOT (end of tape) character (see Appendix D).

Two different ways of formatting and using tapes are found in practice. In one case, the records are variable in length. This allows efficient use of the tape, but it does not permit updating or overwriting of records in place. A format of this type, developed by the IBM Corporation, has become an industry standard. The second possibility is to use fixed-length records, as in tape drives produced by Digital Equipment Corporation. In this case it is possible to update records in place. While this may seem to be a significant advantage, in practice it has turned out to be of little importance. The most common uses of tapes are for backing up information on magnetic disks, for off-line manual transport of information from one computer to another, and for archival storage of data. In these applications, a tape is written from the beginning to the end, so that the size of the records is immaterial.

Magnetic tape cassettes The expanding popularity of microcomputer systems has given impetus to widespread use of smaller magnetic tape units, where the tape and two reels are enclosed in a plastic box. Such units are called cassettes. They offer several advantages relative to standard tape units. Their chief attractiveness lies in their low cost. They are also easier to handle because the tape does not have to be threaded from one reel to another through the transport mechanism. Moreover, fewer difficulties are experienced with particle contaminations caused by manual handling.

The tape used in cassettes is narrower and shorter than in standard tapes. It also has fewer tracks, which means that character data cannot be recorded in parallel across the width of the tape. Instead, it is recorded longitudinally using techniques similar to those discussed in conjunction with magnetic disks. The clock and data information is combined along the same track.

In addition to digital tape cassettes, it is possible to use ordinary audio cassettes. This provides the cheapest form of storage because it makes use of cassette recorders that cost under $100 and cassettes that can be bought for $2 to $3. An audio cassette can store more than 100 Kbytes of data. Audio cassettes are much slower and less reliable than digital cassettes.

A commonly used technique for recording data on audio cassettes is to represent 1s and 0s with 2400-Hz and 1200-Hz square waves, respectively. Each 1 is represented by 8 clock cycles of the 2400-Hz tone, while each 0 is represented by 4 cycles of the 1200-Hz tone, as shown in Figure 9.11. This encoding scheme is known as Kansas City Standard. As seen from the figure, both 0 and 1 have the same bit period. The recording rate, and hence data transmission, is one-quarter of 1200 Hz, which is equivalent to 300 bits/s. Another important point to note is that for each clock pulse there is a transition in the waveform for both 0 and 1. This fact is exploited in the process of reading the tape to recover the clock from the stored information.

From the above discussion it is clear that audio cassettes do not allow · efficient storage of information. Their reliability is sometimes also questioned. But, these drawbacks are offset by their extremely low cost.

We have seen that magnetic tape storage is available in several forms. Numerous tape drives are produced by a variety of manufacturers. Characteristics of some typical units are summarized in Table 9.3.

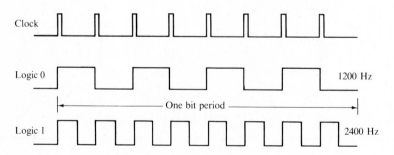

Figure 9.11 Kansas City Standard for audio recording of digital data.

Table 9.3 Characteristics of some commercial magnetic-tape systems

Model	Channels	Tape speed, in/s	Density, bits/in	Transfer rate, (char./s) $\times 10^3$
DEC:				
TU66	9	75	1600	120
TU78	9	125	1600/6250	781
IBM:				
3420-5	9	125	800/1600	200
2420-8	9	200	1600/6250	1250
Telex:*				
6253	9	125	1600/6250	781

*Telex Computer Products, Inc.

9.2.4 Other Developments in Mass Storage Technology

Magnetic disks, drums, and tapes have been used in the majority of mass storage applications since the early days of computers. They offer high storage density combined with fast data transfer rates. However, because of the presence of moving parts, they are vulnerable to mechanical failures. An alternative technology is continually being sought by researchers to obtain equivalent or better performance using only solid-state components. Other alternatives are also being pursued to provide economical means for archival applications where very large amounts of data are to be stored.

Several such alternative technologies have been developed. They include magnetic bubbles, charge-coupled devices, and optical storage. While these technologies have yet to present a serious challenge to magnetic disks and tapes, they offer certain advantages which make them suitable for specialized applications. In what follows, we will discuss briefly the salient characteristics of some of these technologies.

Magnetic bubbles Consider a thin slice of a magnetic material. The characteristics of the magnetic field created by this material are such that, in the absence of external influence, the direction of magnetization of the material tends to be parallel to its surface. The crystals of certain materials, however, strongly favor magnetization in a fixed direction relative to the crystalline axes. Bubble memories are prepared in the form of thin slices of single crystals of such a material. The crystal is grown under controlled conditions and the slices are prepared so that the favored direction of magnetization is perpendicular to the surface of the slice. As a result, magnetization will always be perpendicular to the surface. Different areas of the slice may be magnetized in opposite directions, as shown in Figure 9.12a.

Let us now assume that a uniform magnetic field H_b is applied to the slice of

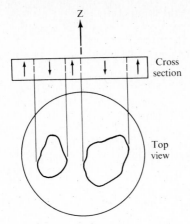

(a) Magnetization in a thin slice of magnetic bubble material

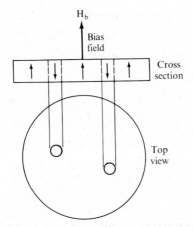

(b) Magnetization after application of bias field   **Figure 9.12** Magnetic bubbles.

Figure 9.12a parallel to the Z-axis. The regions of the slice where magnetization is in the same direction as the H_b field will grow in size and those whose magnetization is in the opposite direction will shrink. At a certain value of H_b, the regions with opposite magnetization collapse into very tiny cylinders, as shown in Figure 9.12b. These cylinders are called magnetic bubbles. They behave as small magnets. They can move about in the slice if attracted or repelled by external magnetic objects. However, they maintain their size and shape as long as the H_b field remains constant.

In a magnetic bubble memory, the H_b field is provided by a permanent magnet surrounding the slice. A soft magnetic material, such as permalloy, is deposited on one side of the slice in a pattern consisting of alternating I's and T's, as shown in Figure 9.13. In addition, a set of coils produces a small magnetic field H_r, which can be made to rotate parallel to the surface of the slice. This field causes the overlay material to be magnetized and attract magnetic bubbles. In

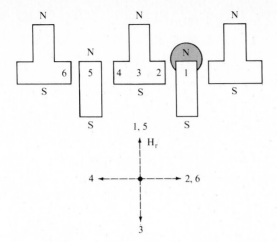

Figure 9.13 T-bar pattern.

the figure, we have assumed that the polarity of the bubbles is such that they are attracted to a north pole.

As the field H_r rotates, the position of the north pole of each element of the pattern changes. Consider the bubble at position 1. It is near the north pole of an I element created by H_r while in direction 1. As the field rotates from direction 1 to direction 2, the pole to which the bubble is attracted moves to the long edge of the I element and becomes weaker in the process. Meanwhile, a much stronger north pole appears at position 2, at the tip of the T element. As a result, the bubble jumps to position 2. As the field continues to rotate, the bubble moves to positions 3 and 4, then jumps to 5, and so on.

The T-bar pattern provides a mechanism for moving bubbles within the slice. Similar patterns, in conjunction with electric current pulses which cause localized changes in the magnetic field, can be used to generate, annihilate, and replicate bubbles. Bubble movement can also be switched from one path to another. The presence of a bubble at a given location can be detected by an appropriate transducer, such as a Hall effect device (a device that generates an electric voltage proportional to magnetic field intensity) or a magnetoresistive element (a component whose electrical resistance changes according to magnetic field intensity). In order to be detected, a magnetic bubble has to be increased in size several hundred times. This can be accomplished by changing the magnitude of the H_b field in the vicinity of the detector.

The above discussion has introduced the basic principles of magnetic bubble technology. We will now discuss briefly the way in which bubble memories are organized and used. The T-bar pattern of Figure 9.13 can be regarded as a row of cells, each consisting of a T element and an adjacent I element. The presence or absence of a bubble within a cell can be used to represent 1 bit of information. As the H_r field rotates, the structure behaves as a shift register in which information is shifted from one cell to the next for each 360° rotation of the field. In a typical magnetic bubble memory, the T-bar pattern is organized to form a

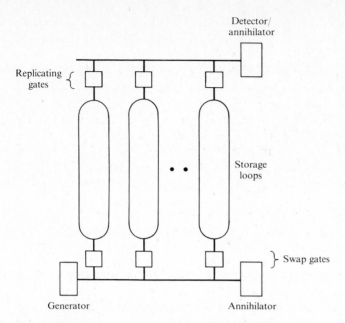

Figure 9.14 Internal organization of a bubble memory.

number of loops, as shown in Figure 9.14. Two tracks enable bubbles to be transferred from a bubble generator to any of the loops and from any loop to the bubble detector/annihilator.

The gate between a loop and the generator track enables bubbles to be swapped between them. During a Write operation, bubbles are transferred from the bubble generator to any of the loops via the corresponding gate. Meanwhile, any bubbles previously stored in that loop are transferred to the generator track and shifted to the bubble annihilator. Once the swap gate is closed, bubbles inside the loop rotate indefinitely around the loop.

A similar procedure is followed during a Read operation. However, the function of the gate between a loop and the detector track is slightly different. Instead of transferring bubbles from one side to the other, this gate splits each bubble inside the loop into two; one continues to travel around the loop, while the other is transferred to the detector track. The latter travels to the detector/annihilator, where it is detected by an appropriate sensor.

The reader will undoubtedly have noticed that the organization of a bubble memory bears considerable resemblance to that of a magnetic disk. The loops of Figure 9.14 are equivalent to the tracks on a disk. Information stored in any of the loops is accessed serially and may be divided into sections equivalent to disk sectors. A typical commercially available bubble memory has 256 loops, each capable of storing 4096 bits, for a total of 1 Mbit. The stored information can be accessed at a rate of 100 Kbit/s. While bubble memories have not been able to compete with magnetic disks, the absence of moving parts makes them attractive in some mobile and airborne applications.

Charge-coupled devices A charge-coupled device (CCD) is a form of dynamic semiconductor memory. It comprises a high-density storage device that can be accessed serially at high speed. A CCD consists of a silicon wafer on which tiny metal electrodes are deposited. When an electrical potential is applied to one of these electrodes, it forms a small pocket in the semiconductor material (the silicon wafer) in which electric charge may be stored for a short time period. By applying an appropriate voltage waveform to the electrodes, the stored charge can be shifted between adjacent pockets. Hence, the structure functions as a shift register.

In order to use CCDs for storing information, the electrodes are organized in loops that incorporate refresh circuitry at regular intervals. The stored information, which is represented by the presence or absence of a charge, circulates continually around the storage loops. As in the case of bubble memories, appropriate structures are used for Read and Write operations.

CCDs are suitable for applications where a high-speed, serially accessed data buffer is needed. For example, they have been used as a cache memory between a magnetic disk and a computer. Because of their volatility, they are not suitable for long-term storage of information.

Optical storage devices The spot of light produced by focussing a laser beam has a diameter of the order of 1 micron. Many devices have been designed using such a spot in the process of storing and accessing information. Typically, the writing mechanism involves the use of a pulse of light to impart a well-controlled amount of heat to a tiny area of a suitable storage medium. The resulting change in temperature causes a change in magnetization of a magnetic material or evaporates a thin layer of metal. The stored information can be accessed by sensing the change in polarization or intensity of a light beam as it is transmitted through the storage medium or reflected from its surface. Elaborate mechanisms that may involve vibrating mirrors or rotating prisms are used to move the light beam to different points of the storage medium. In some devices, the storage medium may also be caused to rotate in a manner similar to a magnetic disk.

Optical storage devices are intended primarily for archival storage applications in which a very high storage density is needed. While some experimental systems have been developed, they are not yet widely used.

9.3 PERSONAL COMPUTERS

Rapidly advancing VLSI technology has resulted in dramatic reductions in the cost of computer hardware. The greatest impact has been in the area of small machines. These developments have led to an expanding market for *personal computers*, which are microcomputer systems suitable for use both at home and in an office environment.

The commercial success of personal computers can be largely attributed to their low cost. They are available in a variety of configurations at prices ranging from a few hundred to a few thousand dollars. Individual models reflect a trade-off between cost and considerations such as computing power, storage capability, and supporting software.

The simplest personal computers comprise a single printed circuit board containing a CPU, a limited amount of main memory, and an ASCII keyboard. They use ordinary television sets as output devices. The digital output information is converted into a radio frequency signal to allow direct attachment to the antenna terminals on a television set.

Minimal software support must be provided even in the simplest home computers. This usually includes a high-level programming language, typically BASIC. In the absence of secondary storage devices, the system software may be placed in a ROM section of the main memory. In some simple systems, a connector to the memory bus is provided to enable insertion of ROM cartridges. Thus, various programs can be made available on different cartridges to be plugged into the computer as required.

Considerable flexibility is gained with the addition of secondary storage, normally consisting of either floppy disks or tape cassettes. It is also useful to have some means for generating hard copy output. This involves either having a dedicated printer or an I/O port connected to another system that has the desired printing capability. As such devices are added to the computer, its cost increases significantly. In larger personal computers, the emphasis shifts from the cost aspect to computing power, versatility, and ease of use. Such machines usually incorporate a dedicated video display.

Let us contemplate the question of what features should be provided in a relatively powerful personal computer selling in the range of $2000 to $5000. The following are some of the most important requirements:

1. A sizeable main memory, at least 64K bytes
2. A dual disk drive, for either floppy or hard disks, to facilitate copying from one disk to another
3. A video display capable of displaying character and graphical images, preferably in color
4. A printer for hard copy output
5. A standard I/O port, probably RS-232-C, for connection to another computer
6. A wide range of available software

Availability of software is of primary importance. In addition to an operating system and some high-level programming languages, a user of a personal computer is likely to be interested in software for word processing, business accounting and even game playing.

Personal computers are self-contained machines that can perform a variety of computational tasks. But, they can also be used as smart terminals, connected to a larger host computer or a computer network. This usage is increasing rapidly because in many office environments there are numerous processing tasks that can be performed locally, with a need for occasional access to a centralized data base or other central computing resources. Personal computers are most suitable for such applications.

9.4 ENGINEERING WORK STATIONS

Automated procedures have become an essential aspect of engineering design work. Manual techniques no longer suffice in a highly competitive technological environment. Automation of the design process is largely based on computerized aids, ranging from relatively straightforward documentation tools to complex simulators used to assess the correctness and performance of the desired products. Such activity is known as *computer-aided design* (CAD).

Let us consider a typical design process in developing an electronic apparatus. Starting with the specifications of the desired apparatus, it is necessary to design the required circuitry. When a satisfactory design has been developed, it is necessary to generate the implementation details in a form that can be used in the manufacturing process. Finally, adequate means for testing the assembled product must be provided. This typically involves deriving an appropriate test procedure.

All of the above steps are facilitated by suitable CAD equipment. The task of designing the circuitry is simplified if the designer can make use of a library of previously developed circuit modules. A new circuit diagram can be drawn on a video display screen. During this process existing library modules may be incorporated into the design. Various sections of the circuit can be replicated, repositioned, and interconnected using simple input commands. The simplest way of checking the expected performance of the circuitry is to simulate its behavior using a simulator program. This despenses with the need for manually breadboarding various parts with physical components and testing the prototype circuit. The process of specifiying a circuit displayed on the screen should automatically result in a circuit description that may be used as input data for a simulator. Any changes in the design are readily made and checked by subsequent simulation. Upon completion of the design, it is necessary to produce a wiring list that can be used to construct the actual physical apparatus. This task is also easily carried out by the computer. The last step is to prepare a procedure for testing the final product. This involves deriving a set of tests, usually in the form of a sequence of input signals and expected output signals, that can be used to verify the correctness of operation of the manufactured apparatus. Again, an appropriate CAD routine can be used for this purpose.

Much of the information generated in a CAD process can be used to automate the manufacturing process as well. This is called computer-aided manufacturing (CAM). The close link between CAD and CAM has led to development of integrated schemes that cover both design and manufacturing automation, often referred to as CAD/CAM techniques.

Successful utilization of CAD methods is contingent on the availability of

CAD facilities. It is obvious that CAD work can be done using a large computer. Indeed, many CAD facilities involve only some graphics terminals connected to a suitable computer. This centralized approach is useful for large organizations which can afford the cost of large computers, either dedicated to CAD functions or time shared for a variety of tasks. In a general time-shared operation, CAD work is likely to place considerable demands on the central computer, thus affecting other users of the system significantly.

A practical alternative is to implement most of the CAD functions within a smaller unit, known as an *engineering work station*. A work station is a rather powerful computer system, usually based on a 16- or 32-bit microprocessor. High-quality graphics capability is an essential requirement. This means that a graphics processor with a high-resolution video display and an extensive drawing and picture manipulation facility must be provided. Sufficient main memory and secondary storage have to be included to allow local handling of most CAD functions.

It is useful to be able to connect a work station to other computing resources. Certain large computational tasks may be better performed on a larger, central computer. This computer may also hold a common data base that can be used by several work stations as needed. Other resources, such as printers and plotters, can also be conveniently shared. Thus, it is useful to connect a work station to other machines, probably by means of a computer network.

The emergence of work stations is one facet of a trend toward distributed computing. In a distributed system, most computational tasks are performed on local machines. These machines are connected to a network that includes a variety of computers and peripheral devices, enabling each machine to have access to other resources when needed.

9.5 CONCLUDING REMARKS

Input/output devices are a fundamental part of a computer system since they constitute the link for feeding information into a computer and for receiving the results. The cost of a large computer justifies the use of a variety of I/O devices in order to maximize the throughput of the system. The choice of I/O device types and the way they are connected to the computer, for example, the number of I/O channels, is an important design decision. The main concern in this decision is that no particular I/O device should create a "bottleneck" by forcing the remainder of the computer system to become idle for long periods of time waiting for an input or output function to be completed. This consideration is closely related to the discussion of operating systems in Chapter 10.

A slightly different situation is encountered in small computer systems. In this case, the cost of peripherals is often a major portion of the total system cost. Thus utilization of the CPU is a less important consideration in the trade-offs of system design. An extreme example of this situation is encountered in microprocessor systems, where the cost of the CPU is very small.

There is very intensive activity in the development of peripheral devices. Every month there are announcements of new devices with improved capabilities or better price/performance ratios. In this chapter we have considered representative technologies and devices that are commercially available. Improvements in VLSI technology have allowed implementation of powerful machines at a relatively low cost, as exemplified by graphic display stations and engineering work stations.

There is abundant literature on the material discussed in this chapter. Most of the up-to-date information is readily available in trade magazines and manufacturers' promotional literature. Also, a considerable number of review articles are published. The list of possible references is large. We will mention only three. The first is a survey of graphic display technology by Hobbs.[9.1] The second is a book by Stone, which gives an excellent discussion of magnetic recording techniques and issues involved in interfacing peripherals into microcomputer systems.[9.2] The third, by Chi, gives a state-of-the-art update on mass storage technology.[9.3]

9.6 PROBLEMS

9.1 The following components are provided:

6-bit binary counter, with Clock and Clear inputs and six outputs
A 3-bit serial-input–parallel-output shift register
A clock which is free running at approximately eight times the input data rate
Logic gates and JK flip-flops with Preset and Clear controls

Design a circuit using the above components to load 3 bits of serial data from an input data line into the shift register. Assume the data to have the format of Figure 9.1, with only 3 bits per character. The circuit you design should have two outputs, A and B. Output A should be set to 1 if a Stop bit is detected following the data bits. Otherwise, output B should be set to 1. Give an explanation of the operation of your design.

9.2 In Section 9.1.1 we defined the term baud and pointed out that in the case of binary signalling the baud rate is the same as the bit rate. Consider now a communications channel where 4-valued signals are used, as indicated in Figure P9.1. If the channel is rated at 9600 baud, what is its capacity in bits per second?

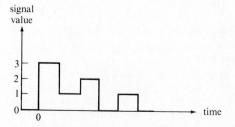

Transmitted pattern: 3, 1, 2, 0, 1, 0   **Figure P9.1**

9.3 Show how Figure 9.2 may be modified so that all 6×8 points of a given character are displayed before moving to the next character.

9.4 Suggest suitable modifications to the CRT display controller of Figure 9.2 to implement a "roll page" feature. That is, upon receiving a special command from the computer, the displayed data moves upward slowly on the screen. Consider the following two cases:

(a) The entire picture on the screen moves upward in steps of one character line at a time.

(b) The picture on the screen moves upward slowly, such that the characters on the top line progressively disappear, while a new line gradually appears at the bottom of the screen. Once started, this process should proceed independently until all data has moved upward one line.

9.5 The display on a CRT screen has to be refreshed at least 30 times per second to remain flicker-free. During each scan, the total time required to illuminate a point on the screen is 1 μs. The beam is then turned off and moved to the next point to be illuminated. On the average, this process takes 3 μs. Because of power-dissipation limitations, the beam cannot be turned on more than 10 percent of the time. Determine the maximum number of points that can be illuminated on the screen.

To illuminate more points than the above maximum, the display may be made to flash at the rate of once every 800 ms. In this case, the display is turned on for 500 ms and off for 300 ms. Determine the maximum number of points that can be illuminated under these conditions.

9.6 A disk pack has nine surfaces. The storage area on each surface has an inner diameter of 22 cm and an outer diameter of 33 cm. The maximum storage density along any track is 1600 bits/cm, and the minimum spacing between tracks is 0.25 mm.

(a) What is the maximum number of bits that can be stored on this pack?

(b) What is the data transfer rate in bytes per second at a rotational speed of 3600 rpm?

(c) Using two 16-bit words, suggest a suitable scheme for specifying the disk address.

(d) The main memory of a computer has a 16-bit word length and 0.5-μs cycle time. Assuming that the disk transfers data to/from the memory on a cycle-stealing basis, what percentage of memory cycles are stolen during the data transfer period?

9.7 The seek time plus rotational delay in accessing a particular data block on a disk is usually much longer than the data flow period for most disk transfer problems. Consider a long sequence of accesses to an IBM 3330 disk drive (see Table 9.1) for either Read or Write operations in which the average block being accessed is 1000 bytes long.

(a) Assuming that the blocks are randomly located on the disk, estimate the average percentage of the total time occupied by seek operations and rotational delays.

(b) Repeat part (a) for the situation where the disk accesses have been arranged such that in 90 percent of the cases the next access will be to a data block on the same cylinder.

9.8 A tape drive has the following parameters:

Bit density	1600 bits/in
Tape speed	200 in/s
Time to reverse direction of motion	225 ms
Minimum time spent at an interrecord gap	3 ms
Average record length	1000 characters

Estimate the percentage gain in time resulting from the ability to read records in both the forward and backward directions. Assume that records are accessed at random and that, on the average, the distance between two records accessed in sequence is four records.

9.9 Consider the operation of a line printer. The paper has to be stationary during the printing process. Assume that the total time required for printing a line is 10 ms. At the end of this period the paper is advanced to bring the next line to the printing position. This process takes T seconds. The speed v of the paper expressed as a function of time may be assumed to have the form

$$v = V_o(1 - \cos \frac{2\pi t}{T})$$

where V_o is a constant. If the maximum acceleration that the paper can sustain without tearing is 65,000 cm/s^2, what is the maximum possible printing rate in lines per minute? Assume line spacing to be 4.2 mm.

9.10 A card reader is capable of reading 1200 cards per minute. The cards are read one column at a time. Estimate the speed at which the card moves, assuming that there is a 5-ms delay between the instants at which the end of one card and the beginning of the next card pass the reading station.

The cards are read using light-emitting diodes and light-sensing circuitry. Estimate the pulse width at the output of the light-sensing circuitry as a punched hole passes through the reading station. Assume a punched hole to be 3 mm high and 1 mm wide.

9.11 Output from the reading station of a card reader is in the form of a 12-bit code known as the Hollerith code. It is required to translate this code into the 7-bit ASCII code before transmitting the information to the computer. This can be done by table look-up, using a ROM. What should the size and organization of this memory be?

The Hollerith code is such that at most 1 bit is equal to 1 in the least significant 7 bits. This fact may be used to compress the code into a smaller number of bits. Show how this may be done and give a logic circuit to implement this code compression. What is the size of the ROM required to implement the translation table in this case?

9.12 Construct a flowchart for a main program and an interrupt-service routine to cause the rectangle drawn by the display program of Figure 9.4 to be increased in size from 150×400 to 190×440 in steps of 2 units, repeatedly. Assume that the computer has a 60-cycle clock which interrupts the computer every sixtieth of a second, at which time the rectangle size is increased. When the rectangle size reaches its maximum, 190×440, it is reset to the minimum size, 150×400, at the next interrupt, and increased again, etc.

9.13 Given that magnetic disks are used as the secondary storage for program and data files in a virtual-memory system, suggest which disk parameter should influence the choice of page size.

9.7 REFERENCES

9.1 Hobbs L.C.: Computer Graphics Display Hardware, *IEEE Computer Graphics,* vol. 1, no. 1, pp. 25–39, Jan. 1981.

9.2 Stone, H.S.: "Microcomputer Interfacing," Addison Wesley, Reading, Mass., 1982.

9.3 Chi C. S.: Advances in Computer Mass Storage Technology, *IEEE Computer*, vol. 15, no. 5, pp. 60–74, May 1982.

TEN

SOFTWARE

The name software refers to all programs that are written to be executed on a computer. These programs may be written in any of a number of different languages. The size of programs has a wide range. Student programs for small numerical problems may consist of only 20 to 50 statements in a high-level, problem-oriented language such as Fortran. At the other end of the scale, the accounting and management information programs that are used by large corporations or governments may have thousands of statements. These examples are from the area that is usually called *application* or *user programs*. They are programs written by people who use computers to solve scientific and business operation problems.

The suppliers of computer systems and services are responsible for the provision of another class of programs, collectively called computer system programs, or *system software*, to distinguish them from user programs. System software includes the programs that translate user programs into machine language programs. Other system programs are used to load these translated programs from secondary storage into the main memory prior to execution. The translators are sometimes called *language processors*. An important component of system software is the set of routines that are used to manage the operation of the physical resources (CPU, main memory, secondary storage, I/O devices, etc.) in a complete computing system. These routines comprise the *operating system* programs.

To reduce the cost of individual user computations, the resources in large computer systems are almost always shared among a number of independent user programs. The purpose of operating system software is to control this resource sharing so that the system is utilized as efficiently as possible, while at the same time it is made easy to use from the customer standpoint. This is an elusive goal, and a large amount of research and development effort has gone into the design and production of operating systems.

This chapter will mainly discuss the function of some of the operating system routines. We will only briefly comment on language processors. System software is a large subject, and one chapter in a book such as this can only introduce the reader to a few of the main ideas. Indeed, many books have been written on topics such as language processors or operating systems. It is very important for any student of computer design to understand the function of system software. The design choices employed in the specification of a particular computer have a direct effect on the ease of constructing efficient operating system software for it. Ideally, the system software should be an integral part of the design of a computer. We will not discuss these topics in enough detail in this chapter to enable the student to actually design any nontrivial system software routines. For that level of treatment, the reader should consult References 10.1 to 10.7.

After a brief discussion of languages and language processors, the remainder of this chapter deals with the basic system software required for:

1. Machine startup and loading of machine language programs from a secondary storage device into the main memory
2. Linking programs that have been prepared separately but that must communicate with each other during execution
3. Supervising the sharing of a single CPU among a number of independent programs

10.1 LANGUAGES AND TRANSLATORS

We have used the assembly language for the PDP-11 minicomputer to give examples in the course of describing instruction sequencing and addressing modes in Chapter 2. The most basic language is machine language, in which programs are represented by a listing of the binary patterns for the machine instructions and data elements (bytes or words). Figure 10.1 shows the machine language version of the assembly language program for multiplication that was given earlier in Figure 7.11. The binary patterns of the machine language program are given in octal notation in the figure.

A machine language program for a specific computer can be executed on that computer without the aid of any other program. However, since programming in machine language is a cumbersome process, programs are usually written in a language that has a more symbolic and stylized form. The simplest of these are assembly languages. Problem-oriented languages such as BASIC, Fortran, PL/I, Cobol, Algol, Pascal, APL, etc., are often called high-level languages. They have a set of operational and control statements which are substantially more powerful than the basic statement types provided in assembly languages.

A program written in any language above machine language is called a

Main memory byte address	Memory word contents (16 bits)	Assembly language program		
212	005000		CLR	R0
214	012703		MOV	#−16.,R3
216	177760			
220	006300	MLOOP:	ASL	R0
222	006101		ROL	R1
224	103002		BCC	NOADD
226	060200		ADD	R2,R0
230	005501		ADC	R1
232	005203	NOADD:	INC	R3
234	001371		BNE	MLOOP
236	000000		HALT	

Figure 10.1 PDP-11 program for multiplication in machine and assembly language.

source program. Source programs are translated into machine language by system programs called *translators*. As discussed in Chapter 2, in the case of assembly languages these translators are called assemblers. When the source program is in a high-level language, the translator is called a *compiler*. The output of the language translation process is called an *object program* or *object code*. In the simplest situation, the object program is in machine language and can be loaded into the main memory and executed directly. Sometimes, parts of large source programs are translated in separate operations into separate object programs. Further processing is required on these object programs to link them together into a single machine language program that can be executed directly. We will discuss some of these aspects in succeeding sections.

A few remarks are in order regarding assembly and high-level languages. Basically, an assembly language is just an orderly and structured set of mnemonics for a corresponding machine language. There are exceptions to this simple viewpoint that merit comment. In some of the more extensive assembly languages, single statements (with parameters) can correspond to short sequences of machine instructions. These types of statements are often called *macroinstructions* or *macros*. The assembler that generates the machine language version of these types of statements automatically expands them into the appropriate sequences of machine instructions. Such an assembler is sometimes called a *macroassembler*.

Assembly languages, even with macro facilities, are closely related to machine languages. On the other hand, high-level languages are independent of the machine language of the computer on which they run. A high-level language has many statements that must be translated into sequences of machine instructions. This is a more complicated process than the expansion of macroinstructions. High-level languages make it easier for programmers to express what they want the computer to do, without having to directly specify how the machine instructions should be assembled to do it. Control structures such as

DO loops, IF · · · THEN · · · ELSE · · · statements, PROCEDURES with parameters, as well as data structures such as ARRAYS, with various data types, characterize these languages.

It is not essential to translate high-level language programs into machine language in order to execute the programs. It is sometimes desirable to perform a translation into an intermediate language form that is then executed by another program called an *interpreter*. The interpreter is a program that reads the program to be interpreted and executes it statement by statement. This is a much slower execution process, but there are situations where the interpretive method is the best choice from the overall system standpoint. For example, interpretive execution of short student jobs that are run only once after being debugged may be the most efficient method. The controlled execution implied by the interpretive technique allows much more extensive and meaningful error diagnostics to be returned to the user at execution time. Interactive computing, in which the user enters a few statements, requests that they be executed and the answers returned to the terminal before proceeding to more computations, is naturally handled by interpretive methods. On the other hand, it is usually best to compile programs into machine language if they are to be run a large number of times using different data. Examples of this are the frequently used mathematical subroutine packages for numerical integration or linear equation solution, and large business data processing programs.

As mentioned in the preamble, we will not discuss the details of the language translation process. The reader should consult References 10.4, 10.5, and 10.7 for such information.

10.2 LOADERS

Let us assume that a program has been translated into machine language form, that is, object code, and stored on a magnetic disk. To execute this program, it must be loaded into the main memory of the computer. In order to load a program into the main memory, we must assume that another program, called a *loader*, is already in the main memory. The execution of the loader performs the proper sequence of I/O operations needed to transfer a machine language program from a specified location on the disk to a specified location in the main memory. Having loaded the object code, the loader starts execution of the object program by branching to its first instruction.

In order to transfer an object program from the disk to the main memory, the loader must know the length of the program and its starting address in the main memory. This information is usually placed in a header preceding the object code on the disk. A loader that transfers object code stored in this format is called an *absolute binary loader*.

The above discussion has sketched the ideas involved in the simplest form of loaders for machine language programs. In many computer systems, particularly larger ones, there is a requirement for a more complex loader, called a *relocating loader*. First, let us motivate the need for such a loader. In the case of the absolute binary loader, the starting point of the program to be loaded is fixed at the time the program is written. In general, the program will run correctly only if it is loaded starting at that particular main memory location. A normal operating environment for many computers is that a number of different programs are in the main memory at any one time. These programs are usually of different sizes so that we would like some flexibility in determining where a particular program is placed at load time. Therefore, the function of a relocating loader is to take a machine language program which was generated on the assumption that it would be loaded starting at some location x, usually chosen as 0 for convenience, and load it starting at location y. In general, such a loader will need to make some changes to the program so that it will run correctly at the new location.

Let us consider the format that an object program must have if it is to be relocatable. When all addresses in a program are specified relative to the program counter, the program will execute correctly no matter where it is placed in the memory. On the other hand, suppose an absolute memory address mode is used somewhere in a program. Such address values are called *address constants*. The relocating loader must adjust these address constants according to where the program is to be loaded. If the object program is generated so that it will run correctly if loaded at location 0, the adjustment simply consists of adding the address of the actual starting location as an offset to all address constants in the program. Obviously, the position of the address constants in the object program must be indicated by the translator. We will see an example of how this can be done in the next section.

Some computers have features that facilitate program relocatability. Suppose all addresses are generated relative to a base register. At execution time, the value in the base register is taken as an offset which is added to the addresses generated by the remainder of the addressing mode information. This machine feature was introduced in Section 3.5. In this case, program relocation can be achieved by simply loading the starting address into the base register. Thus the complexity of address handling by the translator and loader can be greatly reduced by a particular machine organization feature. Virtual-memory systems, as described in Chapter 8, carry the base register relocation idea much further. By introducing the concept of pages and page tables, the operations of loading and relocating pages of a program are deferred until each page is actually referenced during execution. Thus, the job performed by the relocating loader described above is actually performed by the paging and address translation mechanisms in a virtual-memory system.

10.2.1 Machine Startup

When power is turned on in a computer system, some provision is needed to start the process of loading and executing programs. One of the required tasks is to load the loader program into the main memory. A loader is just one of the operating system routines that must be brought into the main memory.

A simple technique used in many computers is to implement a very small portion of the main memory as read-only memory. This ROM contains a few instructions, called a *bootstrap loader*, which are sufficient to transfer the required loader from a fixed location on a secondary storage device into a fixed location in the main memory. This loader is then used to load other operating system routines into the main memory. During the loading process, one of the loaded routines may interact with a CRT terminal operator to determine exactly which set of routines should be loaded for current use.

An alternative approach for machine startup is to incorporate the bootstrap capability directly into the controller of the peripheral device. This controller can then use direct memory access to perform the initial loading.

10.3 LINKERS

Until now we have considered the simple case of loading complete programs that have been translated into machine language as a single unit. In more practical situations, a large program consists of a number of routines that have been written separately, possibly by different people. It is often useful to be able to translate these routines independently into machine language. We will use the term *object module* to denote the output from each of these independent translations. Object modules must be in a format that allows them to be collected together and linked into a single program that can be passed to a loader. This means that the programmer must identify certain symbols as being *external* in the source programs. External symbols are simply those variables or line labels that are referenced by more than one of the separately translated programs or subprograms. The program that links the object modules into a single machine language program that can be passed to a loader is called a *linker*. Let us denote its output as a *load module*. We should note that it is quite common to consolidate the functions of the linker and the loader into one system program called a linking loader. The generation of the load module would then be an intermediate step in the execution of the linking loader.

There are some trade-offs involved here. Instead of trying to link and load separately translated programs, it is sometimes feasible, and perfectly reasonable, to collect all source programs and subprograms required for some composite task and present them as a single entity to the translator which directly generates the load module. The complexity of cross-referencing is then moved back into the translator. In this section, however, we assume that separate translations have been justified.

The easiest starting point is the same as the one taken in the case of the absolute-binary-loader program. We will specify a format for the object modules generated by the separate translations. The major new idea in this format is the specification of external symbols as defined earlier. Figure 10.2 shows a possible format for object modules. This general format starts with a table of external symbols, called the external symbol dictionary (ESD), followed by the machine language listing of the program. A listing of the location of address constants that must be relocated by the loader is placed after the program in a section called the relocation dictionary (RD). In Section 10.2 we said that address

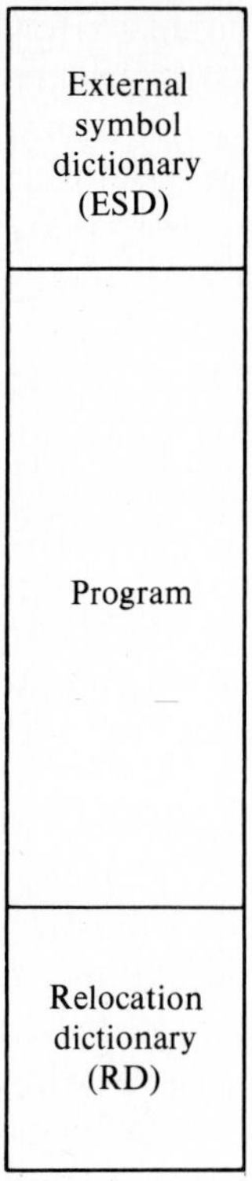

```
┌───────────┐
│ External  │
│  symbol   │
│ dictionary│
│   (ESD)   │
├───────────┤
│           │
│           │
│           │
│ Program   │
│           │
│           │
│           │
├───────────┤
│ Relocation│
│ dictionary│
│   (RD)    │
└───────────┘
```

Figure 10.2 An object module.

constants must be flagged. We are now making this more specific by assuming that these items are identified by a listing of their locations.

Let us take the specific example of two programs A and B that have been translated separately. Program A defines two memory locations DATAWORD1 and DATAWORD2 that are to be accessed by both programs. Program A also calls program B as a subroutine, so it needs to reference the entry point SUBRB of program B. A possible format in which these programs may be presented to the linker is shown in Figure 10.3. An identification tag is included in each line of the ESD. The first line gives the length of the program along with its name, identified by the tag P. The second and third lines in the ESD for program A declare (D) DATAWORD1 and DATAWORD2 as being external. They are the addresses of locations 120 and 121 of this program. The fourth line, SUBRB, is a reference (R) to an address in program B. This reference appears in location 180 of program A. The address SUBRB must be defined in the ESD of program B. When the location of the word labeled SUBRB is determined during the linking process, its value must be entered at word 180 of program A. The fact that this value must be relocated when the final load module is loaded into the main memory is also indicated by entering the address 180 in the RD. Similar comments apply to the object module for program B. An additional example, comprising a local reference represented by the internal address constant

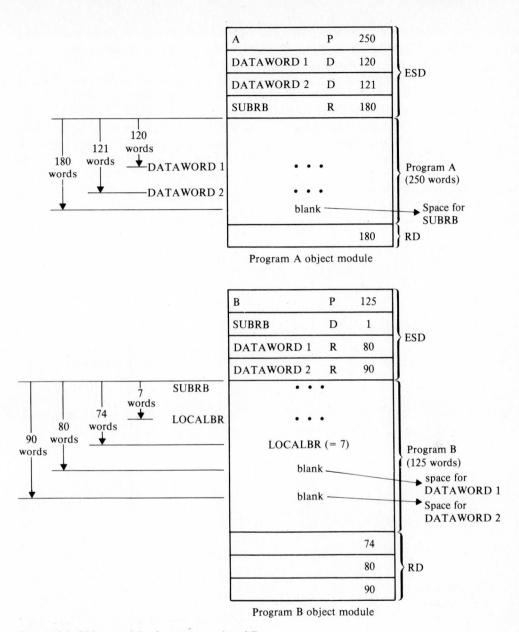

Figure 10.3 Object modules for programs A and B.

LOCALBR, is included in this module. The reference is made in word 74, and this fact is indicated in the RD. The figure shows this address constant to be 7. The other two entries in the RD refer to the locations of the address constants DATAWORD1 and DATAWORD2.

Suppose that these two object modules are presented to the linker in the order A followed by B. The linking process must create a load module consisting of the 375 words of the program bodies of A and B, preceded by a length declaration and followed by a composite RD. It should be easy to convince oneself that there is enough information in the individual ESDs and RDs to create the load module shown in Figure 10.4. For example, the linking process determines that SUBRB is the 251st location of the composite load module. Therefore, the address constant 251 is entered in word 180 of the program body of the load module. Similarly, the address constant 7 in line 74 of the program B module gets changed to address constant 257 (= 250 + 7) when it is entered in

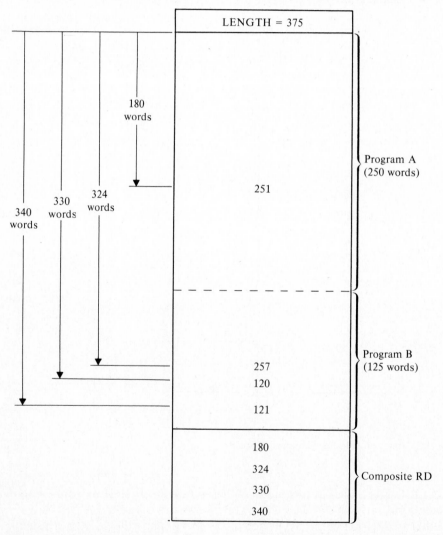

Figure 10.4 Load module generated after linking the object modules for programs A and B.

line 324 (= 250 + 74) of the final load module. This load module can now be passed to the loader program which was discussed in Section 10.2. When a starting address S is specified to the loader, it loads the 375-word program in the main memory beginning at that location. Then it adds the value S − 1 to the constants 251, 257, 120, and 121 in load module locations 180, 324, 330, and 340. The final appearance of the 375-word program in the main memory is shown in Figure 10.5, where a starting address of 3401 has been assumed.

The model of linking and loading that has been presented here is a simplified version of the main ideas involved in the specification of ESDs and RDs. A practical implementation will normally require a number of different classes of external symbols. This provides greater user flexibility in writing programs that must communicate with each other but which are to be translated separately. See Reference 10.6 for more details.

10.4 OPERATING SYSTEMS

In the introduction to this chapter we stated that the resources in a computer system are usually shared among a number of user programs to reduce the cost of computation for the individual user. Resource sharing will reduce costs only if

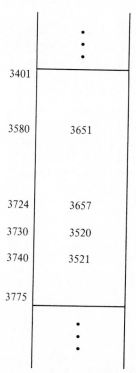

Figure 10.5 Load module of Figure 10.4 placed in the main memory starting at location 3401.

it leads to an increase in system throughput, that is, if more user programs can be run per unit time. The purpose of this section is to discuss the ways that user jobs share the resources and to describe how the operating system programs try to make this sharing efficient, thus resulting in high throughput.

Let us assume that a computer system consists of a CPU, main memory, user terminals, line printer, and magnetic disk storage. The printer and disk communicate with the main memory through two logically independent channels. The channels permit data transfers between the main memory and these peripheral devices to proceed concurrently with the execution of programs by the CPU. It is this possibility for concurrency that must be exploited to achieve a high rate of processing of user programs. A main function of the operating system programs is the scheduling, initiation, and monitoring of both channel and CPU activity.

We will use the term *job* to refer to all the I/O and computation associated with a given user program. Furthermore, it is convenient to use the name *step* to identify phases of input, computation, or output as called for by a job. We will first consider the case where a program and all of its data are stored in disk files. The user initiates execution of this program by entering a job request command at a CRT terminal. The user is not involved in any way while processing proceeds and simply waits for printed output when the job has been completed. When a computer processes a sequence of such jobs, it is said to be operating in a batch processing mode. The case of interactive computing where the user is actively involved during execution, will be discussed later.

A sequence of actions that may occur in a computer system during the processing of a typical job is indicated in Table 10.1. During the first job step, the program is read into the main memory from the disk. If the program is in source form, the operating system will direct the program text to the appropriate compiler for translation to machine language. For our purposes here, we can assume that any processing required to transform the program into executable form is included in computation step C1. This step will also include the initial phase of execution of the program. Execution continues until data input is required at step R2. This data input step requires the disk to transfer the information from some of the data records into the main memory for subsequent

Table 10.1 Example of job sequencing

Job step no.	Operation	System component involved
1	Program input step R1	Disk
2	Computation step C1	CPU
3	Data input step R2	Disk
4	Computation step C2	CPU
5	Data input step R3	Disk
6	Computation step C3	CPU
7	Data output step W1	Line printer

processing during computation step C2. The remainder of the data is read during step R3, and final results are printed in step W1.

There is some opportunity for overlapping I/O with computation in individual jobs. For example, in the job outlined in Table 10.1, the disk could proceed with steps 3 and 5 as soon as step 1 is completed. The data is read into a buffer area in the main memory, using DMA, while computation step C1 is in progress. Output printing in this particular job is the last step. If we assume that it cannot begin until computation step C3 is completed, then there is no chance to overlap output with either input or computation. In other jobs, it might be possible to overlap some output steps with computation steps. What we can now conclude is that some overlapping of I/O and computation is possible within individual jobs. However, the extent of this overlapping is highly variable from job to job.

There are more opportunities for overlapping the activity of the physical resources in the system if we consider the requests of a number of jobs instead of just one job at a time. In such a case it may be possible to read the job file for jobs $N + 1, N + 2, \ldots$ into a main memory buffer area, while computation is proceeding on job N. The files for job N are assumed to have been read earlier. As computation proceeds on job N, output from jobs $\ldots, N - 2, N - 1$ can be transferred from another main memory buffer to the line printer. The jobs are still processed in the order in which they are read into the main memory, but there is a potential gain in efficiency in overlapping processing of adjacent jobs as well as within jobs.

Let us consider some of the details of how overlapping may occur in a specific example. It is convenient to introduce a time line diagram that shows the time required to execute each step of a user job. Figure 10.6a gives the diagrams for the user job of Table 10.1, which we will refer to as job X, and two other jobs, Y and Z. As mentioned above, it is possible to overlap job steps of individual jobs as well as those of different jobs. However, there are limits to the amount of overlapping that can be achieved, since some steps on a given facility cannot be started until associated steps on other facilities are finished. For example, step C2 of job X cannot begin until step R2 is completed for that job. Taking such limitations into account, Figure 10.6b shows the amount of overlapping achievable among the various steps of the three jobs X, Y, and Z. We have assumed that they follow each other in the order stated and that the system begins operation at t_0. Maximum overlapping occurs during time period t_3 to t_4. The CPU idle time from t_1 to t_2 occurs because of the restriction that step C2 of job X cannot be started until step R2 is completed. Similarly, the printer idle time from t_5 to t_6 results from the fact that step W1 for job Z must follow step C2 for job Z.

A few other comments are in order about Figure 10.6b. If the time from t_0 to t_7 is considered as a period of time that occurs after the system has been operating for a while, then output from jobs processed before job X could be printed during the period t_0 to t_3. Also, job files following the files for job Z could be read after t_4.

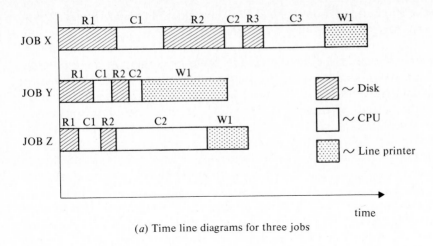

(a) Time line diagrams for three jobs

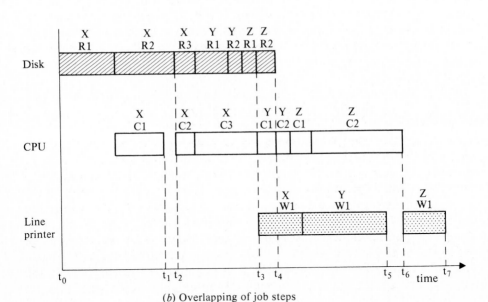

(b) Overlapping of job steps

Figure 10.6 I/O—compute overlap in a batch system.

10.4.1 Spooling

In the above discussion, we have assumed that there is sufficient main memory capacity for the output buffers required to achieve a reasonable level of overlapping. If this is not the case, the extra storage capacity required can be provided by a magnetic disk. We should now consider whether the added overhead of buffering information from the main memory onto the disk, and then back into the main memory as it is needed for sending to the printer, offsets the hoped for overall increase in efficiency. We will not attempt a detailed analysis of the problem. However, it has been found that such systems do achieve increased overall efficiency. The process of buffering output onto the disk and subsequently moving it back into the main memory for transfer to the printer is called *output spooling*. In general, spooling smooths out the wide range of demands by individual jobs on I/O devices so that a steady work load is created for electromechanical devices such as line printers.

10.4.2 Multiprogramming

In batch systems, the CPU is assigned to jobs X, Y, and Z in succession. All computation is completed on job X before computation on job Y is begun, etc.

Now consider a generalization of this situation in which an operating system routine selects a few (maybe three or four) jobs and transfers their programs from a disk into the main memory in preparation for execution. The CPU begins computation (which may include translation, linking to system-supplied subroutines, etc.) on one of these jobs. Then, at some point in the computation, the job requests an I/O operation that results in a disk transfer. The operating system initiates this transfer and then assigns the CPU to one of the other jobs in the main memory.

This situation of having a few jobs in the main memory at any time tends to free the CPU from having to wait for disk transfers (or any other type of independently processed I/O activity). The chances are increased that the CPU can be more highly utilized on user program computations if this is done. The technique is called *multiprogramming*. It clearly involves reasonably complex operating system procedures to achieve the desired efficiency. There is a danger that the required operating system programs themselves may take too much CPU time. However, multiprogramming systems have been successfully employed in practice and are being continually improved.

To give a simple example of activity in a multiprogrammed system, let us again consider the steps of jobs X, Y, and Z in Figure 10.6a. As before, assume that all R1 steps correspond to loading the program from a disk into the main memory. Further, assume that the remaining read steps, R2 and R3, of job X refer to input data on the same disk that held job X, but that steps R2 of jobs Y and Z refer to input from two other secondary storage devices that can operate through other channels concurrently with the first disk. As before, the logical sequence of events for each job must proceed as shown in Figure 10.6a. Suppose that all R1 steps have been performed. Then, any of the C1 steps can be initiated by the operating system. Figure 10.7 shows one possible sequence of events that begins by assigning the CPU to step C1 of job X. When step C1 of X is completed, step R2 of X is begun, and at the same time step C1 of Y is started. The rest of the steps can be easily followed from the diagram. In this example, the CPU is kept busy all the time.

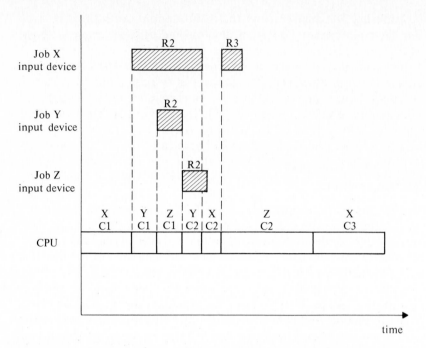

Figure 10.7 Possible sequence of activities in a multiprogramming system.

10.4.3 Operating System Control of Multiprogramming

The previous sections have suggested how multiprogramming can be used to achieve high system throughput of jobs. We gave examples to show how input, computation, and output steps from different jobs could be overlapped. This increases the utilization of the computer system components (I/O devices, channels, CPU) by increasing the amount of parallel activity.

The purpose of this section is to discuss some rudimentary aspects of the operating system routines that are required to schedule, initiate, and monitor the parallel activity. It is common to have a few jobs at various stages of processing in a multiprogramming system. The grouping of jobs for multiprogramming is done by an operating system scheduling routine. This is called *long-term scheduling*, and it is done on the basis of the job control information that the user supplies. The user declares the resources the job will require in job control statements, which typically include estimates for main memory space, CPU time, and peripheral device requirements. Jobs that operate on data files that exist on magnetic tapes or disks also need to specify the particular storage volume (tape or disk) required.

By examining the resource requirements of the jobs, the operating system scheduler routine can group jobs for multiprogramming in an attempt to use the system resources in the most efficient manner. Jobs that require a lot of I/O operations can be grouped with jobs that require a lot of CPU activity so that a balanced demand on all system components is created. There is an aspect of scheduling that is not directly related to system efficiency. Users can often request high-priority service by paying a premium rate. This leads to the establishment of job-priority classes based on service rates. The job priority must also be taken into account by the scheduler.

When job grouping for multiprogramming has been done, the jobs must be loaded into the main memory. This requires the jobs to be assigned to specific parts of the main memory and is referred to as *memory management*. Operating system procedures for this allocation process can be quite complicated and will not be discussed. Once several jobs are in the main memory ready for processing, it is necessary to have an operating system routine that implements *short-term scheduling*. This routine resolves conflicts among memory-resident jobs for CPU time, channel access, etc., as discussed in Section 10.4.2.

In the discussion of operating systems, it is convenient to have a common name for any task that is under the control of the operating system, including any routines that may be executed as part of running a scheduled job. It has become customary to use the word *process* to refer to such tasks. Generally, a process is a basic executable unit under control of the operating system. A complete definition of a process includes the current contents of the processor status word (PSW), the contents of CPU registers, etc. Enough information must be included so that if execution of a process is interrupted, it can be resumed at some later time and proceed correctly. With this informal idea of a process in mind, let us give some examples. Consider a user job that contains the program PROG. During its execution, PROG requests an input operation from a disk via I/O channel A. While the input operation is being performed, execution of PROG is temporarily suspended, and the CPU is assigned to some other job. Upon completion of the input transfer, PROG is ready to resume execution and the CPU is reassigned to it. When computation is completed, a request is made to print some output data. I/O channel B transfers the data to a disk file that accumulates all printing associated with the job. This file will be printed later in a separate operation. There are three processes associated with this job:

P_1 The program PROG
P_2 The input task performed by channel A
P_3 The output task performed by channel B

Individual input and output processes such as P_2 and P_3 are relatively simple from the standpoint of their management by the operating system. Once initiated, they usually run continuously to completion because of the nature of channel operation. On the other hand, processes such as P_1 can have a complicated activity pattern. They may be blocked a number of times by I/O calls or preempted by other higher-priority processes. The result is that a process may go through a number of state transitions between states such as "runnable," "running," and "blocked."

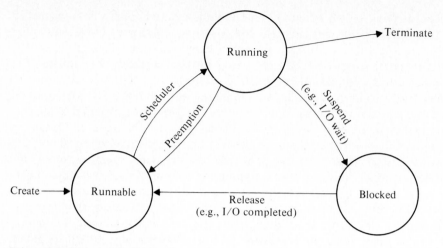

Figure 10.8 Process state diagram.

A useful mechanism for graphically showing the possible state transitions that can occur for a process is the *state diagram*. Figure 10.8 shows a general state diagram. The arrows between states indicate the cause of the transition. One of the responsibilities of the operating system is *process management*, that is, the control of the activities implied by the state diagram model. For example, consider a situation where program X is running while a higher-priority program Y is blocked waiting for an external interrupt. When this interrupt is received, control will be passed to the operating system, and program Y will be released into the runnable state. Since program Y has higher priority than X, the operating system scheduler will suspend execution of program X and resume execution of program Y.

By now, the reader is probably aware that users in multiprogramming systems do not include the actual I/O machine instructions and/or channel commands in their programs. Also, the user does not service the interrupts that result from completion of his or her I/O requests. The user simply requests the operating system to perform an I/O operation and to return control when I/O is completed. The I/O routines of the operating system execute the actual transfer. There are a number of reasons why the individual user does not write the actual I/O routines. First of all, most users only want to specify their input and output operations in simple statements in a high-level language. This type of user cares only about reading in information from disk files and printing out results on a line printer. These users are completely isolated from the mechanics of I/O and multiprogramming. Even in the case of users who could program some of these machine-dependent functions, there is still a need for central control by an operating system to ensure that (1) users do not interfere with each others' data or programs, and (2) no single user unfairly monopolizes the resources and lowers system efficiency. In summary, operating system routines must perform all I/O operations and control the use of shared resources to protect individual jobs and to keep the system throughput high.

We should mention that the CPUs of many computers have both a supervisor mode and a user mode. One difference between supervisor mode and user mode is that certain instructions, such as those that modify the PSW, can only be executed when the CPU is in the supervisor mode. This helps in providing the protection among users mentioned above. In general, when the CPU is in the user mode, it can be interrupted by any peripheral device, causing a transfer to an operating system interrupt-service routine that executes in the supervisory mode. When the CPU is in the supervisory mode, usually only the most time-critical I/O devices can interrupt it.

At this point, we should be more explicit about the role of I/O device interrupt priorities as opposed to the more general concept of user job-process priorities. Priority in scheduling user job processes for the use of shared resources is usually determined by the requirements stated by the user. The operating system determines the job-request priorities based on the job charac-teristics. A possible strategy is as follows: The requests for CPU processing from jobs that require a lot of I/O are given high priority; correspondingly, the I/O requests of jobs that require a lot of CPU processing are given a high priority. The objective of this strategy is to allow jobs to proceed in such a way that they tend toward always being ready to use the resource that they depend on most. In this way, a steady demand on all system resources may be achieved, resulting in maximum component utilization and job throughput. In some cases, as we will see in the next section on interactive systems, scheduling priorities are deter-mined by the urgency of individual process requests, and the system does not have as much freedom in scheduling processes as it does when job throughput is the only performance criterion.

Let us now consider the I/O device interrupt priorities associated with the hardware interrupt requests generated by peripheral devices. These priorities are usually independent of any of the scheduling priorities among user job processes. The device interrupt priorities are determined by the urgency of the response of the servicing routines that are a part of the operating system. These response demands of the devices are a function of their own operating characteristics, and they are independent of the user process demands.

10.4.4 Operating System Control of Interactive Computing

Interactive computing has become a very common method of using a computer. The general idea is that users prepare their programs at a CRT terminal in an *on-line* mode. That is, the user I/O device is under control of the CPU. As characters are entered at the device keyboard, they are either sent directly to the computer, or they are buffered in the terminal and sent to the computer a line at a time. In some cases, simple computations are executed, line by line, as they are entered. In other situations, the user can name a routine, or a function, and then request that it be executed. A number of different languages have been developed for this purpose. Two of the more popular ones are APL and BASIC. A typical time-shared computer can handle anywhere from 5 to 50 user terminals, depending on its computing power and the nature of the user jobs.

In batch processing, the major objective is to achieve high throughput rates. Little importance is attached to the time required to complete an individual job. On the other hand, the main objective in an interactive computing system is to achieve fast response to individual users. This requirement is a more severe constraint on scheduling the use of the CPU than is the case in the general multiprogramming situation. When a user enters a command at a terminal requesting the computer to perform some computation and return an answer, it is important that the computer respond within a few seconds. For purposes of later discussion, let T denote this response delay.

Consider a computer system with a single CPU that performs interactive computation for up to 50 terminals. A scheduling technique called *time-slicing* or *round-robin* servicing can be used to provide the required response times to all users. In this technique, the CPU is assigned to service each terminal in turn for a short interval of time. To meet the response-time requirements, an upper limit must be imposed on these intervals. This upper limit is called a *quantum t*. An interval timer is used to interrupt a user process that tries to execute beyond t seconds. In such a case, control is returned to the operating system, which then assigns a quantum to the next terminal. If there are n active terminals, the value of t can be chosen as $t = T/n$, ignoring operating system overhead for the moment. Consider a specific example where the allowable delay T is at most 2 s and all 50 terminals are active. Then, each user gets 40 ms of computation time every 2 s. On a machine that fetches and executes an instruction every 2 μs on the average, 40 ms of computation time corresponds to the execution of 20,000 instructions. This should be adequate for complete execution of most routines used in interactive computing.

The above numerical example is only an estimate of the computation time assignable to each user every T seconds. A number of details have been overlooked. The parameter T was defined to be the time between the user request for a computation and the response by the computer. We have implied that all the CPU time is assignable to user computations. This is not actually the case. Among other things, CPU time may be required to transfer individual characters from terminals to memory buffers. An alternative is to use a separate I/O processor to collect input characters and assemble them in the memory. Whenever a complete line has been assembled for a terminal, the I/O processor informs the CPU of this fact.

We shall first consider the case where the main CPU performs all tasks related to character collection and buffering. The characters from a specific terminal are collected into an input buffer assigned to that terminal. The computer may also echo back each character to be printed at the terminal immediately after it is received. The echoback must appear to the user to be instantaneous, which means it should be within a small fraction of a second.

The buffering of input strings and the associated echoback of individual characters for all the interactive terminals should be viewed as an independent ongoing operating system process. The same applies to the buffering of output strings that constitute computer responses (answers) and their subsequent display or printing. Interrupts can be used to call the operating system processes associated with receiving and sending characters. Alternatively, the CPU can poll the terminals for individual character transfers. Obviously, this must be done at a much higher rate than the assignment of quanta by the round-robin scheduler.

The tasks of reading and displaying individual characters constitute overhead that decreases the amount of CPU time available for computation. Thus the effective quantum time is less than the previously defined t. However, not all the terminals are likely to request a computation every T seconds. This means that, on the average, each terminal can expect more than one quantum of computation time during every T seconds.

It is instructive to obtain a rough estimate of the time overhead due to individual character handling. A convenient way to proceed is to postulate a "typical" session at a terminal by an "average" user. Consider an engineering student who wishes to perform a calculation associated with determining the voltages in an electric network. Assume that the major calculation involves solving four simultaneous linear equations and that a library routine is available for such a problem. The student enters a maximum of 16 parameters and issues a call to the appropriate routine to get the solution. Each parameter is represented in decimal floating-point format by at most 10 characters. Hence, the student will type at most 160 characters to enter the data for the problem. Assuming that another 40 characters are used in initiating the session and calling the library routine, the student will type about 200 characters in this simple session. The computer responses will consist of four answer values of about 10 characters each and various replies during initiation and termination of the session that might amount to a total of 50 to 60 characters. The computer will then display about 100 characters during the session. Thus a total of 300 characters will be displayed. Let the total elapsed time for the session be 5 min. Hence each terminal represents a character-processing load of 60 characters per minute. If there are 50 active terminals, the total estimated character-processing rate is 3000 characters per minute.

Let us now determine the time required to process a single character. Assume that the system we are considering has interrupt facilities. Upon receiving an interrupt request from a terminal, the current state of the CPU must be saved. Let this procedure take 10 instructions. Servicing of the interrupt consists of identifying the terminal, transferring the character to the appropriate input buffer, adjusting the buffer pointer, and echoing the character back to the terminal printer. This may take another 20 instructions. Finally, about 10 instructions are needed to restore the state of the CPU and branch back to the interrupted program. Therefore, as a rough estimate, 40 instructions are required to process a single character. Assuming that each instruction needs 2 μs for execution, the time required for character handling is $3000 \times 40 \times 2 = 240,000$ μs/min. This represents an overhead of only 0.4 percent.

In the above discussion, we have assumed that a single CPU supports all the processes required to accomplish interactive computing, including the handling of individual characters. Since the latter is an independent task, it may be, and often is, delegated to a separate I/O processor, as suggested earlier. Then the main CPU has to deal with only one interrupt, that from the I/O processor, instead of individual interrupts from the terminals. Although our example calculations showed that this amounted to less than 1 percent of the main CPU time, the situation we chose to examine was very much simplified. All the terminals were assumed to be sending and receiving characters at low rates, and no character translations were performed. I/O processors are used to perform a number of other tasks related to buffering character input and output. There may be different types of terminals, each having different communication protocols. These protocols may represent a considerable overhead, as will be discussed in Chapter 12. The identification of individual terminals and the handling of inbound and outbound character transfers may be much more complicated than we assumed above. Also, character set codes may differ from terminal to terminal. The I/O processor can then be used to translate all codes into some standard format before transferring them to the main computer.

Another practical aspect involves the utilization of computers that provide interactive services. If the interactive computing load does not use all the CPU time available, it is quite feasible to occupy the computer with noninteractive batch processing during the spare time intervals. In such cases, interactive processing should be given higher priority. The batch processing is done at a lower-priority level and is often referred to as background computation.

10.5 CONCLUDING REMARKS

In this chapter, we touched upon some of the aspects of computer system software. The message for the computer designer is that system software is not just another set of programs that are written to run on the machine. System software should be viewed as an integral part of the overall design of a computer system. As such, its requirements should be considered at the outset of the design process so that hardware features can be included to support the running of efficient system software. Operating systems are very complex structures. They require many programmer-years to develop, and they often go through a number of revisions during their lifetime.

10.6 PROBLEMS

10.1 In Section 10.1, it was stated that "high-level" languages have many statements that must be translated into separate sequences of machine instructions.

(a) Suggest how the Fortran DO loop

$$DO \quad 100 \quad I = 1,10,1$$
.
.
.
$$100 \quad CONTINUE$$

may be implemented by machine instructions in the PDP-11 minicomputer.

(b) Repeat part (a) for

$$DO \quad 50 \quad I = J,K,2$$
.
.
.
$$50 \quad CONTINUE$$

10.2 Suggest how the high-level control construct

```
IF A = B
   THEN
      BEGIN
         .
         .        computation 1
         .
      END
   ELSE
      BEGIN
         .
         .        computation 2
         .
      END
"next instruction"
```

may be implemented by machine instructions in the PDP-11.

10.3 An absolute binary loader program is to be designed for a PDP-11 computer. The object code of a program to be loaded and run is located on a magnetic disk. The actual transfer from disk to main memory is to be done by DMA. Knowing that the PDP-11 uses memory-mapped I/O, sketch a PDP-11 assembly language program that initiates the DMA transfer. Assume a disk address format similar to the example shown in Figure 9.8 of Chapter 9. The interrupt generated by the DMA controller is to be handled by an interrupt-service routine that starts execution of the loaded program. Assuming that this routine is a component part of the loader, write out a sequence of instructions for it also. Note that you will need to propose a format for the object code of the program to be loaded in order to answer this question.

10.4 (a) A macroinstruction that multiplies an operand by 10 is to be implemented for the PDP-11. The instruction is coded as MULTEN dst, where dst is specified by any of the applicable addressing modes. Show how this macroinstruction might be expanded into a sequence of PDP-11 instructions. Does your macroinstruction leave the condition code flags in an appropriate state?

(b) Repeat for the macroinstruction DIVTEN dst,R_i which divides the operand at dst by 10, leaving the quotient at dst and the remainder in register R_i.

10.5 (a) Suppose that the object modules in Figure 10.3 are presented to the linker in the order B followed by A. Specify the load module that would be generated. Give your answer in the same format as Figure 10.4.

(b) Show how this load module would appear in the main memory if its starting location is chosen as 2200. Use a format that is similar to Figure 10.5 for your answer.

10.6 Suppose a line printer and a magnetic disk are attached to a computer through two logically independent channels. Lines can be printed at the rate of 900 lines per minute. A complete line consists of 133 eight-bit characters. The disk is a CDC 9760, whose operating characteritics are given in Table 9.1. If the disk is continuously busy handling transfers, actual character moves are made at the stated transfer rate for only about 10 percent of the time. The other 90 percent of the time is used in Read/Write head seek time and rotational display.

Assume that the operating system is able to keep both peripheral devices simultaneously active at their maximum rates. The main memory has a 32-bit word length and a cycle time of 1 μs. What is the average *interference* in this system, where interference is defined by

$$\text{Interference} = \frac{\text{memory cycles stolen by channels}}{\text{total memory cycles available}}$$

Characters are packed or unpacked with respect to 32-bit word quantities by the channel logic.

10.7 Suppose that in a batch system all operations on one job are completed before any operations on the next job are begun. This means that, in terms of Figure 10.6, step R1 of job Y begins after step W1 of job X is completed, and step R1 of job Z begins after step W1 of job Y is completed. However, overlap among the steps of any one job is permitted. For instance, R2 of job X can proceed in parallel with C1 of the same job.

Estimate the amount of extra time needed to execute jobs X, Y, and Z of Figure 10.6a, under the above assumptions as compared to the time t_0 to t_7 required in Figure 10.6b where overlapping among successive jobs is permitted.

10.8 Add an output step W1 to each of the three jobs in Figure 10.7. Assume that there is only one line printer in the system. If a second line printer is added, can it be used to improve throughput in this particular case?

10.9 (a) If a process is suspended or preempted in the sense of Figure 10.8, its "current state" must be saved, where "current state" consists of PSW, CPU registers, etc. Suggest how this may be done.

(b) Is process suspension or preemption any different from program interruption as discussed earlier in conjunction with I/O interrupts?

(c) Since process switching may be a frequent operation, suggest machine hardware features (new instructions, duplicated registers, etc.) that would make it more efficient. Is the stack data structure of any help in this respect?

10.10 In a multiprogramming environment, what is the technique used to avoid intermixing the output lines from several jobs when only a single printer is used?

10.11 Construct a time-diagram example, patterned after Figure 10.6a, to illustrate the reasonableness of the CPU and I/O priority strategy discussed at the end of Section 10.4.3. In constructing this example, use three jobs with different mixes of CPU and I/O activity. In assigning the CPU, assume that preemption can take place; that is, if a job with high CPU priority completes an I/O operation, it is permitted to take the CPU away from (preempt) another job with lower CPU priority that is currently running on the CPU. However, use of a shared I/O device by one job cannot be interrupted by a request for the device from another job that has higher I/O priority. Your solution should consist of showing that the total time needed to complete all three jobs is increased if the priorities are opposite to those of the suggested strategy.

10.12 Two processes PROD (producer) and CONS (consumer) interact with each other through a FIFO queue named BUFFER (see Problem 2.16) in an obvious way—PROD appends data to the queue, 1 byte at a time, by calling an operating system procedure BUFFER.APPEND; and CONS removes data from the queue, 1 byte at a time, by calling an operating system procedure BUFFER.REMOVE. Using the style of Figure 10.8, draw state diagrams for each of the processes PROD and CONS, explicitly labeling the arrows that cause state transitions for the particular case of PROD and CONS interacting through BUFFER.

10.7 REFERENCES

10.1 Shaw, A. C.: "The Logical Design of Operating Systems," Prentice-Hall, Englewood Cliffs, N.J., 1974.
10.2 Brinch Hansen, Per: "Operating System Principles," Prentice-Hall, Englewood Cliffs, N.J., 1973.
10.3 Tsichritzis, D. C., and P. A. Bernstein: "Operating Systems," Academic Press, New York, 1974.
10.4 Gries, D.: "Compiler Construction for Digital Computers," Wiley, New York, 1971.
10.5 McKeeman, W. M., J. J. Horning, and D. B. Wortman: "A Compiler Generator," Prentice-Hall, Englewood Cliffs, N.J., 1970.
10.6 Presser, L., and J. R. White: Linkers and Loaders, *Comput. Surv.,* vol. 4, no. 3, pp. 149–167, Sept. 1972.
10.7 Aho, A. V., and J. D. Ullman: "Principles of Compiler Design," Addison-Wesley, Reading, Mass., 1977.

ELEVEN

MICROPROCESSORS

One of the most significant technological advances of the past two decades has been the emergence of large-scale integrated (LSI) circuits. Improved technology and manufacturing methods have enabled production of very complex circuits on single chips. In the digital-logic domain, this evolution went through the stages of producing standard logic subunits in integrated circuit (IC) packages. The first stage yielded simple gates and flip-flops in small-scale integrated (SSI) chips. This was followed by medium-scale integrated (MSI) chips containing registers, counters, encoders, decoders, etc. The number of distinct elements in any package is largely determined by the required number of external connections to the package. Thus it is typical to find an eight-input to one-output multiplexer or perhaps four flip-flops in a 16-pin package.

As the ability to build ICs with high density of logic elements increased, it became advantageous to consider circuits that require a large number of elements but relatively few external connections. The result was the appearance of more complex packages, such as the arithmetic and logic unit (ALU) chips, capable of performing the usual arithmetic and logic functions on 4-bit operands. The natural continuation of this trend saw the emergence of complete processor elements on a chip in the early 1970s. First, there were chips capable of operating on 4 bits in parallel. Since they had the processing capabilities but not the comparable size and speed of minicomputers, it was reasonable to call the new devices *microprocessors*. Soon thereafter, larger chips became available. At the present time a variety of microprocessor chips are manufactured which operate on 8-bit or 16-bit data in parallel. Moreover, the ever-improving technology has reached the point where very-large-scale integrated (VLSI) circuits can be manufactured to implement a 32-bit microprocessor on a single chip.

Increasing the processing capability of IC chips tends to increase the required number of external connections, resulting in larger packages. It is fairly standard to find 8-bit microprocessors in 40-pin packages. It is more difficult to fit a 16-bit microprocessor into a 40-pin package without time multiplexing the use of some pins. With time multiplexing, one set of pins is used for different functions at different times. Such time sharing is a viable possibility, but it is inevitably achieved at the cost of lower speed of operation and more complex external interfaces. The alternative is to use packages with more than 40 pins. The M68000 microprocessor, which is used as an example in this chapter, has 64 pins.

Early microprocessors were manufactured using p-channel MOS (metal-oxide semiconductor) technology, as it was the first process that enabled effective production of LSI circuits. Other technologies soon became available. While it is beyond the scope of this book to discuss details of various manufacturing processes, we should name a few commonly used methods. The mainstay of present microprocessors is n-channel MOS, which is suitable for low- and medium-speed applications. It allows high density of logic elements on the chip, which is important in systems where it is desired to keep the number of chips to a minimum. CMOS (complementary MOS) technology has been used to fabricate microprocessors that have low power consumption and considerable flexibility in power supply requirements. Higher-performance chips have been manufactured using TTL (transistor-transistor logic) processes, particularly the low-power Schottky process. Very high-performance chips can be produced with ECL (emitter-coupled logic) technology. However, the high performance of ECL and TTL circuits is associated with higher power consumption and lower complexity of the logic circuits on a given chip. Another technology that overlaps some of the above-mentioned ones is I^2L (integrated injection logic). It allows high packing density, as well as low power, and offers a comparatively lower-cost product.

One might expect instruction sets in microprocessors to be limited in scope, creating considerable difficulties when relatively complex programming tasks are to be handled. However, this is not the case. Most microprocessors have surprisingly powerful instruction sets, making them suitable for a great many general-purpose applications.

An obvious difficulty is presented by the short word length when it is restricted to 8 or 16 bits. It was argued in Chapter 3 that adequate bit space for the instructions must be available if a reasonably flexible instruction repertoire is required. When the basic word length is too short, the simplest answer lies in extending instructions over two or more words. This concept, already encountered in the example of PDP-11 minicomputers, is fundamental to the design of microprocessor instruction sets.

11.1 FAMILIES OF MICROPROCESSOR CHIPS

A computer is a complex machine. It is difficult to assemble all its components on a single chip. However, when subdivided into a few well-defined parts, it lends itself to implementation through a set of chips. It is quite feasible to fit the entire CPU on one chip. Other chips are needed to provide the main memory. Further chips are needed for interfacing to input and output devices. All this means that a number of chips are required for construction of a nontrivial machine.

Having established the need for various chips, we should consider the problem of interconnecting them. Since we are talking about low-cost components being used to construct low-cost computers, it is obvious that interconnection requirements must be simple and easy to meet. It is essential that signals generated by one VLSI chip can be used directly as inputs to other VLSI chips. As a solution to this problem, most manufacturers offer complete families of compatible chips. Furthermore, some of the more popular products have emerged as "standards," and their signal characteristics are used as desirable targets for other products. Thus it is not unusual to find compatibility among chips produced by different manufacturers.

As an example of a typical family of chips, let us consider the Motorola M6800[11.1] microprocessor components. Many basic parts are available. They include:

1. M6800 (*microprocessor unit, MPU*) This is a 40-pin CPU chip that processes 8 bits of data in parallel. It uses 16-bit addresses, allowing for memory sizes of up to 64K bytes. There are two 8-bit accumulators and three 16-bit registers serving as a program counter, an index register, and a stack pointer. Instructions are 1 to 3 bytes in length. The instruction set is fairly extensive, and six addressing modes can be used. Interrupt-handling capability is provided. The block diagram of the MPU is shown in Figure 11.1.

2. *PIA (peripheral interface adapter)* The PIA provides a simple means for interfacing peripheral devices to the M6800 bus. It has two I/O ports consisting of two sets of programmable control and data registers. Figure 11.2 gives its block diagram. The two ports are labeled *A* and *B*. Each port provides a separate 8-bit bidirectional data interface and two interrupt control lines for interfacing to peripheral devices. Three internal 8-bit registers are associated with each port. An output register serves as a buffer in output transfers. A data-direction register governs the direction of I/O transfers on an individual line basis. For each bit in the register that is set to 1, the corresponding peripheral data line acts as an output, transferring the contents of the output register to the peripheral device. Similarly, for each bit set to 0, the corresponding peripheral data line acts as an input. There is no internal buffer for input transfers. Instead, the input data is transferred directly to the main MPU bus. The usage of the data-direction register in this fashion allows considerable flexibility in the deployment of the peripheral lines, since it is not necessary to use all of them as either inputs or outputs at any given time. A control register is provided to allow the MPU

Address bus

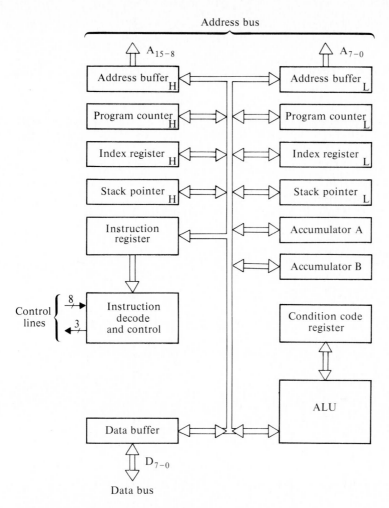

Figure 11.1 Microprocessor unit (MPU).

to control and monitor the status of the I/O and interrupt control lines. All three registers are accessible to the MPU as ordinary addressable locations.
3. *ACIA (asynchronous communications interface adapter)* The ACIA allows simple interfacing to devices that process data in bit-serial fashion. As indicated in Figure 11.3, it contains a transmitter circuit that accepts 8-bit parallel data from the main data bus and sends it to the peripheral device one bit at a time. This is accomplished by means of a "transmit" shift register which can be loaded in parallel. Similarly, a receiver circuit collects serial data from the device and assembles it into an 8-bit word for transfer to the main data bus. The operation of the ACIA can be controlled through a programmable control register.

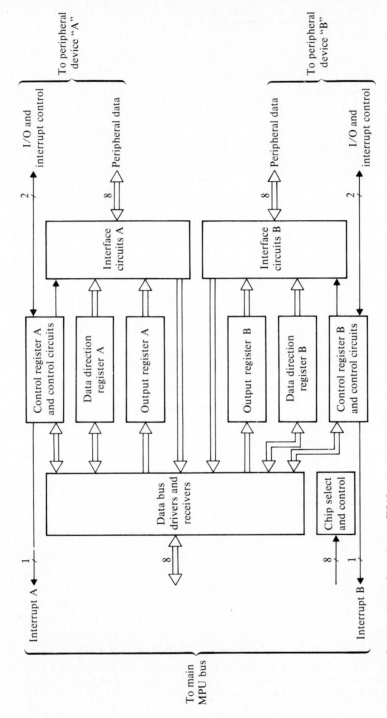

Figure 11.2 Peripheral interface adapter (PIA).

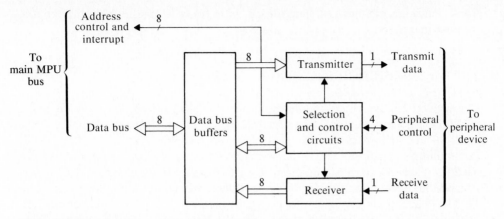

Figure 11.3 Asynchronous communications interface adapter (ACIA).

A number of other chips of a quite general variety are also easily used with such a family of chips. This is particularly the case with memory chips (RAM, ROM, PROM, and EPROM), which can be incorporated into a microprocessor system using the techniques discussed in Chapter 8.

The key characteristic of the chips in a family is their total compatibility. They may be connected to form a simple, yet powerful, system as shown in Figure 11.4. The six chips in this configuration, in conjunction with a clock and a power supply, constitute a complete computer.

As an aid to our discussion, we will consider closely four microprocessors, Motorola's M6800, M6809,[11.2] and M68000[11.3] and Intel's 8085.[11.4] Motorola's microprocessors will be used to illustrate a typical historical progression in microprocessor products from a basic 8-bit chip to a powerful 16-bit microprocessor capable of performance more usually associated with minicomputers. The 8085 is included as a contrast to the M6800, to show an alternative design approach.

All four microprocessors have found great popularity in practical applica-

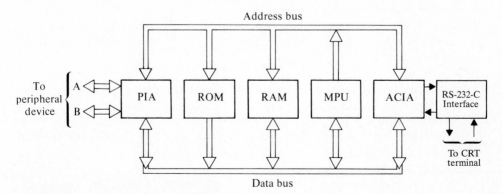

Figure 11.4 A simple microprocessor system.

tions. They are extensively supported with other chips, available from the original manufacturers and other sources.

11.2 M6800 MICROPROCESSOR

The M6800 has been one of the most popular 8-bit microprocessors. It has a register-based architecture, as indicated in the block diagram of Figure 11.1. Most of its arithmetic and logic operations involve one of the two 8-bit accumulators A and B. The index register (IX) and the stack pointer (SP) are used for a specific purpose, and their contents can be manipulated by only a few instructions of the load/store, increment/decrement, and compare types. The M6800 instructions can refer to only one operand in the main memory. In two-operand instructions, one of the operands is always in a CPU register. Thus, the M6800 has the 1½-address format discussed in Section 2.3.

Instructions are from 1 to 3 bytes in length. The first byte is the OP code, which specifies the operation to be performed, the address mode, and the register to be used, if any. The second and third bytes contain either additional addressing information or immediate data. Six addressing modes are available:

Immediate mode. The operand is contained in the second byte of the instruction. Instructions which load the 16-bit IX and SP registers contain the immediate double word in the second and third bytes of the instruction.

Page zero mode. (called direct mode by Motorola) This is a short version of the absolute mode, where the second byte of the instruction specifies an address within page zero, that is, within the lowest 256 bytes of the main memory.

Absolute mode. (called extended mode by Motorola) An absolute address is specified by the second and third bytes of the instruction.

Indexed mode. The second byte of the instruction is added to the contents of the IX register to give the effective address.

Implied register mode. This mode is used in single-byte instructions which specify the address as accumulator A or B, or one of the IX, SP, or condition code registers.

Relative mode. This mode is used in branch instructions. The second byte contains the signed offset to be added to the program counter to obtain the address of the next instruction.

The versatility of these addressing modes is easily appreciated. However, some notable deficiencies are readily identified. Programming tasks are complicated by having a single IX register and only two accumulators. The absence of autoincrement capability in operand addressing leads to increased overhead when the IX and SP registers are to be incremented. Separate instructions have to be used for this purpose.

Table 11.1 shows the instruction set for the M6800. Most of the entries are self-explanatory. Memory reference instructions can involve either of the two accumulators A and B. For example, ADDA performs the addition of the memory operand in location M and the contents of accumulator A, leaving the sum in the latter. An analogous instruction, ADDB, performs the same function involving accumulator B. The two instructions are combined in Table 11.1, as an entry ADDA/B. Similarly, other instructions involving the accumulators are shown as single entries. The symbol "M" represents the effective address of the operand.

Table 11.1 gives the total number of bytes for each instruction in the "#" columns. Another important piece of data pertains to the total number of internal MPU cycles required to execute an instruction. This information is shown in the column labeled "~". Each cycle corresponds to one period of the clock that drives the MPU. A single memory access can be completed within one cycle. Thus execution time is largely determined by the number of bytes that need to be fetched from the memory. However, a secondary consideration arises. Due to the relatively low speed of MOS devices, the time required for an internal MPU arithmetic operation tends to be comparable to memory access time. As a consequence, whenever the computation of an address involves an addition operation, the execution time of the instruction is increased by one cycle for each required 8-bit addition. For example, consider the ADDA instruction in indexed mode. Two bytes are needed to specify the OP code and index offset. To execute this instruction, two cycles are taken for fetching the instruction itself, another two cycles are used to add the offset to the 16-bit IX register, and one cycle is needed to fetch the actual operand from the memory. The final addition of the fetched operand and the contents of accumulator A requires a part of yet another cycle. However, it can be overlapped with the fetching of the first byte of the next instruction, since it only involves transfers internal to the MPU, not affecting the program counter or the address output buffers. Thus the ADDA instruction uses a total of five cycles. Similar situations exist with other instructions.

The number of MPU cycles per instruction gives a good indication of the attainable speed performance of the M6800 microprocessor. It can be driven by a clock in the 2-MHz range. This means that the ADDA instruction in indexed address mode can be processed in approximately 2.5 μs.

The condition code register (CCR) contains six flags:

C   Carry from the most significant bit (bit 7)
V   Arithmetic overflow
Z   Zero
N   Negative
I   Interrupt mask
H   Carry from the bit-3 position (called a half carry)

The first four flags are the condition code bits which are tested by branch instructions. The interrupt mask allows enabling and disabling of interrupt requests. The H flag is useful for processing of binary-coded decimal (BCD)

Table 11.1 M6800 microprocessor instruction set

Operation	Mnemonic	IMMED ~	IMMED #	DIRECT ~	DIRECT #	EXTEND ~	EXTEND #	INDEX ~	INDEX #	IMPLIED ~	IMPLIED #	Performed function	H	I	N	Z	V	C
Add	ADDA/B	2	2	3	2	4	3	5	2			A←[A]+[M]	x		x	x	x	x
Add accumulators	ABA									2	1	A←[A]+[B]	x		x	x	x	x
Add with carry	ADCA/B	2	2	3	2	4	3	5	2			A←[A]+[M]+[C]	x		x	x	x	x
AND	ANDA/B	2	2	3	2	4	3	5	2			A←[A]∧[M]			x	x	0	
Bit test	BITA/B	2	2	3	2	4	3	5	2			[A]∧[M]			x	x	0	
Clear	CLR					6	3	7	2			M←0			0	1	0	0
	CLRA/B									2	1	A←0			0	1	0	0
Compare	CMPA/B	2	2	3	2	4	3	5	2			[A]−[M]			x	x	x	x
Compare accumulators	CBA									2	1	[A]−[B]			x	x	x	x
Complement (1's)	COM					6	3	7	2			M←[M̄]			x	x	0	1
	COMA/B									2	1	A←[Ā]			x	x	0	1
Negate (2's complement)	NEG					6	3	7	2			M←0−[M]			x	x	x	x
	NEGA/B									2	1	A←0−[M]			x	x	x	x
Decimal adjust A	DAA									2	1	Converts binary sum of BCD characters into BCD format			x	x	x	x
Decrement	DEC					6	3	7	2			M←[M]−1			x	x	x	
	DECA/B									2	1	A←[A]−1			x	x	x	
Exclusive OR	EORA/B	2	2	3	2	4	3	5	2			A←[A]⊕[M]			x	x	0	
Increment	INC					6	3	7	2			M←[M]+1			x	x	x	
	INCA/B									2	1	A←[A]+1			x	x	x	

Operation	Mnemonic	Immediate (~/#)	Direct (~/#)	Indexed (~/#)	Extended (~/#)	Inherent (~/#)	Boolean/Arithmetic Operation	H	I	N	Z	V	C
Load accumulator	LDA/B	2/2	3/2	5/2	4/3	—	$A \leftarrow [M]$			x	x	0	
OR (inclusive)	ORA/B	2/2	3/2	5/2	4/3	—	$A \leftarrow [A] \lor [M]$			x	x	0	
Push data	PSHA/B	—	—	—	—	4/1	$M_{SP} \leftarrow [A],\ SP \leftarrow [SP]-1$						
Pull data	PULA/B	—	—	—	—	4/1	$SP \leftarrow [SP]+1,\ A \leftarrow [M_{SP}]$						
Rotate left	ROL, ROLA/B	—	—	7/2	6/3	2/1	M or A: rotate left through C ($C \leftarrow b_7 \cdots b_0 \leftarrow C$)			x	x	x	x
Rotate right	ROR, RORA/B	—	—	7/2	6/3	2/1	M or A: rotate right through C ($C \rightarrow b_7 \cdots b_0 \rightarrow C$)			x	x	x	x
Shift left (arithmetic)	ASL, ASLA/B	—	—	7/2	6/3	2/1	M or A: $C \leftarrow b_7 \cdots b_0 \leftarrow 0$			x	x	x	x
Shift right (arithmetic)	ASR, ASRA/B	—	—	7/2	6/3	2/1	M or A: $b_7 \rightarrow \cdots \rightarrow b_0 \rightarrow C$ (b_7 retained)			x	x	x	x
Shift right (logic)	LSR, LSRA/B	—	—	7/2	6/3	2/1	M or A: $0 \rightarrow b_7 \cdots b_0 \rightarrow C$			0	x	x	x
Store accumulator	STAA/B	—	4/2	6/2	5/3	—	$M \leftarrow [A]$			x	x	0	
Subtract	SUBA/B	2/2	3/2	5/2	4/3	—	$A \leftarrow [A] - [M]$			x	x	x	x
Subtract accumulators	SBA	—	—	—	—	2/1	$A \leftarrow [A] - [B]$			x	x	x	x
Subtract with carry	SBCA/B	2/2	3/2	5/2	4/3	—	$A \leftarrow [A] - [M] - [C]$			x	x	x	x
Transfer accumulators	TAB	—	—	—	—	2/1	$B \leftarrow [A]$			x	x	0	
	TBA	—	—	—	—	2/1	$A \leftarrow [B]$			x	x	0	
Test (zero or minus)	TST, TSTA/B	—	—	7/2	6/3	2/1	$[M] - 0$; $[A] - 0$			x	x	0	0
Compare index register	CMX	3/3	4/2	6/2	5/3	—	$[IX]_H - [M],\ [IX]_L - [M+1]$			x	x	x	
Decrement index register	DEX	—	—	—	—	4/1	$IX \leftarrow [IX] - 1$				x		
Decrement stack pointer	DES	—	—	—	—	4/1	$SP \leftarrow [SP] - 1$						

Table 11.1 (Continued)

Operation	Mnemonic	IMMED ~	IMMED #	DIRECT ~	DIRECT #	EXTEND ~	EXTEND #	INDEX ~	INDEX #	IMPLIED ~	IMPLIED #	Performed function	H	I	N	Z	V	C
Increment index register	INX									4	1	$IX \leftarrow [IX]+1$				x		
Increment stack pointer	INS									4	1	$SP \leftarrow [SP]+1$						
Load index register	LDX	3	3	4	2	5	3	6	2			$IX_H \leftarrow [M], IX_L \leftarrow [M+1]$			x	x	0	
Load stack pointer	LDS	3	3	4	2	5	3	6	2			$SP_H \leftarrow [M], SP_L \leftarrow [M+1]$			x	x	0	
Store index register	STX			5	2	6	3	7	2			$M \leftarrow [IX]_H, (M+1) \leftarrow [IX]_L$			x	x	0	
Store stack pointer	STS			5	2	6	3	7	2			$M \leftarrow [SP]_H, (M+1) \leftarrow [SP]_L$			x	x	0	
Index register to stack pointer	TXS									4	1	$SP \leftarrow [IX]-1$						
Stack pointer to index register	TSX									4	1	$IX \leftarrow [SP]+1$						
Clear carry	CLC									2	1	$C \leftarrow 0$						0
Clear interrupt mask	CLI									2	1	$I \leftarrow 0$		0				
Clear overflow	CLV									2	1	$V \leftarrow 0$					0	
Set carry	SEC									2	1	$C \leftarrow 1$						1
Set interrupt mask	SEI									2	1	$I \leftarrow 1$		1				
Set overflow	SEV									2	1	$V \leftarrow 1$					1	
Accumulator A to CCR	TAP									2	1	$CCR \leftarrow [A]$	x	x	x	x	x	x
CCR to accumulator A	TPA									2	1	$A \leftarrow [CCR]$						

Table 11.1 *(Continued)*

Operation	Mnemonic	RELATIVE ~	RELATIVE #	ABSOL ~	ABSOL #	INDEX ~	INDEX #	IMPLIED ~	IMPLIED #	Branch test
Branch always	BRA	4	2							None
Branch if carry clear	BCC	4	2							$[C] = 0$
Branch if carry set	BCS	4	2							$[C] = 1$
Branch if = zero	BEQ	4	2							$[Z] = 1$
Branch if ≥ zero	BGE	4	2							$[N] \oplus [V] = 0$
Branch if > zero	BGT	4	2							$[Z] \vee ([N] \oplus [V]) = 0$
Branch if higher	BHI	4	2							$[C] \vee [Z] = 0$
Branch if ≤ zero	BLE	4	2							$[Z] \vee ([N] \oplus [V]) = 1$
Branch if lower or same	BLS	4	2							$[C] \vee [Z] = 1$
Branch if < zero	BLT	4	2							$[N] \oplus [V] = 1$
Branch if minus	BMI	4	2							$[N] = 1$
Branch if not equal to zero	BNE	4	2							$[Z] = 0$
Branch if overflow clear	BVC	4	2							$[V] = 0$
Branch if overflow set	BVS	4	2							$[V] = 1$
Branch if plus	BPL	4	2							$[N] = 0$
Branch to subroutine	BSR	8	2							
Jump	JMP			3	3	4	2			
Jump to subroutine	JSR			9	3	8	2			
No operation	NOP							2	1	
Return from interrupt	RTI							10	1	
Return from subroutine	RTS							5	1	
Software interrupt	SWI							12	1	
Wait for interrupt	WAI							9	1	

Notes: ~ = number of cycles needed to execute the instruction; # = number of bytes in the instruction; CCR = condition code register.

data, where two BCD digits are stored in 1 byte, as will be illustrated in a subsequent example.

Table 11.1 indicates which flags are affected by a given instruction. An "x" is used to indicate that a particular flag is set to 1 if the condition represented by it is true, and that it is cleared to 0 otherwise. A 1 or a 0 indicates that the flag is set or cleared, respectively. A blank entry denotes that the corresponding flag is not affected by the instruction. For branch instructions the table shows how the flags are used to form the test conditions.

11.2.1 Example

As an illustration of the use of the M6800 instruction set, let us consider a small program for subtraction of two numbers represented in BCD form. The numbers P and Q are 16 digits long and are stored in locations NUMP and NUMQ on page 0 of the RAM (that is, locations 0–255). Each number spans 8 bytes, with the two most significant digits occupying the lowest-address byte. It is desired to subtract the number at NUMQ from that at NUMP, and to store the result at NUMP.

The main difficulty in performing this subtraction is caused by the fact that a BCD operation is to be carried out using simple binary arithmetic. When 2 bytes containing two BCD digits each are added in an 8-bit binary adder, the result is not necessarily in the correct BCD format. A special instruction, called Decimal Adjust (DAA), can be used to make the required transformation. An algorithm that performs the desired subtraction forms the 10's complement of the subtrahend Q and adds it to the minuend P to obtain the difference. The formation of the complement and the addition step can be combined into a single iterative cycle as indicated in the four-digit example of Figure 11.5. The two numbers are scanned from right to left.

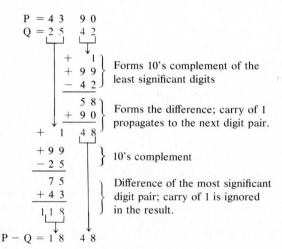

Figure 11.5 An example of BCD subtraction for 4-digit operands.

Location (hex)	Contents (hex)		Assembler format for instructions		Comments
100	CE		LDX	#7	Set IX as a byte number.
101	00				
102	07				
103	0D		SEC		Set carry for 10's complement.
104	86	SLOOP:	LDAA	#$99	Form 10's complement of Q for
105	99				one digit pair.
106	89		ADCA	#0	
107	00				
108	A0		SUBA	NUMQ,X	
109	"NUMQ"				
10A	AB		ADDA	NUMP,X	Form P − Q in binary.
10B	"NUMP"				
10C	19		DAA		Decimal adjust.
10D	A7		STAA	NUMP,X	Store the digit pair of the
10E	"NUMP"				difference into NUMP.
10F	09		DEX		Decrement counter.
110	26		BGE	SLOOP	Loop until last byte is processed.
111	F2				

Figure 11.6 Program for subtraction of 16-digit BCD operands for M6800.

Since the M6800 has only one IX register, it is somewhat awkward to implement the above algorithm using a single pointer to the operands. A possible program is shown in Figure 11.6. The IX register is used as a byte counter and as an incrementable pointer, with the base addresses of P and Q specified as the offset, in indexed address mode. This obviously restricts the usefulness of the program as a potential subroutine if P and Q are not always available in fixed locations. A more general program can easily be written, where the pointers to the operands P and Q are kept in temporary locations in the RAM. Whenever either of the operands is needed, the corresponding pointer must be loaded into the IX register. After fetching the operand, the IX register should be updated to point at the next digit pair and then stored back in the RAM. Thus, during each loop, this process has to be performed twice, first for the Q operand and then for the P operand. The additional overhead involved in fetching and storing the pointers is the price that must be paid to obtain a versatile routine that can handle operands stored anywhere in the RAM.

The program in Figure 11.6 shows the instructions in a format consistent with the M6800 assembler. *Hexadecimal* (hex) notation is used, which is standard in microprocessor systems. The hexadecimal notation is a direct extension of the BCD code given in Appendix D. In this notation, the six 4-bit patterns 1010, 1011, . . ., 1111 are encoded by the capital letters A, B, . . ., F. The first 10 patterns 0000, 0001, . . ., 1001 are encoded by the digits 0, 1, . . ., 9 as in BCD. The hexadecimal notation is very convenient for representing bytes and words in 8-bit, 16-bit, and 32-bit word-length machines because patterns of 8, 16, and 32 bits can be encoded by 2, 4, and 8 hex digits, respectively.

In Figure 11.6 the data is expressed in hex code by placing a "$" sign in front of the numerical value. Immediate operands are indicated by the "#" sign, while indexed addressing is denoted as "OFFSET,X." Actual addresses corresponding to NUMP and NUMQ must, obviously, be used in place of the entries "NUMP" and "NUMQ." The program requires 18 bytes of memory. Using the number of cycles for various instructions as given in Table 11.1, it is readily shown that two 16-digit BCD operands can be subtracted in 245 cycles, where each pass through the basic loop (SLOOP) takes 30 cycles. Assuming a clock frequency of about 2 MHz, it follows that the program can be executed in less than 125 μs.

As a concluding statement in this discussion of the M6800 microprocessor, it is useful to note that some of its features are similar to those found in the PDP-11 minicomputer. The main differences can be attributed directly to the differences in the word length and the pin limitations of the M6800.

11.3 M6809 MICROPROCESSOR

The M6800, like most 8-bit microprocessors that were popular in the mid to late 1970s, has some shortcomings in its architecture. These shortcomings have a direct impact on the ease of use of the microprocessor in practical applications, often resulting in software that is more awkward than it need be. For example, having a single index register can present difficulties in list processing tasks where more than one pointer is needed. Limiting the short form of absolute addressing to the first 256 addressable locations, that is, page zero, is an annoying restriction. The severely restricted scope of arithmetic operations that can be performed on the index register or the stack pointer often proves to be inconvenient. Such shortcomings led to the design of an improved microprocessor of the same class, the M6809.

We will discuss the M6809, assuming that the reader is familiar with the previous discussion of the M6800. The M6809 is fully compatible with the 6800 family of chips. All support chips can be used with it in a straightforward manner. However, the M6809 microprocessor is sufficiently different from the M6800 that programs written for the M6800 cannot be executed on the M6809 without making some modifications. The M6809 is a much more powerful processor. Programs written for it cannot be executed on the M6800 at all.

11.3.1 Register Structure

Figure 11.7 shows the internal registers in the M6809. As in the M6800, there are two 8-bit accumulators A and B. They may be used separately, or they may be

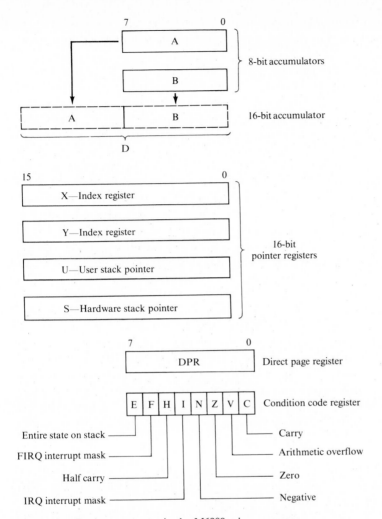

Figure 11.7 Register structure in the M6809 microprocessor.

regarded as a single 16-bit accumulator D. There are two index registers, named X and Y, and two stack pointers, S and U. The stack pointer S is the same as the one in the M6800. It is used to maintain the system stack used in subroutine linkage and interrupt servicing. The second stack pointer U enables the programmer to implement a second stack, called the user stack. This stack provides increased flexibility to the programmer, who may use it for passing subroutine parameters or for organizing temporary storage. Both stack pointers can also be used as extra index registers.

The direct page register (DPR) supports a short form of absolute addressing, as will be explained in the next section. The condition code register (CCR) has eight flags, including the M6800 flags C, V, Z, N, I, and H. Three flags, I, F, and E, are used for handling interrupts. Their use will be explained in Section 11.4.

11.3.2 Addressing Modes

The addressing modes in the M6809 have the same basic structure as those in the M6800, but they include some significant additional facilities. Most notably, the indexed mode is enhanced and autoincrement and autodecrement modes are provided. A summary of the addressing modes, as well as their syntax, is given in Table 11.2.

Two versions of the absolute mode are available. The extended mode uses a 16-bit address specified in the second and third bytes of an instruction. The direct mode makes use of the DPR register. The contents of this register are used as the high-order 8 bits of an address. The low-order 8 bits are specified in the second byte of an instruction. Thus, the direct mode results in shorter instructions than the extended mode.

In the direct mode the addressable space is effectively partitioned into 256 pages pointed at by the 8 bits of the DPR register. Each page is 256 bytes long. Recall that in the case of the M6800 only one page, namely page 0, can be addressed in the direct mode. Setting of the DPR is under programmer control. While there is no single instruction provided for this purpose, the desired page address may be placed into the DPR by first loading it into one of the accumulators and then transferring it into the DPR. At start-up time, that is, when a Reset signal is applied to the microprocessor, the DPR register is cleared to zero. Therefore, it will point at page 0 unless its contents are altered as explained above.

When writing a source program, it is possible to specify whether the extended or the direct mode is to be used, as indicated in Table 11.2. For example, the instruction CLR   >LOC uses the extended mode even if the address LOC is on the page pointed at by the DPR. If neither mode is explicitly specified, then the assembler chooses the direct mode if possible. Thus, in the instruction CLR   LOC, the direct mode will be used if LOC is on the page pointed at by the DPR; otherwise the extended mode will be used. It is important to note that during the assembly process the assembler must know what the contents of the DPR will be at run-time. There exists an assembler command for this purpose that has to be included in the source code.

The indexed, autoincrement, and autodecrement modes can use any of the registers X, Y, S, or U, which are denoted as R in Table 11.2. The autoincrement and autodecrement modes result in updating the value in the register R by either 1 or 2, depending upon whether a 1-byte or a 2-byte operand is involved in the instruction.

The indexed mode is considerably more flexible than in the M6800. The index value (offset) may be specified explicitly within an instruction, or it may be the contents of one of the accumulators A, B, or D.

Table 11.2 Syntax for M6809 Addressing Modes

Mode	Syntax	Addressing function
Implied	Included in the OP code	Operand = [Implied register]
Absolute (extended)	>Value or Value	EA = Value
Absolute short (direct)	<Value or Value	EA = [DPR] ‖ SValue
Immediate	#Value	Operand = Value
Indexed	Value,R SValue,R or ACCUM,R	EA = Value + [R] EA = SValue + [R] EA = [ACCUM] + [R]
Autoincrement	,R+ or ,R++	EA = [R] R←[R] + 1 EA = [R] R←[R] + 2
Autodecrement	,−R or ,−−R	R←[R] − 1 EA = [R] R←[R] − 2 EA = [R]
Relative	Value, PCR	EA = Offset + [PC]
Indexed indirect	[Value,R] [SValue,R] or [ACCUM,R]	EA = [EA indexed]
Autoincrement indirect	[,R++]	EA = [EA autoincrement]
Autodecrement indirect	[,−−R]	EA = [EA autodecrement]
Relative indirect	[Value,PCR]	EA = [EA relative]
Extended indirect	[Value]	EA = [Value]

Notes:
R = X, Y, U, or S register
ACCUM = A, B, or D register
EA = effective address
$a\|b$ = 16-bit number where a is the most significant byte and b is the least significant byte
Value = 16-bit number or a name representing it
SValue = 8-bit number or a name representing it
PC = Program Counter
DPR = Direct Page Register

The first byte of any instruction is the OP code. In the M6800 this byte can indicate all allowable addressing modes, as well as the nature of the operation required. However, a single byte does not provide sufficient bit space to denote all of the possible addressing modes in the M6809. A second byte, called the *post-byte* by Motorola, is appended to the OP-code byte in the case of indexed, autoincrement, autodecrement, relative, and extended indirect modes. The

Table 11.3 Post-byte format in M6809

Post-byte bits 7 6 5 4 3 2 1 0	Assembler syntax	Addressing mode
0 r r q q q q q	Q,R	Indexed with 5-bit signed offset
1 r r 0 0 0 0 0	,R+	Autoincrement
1 r r i 0 0 0 1	,R++	
1 r r 0 0 0 1 0	,−R	Autodecrement
1 r r i 0 0 1 1	,−−R	
1 r r i 0 1 0 0	,R	Indexed with zero offset
1 r r i 0 1 0 1	B,R	Indexed with accumulator offset
1 r r i 0 1 1 0	A,R	
1 r r i 1 0 0 0	SValue, R	Indexed with 8-bit signed offset
1 r r i 1 0 0 1	Value,R	Indexed with 16-bit signed offset
1 r r i 1 0 1 1	D, R	Indexed with register D offset
1 r r i 1 1 0 0	Value,PCR	Relative with 8-bit signed offset
1 r r i 1 1 0 1	Value,PCR	Relative with 16-bit signed offset
1 r r 1 1 1 1 1	[Value]	Extended indirect

Notes: rr specifies register R where $0\ 0 \Rightarrow R = X$
$0\ 1 \Rightarrow R = Y$
$1\ 0 \Rightarrow R = U$
$1\ 1 \Rightarrow R = S$
Q = (q q q q q) is a 5-bit signed number
i = 1 specifies indirect address mode

format for the post-byte is shown in Table 11.3. The table is largely self-explanatory. Note that three different sizes of offsets can be specified in the indexed mode. The shortest is a 5-bit offset that is given within the post-byte. Other possibilities are 8- and 16-bit offsets that are specified in 1 or 2 bytes that follow the post-byte. In all cases the offsets are interpreted as signed 2's-complement numbers. Thus, offsets as large as $\pm 2^{15}$ may be used.

The relative mode is indicated as

Value,PCR

where Value is the desired effective address of the operand, usually expressed as a label. At execution time, this address is generated by adding a signed offset to the current value of the PC. The required offset is computed by the assembler and inserted in the instruction. It occupies 1 or 2 bytes following the post-byte, depending on its size. Note that the assembler recognizes the relative mode by the presence of the symbol PCR (program counter relative). Of course, the execution of an instruction using the relative mode is handled in the same way as the indexed mode.

The other addressing modes in Table 11.2 are self-explanatory. We should point out that indirect versions of several modes which do not exist in the M6800 are provided.

11.3.3 Instruction Set

The instruction set of the M6809 is considerably richer than that of the M6800. It is summarized in Table 11.4. Each instruction is given in all allowable addressing modes, stating the OP codes, the number of bytes, the function performed, and the effect on the flags in the CCR register. In order to save space in the table, some instructions are combined. For example, the Add instruction which uses accumulator A has the mnemonic ADDA, and its OP code for the immediate address mode is 8B. The same instruction using accumulator B has the mnemonic ADDB, and its OP code for the immediate mode is CB. The two instructions are combined in the table as ADDA/B, and the immediate mode OP codes are shown as 8B/CB. The number of bytes required in each addressing mode is also given. Note that the entries for the indexed mode are stated as $n+$. This indicates that at least n bytes are needed, but additional bytes may be involved if 8- or 16-bit offsets are used.

The autoincrement, autodecrement, relative, and indirect addressing modes are not shown explicitly in Table 11.4. They are all implemented by means of the post-byte, as indicated in Table 11.3. The OP-code byte of any instruction using these modes is the same as that for the indexed mode.

The number of cycles needed to execute an instruction is not shown in Table 11.4 because of the lack of space. The discussion of execution times in the previous section on the M6800 is also applicable to the M6809.

The M6809 has a number of useful instructions that are not available in the M6800. When parameters have to be passed to subroutines, it is often convenient to deal with the addresses of operands rather than with the operands directly. Thus, a machine instruction which can determine the address of an operand in a simple way is likely to be valuable. The LEA instructions provide a facility of this type. They load the effective address derived in the indexed addressing mode into a designated 16-bit pointer register. For example, suppose that the address of the sixth entry in a character list pointed at by register Y is to be placed in register X. If Y contains the address of the first entry in the list and each entry occupies 1 byte, then the desired operation can be performed with the instruction

LEAX 5,Y

The effective address is computed as $5 + [Y]$, and loaded into register X.

The LEA instructions are useful for writing position-independent code, where data is addressed relative to the current contents of the program counter. For example, register Y can be loaded with the starting address of a list with the instruction

LEAY LIST,PCR

The fact that a signed number (offset) is added to the register contents in the

Table 11.4 M6809 microprocessor instruction set

| | | Address modes | | | | | |
| | | IMMED | | DIRECT | | EXTEND | |
Operation	Mnemonic	OP	#	OP	#	OP	#
Add	ADDA/B	8B/CB	2	9B/DB	2	BB/FB	3
	ADDD	C3	3	D3	2	F3	3
Add with carry	ADCA/B	89/C9	2	99/D9	2	B9/F9	3
Add accum. B to index register X unsigned	ABX						
AND	ANDA/B	84/C4	2	94/D4	2	B4/F4	3
	ANDCC	1C	2				
	CWAI	3C	2				
Bit test	BITA/B	85/C5	2	95/D5	2	B5/F5	3
Clear	CLR			0F	2	7F	3
	CLRA/B						
Compare	CMPA/B	81/C1	2	91/D1	2	B1/F1	3
	CMPD	1083	4	1093	3	10B3	4
	CMPS	118C	4	119C	3	11BC	4
	CMPU	1183	4	1193	3	11B3	4
	CMPX	8C	3	9C	2	BC	3
	CMPY	108C	4	109C	3	10BC	3
Complement (1's)	COM			03	2	73	3
	COMA/B						
Decimal adjust A	DAA						
Decrement	DEC			0A	2	7A	3
	DECA/B						
Exclusive-OR	EORA/B	88/C8	2	98/D8	2	B8/F8	3
Exchange register contents	EXG (R_1, R_2)						
Increment	INC			0C	2	7C	3
	INCA/B						
Load	LDA/B	86/C6	2	96/D6	2	B6/F6	3
	LDD/U	CC/CE	3	DC/DE	2	FC/FE	3
	LDS	10CE	4	10DE	3	10FE	4
	LDX	8E	3	9E	2	BE	3
	LDY	108E	4	109E	3	10BE	4
Load effective address	LEAS/U						
	LEAX/Y						

Address modes INDEX		Address modes IMPLIED		Performed function	Condition code flags affected H	N	Z	V	C
OP	#	OP	#						
AB/EB	2+			A←[A]+[M]	x	x	x	x	x
E3	2+			D←[D]+[M]	x	x	x	x	x
A9/E9	2+			A←[A]+[M]+[C]	x	x	x	x	x
		3A	1	X←[X]+[B] (unsigned)					
A4/E4	2+			A←[A]∧[M]		x	x	0	
				CCR←[CCR]∧[M]	x	x	x	x	x
				CCR←[CCR]∧[M] store registers on S stack; wait for interrupt	x	x	x	x	x
A5/E5	2+			[A]∧[M]		x	x	0	
6F	2+			M←0		0	1	0	0
		4F/5F	1	A←0		0	1	0	0
A1/E1	2+			[A]−[M]		x	x	x	x
10A3	3+			[D]−[M]		x	x	x	x
11AC	3+			[S]−[M]		x	x	x	x
11A3	3+			[U]−[M]		x	x	x	x
AC	2+			[X]−[M]		x	x	x	x
10AC	3+			[Y]−[M]		x	x	x	x
63	2+			M←[M̄]		x	x	0	1
		43/53	1	A←[Ā]		x	x	0	1
		19	1	Converts binary sum of BCD characters into BCD format		x	x	0	x
6A	2+			M←[M]−1		x	x	x	
		4A/5A	1	A←[A]−1		x	x	x	
A8/E8	2+			A←[A]⊕[M]		x	x	0	
		1E	2	R₁↔R₂					
6C	2+			M←[M]+1		x	x	x	
		4C/5C	1	A←[A]+1		x	x	x	
A6/E6	2+			A←[M]		x	x	0	
EC/EE	2+			D←[M]		x	x	0	
10EE	3+			S←[M]		x	x	0	
AE	2+			X←[M]		x	x	0	
10AE	3+			Y←[M]		x	x	0	
32/33	2+			S←EA					
30/31	2+			X←EA	x				

Table 11.4 M6809 microprocessor instruction set *(Continued)*

		Address modes					
		IMMED		DIRECT		EXTEND	
Operation	Mnemonic	OP	#	OP	#	OP	#
Multiply	MUL						
Negate (2's complement)	NEG NEGA/B			00	2	70	3
No operation	NOP						
OR (inclusive)	ORA/B ORCC	8A/CA 1A	2 2	9A/DA	2	BA/FA	3
Push	PSHS/U (reg. list)						
Pull	PULS/U (reg. list)						
Rotate left	ROL ROLA/B			09	2	79	3
Rotate right	ROR RORA/B			06	2	76	3
Shift left (arithmetic)	ASL ASLA/B			08	2	78	3
Shift right (arithmetic)	ASR ASRA/B			07	2	77	3
Shift left (logic)	LSL LSLA/B			08	2	78	3
Shift right (logic)	LSR LSRA/B			04	2	74	3
Sign extend B into A	SEX						
Store	STA/B STD STS STU/X STY			97/D7 DD 10DF DF/9F 109F	2 2 3 2 3	B7/F7 FD 10FF FF/BF 10BF	3 3 4 3 4
Subtract	SUBA/B SUBD	80/C0 83	2 3	90/D0 93	2 2	B0/F0 B3	3 3
Subtract with carry	SBCA/B	82/C2	2	92/D2	2	B2/F2	3
Transfer register to register	TFR (R_1,R_2)						
Test	TST TSTA/B			0D	2	7D	3

Address modes				Performed function	Condition code flags affected				
INDEX		IMPLIED			H	N	Z	V	C
OP	#	OP	#						
		3D	1	D←[A]×[B] (unsigned)		x			x
60	2+			M←0−[M]		x	x	x	x
		40/50	1	A←0−[A]		x	x	x	x
		12	1	No operation					
AA/EA	2+			A←[A]∨[M]		x	x	0	
				CCR←[CCR]∨[M]	x	x	x	x	x
		34/36	2	Push registers on S stack					
		35/37	2	Pull registers from S stack					
69	2+			M (C←b7...b0←)		x	x	x	x
		49/59	1	A		x	x	x	x
66	2+			M (→C→b7...b0)		x	x		x
		46/56	1	A		x	x		x
68	2+			M (C←b7...b0←0)		x	x	x	x
		48/58	1	A		x	x	x	x
67	2+			M (b7...b0→C)		x	x		x
		47/57	1	A		x	x		x
68	2+			M (C←b7...b0←0)		x	x	x	x
		48/58	1	A		x	x	x	x
64	2+			M (b7...b0→C)	0	x			x
		44/54	1	A	0	x			x
		1D	1	Set all bits in A to equal the sign bit in B		x	x	0	
A7/E7	2+			M←[A]		x	x	0	
ED	2+			M←[D]		x	x	0	
10EF	3+			M←[S]		x	x	0	
EF/AF	2+			M←[U]		x	x	0	
10AF	3+			M←[Y]		x	x	0	
A0/E0	2+			A←[A]−[M]		x	x	x	x
A3	2+			D←[D]−[M]		x	x	x	x
A2/E2	2+			A←[A]−[M]−[C]		x	x	x	x
		1F	2	R₂←[R₁]					
6D	2+			[M]−0		x	x	0	
		4D/5D	1	[A]−0		x	x	0	

Table 11.4 (*Continued*)

Operation	Mnemonic	Address modes										Branch test
		RELATIVE		DIRECT		EXTEND		INDEX		IMPLIED		
		OP	#	OP	#	OP	#	OP	#	OP	#	
Branch always	BRA	20	2									None
	LBRA	16	3									
Branch if carry clear	BCC	24	2									$[C] = 0$
	LBCC	1024	4									
Branch if carry set	BCS	25	2									$[C] = 1$
	LBCS	1025	4									
Branch if $= 0$	BEQ	27	2									$[Z] = 1$
	LBEQ	1027	4									
Branch if ≥ 0	BGE	2C	2									$[N] \oplus [V] = 0$
	LBGE	102C	4									
Branch if > 0	BGT	2E	2									$[Z] \vee ([N] \oplus [V]) = 0$
	LBGT	102E	4									
Branch if higher	BHI	22	2									$[C] \vee [Z] = 0$
	LBHI	1022	4									
Branch if higher or same	BHS	24	2									$[C] = 0$
	LBHS	1024	4									
Branch if ≤ 0	BLE	2F	2									$[Z] \vee ([N] \oplus [V]) = 1$
	LBLE	102F	4									
Branch if lower	BLO	25	2									$[C] = 1$
	LBLO	1025	4									
Branch if lower or same	BLS	23	2									$[C] \vee [Z] = 1$
	LBLS	1023	4									

Operation	Mnemonic	Relative OP	#	Direct OP	#	Extended OP	#	Indexed OP	#	Inherent OP	#	Condition
Branch if < 0	BLT / LBLT	2D / 102D	2 / 4									$[N \vee V] = 1$
Branch if minus	BMI / LBMI	2B / 102B	2 / 4									$[N] = 1$
Branch if ≠ 0	BNE / LBNE	26 / 1026	2 / 4									$[Z] = 0$
Branch if plus	BPL / LBPL	2A / 102A	2 / 4									$[N] = 0$
Branch never	BRN / LBRN	21 / 1021	2 / 4									None
Branch if overflow clear	BVC / LBVC	28 / 1028	2 / 4									$[V] = 0$
Branch if overflow set	BVS / LBVS	29 / 1029	2 / 4									$[V] = 1$
Branch to subroutine	BSR / LBSR	8D / 17	2 / 3									
Jump	JMP			0E	2	7E	3	6E	2+			
Jump to subroutine	JSR			9D	2	BD	3	AD	2+			
Return from interrupt	RTI									3B	1	
Return from subroutine	RTS									39	1	
Software interrupt	SWI / SWI2 / SWI3									3F / 103F / 113F	1 / 2 / 2	
Wait for interrupt	SYNC									13	1	

Notes: OP = OP code; # = number of bytes in the instruction; EA = effective address; For two-byte operands: R ← [M] implies R_H ← [M] and R_L ← [M + 1]

LEA instructions makes these instructions suitable for doing addition and subtraction on the pointer registers. A register, say X, may be decremented with the instruction

$$\text{LEAX} \quad -1,X$$

One of the deficiencies of the M6800 is that its branch instructions use only 1 byte to specify a signed offset from the program counter. This means that the range of the offset is limited to $-128 \le \text{offset} \le +127$. In the M6809, a much wider range of branching is possible, since for each branch condition two instructions are provided: a branch with an 8-bit signed offset and a long branch with a 16-bit signed offset.

Most instructions that use the implied addressing mode are only 1 byte long. There are four exceptions where it is necessary to append a second byte to indicate the registers involved. In EXG and TFR instructions registers R_1 and R_2 may be any pair of 8-bit registers or any pair of 16-bit registers. The assembler syntax in this case is

$$\text{EXG} \quad R1,R2$$

In the PSH and PUL instructions, the second byte indicates which of the eight CPU registers are to be pushed on the stack or pulled from the stack. Bits b_7 to b_0 are used to specify PC, U or S, Y, X, DP, B, A, and CCR, in that order. This is also the order in which the registers are stored on the stack. Some or all of these registers are transferred, as denoted by the instruction. For example, the instruction

$$\text{PSHS} \quad \text{PC,U,B,A}$$

pushes the four indicated registers on the stack. When assembled, the second byte of this instruction would have bits b_7, b_6, b_2, and b_1 set to 1, and the remaining bits equal to 0.

Comparison of Tables 11.1 and 11.4 reveals that the M6809 includes most M6800 instructions. Some M6800 instructions are not included directly in the M6809 set, but their functional capability is available in different forms. For example, the M6800 instructions that increment and decrement the index register and the stack pointer can be realized with the LEA instructions as explained above.

11.3.4 Example

Let us reconsider the BCD subtraction example from the previous section. Figure 11.8 shows how this task can be implemented using the M6809. The program uses the index registers X and Y as pointers to the BCD operands involved in the process. This provides two significant advantages over the M6800 implementation in Figure 11.6. Firstly, the program can be used as a subroutine, where it is only necessary to initialize the X and Y registers with the memory addresses of the BCD operands. Secondly, this program does not have the

Location (hex)	Contents (hex)	Assembler format for instructions		Comments
		NUMP	EQU $2000	
		NUMQ	EQU $3000	
			ORG $100	
100	8E		LDX #NUMP	Register X points to NUMP.
101	20			
102	00			
103	10		LDY #NUMQ	Register Y points to NUMQ.
104	8E			
105	30			
106	00			
107	C6		LDB #7	Set B as a byte counter.
108	07			
109	1A		ORCC #1	Set carry for 10's complement.
10A	01			
10B	86	SLOOP	LDA #$99	Form 10's complement of Q for one digit pair.
10C	99			
10D	89		ADCA #0	
10E	00			
10F	A0		SUBA B,Y	Form P − Q in binary.
110	A5			
111	AB		ADDA B,X	
112	85			
113	19		DAA	Decimal adjust.
114	A7		STA B,X	Store the digit pair of the difference into NUMP.
115	85			
116	5A		DECB	
117	2C		BGE SLOOP	Loop until last byte is processed.
118	F2			

Figure 11.8 Program for subtraction of 16-digit BCD operands for M6809.

restriction of requiring the BCD operands to be stored on page 0 in the memory. This restriction in the previous example was due to the fact that the M6800 indexed addressing mode allows only a 1-byte offset from the value in the index register. The index register was used to scan across both numbers P and Q, where the contents of IX was the distance in bytes from the addresses of the high-order two digits of these numbers. Then, using the 8-bit offsets in the indexed mode for these addresses means that the numbers must be on page 0. Of course, this restriction could have been avoided in the program of Figure 11.6 by loading and storing the IX register twice during each iteration, using two memory locations to hold the updated addresses of each digit pair of P and Q as they are being scanned. However, such a change would increase both the memory space needed and the execution time.

In the M6809 program in Figure 11.8, the BCD numbers and the program itself are placed in specific memory locations by the three assembler commands at the beginning of the program. This was done to enable the reader to see what the actual assembled object code would look like when loaded in the memory. Note that the memory addresses and their contents are shown in the figure.

11.4 INPUT/OUTPUT IN MICROPROCESSOR SYSTEMS

A user of a microprocessor system will derive many benefits from a good understanding of its hardware characteristics. Perhaps the most important hardware aspect is the I/O structure. A thorough appreciation of the I/O details, from both the software and hardware points of view, is likely to prove beneficial in many ways. This section will deal with I/O in microprocessor systems in some detail. Applicable techniques and typical interfaces will be discussed. In order to give the reader a feeling for the practical complexity of I/O structures, some detailed examples using the M6809 microprocesor will be given.

11.4.1 Control of I/O Activity

Two basic schemes for controlling I/O activity were discussed in Chapter 6. The first involved continuous checking of the status of an I/O device by the CPU. The second was based on interrupts raised by a device to indicate changes in its status. These schemes are applicable to all computers, regardless of size, and are commonly used in microprocessor systems.

Continuous status checking is the simplest to implement. It requires the I/O device status information to be available in the I/O interface in a form suitable for reading by the CPU. A practical way of realizing this scheme is to include one or more status registers which can be accessed as addressable locations in the I/O interface. The actual arrangement is influenced mostly by the nature of the I/O devices and the structure of the interface chips used. It is essentially independent of the choice of the microprocessor (that is, the CPU) because most microprocessors are capable of executing simple instructions to poll these addressable locations.

Interrupt-driven I/O is more complex. The interrupt mechanism that can be implemented is largely dependent upon the corresponding capability of the microprocessor used. Varying degrees of interrupt-handling capability are found in commercially available microprocessors. While the fundamental principles are those outlined in Chapter 6, the scope of interrupt structure and capability may differ considerably for different microprocessors.

Let us consider the interrupt characteristics of the M6809 microprocessor. The M6809 chip has four input connections, that is, pins, dedicated to interrupts. An active signal on one of these inputs indicates an interrupt request. The four interrupt inputs are: Reset, interrupt request (IRQ), fast interrupt request (FIRQ), and nonmaskable interrupt (NMI). We should note that the active signals on these inputs are negative-going signals. It is customary in the technical literature to indicate this fact by writing a bar (as in complementation) over the names of such inputs. Thus, the M6809 interrupt inputs are denoted as $\overline{\text{Reset}}$, $\overline{\text{IRQ}}$, $\overline{\text{FIRQ}}$, and $\overline{\text{NMI}}$.

The IRQ is the most basic maskable interrupt and is found in almost all computers. It is enabled or disabled by setting the I flag (bit 4) in the CCR register to 0 or 1, respectively. If an IRQ request arrives when the I flag is 0, the M6809 will set the I flag to 1 (disabling further IRQ requests) and store its entire state on the S stack. Then, it will enter the interrupt-service routine.

The entire state includes all registers in the processor. It takes considerable time to store these registers. In some real-time applications it is impractical to have to spend this time in saving the registers, particularly if the interrupt-service routine will not affect the contents of most registers. A faster response can be obtained with the FIRQ request. In this case, only the contents of the program counter and the CCR register are stored on the stack. The FIRQ interrupt is masked with the F flag (bit 6) in the CCR in the same way as the IRQ interrupt is masked by the I flag. Since the FIRQ has higher priority than the IRQ, its occurrence sets the I flag, as well as the F flag, to 1.

The difference between the IRQ and the FIRQ is the number of registers saved. Since both interrupts are handled by interrupt-service routines of similar type, routines that end with an RTI (Return-from-Interrupt) instruction, it is essential to have some mechanism for remembering the type of interrupt that has occurred. This is done by including the E flag (bit 7) in the CCR. In response to an IRQ request, it is set to 1 before the contents of the CCR are stored, as part of the entire state. It is cleared to 0 if an FIRQ occurs. Then, when a Return-from-Interrupt is performed, after the completion of the interrupt-service routine, the state of bit 7 in the status word that is reloaded into the CCR indicates whether or not all processor registers were saved and hence must be reloaded.

The M6809 also provides a nonmaskable interrupt NMI. This interrupt request cannot be ignored. The interrupt sequence starts when the M6809 detects a negative-going transition on its NMI input. Thus, the NMI is an edge-triggered interrupt. This means that it is dangerous to connect more than one device to the NMI input because if two or more devices activate the NMI line at the same time, only one interrupt request will be recognized. The NMI interrupt sets both I and F flags to 1, giving it higher priority than either IRQ or FIRQ.

The highest priority interrupt is Reset. Its activation resets the M6809 to the initial state. It is used to start the operation of a microprocessor system at power-up time or in cases where the computation has gone hopelessly astray and system software cannot be used to recover from the inadvertently reached, undesired state. Activation of the Reset input disables IRQ and FIRQ interrupts by setting I and F flags to 1, clears the contents of the DPR register, and then starts the execution of the Reset routine. The reader should note that while we have referred to Reset as an interrupt, its function is somewhat different. When Reset is activated, the current state of the CPU is abandoned. Hence, upon completion of the Reset routine, no RTI instruction can be meaningfully executed.

In addition to the hardware interrupts, the M6809 has three software interrupts generated by the execution of machine instructions SWI, SWI2, and SWI3. The entire processor state is saved on the stack for these interrupts. The SWI interrupt has higher priority than IRQ or FIRQ, but SWI2 and SWI3 have lower priority.

An interrupt-service routine is associated with each interrupt. The starting addresses of these routines are stored in predetermined locations in the memory, as shown in Figure 11.9. Two bytes are needed to store each 16-bit address.

The M6809 has no hardware means for distinguishing interrupt requests coming from two or more devices connected to the same interrupt input. Software polling may be used to identify the interrupting devices.

11.4.2 I/O Interface Circuits

Chapter 6 dealt with the general problem of interfacing I/O devices to a computer bus. In the microprocessor environment it is common to use interface chips, such as the PIA and the ACIA described in Section 11.1. In this section we will consider a parallel interface circuit, along the lines of the PIA, to illustrate in more detail the nature and complexity of interfacing techniques.

The diagram in Figure 11.2 shows a parallel interface, having two ports that handle 8 bits of data each. A port includes input and output data paths and

Interrupt	Memory location of interrupt vector
Reset	FFFE, FFFF
NMI	FFFC, FFFD
SWI	FFFA, FFFB
IRQ	FFF8, FFF9
FIRQ	FFF6, FFF7
SWI2	FFF4, FFF5
SWI3	FFF2, FFF3

Figure 11.9 Memory locations where addresses of interrupt-service routines are stored in M6809.

control information, all of which are accessible as addressable memory locations. Instead of pursuing the PIA example, we will define a simplified version of a typical interface that will allow us to discuss the relevant issues without having to worry about peculiarities of a specific product.

Figure 11.10 shows the block diagram of a parallel interface circuit (PIC). It has two 8-bit I/O ports, labelled A and B. Each port has three registers directly associated with it. The input (IR) and output (OR) registers hold 8-bit data during input and output transfers. A data direction register (DDR) determines the direction of the I/O transfer for each data line in a port. If bit k ($k = 0, 1, \ldots, 7$) in the DDRA (DDRB) is 0, then line k in port A(B) acts as an input line. If this bit is 1, then the corresponding line acts as an output line.

There are two control lines used with each port. CA1(CB1) is an input line that may, for example, be used by an I/O device to indicate its busy/idle status. CA2(CB2) is a bidirectional line for exchange of control signals between the PIC and a connected device. The nature of signals on these control lines is determined by the contents of the control signal register (CSR), as will be explained later.

The control lines can be used by the I/O devices to raise interrupt requests. The status of these lines is recorded in the status flag register (SFR). This information is used to activate the $\overline{\text{IRQ}}$ (interrupt-request) line of the microprocessor bus. The activation of the $\overline{\text{IRQ}}$ line is dependent upon the setting of bits in the interrupt-enable register (IER).

On the processor bus side, the PIC has eight data bus drivers and receivers,

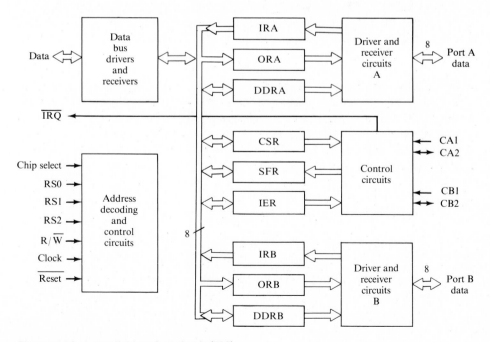

Figure 11.10 A parallel interface circuit (PIC).

as well as address decoding and control circuits. The addressing information consists of a chip select input, register select (RS) inputs which identify specific registers, and the R/$\overline{\text{W}}$ input that indicates whether a read or a write operation is required. The clock input allows synchronization of operations in the PIC with the rest of the system. The $\overline{\text{Reset}}$ input is used to clear all registers in the PIC, and it is usually connected to the reset inputs of all other units in the system, including the one in the CPU.

The registers in the PIC are addressable as memory locations. Figure 11.11 shows a map of the registers along with the addressing codes that distinguish them. Since there are nine registers, it is necessary to use four input signals to specify any given register. The three register select signals, RS0, RS1, and RS2, and the R/$\overline{\text{W}}$ control input are used for this purpose. Note that the same value of RS inputs is used to refer to both the input and the output registers in each port. They are distinguished by the value of the R/$\overline{\text{W}}$ input.

In order to access the PIC from the microprocessor bus, the chip select input must be activated. A decoder circuit may be used for this purpose, in which case the high-order 13 bits of a 16-bit address are the inputs to the decoder. When an address assigned to a PIC register appears on the bus, the decoder output activates the chip select input. The remaining three address lines are connected directly to the RS0, RS1, and RS2 inputs.

A set of distinct input, output, and data-direction registers is included in each port. Additional control and status information is incorporated into CSR, SFR, and IER registers, which serve both ports as indicated in the figure.

The exact meaning of the bits in the PIC registers is described in Figure 11.12. The figure deals only with the bits pertaining to port A, but it is assumed that the same meaning applies to the corresponding bits for port B. Most entries in this figure are self-explanatory. Note that interrupt requests can be generated through the CA1(CB1) and CA2(CB2) control lines. Thus, there are four possible sources of interrupt requests, each of which can be disabled (masked) by clearing the corresponding bit in the IER register. An IRQ request to the CPU is made if an enabled interrupt request appears on a control line. It is useful to be able to easily set or clear individual bits in the IER without disturbing the rest of the bits. This can be done with the aid of bit 7 in the IER. When this Set/$\overline{\text{Clear}}$ bit is a 1 in an 8-bit word that the CPU writes into the IER, then for each 1 in bit positions 0 through 3 of the word, the corresponding IER bit is set to 1, while the state of other bits remains unchanged. Similarly, when bit 7 is a 0, then for each 1 in a word written into the IER the corresponding IER bit is cleared to 0.

Control lines CA2 and CB2 can be used in a very flexible fashion. Figure 11.13 gives a description of the possible modes for CA2. The mode information for CA2 is specified in bits 1 through 3 of the CSR register. The CB2 line has the same modes of operation, specified by CSR bits 5 through 7. The description of the modes in the figure should be self-explanatory. Note that an interrupt request can be raised by either a positive or a negative transition on the CA2 line. The interrupt flags in the SFR can be cleared either by performing a data

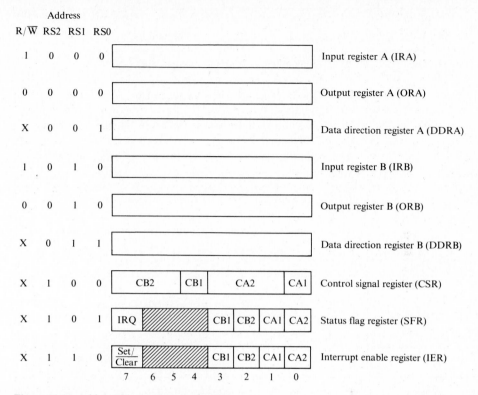

Figure 11.11 Addressable registers in the PIC.

transfer to or from the port, or by writing new control information into the SFR. Other modes allow for implementation of handshake control and an acknowledgement scheme where a pulse, one clock cycle in duration, is sent to the connected device. It is also possible to set the state of the CA2 line directly from the CPU, independent of the device connected to it.

In order to show how a chip having the structure of the PIC may be used in a microprocessor system, we will give two simple examples.

11.4.3 Example 1

Let us assume that a keyboard is to be connected to a printer, so that 8-bit encoded characters can be transferred from the keyboard to the printer. The keyboard has eight data pins that display the encoded character corresponding to a pressed key. It also has one control line to indicate that valid data is available on the data pins. The printer has eight data input connections and two control lines. One control line informs the printer that data is available, and the other indicates the busy/idle status of the printer.

Bit position	Bit state	Function
DDRA$_k$ (k = 0, 1, . . ., 7)	0	Line k in port A acts as an input line.
	1	Line k in port A acts as an output line.
CSR$_0$	0	Negative (high to low) is the active transition on the CA1 line.
	1	Positive (low to high) is the active transition on the CA1 line.
SFR$_0$	0	Indicates that no active transition has been received on the CA2 line.
	1	Indicates that an active transition has been received on the CA2 line.
SFR$_1$	0	Indicates that no active transition has been received on the CA1 line.
	1	Indicates that an active transition has been received on the CA1 line. This flag is cleared by reading from IRA or writing into ORA.
SFR$_7$	IRQ	IRQ = SFR$_3$·IER$_3$ + SFR$_2$·IER$_2$ + SFR$_1$·IER$_1$ + SFR$_0$·IER$_0$
IER$_{0,1}$	0	Disable the corresponding interrupt.
	1	Enable the corresponding interrupt.
IER$_7$	0, 1	Used to control the setting or clearing of bits in the IER. See the explanation in the text.

Figure 11.12 Meaning of bits in PIC, for port A.

The desired connection may be achieved with the aid of a PIC, as shown in Figure 11.14. The keyboard is connected to port A, with the CA1 line serving to indicate the availability of the data. The printer is connected to port B, with control lines CB1 and CB2 indicating the availability of data and the status of the printer. An M6809 microprocessor is the CPU used to execute the required transfers. The task to be implemented is:

- The keyboard indicates that valid data is ready on its data pins by a positive-going signal on the Data Ready line.
- The CPU polls the status of the keyboard to determine when the data is available.
- The CPU transfers the 8-bit character to the printer and informs it that data is available for printing.

CSR_3	CSR_2	CSR_1	Mode
0	0	0	Automatic flag clear—SFR_0 is set by a negative transition on the CA2 line; it is cleared by reading from IRA or writing into ORA.
0	0	1	Independent flag clear—SFR_0 is set by a negative transition on the CA2 line; it is cleared by writing into SFR_0.
0	1	0	Automatic flag clear—SFR_0 is set by a positive transition on the CA2 line; it is cleared by reading from IRA or writing into ORA.
0	1	1	Independent flag clear—SFR_0 is set by a positive transition on the CA2 line; it is cleared by writing into SFR_0.
1	0	0	Handshake mode—CA2 goes low upon reading from IRA or writing into ORA; it is restored high by an active transition on the CA1 line.
1	0	1	Pulse acknowledgment mode—CA2 goes low for one clock cycle after reading from IRA or writing into ORA.
1	1	0	Direct CA2 control mode—CA2 is held low.
1	1	1	Direct CA2 control mode—CA2 is held high.

Figure 11.13 Modes of control for the CA2 line in PIC.

- The printer indicates its availability to receive another character by a negative-going signal on the Printer Ready line.

In order to meet these requirements, the PIC must be initialized as follows:

Port A

- Data lines of port A must be configured as inputs; therefore all bits in DDRA must be cleared to 0.
- CA1 is used as the Data Ready line. It must be conditioned to respond to positive transitions from the keyboard. Thus, the control bit CSR_0 must be set to 1, as shown in Figure 11.12.

Port B

- Data lines of port B must be configured as outputs; therefore all bits in DDRB must be set to 1.
- CB2 is used as the Data Available line. A full handshake between the PIC and the printer is required. Thus, the handshake mode in Figure 11.13 is chosen, which requires the setting of control bits $CSR_7 = 1$, $CSR_6 = 0$, and $CSR_5 = 0$.
- CB1 is used as the Printer Ready line. It must be conditioned to recognize negative transitions, thus $CSR_4 = 0$.

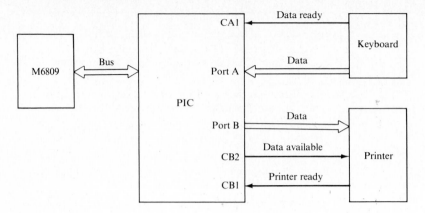

Figure 11.14 A parallel interface circuit connecting a keyboard to a printer.

This means that the desired CSR bit assignment is

$$1\ 0\ 0\ 0\ 0\ 0\ 0\ 1 \rightarrow 81_{16}$$

Note that CA2 is not used; hence it can be specified in any mode (0 in our example).

An M6809 program capable of performing the required task is given in Figure 11.15. It includes an initializing sequence that configures the PIC according to the above stated requirements. Note that it also disables interrupts because CPU polling of the device status is the specified I/O mode of operation.

The reader should note that the chosen example is merely intended to illustrate how a typical commercially available parallel interface integrated circuit may be used to connect to input and output devices. The actual arrangement of transferring characters directly from a keyboard to a printer is unlikely to be of significant value. In practical applications, the CPU would perform some manipulation on the input characters before sending the results to a printer.

11.4.4 Example 2

In the previous example, we considered a simple connection to a keyboard and a printer, where the CPU controlled the I/O activity by polling the status of both devices. Let us modify the arrangement by using interrupts in dealing with the keyboard. Let the required operation be as follows.

A line of alphanumeric characters is to be read from the keyboard and stored in the main memory. The availability of a new character is indicated to the CPU by an IRQ interrupt. When a carriage return is encountered, the stored line of text is processed by calling a subroutine LINE. Processed results are printed on the printer.

*Initializing sequence for the PIC

```
            LDA     #$0F        Disable interrupts.
            STA     IER
            CLR     DDRA        Port A lines are inputs.
            LDA     #$FF
            STA     DDRB        Port B lines are outputs.
            LDA     #$81        Load the required pattern into the CSR.
            STA     CSR
                     ⋮
```

*Transfer one character from keyboard to printer

```
WAITR       LDA     SFR         Test keyboard status, on line CA1.
            ANDA    #$02
            BEQ     WAITR       Wait if character not ready.
            LDB     IRA         Read character from keyboard.
WAITW       LDA     SFR         Test printer status, on line CB1.
            ANDA    #$08
            BEQ     WAITW       Wait if printer not ready.
            STB     ORB         Send the character to printer.
                     ⋮
```

Figure 11.15 A program for Example 1.

The physical connection can be made as in Figure 11.14. Moreover, the control signalling between the PIC and the I/O devices will be the same as in Example 1. However, in the present case an active transition on the CA1 line will be used to raise an IRQ interrupt request.

The required initializing sequence is shown in Figure 11.16. It configures port A as input and port B as output, and sets up the control lines as in Example 1. Assuming that the first line is to be stored in a main memory buffer starting at location LOC, this address is placed in a pointer location MEMADR which will subsequently be updated to contain the address where the next character is to be stored. Next, interrupts generated by active transitions on the CA1 line are enabled. Note that this is done by writing a word with bits 7 and 1 equal to 1 ($= 82_{16}$), into the IER. Finally, the IRQ interrupt mask bit in the CCR register is cleared.

An interrupt-service routine is also shown in the figure. It first checks to see if the IRQ request was caused by the CA1 line. Should the request be from some other source, either in the same PIC or another device that may be connected to the $\overline{\text{IRQ}}$ input of the M6809, a branch is made to the routine OTHER. Index register X is used in the autoincrement mode to access successive memory locations in transferring characters from the IRA into the memory buffer. Upon encountering a carriage return ($= 0D_{16}$), a call to the line processing subroutine LINE is made.

The reader should compare this example with that presented in Figure 6.11. Both examples deal with the same task of reading a line from a keyboard. Their

```
*Initialization sequence for the PIC
              LDA      #$0F          Disable interrupts.
              STA      IER
              CLR      DDRA          Port A lines are inputs.
              LDA      #$FF
              STA      DDRB          Port B lines are outputs.
              LDA      #$81          Load the required pattern
              STA      CSR             into the CSR.
              LDX      #LOC          Place the starting address of
              STX      MEMADR          the memory buffer in MEMADR.
              LDA      #$82          Enable interrupt requests
              STA      IER             on the CA1 line.
              ANDCC    #%11101111    Clear IRQ mask in CCR.
                •
                •
                •
```

```
*Interrupt-service routine for reading one character.

KBDINT   LDA      SFR          Check if the interrupt was
         ANDA     #$02            originated by the CA1 line.
         BEQ      OTHER        Some other interrupt occurred.
         LDX      MEMADR       Use register X as a buffer pointer.
         LDA      IRA          Tranfer a character into the
         STA      ,X+            memory buffer.
         STX      MEMADR       Store the updated pointer value.
         CMPA     #$0D         Check if carriage return.
         BNE      DONE
         BSR      LINE         Process input line.
DONE     RTI
OTHER    Check for other sources of interrupts.
```

Figure 11.16 Initializing sequence and interrupt-service routine for Example 2.

implementations reflect the differences in structure of the M6809 and the PDP-11 computers.

11.4.5 Commercial Interface Chips

In order to simplify the discussion and focus on the most basic aspects of I/O interfacing, we defined the PIC. While the PIC is not a commercial product, it has a structure that corresponds closely to Motorola's PIA. It also resembles the main part of the VIA (Versatile Interface Adapter), produced by Synertek.[11.5] In addition to two parallel ports, the VIA contains a serial port and two timers. The serial port allows connection to devices that can handle data in a bit-serial manner only. The timers consist of counters that can be used for counting externally produced pulses and for generation of programmable-frequency square wave signals.

Numerous other interface chips are available. They support various forms of serial and parallel data transfer schemes. Many of these chips incorporate useful timing capabilities. These I/O interface chips can often be used with a number of different microprocessors. Their versatility is an important characterisitic.

11.5 MOTOROLA M68000 MICROPROCESSOR

The development of microprocessors has been spectacular. Four-bit micro-processors have been used in consumer products such as pocket calculators and digital watches, as well as in industrial machine controllers. More complex applications cannot be supported adequately by these rather limited processors. Eight-bit microprocessors, such as the M6800, the M6809, Intel's 8085, and Zilog's Z80[11.6] are highly suitable for use in a host of applications, including personal computers, word processors, graphics terminals, video games, measuring instruments, and telephone switchboards. However, the 8-bit word length is restrictive enough to make these devices unsuitable for more demanding applications traditionally requiring the use of minicomputers.

By 1980 the advances in VLSI technology made it possible to fabricate 16-bit microprocessors. Some well-known examples are Motorola's M68000, Intel's 8086,[11.7] Zilog's Z8000,[11.8] and National's 16032.[11.9] These are powerful and sophisticated processors with sizeable addressing space. They are capable of performing computing tasks usually associated with minicomputers and perhaps even larger computers. In this section we will examine some features of the M68000, as an illustration of this class of processors. The full instruction set for the M68000 is given in Appendix C.

11.5.1 M68000 Structure

One of the important requirements of any computer is that it should be easy to use. This means that writing application programs for it should be made as easy as possible, which in turn implies that programs should be written mostly in high-level languages. A primary design consideration for any processor is that it be suitable for use with one or more high-level programming languages. This means that it should be easy for a compiler to generate efficient object code for source programs written in a high-level language. While 8-bit microprocessors have been severely handicapped in this respect by their size, their 16-bit successors have reached the point where the desired features can be readily provided. As discussed in Section 3.3, these features include a large addressable space, flexible addressing modes, a reasonably large number of CPU registers, and a set of instructions that facilitate implementation of high-level language constructs.

The M68000 was designed with the objective of facilitating both assembly and high-level language programming. It uses 24-bit addresses, resulting in a 16M-byte addressable space. External data is handled in words of 16 bits. Thus, the M68000 chip needs 40 pins just to accommodate the address and data lines.

A number of control lines are also necessary. The total number of pins is 64, requiring a relatively large IC package.

The register structure of the M68000 is shown in Figure 11.17. The registers are 32 bits long. In order to allow some flexibility, it is possible to deal with shorter operands in a register. In particular, *byte* operands and 16-bit *word* operands can be used, in addition to 32-bit *long-word* operands. The word and long-word operands can be used in all data and address registers, while byte operands may be used only in data registers. Byte and word operands are always located in the low-order bit positions of a register, as indicated in Figure 11.17. They can be used by instructions without altering the contents of the remaining high-order bits of a register. They can also have their values sign-extended into the high-order bits.

The data registers serve as general-purpose accumulators and as counters. The address registers normally hold addresses, thus serving as location pointers. Both data and address registers can also be used as index registers.

One address register, A_7, has the special function of being a stack pointer. In fact, there are two stack pointers, both addressable as A_7. The M68000 has two basic modes of operation, called the *supervisor* and *user* modes. In the supervisor mode all instructions can be used, while in the user mode certain instructions are not allowed. The supervisor and user stack pointers, shown in Figure 11.17, are associated with their respective modes. Thus, two separate stacks are maintained. The mode of operation determines which pointer is used when register A_7 is named in an instruction.

The address registers and address calculations involve 32 bits. However, having derived the 32-bit effective address of an operand, only the least significant 24 bits are used and transmitted on the address bus. Recall that the M68000 processor chip has 24 address pins. The program counter, like the address registers, contains 32 bits, but only 24 are used to address the main memory.

The last register shown in Figure 11.17 is the status register SR. It contains standard condition code flags C, V, Z, and N, as well as the "extend" flag X. The latter flag is used to facilitate implementation of multiple precision arithmetic operations. It is affected only by the arithmetic instructions.

Bits b_{10-8} of the SR register are the interrupt mask. Their value, 0 to 7, determines the priority levels of interrupts that will be accepted by the processor. At any given time the processor will respond only to those interrupts whose priority level is above that denoted by the interrupt mask.

The S bit in the SR determines the choice between the supervisor and user modes of operation of the M68000. When it is set to 1, the processor operates in the supervisor mode. When S = 0, the processor is in the user mode.

The last bit in the SR to be discussed is the trace bit T, which is used for program debugging purposes. The task of debugging a program is often arduous. The detection of subtle errors frequently hinges upon the availability of detailed information that the programmer can obtain during execution of an erroneous program. We have not yet discussed the problem of debugging machine language programs. This is an important practical issue. Since the existence of a trace bit

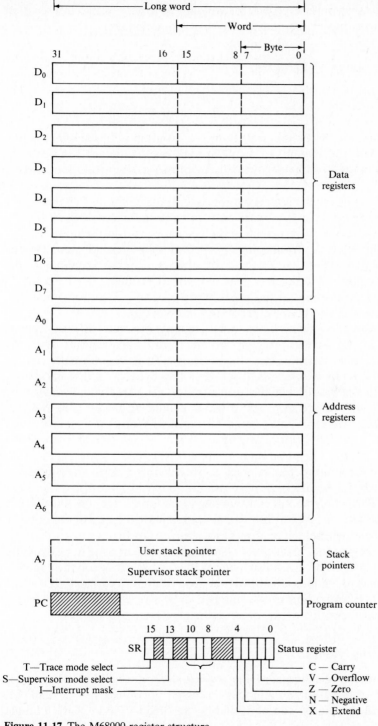

Figure 11.17 The M68000 register structure.

in a processor is useful in this respect, we will digress briefly from our discussion of the M68000 to consider the question of program debugging.

Commonly used tools for debugging are:

- Single-step execution of a program
- Breakpoints
- Program trace
- Memory dump

The single-step feature stops the execution of a program after each instruction and usually displays the contents of the CPU registers. Execution is resumed by a programmer-initiated command, typically by pressing a control key on a CRT terminal.

Single stepping through a long program is time consuming. Often it is better to stop the execution of a program only in certain places chosen by the programmer. System software usually provides a mechanism for doing this by means of breakpoints. A breakpoint is inserted in a desired place by the programmer. When the execution of a program reaches a breakpoint, the execution is stopped, enabling the programmer to examine the contents of registers or memory locations at this point in the program. The breakpoints are normally implemented as software generated interrupts.

Another useful possibility is to have the contents of some CPU registers or memory locations displayed, probably in the form of a printout, after the execution of each instruction. Thus, the program is executed normally, except for producing the extra information displayed. This type of facility is called a *trace*. It is particularly useful if the programmer has some simple means of designating the sections of the program which should be traced. The M68000 provides this means with the T flag in the SR register. When this flag is set to 1, the processor is in the trace mode, forcing a software generated interrupt at the end of each instruction. The programmer can write the desired interrupt-service routine to suit the requirements. A trace facility of this kind is not commonly available in microprocessors. It is more usually found in larger machines. For example, in PDP-11 minicomputers a *trap* flag in the processor status word (see Section 3.1.1) is used for this purpose. We should note that the existence of the T flag also facilitates the implementation of the single-step feature.

The last debugging tool that should be mentioned to complete our discussion is a memory dump. This involves displaying at the time of execution the contents of the main memory locations affected by the troublesome sections of a program being debugged. Examination of the dumped data is a tedious process, but it provides a useful alternative when other debugging attempts fail.

11.5.2 Addressing Modes

The M68000 addressing modes provide a great deal of flexibility in accessing operands. Most of the addressing modes discussed previously for the PDP-11, the VAX-11, and the M6809 can be found in the M68000. Two of the notable characteristics are the existence of a powerful indexing mode and the general absence of indirect modes, with only the register indirect mode being included. A brief discussion of the addressing modes provided is given below.

Immediate mode. The operand is contained in the instruction. There are four sizes of operands that can be specified. The byte, word, and long-word operands are given in the bytes that follow the OP-code word. The fourth type of immediate operand, consisting of very small numbers, can be included in some instructions directly in the OP-code word.

Absolute mode. The absolute address of an operand is given in the instruction, following the OP code. There are two versions of this mode, long and short. In the long mode a 24-bit address is specified explicitly. In the short mode a 16-bit value is given in the instruction to be used as the low-order 16 bits of an address. The sign bit of this value is extended to provide the high-order 8 bits of the address. Since the sign bit is either 0 or 1, it follows that in the short mode only two pages of the addressable space can be accessed. These are the 0 page and the $FF8_{16}$ page, each consisting of 32K bytes.

Register mode. The operand is in a CPU register specified in the instruction.

Register indirect mode. The effective address of the operand is the contents of an address register specified in the instruction.

Autoincrement mode. The effective address of the operand is the contents of an address register A_n specified in the instruction. After the operand is accessed, the contents of A_n are incremented by 1, 2, or 4, depending, respectively, upon whether a byte, a word, or a long-word operand is involved.

Autodecrement mode. An address register A_n specified in the instruction is decremented by 1, 2, or 4, depending, respectively, upon whether a byte, a word, or a long-word operand is involved. Then, the effective address of the operand is the new contents of A_n.

Basic indexed mode. A 16-bit signed offset (displacement) and an address register A_n are specified in the instruction. The sum of this offset and the contents of A_n is the effective address of the operand.

Full indexed mode. An 8-bit signed offset, an address register A_n, and an index register R_k (either an address or a data register) are given in the instruction. The effective address of the operand is the sum of the offset and the contents of registers A_n and R_k. Either all 32 bits or the sign-extended low-order 16 bits of R_k are used in the derivation of the address. In the former case the specification of R_k in the assembler syntax must be stated as Rk.L, while the latter is the default case, which can also be indicated as Rk.W.

Basic relative mode. This is the same mode as the basic indexed mode except that the program counter is used instead of an address register A_n.

Full relative mode. This is the same mode as the full indexed mode except that the program counter is used instead of an address register A_n.

The addressing modes and their assembler syntax are summarized in Table 11.5.

Table 11.5 M68000 Addressing Modes

Name	Assembler syntax	Addressing function
Immediate	#Value	Operand = Value
Absolute short	Value	EA = Sign Extended WValue
Absolute long	Value	EA = Value
Register	Rn	EA = R_n that is, Operand = $[R_n]$
Register indirect	(An)	EA = $[A_n]$
Autoincrement	(An)+	EA = $[A_n]$; Increment A_n
Autodecrement	−(An)	Decrement A_n; EA = $[A_n]$
Indexed basic	WValue(An)	EA = WValue + $[A_n]$
Indexed full	BValue(An,Rk.S)	EA = BValue + $[A_n]$ + $[R_k]$
Relative basic	WValue(PC) or Label	EA = WValue + [PC]
Relative full	BValue(PC,Rk.S) or Label (Rk)	EA = BValue + [PC] + $[R_k]$

Notes: EA = effective address
　　 Value = a number given either explicitly or represented by a label
　BValue = an 8-bit Value
WValue = a 16-bit Value
　　　A_n = an address register
　　　R_n = an address or a data register
　　　 S = a size indicator: W for sign-extended 16-bit word and L for
　　　　　 32-bit long word

The reader will have noted that the M68000 addressing modes encompass most of the addressing capability of the PDP-11. Useful additions include the full indexed mode and the variable size immediate mode. The motivation for these modes has been discussed in conjunction with the VAX-11 in Section 3.4.2.

11.5.3 Instruction Set

The M68000 instruction set reflects the stated objective of efficiently supporting high-level programming languages. It provides an extensive set of instructions. Most instructions can operate on any of the three possible sizes of operands. All addressing modes can be used in a uniform way with most instructions. Instruction sets which exhibit this useful feature are often said to be "orthogonal."

The format of two-operand instructions in the M68000 is considerably different from that in the M6800 or the M6809. Instead of indicating one register operand in the OP code itself, both operands are specified in operand fields in a manner similar to that used in the PDP-11. The format is

OP   src,dst

where the operation OP is performed using the source and destination operands, and the result is placed in the destination location.

    Most two-operand instructions require one operand to be specified as the contents of a CPU register, while the other operand may be given in any addressing mode. General operations on two operands in the main memory are not available. A few instructions can involve two memory operands. The most flexible of these is the MOVE instruction, where both the source and destination operands may be specified using any addressing mode. Other instructions allow specification of memory operands in a very restricted manner. For example, two memory operands can be compared with the instruction

CMPM   (Ai)+,(Aj)+

where address registers A_i and A_j are pointers to the operands. The autoincrement mode is the only addressing mode allowed in this instruction. Another example is the instruction

ABCD   −(Ai),−(Aj)

which adds two byte-sized operands encoded in binary-coded decimal (BCD) format. There is also an equivalent instruction for BCD subtraction. Since several bytes are likely to be needed for a given BCD number and such numbers are stored with the least significant digit in the high-address location, it is sensible to use the autodecrement mode in processing them. Indeed, the only other addressing mode allowed in the ABCD instruction is where both operands are in data registers.

    Instructions can operate on byte, word, or long-word operands. In assembler notation this is indicated by appending letters B, W, or L to the operation mnemonic. Thus, the instruction

ADD.B   D0,D1

adds the least significant 8 bits in registers D_0 and D_1, and leaves the result in D_1. The most significant 3 bytes of register D_1 are not affected by this instruction. If there is a carry-out from bit position 7, the C flag is set. If the operand size is not specified by an appended suffix, the Motorola assembler uses the word size by default.

    In addition to two-operand instructions, the M68000 instruction set includes the usual one-operand instructions, as well as a number of program control instructions. Some of the instructions are considerably more powerful than the ones we have encountered in 8-bit microprocessors. They are of the type more usually associated with larger processors.

    We will not discuss the M68000 instruction set in full detail. But, in order to give the reader some indication of its scope, we will look at two previous

```
NUMP        EQU         $2000
NUMQ        EQU         $3000

            ORG         $100
            MOVEA.L     #NUMP,A0
            MOVEA.L     #NUMQ,A1
            MOVEQ       #7,D1
            BSR         BCDSUB
                          .
                          .
                          .
BCDSUB      LEA         1(A0,D1.W),A0
            LEA         1(A1,D1.W),A1
            MOVE        #0,CCR
SLOOP       SBCD.B      -(A1),-(A0)
            DBRA        D1,SLOOP
            RTS
```

Figure 11.18 Program for subtraction of 16-digit BCD operands for M68000.

examples. First, let us reconsider the BCD subtraction example of Figure 11.8. A possible M68000 program for this task is shown in Figure 11.18. The subroutine in this figure is much shorter than the one for the M6809. This is due to the existence of an instruction that performs the required decimal subtraction directly.

Address registers A_0 and A_1 are used as pointers to numbers P and Q. They are initially set to point at the least significant bytes of P and Q, using the LEA (Load Effective Address) instructions in the full indexed mode. Data register D_1 is used as the byte counter to control the number of passes through the subtract loop. Note that this loop consists of only two instructions. The SBCD (Subtract Binary-Coded Decimal) instruction performs the required subtraction. The DBRA (Decrement and Branch) instruction allows simple termination of the loop. The contents of the source register, D_1 in our example, are decremented, and if the result is equal to -1, the next instruction in the straight-line sequence is executed; otherwise a branch is made to the branch location.

The SBCD instruction uses byte operands only, where both operands are in the main memory. The operation performed is

$$dst \leftarrow [dst] - [src] - [X]$$

The source and destination operands have two BCD digits per byte. The value of the extend flag X is subtracted, along with the two digits of the source operand, from the destination operand. If a borrow is generated as a result of this subtraction, then the C and X flags are set to 1; otherwise both flags are cleared to 0. The X flag is generally useful in multiple precision arithmetic. It is only affected by arithmetic instructions, while the C flag is affected by many other instructions. Thus, the X flag provides a means for retaining the "carry-out" information generated in arithmetic operations on segments of long numbers. This is convenient in program loops where the value of the C flag may be altered by other nonarithmetic instructions. Note that the X flag must be cleared prior to entering the SLOOP, which is accomplished by the special form of the Move instruction, called MOVE to CCR. This instruction moves the source operand into the condition code portion of the status register, namely, its least significant byte, referred to as the CCR.

The calling program in the example makes straightforward use of instructions whose meaning should be obvious to the reader. Note that the MOVEA instruction is used to move addresses. The MOVEQ (Move Quick) instruction moves a sign-extended 8-bit operand into a data register.

The second example is given in Figure 11.19. It is a byte-sorting program, which is based on the algorithm in Figure 2.16a. There is one difference in that the list is scanned in reverse order to simplify termination of loops by comparing loop indexes to zero. The program is given in the form of a subroutine.

The parameters, comprising the length and the starting address of the list, are passed by specifying them immediately following the subroutine call instruction in the calling program. The subroutine uses data registers D_1 and D_2

```
              . . . . . . . . . .
              JSR         SORTSUB              Call subroutine.
              DC.L        N                    Parameters for
              DC.L        LIST                    the subroutine.
              "next instruction"
              . . . . . . . . . .

SORTSUB       MOVEM.L     A1−A2/D1−D3,−(A7)     Save registers.
              MOVEA.L     20(A7),A2            A2 points to
                                                 parameter list.
              MOVEM.L     (A2)+,A1/D1          Load parameters.
              MOVE.L      A2,20(A7)            Adjust return address.
              SUBQ.W      #1,D1                Set index j.

OUTER         MOVE.L      D1,D2                Set index k.
              SUBQ.W      #1,D2

INNER         MOVE.B      (A1,D1.W),D3         Current minimum
                                                 value in D3.
              CMP.B       (A1,D2.W),D3         Compare L(j) and
                                                 L(k).
              BHS.S       NEXT
              MOVE.B      (A1,D2.W),(A1,D1.W)  Interchange
              MOVE.B      D3,(A1,D2.W)            L(j) and L(k).

NEXT          DBRA        D2,INNER             Decrement counters
              SUBQ.W      #1,D1                   and branch back
              BGT.S       OUTER                   if not finished.

              MOVEM.L     (A7)+,A1−A2/D1−D3    Restore registers.

              RTS
```

Figure 11.19 A byte-sort program for M68000.

to hold index values J and K. The address of the first entry in the list is held in address register A_1. At the start of the subroutine, the contents of all registers used are saved on the stack in order to make the subroutine suitable for general use. This is accomplished with the MOVEM (Move Multiple registers) instruction, where the required registers are indicated in the source operand field. The saved registers are A_1, A_2, D_1, D_2, and D_3. Next, address register A_2 is set up as a pointer to the parameter list. This requires loading it with the updated value of the program counter that was stored on the stack as the return address during execution of the subroutine call instruction. Since five registers were saved, each having 4 bytes, this return address is found 20 bytes from the present top of the stack. After the two long-word parameters are loaded into their respective registers, the correct return address must replace the previously stored value of the program counter.

Sorting is done by comparing entries in the list with the current minimum value. Whenever a smaller value is encountered, it is swapped with the top entry in the sublist. The minimum value is held in data register D_3 because the M68000 does not have a Compare instruction that allows the desired comparison to be performed conveniently on two operands in the main memory.

The use of short immediate operands is illustrated in the SUBQ (Subtract Quick) instruction, which subtracts a 3-bit immediate operand from the destination operand. The instruction occupies only 2 bytes of memory space. The conditional branch instructions BHS (Branch if Higher or Same) and BGT (Branch if Greater Than) transfer program control, as implied by their names. Two forms of branch instructions can be specified. Our example uses the short form, denoted by appending S to the mnemonic, where an 8-bit signed offset is used. The long form makes use of a 16-bit signed offset, requiring an extra word for the instruction.

The inner loop is terminated by the DBRA instruction, whose meaning was explained in conjunction with the previous example. However, the same instruction cannot be used to terminate the outer loop because the final value for K is $+1$, rather than 0. After the sort is completed, the contents of the registers used in the subroutine are restored from the stack.

The reader should compare the above examples with the programs illustrating the same tasks for other previously discussed processors. It is obvious that the M68000 is superior to both the M6800 and the M6809. Comparison of the byte-sorting example with those for the PDP-11 in Section 2.5.6 and the VAX-11 in Section 3.4.4 will indicate that the M68000 has many of the features of such powerful processors. Indeed, the term microprocessor is fitting for this kind of processor only because of its small physical size and very low cost.

11.6 INTEL 8085 MICROPROCESSOR

So far we have considered three microprocessors produced by Motorola as representative examples of commercial products. These microprocessors have a register structure and addressing mechanisms that show many similarities to the previously discussed PDP-11 and VAX-11 computers. However, it would be wrong to suggest that all microprocessors exhibit the same characteristics. In this section we will describe an interesting alternative found in the Intel 8085 microprocessor (and its predecessor the 8080).

The 8085 is one of a family of compatible chips, including RAM, ROM, peripheral and communication interfaces, etc. We will concentrate our discussion on the 8085 CPU. It is a 40-pin chip which processes data in 8-bit parallel fashion. Memory and I/O device addressing is done using 16-bit addresses.

The register structure of the 8085 is shown in Figure 11.20. There is an 8-bit accumulator, a 16-bit stack pointer, a 16-bit program counter, and a condition code register.

Addressing in the 8085 is based on the "pointer" concept. Six 8-bit registers B, C, D, E, H, and L are used in pairs (B, C), (D, E), and (H, L) for addressing purposes. That is, the 16-bit contents of a register pair may be used directly as an address of an operand in the memory. The (H, L) pair is most frequently used, while the other two are restricted to a relatively small number of instructions. Data may be transferred to and from the registers either in 8-bit words individually or in 16-bit quantities involving register pairs. Using register pairs for operand addressing allows implementation of a considerable number of useful single-byte instructions, with the aim of reducing the execution time and memory space requirements. Of course, pointer addressing alone would be rather restrictive for memory accesses. Thus two other addressing modes are provided, immediate and absolute. As in most microprocessors, immediate data and absolute addresses are included in the second and third bytes of an instruction. Therefore, there is a total of five address modes:

Immediate mode. The operand is contained in the second byte of the instruction. Instructions which load 16-bit registers (or register pairs) have the immediate operand in the second and third bytes.

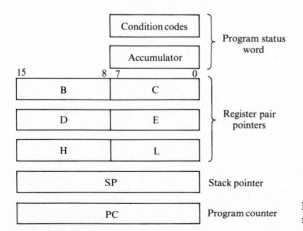

Figure 11.20 Registers in the 8085 microprocessor.

Table 11.6 Instruction set for Intel 8085 microprocessor

Operation	Mnemonic	IMMED		ABSOL		REG		REG IND.		IMPLIED		Performed function	Condition code flags affected				
		~	#	~	#	~	#	~	#	~	#		Z	S	P	C	H
Move	MOV					4	1	7	1			$dst \leftarrow [src]$					
Move immediate	MVI					7	2	10	2			$dst \leftarrow [Byte_2]$					
Load register pair immediate	LXI	10	3									$RP \leftarrow [Byte_3, Byte_2]$					
Load accumulator direct	LDA			13	3							$A \leftarrow [[Byte_3, Byte_2]]$					
Store accumulator direct	STA			13	3							$[Byte_3, Byte_2] \leftarrow [A]$					
Load H and L direct	LHLD			16	3							$L \leftarrow [[Byte_3, Byte_2]]$; $H \leftarrow [[Byte_3, Byte_2] + 1]$					
Store H and L direct	SHLD			16	3							$[Byte_3, Byte_2] \leftarrow [L]$; $[Byte_3, Byte_2] + 1 \leftarrow [H]$					
Load accumulator indirect	LDAX							7	1			$A \leftarrow [[RP]]$					
Store accumulator indirect	STAX							7	1			$[RP] \leftarrow [A]$					
Exchange H, L with D, E	XCHG									4	1	$[H] \leftrightarrow [D], [L] \leftrightarrow [E]$					
Add	ADD					4	1	7	1			$A \leftarrow [A] + [src]$	x	x	x	x	x
Add immediate	ADI	7	2									$A \leftarrow [A] + [Byte_2]$	x	x	x	x	x
Add with carry	ADC					4	1	7	1			$A \leftarrow [A] + [src] + [Carry]$	x	x	x	x	x
Add immediate with carry	ACI	7	2									$A \leftarrow [A] + [Byte_2] + [Carry]$	x	x	x	x	x
Subtract	SUB					4	1	7	1			$A \leftarrow [A] - [src]$	x	x	x	x	x
Subtract immediate	SUI	7	2									$A \leftarrow [A] - [Byte_2]$	x	x	x	x	x
Subtract with borrow	SBB					4	1	7	1			$A \leftarrow [A] - [src] - [Carry]$	x	x	x	x	x
Subtract immediate with borrow	SBI	7	2									$A \leftarrow [A] - [Byte_2] - [Carry]$	x	x	x	x	x
Increment	INR					4	1	10	1			$src \leftarrow [src] + 1$	x	x	x		x
Decrement	DCR					4	1	10	1			$src \leftarrow [src] - 1$	x	x	x		x
Increment register pair	INX					6	1					$RP \leftarrow [RP] + 1$					
Decrement register pair	DCX					6	1					$RP \leftarrow [RP] - 1$					
Add register pair to H,L	DAD					10	1					$H,L \leftarrow [H,L] + [RP]$				x	
Decimal adjust	DAA									4	1	Converts binary number in A into BCD format	x	x	x	x	x

Operation	Mnemonic	Bytes	Machine cycles	T-states	Operation performed	S	Z	AC	P	CY
AND	ANA	1	1	4	$A \leftarrow [A] \land [src]$	x	x	x	x	0
AND immediate	ANI	2	2	7	$A \leftarrow [A] \land [Byte_2]$	x	x	x	x	0
Exclusive OR	XRA	1	1	4	$A \leftarrow [A] \oplus [src]$	x	x	x	x	0
Exclusive OR immediate	XRI	2	2	7	$A \leftarrow [A] \oplus [Byte_2]$	x	x	x	x	0
OR (inclusive)	ORA	1	1	4	$A \leftarrow [A] \lor [src]$	x	x	x	x	0
OR immediate	ORI	2	2	7	$A \leftarrow [A] \lor [Byte_2]$	x	x	x	x	0
Compare	CMP	1	1	4	$[A] - [src]$	x	x	x	x	x
Compare immediate	CPI	2	2	7	$[A] - [Byte_2]$	x	x	x	x	x
Rotate left	RLC	1	1	4	$Carry \; A_7 \cdots A_0$ (rotate left)					x
Rotate right	RRC	1	1	4	$A_7 \cdots A_0 \; Carry$ (rotate right)					x
Rotate left through carry	RAL	1	1	4	$Carry \; A_7 \cdots A_0$ (rotate left through carry)					x
Rotate right through carry	RAR	1	1	4	$Carry \; A_7 \cdots A_0$ (rotate right through carry)					x
Complement accumulator	CMA	1	1	4	$A \leftarrow [\overline{A}]$					
Complement carry	CMC	1	1	4	$Carry \leftarrow [\overline{Carry}]$					x
Set carry	STC	1	1	4	$Carry \leftarrow 1$					x
Push register pair into stack	PUSH	1	3	12	$[SP]-1 \leftarrow [RP]$, $SP \leftarrow [SP]-2$					
Pop register pair	POP	1	3	10	$RP \leftarrow [[SP]]$, $SP \leftarrow [SP]+2$					
Exchange stack with H,L	XTHL	1	5	18	$[L] \leftrightarrow [[SP]]$, $[H] \leftrightarrow [[SP]+1]$					
Move H,L to SP	SPHL	1	1	6	$SP \leftarrow [H,L]$					
Input	IN	2	3	10	$A \leftarrow [I/O\ port]$					
Output	OUT	2	3	10	$I/O\ port \leftarrow [A]$					
Enable interrupts	EI	1	1	4	Enables interrupt system					
Disable interrupts	DI	1	1	4	Disables interrupt system					
Read interrupt mask	RIM	1	1	4	$A \leftarrow [Interrupt\ mask]$					
Set interrupt mask	SIM	1	1	4	$Interrupt\ mask \leftarrow [A]$					
Halt	HLT	1	1	7	Halts processor					
No operation	NOP	1	1	4	No operation performed					

Table 11.6 *(Continued)*

Operation	Mnemonic	ABSOL ~	ABSOL #	IMPLIED ~	IMPLIED #	Condition test	Performed function
Jump unconditionally	JMP	10	3			None	If condition test is true
Jump if carry set	JC	10	3			Carry=1	then
Jump if carry clear	JNC	10	3			Carry=0	PC←[Byte$_3$, Byte$_2$]
Jump if zero	JZ	10	3			Z=1	
Jump if not zero	JNZ	10	3			Z=0	
Jump if positive	JP	10	3			S=0	
Jump if minus	JM	10	3			S=1	
Jump if parity even	JPE	10	3			P=1	
Jump if parity odd	JPO	10	3			P=0	
Call unconditionally	CALL	18	3			None	If condition test is true
Call if carry set	CC	18	3			Carry=1	then [SP]−1←[PC]
Call if carry clear	CNC	18	3			Carry=0	SP←[SP]−2
Call if zero	CZ	18	3			Z=1	PC←[Byte$_3$, Byte$_2$]
Call if not zero	CNZ	18	3			Z=0	
Call if positive	CP	18	3			S=0	
Call if minus	CM	18	3			S=1	
Call if parity even	CPE	18	3			P=1	
Call if parity odd	CPO	18	3			P=0	
Return unconditionally	RET			10	1	None	If condition test is true
Return if carry set	RC			12	1	Carry=1	then PC←[[SP]]
Return if carry clear	RNC			12	1	Carry=0	SP←[SP]+2
Return if zero	RZ			12	1	Z=1	
Return if not zero	RNZ			12	1	Z=0	
Return if positive	RP			12	1	S=0	
Return if minus	RM			12	1	S=1	
Return if parity even	RPE			12	1	P=1	
Return if parity odd	RPO			12	1	P=0	
Restart	RST			12	1		[SP]−1←[PC] SP←[SP]−2 PC←8×[b$_5$b$_4$b$_3$]
Move H,L to PC	PCHL			6	1		PC←[H,L]

Notes: ~ = number of states needed to execute the instruction; # = number of bytes in the instruction; RP = register pair (B,C), (D,E), or (H,L)

Absolute mode. The absolute address is specified by the second and third bytes of the instruction.

Register mode. A single register or a register pair is specified.

Register indirect mode. The operand address is given by the contents of a register pair which is specified in the first byte of the instruction.

Implied mode. The first byte of the instruction indicates the address as being the accumulator, stack pointer, or condition code register.

There are five conditon code flags:

H   Carry from the bit-3 position (half carry)
C   Carry from the most significant bit (bit 7)
P   Parity bit, which is set to 1 if the result of an operation has even parity
     (that is, if the modulo 2 sum of the bits of the result is zero)
S   Sign bit, which is set to 1 if the most significant bit (bit 7) of the result
     of an operation is 1
Z   Zero-result bit

The contents of the condition code register appear as a status byte, which, in conjunction with the contents of the accumulator, forms the program status word (PSW).

Table 11.6 shows the instruction set of the 8085 microprocessor. It is apparent that the set is quite extensive. It is particularly impressive to see the large number of program control instructions, including a full complement of conditional and unconditional Call-Subroutine and Return-from-Subroutine instructions. Columns under the label "#" give the number of bytes in an instruction for the particular address mode. To provide an indication of speed capability, the columns under the "~" sign show the number of internal machine states needed to execute an instruction. In this case the states correspond directly to the main clock, where the states are delineated by successive low-to-high transitions of the clock. A typical clock rate is 5 MHz, which means that each state has a duration of 0.2 μs.

To illustrate the applicability of some of the 8085 instructions, let us reconsider the BCD subtraction example of Section 11.2.1. This task can be implemented with the program in Figure 11.21, using the same algorithm as before. Register pairs (H, L) and (D, E) are used as pointers to the operands P and Q. Since the (H, L) pair must be used in MOV instructions, it is necessary to interchange its contents with the (D, E) pair twice during each iteration. This is conveniently achieved with the XCHG instruction. Using this addressing mechanism it is not necessary to place any restrictions on the location of the operands P and Q. A total of 25 bytes of memory space is needed for the program. Program execution requires 615 internal machine states to subtract two 16-digit BCD numbers. If the processor is driven by a 5-MHz clock, this means that the program can be executed in 123 μs. These memory-space and execution-time numbers are roughly similar to those for the program in Figure 11.6, suggesting that the Intel 8085 and the M6800 microprocessors are comparable in performance. Of course, such conclusions should never be made on the basis of a single example. Proper assessment of the relative merits of processors can only be made by testing them on a number of well-chosen *benchmark* tasks. Indeed, the above two microprocessors tend to be quite dissimilar, with the Intel 8085 being suitable for numerical and list-processing applications, and the M6800 appearing to have an edge in other, non-numerical applications.

The 8085 has an interesting interrupt mechanism. It includes one non-maskable and three maskable interrupts of the type discussed in conjunction

Location (hex)	Contents (hex)	Assembler format for instructions		Comment
100	11	LXI	D,NUMP	Load address of P into (D, E)
101	"NUMP"$_L$			register pair
102	"NUMP"$_H$			
103	21	LXI	H,NUMQ	Load address of Q into (H, L)
104	"NUMQ"$_L$			register pair
105	"NUMQ"$_H$			
106	0E	MVI	C,8	Set the counter for 8 iterations
107	08			
108	37	STC		Set carry for 10's complement
109	3E	SLOOP: MVI	A,99	Form 10's complement of Q for one
10A	99			digit pair
10B	CE	ACI	0	
10C	00			
10D	96	SUB	M	
10E	EB	XCHG		Exchange (D, E) and (H, L)
10F	86	ADD	M	Form P - Q in binary
110	27	DAA		Decimal adjust
111	77	MOV	M,A	Store result in NUMP
112	EB	XCHG		Set the (H, L) pointer to NUMQ
113	13	INX	D	Increment the pointers in (D, E) and
114	23	INX	H	(H, L)
115	0D	DCR	C	Decrement counter
116	C2	JNZ	SLOOP	Loop until last byte is processed
117	09			
118	01			

Figure 11.21 Program for subtraction of 16-digit BCD operands, using Intel 8085 instruction set.

with the M6800 and M6809. It also has another interrupt input that provides a means for implementing a vectored interrupt scheme (described in Section 6.4.3), where an I/O device can send the starting address of the interrupt-service program to the CPU. We will give a brief description of this scheme. In the 8085 there is a special instruction called RST (Restart) that is used for this purpose. A vectored interrupt sequence is started when an I/O device raises an interrupt request. When the CPU acknowledges the interrupt request, the I/O device places 1 byte of data that is in fact the binary code for the RST instruction on the processor data bus. The RST instruction is then gated into the instruction register. Its execution results in storing the contents of the PC on the stack, updating the SP, and setting the new value of the PC to eight times the value of bits $b_5 b_4 b_3$ in the RST instruction. Thus the PC is set to point at a memory location, whose decimal address may be one of the following: 0, 8, 16, 24, 32, 40, 48, or 56. These locations can then be used as starting points of interrupt-service routines. It is apparent that in this scheme the RST instruction is used as a simple call to the interrupt-service routines, where the address of a particular routine is specified by the I/O device through the setting of bit positions 5, 4, and 3. Upon completion of the interrupt routine, control may be returned to the program that was interrupted in the same manner as a return from an ordinary subroutine would be performed.

We have discussed the 8085 microprocessor to give an example of an alternative design. The 8085 has found wide acceptance in practice. It is interesting to note that when the Intel Company produced a 16-bit microprocessor, the 8086, they decided to incorporate the 8085 features into it. The 8086 has a greatly expanded set of registers and addressing capability, but it provides a mode where it functions as an 8085. The intent is to make it suitable for applications where considerable 8085 software exists, but a more powerful CPU would be useful.

11.7 SINGLE-CHIP MICROCOMPUTERS

The microprocessors discussed in the preceding sections are CPUs implemented on a single chip. In order to realize a useful microcomputer, these microprocessors must be connected to some memory and I/O interface chips. Thus, several chips are needed to construct a microcomputer.

There are many applications where a microcomputer can be employed advantageously but where only a small amount of software and data are involved. This is the case in microcomputer-controlled instruments, simple pocket calculators, hand-held video games, digital watches, etc. The limited memory and I/O requirements of such applications have given impetus to the development of single-chip microcomputers.

A typical single-chip microcomputer contains the CPU, some RAM and ROM (or EPROM) storage, and one or more I/O ports for connection to I/O devices. All of this circuitry is implemented on a single chip. If a microcomputer is to be mounted in a 40-pin package, it is apparent that separate pins for address, data, I/O, and control information cannot be provided. An obvious solution is to multiplex the use of some pins. The use of the pins at a given time is defined by software. For example, in one mode some pins may be used for I/O and control purposes, while in another mode the same pins may carry the addressing and data information. The latter mode allows the addition of external memory and I/O chips.

Intel's 8051[11.10] is a good example of a single-chip microcomputer. It includes 128 bytes of RAM, 4K bytes of ROM, two 16-bit timers, and four I/O ports that can provide up to 32 I/O lines. It has an extensive instruction set, which includes Multiply and Divide instructions. Its ROM is mask-programmable at the time of manufacture. There exists another version of this microcomputer, named the 8751, in which the ROM is replaced with an EPROM of the same size to allow user programmability.

Motorola's M68705R3[11.11] is another interesting example. It has an M6800-based instruction set. It includes 112 bytes of RAM, 3776 bytes of EPROM, and 4 I/O ports that provide 24 I/O lines. It also includes an 8-bit analog/digital converter to facilitate connection of up to four analog inputs.

Single-chip microcomputers are versatile devices. They can be used as self-contained units in a variety of applications. They can also be used with additional memory and I/O chips in expanded systems.

11.8 APPLICATIONS OF MICROPROCESSORS

The scope for using microprocessors in product applications is virtually limitless. Their initial impact occurred in the area of calculators. The heart of a typical hand calculator is a microprocessor, which allows implementation of many useful features at low cost. This was a very natural application, soon followed by many others. A related, but more challenging, possibility is to build a larger general-purpose minicomputer with a microprocessor as its driving element. While the speed performance of such minicomputers is likely to be worse than that of machines designed in a conventional way, they are inevitably going to be lower-priced. Good examples of this approach are the DEC LSI-11,[11.12] which is a model of the PDP-11 line, and numerous word processors and personal computers.

Microprocessors have found their way into the standard equipment in computer systems. They are used in controllers for magnetic disks, as well as in "intelligent" terminals. Data acquisition systems may be simplified by using microprocessors at remote points as data-gathering devices. This allows some preprocessing before sending data to the main computer.

Most machines that require extensive control circuits provide an environment for advantageous usage of microprocessors. These include point-of-sale terminals and business machines in general. A number of application possibilities exist in the home, where microprocessors can control sophisticated appliances, security systems, temperature, and lighting, as well as providing a means for entertainment through real-time participation games.

Microprocessors can be used to build surprisingly complex systems. An example is provided by private telephone exchanges, usually called PABX (private automatic branch exchange) systems. A considerable number of telephone lines (200 or more) can be controlled by a single microprocessor. Such systems can provide numerous operational features that would be difficult to implement without computer control.

Another area that shows great promise is instrumentation. Sophisticated electronics is necessary in many instruments, having an adverse effect on their price. Much of this electronic circuitry can often be replaced with a microprocessor, reducing the cost of the product and usually increasing its versatility.

This leads us to one general-applications area that warrants a few further comments. Many machines, instruments, and processes involve electronic control circuits. These logic circuits may be built into a machine or an instrument or they may be a part of a separate "control panel." Their main function is to govern the sequencing of tasks that must be performed. This is similar to functions performed by control circuits in a typical computer. In Chapters 4 and 5 we argued that such control can be implemented effectively through a microprogrammed control structure, which replaces hardwired circuits with a control store. The approach is readily extended to a more general environment. Electronic control circuits can be replaced with instructions in a "control memory," which are executed by a microprocessor that generates the signals that would otherwise be produced by the control circuits. This strategy of replacing hardwired electronics with microprocessor and memory chips usually results in significant cost reductions. Since we are replacing circuits of fixed structure, it is reasonable to assume that the control memory will consist primarily of ROM chips. The advantages of using microprocessors in this way are numerous. In addition to lower cost, the design process is simplified as there are fewer components to be dealt with. Many design errors can be corrected and new options added simply by changing the contents of the control memory. The only possible problem arises when the speed of operation is a critical factor. Microprogrammed control cannot match the speed of hardwired circuits. However, in many applications the required speed performance is well within the bounds attainable using microprocessors.

The above application of replacement of hardwired electronics by a microprocessor emphasizes the use of ROM chips in the main memory. However, this is a more general phenomenon. In most applications, a micro-processor is used to perform relatively fixed tasks, which suggests that a considerable part of the main memory is likely to consist of ROM components.

11.9 CONCLUDING REMARKS

The progress in VLSI technology has been very rapid. Its impact upon microprocessors is, understandably, very pronounced. Every year a number of new chips are developed and marketed. They tend to be increasingly more versatile and powerful. This has led to a situation where any given microproces-sor is likely to have a relatively short "lifetime," as it inevitably becomes obsolete in view of newer products.

It is perhaps dangerous to refer to any particular microprocessor in a discussion of the topic. We made use of four specific examples in this chapter. They helped to illustrate the concepts involved in microprocessors in general. Thus, while they may become obsolete soon, the basic principles will remain useful and will continue to be found in other products. Problems associated with pin limitations will certainly influence the design of microprocessors for years to come.

11.10 PROBLEMS

11.1 Figure 2.16 shows a byte-sorting program. Write a program to perform the same task using the M6800 microprocessor. How many bytes of storage are needed for your program? How long would it take to execute?

11.2 Repeat Problem 11.1 using the Intel 8085 microprocessor.

11.3 Comment on the relative merits of the M6800 and Intel 8085 microprocessors with respect to the above byte-sorting tasks.

11.4 Write an M6800 program to multiply two 16-bit signed numbers, using the Booth algorithm from Section 7.7. Assume that the multiplicand, multiplier, and the resultant 32-bit product occupy 8 consecutive bytes of RAM.

11.5 Repeat Problem 11.4 for the Intel 8085 microprocessor.

11.6 Write an M6800 program to convert a two-digit BCD number stored in 1 byte into an 8-bit binary number.

11.7 Repeat Problem 11.6 for the Intel 8085 microprocessor.

11.8 A string of n 8-bit characters is stored in consecutive locations of a RAM. The string starts at location STRING. Another string of m characters is stored in consecutive locations of the RAM, starting at location SUBSTRING. Assuming that $m < n$, write an M6800 program that will determine if the substring occurs anywhere within the first string. If a matching substring is found, the address of its first character must be placed in the memory location STADDR, which is otherwise cleared to 0.

11.9 Repeat Problem 11.8 for the Intel 8085 microprocessor.

11.10 In the program of Figure 11.6, the memory locations "NUMP" and "NUMQ" were referenced within the program as absolute addresses. This may not be desirable if the program is to be used as a subroutine to operate on numbers P and Q that are not necessarily stored in predetermined locations. This is particularly true if the program is to be resident in a ROM, where its contents cannot be modified. Rewrite the given program without such absolute references to P and Q. How do your modifications affect the time of execution?

How would a similar requirement affect the Intel 8085 program of Figure 11.21?

11.11 In view of your experiences with the above problems, suggest possible design changes, if any, in the M6800 and Intel 8085 microprocessors that would enhance their processing capability. In the case of M6800, has the M6809 included any of the desirable changes?

11.12 Consider an M6800 system that has four peripheral devices connected to two PICs (described in Section 11.4.2), one device per each port of a PIC. All four devices can raise interrupts. Interrupt requests are wire-ORed and appear as an IRQ signal on the corresponding pin of the microprocessor.

An interrupt cannot be acknowledged until the execution of the current instruction is completed. Estimate the maximum delay that the lowest-priority device will experience before its request is serviced, given that it is the only interrupting device and that the interrupt mask (bit I in the condition code register) is not set. Note that prior to servicing any interrupt request, the M6800 will automatically store the contents of its internal registers on the stack, which takes nine cycles.

11.13 Two 7-segment displays are connected to an M6809 system, one to each port of a PIC (described in Section 11.4.2). The displays have the organization indicated in Figure A.33, but a BCD–to–7-segment decoder circuit is not used. Write a program capable of displaying 10 two-digit BCD numbers stored (two numbers per byte) in a list in RAM. Each number should be displayed for approximately 2 seconds.

11.14 Repeat Problem 11.13 for the M68000 microprocessor.

11.15 Write an M6809 program that reverses the order of bits in accumulator A. For example, if the starting pattern in the accumulator is 10110100, the result left in the accumulator should be 00101101.

11.16 Repeat Problem 11.15 for the M68000 microprocessor. Assume that all 32 bits of data register D_1 are to be reversed.

11.17 Assume that a given text is stored in the main memory starting at location 1000_{16}. The text consists of a string of ASCII characters. Each character occupies 1 byte, consisting of the 7-bit ASCII code (see Appendix D) and a 0 in the most significant bit position. The character string is terminated by the NULL character, which is encoded as 00_{16}. Write an M6809 program which counts the number of occurrences of the definite article 'the' in the stored text.

11.18 Repeat Problem 11.17 for the M68000 microprocessor.

11.19 Generalize the program written in answer to Problem 11.17 to make it capable of finding a particular string of characters in a given text. Write the program as a subroutine, where the starting addresses of both the text and the buffer that holds the string that is to be searched for are passed as parameters.

11.20 Repeat Problem 11.19 for the M68000 microprocessor.

11.21 A commonly used input device is a hexadecimal keypad. It has 16 keys corresponding to the 16 hex digits. Internally, the hex keypad consists of four row wires (R0,R1,R2,R3) and four column wires (C0,C1,C2,C3) in a matrix arrangement. The wires are normally isolated from each other. When a key is pressed, it activates a mechanical switch which connects one of the row wires to one of the column wires. Assume that the keys corresponding to the hex digits 0,1, . . . , 9,A, . . . ,E,F establish connection between the row/column pairs R0/C0, R0/C1, . . . , R2/C1, R2/C2, . . . , R3/C2, R3/C3, respectively.

Let the hex keypad be connected to one of the ports of a PIC (described in Section 11.4.2). Then, the closure of any switch can be detected by writing a 0 to all row wires and by reading the column wires, and vice versa. Write an M6809 program capable of reading the keys pressed on the keypad.

11.22 One of the problems with mechanical switches is that their contacts often bounce (open and close several times) before making a firm electrical connection. This can lead to the reading of more than one digit for a single pressing of a key on a keypad. Modify your program for Problem 11.21 to 'debounce' the switches on the keypad, to prevent the unwanted reading of digits.

11.23 Repeat Problem 11.21 for the M68000 microprocessor.

11.24 Repeat Problem 11.22 for the M68000 microprocessor.

11.25 Design an M6809 system, in conjuction with a PIC (described in Section 11.4.2), for the following application.

Two devices are to be connected to the system. One device, D_1, is a timer circuit which generates a 100-μs-long negative-going pulse once every second. The second device, D_2, is a part of a controller which needs the exact time of day. Whenever it requires the time of day, D_2 raises an interrupt request to the microcomputer by means of a positive-going signal. This signal remains high until the end of the transfer of data that represents the time of day. The required data consists of 6 bytes in ASCII code, where 2 bytes are used to denote each of the number of hours, minutes, and seconds. Each byte transmitted to D_2 is to be accompanied by a pulse on a control wire indicating that valid data is available on the 8 data lines.

Note that the M6809 must maintain the necessary information about the time. This feature in a computer system is often referred to as a *real-time clock*.

11.26 Write an M6809 program to multiply two matrices, using the approach explained in Section 3.3.

11.27 Repeat Problem 11.26 for the M68000 microprocessor.

11.11 REFERENCES

11.1 "M6800 Microprocessor Manual," Motorola Inc., 1975.
11.2 "MC6809 Microprocessor Manual," Motorola Inc., 1979.

11.3 "MC68000 16-bit Microprocessor User's Manual," Motorola Inc., 1980.

11.4 "MCS-85 User's Manual," Intel Corp., 1977.

11.5 "Versatile Interface Adapter (VIA)," Synertek Inc., 1979.

11.6 "Z80 Product Specification," Zilog Inc., 1977.

11.7 "The 8086 Family User's Manual," Intel Corp., 1979.

11.8 "Z8000 Product Specification," Zilog Inc., 1979.

11.9 "NS16032 High-Performance Microprocessors," National Semiconductor Corp., 1982.

11.10 "MCS-51 Family of Single Chip Microcomputers User's Manual," Intel Corp., 1981.

11.11 "MC68705R3 8-bit EPROM Microcomputer Unit with A/D," Motorola Inc., 1981.

11.12 Sebern, M. J.: A Minicomputer-Compatible Microcomputer System: The DEC LSI-11, *Proc. IEEE,* vol. 64, no. 6, pp. 881–888, June 1976.

COMPUTER COMMUNICATIONS

In the discussion of interface design in Chapter 6, it was implicitly assumed that input and output devices are in physical proximity to the CPU. From the implementation point of view, the main constraint on the location of I/O devices relates to the distance over which the I/O bus signals need to travel. Longer distances mean longer propagation delays, hence slower speed. The total length of the I/O bus is typically limited to a few meters. This is the length required to connect all the I/O interfaces. The interfaces are connected to their respective peripheral devices via cables which may be somewhat longer (3 to 10 m). The format of data transfer along these cables depends upon the nature of the device. In the case of high-speed devices, the information is usually transferred in parallel, thus requiring multiconductor cables. Slow devices, on the other hand, may use a serial link, with an asynchronous start-stop transmission format similar to that discussed in Section 9.1.1.

There are a large number of computer applications in which the usefulness of a computer system can be enhanced considerably if some of the I/O devices can be situated at remote locations. This, in fact, generates a whole set of applications that would not otherwise be possible. Consider, for example, the following situations:

1. *Remote terminals.* A computer system is typically accessed from terminals placed in user-convenient locations. They are likely to be scattered throughout a building or a plant site. Sometimes, access to a computer from different points in a city or even from different cities is required. In all of these cases, a communication facility is needed to transfer data between the computer and the terminals.

2. *Computer-to-computer communication*. Often, it is necessary to transfer data from one computer to another. For example, it has been pointed out in Chapter 9 that intelligent terminals and work stations are computers in their own right. However, they are often connected to other computers that provide file storage facilities, additional computing power, and access to specialized resources. The required connections are achieved through a communications network. Networks that span a small geographic area, with distances not exceeding a few kilometers, are called *local area networks*. Networks that cover larger areas, involving distances up to thousands of kilometers, are referred to as *long-haul networks*, or *wide area networks*. Such networks provide service nationally or internationally.

Terminal-to-computer and computer-to-computer data transfers impose different requirements on a communication network. The former are characterized by small amounts of data being transmitted at a time. Moreover, their interactive nature requires short delays. On the other hand, communication between two computers often involves large files, transferred at high speed. A computer communication network should enable both types of traffic to be handled efficiently and economically.

Terminal networks, local area networks, and long-haul networks represent three distinct types of data communication networks, each characterized by its own speed of transmission, type of transmission lines, and organization. These and other details are the subject of this chapter. We shall start by considering the means available for communication with a single remote terminal, followed by a discussion of multiplexing of a number of remote terminals. At the end of the chapter a brief introduction will be given to "resource-sharing" networks that allow exchange of data among several computers.

12.1 COMMUNICATION WITH A REMOTE TERMINAL

When an I/O terminal and the main computer are situated a considerable distance apart, the straightforward connection between them may become impractical. Consider first a terminal that requires parallel data transfer, as is the case with many high-speed line printers. The cost of cables may become excessive. Moreover, as the length of the cable increases, so does the data skew (see Section 6.5.1). This places an upper limit on the data rate, thus eliminating the main advantage of parallel transmission. A more reasonable approach is to convert the parallel data to a serial format at the transmitting end and back to the parallel format at the receiving end. This approach is normally used with remote terminals, irrespective of the nature of the I/O device.

Two important aspects of serial transmission of digital data need to be considered, namely:

- The nature of the transmitted signal
- The format of transmission

A detailed presentation of these topics as they relate to the type and characteristics of the transmission line is beyond the scope of this book. However, a brief discussion is given below of those aspects that reflect directly on the design of computer systems.

12.1.1 Transmission of Digital Data

The simplest transmission line arrangement suitable for digital data is a *current loop*. As shown in Figure 12.1a, the transmitter is a simple ON/OFF switch. The receiver is arranged such that when the transmitter switch is closed, a current I of 20 mA flows in the circuit. The terms *mark* and *space* are used to describe the situations when the transmitter switch is closed ($I = 20$ mA) and open ($I = 0$), corresponding to logic values 1 and 0, respectively. The receiver senses the state of the line and generates an output logic signal. The scheme of Figure 12.1 enables installation of terminals either locally or hundreds of meters away, where four wires are used to enable transmission in both directions. Data transmission is in the asynchronous start-stop format described in Section 9.1.1.

Some precautions are often necessary when transmitting signals over long distances. Long cables are likely to pick up electric noise from the environment.

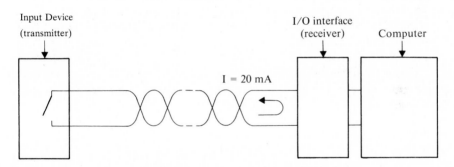

(*a*) Data transmission using a current loop

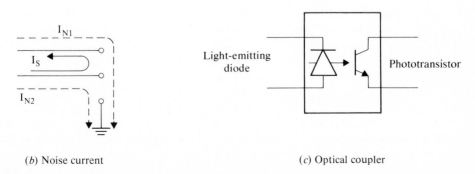

(*b*) Noise current   (*c*) Optical coupler

Figure12.1 Connection of a remote device using a current loop.

The receiver at the end of a long cable may detect signals on the line, even when nothing is being transmitted at the sending end. These signals may be picked up from nearby communication or power cables. If, at the receiver, the noise signal level is comparable to that of the transmitted signals, the receiver cannot separate them, and errors will occur. An effective and economical way for separating the two components of the received signal is to take advantage of some of the differences in the characteristics of the noise current and the transmitted signal current. The most important difference is illustrated in Figure 12.1b. While signal current flows around the loop, noise currents flow from either side of the loop to ground. Hence, the receiver should be designed to detect only the component of the current that flows around the loop, which has the magnitude $I_S + I_{N2} - I_{N1}$. Moreover, the transmission line should be designed such that the two currents I_{N1} and I_{N2} are as close to each other as possible. In other words, the transmission line should be *balanced*. Considerable balancing can be achieved through the use of a twisted pair of wires to form the transmission line. The average value of I_{N1} and I_{N2} is usually referred to as the *common-mode* signal, while the loop current constitutes the *differential-mode* signal. A receiver amplifier that is sensitive to the differential component only is referred to as a differential amplifier. Such amplifiers are capable of detecting differential-mode signals that are thousands of times smaller than the common-mode component.

Another important precaution regards the protection of semiconductor circuits whenever such circuits are used as a part of the receiver or the transmitter. Semiconductor circuits can be designed to withstand a few tens of volts or even a few hundreds of volts before they break down. However, equipment connected to a long cable is subject to large voltage surges that may result, for example, from lightning strikes. Voltages of 1000 V or higher may be encountered in such situations. Thus it is necessary to isolate the sensitive circuitry from the lines that may carry such high voltages. A device that is highly suitable for this purpose is the *optical isolator*, represented schematically in Figure 12.1c. An optical source (light-emitting diode) and an optical sensor (phototransistor) are contained in a small sealed package. The transistor is equivalent to an open switch. When the loop current flows through the diode, the emitted light causes the transistor to become conducting. Thus the receiver circuitry can sense the presence or absence of loop current without direct electric connection to the transmission line. It should also be noted that the diode carries only the loop current and is not affected by the common-mode component. Therefore, in addition to providing the required protection, the optical isolator enables rejection of the common-mode noise currents on the line.

Figure 12.1a requires the link to allow transmission of dc (direct current) signals. If the transmission link is a part of the public telephone network, this is usually not possible to achieve. A *voice-grade* link will only allow signals with frequencies in the range of 300 to 3600 Hz to be transmitted without excessive attenuation. Unless special arrangements are made with the telephone company, no dc path exists between the two ends of a telephone connection (because of the intervening central office equipment). This means that to transmit data on such links an encoding scheme has to be used to represent the 0 and 1 logic values by signals whose frequencies lie within the transmission band of the line.[12.1] This function is performed by a *modem* (MOdulator-DEModulator) which is installed at each end of the line. The modem and its associated control circuitry are often referred to as a *data set*.

Two transmission channels can be established on a single line by an appropriate choice of the transmission frequencies for each direction. A commonly used scheme, referred to as frequency-shift keying (FSK), is shown in Figure 12.2. One of the channels is used for transmission in one direction, and the other is used for the opposite direction.

The scheme of Figure 12.2 does not necessarily imply that the modems are hardwired to the telephone line. It is also possible to connect them to the line via a standard telephone set by using an *acoustic coupler*. The coupler consists of a microphone-speaker pair physically mounted to match the standard telephone handset, as shown in Figure 12.3. Output signals from the modem are fed to the speaker, which is acoustically coupled to the transmitter in the handset.

	Frequency, Hz	
Logic state	0 (space)	1 (mark)
Channel 1	1075	1275
Channel 2	2025	2225

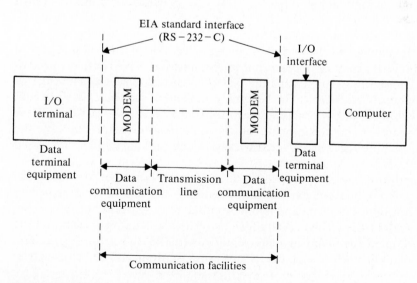

Figure 12.2 Remote connection of an I/O terminal over a dedicated telephone line using frequency-shift keying.

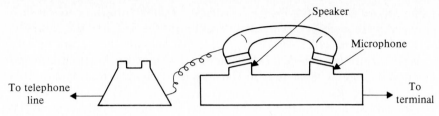

Figure 12.3 Acoustic coupling.

Similarly, sound signals from the telephone receiver are picked up by the microphone and transmitted as electric signals to the modem.

12.1.2 Synchronous and Asynchronous Transmission

The asynchronous start-stop format mentioned earlier is most commonly used for communication with remote terminals, particularly over the dialed public network. However, for higher-speed devices this transmission format is wasteful of the line bandwidth,[1] because of the need to transmit the start and stop bits for every character. Better utilization of the transmission link can be attained through the use of synchronous transmission. In this case, a continuously running clock is used for timing of the transmission of consecutive bits. At the receiving end, a clock having the same frequency and a fixed phase relationship to the transmitting clock must be used to sample the received signal. Special modulation techniques, similar to those discussed in connection with magnetic recording in Chapter 9, may be used to transmit the frequency and phase information from the sending to the receiving end. A detailed discussion of such techniques is given in Reference 12.1.

In asynchronous transmission, Start and Stop bits enable the receiver to locate the beginning and the end of each character. An alternative mechanism must be provided when using synchronous transmission. This is usually accomplished by transmitting data in separate blocks consisting of several hundreds or several thousands of bits each. The beginning and end of each block are marked, and data within a block is organized according to a known set of rules. These rules constitute an important part of the *data link protocol* used by the transmitter and the receiver. Synchronous data link protocols will be discussed in Section 12.3.

The need for a modem when using telephone lines or other long transmission links was pointed out earlier. Some modems are especially designed to support synchronous transmission by incorporating the function of clock recovery. They present the receiving data terminal with the data bit stream and the clock on separate lines. Many modems require a significant "start-up" time. This time is needed to complete such operations as transmitting and detecting carrier

---

[1]Line bandwidth roughly corresponds to the transmission capacity of the line in bits per second.

Table 12.1 Summary of the characteristics of some commercially available modems[12.3]

Model	Speed, bits/s	Synch./Asynch.	Start-up time. ms
103A	up to 300	Asynch.	NA
202S	1200	Asynch.	NA
202T	1800	Asynch.	NA
212A	0 to 1200	Asynch.	NA
201C	2400	Synch.	7
208A	4800	Synch.	50
209A	9600	Synch.	8

frequencies and establishing synchronization. In some modems, the start-up time is also used to adapt the modem circuits to the current transmission properties of the link. Typical characterisitics of some commercially available modems are given in Table 12.1.

12.1.3 Full- and Half-Duplex Links

In general, a communication link may be one of three types:

1. *Simplex* allows transmission in one direction only.
2. *Half duplex (HDX)* allows transmission in either direction, but not at the same time.
3. *Full duplex (FDX)* allows simultaneous transmission in both directions.

The simplex configuration is useful only if the remote location contains an input or an output device, but not both. Hence, it is seldom used. The choice between half and full duplex is basically a trade-off between economy and speed of transmission.

With a transmission scheme such as the current loop, a pair of wires enables transmission in one direction only, that is, simplex operation. To obtain a half-duplex link, it is necessary to use switches at both ends to connect either the transmitter or the receiver, but not both, to the line. When transmission in one direction is completed, the switches are reversed to enable transmission in the reverse direction. Control of the position of the switches is a part of the function of the devices at each end of the line.

Full-duplex operation can be achieved on a four-wire link, with two wires dedicated to each direction of transmission. Alternatively, a two-wire link with two nonoverlapping frequency bands can be used to create two independent transmission channels, one for each direction. An example of a full-duplex link was given in Figure 12.2, where the two channels have the signaling frequencies 1275/1075 and 2225/2025 Hz.

In the case of synchronous half-duplex operation, a time delay is encountered whenever the direction of transmission is reversed, because the transmitting modem may have to transmit an initializing sequence of signals to allow the receiving end to adapt to the conditions of the channel. The amount of delay encountered depends upon the modem and the transmission facilities and may be anywhere from a few milliseconds to several hundred milliseconds.

The above discussion relates directly to the characteristics of the transmission link and the modems. Other important factors that influence the choice between half- and full-duplex operation are the nature of the data traffic and the means by which the system reacts to the occurrence of errors during transmission. The former is discussed below; the latter will be dealt with in Section 12.2.

A large number of computer applications require the computer to receive input data, perform some processing, and then return output data. Basically, this is half-duplex operation. A half-duplex link will not only satisfy the requirements for such an application, but it will also enable data transmission to take place at the maximum possible speed. However, if the messages exchanged between the two ends are short and frequent, the delay encountered in reversing the direction of transmission becomes significant. For that reason alone, many such applications utilize full-duplex transmission facilities, although actual data transmission never takes place in both directions at the same time.

There are situations, however, where simultaneous transmission in both directions can be used to considerable advantage. Again, let us consider the system of Figure 12.2, with the remote terminal being a simple CRT terminal. Each character entered at the keyboard should be echoed back to be displayed on the screen. This may be done locally, for example, by the control circuitry of the terminal, or remotely by the computer or its peripherals. The latter provides an automatic checking capability to ensure that no errors have been introduced during transmission. If a half-duplex link is used in such a case, transmission of the next character must be delayed until the first character has been echoed back. No such restriction is necessary with full-duplex operation. Another example can be found in high-speed computer communication networks. Messages traveling in opposite directions on any given link often bear no relation to each other; hence, they can be transmitted simultaneously.

12.1.4 Standard Communications Interface

To allow interconnection of equipment made by different manufacturers, it is useful to develop standards that define how these devices may be interconnected. Such standards should define both the physical and functional characteristics of the interface. As pointed out in Section 6.6, a standard interface refers to the dividing line, or the collection of points at which two instruments are connected together. One such standard that has gained acceptance is the EIA (Electronics Industry Association) Standard RS-232-C. Outside North America, it is known as the CCITT (Comité Consultatif International Télégraphique et Téléphonique) recommendation V24. It completely specifies the interface between data communication devices (for example, modems) and data terminal equipment

**Table 12.2 Summary of the EIA Standard RS-232-C signals
(CCITT recommendation V24)**

Name			
EIA	CCITT	Pin* no.	Function
AA	101	1	Protective ground
AB	102	7	Signal ground–common return
BA	103	2	Transmitted data
BB	104	3	Received data
CA	105	4	Request to send
CB	106	5	Clear to send
CC	107	6	Data set ready
CD	108.2	20	Data terminal ready
CE	125	22	Ring indicator
CF	109	8	Received line signal detector
CG	110	21	Signal quality detector
CH	111	23§	Data signal rate selector (from DTE† to DCE‡)
CI	112	23§	Data signal rate selector (from DCE‡ to DTE†)
DA	113	24	Transmitter signal element timing (DTE†)
DB	114	15	Transmitter signal element timing (DCE‡)
DD	115	17	Receiver signal element timing (DCE‡)
SBA	118	14	Secondary transmitted data
SBB	119	16	Secondary received data
SCA	120	19	Secondary request to send
SCB	121	13	Secondary clear to send
SCF	122	12	Secondary received line signal detector

*Pins 9 and 10 are used for testing purposes and pins 11, 18, and 25 are spare.
†Data terminal equipment.
‡Data communication equipment.
§The signal on this pin is given a different name, depending upon its direction.

(for example, the computer and the I/O terminal in Figure 12.2). The RS-232-C interface consists of 25 connection points, which are described in Table 12.2.

For illustration purposes, let us discuss a simple, but frequently encountered example. Consider the link of Figure 12.2, assuming the remote terminal to be a CRT terminal and the connection to be over the dialed telephone network. The data set on the computer side, which we will refer to as data set A, is capable of going on- and off-hook under computer control as well as detecting the ringing signal on the telephone line. A simpler data set is used on the I/O terminal side, with manual dialing and acoustic coupling. Figure 12.4 gives the sequence of logic signals needed to establish a connection, transmit data, and terminate the connection. The steps involved in this process are described briefly below.

1. When the computer is ready to accept a call, it sets the data terminal ready signal (CD) to 1.
2. Data set A monitors the telephone line, and when it detects the ringing current, indicating an incoming call, it signals the computer by setting the

Step no.	Terminal	Interface signals	Data set B	Data set A	Interface signals	Computer
1				Enable automatic answering	CD	←1
2	Dialed digits →			1 →	CE	
				Goes off-hook		
3		CF	←1	←2225 Hz	CC	
					CA	←1
4	Push button (equivalent to 1 →)	CA	1275 Hz →	1 →	CB	
		CB	←1	1 →	CF	
		CC	←1			
5	Output data ←	BB	←data	←2225–2025 Hz	BA	←output data
	Input data →	BA	1275–1075 Hz →	Data →	BB	→input data
6		CF	←0	Drop 2225 Hz and disconnect	CA	←0
					CD	←0
7	(0 →)	CA	Drop 1275	0 →	CF	
				0 →	CC	
				0 →	CB	
8	Terminate connection	CB	←0		CD	←1
		CC	←0			

Figure 12.4 RS-232-C standard signaling sequence.

ring indicator (CE) to 1. If CD = 1 at the time the ringing current is detected, the data set automatically answers the call by going off-hook. Then, it sets the data set ready (CC) signal to 1.

3. The computer instructs data set A to start transmitting the frequency representing a mark condition (2225 Hz) by setting request to send (CA) to 1. When this is accomplished, data set A responds by setting clear to send (CB) to 1. The detection of the mark frequency at data set B causes it to set the received line signal detector (CF) to 1, and turn on a front panel indicator light.

4. The user responds by pressing a button on the front panel of the data set, which is equivalent to setting CA to 1, causing transmission of the 1275-Hz signal. Data set B then sets CB and CC to 1. When data set A detects the 1275-Hz frequency, it sets CF to 1.

5. A full-duplex link is now established between the computer and the remote terminal. The computer can transfer data to and from the remote terminal in the same way as in the case of local terminals. Interface pins BA (transmitted data) and BB (received data) are used for this purpose, while all other signals in the interface remain unchanged.

6. When the user signs off, the computer sets the request to send and data terminal ready signals (CA and CD) to 0, causing data set A to drop the mark condition and disconnect from the line. Signals CB, CF, and CC are set to 0 by data set A. When data set B senses the disappearance of the mark condition on the line, it sets the received line signal detector (CF) to 0.

7. Data set B responds by removing its mark frequency from the line and setting CB and CC to 0. The user terminates the connection by going on-hook.

8. The computer sets data terminal ready (CD) to 1, in preparation for a new call.

We should point out that the above description pertains specifically to the case of a transmission link involving a modem. The RS-232-C interface is much more general because it can be used to provide a serial connection between any two digital devices. Of course, the interpretation of individual signals such as CA and CD depends on the functional capabilities of the devices involved. When these signals are not needed, they are simply ignored by both devices. In some situations, a device such as a computer requires an active signal on certain lines, for example, on the data terminal ready (CD) line. If the terminal connected to the computer does not generate an active signal on this line, the interface wiring should provide the required active level.

12.2 ERROR CONTROL

In the previous section, some elementary concepts related to communication between a computer and a remote terminal were introduced. Such communication takes place in much the same way as with local terminals. So far, only one substantial difference between the two cases has been encountered; namely, the remote terminal requires some means for establishing and breaking the connection with the computer, while such means are usually not needed for local terminals. With the latter, the link exists, in effect, as long as power is supplied to the equipment. The next and even more fundamental difference between local and remote peripherals is that errors are much more likely to occur during communication with a remote peripheral. The detection of these errors and the provision of some means for recovery are important functions of the communications hardware and software.

The functions related to the control of data transfer over a communication link are referred to as *data link control* (DLC). In addition to error control, the DLC functions include synchronization of the transmitting and receiving clocks, control of the direction of transmission on half-duplex links, and addressing of terminals on multipoint lines, as will be discussed in Section 12.3. At the computer end, many of these functions may be performed by the computer itself. However, when a large number of terminals is involved, it becomes advantageous to introduce a dedicated *communications controller*, which is separate from the computer and connected to it as an I/O peripheral. Such a controller may either have a fixed hardwired structure or operate under stored program control. At the remote end, a terminal may include a microprocessor which performs all DLC functions. The microprocessor may also be used to convert from one character code to another or to assist in the preparation of the user's messages via text editing. A terminal offering such capabilities is usually referred to as an *intelligent terminal*.

In this section we will start with a brief presentation of error-detection techniques, followed by a discussion of the procedures used for error correction or retransmission of the erroneous message.

12.2.1 Detection of Transmission Errors

The simplest method for error detection is the use of *parity* bits. Parity bits may be inserted in the data stream in a variety of ways. For example, a parity bit may be added to each character to form either odd or even parity. For a 7-bit character $b_6 b_5 \ldots b_0$, an even-parity bit P may be transmitted as an eighth bit, where

$$P = b_6 \oplus b_5 \oplus \ldots \oplus b_0$$

The symbol $\oplus$ denotes the *Exclusive-OR*, or *modulo 2 sum*, function. If odd parity is used, P is replaced by $\bar{P}(= 1 \oplus P)$. The receiving end can easily check whether each of the received characters has the appropriate parity. If a character with the wrong parity is received, a transmission error has occurred. This form of error checking is usually referred to as *vertical redundancy checking* (VRC). Another parity scheme referred to as *longitudinal redundancy checking* (LRC) introduces a single checking character at the end of a group of characters that

	P	Data						
	0	1	0	1	1	0	0	1
	0	0	1	0	0	1	0	0
	0	1	1	1	0	0	0	1
	0	1	0	0	1	1	1	0
VRC parity bits	1	0	1	0	1	0	1	0
(even parity)	1	0	0	1	0	1	1	0
	0	1	0	0	1	1	0	1
	1	1	1	0	0	1	1	1
	1	1	0	1	0	1	0	0

1 0 1 0 1 0 0 ◄———LRC check sum

Figure 12.5 Use of VRC and LRC parity checking.

constitute a message. For example, a message consisting of a group of 7-bit characters is followed by a 7-bit *check sum* $P_6P_5 \ldots P_0$. Each of the parity bits P_6 to P_0 is equal to the modulo 2 sum of all the corresponding bit positions in the characters of the message. The VRC and LRC schemes may be combined as shown in Figure 12.5 to enhance the error-detection capability.

The above error-detection schemes are very useful when bit errors occur as isolated events. Unfortunately, errors on telephone channels usually occur in "bursts," particularly at higher transmission speeds. As an example, switching transients on near-by power lines may cause errors in a number of consecutive bits. The bursty nature of errors on telephone lines limits the usefulness of the VRC and LRC schemes. A number of other error-detection schemes have been developed for use in such environments. A powerful and commonly used scheme is the *cyclic-redundancy-checking* (CRC) technique. Similar to LRC, the CRC scheme uses a check sum at the end of the message. The check sum is generated by computing the modulo 2 sum of the message bits after grouping them in a special way. The number of bits in the check sum is usually 8 or 16, depending upon the length of the message and the desired error-detection capability. A thorough treatment of this subject may be found in Reference 12.4.

12.2.2 Procedures for Recovery from Transmission Errors

In general, recovery from transmission errors may be achieved in one of two ways:[12.5]

1. By including enough redundancy to enable the receiver to reconstruct the transmitted message even when some of the received bits are in error. This approach is referred to as *forward error correction* (FEC).
2. By using an error-detection scheme and requesting retransmission when an error is detected. This approach is referred to as *automatic repeat request* (ARQ).

A well-known example of FEC codes are the Hamming codes, which are a special case of the CRC techniques. One problem with error-correcting codes is that they require a large number of additional check bits. For example, a 7-bit message containing 4 bits of information and 3 check bits enables the receiver to reconstruct the original message after the occurrence of an error in 1 bit. In general, n check bits enable correction of a 1-bit error in a message that is $2^n - 1$ bits long (including the check bits). More check bits are necessary if it is required to have the capability for correcting errors in more than 1 bit. For this reason, such codes are only suitable for use on channels that have very low error rates or when a reverse channel is not available to request retransmission. Examples of the use of forward error correction can be found in radio and satellite communications.

The most commonly used scheme for error control on telephone channels is ARQ, which is described below in some detail.

ARQ protocols The simplest of these protocols is referred to as *stop-and-wait* ARQ. After the sending end completes transmission of a message, it stops and waits until either a positive or a negative acknowledgment is received from the remote end. An acknowledgment is a coded message that the receiving end sends to the sending end when the reception of a message is completed. A positive acknowledgment indicates that no errors have been detected. That is, the check sum computed by the receiver matches that at the end of the message. A negative acknowledgment indicates an error condition, and it is interpreted by the sending end as a request for retransmission of the same message. A system using this protocol should also allow for the possibility that, for some reason, the acknowledgment message does not reach the sending end. In order to guard against the transmiter waiting indefinitely for a reply, a watchdog timer should be used. After a time-out period, the sender assumes that its message has been lost and starts retransmission. This may be attempted a few times, after which the sender assumes that the transmission link is broken.

The stop-and-wait system is very simple to implement and can be used with either full- or half-duplex lines. Its main disadvantage, however, is that line utilization is low, since considerable time is spent waiting for acknowledgments. The situation is depicted in Figure 12.6, where T is the message transmission time and W is the waiting time before the next message can be transmitted. Thus message transmission takes place only $T/(T + W)$ of the available time. Furthermore, if we assume that P is the probability of an erroneous message, only $1 - P$ of the transmitted messages are received correctly. The remaining messages are discarded by the receiving end because of the presence of errors. Thus we can define a transmission efficiency factor η as

$$\eta = \frac{T}{T + W} (1 - P)$$

Let the speed of transmission be v bits/s and the message length be n bits; then,

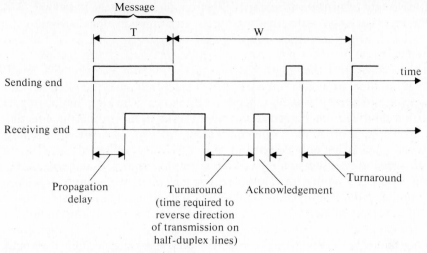

Figure 12.6 Stop-and-wait ARQ scheme.

$$\eta = \frac{n/v}{n/v + W}(1 - P)$$

$$= \frac{n}{n + Wv}(1 - P)$$

It can be easily seen from Figure 12.6 that the waiting time W consists of three components: the round-trip propagation delay, the time required to reverse the direction of transmission twice, and the transmission time of the acknowledgment message. As an example, let us consider a 4800-bit/s communication link over the public telephone network. The propagation delay may be estimated at 4 ms/100 mi. The turnaround time varies considerably and will be assumed to be 150 ms. The transmission time for the acknowledgment message is a function of the number of characters it contains. Since this involves the transmission of only a few characters, the transmission time is short and may be neglected. Assuming a 300-mi link, we obtain

$$W = 2(4 \times 3 + 150) = 324 \text{ ms}$$

Next, let us consider the probability of error P. Obviously, this is a function of the message length n. For n in the range of 10 to 10^4 bits, a rough estimate for P for a 4800-bit/s link may be obtained from the equation[12.6]

$$P = 0.15 \times 10^{-4}n$$

Then, for a message length of 1000 bits, we obtain

$$\eta = \frac{1000(1 - 0.015)}{1000 + 0.324 \times 4800} = 0.39$$

The effective rate of transmission under these conditions is $0.39 \times 4800 = 1870$ bits/s. For message lengths such that $P \ll 1$, the transmission efficiency improves as the message length increases. For $n = 200$, η drops to 0.11, while for $n = 5000$, $\eta = 0.71$.

Let us now consider the effect of increasing the modem speed to 9600 bits/s. The new value for η for a 1000-bit message becomes 0.24, and the effective rate of transmission increases to $0.24 \times 9600 = 2300$ bits/s. Thus it is interesting to observe that doubling the transmission speed results in increasing the effective rate of transmission by only 23 percent (from 1870 to 2300 bits/s), because transmission takes place only 24 percent of the time at the higher speed.

From the above discussion, it can be seen that the stop-and-wait ARQ scheme is inherently inefficient. However, because of its simplicity it is widely used. Note that if the transmission facilities are full duplex, the turnaround time is reduced to zero. Since this is the dominant parameter in the above example, a significant increase in the transmission efficiency can be expected. In fact, for a 4800-bit/s link and for $n = 200$, 1000, and 5000 bits, η is equal to 0.63, 0.90, and 0.97, respectively.

For long-distance transmission, the efficiency of the stop-and-wait scheme is low, even with full-duplex transmission. Significant improvement can be achieved if the wait period is eliminated, which is the case with the continuous-ARQ scheme described briefly below.

Continuous ARQ With full-duplex facilities, the transmitting end may continue sending messages without waiting for the arrival of acknowledgments. When a negative acknowledgment is received, the sending end starts retransmitting the messages that were received in error. This implies that:

1. Messages are kept in memory buffers until the corresponding acknowledgments are received.
2. Messages and their acknowledgments should be numbered so that the transmitting end can retransmit the correct messages.

The continuous-ARQ method is considerably more involved than the stop-and-wait scheme. It is used in situations where line utilization and overall throughput are important factors.

12.3 MULTITERMINAL CONFIGURATIONS

We now consider the problem of connecting a number of remote terminals to a computer. Four possible configurations suitable for this purpose are given in Figure 12.7. These are:

• The star configuration
• The multipoint line
• The loop configuration
• The tree configuration

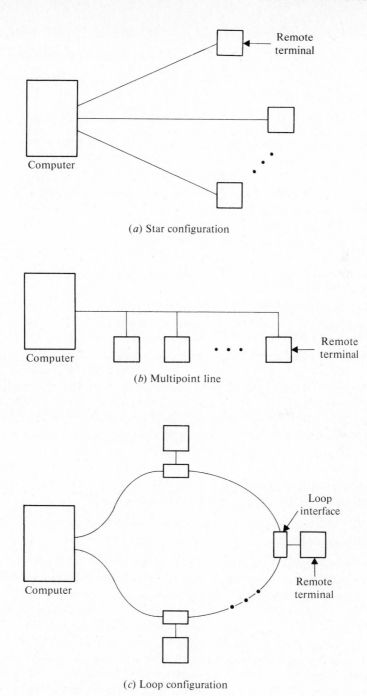

(*a*) Star configuration

(*b*) Multipoint line

(*c*) Loop configuration

Figure 12.7 Connection of remote terminals.

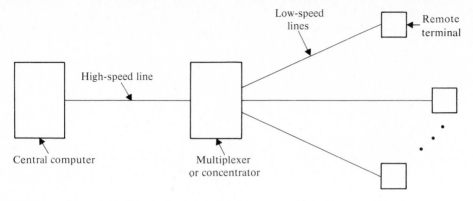

(*d*) Tree configuration (only one branch shown)

Figure 12.7 *(Continued)*

12.3.1 Star Configuration

This is the simplest configuration. A separate transmission link is used between each terminal and the computer, as shown in Figure 12.7a. The links in such a network may be either dedicated transmission lines or a part of the dialed telephone network. Each link has a configuration similar to that of Figure 12.2 and may be connected to the computer via a separate I/O interface. When the number of remote terminals is large, it becomes advantageous to connect the lines to the main computer via a *multiplexer*. The multiplexer collects data characters from individual lines and presents them to the computer, together with an address identifying the source terminal. During output a reverse process takes place. That is, the computer sends a data character and a line address to the multiplexer, which, in turn, transmits the character to the appropriate terminal. Multiplexing is usually one of the functions performed by a communications controller, if one exists.

12.3.2 Multipoint Lines

The second configuration (Figure 12.7b) is the *multipoint*, or *multidrop*, line. In this case, a single transmission line is used for connecting a number of terminals, which can lead to a substantial saving in cabling costs. However, it introduces some new problems related to the way in which a communication path is established between the computer and one of the terminals. In the following discussion we will assume that full-duplex operation is possible, which is usually the case with multipoint lines. This means that at any given time the computer can be transmitting to one or more terminals and receiving from one terminal. A control scheme (protocol) has to be established to deal with:

   a. Addressing of individual terminals
   b. Scheduling the use of the transmission line

a. Addressing of individual terminals When the computer transmits a message, it should be able to select only one of the terminals to receive this message. This is accomplished by transmitting the message preceded by the terminal address. Thus a protocol is required to allow all devices connected to the line to unambiguously identify the address and data components of a message. Two such protocols are described below.

ASCII data link control This protocol[12.7] is used on synchronous transmission links, both for point-to-point and multipoint connections. It is based on transmitting the address, control, and data bits as 7- or 8-bit characters. The standard ASCII 7-bit character set is given in Appendix D. The 8-bit code usually consists of the standard 7-bit code plus one parity bit. A few characters are reserved for establishing character synchronization and identifying various sections of a transmitted message.

Let us consider first the problem of character synchronization. Since transmission on a communication link is in the bit-serial mode, the receiver needs to identify the beginning and end of each character. The character SYN is used for this purpose. The binary code for this character is 0010110, which has the property that upon circular shifting the code repeats itself only after a full 7-bit cycle. This means that if a sequence of SYN characters is transmitted, the receiver can unambiguously identify their boundaries, thus establishing character synchronization for subsequent characters.

Having established the character boundaries, it remains for the receiver to separate the address, control, and data components of a message. The message can be divided into two parts: the *message header* consisting of the address and control information, and the *message text*, which is the actual data transmitted. Special characters are used to identify each part. The exact format of the message, and the particular characters used as "delimiters," vary from one application to another. An example of a full ASCII message is given in Figure 12.8. In this case, the characters SOH (start of header), STX (start of text), and ETX (end of text) are used to identify the beginning and end of the header and text.

This simple ASCII scheme can be used for addressing terminals on a multipoint line. However, it has a few limitations, as follows:

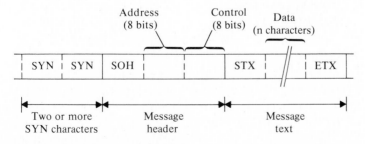

Figure 12.8 A typical ASCII message.

1. The user is restricted to transmitting 8-bit entities.
2. The user is prohibited from using the codes corresponding to the reserved control characters. In the case of traffic consisting of printing characters this is not an important limitation, since the control characters are always chosen from the 32 nonprinting characters of the ASCII code (see Appendix D). If the user wishes to transmit all possible codes, for example, in the case of transmitting binary numbers rather than ASCII characters, it is necessary to make the line control protocol "transparent." This can be achieved by a slight modification to the ASCII protocol, based on the use of the character DLE (data link escape). Control characters can be uniquely identified if they are always preceded by DLE. In the text portion of the message, any occurrence of the DLE character is duplicated by the transmitting end. At the receiving end, the first DLE character is always dropped. If the next character is another DLE, it is regarded as part of the text. Otherwise, it is treated as a control character. An example of the use of this scheme can be found in the ARPA network.[12.8]
3. The protocol does not guarantee the occurrence of 0 to 1 transitions in the user's text. Thus a transmission scheme has to be used that does not depend on these transitions for recovering the clock at the receiving end.

High-level data link control (HDLC) This control protocol[12.9] overcomes the difficulties encountered in the ASCII scheme. It has been recommended by the International Standards Organization (ISO) as an international standard for control of communication lines. With minor variations, it is also known as SDLC (synchronous data link control), ADCCP (advanced data communication control procedure), and LAP (link-access protocol). This scheme has two basic characteristics:

1. The notion of a fixed-size character being a fundamental transmission unit is discarded.
2. A unique 8-bit combination, referred to as a "flag," is introduced to serve as the only delimiter in the system. The uniqueness of this flag is guaranteed in a way that is transparent to the user.

The format of a message using this protocol is given in Figure 12.9. The flag has the code 01111110. The same flag is used to indicate the beginning and the end of a message. Any number of flags may be transmitted between messages for

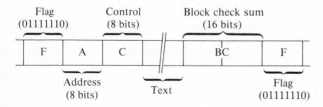

Figure 12.9 High-level data link protocol.

synchronization purposes. Whenever five consecutive 1s appear in the user's message, the transmitting end automatically inserts a 0. Similarly, the receiving end automatically discards a 0 following five 1s. Therefore, six consecutive 1s is a unique code encountered only in the flag. Recovery of the transmission clock at the receiving end is also facilitated by the encoding scheme used. A 0 is encoded as a state change on the line, that is, by either a high to low or a low to high transition, and a 1 is transmitted by maintaining the same state as in the preceding bit period. Hence, since the maximum length of a string of 1s is 6 bits, a special circuit, such as a phase-locked loop, can be used to reconstruct the transmission clock from the received signal. The scheme is transparent, since the user need not be aware of the insertion and deletion of 0s. This function is automatically performed by the transmitting and receiving hardware.

The address and control fields have a fixed length of 8 bits each. These are followed by the message text which may consist of any number of bits. The last 16 bits in the message consist of a CRC check sum for error-detection purposes.

b. Scheduling the use of the transmission line Let us consider the situation when some of the terminals of Figure 12.7b are ready to transmit data to the computer. Obviously, only one terminal can be allowed to transmit at any given time. Coordination of this process has to be under control of the computer. Three commonly used schemes for this purpose are "roll polling," "hub polling," and "contention."

Roll polling This is the simplest of the control procedures for a multipoint line. The computer starts by transmitting a short poll message to one of the terminals. If the terminal is ready for transmission, it responds by transmitting its data. Otherwise, it transmits a "not ready" message. The computer then polls the next terminal, and so on. In this scheme, the computer transmits and all terminals receive on the outbound channel of the full-duplex link. The selected terminal transmits and the computer receives on the inbound channel. Thus, outbound messages, other than poll messages, may be overlapped with terminal-to-computer transmission.

Hub polling This is a modification of the roll-polling scheme aimed at reducing the polling overhead.[12.10] The hub-polling procedure is illustrated in Figure 12.10. The computer starts by sending a poll message on the outbound channel to terminal 1. If this terminal is ready for transmission, it responds, as before, by transmitting its message. However, if it is not ready, it transmits the poll message to terminal 2 on the inbound channel. This can be accomplished simply by inserting the address of terminal 2 into the address space of the poll message. Thus, terminal 2 must be able to receive messages on the inbound channel. Of course, all terminals must also be able to receive messages from the computer on the outbound channel. When any terminal finishes transmitting a message, it should send the poll message to the next terminal on the inbound channel.

The hub-polling scheme results in a significant reduction in the polling

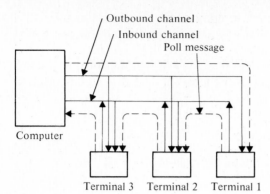

Terminal 3   Terminal 2   Terminal 1   **Figure 12.10** Hub polling.

overhead. The computer only initiates the polling process by sending a poll message on the outbound channel. While polling proceeds on the inbound channel, the computer is free to use the outbound channel for sending output messages. Moreover, if propagation delay is taken into consideration, it can be shown that the delay involved in polling all the terminals on the line is substantially decreased in comparison with the roll-polling scheme.

Contention When terminal traffic is light, the probability of more than one terminal becoming ready for transmission at the same time is fairly low. This is sometimes exploited by allowing terminals to start transmitting as soon as they have a message ready, preceding their messages with an identifying address. Whenever the computer receives garbled data resulting from more than one terminal starting transmission at the same time, it issues a "stop" command causing all terminals to stop transmission. It then starts polling terminals in order. This method is obviously inefficient at times of high terminal activity. Therefore, the messages "enable transmission" and "disable transmission" are usually provided to enable the computer to switch between the polling and contention modes of operation. This scheme is known as ALOHA, because it was first used in the ALOHA network at the University of Hawaii.[12.11]

12.3.3 Loop Organization

The main difference between the loop configuration of Figure 12.7c and the multipoint line is that the loop consists of separate point-to-point links interconnecting the loop interfaces. Transmission around the loop always takes place in the same direction, that is, either clockwise or counterclockwise. Thus, all line segments operate in the simplex mode. Data received at the input side of a loop interface is either sent to the corresponding terminal or transmitted, after some delay, on the next segment of the loop. The loop interface may also transmit data received from its associated terminal. Obviously, a loop protocol is required to determine when an interface can place this data on the loop, and the format in which this transmission can take place. An example of such a protocol is found in terminal loops used with some IBM equipment.[12.12]

12.3.4 Tree Configuration

In this configuration, Figure 12.7*d*, terminals are not connected directly to the central computer. Instead, they are connected to an intermediate node, which, in turn, is connected to the computer via a high-speed link. A hardwired controller or a small computer is used at this node to collect characters or messages from individual terminals and transmit them to the central computer, together with some means for identifying their sources. Depending on its mode of operation, the node controller is referred to as either a multiplexer or a concentrator.

Multiplexers Let us consider the case where *n* terminals are connected to the intermediate node. A multiplexer, in effect, uses the high-speed line to establish the equivalent of *n* independent links to the central computer.[12.13] Each of these links has a capacity equal to that of one of the low-speed lines connecting the multiplexer to the terminals. The multiplexer assigns one link to each terminal, thus creating a direct link between the terminal and the central computer. Two multiplexing techniques are discussed below: *frequency-division multiplexing* (FDM) and *synchronous time-division multiplexing* (STDM).

The FDM technique has long been used in voice communications on the telephone network, where individual voice signals are combined for transmission on high-speed lines between central offices. Essentially the same technique can be used for combining the signals received on the low-speed lines of Figure 12.7*d*. The transmission frequency band of the high-speed line is divided into frequency slots or channels. Individual line signals are then shifted in frequency to fit into these slots. This process is called *modulation*. The reverse process, *demodulation*, takes place at the receiving end. The combined signal which is transmitted on the high-speed line is depicted in Figure 12.11. The frequency separation between channels is required to guarantee that transmission over one channel does not interfere with a neighboring channel. Note that no further addressing information is required during transmission, since individual terminals are identified by the frequency slot they occupy.

The FDM scheme is simple to implement. Its main disadvantage is that it

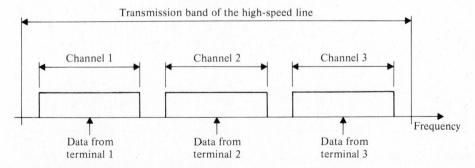

Figure 12.11 Frequency-division multiplexing.

does not provide for full utilization of the transmission capacity of the line, due to the need for separation of the channels. In general, FDM is used only in relatively low-speed applications, where it is desirable to keep the cost of the multiplexing equipment to a minimum. In higher-performance systems, the STDM scheme is more attractive.

The STDM scheme requires the time for transmitting one character on the high-speed line to be less than $(1/n)$th of the corresponding transmission time on the low-speed lines. Its implementation is based on the use of a multiplexer whose organization is indicated in Figure 12.12. The multiplexer consists of a switch that continuously scans the low-speed lines in such a way that one character is transmitted from line 1, followed by one character from line 2, and so on. When line n is reached the scanning process is repeated. Usually, a special framing character is transmitted at the beginning of each scan to enable the receiving end to identify the data from individual lines. The first character following the framing character belongs to line 1, the second character belongs to line 2, and so on. The resulting transmission format is shown in Figure 12.13. In effect, the time period corresponding to one transmission frame is divided

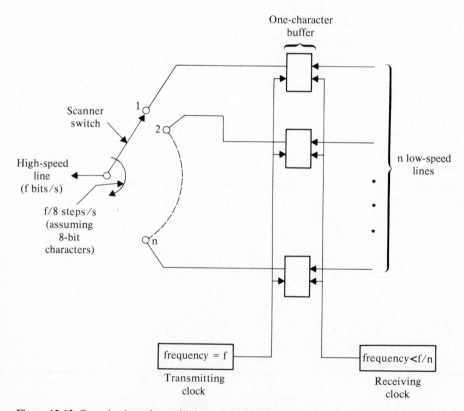

Figure 12.12 Organization of a multiplexer for STDM.

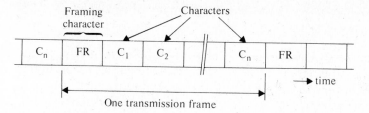

Figure 12.13 Transmission format in synchronous time-division multiplexing.

into $n + 1$ time slots. The first of these slots is always occupied by the framing character. The next n slots provide n independent channels which are assigned to the n low-speed lines. As in the case of FDM, no further addressing information is needed, since individual lines are identified by their relative positions within the transmission frame.

We should note that when the scanner switch is connected to any line i, it is possible that the character buffer for that particular line is empty. In this case, the multiplexer transmits a "Null" character. The receiving end automatically discards Null characters. Thus, proper operation of the system requires two characters to be reserved for the frame and null functions. Hence, these characters must not be included in the character set that the terminals transmit.

It is interesting to investigate the operation of the character buffers in Figure 12.12. These buffers perform an important function related to the coupling of two transmission lines operating at different speeds. The double-buffer arrangement of Figure 12.14 is needed for this purpose. Bits from the low-speed line are shifted serially into an input buffer. When a complete character has been received it is transferred to the output buffer, where it is stored until it can be transmitted in the appropriate time slot. Meanwhile, the next character is assembled in the input buffer. The figure shows the buffers needed for transmission from the terminal to the computer. For full-duplex operation, a similar arrangement is required for transmission in the opposite direction.

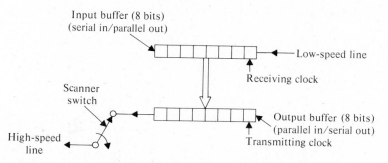

Figure 12.14 Double-buffer arrangement for the multiplexer of Figure 12.12, assuming 8-bit characters and one character per time slot.

The STDM scheme allows better utilization of the transmission facilities than FDM. However, it is still necessary to have the capacity of the high-speed line at least slightly higher than the sum of the capacities of all the low-speed lines. Since the remote terminals are seldom all busy at the same time, and since terminal operation involves long periods of inactivity, a significant proportion of the time slots will be wasted. If empty time slots are used to transmit data from other terminals, a considerable reduction in the capacity requirement for the high-speed line can be achieved. Node controllers that allow such flexibility are referred to as *concentrators*. In this case, the transmission capacity of the high-speed line can be less than the sum of the capacities of the low-speed lines.

Concentrators To enable utilization of the unused time slots in the STDM scheme, it is necessary to discard the fixed assignments of Figure 12.13. Let time slots be assigned only to inputs that have data ready for transmission. In such a case, the use of a fixed transmission frame and addressing by position within it are no longer possible. One alternative is to use a part of each time slot as an address field. A framing character is also required to establish the beginning of each time slot. Obviously the length of the time slot, and, hence, the number of characters per slot, must be increased considerably relative to that of Figure 12.12 if the framing and addressing overhead is to be kept to a minimum. The technique is generally known as *asynchronous time-division multiplexing* (ATDM).[12,13] The resulting transmission format is given in Figure 12.15.

The organization of the STDM multiplexer in Figure 12.12, with minor modifications, can be used for ATDM purposes. First, the scanner switch should be controlled such that it can skip positions whose output buffers are empty. Second, the size of the character buffers should be increased to correspond to at least the number of characters transmitted in one time slot. An organization that is well suited to this application is the queue, or first-in first-out (FIFO) buffer. A hardwired FIFO buffer may have the structure shown in Figure 12.16. After a character is assembled in the input buffer, it is entered into the top position of the FIFO buffer. The control hardware automatically shifts the character downward through successive character positions in the buffer until it reaches the lowest unoccupied position. When the output buffer is emptied, the character occupying the lowest location is shifted out, causing all characters in the FIFO buffer to move downward one position. Thus the FIFO buffer of a given line is filled at the low input rate until a time slot is assigned to this line. At this time a number of characters corresponding to the contents of one time slot are transmitted at the high output rate.

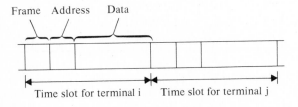

Time slot for terminal i   Time slot for terminal j

Figure 12.15 Asynchronous time-division multiplexing.

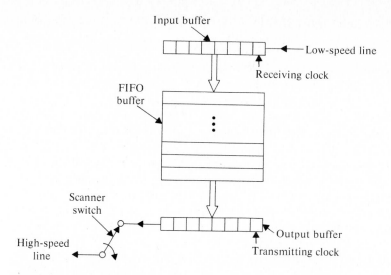

Figure 12.16 Use of FIFO buffers as line buffers in a concentrator.

The maximum length of the queue in any line buffer is a function of the input traffic on this line and of the output rate, which is also affected by traffic on other lines. The size of the FIFO buffer should be chosen to accommodate the expected maximum length. If under extreme conditions this is exceeded, some characters will be lost. The system design should provide some means for rectifying these situations or preventing them from happening.

The above discussion referred to a hardware implementation of the multiplexer and concentrator functions. These functions are often performed by a microprocessor unit. In this case the input, output, and FIFO functions are implemented in software, and the data is stored in the main memory. In addition to being cost effective, this approach provides considerable flexibility in the design.

12.3.5 Hierarchy of Control

Before proceeding to more complex networks, we will pause briefly to examine what we have encountered so far regarding the control of data transfer in a computer network. Let us refer again to the tree configuration of Figure 12.7*d*. The need for addressing discussed in the previous section, and represented in Figure 12.15, is required to route data received from remote terminals to the central computer. This is in addition to any protocols that are needed to control data flow over the high-speed link, which may still use any of the data link control procedures discussed in Section 12.3.2. In fact, the message format of Figure 12.15 is a "substructure" for the text portion of Figures 12.8 or 12.9.

We have identified two levels of control in a tree network. One level deals with data transfer between the concentrator and the central computer, and a higher level handles the routing of data to and from individual terminals. A still higher level is needed for handling the text received by the central computer from an individual user. For example, consider a user who is communicating with an interactive operating system. All commands, data, or control characters that are needed for this communication are simply treated as text by the other two levels. The user need not be aware of any of the details of the first two levels except for the possible restriction on the transmission of some reserved characters. This hierarchy of control, and the requirement that lower levels of protocol be transparent to higher levels, are important features of a properly designed computer communications network.[12.14, 12.15] The requirement for independence between various levels becomes more important as the size and complexity of the network increases. Independence allows each level to be developed or updated from time to time without affecting other levels in the network. The term *hierarchical networks* is used to describe computer networks where a hierarchy of levels can be clearly identified in the control structure of the network. Individual levels are often referred to as *protocol layers*.

12.4 CIRCUIT AND MESSAGE SWITCHING

The previous discussion dealt with networks that connect a number of peripherals to a single central computer. We will now consider a more general class of networks which interconnect an arbitrary selection of terminals and computers. Data transfer may take place between a terminal and a computer or between two computers. The service provided by such a network is akin to that provided by the public telephone network. Indeed, the latter can be, and sometimes is, used for this purpose. The dialed connection discussed in Section 12.1 is an example of such a use. However, there are several advantages in using networks designed specifically for computer communications, because of the special nature of this type of communication. In this case, the dialed network can still be useful for back-up purposes.

Two fundamental differences can be readily identified between voice communications, for which the telephone network is designed, and computer communications. These are:

- Computer traffic is bursty in nature.
- Computers are far less tolerant of transmission errors.

In the telephone network, a transmission path is established between the calling and the called parties soon after dialing. The facilities involved are dedicated to this call throughout its duration. That is, they cannot be shared with other users, even during long periods of silence. Such schemes for connecting two points are referred to as *circuit* or *line switching*. In the case of computer communications, the majority of the network traffic consists of short bursts of data separated by relatively long periods of inactivity. When this type of traffic is carried on a circuit-switched network, the utilization of the transmission facilities is very low. A possible alternative is to place a separate call for each burst of data. However, this is likely to be inefficient, since the setup time (that is, the time required to establish a call) is often long in comparison with the transmission time of a burst of data. A better alternative is to design a network that operates on the basis of dynamic allocation of resources. That is, a number of users should be able to share the use of the transmission hardware on a demand basis.

A scheme which satisfies this requirement is known as *message switching*. A source of data presents its message, preceded by the address of its intended destination, to the communications network. The network temporarily stores the message at the node where the message is received. Then it selects an appropriate route for the message depending upon the destination address and upon the current traffic in the network. As the message is transferred along this route, it is stored at each node until a transmission link to the next node is available. This mode of operation is called *store-and-forward* . It represents an extension of the ideas presented in Section 12.3 regarding the use of ATDM in the concentrator application.

The other important difference between the telephone network and a computer network relates to their error performance. As mentioned in Section 12.2, fairly complex procedures are required to enable error-free transfer of data. In a network designed specifically for computer communications, such procedures can be incorporated as an integral part of the network protocols.

12.4.1 Network Design Considerations

Let us consider a network, such as that shown in Figure 12.17, which is used to interconnect a number of terminals and computers. The network is capable of

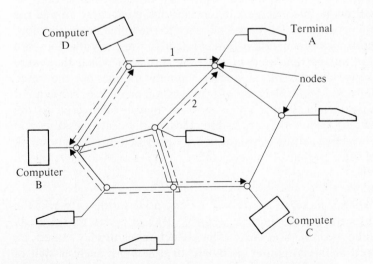

Figure 12.17 An example of an 8-node store-and-forward network.

providing communication paths between any pair of users. For example, terminal A may want to communicate with computer B, and, at the same time, data transfer may take place between computers C and D. The store-and-forward mode of operation requires the controller at each node of the network to perform the following functions:

- Store a message.
- Select an appropriate outgoing link, based on the destination address.
- Transmit the message when this link is free.

These tasks are in addition to error control and other DLC functions required to transfer a message between any two nodes. Because of the complexity of these tasks, a small computer is normally used as the node controller. We will present briefly a number of important issues related to the operation of a message-switching network.

Type of service In a telephone network, a connection exists between the calling and the called parties which is maintained until the call is terminated. A number of network resources are dedicated to this connection to provide a transmission path between the two ends. In the case of message switching, two types of networks can be identified. In the first, the network service appears to the user very much like that provided by a telephone network. After establishing a connection, two users can exchange messages for any period of time, then close down the connection. The network nodes keep track of the connection by means of table entries at various nodes. Thus, user messages need not carry the address of their destination. Such a logical connection between two users is called a *virtual circuit*. Note that actual physical transmission links are allocated to the connection only while a message is being transmitted.

In the second type of network, the concept of a connection is discarded, at least as far as the network is concerned. Each message must carry an address which is used by the network to deliver the message to the intended destination. Since individual messages are handled independently, the network does not guarantee that they will be delivered in the same order in which they were presented to the network by the source. In fact, the network does not guarantee that they will be delivered at all. Because of transmission errors and subsequent retransmissions, several copies of a given message may be delivered to the destination. It is up to the network users to detect lost or duplicate messages and take appropriate corrective action. Since the service provided by such a network bears some resemblance to that of the post office, it is referred to as *datagram* service.

Message routing When a message is received by any node in the network, the node processor inspects the destination address field in order to select an appropriate outgoing transmission link. This selection is usually based on routing tables stored in the computer memory. In a network such as that of

Figure 12.17, a number of alternative routes exist between any two points. For example, paths 1 and 2 are possible choices for a message from terminal A to computer B. It is advantageous to have as much flexibility as possible in choosing a suitable path, taking into account such considerations as broken links, heavily loaded links or nodes, etc.

Control of data flow Congestion in the network (the situation when a large percentage of the buffer space is occupied) can lead to undesirable results.[12.16, 12.17] Consider two node computers X and Y exchanging messages. Messages arriving at each computer destined for the other are buffered in an output queue. As the traffic increases, the lengths of both output queues increase until they occupy all the buffer space available. At this point no further message transfers can take place between the two computers. Computer X cannot accept any message from Y, or from any other computer, since it has no buffer space available to store the message. Similarly, computer Y cannot accept any messages from X. A *deadlock* is said to have occurred, and message traffic stops. To avoid the occurrence of such deadlocks, the buffer allocation scheme in computer Y should ensure that at least one message buffer space is always available for receiving messages from computer X, and vice versa.

In general, network protocols must be provided to control the flow of messages into the network. In addition to preventing the occurrence of deadlocks, these protocols protect against the occurrence of excessive delays.

Choice of message length Message length is an important parameter that has a significant effect on network performance. The statistical distribution of message length depends upon the application. For example, in interactive traffic, messages are relatively short and limited to a maximum, such as the length of a line of text on a terminal. On the other hand, when transferring data files from one computer to another, messages can be very long. In a store-and-forward network, long messages require a large amount of buffer storage and may adversely affect the network throughput. They also require long transmission time, thus leading to slower response time for other users. This is highly undesirable if the network also services interactive terminals. Very short messages lead to inefficient operation, because network overhead, for example, addressing, routing, and acknowledgments, is independent of the message length. Thus there is an optimal message length that provides an acceptable compromise between efficiency and response time.

It is not convenient to force the network user to limit all messages to the optimal length required by the network. This suggests the following mode of operation. Variable-length messages may be accepted by the network at the source point. Then, prior to transmitting them through the network, each message is broken down into smaller messages that correspond to the optimal message length in the network. These shorter messages can now be transmitted through the network, and, when they reach the destination point, they are reassembled into the original format and delivered to the receiver. Such short messages that travel through the network are referred to as *packets*, and the technique is known as *packet switching*. Networks using this approach can transfer long messages without a significant degradation in service to users with short messages. A maximum message length is usually imposed because of buffer storage limitations. This maximum can be several times the packet length.

12.4.2 Network Control

A number of functions have been identified that are related to the transfer of data via a message-switching network. They include establishing a connection, selecting suitable routes, and regulating message flow between any two points. The decisions involved in performing these functions require information about the status of various parts of the network. A simple way to accomplish this is to arrange for the status information to be sent from the individual node processors to a central processor, which performs all control functions for the network. For example, this processor can keep track of all current connections in the network. For every new connection, it selects a suitable route and sends the appropriate routing-table entries to all node processors on this route.[12.18]

An alternative approach is to distribute the control functions among the node processors, eliminating the need for a central control processor. Distributed control allows a more dynamic routing strategy to be implemented. A good example of this approach to network control is the ARPA network.[12.19]

An interesting aspect of distributed control is the way in which routing of packets may be accomplished. We will illustrate this by discussing a possible routing strategy for the network shown in Figure 12.18. Let us assume that this is a packet-switching network. Each packet is preceded by a header containing its destination address and is transmitted independently through the network. An individual node need not know the entire route of a packet. However, it should have sufficient information about the state of the network to decide which of its immediate neighbors is to receive a given packet. This information is kept in the form of a routing table such as that shown in Figure 12.19. For each destination in the network, the first entry in the table gives the next node to which a packet

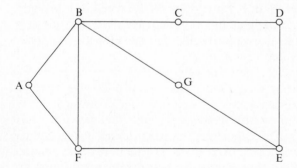

Figure 12.18 Network configuration used for generation of the routing table in Figure 12.19.

Destination	Next node	No. of links
A	A	1
B	B	0
C	C	1
D	C	2
E	G	2
F	F	1
G	G	1

Figure 12.19 Routing table at node B of Figure 12.18

with this destination address should be sent. The second entry gives the number of links through which the packet is expected to travel before it reaches its destination.

The entries in the routing tables are updated regularly to reflect any changes in the status of individual links. Whenever a node detects that the link to one of its neighbors is broken, it records this in its routing table by inserting a large number in the number-of-links column in the entry corresponding to this destination. For example, when node B detects that link BC is broken, it enters a large number, for example, 10, corresponding to destination C. To pass this information to other nodes, all nodes transmit their routing tables to their neighbors on a regular basis. When a node receives a neighbor's table, it adds 1 to all entries in the number-of-links column and compares the results with the corresponding entries in its own table. It then retains the smaller of the two values for each destination and updates the next-node entry accordingly. As this process is repeated a number of times at all nodes, the routing tables are updated to contain entries corresponding to the shortest routes, given the current status of the network. The reader is urged to study Problem 12.14 at the end of this chapter for further illustration.

The routing strategy described above was first used in the ARPA network.[12.8] After extensive observation and testing, a number of difficulties were identified, and a new routing algorithm was introduced. In the new algorithm, each node periodically measures the average delay to its neighbors and sends this information to all other nodes. Thus, all nodes will always have complete knowledge of the delays on all links in the network. This enables them to independently compute the best route for each packet. We should note that while this algorithm is conceptually very simple, the details of its implementation are considerably more involved.[12.20]

12.5 LOCAL AREA NETWORKS

As discussed in the introduction to this chapter, a local area network is a computer network which is limited to a geographically small area. It interconnects computers, terminals, and other digital devices within a plant site, a university campus, an office building, etc.

Most local area networks use one of three topologies: star, ring, or bus. Star networks use a central switch, similar to the PABX (private automatic branch exchange) equipment used for local telephones in a business office. A ring network has the general topology of Figure 12.7c, without the controlling computer. In the loop of that figure all messages flow either to or from the controlling computer. In a ring network, any device can communicate directly with any other device.

One of the simplest ring structures is a *slotted ring*, where data transmission around the ring is divided into time slots. These slots are separated by special framing characters that serve the same function as the flag in the HDLC protocol. A bit following the framing character indicates whether the slot contains data. When a device is ready to transmit data, it waits for the arrival of an empty slot. Then it starts transmitting its data, preceded by a destination address naming the device that should receive this data, and its own address. It also sets the full/empty bit to indicate that the slot is full. The format of a transmission frame is given in Figure 12.20. Each ring interface continuously monitors the slots traveling around the ring and inspects the destination address portion of each slot marked "full." If this address is its own, it delivers the contents of the frame to the device connected to it. The slot status bit may be changed back to "empty" by either the destination or the source device interface. Each possibility has some advantages (see Problem 12.16).

A slotted ring is functionally equivalent to a circular conveyor belt carrying empty bins. Any station alongside the belt can fill an empty bin and tag it with a destination address. When this bin arrives at the destination station, its contents are delivered. Then, the tag is removed so that the bin can be used by another station.

An alternative structure for a ring network is known as a *token ring*. The main difference between a token ring and a slotted ring is the means by which a particular device is given permission to transmit. In a token ring, a single, appropriately encoded flag, or token, circulates continuously around the ring. The arrival of the token at a ring station represents permission to transmit. If the station has nothing to transmit, it forwards the token to the next station downstream with as little delay as possible. If, on the other hand, the station has data ready for transmission, it inhibits the propagation of the token. Instead it transmits a packet of information. The packet is transmitted around the ring in the normal fashion. Its contents are read as it travels past the destination station. The packet continues to travel around the ring until it reaches the source station,

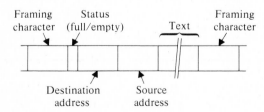

Framing character   Status (full/empty)   Text   Framing character

Destination address   Source address

Figure 12.20 Format of a transmission frame on a slotted ring.

where it is discarded. When the source station completes transmitting a packet, it releases the permission token, which again starts to circulate around the ring. The packet size on a token ring is variable and is limited only by the amount of buffer memory available in each station. A recommended standard for the operation of token rings has been developed by the IEEE.[12.21].

Operation of either the slotted ring or the token ring is critically dependent upon proper maintenance of the timing flags or tokens. If a flag is lost or a duplicate appears as a result of noise or malfunctioning of an interface, the proper timing structure must be restored. This function is performed by a controller station.

Finally let us consider bus-organized local area networks. We will discuss briefly a commercially available network known as *Ethernet*.[12.22]

12.5.1 Ethernet

The Ethernet structure is depicted in Figure 12.21. The transmission medium consists of a special coaxial cable, up to 2.5 km long. A computer, or any other device, is connected to the coaxial cable by means of a controller and a transceiver unit. The controller is responsible for implementing the Ethernet access protocol. The transceiver (transmitter-receiver) unit incorporates the circuits needed for transmitting and receiving data. Data is transmitted using Manchester encoding (see Section 9.2.1), with a bit rate of 10 Mbits/s.

The access protocol used in Ethernet represents a variation of the ALOHA contention scheme described in Section 12.3.2. An analysis of the simple ALOHA scheme indicates that only about 18 percent of the capacity of the transmission medium is available for useful transmission.[12.23] The remaining 82 percent is lost because of the fact that a given packet may have to be transmitted several times before it is received successfully. This is caused by the high probability of collision, that is, that two or more devices transmit at the same time, under heavy traffic conditions. In the Ethernet scheme, the probability of collision is reduced significantly by introducing two additional features: carrier sensing and collision detection. Carrier sensing refers to the ability of the controller to sense the fact that another device is transmitting. When it has a packet to transmit, the controller first checks to see if the transmission medium is already in use. If so, it waits until the current transmission ends, thus avoiding a sure collision.

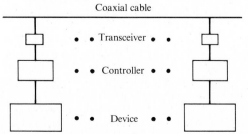

Figure 12.21 An Ethernet network.

Carrier sensing does not eliminate collisions completely. When the bus is not in use, it is possible for two devices to start transmission at the same time. The collision detection feature enables the controller to listen to its own transmission to determine whether it is being corrupted by transmission from another device. If it detects a collision, it aborts transmission immediately and reschedules it for a later time. By aborting the transmission, a period of time is saved which would otherwise be lost in completing a transmission that has already been destroyed. Another advantage of collision detection is that the controller knows immediately that retransmission is needed. Otherwise, it would have to wait for an acknowledgment, then start retransmission when no acknowledgment is received after a time-out period. Because of the carrier sensing and collision detection features, the Ethernet access protocol is referred to as a *carrier-sense, multiple access with collision detection (CSMA/CD)* protocol.

An important consideration in a network that uses a CSMA/CD scheme is the algorithm used for rescheduling transmission following the occurrence of a collision. The objective is to minimize the probability that the devices involved will again collide when they attempt retransmission. In Ethernet, a random delay is introduced by each controller before attempting retransmission. It is still possible for a second collision to occur, perhaps with a different device. The likelihood of a second collision increases when the network is heavily loaded. In order to reduce the probablity of repeated collisions when attempting to retransmit a given message, the average of the random retransmission delay introduced by the controller is doubled after each successive attempt at retransmission. The scheme is known as random delay with binary exponential back-off.

The Ethernet packet format is shown in Figure 12.22. It starts with a 64-bit preamble. The preamble consists of alternating 1s and 0s and ends with two consecutive 1s. This is needed by the receiver to recover the transmission clock. The preamble is followed by the destination and source addresses, each 48 bits long. This rather large address space has been used to enable every Ethernet controller anywhere in the world to have its own unique address. To ensure uniqueness, addresses are assigned to Ethernet users from a central registry. The type field indicates the nature of the packet. For example, it may indicate whether the packet contains user data or control information to be interpreted by the controller. The type field is followed by a variable-length data field and a 32-bit error check sum. The data field is limited to a maximum of 1500 bytes.

The format of the Ethernet packet makes it well suited for transmission of long files between computers. Since each packet contains 208 bits of overhead,

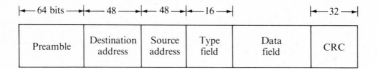

Figure 12.22 Ethernet packet format.

this format becomes inefficient when short terminal traffic is involved. For this reason, terminals are usually connected to Ethernet via concentrators similar to those discussed in Section 12.3.4.

We should note that Ethernet conforms to the IEEE standard for local area networks using the CSMA/CD bus access scheme.[12.21]

12.6 CONCLUDING REMARKS

This chapter has presented an overview of the concepts involved in computer communication networks. Applications of such networks are virtually limitless. They cover widely differing areas, such as scientific research, banking, library services, medical services, weather forecasting, etc. Many networks have been implemented and many others are in the planning stages. Interconnection of these networks is an important topic that has not been dealt with in this chapter. Ground, underwater, and satellite communications links are being used for this purpose. Other important issues include economic, regulatory, and reliability considerations. The interested reader should consult References 12.23 to 12.25 for further discussions of these topics.

12.7 PROBLEMS

12.1 Design a transistor circuit to implement the driver and receiver required for the 20-mA current loop of Figure 12.1. Assume that the maximum loop resistance is 1000 Ω. Your circuits should be compatible with TTL logic.

12.2 Show how you may add optical isolation to the circuit of Problem 12.1.

12.3 Consider a modem connected to a PDP-11 computer through an RS-232-C interface. Assume that the control signals associated with this interface can be accessed by the computer via an I/O register, as shown in Figure P12.1. Write a computer program to implement the control sequence required to establish a telephone connection according to steps 1 to 4 of Figure 12.4.

12.4 Ten terminals are connected to a computer via a single, full-duplex, multipoint line. The computer periodically polls each terminal for input data. Estimate the time required for a complete polling cycle, not including data transmission, for both the roll-polling and hub-polling schemes described in Section 12.3.2. Assume the following parameters:

Distance between two terminals	5 km
Distance between computer and first terminal	10 km

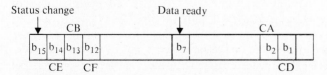

Figure P12.1 Organization of one of the status registers for the modem interface. The status change bit (b_{15}) is set to 1 whenever there is a change in the state of bits b_{12} or b_{13}, or when b_{14} is set to 1. It is cleared when this register is accessed by the CPU.

Propagation delay	3 ms/100 km
Transmission speed	2400 bits/s
Length of poll message	40 bits
Length of reply message	40 bits

12.5 Ten terminals are connected to a computer in a multipoint line configuration. Transmission of data from the terminals to the computer is on a contention basis. On the average, each terminal transmits data for 100 ms in every 10-s period. The time required for any terminal to recognize that another terminal is transmitting is 5 ms. Estimate the probability of two terminals starting transmission at the same time. When a terminal tries to use the line and finds the line busy, it will retry later. How does the retry strategy affect the above probability?

12.6 Consider a half-duplex communication link between two computers that are 400 km apart. The parameters for this link are as follows:

Propagation delay	3 ms/100 km
Turnaround time	50 ms
Transmission speed	4800 bits/s
Length of Acknowledge message	40 bits
Probability of error in a transmission block	$2 \times 10^{-5}n$

where n is the number of bits in a transmission block. Assume that the stop-and-wait ARQ protocol is used. Plot a curve for the effective transmission rate over this link versus the block size n, for n in the range 100 to 30,000 bits. Estimate the block size that results in a maximum effective transmission rate.

12.7 Repeat Problem 12.6 assuming that the transmission speed is doubled, with all other parameters remaining the same.

12.8 The communication link of Problem 12.6 is operated in a full-duplex mode. Calculate the resulting percentage increase in the effective transmission rate over this link for $n = 1000$.

12.9 Consider a continuous-ARQ transmission scheme. Assume that when an error is detected all messages are retransmitted, starting with the message where the error is detected.

(a) Give a diagram similar to that of Figure 12.6, showing the transmission sequence when an error is detected.

(b) Derive an expression for the transmission efficiency factor η in this case.

12.10 Consider a synchronous time-division multiplexing scheme similar to that of Figure 12.13. Assume that each transmission frame contains character data from 15 different devices and that each character is 8 bits long. The framing character is also 8 bits long.

(a) What is the effective data rate for each of the 16 devices if the transmission speed on the high-speed line is 1200 bits/s?

(b) If only 3 of the 15 devices may be transmitting data at any given time, what data rate can they have?

12.11 The transmission scheme of Problem 12.10 is replaced by an asynchronous time-division multiplexing scheme.

(a) Suggest a suitable format for transmission.

(b) What is the average data rate for each device when only 3 out of the 15 devices are transmitting? Assume that, on the average, five data characters are transmitted in each time slot.

12.12 It is required to implement the FIFO buffer of Figure 12.16 using random-access memory and control logic. Give a block diagram showing how this may be accomplished.

12.13 Consider the routing table of Figure 12.19 for node B of the network of Figure 12.18. Construct similar routing tables for nodes A, D, and F.

12.14 Assume that link AB in the network of Figure 12.18 is broken. When this information is received at node B, the entry corresponding to destination A in the routing table of Figure 12.19 is updated as follows:

$$A \qquad X \qquad X$$

where X stands for unknown. Assume that the table at node D has the following entry:

$$A \qquad C \qquad 3$$

Show a possible sequence of table transfers between neighboring nodes that will result in the above entry at node D being updated so that messages are rerouted to avoid the broken link.

12.15 Consider the following scheme for routing messages in a multiconnected network. When a message is received at any node, its address field is inspected. If the message is addressed to that node, it is accepted. Otherwise, copies of the message are transmitted to all neighboring nodes. This scheme is called "flooding." It will obviously result in multiple copies of a given message arriving at the destination. Assume that this scheme is used in the network of Figure 12.18 and that a message originates at node A addressed for node G. What sequence of transmissions will result in the first arrival of that message at node G? Suggest how the flooding scheme may be used for establishing the shortest route between any two points in a network using distributed control.

12.16 Consider a ring network using the slotted format discussed in Section 12.5. Assume that the width of the framing character in Figure 12.20 is equal to 2 bit periods, and that network addresses are 8 bits long.

    a) What is the minimum delay through a ring interface, assuming a full slot is changed to empty by the destination?

    b) Suggest a mechanism which enables the source rather than the destination to remove its packet after it has travelled around the ring. The delay through a ring interface should be as short as possible (i.e. the interface should not have to wait until it reads the source address to recognize its own packet).

12.8 REFERENCES

12.1. Davey, J. R.: Modems, *Proc. IEEE*, vol. 60, pp. 1284–1292, November 1972.

12.2. Abramson, N., and R. F. Kuo (eds.): "Computer Communication Networks," Prentice-Hall, Englewood Cliffs, N.J., 1973.

12.3. Staff report: Guide to Modems, *Comput. Decisions*, pp. 36–40, October 1973.

12.4. Peterson, W. W.: "Error-Correcting Codes," M.I.T., Cambridge, MA, 1961.

12.5. Burton, H. O., and D. D. Sullivan: Errors and Error Control, *Proc, IEEE*, vol. 60, pp. 1293–1301, November 1972.

12.6. Balkovic, M. D., H. W. Klancer, S. W. Klare, and W. G. McGruther: High-Speed Voiceband Data Transmission Performance on the Switched Telecommunications Network, *Bell Syst. Tech. J.*, vol. 50, no. 4, pp. 1349–1384, April 1971.

12.7. Gray, J. P.: Line Control Procedures, *Proc. IEEE*, vol. 60, pp. 1301–1312, November 1972.

12.8. Heart, F. E., R. E. Kahn, S. M. Ornstein, W. R. Crowther, and D. C. Walden: The Interface Message Processor for the ARPA Computer Network, *AFIPS Proc.*, vol. 36, SJCC, pp. 243–254, 1972.

12.9. Donnan, R. A., and J. R. Kersey: Synchronous Data Link Control: A Perspective, *IBM Syst. J.*, pp. 140–162, May 1974.

12.10. Knight, J. R.: A Case Study: Airlines Reservations Systems, *Proc. IEEE*, vol. 60, pp. 1423–1431, November 1972.

12.11. Abramson, N., and F. Kuo (eds.): The Aloha System, "Computer Networks," Prentice-Hall, Englewood Cliffs, N.J., 1973, chap. 14.

12.12. Steward, E. H.: A Loop Transmission System, *Proc Intrnl. Conf. on Commun.*, pp. 36–1 to 36–9, June 1970.

12.13. Doll, D. R.: Multiplexing and Concentration, *Proc. IEEE*, vol. 60, pp. 1313–1321, November 1972.

12.14. Rybczynski, A.: X.25 Interface for End-to-End Characteristics of Virtual-Circuit Based Services in Public Networks, *IEEE Trans. Commun.*, vol. COM-28, no. 4, pp. 550–510, April 1980.

12.15. Cerf, V. G., and P. T. Kirstein: Issues in Packet-Network Interconnection, *Proc. IEEE*, vol. 66, no. 11, pp. 1386–1408, November 1978.

12.16. Kahn, R. E., and W. R. Crowther: Flow Control in a Resource Sharing Computer Network, *IEEE Trans. Commun.*, vol. COM-20, no. 3, pp. 539-546, June 1972.

12.17. Kleinrock, L.: Computer-Communication Networks: Measurement, Flow Control, and ARPANET Traps, "Queueing Systems," vol. II, Wiley, New York, 1978, chap. 6.

12.18. Schwartz, M., R. R. Boorstyn, and R. L. Pickholtz: Terminal-Oriented Computer Communication Networks, *Proc. IEEE*, vol. 60, pp. 1408–1423, November 1972.

12.19. Kahn, R. E.: Resource Sharing Computer Communications Network, *Proc. IEEE,* vol. 60, pp. 1397–1407, November 1972.

12.20. McQuillan, J. M., I. Richer, and E. C. Rosen: The New Routing Algorithm for the ARPANET, *IEEE Trans. Commun.*, vol. COM-28, no. 5, pp. 711–719, May 1980.

12.21. *IEEE Local Area Network Standard 802, Draft D*, November/December 1982.

12.22. Shock, J. F., Y. K. Dalal, D. D. Redell, and R. C. Crane: Evolution of the Ethernet Local Computer Network, *Computer*, vol. 15, no. 8, pp. 10-27, August 1982.

12.23. Franta, W. R. and I. Chlamtac: "Local Networks, " Lexington Books, Lexington, Mass. 1981.

12.24. Tanenbaum, A. S.: "Computer Networks," Prentice-Hall, Englewood Cliffs, N.J., 1981.

12.25. Ahuja, V. C.: "Design and Analysis of Computer Communication Networks," McGraw-Hill, New York, 1982.

12.26. Chou, W. (ed.): "Computer Communications," vol. I., Prentice-Hall, Englewood Cliffs, N.J., 1983.

LOGIC CIRCUITS

Information in digital computers is represented and processed by electronic networks called *logic circuits*. The circuits operate on *binary variables* that assume one of two distinct values, usually called 0 and 1. In this appendix we will give a concise presentation of logic functions and circuits for their implementation, including a brief review of integrated circuit technology.

A.1 BASIC LOGIC FUNCTIONS

It is helpful to introduce the topic of binary logic by examining a practical problem that arises in all homes. Consider a light bulb whose On-Off condition is to be controlled by two switches x_1 and x_2. Each switch can be in one of two possible positions, 0 or 1, as shown in Figure A.1a. Thus it can be represented by a binary variable. We will let the switch names serve as the names of the associated binary variables. The figure also shows an electrical power supply and a light bulb. The way the switch terminals are interconnected determines how the switches control the light. The light will be On only if a closed path exists from the power supply through the switch network to the light bulb. Let a binary variable f represent the condition of the light. If the light is On, $f = 1$, and if the light is Off, $f = 0$. Thus $f = 1$ means that there is at least one closed path through the network, and $f = 0$ means that there is no closed path. Clearly, f is a function of the two variables x_1 and x_2.

Let us consider some possibilities for controlling the light. First, suppose that the light is to be On if either switch is in the 1 position; that is, $f = 1$ if

$$x_1 = 1 \quad \text{and} \quad x_2 = 0$$

or

$$x_1 = 0 \quad \text{and} \quad x_2 = 1$$

or

$$x_1 = x_2 = 1$$

493

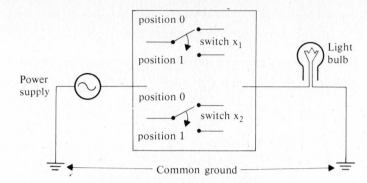

(*a*) Light bulb controlled by two switches

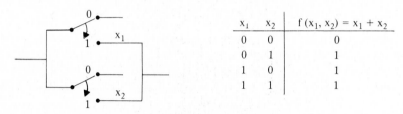

x_1	x_2	$f(x_1, x_2) = x_1 + x_2$
0	0	0
0	1	1
1	0	1
1	1	1

(*b*) Parallel connection (OR control)

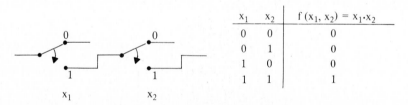

x_1	x_2	$f(x_1, x_2) = x_1 \cdot x_2$
0	0	0
0	1	0
1	0	0
1	1	1

(*c*) Series connection (AND control)

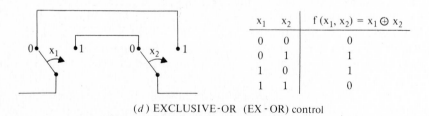

x_1	x_2	$f(x_1, x_2) = x_1 \oplus x_2$
0	0	0
0	1	1
1	0	1
1	1	0

(*d*) EXCLUSIVE-OR (EX - OR) control

Figure A.1 Light switch example.

The connections that implement this type of control are shown in Figure A.1b. A logic *truth table* that represents this situation is shown beside the wiring diagram. The table lists all possible switch settings, along with the value of f for each setting. In logic terms, this table represents the OR function of the two variables x_1 and x_2. The operation is represented algebraically by a "+" sign or a "$\vee$" sign, so that

$$f = x_1 + x_2 = x_1 \vee x_2$$

We also say that x_1 and x_2 are the *input* variables and f is the *output* function.

We should point out some basic properties of the OR operation. It is commutative; that is,

$$x_1 + x_2 = x_2 + x_1$$

It can be extended to n variables, so that

$$f = x_1 + x_2 + \cdots + x_n$$

has the value 1 if any of the x_i variables has the value 1. This represents the effect of connecting more switches in parallel with the two switches in Figure A.1b. Also, inspection of the truth table shows that

$$1 + x = 1$$

and

$$0 + x = x$$

Now, suppose that the light is to be On only when both switches are in the 1 position. The connections for this, along with the corresponding truth-table representation, are shown in Figure A.1c. This is the AND function, denoted as

$$f = x_1 \cdot x_2 = x_1 \wedge x_2$$

Some basic properties of the AND operation are

$$x_1 \cdot x_2 = x_2 \cdot x_1$$

$$1 \cdot x = x$$

and

$$0 \cdot x = 0$$

The AND function also extends to n variables, with

$$f = x_1 \cdot x_2 \cdot \cdots \cdot x_n$$

having the value 1 only if all the x_i variables have the value 1. This represents the case where more switches are connected in series with the two switches in Figure A.1c.

The final possibility that we will discuss for the way the switches determine the light status is actually the most common situation. If we assume that the switches are at either end of a stairway, the most practical requirement is that it should be possible to turn the light On or Off from either switch position. That is, if the light is On, changing either switch position should turn it Off; and correspondingly, if it is Off, changing either switch position should turn it On. Assume that the light is Off when both switches are in the 0 position. Then, changing either switch to the 1 position should turn the light On. Now suppose that the light is On with $x_1 = 1$ and $x_2 = 0$. Switching x_1 back to 0 will obviously turn the light Off. Furthermore, it must be possible to turn the light Off by changing x_2 to 1; that is, $f = 0$ if $x_1 = x_2 = 1$. The connections to implement this type of control are shown in Figure A.1d. The corresponding logic operation is called the EXCLUSIVE-OR (EX-OR) function. Some of its properties are

$$x_1 \oplus x_2 = x_2 \oplus x_1$$

$$1 \oplus x = \overline{x}$$

and
$$0 \oplus x = x$$

where $\overline{x}$ denotes the NOT function of the variable x. This single-variable function, $f = \overline{x}$, has the value 1 if $x = 0$ and the value 0 if $x = 1$. We say that the input x is being *inverted* or *complemented*.

A.1.1 Electronic Logic Gates

The use of switches, closed or open electrical paths, and light bulbs to illustrate the idea of logic variables and functions is convenient because of their familiarity and simplicity. The logic concepts that have been introduced are equally applicable to the electronic circuits that are used to process information in digital computers. The physical variables are electric voltages and currents instead of switch positions and closed or open paths. For example, consider a circuit that is designed to operate on inputs that are at either +5 or 0 V. The circuit outputs are also at either +5 or 0 V. Now, if we say that +5 V represents logic 1 and that 0 V represents logic 0, then we can describe what the circuit does by specifying the truth table for the logic operation that it performs.

It is possible to design reasonably simple electronic circuits, using standard components such as resistors and transistors, that perform logic operations such as AND, OR, EX-OR, and NOT. It is customary to use the name *gates* for these basic logic circuits. Standard symbols for the above gates are shown in Figure A.2. A somewhat more compact graphical notation for the NOT operation is used when inversion is applied to a logic-gate input or output. In such cases, the inversion is denoted by a small circle.

The electronic implementation of logic gates will be discussed in Section A.5. We will now proceed to discuss how basic gates can be used to construct logic networks that implement more complex logic functions.

A.2 SYNTHESIS OF LOGIC FUNCTIONS USING AND, OR, AND NOT GATES

Consider the network composed of two AND gates and an OR gate that is shown in Figure A.3a. It can be represented by the expression

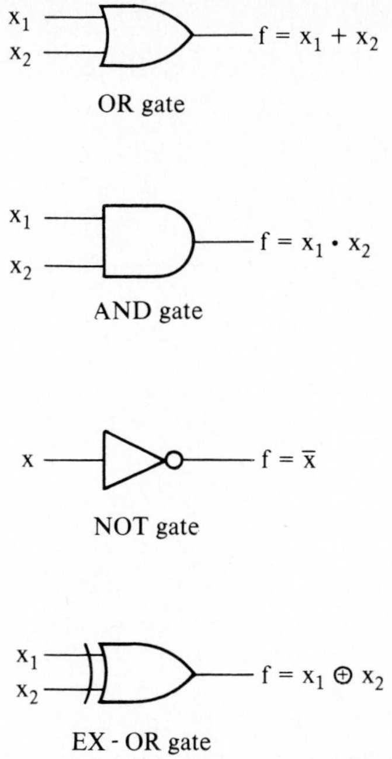

OR gate

AND gate

NOT gate

EX - OR gate

Figure A.2 Standard logic gate symbols.

$$f = \overline{x}_1 \cdot x_2 + x_1 \cdot \overline{x}_2$$

The construction of the truth table for this network expression is shown in Figure A.3b. First, the values of the AND terms are determined for each input valuation. Then the values of the function f are determined using the OR operation. The truth table for f is identical to the truth table for the EX-OR function. Therefore, the three-gate network in Figure A.3a is an implementation of the EX-OR function using AND, OR, and NOT gates. The logic expression $\overline{x}_1 \cdot x_2 + x_1 \cdot \overline{x}_2$ is called a *sum-of-products* form because the OR operation is sometimes called the "sum" function and the AND operation the "product" function.

We should note that it would be more proper to write

$$f = ((\overline{x}_1) \cdot x_2) + (x_1 \cdot (\overline{x}_2))$$

to indicate the order of applying the operations in the expression. To simplify the appearance of such expressions, we define a hierarchy among the three operations AND, OR, and NOT. In the absence of parentheses, operations in a logic expression should be performed in the following order: NOT, followed by AND, followed by OR. Furthermore, it is customary to omit the "·" operator whenever there is no ambiguity.

Returning to the sum-of-products form, we will now explain how any logic function can be synthesized in this form directly from its truth table. Consider the truth table of Table A.1, and suppose we wish to synthesize the function f_1 using AND, OR, and NOT gates. For each row of the table where $f_1 = 1$, we

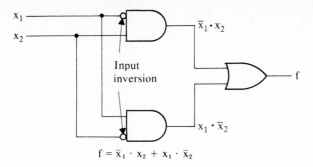

$$f = \overline{x}_1 \cdot x_2 + x_1 \cdot \overline{x}_2$$

(a) Network for the EX-OR function

x_1	x_2	$\overline{x}_1 \cdot x_2$	$x_1 \cdot \overline{x}_2$	$f = \overline{x}_1 \cdot x_2 + x_1 \cdot \overline{x}_2$ = $x_1 \oplus x_2$
0	0	0	0	0
0	1	1	0	1
1	0	0	1	1
1	1	0	0	0

(b) Truth table construction for $\overline{x}_1 \cdot x_2 + x_1 \cdot \overline{x}_2$

Figure A.3 Implementation of the EX-OR function using AND, OR, and NOT gates.

include a product (AND) term in the sum-of-products form. The product term includes all three input variables. The NOT operator is applied to these variables individually so that the term is 1 only when the variables have the particular valuation that corresponds to that row of the truth table. This means that if $x_i = 0$, then $\overline{x}_i$ is entered in the product term, while if $x_i = 1$, then x_i is entered. For example, the fourth row of the table has the function entry 1 for the input valuation

$$(x_1, x_2, x_3) = (0, 1, 1)$$

The product term corresponding to this is $\overline{x}_1 x_2 x_3$. Doing this for all rows where the function f_1 has the value 1 leads to

$$f_1 = \overline{x}_1 \overline{x}_2 \overline{x}_3 + \overline{x}_1 \overline{x}_2 x_3 + \overline{x}_1 x_2 x_3 + x_1 x_2 x_3$$

Table A.1 Two 3-variable functions

x_1	x_2	x_3	f_1	f_2
0	0	0	1	1
0	0	1	1	1
0	1	0	0	1
0	1	1	1	0
1	0	0	0	1
1	0	1	0	1
1	1	0	0	0
1	1	1	1	0

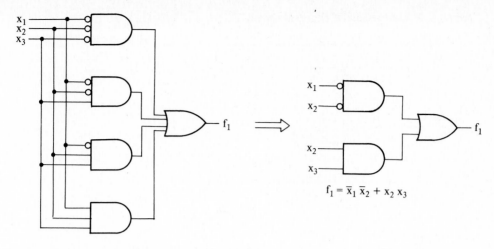

$$f_1 = \overline{x}_1 \, \overline{x}_2 \, \overline{x}_3 + \overline{x}_1 \, \overline{x}_2 \, x_3 + \overline{x}_1 \, x_2 \, x_3 + x_1 \, x_2 \, x_3$$

Figure A.4 A logic network for f_1 of Table A.1 and an equivalent minimal network.

The logic network corresponding to this expression is shown on the left side in Figure A.4. As another example, the sum-of-products expression for the EX-OR function can be derived from its truth table by this technique. This approach can be used to derive sum-of-products expressions and the corresponding logic networks for truth tables of any size.

A.3 MINIMIZATION OF LOGIC EXPRESSIONS

We have shown how to derive one sum-of-products expression for each truth table. In fact, there are many equivalent expressions and logic networks for any particular truth table. Two logic expressions or logic-gate networks are equivalent if they have identical truth tables. An expression that is equivalent to the sum-of-products expression that we derived for f_1 in the previous section is

$$\overline{x}_1 \overline{x}_2 + x_2 x_3$$

To prove this, we construct the truth table for the simpler expression and show that it is identical to the truth table for f_1 in Table A.1. This is done in Table A.2. The construction of the table for $\overline{x}_1 \overline{x}_2 + x_2 x_3$ is done in three steps. First, the value of the product term $\overline{x}_1 \overline{x}_2$ is computed for each valuation of the inputs. Then $x_2 x_3$ is evaluated. Finally, these two columns are ORed together to obtain the truth table for the expression. This truth table is identical to the truth table for f_1 given in Table A.1.

To simplify logic expressions we will perform a series of algebraic manipulations. The new logic rules that we will use in these manipulations are the distributive rule

Table A.2 Evaluation of the expression $\overline{x}_1\overline{x}_2 + x_2x_3$

x_1	x_2	x_3	$\overline{x}_1\overline{x}_2$	x_2x_3	$\overline{x}_1\overline{x}_2 + x_2x_3 = f_1$
0	0	0	1	0	1
0	0	1	1	0	1
0	1	0	0	0	0
0	1	1	0	1	1
1	0	0	0	0	0
1	0	1	0	0	0
1	1	0	0	0	0
1	1	1	0	1	1

$$w(y + z) = wy + wz$$

and the identity

$$w + \overline{w} = 1$$

Table A.3 shows the truth-table proof of the distributive rule. It should now be clear that rules such as this can always be proved by constructing the truth tables for the left-hand side and the right-hand side to show that they are identical. Logic rules, such as the distributive rule, are sometimes called *identities*. Although we will not need to use it here, there is another form of distributive rule that we should include for completeness, namely,

$$w + yz = (w + y)(w + z)$$

The objective in logic minimization is to reduce the cost of implementation of a given logic function according to some criterion. More particularly, we wish to start with a sum-of-products expression, derived from a truth table, and simplify it to an equivalent *minimal sum-of-products* expression. To define the criterion for minimization, it is necessary to introduce a size or cost measure for a sum-of-products expression. The usual cost measure is a count of the total number of gates and gate inputs required in implementing the expression in the form shown in Figure A.4. For example, the larger expression in this figure has a

Table A.3 Truth-table technique for proving equivalence of expressions

w	y	z	$y + z$	Left-hand side $w(y + z)$	wy	wz	Right-hand side $wy + wz$
0	0	0	0	0	0	0	0
0	0	1	1	0	0	0	0
0	1	0	1	0	0	0	0
0	1	1	1	0	0	0	0
1	0	0	0	0	0	0	0
1	0	1	1	1	0	1	1
1	1	0	1	1	1	0	1
1	1	1	1	1	1	1	1

cost of 21, composed of a total of 5 gates and a total of 16 gate inputs. Input inversions are ignored in this counting process. The cost of the simpler expression is 9, composed of 3 gates and 6 inputs. We are now in a position to state that a sum-of-products expression is minimal if there is no other equivalent sum-of-products expression with a lower cost. In the simple examples that we will deal with, it is usually reasonably clear when we have arrived at a minimal expression. Thus we will not give rigorous proofs of minimality.

The general strategy in performing algebraic manipulations on a given expression in order to simplify it is as follows. First, group product terms in pairs that differ only in that some variable appears complemented ($\bar{x}$) in one term and true (x) in the other. When the common subproduct consisting of the other variables is factored out of the pair by the distributive rule, we are left with the term $x + \bar{x}$ that has the value 1. Applying this procedure to the first expression for f_1, we obtain

$$f_1 = \bar{x}_1\bar{x}_2\bar{x}_3 + \bar{x}_1\bar{x}_2x_3 + \bar{x}_1x_2x_3 + x_1x_2x_3$$

$$= \bar{x}_1\bar{x}_2(\bar{x}_3 + x_3) + (\bar{x}_1 + x_1)x_2x_3$$

$$= \bar{x}_1\bar{x}_2 \cdot 1 + 1 \cdot x_2x_3$$

$$= \bar{x}_1\bar{x}_2 + x_2x_3$$

This expression is minimal. The network corresponding to it is shown in Figure A.4.

The grouping of terms in pairs, so that minimization can lead to the simplest expression, is not always as obvious as in the above example. A rule that is often helpful is

$$w + w = w$$

This allows us to repeat product terms so that a particular term can be combined with more than one other term in the factoring process. As an example of this, consider function f_2 in Table A.1. The sum-of-products expression that can be derived for it directly from the truth table is

$$f_2 = \bar{x}_1\bar{x}_2\bar{x}_3 + \bar{x}_1\bar{x}_2x_3 + \bar{x}_1x_2\bar{x}_3 + x_1\bar{x}_2\bar{x}_3 + x_1\bar{x}_2x_3$$

By repeating the first product term $\bar{x}_1\bar{x}_2\bar{x}_3$ and interchanging the order of terms (by the commutative rule), we obtain

$$f_2 = \bar{x}_1\bar{x}_2\bar{x}_3 + \bar{x}_1\bar{x}_2x_3 + x_1\bar{x}_2\bar{x}_3 + x_1\bar{x}_2x_3 + \bar{x}_1\bar{x}_2\bar{x}_3 + \bar{x}_1x_2\bar{x}_3$$

Grouping the terms in pairs and factoring yields

$$f_2 = \bar{x}_1\bar{x}_2(\bar{x}_3 + x_3) + x_1\bar{x}_2(\bar{x}_3 + x_3) + \bar{x}_1(\bar{x}_2 + x_2)\bar{x}_3$$

$$= \bar{x}_1\bar{x}_2 + x_1\bar{x}_2 + \bar{x}_1\bar{x}_3$$

The first pair of terms again reduces by factoring, and we obtain the minimal expression

$$f_2 = \bar{x}_2 + \bar{x}_1\bar{x}_3$$

This completes our discussion of algebraic simplification of logic expres-

Table A.4 Rules of binary logic

Name	Algebraic identity	
Commutative	$w + y = y + w$	$wy = yw$
Associative	$(w + y) + z = w + (y + z)$	$(wy)z = w(yz)$
Distributive	$w + yz = (w + y)(w + z)$	$w(y + z) = wy + wz$
Idempotent	$w + w = w$	$ww = w$
Involution	$\overline{\overline{w}} = w$	
Complement	$w + \overline{w} = 1$	$w\overline{w} = 0$
de Morgan	$\overline{w + y} = \overline{w}\overline{y}$	$\overline{wy} = \overline{w} + \overline{y}$
	$1 + w = 1$	$0 \cdot w = 0$
	$0 + w = w$	$1 \cdot w = w$

sions. The obvious practical application of this mathematical exercise stems from the fact that networks with fewer gates and inputs are cheaper and easier to implement. Therefore, it is of economic interest to be able to determine the minimal expression that is equivalent to a given expression. The rules that we have used in manipulating logic expressions are summarized in Table A.4. They are arranged in pairs to show their symmetry as they apply to both the AND and OR functions. So far, we have not had occasion to use either the involution or de Morgan's rules, but they will be found useful in the next section.

A.3.1 Minimization Using Karnaugh Maps

In our algebraic minimization of the functions f_1 and f_2 of Table A.1, it was necessary to "guess" the best way to proceed at certain points. For instance, deciding to repeat the term $\overline{x}_1\overline{x}_2\overline{x}_3$ as the first step in minimizing f_2 is not obvious. There is a geometric technique that can be used to quickly derive minimal expressions for logic functions of a few variables. The technique depends on a different form for presentation of the truth table, a form called the *Karnaugh map*. For three-variable functions, the map is a rectangle composed of eight squares arranged in two rows of four squares each, as shown in Figure A.5a. Each square of the map corresponds to a particular valuation of the input variables. For example, the third square of the top row represents the valuation $(x_1, x_2, x_3) = (1, 1, 0)$. Since there are eight rows in a three-variable truth table, the map obviously requires eight squares. The entries in the squares are the function values for the corresponding input valuations.

The key idea in the formation of the map is that horizontally and vertically adjacent squares correspond to input valuations that differ in one variable only. When two adjacent squares contain 1s, they indicate the possibility of an algebraic simplification. In the map for f_2 in Figure A.5a, the two 1 values in the left two squares of the top row correspond to the product terms $\overline{x}_1\overline{x}_2\overline{x}_3$ and $\overline{x}_1x_2\overline{x}_3$. As we have already seen, the simplification

$$\overline{x}_1\overline{x}_2\overline{x}_3 + \overline{x}_1x_2\overline{x}_3 = \overline{x}_1\overline{x}_3$$

was performed in minimizing the algebraic expression for f_2. This simplification

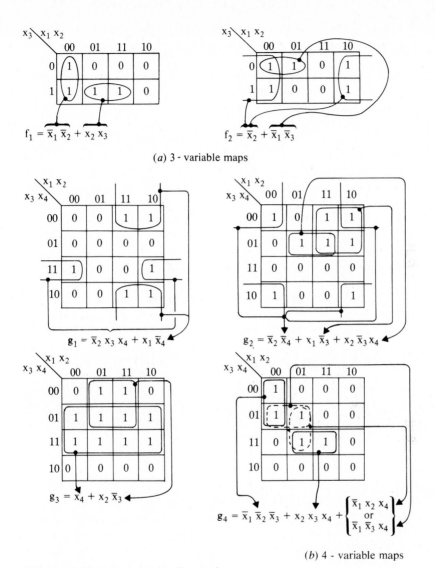

(a) 3 - variable maps

(b) 4 - variable maps

Figure A.5 Minimization using Karnaugh maps.

can be obtained directly from the map by grouping the two 1s as shown. The product term that corresponds to a group of squares is the product of the input variables whose values are constant on these squares. If the value of input variable x_i is 0 for all 1s of a group, then $\bar{x}_i$ is entered in the product, while if x_i has the value 1 for all 1s of the group, then x_i is entered in the product. Adjacency of two squares includes the fact that the left-end squares are adjacent to the right-end squares. Continuing with our discussion of f_2, the group of four 1s consisting of the left-end column and the right-end column simplifies to the single-variable term $\bar{x}_2$, because x_2 is the only variable whose value remains constant over the group, and all possible values of the other two variables occur in the group.

Karnaugh maps can be used for more than three variables. A Karnaugh map for four variables can be obtained from 2 three-variable maps. Examples of four-variable maps are shown in Figure A.5*b*, along with minimal expressions for the functions represented by the maps. In addition to two- and four-square groupings, it is now possible to form eight-square groupings. Such a grouping is illustrated in the map for g_3. Note that the four corner squares constitute a valid group of four, and are represented by the product term $\bar{x}_2\bar{x}_4$ in g_2. As in the case of three-variable maps, the term that corresponds to a group of squares is the product of the variables whose values do not change over the group. For example, the grouping of four 1s in the upper right-hand corner of the map for g_2 is represented by the product term $x_1\bar{x}_3$, because $x_1 = 1$ and $x_3 = 0$ over the group. The variables x_2 and x_4 have all the possible combinations of values over this group. It is also possible to use Karnaugh maps for five-variable functions. In this case, 2 four-variable maps are used, one of them corresponding to the 0 value for the fifth variable and the other corresponding to the 1 value.

The general procedure for forming groups of two, four, eight, etc., in Karnaugh maps is readily derived. Two adjacent pairs of 1s can be combined to form a group of four. Similarly, two adjacent groups of four can be combined to form a group of eight, and so on. In general, the number of squares in any valid group must be equal to 2^k, where k is an integer.

We will now consider a procedure for using Karnaugh maps to obtain minimal sum-of-products expressions. As can be seen in the maps of Figure A.5, a large group of 1s corresponds to a small product term. Thus, a simple gate implementation results from covering all the 1s in the map with as few groups as possible. In general, we should choose the smallest set of groups, picking large ones wherever possible, that cover all the 1s in the map. Consider, for example, the function g_2 in Figure A.5*b*. As we have already seen, the 1s in the four corners constitute a group of four that is represented by the product term $\bar{x}_2\bar{x}_4$. Another group of four exists in the upper right-hand corner and is represented by the term $x_1\bar{x}_3$. This covers all the 1s in the map except for the 1 in the square where $(x_1, x_2, x_3, x_4) = (0, 1, 0, 1)$. The largest group of 1s that includes this square is the two-square group represented by the term $x_2\bar{x}_3x_4$. Therefore the minimal expression for g_2 is

$$g_2 = \bar{x}_2\bar{x}_4 + x_1\bar{x}_3 + x_2\bar{x}_3x_4$$

In a similar manner, minimal expressions can be derived for the other functions shown in the figure. Note that in the case of g_4 there are two possible minimal expressions, one including the term $\bar{x}_1x_2x_4$ and the other including the term $\bar{x}_1\bar{x}_3x_4$. It is often the case that a given function has more than one minimal expression.

In all our examples, it is relatively easy to derive minimal expressions. In general, there are formal algorithms for this process,[A.1 to A.6] but we will not consider them here.

A.3.2 Don't-Care Conditions

In many situations, some valuations of the inputs to a digital circuit never occur. For example, consider the binary-coded decimal (BCD) number representation. Four binary variables b_3, b_2, b_1, and b_0 are used to represent the decimal digits 0 through 9 as shown in Figure A.6. These four variables have a total of 16 distinct valuations, only 10 of which are used for representing the decimal digits. The remaining valuations are not used. Therefore, any logic circuit that processes BCD data will never encounter any of these six valuations at its inputs.

Decimal digit represented	Binary coding b_3 b_2 b_1 b_0				f
0	0	0	0	0	0
1	0	0	0	1	0
2	0	0	1	0	0
3	0	0	1	1	1
4	0	1	0	0	0
5	0	1	0	1	0
6	0	1	1	0	1
7	0	1	1	1	0
8	1	0	0	0	0
9	1	0	0	1	1
unused {	1	0	1	0	d
	1	0	1	1	d
	1	1	0	0	d
	1	1	0	1	d
	1	1	1	0	d
	1	1	1	1	d

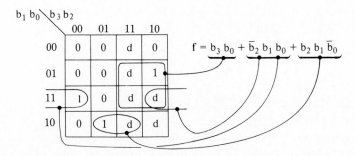

$$f = b_3 \, b_0 + \bar{b}_2 \, b_1 \, b_0 + b_2 \, b_1 \, \bar{b}_0$$

Figure A.6 Four-variable Karnaugh map illustrating don't-cares.

Figure A.6 gives the truth table for a particular function that may be performed on a BCD digit. We do not care what the function values are for the unused input valuations. Hence, they are called *don't-cares* and are denoted as such by the letter d in the truth table. To obtain a circuit implementation, the function values corresponding to don't-care conditions can be arbitrarily assigned to be either 0 or 1. The best way to assign them is in such a manner as to lead toward a minimal logic-gate implementation. We should interpret don't-cares as 1s whenever they can be used to enlarge a group of 1s. Since larger groups correspond to smaller product terms, minimization is enhanced by the judicious inclusion of don't-care entries.

The function in Figure A.6 represents the following processing on a decimal digit input: The output f is to have the value 1 whenever the inputs represent a nonzero digit that is evenly divisible by 3. Three groups are necessary to cover the three 1s of the map, and don't-cares have been used to enlarge these groups as much as possible.

A.4 SYNTHESIS WITH NAND AND NOR GATES

We will now consider two other basic logic gates, called NAND and NOR, which are extensively used in practice because of their simple electronic realizations. The truth table for these gates is shown in Figure A.7. They implement the equivalent of the AND and OR functions followed by the NOT function, which is the motivation for the names and standard logic symbols for these gates. Letting the arrows "↑" and "↓" denote the NAND and NOR operators, respectively, and using de Morgan's rule in Table A.4, we have

$$x_1 \uparrow x_2 = \overline{x_1 x_2} = \overline{x}_1 + \overline{x}_2$$

and

$$x_1 \downarrow x_2 = \overline{x_1 + x_2} = \overline{x}_1 \overline{x}_2$$

x_1	x_2	f
0	0	1
0	1	1
1	0	1
1	1	0

$f = x_1 \uparrow x_2 = \overline{x_1 x_2} = \overline{x}_1 + \overline{x}_2$

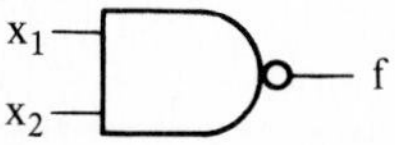

x_1	x_2	f
0	0	1
0	1	0
1	0	0
1	1	0

$f = x_1 \downarrow x_2 = \overline{x_1 + x_2} = \overline{x}_1 \overline{x}_2$

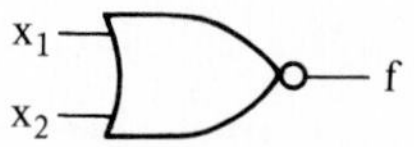

(a) NAND

(b) NOR

Figure A.7 NAND and NOR gates.

NAND and NOR gates with more than two input variables are available, and they operate according to the obvious generalization of de Morgan's law as

$$x_1 \uparrow x_2 \uparrow \cdots \uparrow x_n = \overline{x_1 x_2 \cdots x_n} = \overline{x}_1 + \overline{x}_2 + \cdots + \overline{x}_n$$

and $\quad x_1 \downarrow x_2 \downarrow \cdots \downarrow x_n = \overline{x_1 + x_2 + \cdots + x_n} = \overline{x}_1 \overline{x}_2 \cdots \overline{x}_n$

Logic design with NAND and NOR gates is not as straightforward as is the case in using AND, OR, and NOT gates. One of the main difficulties in the design process is that the associative rule is not valid for NAND and NOR operations. We will expand on this problem later. First, however, let us describe a simple, general procedure for synthesizing any logic function using only NAND gates. There is a direct way to translate a logic network expressed in sum-of-products form into an equivalent network composed only of NAND gates. The procedure is easily illustrated with the aid of an example. Consider the following algebraic manipulation of a logic expression corresponding to a four-input network composed of 3 two-input NAND gates:

$$(x_1 \uparrow x_2) \uparrow (x_3 \uparrow x_4) = \overline{(\overline{x_1 x_2})(\overline{x_3 x_4})}$$

$$= \overline{\overline{x_1 x_2}} + \overline{\overline{x_3 x_4}}$$

$$= x_1 x_2 + x_3 x_4$$

We have used de Morgan's rule and the involution rule in this derivation. Figure A.8 shows the logic network equivalent of this derivation. Since any logic function can be synthesized in a sum-of-products (AND-OR) form, and the above derivation is obviously reversible, we then have the result that any logic function can be synthesized in the NAND-NAND form. It is easily seen that this result is true for functions of any number of variables. The required number of

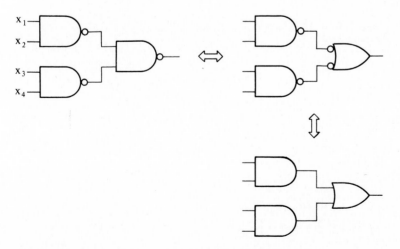

Figure A.8 NAND-NAND synthesis of an AND-OR network.

inputs to the NAND gates is obviously the same as the number of inputs to the corresponding AND or OR gates.

Let us return to the comment that the nonassociativity of the NAND operator can be an annoyance. In designing logic networks with NAND gates using the procedure illustrated in Figure A.8, a requirement for a NAND gate with more inputs than can be found on standard commercially available gates may arise. If this happens when one is using AND and OR gates, there is no problem. Because the AND or OR operators are associative, a straightforward cascade of limited fan-in gates can be used. The case of implementing three-input AND and OR functions with two-input gates is shown in Figure A.9a. The solution is not as simple in the case of NAND gates. For example, a three-input NAND function cannot be implemented by a cascade of 2 two-input NAND gates. Three gates are needed, as shown in Figure A.9b.

A discussion of the implementation of logic functions using only NOR gates proceeds in a similar manner. Any logic function can be synthesized in a product-of-sums (OR-AND) form. Such networks can be implemented by equivalent NOR-NOR networks.

The above discussion introduced some basic concepts in logic design. Detailed discussion of the subject can be found in any of a number of textbooks.[A.1 to A.4]

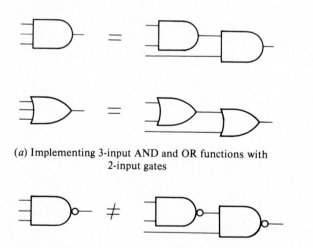

(a) Implementing 3-input AND and OR functions with 2-input gates

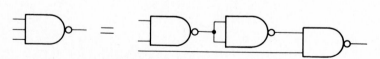

(b) Implementing a 3-input NAND function with 2-input gates

Figure A.9 Cascading of gates.

A.5 PRACTICAL IMPLEMENTATION OF LOGIC GATES

Let us now turn our attention to the means by which logic variables may be represented and logic functions implemented in practice. The choice of a parameter to represent logic variables is obviously technology-dependent. In electronic circuits, either voltage or current levels can be used for this purpose.

To establish a correspondence between voltage levels and logic values or states, the concept of a *threshold* may be used. Voltages above a given threshold may be taken to represent one logic value, while voltages below that threshold represent the other. In practical situations, the voltage at any point in an electronic circuit undergoes small random variations due to a variety of reasons. Because of this "noise," the logic state corresponding to a voltage level near the threshold cannot be reliably determined. To avoid such ambiguity, a "forbidden range" should be established as shown in Figure A.10. In this case, voltages below $V_{0,max}$ represent the 0 value, and voltages above $V_{1,min}$ represent the 1 value. In subsequent discussion, we will often use the terms "low" and "high" to represent the voltage levels corresponding to logic values 0 and 1, respectively.

Consider the circuits in Figure A.11. When switch S in Figure A.11a is closed, the output voltage V_{out} is equal to 0 (ground). On the other hand, when S is open, V_{out} is equal to the supply voltage. The same effect can be obtained in Figure A.11b, where a transistor Q is used to replace the switch S. When no current is supplied to the base of the transistor, that is, when the input voltage $V_{in} = 0$, the transistor is equivalent to an open switch, and $V_{out} = V_{supply}$. As V_{in} increases, V_{out} starts to drop until V_{out} is very close to 0. The rate at which this happens is a function of the values of resistors R_1 and R_2 and the characteristics of the transistor. Through proper choice of these components, it is possible to establish the two levels $V_{1,min}$ and $V_{0,max}$ so that

$$\text{If } V_{in} \leq V_{0,max}, \text{ then } V_{out} > V_{1,min}$$

and

$$\text{if } V_{in} \geq V_{1,min}, \text{ then } V_{out} < V_{0,max}$$

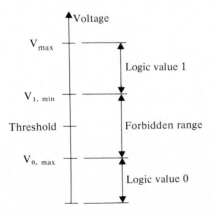

Figure A.10 Representation of logic values by voltage levels.

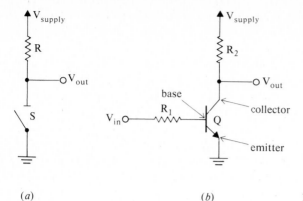

(a)   (b)   **Figure A.11** An inverter circuit.

Under these conditions, the circuit performs the function of a logic NOT gate.

We can now proceed to discuss the implementation of more complex logic functions. Figure A.12 shows a circuit realization for a NOR gate. In this case, V_{out} in Figure A.12a is high only when both switches S_a and S_b are open. Similarly, V_{out} in Figure A.12b is high only when both inputs V_a and V_b are low. Thus the circuit is equivalent to a NOR gate, where V_a and V_b correspond to two logic variables x_1 and x_2. It is easily verified that a NAND gate can be obtained by connecting the transistors as shown in Figure A.13. The logic functions AND and OR can be implemented by using NAND and NOR gates, respectively, followed by the inverter of Figure A.11. The circuits of Figures A.11 to A.13 form a "logic family" that is generally referred to as *resistor-transistor logic* (RTL).

It is interesting to note that in the RTL family, NAND and NOR gates are simpler in their circuit implementation than AND and OR gates. It will be seen shortly that the same applies to most other logic families, with the notable exception of emitter-coupled logic. Hence, it is not surprising to find that

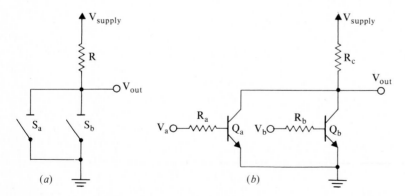

Figure A.12 A transistor circuit implementation for a NOR gate.

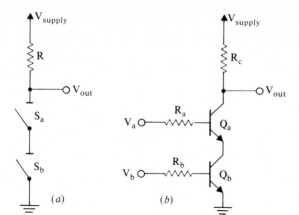

Figure **A.13** A transistor circuit implementation for a NAND gate.

practical realizations of logic functions use NAND and NOR gates extensively. Many of the examples given in this book show circuits consisting of AND, OR, and NOT gates, for ease of understanding. In practice, logic circuits contain all five types.

A.5.1 Logic Families

The RTL circuits of Figures A.11 to A.13 are very simple. However, their use is subject to a number of limitations arising from their electrical characteristics. A number of other logic families have been developed to overcome these limitations. Of course, all logic families perform the same logic functions. They differ only in their electrical and physical characteristics. Although we do not intend to study these characteristics in detail, we will present a summary of those parameters that affect the choice of the logic family to be used in a given application.

Circuits belonging to different logic families exhibit a number of trade-offs among three basic properties: speed, power, and packaging density. Speed is measured by the rate at which state changes can take place at the output of any logic element. A related parameter is the *propagation delay*, which is defined in Figure A.14. When a state change takes place at a gate input, a finite delay is encountered before the corresponding change at the gate output is observed. The propagation delay is usually measured between the 50 percent points, as defined in the figure. Another important parameter is the *transition time*, which is normally measured between the 10 and 90 percent points on the waveform, as shown. The maximum speed at which a logic circuit can be operated decreases as the propagation delay through different paths within that circuit increases. The delay along any path is the sum of individual gate delays along this path.

Power consumption is the next parameter in the characterization of logic families. High power consumption leads to complex and costly packaging to enable dissipation of the heat produced. The cost of the power supply is also

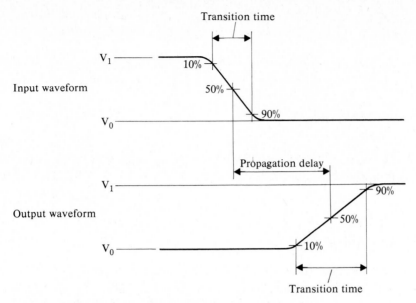

Figure A.14 Definition of propagation delay and transition time.

increased. Power consumption is particularly significant in the case of *very large-scale integration* (VLSI). This is the case when a logic subsystem consisting of a large number of gates is assembled on a single integrated circuit chip. Power dissipation places an upper limit on the number of gates that can be used in such a situation.

For a general circuit configuration, such as that of Figure A.11, it is possible to obtain a number of designs that differ in their speed and power characteristics. However, as the speed capability increases, so will the power consumption. Roughly, the product of power dissipation per gate and propagation delay remains constant. This power-delay product is often used as a figure of merit that describes the capabilities of a given logic family.

It has already been pointed out that power consumption influences the packaging density. Other factors that affect packaging density are the number of components in the circuit and the shape and size of these components. The development of VLSI is closely linked to the development of circuit configurations and to manufacturing techniques that allow high packaging densities. A figure of merit that takes packaging density into consideration is the power-delay-area product, where the area is that of a typical gate on a VLSI chip.

In addition to the three basic characteristics presented above, a number of other important properties should be taken into consideration when comparing logic families. These include:

Noise immunity, which refers to the ability to reject interference from neighboring circuits

Drive requirement, which is the electrical load presented by a gate input to the circuit preceding it (for example, the input current in the circuit of Figure A.11)

Drive capability, which is the maximum amount of current that can be drawn from a gate output without serious degradation of its performance

The combination of drive requirement and drive capability determines two important parameters, namely,

Fan-in, which is the maximum number of inputs that a logic gate can have
Fan-out, which is the maximum number of gates that can be driven from the output of a single gate

With the above considerations in mind, we shall now present a review of some of the commonly used logic families.

Transistor-transistor logic (TTL) A TTL configuration for a NAND gate is shown in Figure A.15a. To understand the operation of this gate, let us consider the circuit of Figure A.15b. This circuit belongs to an earlier logic family known as *diode-transistor logic* (DTL). First, consider the case when the two inputs V_a and V_b are high. Since a diode conducts current only in the forward direction, no appreciable current flows through $D1$ or $D2$. Diode $D3$, however, is forward-biased and allows a current I_b to flow to the base of transistor Q. Thus Q is turned On, and V_{out} is close to ground, indicating a logic value of 0. If either V_a or V_b drops to the 0 state, the corresponding diode starts to conduct. This causes the voltage at point P to drop to a value below that required to maintain the flow of I_b. Thus transistor Q turns Off, and V_{out} rises to the supply voltage. In other words, this circuit performs a NAND function.

When the above DTL circuit is implemented in an integrated circuit form, the three diodes $D1$, $D2$, and $D3$ can be combined to form transistor Q_1 of Figure A.15a, reducing the chip area required for the gate. This also leads to an improvement in performance, because of the higher speed with which transistor Q_2 can be changed from the On to the Off state. Detailed discussion of these properties can be found in texts on electronics.[A.7, A.8] The logic family based on the circuit configuration of Figure A.15a is referred to as *transistor-transistor logic.*

To enhance the output drive capability of the circuit of Figure A.15a and, hence, to improve the fan-out, a driver stage is usually added. This yields the standard TTL circuit configuration given in Figure A.16. The output stage contains two transistors Q_3 and Q_4. When the output is in the 0 state, transistor Q_3 is Off and transistor Q_4 is On. Conversely, when the output is in the 1 state, Q_3 is On and Q_4 is Off. This allows higher load currents to be handled without excessive power dissipation or reduction in speed.

The 0 and 1 voltage levels for the TTL logic family are defined in Figure A.17. It is important to note that the values of $V_{0,max}$ and $V_{1,min}$ defined earlier are

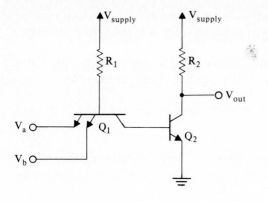

(*a*) TTL

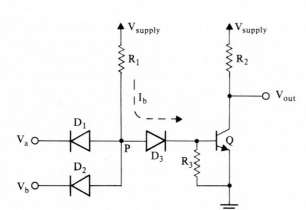

(*b*) DTL

Figure A.15 TTL and DTL gates.

different for the input and output sides of the gate. This is necessary to guarantee that the output of a gate will not lie within the forbidden range of the input to the next gate, even in the presence of a small amount of noise. The difference between the corresponding levels for the input and output defines the *noise margins* for the logic family. In the case of TTL, the noise margin for both the 0 and 1 states is 0.4 V.

The TTL logic family has been the workhorse in computer and logic applications for a long time. A number of variations of the circuit in Figure A.16 have evolved for low-power or high-speed applications. One important variation is known as low-power Schottky TTL. It uses Schottky transistors, which are characterized by very short turn-off time (transistor turn-off time is the limiting factor for the speed of standard TTL). This circuit combines low power and high speed and is particularly suited for VLSI applications. It has a typical propaga-

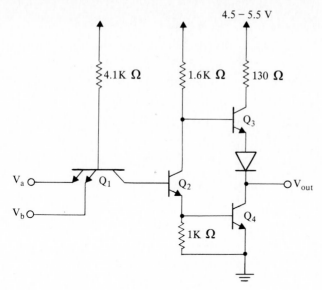

4.5 – 5.5 V

4.1K Ω   1.6K Ω   130 Ω

Q_3

V_a Q_1 Q_2 V_{out}

V_b Q_4

1K Ω

Figure A.16 A standard TTL gate.

tion delay of 8 ns and power dissipation of 4 mW (milliwatts) per gate. The corresponding figures for standard TTL are 10 ns and 10 mW, respectively.

Complementary metal-oxide semiconductor (CMOS) logic A number of logic families have been developed using metal-oxide semiconductor (MOS) transistors instead of the bipolar transistors used in TTL. For the purposes of this review, the reader need not be concerned with the differences between various types of transistors. Interested readers may consult References A.7 and A.8. Depending on the manufacturing process, MOS transistors are known as either p- or n-channel transistors. In general, MOS circuits operate at lower speeds in comparison with bipolar circuits. Their major advantage, however, is that they are well-suited to VLSI. Logic families based on either p- or n-channel

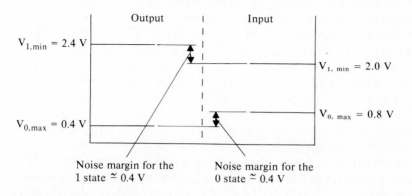

Output   Input

$V_{1,min} = 2.4$ V

$V_{1, min} = 2.0$ V

$V_{0, max} = 0.8$ V

$V_{0,max} = 0.4$ V

Noise margin for the   Noise margin for the
1 state ≃ 0.4 V   0 state ≃ 0.4 V

Figure A.17 TTL logic levels.

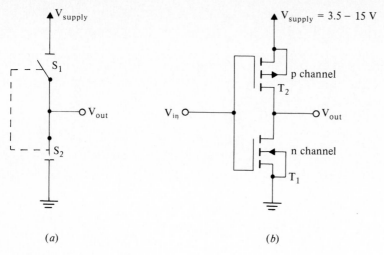

Figure A.18 A CMOS inverter.

transistors are extensively used in VLSI applications. Important examples of this are the memory and microprocessor chips discussed in Chapters 8 and 11.

A logic family that combines p- and n-channel MOS transistors on the same chip is known as the *complementary MOS* or CMOS family. The circuit configuration for a CMOS inverter is given in Figure A.18*b*. Operation of this inverter circuit is similar to that of the circuit in Figure A.18*a*, where the two switches S_1 and S_2 are linked such that when switch S_1 is closed, switch S_2 is open, and vice versa. In the CMOS circuit, when V_{in} is high, the n-channel transistor is On and the p-channel transistor is Off. Thus the output terminal is at 0 V. As the input voltage changes from high to low, the p-channel transistor starts to conduct, and the n-channel transistor turns Off, causing V_{out} to rise to the supply voltage. Extension of this circuit to obtain NAND and NOR functions is straightforward. A NOR gate is illustrated in Figure A.19.

Advantages of CMOS logic circuits include high noise immunity and low power consumption. The noise immunity occurs because the noise margin for the basic inverter circuit of Figure A.18 is roughly equal to a third of the supply voltage. With V_{supply} in the range of 3.5 to 15 V, the noise margin is in the range of 1 to 5 V. The low power of CMOS circuits can be appreciated by inspection of Figure A.18. Consider first the case where V_{in} is held near either 0 or V_{supply}. Since in either case one of the two transistors is in the nonconducting mode, no steady flow of current takes place from the power supply to ground. Only a very small amount of "leakage" current exists, thus leading to very low power dissipation. However, while switching between the two logic states, there is a short period of time when both transistors are in the conducting mode. This leads to a short current pulse being observed at the power supply associated with every change of state. Therefore, in CMOS circuits, power dissipation is dependent on the rate at which state changes take place. In fact, it increases

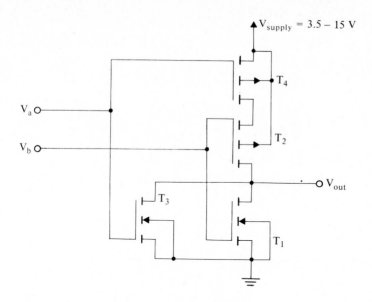

Figure A.19 A two-input CMOS NOR gate.

linearly with the frequency of operation. At 1 MHz, power dissipation is about 1 mW per gate. In comparision with TTL, a considerable saving in power is achieved up to frequencies of a few megaherz. Propagation delay for CMOS gates is in the range of 25 to 100 ns.

Emitter-coupled logic (ECL) This logic family provides the highest-speed logic devices that are presently commercially available. ECL gates have propagation delays of the order of 1 or 2 ns. The basic configuration of an ECL NOT gate is illustrated in Figure A.20. In this figure, current flows from the ground terminal to a negative power supply. Operation of the circuit can be described as follows. When the input voltage V_{in} is below the fixed reference voltage V_{ref}, transistor Q_2 is in the conducting mode and transistor Q_1 is turned Off. Thus a current I flows through resistor R_2. When V_{in} rises above V_{ref}, the situation is reversed, causing the same current I to flow through R_1. Only a small change in V_{in}, of the order of a few tenths of a volt, is required for this change of state to take place. As V_{in} rises from its low state (V_L) to its high state (V_H), the voltage at point P drops from 0 to $-IR_1$. A simple voltage-level-shifting network produces output voltages of V_H and V_L when point P is at 0 and $-IR_1$, respectively.

In summary, state changes in the circuit of Figure A.20 take place by "steering" the current I from one branch of the circuit to the other. This is in contrast to switching the supply current On and Off as in the case of RTL and TTL families. The use of current steering and the attendant low-voltage changes are the main reasons for the high speed of ECL logic. We should note, however, that this is accomplished at the expense of increased power consumption. For a 2-ns gate, power dissipation is about 25 mW.

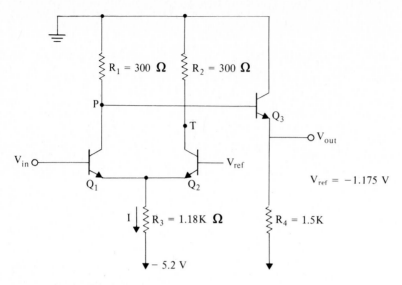

Figure A.20 An ECL logic inverter.

The logic levels for the ECL family are as follows.

Output:
$$V_{1,min} = -0.850 \text{ V}$$
$$V_{0,max} = -1.500 \text{ V}$$

Input:
$$V_{1,min} = -1.025 \text{ V}$$
$$V_{0,max} = -1.325 \text{ V}$$

Therefore the noise margin for both the 0 and 1 states is 0.175 V.

It is interesting to note that the state of point T in the circuit of Figure A.20 is always the complement of that of point P. Thus, at the small expense of an extra level-shifting network, both the output and its complement can be made available. This is illustrated in Figure A.21, which gives the organization of an ECL OR-NOR circuit. The two outputs are represented symbolically as shown in the figure.

A comparison of the three logic families presented in this brief review is given in Table A.5.

A.5.2 Integrated Circuit Packages

Individual logic gates are commercially available in integrated circuit (IC) form. An IC chip is mounted inside a sealed protective package, which has a number of metallic pins for external connections. Standard IC packages are available with different numbers of pins. A typical package containing four NAND gates is shown in Figure A.22. The four gates utilize common power supply and ground

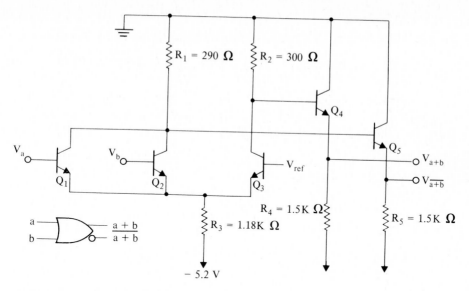

Figure A.21 An ECL OR-NOR gate.

pins. Such ICs comprising only a few logic gates are referred to as *small-scale integrated* (SSI) circuits.

We should note that the speed and power dissipation figures given in this section apply to gates in SSI form. In any VLSI implementation, these figures can be considerably smaller. Moreover, they may vary from gate to gate depending upon size and geometry.

A.6 FLIP-FLOPS

In the majority of applications of digital logic, there is a need for storing information. For example, in the familiar problem of a combinational lock, it is

Table A.5 Comparison of logic families

Logic family	Typical gate delay, ns	Power dissipation, mw	Propagation delay-power product, pJ
RTL	12	12	144
Standard TTL	10	10	100
Low-power TTL	33	1	33
Schottky TTL	4	35	140
Low-power Schottky TTL	8	4	32
CMOS	70	1 (at 1 MHz)	70
ECL	2	25	50

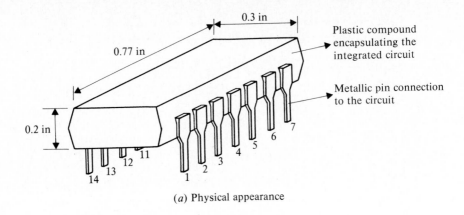

(*a*) Physical appearance

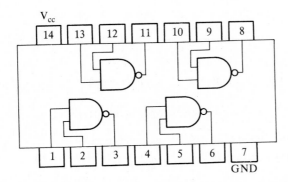

(*b*) Schematic of an integrated circuit providing 4 two-input NAND gates

Figure A.22 A 14-pin integrated circuit.

necessary to remember the sequence in which the digits are dialed in order to decide whether to open the lock. Another important example is the storage of programs and data in the memory of a digital computer.

The basic electronic element for storing binary information is termed a *flip-flop*. Consider the two cross-coupled NOR gates in Figure A.23*a*. Let us examine this circuit, starting with the situation where R = 1 and S = 0. Simple analysis shows that $Q_a = 0$ and $Q_b = 1$. Under this condition, both inputs to gate G_a are equal to 1. Thus, if R is changed to 0, no change will take place at the outputs Q_a and Q_b. Now, if S is set to 1 with R equal to 0, Q_a and Q_b will become 1 and 0, respectively, and will continue in this state after S is returned to 0. Hence this logic circuit constitutes a memory element, or a flip-flop, that "remembers" which of the two inputs S and R was most recently equal to 1. A truth table for this flip-flop is given in Figure A.23*b*. Some typical waveforms that characterize the flip-flop are shown in Figure A.23*c*. The arrows in Figure A.23*c* indicate the cause-effect relationships between the signals. Note that

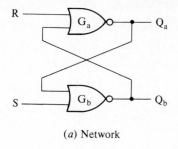

(*a*) Network

S	R	Q_a	Q_b
0	0	0/1	1/0
0	1	0	1
1	0	1	0
1	1	0	0

(*b*) Truth table

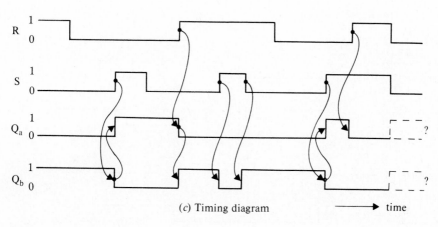

(*c*) Timing diagram   → time

Figure A.23 An RS flip-flop.

when both the R and S inputs change from 1 to 0 at the same time, the resulting state is undefined. In practice, the flip-flop will assume one of its two stable states depending upon any asymmetry in the circuit. As a result of this ambiguity, the input valuation R = S = 1 is not used in most applications of RS flip-flops.

Because of the nature of operation of the above circuit, the S and R lines are referred to as the set and reset inputs, and Q_a and Q_b are usually represented by Q and $\overline{Q}$, respectively. Furthermore, the circuit is called an *RS flip-flop*. We should note that, in this context, $\overline{Q}$ should be regarded merely as a symbol representing the second output of the flip-flop, rather than the complement of Q, since the input valuation R = S = 1 yields Q = $\overline{Q}$ = 0.

A.6.1 Clocked Flip-Flops

A large number of applications require that the time at which a flip-flop is set or reset be controlled from an input other than R and S, termed a clock input. The resulting configuration is called a *clocked RS flip-flop*. A logic circuit and

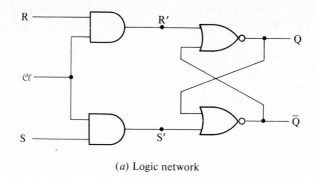

(a) Logic network

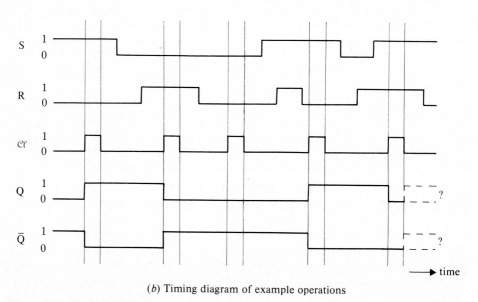

(b) Timing diagram of example operations

Figure A.24 Clocked RS flip-flop.

characteristic waveforms for such a flip-flop are given in Figure A.24. When the clock Cl is equal to 1, points S' and R' follow the inputs S and R, respectively. On the other hand, when $Cl = 0$, the S' and R' points are equal to 0, and no change in the state of the flip-flop can take place.

In the technical literature, the basic storage element consisting of two cross-coupled NOR gates, such as the one in Figure A.23a, is often called a *latch*. The term flip-flop is then used to denote a circuit where a clock input is included, such as the one in Figure A.24a.

So far we have used truth tables to describe the behavior of logic circuits. A truth table gives the output of a network for various input valuations. Logic circuits whose outputs are uniquely defined for each input valuation are referred to as *combinational circuits*. This is the class of circuits discussed in Sections A.1 to A.4. When memory elements are present, a different class of circuits is obtained. The output of such circuits is a function not only of the present valuation of the input variables but also of their previous behavior. An example of this is shown in Figure A.23. These types of circuits are called *sequential circuits*.

Because of the memory property of a flip-flop, its truth table should be modified to show the effect of its present state. Table A.6 describes the behavior of the clocked RS flip-flop, where Q_n denotes its present state. The next state, Q_{n+1}, is reached at the end of a clock pulse. We should note that the undefined state following a clock pulse with the input valuation S = R = 1 appears explicitly when the table is written in this form.

A second type of flip-flop, called the *D flip-flop*, is given in Figure A.25. In this case, the two signals S and R are derived from a single input D. Upon arrival of the clock, the Q output is set to 1 if D = 1, or reset to 0 if D = 0. This means that the D flip-flop samples the D input at the time the clock is high and stores that information until a subsequent clock pulse arrives.

A.6.2 Master-Slave and Edge-Triggered Flip-Flops

In the circuit of Figure A.24 we assumed that while $C\ell = 1$ the inputs S and R do not change. Inspection of the circuit reveals that any change in the S or R inputs during this time will be followed immediately by a corresponding change in the output. Similarly, for the circuit of Figure A.25, Q = D as long as $C\ell = 1$. This is undesirable in many cases, particularly in circuits involving counters and shift registers, which will be discussed later. In such circuits, immediate propagation of logic conditions from the data inputs (R, S, or D) to the flip-flop outputs cannot be tolerated. The concept of a *master-slave* organization eliminates this problem. Two flip-flops can be connected to form a master-slave RS flip-flop, as shown in Figure A.26a. The first, referred to as the master, is connected to the input lines when $C\ell = 1$. A 1 to 0 transition of the clock isolates the master from the input and transfers the contents of the master stage to the slave stage. The thresholds at which logic transitions occur in particular gates are arranged as shown in Figure A.26b. It is easily seen that, at all times, no direct path exists from the inputs to the outputs.

It should be noted that while $C\ell = 1$ the state of the master stage is

Table A.6 Truth table for a clocked RS flip-flop

S	R	Q_{n+1}
0	0	Q_n (no change in state)
0	1	0
1	0	1
1	1	X (undefined)

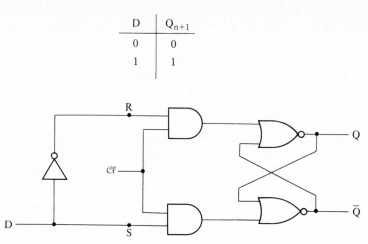

D	Q_{n+1}
0	0
1	1

Figure A.25 D flip-flop.

immediately affected by changes in the inputs S and R. The function of the slave stage is to hold the output of the flip-flop while the master stage is being set up to the next-state value as determined by the S and R inputs. In most applications, this means that the S and R inputs should have reached the correct levels for determining the next state before the 0 to 1 transition on $C\ell$ and should hold these levels while $C\ell = 1$. The new state is then transferred from the master to the slave after the 1 to 0 transition on $C\ell$. At this point, the master stage has been isolated from the inputs so that further changes in the S and R inputs will not affect this transfer. The master-stage outputs Q' and $\overline{Q}'$ are the slave-stage inputs S' and R', respectively, as shown in the figure. Examples of state transitions for various S and R input combinations are shown in Figure A.26c.

Another very useful type of flip-flop is the *JK flip-flop*. A truth table defining its operation is given in Table A.7. The first three entries in this table exhibit the same behavior as those in Table A.6, where J and K correspond to S and R, respectively. For the input valuation J = K = 1, the next state is defined as the complement of the present state of the flip-flop. That is, when J = K = 1, the flip-flop functions as a *toggle*, or a modulo 2 counter. A JK flip-flop can be implemented using an RS flip-flop connected such that

$$S = J\overline{Q} \quad \text{and} \quad R = KQ$$

This means that feedback connections are required from the outputs Q and $\overline{Q}$ to the inputs R and S. It is important, therefore, that the flip-flop does not allow input changes to be propagated immediately to the output. Otherwise, a steady state can never be reached when J = K = 1, since a change in the output causes a change in the input, which leads to a further change in the output, and so on. In other words, the circuit will oscillate. A master-slave organization can be used to guarantee proper operation. Figure A.27a gives an implementation of a master-slave JK flip-flop derived by adding the appropriate feedback connec-

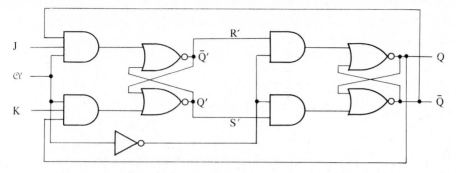

(*a*) Implementation of a JK flip-flop from a master-slave RS flip-flop

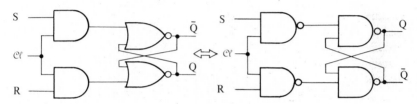

(b) NAND gate implementation of a clocked RS flip-flop

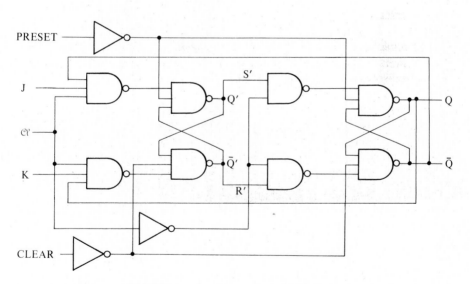

(*c*) NAND gate implementation of a JK flip-flop

Figure A.27 Master-slave JK flip-flops.

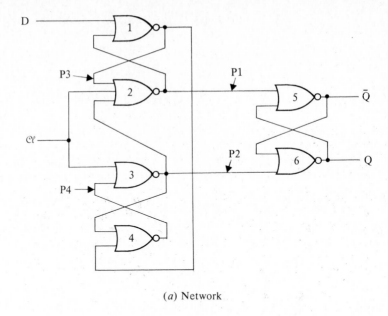

(a) Network

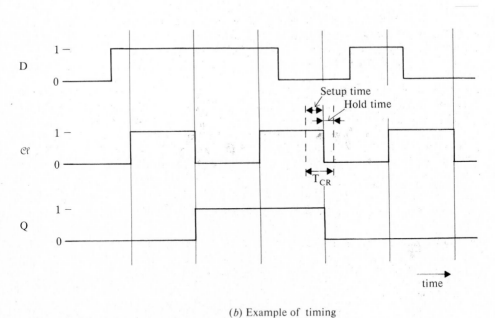

(b) Example of timing

Figure A.28 A negative edge-triggered D flip-flop.

suppose D = 1, at the trailing edge of $\mathcal{Cl}$. The 1 at P1 means further changes at D cannot affect the output of gate 1 which is maintained at 0.

When $\mathcal{Cl}$ goes to 1 at the start of the next clock pulse, points P1 and P2 are again forced to 0, isolating the output from the remainder of the circuit. Then points P3 and P4 follow changes at D as described above.

An example of the operation of this type of D flip-flop is shown in Figure A.28b. The state acquired by the flip-flop upon the 1 to 0 transition of $C\ell$ is equal to the value on the D input immediately preceding this transition. However, there is a critical time period T_{CR} around the trailing edge of $C\ell$ during which the value on D should not change. This region is split into two parts, the *setup time* before the clock edge, and the *hold time* after the clock edge, as shown in the figure.

Other flip-flop types are available in the edge-triggered configuration, but we will not discuss any of their details.

We have introduced a number of flip-flop configurations that differ in their data input and clock requirements. The data input can take the form of RS, D, or JK inputs. Clocking may consist of simple input gating, edge-triggering, or a master-slave arrangement. This gives considerable flexibility in the choice of a particular type of flip-flop for a given application. In general, the input configuration is chosen to simplify any external logic circuitry that may be required. Choice of the clocking arrangement is dependent on the timing constraints.

Flip-flops are available in IC form with two or four flip-flops to a package. The number of flip-flops in a package is limited by the number of pins available, which is either 14 or 16 for SSI circuits. A variety of ICs are also available which contain a number of gates and flip-flops connected to implement small logic subsystems. Such ICs represent *medium-scale integration* (MSI). Some examples of MSI circuits will be given in the following sections.

A.7 REGISTERS

Individual flip-flops can be used to store a few bits. However, in machines where data is handled in words consisting of a number of bits (perhaps as many as 64), it is more convenient to have larger devices capable of holding several bits of data. Such devices are usually called *registers*. The simplest form of a register in a single IC package consists of a few flip-flops whose operation is synchronized by a common clock signal. In a 24-pin MSI package one may find as many as 10 D-type flip-flops.

The number of pins in an IC package is often the factor that determines the number of circuits that can be usefully included on an IC chip. If a register consists of individual flip-flops and if each flip-flop needs a certain number of input and output connections, then it is apparent that pin limitation constrains the size of the register. An interesting and useful alternative is to put more than one register on a single chip, sharing some of the external connections. Thus a "register file" is obtained. It contains an array of flip-flops organized into several register sections. A typical configuration may involve four 4-bit sections, or perhaps eight 2-bit sections. The chip must obviously have some inputs that can select the desired section. Such register files provide economical means for the implementation of general-purpose registers in computers. We should note that the concept of register files is readily extendable to larger-scale circuits, where they in effect become full-fledged memory chips that may store thousands of bits of data. Of course, the access circuitry in memory chips is considerably more complex. See Chapter 8 for details.

A.8 SHIFT REGISTERS

Processing of digital data often requires the capability to shift and rotate the data. Thus it is necessary to provide the hardware with this facility. A simple mechanism for realizing both operations is to devise a register whose contents may be shifted, to the right or left, one bit position at a time. As an example, consider the 4-bit shift register in Figure A.29. It consists of JK flip-flops connected so that each clock pulse will cause transfer of the contents (state) of F_i to F_{i+1}, thus effecting a "right shift." Data is shifted serially into and out of the register.

A key requirement for proper operation of a shift register is that its contents be shifted exactly one position for each clock pulse. This places a constraint on the type of flip-flops that can be used. Flip-flops having simple input gating, as in Figures A.24 or A.25, are not suitable for this purpose. While the clock is high, the data applied to the input of a flip-flop quickly propagates to its output. From there, it propagates through the next flip-flop in the same manner. Hence there is no control over the number of shifts that will take place during a single clock pulse. This number depends upon the propagation delays of the flip-flops and the duration of the clock pulse. The solution to the problem is to use either the master-slave or the edge-triggered flip-flops described in Section A.6.2. In the remainder of this appendix we will assume that one of these two types is used.

A particularly useful form of a shift register is one that can be loaded and read in parallel. This can be accomplished with some additional gating as illustrated in Figure A.30. Hence, a 4-bit register is constructed with RS flip-flops. It can be loaded either serially or in parallel. When the register is clocked, a shift takes place if Shift/Load = 1; otherwise a parallel load is performed.

Shift registers of this type are commercially available in many different configurations. A typical IC package may realize an 8-bit register. In addition to providing the shifting in one direction, it is not difficult to obtain the ability to

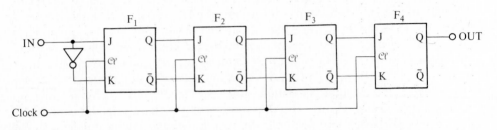

Figure A.29 A simple shift register.

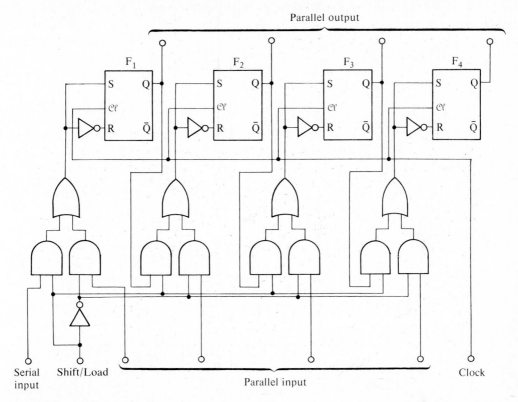

Figure A.30 Parallel-access shift register.

shift in the opposite direction as well by means of some extra logic. One readily finds shift-register chips that allow parallel data access and shifting in either direction.

A.9 COUNTERS

In the preceding section we discussed the applicability of flip-flops in the construction of shift registers. They are equally useful in the implementation of *counter* circuits. It is hardly necessary to justify the need for counters in digital machines. In addition to being a hardware mechanism for realizing ordinary counting functions, they are also used to generate control and timing signals. A counter driven by a high-frequency clock can be used to produce signals whose frequencies are submultiples of the original clock frequency. In such applications a counter is said to be functioning as a *scaler*.

A simple four-stage (or 4-bit) counter constructed with JK flip-flops is given in Figure A.31. Recall that when the J and K inputs are both equal to 1, the flip-flop acts as a toggle; that is, its state changes with each successive clock pulse. Thus two clock pulses will result in F_1 changing from the 1 (0) state into

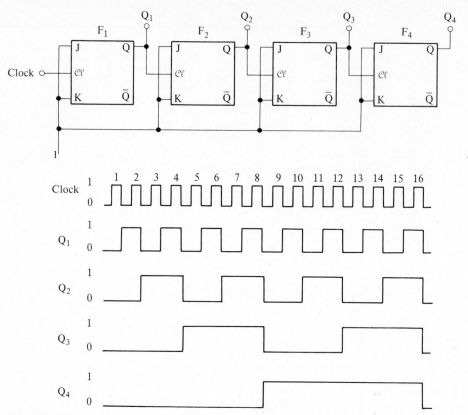

Figure A.31 A four-stage counter and associated signal waveforms.

the 0 (1) state and back into the 1 (0) state. This means that the output waveform of F_1, denoted in the figure as Q_1, has half the frequency of the clock. Similarly, since F_2 is driven by the output of F_1, the waveform at Q_2 has half the frequency of Q_1, or one-fourth the frequency of the clock. Note that we have assumed that the trailing edge of the clock input to each flip-flop triggers the change of its state.

The above counter is often called a "ripple" counter because the effect of an input clock pulse ripples through the counter. For example, the trailing edge of pulse 8 will change the state of F_1 from 1 to 0. This change in Q_1 will then force Q_2 from 1 to 0. Next Q_3 is changed from 1 to 0, which in turn forces Q_4 from 0 to 1. If each flip-flop introduces some delay Δ, then the delay in setting Q_4 is 4Δ. Such delays can be a problem when very fast operation of counter circuits is required. However, in many applications they are small in comparison with the length of the clock pulses and can be neglected.

With the addition of some extra logic gates, it is possible to construct a "synchronous" counter, where each stage is under the control of the common clock, so that all flip-flops can change their states simultaneously. Such counters are capable of operation at higher speed, as the total propagation delay is reduced considerably.

A.10 DECODERS

Much of the information in computers is handled in a highly encoded form. In an instruction, an n-bit field may be used to denote 1 out of 2^n possible choices for the action to be taken. To perform the desired action, the encoded instruction must first be decoded. A circuit capable of accepting an n-variable input and generating the corresponding output signal on one out of 2^n output lines is called a *decoder*. A simple example of a two-input to four-output decoder is given in Figure A.32. One of the four output lines is selected by the inputs x_1 and x_2 as indicated in the figure. The selected output has the logic value 1, while the remaining outputs have the value 0.

So far, we have considered only the simplest kind of decoders. Many others exist. For example, using information in BCD form often requires decoding circuits where a four-variable BCD input is used to select 1 out of 10 possible outputs. As another specific example let us consider a decoder suitable for driving a seven-segment display. Figure A.33 shows the structure of a seven-segment element used for display purposes. It is easily seen that any decimal number from 0 to 9 can be displayed with this element simply by turning some segments On (light), while leaving others Off (dark). The necessary functions are indicated in the table. They can be realized using the decoding circuit shown in the figure. Note that the circuit is constructed with NAND gates. The reader is encouraged to verify that the circuit indeed implements the required functions.

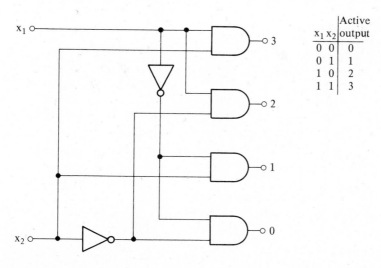

x_1 x_2	Active output
0 0	0
0 1	1
1 0	2
1 1	3

Figure A.32 A two-input to four-output decoder.

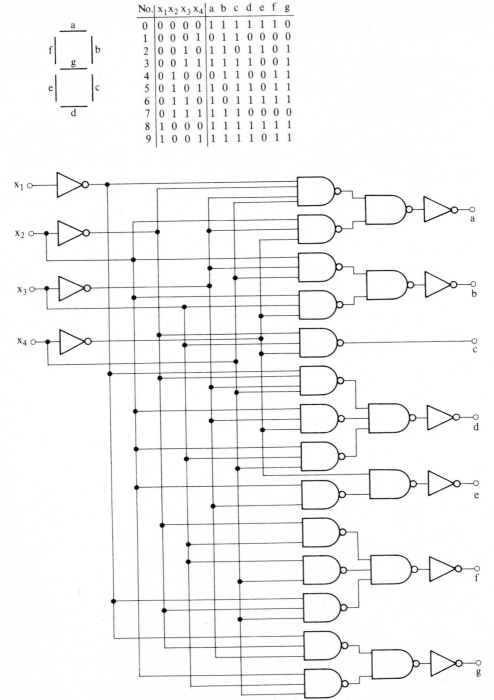

No.	x_1	x_2	x_3	x_4	a	b	c	d	e	f	g
0	0	0	0	0	1	1	1	1	1	1	0
1	0	0	0	1	0	1	1	0	0	0	0
2	0	0	1	0	1	1	0	1	1	0	1
3	0	0	1	1	1	1	1	1	0	0	1
4	0	1	0	0	0	1	1	0	0	1	1
5	0	1	0	1	1	0	1	1	0	1	1
6	0	1	1	0	1	0	1	1	1	1	1
7	0	1	1	1	1	1	1	0	0	0	0
8	1	0	0	0	1	1	1	1	1	1	1
9	1	0	0	1	1	1	1	1	0	1	1

Figure A.33 A BCD to seven-segment display decoder.

A.11 MULTIPLEXERS

In the preceding section we saw that decoders select one output line on the basis of input signals. The selected output line has a logic value 1, while the other outputs have the value 0. There exists another class of very useful selector circuits, where any one of n inputs can be selected to appear as the output. The choice is governed by a set of "select" inputs. Such circuits are called *multiplexers*. An example of a multiplexer circuit is shown in Figure A.34. It has two select inputs w_1 and w_2. Their four possible valuations are used to select one of four inputs x_1, x_2, x_3, or x_4, so that the selected input appears as the output z. A simple logic circuit that can implement the required operation is also given. Obviously, the same structure can be used to realize larger multiplexers, where k

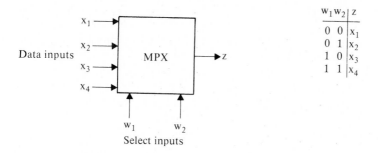

w_1	w_2	z
0	0	x_1
0	1	x_2
1	0	x_3
1	1	x_4

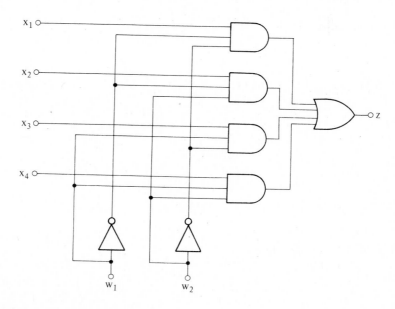

Figure A.34 A four-input multiplexer.

select inputs are used to connect one of the 2^k data inputs to the output. Many such circuits are available in IC form.

The obvious application of multiplexers is in gating of data that may come from a number of different sources. For example, if a 16-bit data register is to be loaded from one of four distinct sources, this can be accomplished with 16 four-input multiplexers that come in eight IC packages.

Multiplexers are also very useful as basic elements for implementing logic functions. Consider a function f defined by the truth table of Figure A.35. It can be represented as shown by factoring out the variables x_1 and x_2. Note that for each valuation of x_1 and x_2, the function f corresponds to one of four terms: 0, 1, x_3, or $\overline{x}_3$. This suggests the possibility of using a four-input multiplexer circuit, where x_1 and x_2 are the two select inputs that choose one of the four data inputs. Then, if the data inputs are connected to 0, 1, x_3, or $\overline{x}_3$, as required by the truth table, the output of the multiplexer will correspond to the function f. The approach is completely general. Any function of three variables can be realized with a single four-input multiplexer. Similarly, any function of four variables can be implemented with an eight-input multiplexer, etc.

Using multiplexers in this fashion is a straightforward approach, which often reduces the total number of ICs needed to realize a given function. If the function of Figure A.35 is constructed with AND, OR, and NOT gates, its minimal form is

$$f = x_1\overline{x}_2 + x_1\overline{x}_3 + \overline{x}_1x_2x_3$$

which implies a network of three AND gates and one OR gate. Thus parts of more than one IC are needed for this implementation. In general, the multiplexer approach is more attractive for functions that do not yield simple sum-of-

x_1	x_2	x_3	f
0	0	0	0
0	0	1	0
0	1	0	0
0	1	1	1
1	0	0	1
1	0	1	1
1	1	0	1
1	1	1	0

$\Longrightarrow$

x_1	x_2	f
0	0	0
0	1	x_3
1	0	1
1	1	$\overline{x}_3$

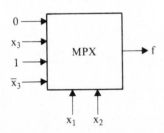

Figure **A.35** Multiplexer implementation of a logic function.

products expressions. Of course, the relative merits of the two approaches should be judged by the number of ICs needed to implement a given function.

A.12 PROGRAMMABLE LOGIC ARRAYS (PLAs)

Sections A.2 and A.3 showed how a given switching function can be represented in terms of sum-of-products expressions and implemented in terms of the corresponding AND-OR gate networks. Section A.11 showed how multiplexers can used to realize switching functions. In this section we will consider another class of ICs that can be used for the same purpose. These circuits consist of arrays of switching elements that can be programmed to allow implementation of sum-of-products expressions. They are called *programmable logic arrays*.

Figure A.36 shows the block diagram of a PLA. It has n input variables $(x_1, \ldots, x_n)$ and m outputs $(f_1, \ldots, f_m)$. Each function f_i is realized as a sum of product terms that involve the input variables. The variables $x_1, \ldots, x_n$ are presented in true and complemented form to the AND array, where up to k product terms are formed. These are then gated into the OR array, where the output functions are formed. Some of the product terms may be used in the synthesis of more than one of the output functions.

Let us consider a specific example of a three-input two-output PLA, where the output functions are

$$f_1 = x_1x_2 + x_1\bar{x}_3 + \bar{x}_1\bar{x}_2x_3$$

and

$$f_2 = x_1x_2 + x_1x_3 + \bar{x}_1\bar{x}_2x_3$$

Its structure can be modeled by an equivalent logic-gate network as shown in Figure A.37. Note that only four product terms are needed, since two of them can be shared by both functions. A simplified circuit for a PLA programmed to implement these functions is given in Figure A.38. Diodes are used to implement the product terms in the AND array and to realize the desired sums in the OR array. The operation of this circuit follows the principles described in

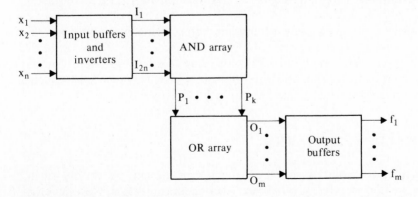

Figure A.36 A block diagram for a PLA.

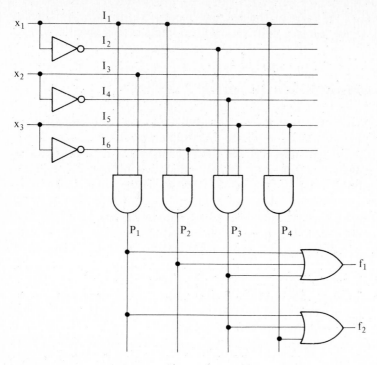

$$f_1 = x_1 x_2 + x_1 \bar{x}_3 + \bar{x}_1 \bar{x}_2 x_3$$
$$f_2 = x_1 x_2 + x_1 x_3 + \bar{x}_1 \bar{x}_2 x_3$$

Figure A.37 Logic gate equivalent of an example PLA.

Section A.5.1. Note that the absence of a diode at any given crosspoint merely indicates that the corresponding variable does not appear in the particular product term.

A PLA has switching elements available at each crosspoint of both AND and OR arrays. However, they do not provide an actual conducting path until they are programmed. Programming is typically the last step in the manufacturing process.

PLAs provide a simple way of implementing switching functions. The number of functions that can be implemented is dependent upon the size of the PLA. For example, one can obtain a PLA that has 14 input variables, 8 output functions, and up to 48 internal product terms in the AND array. Clearly, such a device can be used to realize a fairly complex logic network.

A.13 CONCLUDING REMARKS

IC technology has revolutionized the art of logic design. A variety of IC components are commercially available at ever decreasing costs. New developments and technological improvements are constantly adding to this collection.

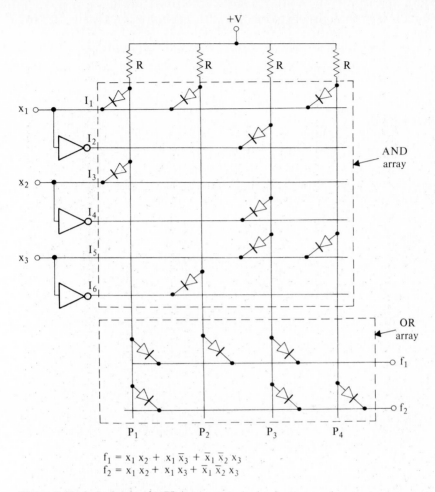

$$f_1 = x_1 x_2 + x_1 \bar{x}_3 + \bar{x}_1 \bar{x}_2 x_3$$
$$f_2 = x_1 x_2 + x_1 x_3 + \bar{x}_1 \bar{x}_2 x_3$$

Figure A.38 An example of a PLA.

In this appendix we introduced a number of the basic components that are useful in the design of digital systems. Several others are discussed in the main body of the book. For example, ICs that implement arithmetic functions are dealt with in Chapter 7. Very large-scale integrated (VLSI) circuits as used in the microprocessor environment are treated in Chapter 11. In these cases, it is more natural to talk about particular components within the framework of their typical applications.

From the designer's point of view, the obvious parameter to keep in mind is the cost of the resultant circuits. This implies that the number of IC packages used should be as low as possible.

While the component cost in a digital system is a significant factor, two other design objectives are becoming increasingly more important. The ability to easily test the resultant circuits simplifies the task of proving that newly produced equipment works correctly, as well as repairing it in the case of failure.

Furthermore, it is often desirable to increase the reliability of a system with the help of additional redundant logic circuits (for example, by duplicating some parts). Both these objectives are likely to lead to increased component cost. It is the designer's job to arrive at a satisfactory trade-off between these considerations.

A.14 PROBLEMS

A.1 Implement the COINCIDENCE function in sum-of-products form, where COINCIDENCE = EX-OR.

A.2 Prove the following identities by algebraic manipulation and also by using truth tables.

(a) $a \oplus b \oplus c = \overline{a}\overline{b}\overline{c} + a\overline{b}c + \overline{a}bc + ab\overline{c}$

(b) $x + w\overline{x} = x + w$

(c) $x_1\overline{x}_2 + \overline{x}_2x_3 + x_3\overline{x}_1 = x_1\overline{x}_2 + x_3\overline{x}_1$

A.3 Derive minimal sum-of-products forms for the 4 three-variable functions f_1, f_2, f_3, f_4.

x_1	x_2	x_3	f_1	f_2	f_3	f_4
0	0	0	1	1	d	0
0	0	1	1	1	1	1
0	1	0	0	1	0	1
0	1	1	0	1	1	d
1	0	0	1	0	d	d
1	0	1	0	0	0	d
1	1	0	1	0	1	1
1	1	1	1	1	1	0

Is there more than one minimal form for any of these functions? If so, derive all of them.

A.4 Two 2-bit numbers $A = a_1a_0$ and $B = b_1b_0$ are to be compared by a four-variable function $f(a_1, a_0, b_1, b_0)$. The function f is to have the value 1 whenever

$$v(A) \leq v(B)$$

where $v(X) = x_1 \times 2^1 + x_0 \times 2^0$ for any 2-bit number. Assume that the variables A and B are such that $|v(A) - v(B)| \leq 2$. Synthesize f using as few gates as possible.

A.5 A number code where consecutive numbers are represented by binary patterns that differ in one bit position only is called a Gray code. A truth table for a 3-bit Gray-code to binary-code converter is shown.

3-bit Gray code inputs			Binary code outputs		
a	b	c	f_1	f_2	f_3
0	0	0	0	0	0
0	0	1	0	0	1
0	1	1	0	1	0
0	1	0	0	1	1
1	1	0	1	0	0
1	1	1	1	0	1
1	0	1	1	1	0
1	0	0	1	1	1

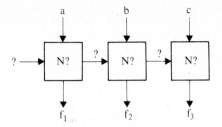

f_1 f_2 f_3 **Figure PA.1** Code conversion network.

(a) Implement the three functions f_1, f_2, f_3 using only NAND gates.

(b) A lower-cost network for performing this code conversion can be derived by noting the following relationships between the input and output variables.

$$f_1 = a$$

$$f_2 = f_1 \oplus b$$

$$f_3 = f_2 \oplus c$$

Using these relationships, specify the contents of a combinational network N that can be repeated, as shown in Figure PA.1, to implement the conversion. Compare the total number of NAND gates required to implement the conversion in this form to the number required in part (a).

A.6 In the production of ICs it is desirable to have circuits with as few wire crossovers as possible. Implement the EX-OR function with NAND gates only, so that there are no wire crossovers inside the box shown in Figure PA.2.

A.7 Figure A.33 defines a BCD to seven-segment display decoder. Give an implementation for this truth table using AND, OR, and NOT gates. Verify that the same functions are implemented correctly by the NAND-gate circuits shown in the figure.

A.8 In the logic network shown in Figure PA.3, gate 3 fails and produces the logic value 1 at its output F1 regardless of the inputs. Redraw the network, making simplifications wherever possible, to obtain a new network that is equivalent to the given faulty network and contains as few gates as possible. Repeat this problem, assuming that the fault is at position F2 and that it is stuck at a logic value 0.

A.9 The circuit configuration for a CMOS two-input NOR gate is given in Figure A.19. Show how the four MOS transistors can be connected to obtain a two-input NAND gate.

A.10 Consider the DTL circuit in Figure A.15. Assume that the voltage drop across each diode is 0.7 V when the diode is conducting. Furthermore, assume that the transistor is turned Off when the base-emitter voltage V_{BE} is less than 0.4 V. When the transistor is turned fully On, the collector-emitter voltage is 0.2 V and $V_{BE} = 0.7$ V. For V_{BE} between 0.4 and 0.7 V, the transistor is partially conducting. Plot the I/O characteristics for this circuit with the two inputs tied together. Suggest suitable values for $V_{1.min}$ and $V_{0,max}$ at the input for proper operation as a logic inverter.

A.11 The ECL logic family provides considerable flexibility in implementing logic functions by allowing gate outputs to be tied together. By inspection of the circuit configuration for an ECL NOR gate, derive the logic expressions for the functions f_1 to f_4 in Figure PA.4.

A.12 Logic circuits for JK master-slave flip-flops are given in Figure A.27. Draw the waveforms at S', R', Q, and $\overline{Q}$ for the input waveforms shown in Figure PA.5, assuming that the flip-flop is initially in the 0 state.

$f = a \oplus b$

Figure PA.2 Combinational network for the EX-OR function.

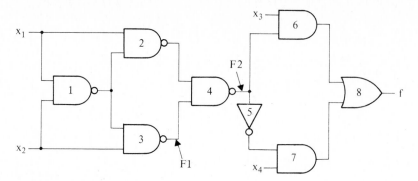

Figure PA.3 A faulty network.

A.13 Derive the truth table for the NAND-gate circuit in Figure PA.6. Compare it to the truth table in Figure A.23*b*, and then verify that the equivalence shown in Figure A.27*b* is correct.

A.14 Compute both the setup time and the hold time, in terms of NOR-gate delays, for the negative edge-triggered D flip-flop shown in Figure A.28.

A.15 Figure A.29 shows a shift-register network, which shifts the data to the right, one place at a time, under the control of a clock signal. Modify this shift register to make it capable of shifting data either one or two places at a time under the control of the clock and an additional control input ONE/TWO.

A.16 It is required to design a 4-bit shift register that has three inputs: INITIALIZE, RIGHT/ LEFT, and CLOCK. When INITIALIZE is set to 1, the binary number 1000 should be loaded in the register independently of the clock input. When INITIALIZE = 0, pulses at the CLOCK input should rotate this pattern to the right or to the left when the RIGHT/LEFT input is equal to 1 or 0, respectively. Give a suitable design for this register using JK flip-flops that have PRESET and CLEAR inputs as shown in Figure A.27.

A.17 Derive a three-input to eight-output decoder network, with the restriction that the gates to be used cannot have more than two inputs.

A.18 JK flip-flops are useful in constructing counters because of their "toggle" effect when J = K = 1. Isolating this feature in a separate storage circuit leads to a "T" flip-flop, shown in Figure PA.7.
    (*a*) Derive a T flip-flop using a D flip-flop and any additional logic gates that may be required.
    (*b*) Construct a modulo 8 counter using the T flip-flops.

A.19 Figure A.31 shows a four-stage "up counter." A counter that counts in the opposite direction, that is, 15, 14, . . . , 1, 0, 15, . . . , is called a "down counter." A counter capable of counting in both directions, under the control of an UP/DOWN signal is called an "up-down counter." Show a logic diagram for a four-stage up-down counter which can also be preset to any state through parallel loading of its flip-flops from an external source. A LOAD/COUNT control is used to determine whether the counter is being loaded or is operating as a counter.

A.20 In digital systems it is often necessary to be able to load a register from a number of different

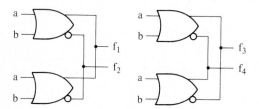

Figure PA.4 Wired output configurations.

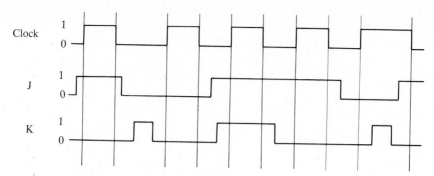

Clock

J

K

Figure PA.5 Input waveforms for a JK flip-flop.

sources. Section A.11 suggested that multiplexer circuits can be used for this purpose very conveniently. However, suppose that the required gating is to be accomplished using AND, OR, and NOT gates in separate IC packages. Let these gates have fan-out of 10. How many such gates would be needed in a circuit that would permit loading a 16-bit register from one of four distinct sources?

A.21 A switching function to be implemented is described by the expression

$$f(x_1, x_2, x_3, x_4) = x_1 x_3 \bar{x}_4 + \bar{x}_1 \bar{x}_3 x_4 + x_2 x_3 x_4 + \bar{x}_2 \bar{x}_3 \bar{x}_4$$

(a) Show an implementation for f in terms of an eight-input multiplexer circuit.
(b) Can f be realized with a four-input multiplexer circuit? If so, show how.

A.22 Repeat problem A.21 for

$$f(x_1, x_2, x_3, x_4) = x_1 \bar{x}_2 x_3 + x_2 x_3 x_4 + \bar{x}_1 \bar{x}_4$$

A.23 Find the simplest sum-of-products form for the function f using the don't-care condition d, where

$$f = x_1(x_2 \bar{x}_3 + x_2 x_3 + \bar{x}_2 \bar{x}_3 x_4) + x_2 \bar{x}_4(\bar{x}_3 + x_1)$$

and $d = x_1 \bar{x}_2(x_3 x_4 + \bar{x}_3 \bar{x}_4) + \bar{x}_1 \bar{x}_3 x_4$

A.24 Implement the following function with no more than six NAND gates, each having three imputs:

$$f = xy + xyz + \bar{x} \bar{y} \bar{z} w + \bar{x} \bar{y} z \bar{w}$$

Assume that both true and complemented inputs are available.

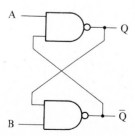

A

Q

B

$\bar{Q}$

Figure PA.6 NAND flip-flop.

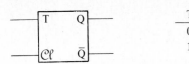

T	Q_{n+1}
0	Q_n
1	$\bar{Q}_n$

Figure PA.7 A T flip-flop.

A.25 Show how to implement the following function using 6 or fewer two-input NAND gates. Complemented input variables are not available.

$$f = xy + \bar{z} + \bar{x}w$$

A.26 Implement the following function as economically as possible using only NAND gates. Assume that complemented input variables are not available.

$$f = (x_1 + x_3)(\bar{x}_2 + \bar{x}_4)$$

A.27 Repeat Problem A.4 for $f = 1$ whenever

$$v(A) > v(B)$$

subject to the input constraint

$$v(A) + v(B) \leq 4$$

A.15 REFERENCES

A.1. Kohavi, Z.: "Switching and Finite Automata Theory," 2d ed., McGraw-Hill, New York, 1978.
A.2. Dietmeyer, D. L.: "Logical Design of Digital Systems," 2d ed., Allyn and Bacon, Boston, 1978.
A.3. Hill, F. J., and G. R. Peterson: "Introduction to Switching Theory and Logical Design," 3d ed., Wiley, New York, 1981.
A.4. McCluskey, E. J.: "Introduction to the Theory of Switching Circuits," McGraw-Hill, New York, 1965.
A.5. Mano, M. Morris: "Digital Logic and Computer Design," Prentice-Hall, Inc., Englewood Cliffs, N.J., 1979.
A.6. Fletcher, William I.: "An Engineering Approach to Digital Design," Prentice-Hall, Inc., Englewood Cliffs, N.J. 1980.
A.7. Taub, H., and D. Schilling: "Digital Integrated Electronics," McGraw-Hill, New York, 1977.
A.8. Sedra, Adel S., and K. C. Smith: "Microelectronic Circuits," Holt, Rinehart, and Winston, New York, N.Y., 1982.

INSTRUCTION SET FOR PDP-11
MINICOMPUTERS

This appendix contains a list of instructions used in PDP-11 minicomputers. There are a number of different models of these computers involving differing instruction sets. In general, larger models have all the instructions found in the smaller ones, plus some additional instructions that are either standard or a part of an optional feature. For illustrative purposes in this book, it is adequate to consider a relatively basic set. The instruction set given in this appendix can be found in most models of the PDP-11 computer.

The addressing scheme for the PDP-11 was fully described in Chapter 2 and will not be repeated here. The instructions are listed below in tabular form, with most entries being self-explanatory. However, some notational abbreviations are used to keep the table as compact as possible. Instructions that have both word and byte formats are combined as single entries; for example, MOV and MOVB are shown as MOV {B}. Such instructions are distinguished by the most significant bit of the OP code, which is 0 in the case of a word instruction and 1 for a byte instruction. This fact is denoted by the character "β." Manipulation of the condition codes is indicated for each instruction, where they are affected. In a typical statement it may be indicated that a flag corresponding to a particular condition code is set to 1 if a given condition is met. It is implicitly assumed that the flag is reset or cleared to 0 if this condition is not met. Thus, instead of writing in full "Condition Code Z: set if result = 0; cleared otherwise," we will show simply "Z: set if result = 0."

Following is a summary of the symbols and abbreviations used:

β   0 for word and 1 for byte instructions
MSB   Most significant bit
PC   Program counter
SP   Stack pointer (that is, register 6)
PSW   Processor status word
temp Internal temporary storage register in the CPU
∧   Logical AND operation
∨   Logical OR operation
⊕   Logical EXCLUSIVE-OR operation
[ ]   Denotes the contents of the register or memory location specified

TWO-OPERAND INSTRUCTIONS

There are two formats for two-operand instructions. The first one allows complete freedom in specifying the source and destination operands, using any of the addressing modes. The format is

OP code	src	dst
15　12	11　6	5　0

It is used in the following instructions:

Mnemonic (name)	OP code (octal)	Operation performed	Condition codes
MOV{B} (Move)	β1	dst ← [src] In MOVB, if dst is a register, then MSB of the low-order byte is extended into the high-order byte	N set if [src] < 0 Z set if [src] = 0 V reset C not affected
ADD (Add)	06	dst ← [src] + [dst]	N set if result < 0 Z set if result = 0 V set if arithmetic overflow occurs C set if carry from MSB of result occurs
SUB (Subtract)	16	dst ← [dst] − [src]	N, Z, V same as in ADD C set if no carry from MSB of result occurs
CMP{B} (Compare)	β2	[src] − [dst] Neither of the operands is affected	Same as in SUB

Mnemonic (name)	OP code (octal)	Operation performed	Condition codes
BIT{B} (Bit test)	$\beta 3$	$[\text{src}] \wedge [\text{dst}]$ Neither of the operands is affected	N set if MSB of result = 1 Z set if result = 0 V reset C not affected
BIC{B} (Bit clear)	$\beta 4$	$\text{dst} \leftarrow \overline{[\text{src}]} \wedge [\text{dst}]$	Same as in BIT
BIS{B} (Bit set)	$\beta 5$	$\text{dst} \leftarrow [\text{src}] \vee [\text{dst}]$	Same as in BIT

The second format for two-operand instructions allows full flexibility in specifying only one operand, either the source or the destination. The second operand is restricted to be in one of the registers, thus requiring only a 3-bit field to specify it. The format is

OP code	reg	src/dst
15	9 8 6 5	0

It is used in the following instructions:

Mnemonic (name)	Op code (octal)	Operation performed	Condition codes
XOR (Exclusive-OR)	074	$\text{dst} \leftarrow [\text{reg}] \oplus [\text{dst}]$	Same as in BIT
MUL (Multiply)	070	reg, reg $\vee$ 1 $\leftarrow [\text{reg}] \times [\text{src}]$ The double-length product is stored in reg and the next higher-numbered register if reg is even. If reg is odd, then only the low-order word is stored in reg.	N set if product < 0 Z set if product = 0 V reset C set if result is not within the range -2^{15} to $2^{15}-1$.
DIV (Divide)	071	reg, reg $\vee$ 1 $\leftarrow$ [reg, reg $\vee$ 1] $\div [\text{src}]$ reg must be even, quotient goes to reg and remainder to the next higher-numbered register (that is, reg $\vee$ 1)	N set if quotient < 0 Z set if quotient = 0 V set if $[\text{src}] = 0$ or if $|[\text{reg}]| > |[\text{src}]|$ C set if divide by 0 is attempted
ASH (Arithmetic shift)	072	Contents of reg are shifted right or left according to the count in the low-order 6 bits of src. Negative	N set if result < 0 Z set if result = 0 V set if MSB of reg changed during shifting

Mnemonic (name)	OP code (octal)	Operation performed	Condition codes
		count results in right shift and positive in left shift	C loaded by the last bit shifted out of reg

or

Mnemonic (name)	OP code (octal)	Operation performed	Condition codes
ASHC (Arithmetic shift combined)	073	Contents of a double-word operand in reg, reg $\vee$ 1 are shifted right or left in a way analogous to the ASH instruction	Same as in ASH

ONE-OPERAND INSTRUCTIONS

The format for one-operand instructions is

OP code		dst
15	6 5	0

The operand can be specified using any of the addressing modes. Instructions in this group are:

Mnemonic (Name)	OP code (octal)	Operation performed	Condition codes
CLR{B} (clear)	β050	dst ← 0	N, V, C reset Z set
COM{B} [Complement (1's)]	β051	dst ← $\overline{[dst]}$	N set if MSB of result is 1 Z set if result = 0 V reset C set
INC{B} (Increment)	β052	dst ← [dst] + 1	N set if result < 0 Z set if result = 0 V set if [dst] was 077777 C not affected
DEC{B} (Decrement)	β053	dst ← [dst] − 1	N, Z, C same as in INC V set if [dst] was 100000

Mnemonic (name)	OP code (octal)	Operation performed	Condition codes
NEG{B} [Negate (2's compl.)]	$\beta054$	dst $\leftarrow -$ [dst]	N, Z same as in INC V set if result = 100000 C reset if result = 0, set otherwise
ADC{B} (Add carry)	$\beta055$	dst $\leftarrow$ [dst] + [C]	N, Z, V, C same as in ADD
SBC{B} (Subtract carry)	$\beta056$	dst $\leftarrow$ [dst] $-$ [C]	N, Z, V, C same as in SUB
TST{B} (Test)	$\beta057$	dst $\leftarrow$ [dst]	N, Z same as in INC V, C reset
ROR{B} (Rotate right one place)	$\beta060$	(diagram: C → bits 15..0 rotate right; byte form bits 7..0 (15) (8))	N, Z same as in ASH V set to N $\oplus$ C
ROL{B} (Rotate left one place)	$\beta061$	(diagram: C ← bits 15..0 rotate left; byte form bits 7..0 (15) (8))	N, Z, V same as in ROR
ASR{B} (Arithmetic shift right one place)	$\beta062$	(diagram: bits 15..0 → C; byte form bits 7..0 → C (15) (8))	N, Z, V same as in ROR
ASL{B} (Arithmetic shift left one place)	$\beta063$	(diagram: C ← bits 15..0 ← 0; byte form C ← bits 7..0 ← 0 (15) (8))	N, Z, V same as in ROR
SWAB (Swap bytes)	0003	dst$_{15-8}$ $\leftarrow$ [dst$_{7-0}$] dst$_{7-0}$ $\leftarrow$ [dst$_{15-8}$]	N set if b_7 of result set Z set if low-order byte of result = 0 V, C reset
SXT (Sign extended)	0067	dst $\leftarrow$ 0 if [N] = 0 dst $\leftarrow -1$ if [N] = 1	N, C not affected Z set if [N] = 0 V reset

BRANCH INSTRUCTIONS

Branch instructions use the format

OP code	Offset
15 8	7 0

If the branch condition is satisfied, the new value of the program counter is PC ←[updated PC] + 2 × Offset, where the updated PC is equal to the address of the branch instruction plus 2, and the Offset is interpreted as a signed 8-bit number. Condition codes are not affected by the branch instructions.

Mnemonic	Name	OP code (binary)	Branch condition
BR	Branch unconditionally	00000001	None
BNE	Branch if $\neq 0$	00000010	$Z = 0$
BEQ	Branch if $= 0$	00000011	$Z = 1$
BPL	Branch if plus	10000000	$N = 0$
BMI	Branch if minus	10000001	$N = 1$
BVC	Branch if overflow clear	10000100	$V = 0$
BVS	Branch if overflow set	10000101	$V = 1$
BCC	Branch if carry clear	10000110	$C = 0$
BCS	Branch if carry set	10000111	$C = 1$
BGE	Branch if ≥ 0	00000100	$N \oplus V = 0$
BLT	Branch if < 0	00000101	$N \oplus V = 1$
BGT	Branch if > 0	00000110	$Z \vee (N \oplus V) = 0$
BLE	Branch if ≤ 0	00000111	$Z \vee (N \oplus V) = 1$
BHI	Branch if higher	10000010	$C \vee Z = 0$
BLOS	Branch if lower or same	10000011	$C \vee Z = 1$
BHIS*	Branch if higher or same	10000110	$C = 0$
BLO*	Branch if lower	10000111	$C = 1$

*Instructions BHIS and BLO are the same as BCC and BCS. These mnemonics are included for convenience purposes only.

The instructions BHI, BLOS, BHIS, and BLO are normally used after a Compare instruction. They are based on interpreting the data which caused the setting of the condition codes as positive 16-bit integers. This is in contrast to the instructions BGE, BLT, BGT, and BLE, which are based on interpreting the data as 16-bit signed integers in 2's-complement representation.

JUMP AND SUBROUTINE INSTRUCTIONS

In the description of bit patterns for this group of instructions the following notation is used:

DD   Represents a 6-bit destination (dst) in any of the standard addressing modes

R   Represents a general-purpose register (reg)

QQ   Represents a 6-bit positive number

The condition codes are not affected by these instructions.

Mnemonic	Name	Code (octal)	Operation performed
JMP	Jump	0001DD	PC ← dst
JSR	Jump to subroutine	004RDD	temp ← dst SP ← [SP] − 2 [SP] ← [reg] reg ← [PC] PC ← [temp]
RTS	Return from subroutine	00020R	PC ← [reg] reg ← [[SP]] SP ← [SP] + 2
MARK	Mark	0064QQ	SP ← [SP] + 2 × QQ PC ← [reg 5] reg 5 ← [[SP]] SP ← [SP] + 2
SOB	Subtract one and branch	077RQQ	reg ← [reg] − 1 If result ≠ 0, then PC ← [PC] − 2 × QQ

The MARK instruction is used to facilitate return from subroutines when subroutine parameters are to be removed from the processor stack. The SOB instruction provides a convenient means for controlling program loops.

TRAP AND INTERRUPT INSTRUCTIONS

Mnemonic	Name	Code (octal)	Operation performed	Condition codes
RTI	Return from interrupt	000002	PC ← [[SP]] SP ← [SP] + 2 PSW ← [[SP]] SP ← [SP] + 2	N, Z, V, C loaded from the processor stack
TRAP	Trap	104400–104477	SP ← [SP] − 2 [SP] ← [PSW] SP ← [SP] − 2 [SP] ← [PC] PC ← [loc. 34] PSW ← [loc. 36]	N, Z, V, C loaded from the trap vector

There are four other trap and return from interrupt instructions, for which the reader may consult the manufacturer's manuals. Note that trap instructions are, in effect, software-generated interrupts. The new values for the PC and PSW are obtained from a two-word trap vector at a fixed memory location. The above trap instruction is defined by the high-order byte only, while the low-order byte may be used to transmit data to the trap routine.

CONDITION CODE INSTRUCTIONS

A set of 10 instructions is provided to enable setting and resetting of condition codes. Their format is

0	0	0	0	0	0	0	0	1	0	1	0/1	N	Z	V	C

15   0

Condition codes N, Z, V, and C are manipulated if the corresponding bits in positions b_3 to b_0 are set. The selected condition codes are set if $b_4 = 1$ and reset if $b_4 = 0$. Note that all 16 bits of these instructions, in effect, constitute an OP code.

Mnemonic	Name	OP code (octal)
CLC	Clear C	000241
CLV	Clear V	000242
CLZ	Clear Z	000244
CLN	Clear N	000250
SEC	Set C	000261
SEV	Set V	000262
SEZ	Set Z	000264
SEN	Set N	000270
SCC	Set all condition codes	000277
CCC	Clear all condition codes	000257

MISCELLANEOUS INSTRUCTIONS

These instructions are used for control purposes and do not affect the condition codes:

Mnemonic	Name	OP code (octal)	Function
HALT	Halt	000000	Stops the processor
WAIT	Wait for interrupt	000001	Causes the processor to wait for an external interrupt
RESET	Reset external bus	000005	All devices on the Unibus are reset
NOP	No operation	000240	No operation is performed

INSTRUCTION SET FOR MOTOROLA 68000 MICROPROCESSOR

This appendix contains a summary of the instructions for the M68000 micro-processor. An introductory discussion of the main characteristics of this microprocessor was presented in Chapter 11. It included a description of the register structure and the addressing modes, summarized in Figure 11.17 and Table 11.5, respectively. Note that Table 11.5 includes the assembler syntax for the addressing modes.

The general format for encoding the address field for an operand is shown in Table C.1. A 6-bit field is used to specify the addressing mode and the register involved. In the modes where it is not necessary to specify a particular register, the register field is used as an extension of the mode field having the bit patterns shown in the table.

The names of addressing modes in Table C.1 are consistent with those used in this book. We should caution the reader that some of these names are different from those used in Motorola literature. Since the reader will undoubt-edly find it useful to consult the manufacturer's data sheets and user manuals, we should point out the differences in the terminology used. The differences are summarized in Table C.2. It is apparent that the Motorola terminology is highly descriptive, but somewhat awkward to use for discussion purposes.

The M68000 instructions are presented in this appendix in the form of a table. In order to keep the table reasonably small, extensive notational abbreviations are used. Table C.3 gives the notational symbols and their meaning. Note that symbols which correspond to bit patterns in the OP-code field have one letter for each bit position involved.

Table C.4 provides a complete listing of the available instructions. The addressing modes allowed for each instruction are indicated in a matrix format.

Table C.1 Address field encoding for M68000

Address field

Mode		Register	
5	4 3	2 1	0

Addressing mode	Mode field	Register field
Data register direct	000	Register number
Address register direct	001	Register number
Address register indirect	010	Register number
Autoincrement	011	Register number
Autodecrement	100	Register number
Indexed basic	101	Register number
Indexed full	110	Register number
Absolute short	111	000
Absolute long	111	001
Relative basic	111	010
Relative full	111	011
Immediate or status register	111	100

Table C.2 Differences from Motorola terminology

Terminology used in this text	Motorola terminology
Autoincrement	Address register indirect with postincrement
Autodecrement	Address register indirect with predecrement
Indexed basic	Address register indirect with displacement
Indexed full	Address register indirect with index
Relative basic	Program counter with displacement
Relative full	Program counter with index

Table C.3 Notation for Table C.4

Symbol	Meaning
s	Source operand
d	Destination operand
An	Address register n
Dn	Data register n
Xn	An address or data register, used as an index register
PC	Program counter
SP	Stack pointer
SR	Status register
CCR	Condition code flags in SR
AAA	Address register number
DDD	Data register number
rrr	Source register number
RRR	Destination register number
eeeeee	Effective address of the source operand
EEEEEE	Effective address of the destination operand
MMM	Effective address mode of destination
CCCC	Specification for a condition code test
P . . . P	Displacement
Q . . . Q	Quick immediate data
SS	Size: $00 \equiv$ byte, $01 \equiv$ word, $10 \equiv$ long word
VVVV	Trap vector number
u	Condition code flag state is undefined (meaningless)
d(An)	Indexed basic addressing mode
d(An,Xi)	Indexed full addressing mode
d(PC)	Relative basic addressing mode
d(PC,Xi)	Relative full addressing mode

For each source (destination) addressing mode provided, all destination (source) addressing modes permitted are denoted with an x. For example, for the AND instruction, if the source is a data register, the destination mode may be any of (An), (An)+, −(An), d(An,Xi), Abs.W, or Abs.L. Moreover, if the destination is a data register, the source can be specified in any of the 11 modes shown in the table.

The OP-code column shows the actual bit pattern of the first 16-bit word of an instruction. Instructions that have immediate source data use a second word

Table C.4 M68000 instruction set

Mnemonic (Name)	Size	Addressing mode	Dn	An	(An)	(An)+	-(An)	d(An)	d(An,Xi)	Abs.W	Abs.L	d(PC)	d(PC,Xi)	Immed	SR or CCR
ABCD (Add BCD)	B	s = Dn, d =	x												
		s = -(An), d =					x								
ADD (Add)	B,W,L	s = Dn, d =			x	x	x	x	x	x	x				
		d = Dn, s =	x	x	x	x	x	x	x	x	x	x	x	x	
ADDA (Add address)	W	d = An, s =	x	x	x	x	x	x	x	x	x	x	x	x	
	L	d = An, s =	x	x	x	x	x	x	x	x	x	x	x	x	
ADDI (Add immediate)	B,W,L	s = Immed, d =	x		x	x	x	x	x	x	x				
ADDQ (Add quick)	B,W,L	s = Immed3, d =	x	x	x	x	x	x	x	x	x				
ADDX (Add extended)	B,W,L	s = Dn, d =	x												
		s = -(An), d =					x								
AND (Logical AND)	B,W,L	s = Dn, d =			x	x	x	x	x	x	x				
		d = Dn, s =	x		x	x	x	x	x	x	x	x	x	x	
ANDI (AND immediate)	B,W,L	s = Immed, d =	x		x	x	x	x	x	x					x
ASL (Arithmetic shift left)	B,W,L	count = [Dn], d =	x												
		count = QQQ, d =	x												
		count = 1, d =			x	x	x	x	x	x					
ASR (Arithmetic shift right)	B,W,L	count = [Dn], d =	x												
		count = QQQ, d =	x												
		count = 1, d =			x	x	x	x	x	x					
BCHG* (Test a bit and change it)	B	bit# = [Dn], d =			x	x	x	x	x	x	x				
		bit# = Immed, d =			x	x	x	x	x	x	x				
	L	bit# = [Dn], d =	x												
		bit# = Immed, d =	x												
BCLR* (Test a bit and clear it)	B	bit# = [Dn], d =			x	x	x	x	x	x	x				
		bit# = Immed, d =			x	x	x	x	x	x	x				
	L	bit# = [Dn], d =	x												
		bit# = Immed, d =	x												

OP code $b_{15} \ldots b_0$	Operation performed	Condition flags				
		X	N	Z	V	C
1100 RRR1 0000 0rrr 1100 RRR1 0000 lrrr	d ← [s] + [d] + [X] Binary-coded decimal addition	x	u	x	u	x
1101 DDD0 SSEE EEEE 1101 DDD1 SSee eeee	d ← [Dn] + [d] Dn ← [s] + [Dn]	x x	x x	x x	x x	x x
1101 AAA0 11ee eeee 1101 AAA1 11ee eeee	An ← [s] + [An]					
0000 0110 SSEE EEEE	d ← s + [d]	x	x	x	x	x
0101 QQQ0 SSEE EEEE	d ← QQQ + [d]	x	x	x	x	x
1101 RRR1 SS00 0rrr 1101 RRR1 SS00 1rrr	d ← [s] + [d] + [X] Multiprecision addition	x	x	x	x	x
1100 DDD1 SSEE EEEE 1100 DDD0 SSee eeee	d ← [Dn] ∧ [d]		x	x	0	0
0000 0010 SSEE EEEE	d ← s ∧ [d]		x	x	0	0
1110 rrrl SS10 0DDD 1110 QQQ1 SS00 0DDD 1110 0001 11EE EEEE	C ← operand ← 0 X ←	x	x	x	x	x
1110 rrr0 SS10 0DDD 1110 QQQ0 SS00 0DDD 1110 0000 11EE EEEE	operand → C → X	x	x	x	x	x
0000 rrr1 01EE EEEE 0000 1000 01EE EEEE 0000 rrr1 01EE EEEE 0000 1000 01EE EEEE	Z ← $\overline{\text{(bit\# of d)}}$; then complement the tested bit in d.			x		
0000 rrr1 10EE EEEE 0000 1000 10EE EEEE 0000 rrr1 10EE EEEE 0000 1000 10EE EEEE	Z ← $\overline{\text{(bit\# of d)}}$; then clear the tested bit in d.			x		

Table C.4 *(Continued)*

Mnemonic (Name)	Size	Addressing mode	Dn	An	(An)	(An)+	-(An)	d(An)	d(An,Xi)	Abs.W	Abs.L	d(PC)	d(PC,Xi)	Immed	SR or CCR
BSET* (Test a bit and set it)	B	bit# = [Dn] d =			x	x	x	x	x	x	x				
		bit# = Immed d =			x	x	x	x	x	x	x				
	L	bit# = [Dn] d =	x												
		bit# = Immed d =	x												
BTST* (Test a bit)	B	bit# = [Dn] d =			x	x	x	x	x	x	x				
		bit# = Immed d =			x	x	x	x	x	x	x				
	L	bit# = [Dn] d =	x												
		bit# = Immed d =	x												
CHK (Check register against bounds)	W	d = Dn s =	x		x	x	x	x	x	x	x	x	x	x	
CLR (Clear)	B,W,L	d =	x		x	x	x	x	x	x	x				
CMP (Compare)	B,W,L	d = Dn s =	x	x	x	x	x	x	x	x	x	x	x	x	
CMPA (Compare address)	W	d = An s =	x	x	x	x	x	x	x	x	x	x	x	x	
	L	d = An s =	x	x	x	x	x	x	x	x	x	x	x	x	
CMPI (Compare immediate)	B,W,L	s = Immed d =	x		x	x	x	x	x	x	x				
CMPM (Compare memory)	B,W,L	s = (An) + d =				x									
DIVS (Divide signed)	W	d = Dn s =	x		x	x	x	x	x	x	x	x	x	x	
DIVU (Divide unsigned)	W	d = Dn s =	x		x	x	x	x	x	x	x	x	x	x	
EOR (Exclusive OR)	B,W,L	S = Dn d =	x		x	x	x	x	x	x	x				
EORI (Exclusive OR immediate)	B,W,L	S = Immed d =	x		x	x	x	x	x	x	x				x
EXG (Exchange)	L	S = Dn d =	x	x											
		s = An d =	x	x											
EXT (Sign extend)	W	d =	x												
	L	d =	x												

OP code $b_{15} \ldots b_0$	Operation performed	X	N	Z	V	C
0000 rrr1 11EE EEEE 0000 1000 11EE EEEE 0000 rrr1 11EE EEEE 0000 1000 11EE EEEE	Z ← $\overline{(\text{bit\# of d})}$; then set to 1 the tested bit in d.			x		
0000 rrr1 00EE EEEE 0000 1000 00EE EEEE 0000 rrr1 00EE EEEE 0000 1000 00EE EEEE	Z ← $\overline{(\text{bit\# of d})}$			x		
0100 DDD1 10ee eeee	If [Dn] < 0 or [Dn] > [s], then raise an interrupt.		x	u	u	u
0100 0010 SSEE EEEE	d ← 0		0	1	0	0
1011 DDD0 SSee eeee	[d] − [s]		x	x	x	x
1011 AAA0 11ee eeee 1011 AAA1 11ee eeee	[An] − [s]		x	x	x	x
0000 1100 SSEE EEEE	[d] − [s]		x	x	x	x
1011 RRR1 SS00 1rrr	[d] − [s]		x	x	x	x
1000 DDD1 11ee eeee	d ← [d] ÷ [s], using 32 bits of s and 16 bits of d.		x	x	x	0
1000 DDD0 11ee eeee	d ← [d] ÷ [s], using 32 bits of s and 16 bits of d.		x	x	x	0
1011 rrr1 SSEE EEEE	d ← [Dn] $\oplus$ [d]		x	x	0	0
0000 1010 SSEE EEEE	d ← s $\oplus$ [d]		x	x	0	0
1100 DDD1 0100 0DDD 1100 AAA1 0100 1AAA 1100 DDD1 1000 1AAA	[s] ↔ [d]					
0100 1000 1000 0DDD 0100 1000 1100 0DDD	(bits 8–15 of d) ← (bit 7 of d) (bits 16–31 of d) ← (bit 15 of d)		x x	x x	0 0	0 0

Table C.4 *(Continued)*

Mnemonic (Name)	Size	Addressing mode		Dn	An	(An)	(An)+	-(An)	d(An)	d(An,Xi)	Abs.W	Abs.L	d(PC)	d(PC,Xi)	Immed	SR or CCR
JMP (Jump)			d =		x				x	x	x	x	x	x		
JSR (Jump to subroutine)			d =		x				x	x	x	x	x	x		
LEA (Load effective address)	L	d = An	s =		x				x	x	x	x	x	x		
LINK (Link and allocate)		disp = Immed	s =	x												
LSL (Logical shift left)	B,W,L	count = [Dn]	d =	x												
		count = QQQ	d =	x												
	W	count = 1	d =			x	x	x	x	x	x	x				
LSR (Logical shift right)	B,W,L	count = [Dn]	d =	x												
		count = QQQ	d =	x												
		count = 1	d =			x	x	x	x	x	x	x				
MOVE (Move)	B,W,L	s = Dn	d =	x	x	x	x	x	x	x	x	x				
		s = An	d =	x	x	x	x	x	x	x	x	x				
		s = (An)	d =	x	x	x	x	x	x	x	x	x				
		s = (An) +	d =	x	x	x	x	x	x	x	x	x				
		s = − (An)	d =	x	x	x	x	x	x	x	x	x				
		s = d(An)	d =	x	x	x	x	x	x	x	x	x				
		s = d(An,Xi)	d =	x	x	x	x	x	x	x	x	x				
		s = Abs.W	d =	x	x	x	x	x	x	x	x	x				
		s = Abs.L	d =	x	x	x	x	x	x	x	x	x				
		s = d(PC)	d =	x	x	x	x	x	x	x	x	x				
		s = d(PC,Xi)	d =	x	x	x	x	x	x	x	x	x				
		s = Immed	d =	x	x	x	x	x	x	x	x	x				
	W	d = CCR	s =	x	x	x	x	x	x	x	x	x	x	x	x	
		d = SR	s =	x	x	x	x	x	x	x	x	x	x	x	x	
		s = SR	d =	x		x	x	x	x	x	x	x				
	L	s = SP	d =		x											
		d = SP	s =		x											
MOVEA (Move address)	W,L	d = An	s =	x	x	x	x	x	x	x	x	x	x	x	x	

OP code $b_{15} \ldots b_0$	Operation performed	Condition flags				
		X	N	Z	V	C
0100 1110 11EE EEEE	PC ← [d]					
0100 1110 10EE EEEE	SP ← [SP] − 2; [SP] ← [PC]; PC ← [d]					
0100 AAA1 11ee eeee	An ← effective address of s					
0100 1110 0101 0AAA	SP ← [SP] − 2; [SP] ← [An]; An ← [SP]; SP ← [SP] + disp					
1110 rrr1 SS10 1DDD 1110 QQQ1 SS00 1DDD 1110 0011 11EE EEEE	[C]← operand ← 0 [X]←	x	x	x	0	x
1110 rrr0 SS10 1DDD 1110 QQQ0 SS00 1DDD 1110 0010 11EE EEEE	0⟶ operand ⟶[C] ⟶[X]	x	x	x	0	x
00SS RRRM MMee eeee	d ← [s]		x	x	0	0
0100 0100 11ee eeee 0100 0110 11ee eeee 0100 0000 11EE EEEE 0100 1110 0110 1AAA 0100 1110 0110 0AAA	CCR ← [s] SR ← [s] d ← [SR] d ← [SP] SP ← [d]	x x	x x	x x	x x	x x
00SS AAA0 01ee eeee	An ← [s]					

Table C.4 *(Continued)*

Mnemonic (Name)	Size	Addressing mode	Dn	An	(An)	(An)+	-(An)	d(An)	d(An,Xi)	Abs.W	Abs.L	d(PC)	d(PC,Xi)	Immed	SR or CCR
MOVEM* (Move multiple registers)	W	s = Xn d =			x		x	x	x	x	x				
		d = Xn s =			x	x		x	x	x	x	x	x		
	L	s = Xn d =			x		x	x	x	x	x				
		d = Xn s =			x	x		x	x	x	x	x	x		
MOVEP* (Move peripheral data)	W	s = Dn d =						x							
	L	s = Dn d =						x							
	W	s = d(An) d =	x												
	L	s = d(An) d =	x												
MOVEQ (Move quick)	L	s = Immed8 d =	x												
MULS (Multiply signed)	W	d = Dn s =	x		x	x	x	x	x	x	x	x	x	x	
MULU (Multiply unsigned)	W	d = Dn s =	x		x	x	x	x	x	x	x	x	x	x	
NBCD (Negate BCD)	B	d =	x		x	x	x	x	x	x	x				
NEG (Negate)	B,W,L	d =	x		x	x	x	x	x	x	x				
NEGX (Negate extended)	B,W,L	d =	x		x	x	x	x	x	x	x				
NOP (No operation)															
NOT (Complement)	B,W,L	d =	x		x	x	x	x	x	x	x				
OR (Logical OR)	B,W,L	s = Dn d =			x	x	x	x	x	x	x				
		d = Dn s =	x		x	x	x	x	x	x	x	x	x	x	
ORI (OR immediate)	B,W,L	s = Immed d =	x		x	x	x	x	x	x	x				x
PEA (Push effective address)	L	s =			x			x	x	x	x	x	x		

OP code $b_{15} \ldots b_0$	Operation performed	Condition flags				
		X	N	Z	V	C
0100 1000 10EE EEEE 0100 1100 10ee eeee 0100 1000 11EE EEEE 0100 1100 11ee eeee	d ← [Xn]　　A second word is Xn ← [s]　　used to specify d ← [Xn]　　the registers Xn ← [s]　　involved.					
0000 DDD1 1000 1AAA 0000 DDD1 1100 1AAA 0000 DDD1 0000 1AAA 0000 DDD1 0100 1AAA	Alternate bytes of d ← [Dn] Dn ← alternate bytes of d					
0111 DDD0 QQQQ QQQQ	Dn ← QQQQQQQQ		x	x	0	0
1100 DDD1 11ee eeee	Dn ← [s] × [Dn]		x	x	0	0
1100 DDD0 11ee eeee	Dn ← [s] × [Dn]		x	x	0	0
0100 1000 00EE EEEE	d ←0− [d] − [X] using BCD arithmetic.	x	u	x	u	x
0100 0100 SSEE EEEE	d ← 0 − [d]	x	x	x	x	x
0100 0000 SSEE EEEE	d ← 0 − [d] − [X]	x	x	x	x	x
0100 1110 0111 0001	none					
0100 0110 SSEE EEEE	d ← $\overline{[d]}$		x	x	0	0
1000 DDD1 SSEE EEEE 1000 DDD0 SSee eeee	d ← [s] ∨ [d]		x	x	0	0
0000 0000 SSEE EEEE	d ← s ∨ [d]		x	x	0	0
0100 1000 01ee eeee	SP ← [SP] − 2; [SP] ← effective address of s					

Table C.4 *(Continued)*

Mnemonic (Name)	Size	Addressing mode		Dn	An	(An)	(An)+	-(An)	d(An)	d(An,Xi)	Abs.W	Abs.L	d(PC)	d(PC,Xi)	Immed	SR or CCR
RESET																
ROL (Rotate left without X)	B,W,L	count = [Dn]	d =	x												
		count = QQQ	d =	x												
	W	count = 1	d =			x	x	x	x	x	x	x				
ROR (Rotate right without X)	B,W,L	count = [Dn]	d =	x												
		count = QQQ	d =	x												
	W	count =1				x	x	x	x	x	x	x				
ROXL (Rotate left with X)	B,W,L	count = [Dn]	d =	x												
		count = QQQ	d =													
		count = 1	d =	x												
	W					x	x	x	x	x	x	x				
ROXR (Rotate right with X)	B,W,L	count = [Dn]	d =	x												
		count = QQQ	d =	x												
	W	count = 1	d =			x	x	x	x	x	x	x				
RTE (Return from exception)																
RTR (Return and restore CCR)																
RTS (Return from subroutine)																
SBCD (Subtract BCD)	B	s = Dn	d =	x												
		s = - (An)	d =					x								
Scc (Set on condition)	B		d =	x		x	x	x	x	x	x	x				

OP code $b_{15} \ldots b_0$	Operation performed	Condition flags				
		X	N	Z	V	C
0100 1110 0111 0000	Assert RESET output line.					
1110 rrrl SS11 1DDD 1110 QQQ1 SS01 1DDD 1110 0111 11EE EEEE	[C] ← operand ← (loop)		x	x	0	x
1100 rrrl SS11 1DDD 1110 QQQ0 SS01 1DDD 1110 0111 11EE EEEE	(loop) → operand → [C]		x	x	0	x
1110 rrrl SS11 0DDD 1110 QQQ1 SS01 0DDD 1110 0101 11EE EEEE	[C] ← operand ← [X]	x	x	x	0	x
1110 rrr0 SS11 0DDD 1110 QQQ0 SS01 0DDD 1110 0100 11EE EEEE	[X] → operand → [C]	x	x	x	0	x
0100 1110 0111 0011	SR ← [[SP]]; SP ← [SP] + 2; PC ← [[SP]]; SP ← [SP] + 2	x	x	x	x	x
0100 1110 0111 0111	CCR ← [[SP]]; SP ← [SP] + 2; PC ← [[SP]]; SP ← [SP] + 2	x	x	x	x	x
0100 1110 0111 0101	PC ← [[SP]]; SP ← [SP] + 2					
1000 RRR1 0000 0rrr 1000 RRR1 0000 1rrr	d ← [d] − [s] −[X] Binary-coded decimal subtraction	x	u	x	u	x
0101 CCCC 11EE EEEE	Set all 8 bits of d to 1 if cc is true, otherwise clear them to 0.					

Table C.4 *(Continued)*

Mnemonic (Name)	Size	Addressing mode		Dn	An	(An)	(An)+	-(An)	d(An)	d(An,Xi)	Abs.W	Abs.L	d(PC)	d(PC,Xi)	Immed	SR or CCR
STOP (Load SR and stop)		s =													x	
SUB (Subtract)	B,W,L	s = Dn d = Dn	d = s =	 x	 x	x x	x x	x x	x x	x x	x x	x x	 x	 x	 x	
SUBA (Subtract address)	W L	d = An d = An	s = s =	x x	x x	x x	x x	x x	x x	x x	x x	x x	x x	x x	x x	
SUBI (Subtract immediate)	B,W,L	s = Immed	d =	x		x	x	x	x	x	x	x				
SUBQ (Subtract quick)	B,W,L	s = Immed 3	d =	x	x	x	x	x	x	x	x	x				
SUBX (Subtract extended)	B,W,L	s = Dn s = - (An)	d = d =	x 				 x								
SWAP (Swap register halves)	W		d =	x												
TAS (Test and set)	B		d =	x		x	x	x	x	x	x	x				
TRAP (Trap)																
TRAPV (Trap on overflow)																
TST (Test)	B,W,L		d =	x		x	x	x	x	x	x	x				
UNLK (Unlink)					x											

OP code $b_{15} \ldots b_0$	Operation performed	X	N	Z	V	C
0100 1110 0111 0010	SR ← s; Wait for interrupt.	x	x	x	x	x
1001 DDD1 SSEE EEEE 1001 DDD0 SSee eeee	d ← [d] − [s]	x	x	x	x	x
1001 AAA0 11ee eeee 1001 AAA1 11ee eeee	An ← [An] − [s]					
0000 0100 SSEE EEEE	d ← [d] − s	x	x	x	x	x
0101 QQQ1 SSEE EEEE	d ← [d] − QQQ	x	x	x	x	x
1001 RRR1 SS00 0rrr 1001 RRR1 SS00 1rrr	d ← [d] − [s] − [X]	x	x	x	x	x
0100 1000 0100 0DDD	$[Dn]_{31\text{-}16} \leftrightarrow [Dn]_{15\text{-}0}$		x	x	0	0
0100 1010 11EE EEEE	Test d and set N and Z flags: set bit 7 of d to 1.		x	x	0	0
0100 1110 0100 VVVV	SP ← [SP] − 2; [SP] ← [PC]; SP ← [SP] −2; [SP] ← [SR]; PC ← vector					

0100 1110 0111 0110	If V = 1, then
	    SP ← [SP] −2;
	    [SP] ← [PC];
	    SP ← [SP] − 2;
	    [SP] ← [SR];
	    PC ← TRAPV vector					

0100 1010 SSEE EEEE	Test d and set N and Z flags.		x	x	0	0
0100 1110 0101 1AAA	SP ← [An]; An ← [[SP]]; SP ← [SP] + 2					

for 8- and 16-bit operands, and a second and third word for 32-bit operands. For the indexed and relative addressing modes, the required index value (displacement) is given in the word that follows the OP code.

Shift and rotate instructions can specify a count of the number of bit positions by which the operand is to be shifted or rotated. The count can be given as the contents of a data register, or as an immediate 3-bit value within the OP code. However, if a memory operand is involved, then the count is always equal to 1.

Branch instructions are listed in Table C.5. The branch offset (displacement) is a signed 2's-complement number that specifies the relative distance in bytes. For conditional branch instructions, as well as for Scc (set on condition) instructions, the condition code suffix possibilities (cc) are shown in Table C.6. The table also indicates the condition that is tested to determine if a branch is to be taken.

The operation performed for a given instruction is indicated in Tables C.4 and C.5. For most instructions the action taken is obvious. However, for a few instructions, additional comments are in order. The instructions labeled with an asterisk in the mnemonic column are discussed further in the following paragraphs.

BCHG, BCLR, BSET, and BTST All of these instructions test a specified bit of the destination operand. The number of the bit position to be tested (bit#) is

Table C.5 M68000 branch instructions

Mnemonic (Name)	Displacement size	OP code	Operation performed
BRA (Branch always)	8	0110 0000 PPPP PPPP	PC ← [PC] + disp
	16	0110 0000 0000 0000 PPPP PPPP PPPP PPPP	
BCC (Branch conditionally)	8	0110 CCCC PPPP PPPP	If cc is true, then
	16	0110 CCCC 0000 0000 PPPP PPPP PPPP PPPP	PC ← [PC] + disp
BSR (Branch to subroutine)	8	0110 0001 PPPP PPPP	SP ← [SP] − 2; [SP] ← [PC];
	16	0110 0001 0000 0000 PPPP PPPP PPPP PPPP	PC ← [PC] + disp
DBcc (Decrement and branch conditionally)	16	0101 CCCC 1100 1DDD PPPP PPPP PPPP PPPP	If cc is false, then Dn ← [Dn] − 1; If [Dn] ≠ −1, then PC ← [PC] + disp
DBRA (Decrement and branch)	The assembler interprets this instruction as DBF (see the DBcc entry).		

Table C.6 Condition codes for Bcc, DBcc, and Scc instructions

Machine code CCCC	Condition suffix cc	Name	Test condition
0000*	T	True	Always true
0001*	F	False	Always false
0010	HI	High	$C \vee Z = 0$
0011	LS	Low or same	$C \vee Z = 1$
0100	CC	Carry clear	$C = 0$
0101	CS	Carry set	$C = 1$
0110	NE	Not equal	$Z = 0$
0111	EQ	Equal	$Z = 1$
1000	VC	Overflow clear	$V = 0$
1001	VS	Overflow set	$V = 1$
1010	PL	Plus	$N = 0$
1011	MI	Minus	$N = 1$
1100	GE	Greater or equal	$N \oplus V = 0$
1101	LT	Less than	$N \oplus V = 1$
1110	GT	Greater than	$Z \vee (N \oplus V) = 0$
1111	LE	Less or equal	$Z \vee (N \oplus V) = 1$

*T and F suffixes cannot be used in the Bcc instruction.

indicated either as the contents of a data register or as an immediate value within the instruction. The test is made by loading the complement of the tested bit into the condition flag Z.

MOVEM This instruction moves the contents of one or more registers to or from consecutive memory locations. The registers involved in the transfer are specified in the second word of the instruction. Bits 0 to 7 correspond to D0 to D7 and bits 8 to 15, to A0 to A7, respectively. This arrangement is valid for all addressing modes except the autodecrement mode, in which case the order of registers is reversed.

MOVEP This instruction is useful for data transfers between the M68000 and 8-bit peripheral devices. The data is transferred in bytes, with the memory address incremented by 2 after each byte. Thus, if the starting address is even, all bytes are transferred to or from even numbered address locations by means of the high-order eight lines of the data bus. Similarly, if the starting address is odd, then all transfers are done via the low-order eight lines of the data bus. The high-order byte of a data register is transferred first and the low-order byte last.

As pointed out in Chapter 11, the M68000 has two basic modes of operation. In the supervisor mode all instructions can be used. In the user mode, some instructions cannot be executed. Instructions which can be used in the supervisor mode only are called *privileged* instructions. These are:

- ANDI, EORI, ORI, and MOVE instructions when the destination is the status register SR
- MOVE instruction which moves the contents of the user stack pointer to or from an address register
- RESET, RTE, and STOP instructions

The information presented in this appendix should enable the reader to write and debug assembly language programs for the M68000. The size and structure of assembled instructions can be determined on the basis of the OP codes given and the addressing modes employed. Lack of space has prevented inclusion of timing information, such as the number of machine cycles needed to execute a given instruction. This information, as well as further details about the instruction set, can be found in the manufacturer's literature.

CHARACTER CODES AND NUMBER CONVERSION

D.1 CHARACTER CODES

Information storage and processing in digital computers involves coding the individual items of information by using a number of binary variables. In most scientific computers, positive and negative numbers are represented in some variation of the binary number system. The most usual formats are presented in Chapter 7, where both integer and floating-point numbers are discussed.

In computers that are used mainly for business data processing, it is useful to represent and process numbers in the base-10 (decimal) format. Table D.1 gives the most usual coding for individual digits, called the binary-coded decimal (BCD) code. This code is simply the first 10 values (0–9) of the 4-bit binary number system. Strings of these 4-bit code values can be used to represent any desired range of positive and negative integers, with an appropriate code being used for the sign position.

Alphabetic characters (A–Z), operators, punctuation symbols, and control characters (+ − / , : ; LF CR EOT), as well as numbers, need to be represented for text storage and editing and high-level language input, processing, and output operations. Two standard codes for this purpose are the American Standards Committee on Information Interchange (ASCII) code and the Extended Binary Coded Decimal Interchange Code (EBCDIC). The standard ASCII code is a 7-bit code, and the EBCDIC code is an 8-bit code. Tables D.2 and D.3 show the standard ASCII and EBCDIC codes, respectively.

Table D.1 BCD encoding of decimal digits

Decimal digit	BCD code
0	0000
1	0001
2	0010
3	0011
4	0100
5	0101
6	0110
7	0111
8	1000
9	1001

Table D-2 The 7-bit ASCII code

Bit positions 3210	Bit positions 654							
	000	001	010	011	100	101	110	111
0000	NUL	DLE	SPACE	0	@	P	'	p
0001	SOH	DC1	!	1	A	Q	a	q
0010	STX	DC2	"	2	B	R	b	r
0011	ETX	DC3	#	3	C	S	c	s
0100	EOT	DC4	$	4	D	T	d	t
0101	ENQ	NAK	%	5	E	U	e	u
0110	ACK	SYN	&	6	F	V	f	v
0111	BEL	ETB	'	7	G	W	g	w
1000	BS	CAN	(	8	H	X	h	x
1001	HT	EM	)	9	I	Y	i	y
1010	LF	SUB	*	:	J	Z	j	z
1011	VT	ESC	+	;	K	[	k	{
1100	FF	FS	,	<	L	\	1		
1101	CR	GS	–	=	M	]	m	}
1110	SO	RS	.	>	N	^	n	~
1111	SI	US	/	?	O	—	o	DEL

NUL	Null/Idle	SI	Shift in
SOH	Start of header	DLE	Data link escape
STX	Start of text	DC1-DC4	Device control
ETX	End of text	NAK	Negative acknowledgement
EOT	End of transmission	SYN	Synchronous idle
ENQ	Enquiry	ETB	End of transmitted block
ACK	Acknowledgement	CAN	Cancel (error in data)
BEL	Audible signal	EM	End of medium
BS	Back space	SUB	Special sequence
HT	Horizontal tab	ESC	Escape
LF	Line feed	FS	File separator
VT	Vertical tab	GS	Group separator
FF	Form feed	RS	Record separator
CR	Carriage return	US	Unit separator
SO	Shift out	DEL	Delete/Idle

Bit positions of code format = | 6 | 5 | 4 | 3 | 2 | 1 | 0 |

Table D-3 The 8-bit EBCDIC code

Bit positions 3210	Bit positions 7654															
	0000	0001	0010	0011	0100	0101	0110	0111	1000	1001	1010	1011	1100	1101	1110	1111
0000	NULL				SP	&	—									0
0001							/		a	j			A	J		1
0010									b	k	s		B	K	S	2
0011									c	l	t		C	L	T	3
0100	PF	RES	BYP	PN	¢	!		:	d	m	u		D	M	U	4
0101	HT	NL	LF	RS	.	$	,	#	e	n	v		E	N	V	5
0110	LC	BS	EOB	UC	<	*	%	@	f	o	w		F	O	W	6
0111	DEL	IL	PRE	EOT	(	)	_	'	g	p	x		G	P	X	7
1000					+	;	>	=	h	q	y		H	Q	Y	8
1001					|	¬	?	"	i	r	z		I	R	Z	9
1010			SM													
1011																
1100																
1101																
1110																
1111																

NULL	Null/Idle	NL	New line	PRE	Prefix
PF	Punch off	BS	Backspace	SM	Set mode
HT	Horizontal tab	IL	Idle	PN	Punch on
LC	Lower case	BYP	Bypass	RS	Reader stop
DEL	Delete	LF	Line feed	UC	Upper case
RES	Restore	EOB	End of block	EOT	End of transmission
				SP	Space

Bit positions of code format = | 7 | 6 | 5 | 4 | 3 | 2 | 1 | 0 |

In many applications it is preferable to use 8-bit quantities, thus the basic ASCII code is often extended to 8-bits. A common way of doing this is to set the high-order bit position (bit 7) to zero. Another popular possibility is to use bit 7 as a parity bit for the encoded character. .

Some comments about the structure of the ASCII and EBCDIC codes are helpful. Note that in both codes the low-order 4 bits of the decimal character codes (0–9) are the BCD codes of Table D.1. This facilitates two operations. First, the comparison of two characters that represent decimal digits to determine which is larger can be done with the same type of logic circuits that are used to perform the standard arithmetic operations on binary numbers. This is helpful when strings of decimal numbers need to be sorted into numerical order. Second, when it is determined by context that consecutive 7- or 8-bit codes in some input string represent a decimal number that is to be stored and processed as a single entity, then it is sometimes practical to remove the leftmost 3 or 4 bits of each digit code and compress the number being represented into a string of 4-bit BCD digits. Of course, this compression or packing of data requires starting and ending delimiters, but it is justified in many situations where storage space requirements are a concern. Similar comments apply to the codes for the alphabetic characters. The fact that their binary bit patterns are in numerical sequence facilitates alphabetic sorting.

D.2 DECIMAL TO BINARY CONVERSION

This section will show how to convert a fixed-point decimal number to its binary equivalent. The value represented by the binary number

$$B = b_n b_{n-1} \cdots b_0 \, . \, b_{-1} b_{-2} \cdots b_{-m}$$

is given by

$$V(B) = b_n \times 2^n + b_{n-1} \times 2^{n-1} + \cdots + b_0 \times 2^0$$
$$+ b_{-1} \times 2^{-1} + b_{-2} \times 2^{-2} + \cdots + b_{-m} \times 2^{-m}$$

To convert a fixed-point decimal number into binary, the integer and fraction parts are handled separately. First, the integer part is converted as follows. It is divided by 2. The remainder is the least significant bit of the integer part of the binary representation. The quotient is again divided by 2, and the remainder is the next bit of the binary representation. The process is repeated up to and including the step in which the quotient becomes 0.

Second, the fraction part is converted by multiplying it by 2. The part of the product to the left of the decimal point (which is either 0 or 1) is a bit in the binary representation. The fractional part of the product is again multiplied by 2, generating the next bit of the binary representation. The first bit generated is the bit immediately to the right of the binary point. The next bit generated is the

Convert $(927.45)_{10}$

$\frac{927}{2} = 463 + \frac{1}{2} \quad \longrightarrow 1 \text{ LSB}$

$\frac{463}{2} = 231 + \frac{1}{2} \quad \longrightarrow 1$

$\frac{231}{2} = 115 + \frac{1}{2} \quad \longrightarrow 1$

$\frac{115}{2} = 57 \ + \frac{1}{2} \quad \longrightarrow 1$

$\frac{57}{2} = 28 \ + \frac{1}{2} \quad \longrightarrow 1$

$\frac{28}{2} = 14 \ + \frac{0}{2} \quad \longrightarrow 0$

$\frac{14}{2} = \ 7 \ + \frac{0}{2} \quad \longrightarrow 0$

$\frac{7}{2} = \ 3 \ + \frac{1}{2} \quad \longrightarrow 1$

$\frac{3}{2} = \ 1 \ + \frac{1}{2} \quad \longrightarrow 1$

$\frac{1}{2} = \ 0 \ + \frac{1}{2} \quad \longrightarrow 1 \text{MSB}$

$0.45 \times 2 \ = \ 0.09 \quad \longrightarrow \ 0 \text{ MSB}$

$0.09 \times 2 \ = \ 1.80 \quad \longrightarrow 1$

$0.80 \times 2 \ = \ 1.60 \quad \longrightarrow 1$

$0.60 \times 2 \ = \ 1.20 \quad \longrightarrow \ 1$

$0.20 \times 2 \ = \ 0.40 \quad \longrightarrow 0$

$0.40 \times 2 \ = \ 0.80 \quad \longrightarrow 0$

$0.80 \times 2 \ = \ 1.60 \quad \longrightarrow 1 \text{ LSB}$

$(927.45)_{10} = (1110011111.0111001\cdots)_2$ **Figure D.1** Conversion from decimal to binary.

second bit to the right, and so on. The process is repeated until the required accuracy is attained.

Figure D.1 shows an example of conversion from $(927.45)_{10}$ to binary. Note that conversion of the integer part is always exact, but the binary fraction for an exact decimal fraction may not be exact. For example, the fraction $(0.45)_{10}$ used in Figure D.1 does not have an exact binary equivalent. This is obvious from the pattern developing in the figure. In such cases, the binary fraction is generated to some desired level of accuracy. In general, the maximum absolute error e in generating a k-bit fractional representation is bounded as $e \leq 2^{-k}$. Of course, some decimal fractions have an exact binary representation. For example, $(0.25)_{10} = (0.01)_2$.

BIBLIOGRAPHY

Abd-alla, A. M., and A. C. Meltzer: "Principles of Digital Computer Design," Prentice-Hall, Englewood Cliffs, NJ, 1976.

Abrams, M. D., and P. G. Stein: "Computer Hardware and Software: An Interdisciplinary Introduction," Addison-Wesley,Reading, MA, 1973.

Baer, J.-L.: "Computer Systems Architecture," Computer Science Press, Potomac, Maryland, 1980.

Bartee, T. C.: "Digital Computer Fundamentals," 4th ed., McGraw-Hill, New York, 1977.

Bell, C. G., J. C. Mudge, and J. E. McNamara: "Computer Engineering," Digital Press, Bedford, MA, 1978.

Bell, C. G., and A. Newell: "Computer Structures: Readings and Examples," McGraw-Hill, New York, 1971.

Bowen, B. A., and R. J. A. Buhr: "The Logical Design of Multiple-Microprocessor Systems," Prentice-Hall, Englewood Cliffs, NJ, 1980.

Chirlian, P. M.: "Analysis and Design of Digital Circuits and Computer Systems," Matrix, Champaign, IL, 1976.

Chu, Y.: "Computer Organization and Microprogramming," Prentice-Hall, Englewood Cliffs, NJ, 1972.

Eckhouse, R. H.: "Minicomputer Systems: Organization and Programming," Prentice-Hall, Englewood Cliffs, NJ, 1975.

Flores, I.: "Computer Organization," Prentice-Hall, Englewood Cliffs, NJ, 1969.

Foster, C. C.: "Computer Architecture," Van Nostrand Reinhold, New York, 1970.

Gear, C. W.: "Computer Organization and Programming," 3d ed., McGraw-Hill, New York, 1980.

Gschwind, H. W. and E. J. McCluskey: "Design of Digital Computers," Springer-Verlag, New York, 1975.

Hayes, J. P.: "Computer Architecture and Organization," 2d ed., McGraw-Hill, New York, 1984.

Hayes, J. P.: "Digital System Design and Microprocessors," McGraw-Hill, New York, 1984.

Hellerman, H.: "Digital Computer System Principles," 2d ed., McGraw-Hill, New York, 1973.

Hilburn, J. L., and P. N. Julich: "Microcomputers/microprocessors: Hardware, Software, and Applications," Prentice-Hall, Englewood Cliffs, NJ, 1976.

Hill, F. J., and G. R. Peterson: "Digital Systems: Hardware Organization and Design," 2d ed., Wiley, New York, 1978.

Husson, S.: "Microprogramming: Principles and Practices," Prentice-Hall, Englewood Cliffs, NJ, 1970.

Hwang, K., and F. A. Briggs: "Parallel Computer Architecture," McGraw-Hill, New York, 1984.

Katzan, H., Jr.: "Computer Systems Organization and Programming," Science Research, Chicago, 1976.

Kogge, P. M.: "The Architecture of Pipelined Computers," McGraw-Hill, New York, 1981.

Langdon, G. G., Jr.: "Computer Design," Computeach Press, Inc., San Jose, CA, 1982.

Lewin, D.: "Theory and Design of Digital Computers," Nelson, London, 1972.

Mano, M. M.: "Computer System Architecture." 2d ed., Prentice-Hall, Englewood Cliffs, NJ, 1982.

Nashelsky, L.: "Introduction to Digital Computer Technology," 2d ed., John Wiley & Sons, New York, 1977.

O'Malley, J.: "Introduction to the Digital Computer," Holt, New York, 1972.

Osborne, A.: "An Introduction to Microcomputers, Vol. 2: Some Real Products," Adam Osborne and Associates, Berkeley, CA, 1976.

Pfleeger, C. P.: "Machine Organization," John Wiley & Sons, New York, 1982.

Poppelbaum, W. J.: "Computer Hardware Theory," McGraw-Hill, New York, 1972.

Siewiorek, D. P., C. G. Gell, and A. Newell: "Computer Structures: Principles and Examples," McGraw-Hill, New York, 1982.

Sloan, M. E.: "Computer Hardware and Organization," Science Research, Chicago, 1976.

Sobel, H. S.: "Introduction to Digital Computer Design," Addison-Wesley, Reading, MA, 1970.

Stone, H. S. (ed.): "Introduction to Computer Architecture," 2d ed., Science Research, Chicago, 1980.

Stone, H. S.: "Microcomputer Interfacing," Addison-Wesley, Reading, MA, 1982.

Stone, H. S., and D. P. Siewiorek: "Introduction to Computer Organization and Data Structures: PDP-11 Edition," McGraw-Hill, New York, 1975.

Tanenbaum, A. S.: "Structured Computer Organization," 2d ed., Prentice-Hall, Englewood Cliffs, NJ, 1984.

Wakerly, J.: "Microcomputer Architecture and Programming," John Wiley & Sons, New York, 1981.

Weitzman, C.: "Distributed Micro/Minicomputer Systems," Prentice-Hall, Englewood Cliffs, NJ, 1980.

INDEX